Legal Aid Handbook

Legalaidhandbook.com

Legal Aid Handbook 2020/21 is supported by legalaidhandbook.com

Readers will have access to a supporting website with regular news, updates and case reports and a comprehensive resources page.

Register to receive email updates at legalaidhandbook.com

Follow the Handbook on Twitter @legalaidhbk

The purpose of Legal Action Group is to promote equal access to justice for all members of society who are socially, economically or otherwise disadvantaged. To this end, it seeks to improve law and practice, the administration of justice and legal services.

Legal Aid Handbook 2020/21

Edited by Vicky Ling, Sue James

and Carol Storer

with Anthony Edwards

 Legal Action Group
2020

This edition published in Great Britain 2020
by LAG Education and Service Trust Limited
National Pro Bono Centre, 48 Chancery Lane, London WC2A 1JF
www.lag.org.uk

British Library Cataloguing in Publication Data
a CIP catalogue record for this book is available from the British Library.

print ISBN 978 1 912273 89 8
eBook ISBN 978 1 912273 90 4
bundle (print and eBook) ISBN 978 1 912273 91 1

Typeset by Refinecatch Ltd, Bungay, Suffolk
Printed in Great Britain by Hobbs the Printers, Totton, Hampshire

This book is dedicated to the memory of Andrew Wilson,
a fine lawyer who believed passionately in justice for all, fought
tenaciously for his clients, and inspired all who worked with him.

Preface

This edition will be the first without Simon Pugh, after fifteen years as general editor. His commitment and dedication to legal aid work has been exceptional. He will be missed.

Our thanks as always to Esther Pilger of Legal Action Group (LAG) for her unwavering support and smile. Steve Hynes stepped down as LAG's director this year, but we are pleased that Steve has continued his contribution to the handbook with his usual analysis of legal aid policy.

We welcome Carol Storer as both general editor and also interim director of LAG. We were fortunate that after a decade of leading LAPG, and with her incredible knowledge on legal aid, that she agreed to join us.

Special thanks have to go to the legal aid practitioners who continue to work in legal aid. These are challenging times. You do a brilliant job in difficult circumstances. We hope that the Handbook is a tool that you will continue to use to support your work.

The Handbook grows in size as the legal aid scheme becomes ever more complicated. We have two new chapters for this edition – a public law chapter edited by Silvia Nicolaou Garcia and a chapter on costs appeals by Paul Keeley. We are pleased to have new editors – Polly Brendon on exceptional case funding, Samantha Little on advocacy in family cases, Simon Mullings on housing and Hilton von Herbert and Daniel M Grütters on immigration. All experts in their fields.

We have endeavoured to give as complete an account of the legal aid scheme, as at 1 January 2020, as we can. Any errors or omissions are, of course, our responsibility. The Handbook's supporting website, www.legalaidhandbook.com, will continue to be used for updates, news alerts and other material of interest. Readers can sign up to receive updates and alerts and follow us on Twitter @legalaidhbk.

Comments and contributions are always welcome. We want the Handbook to be both practical and relevant. Readers can contact us at admin@legalaidhandbook.com or via Legal Action Group at lag@lag.org.uk

Vicky Ling, Sue James and Carol Storer
January 2020

Contributors

Vicky Ling is a Chartered Quality Professional and management consultant. Vicky worked for the Legal Aid Board in the early 1990s at the inception of 'franchising', has experience of managing organisations with legal aid contracts and has written and lectured extensively on legal aid practice management.

Vicky is a founder member of the Law Consultancy Network, an international team of highly experienced law firm management consultants and is an associate at Infolegal, providing compliance and practice advice. She has advised hundreds of firms of solicitors and not-for-profit organisations on all aspects of legal aid contracts and quality standards.

Sue James is director and solicitor at Hammersmith and Fulham Law Centre and a specialist in housing law. In 2017 she won the Legal Aid Lawyer of the Year Outstanding Achievement Award. She is a founding trustee at Ealing Law Centre which opened in 2013 and has worked in law centres for most of her career. She is a member of the campaigning group Justice Alliance and is a regular speaker on legal aid and access to justice. Sue also writes a regular column for *Legal Action* and writes regular articles for other journals.

Carol Storer OBE is interim director of Legal Action Group. Carol worked as a solicitor for many years, working in a law centre, local authority, private practice and Shelter before becoming director of Legal Aid Practitioners Group where she worked for ten years.

Carol served as a commissioner on the Bach Commission which produced 'The Right to Justice' report in September 2017. Carol chairs The Law Society's Access to Justice Committee and is a trustee of Coram Children's Legal Centre.

Polly Brendon is a solicitor specialising in public law and human rights. Since January 2020 she has been head of the legal advice and welfare team at the charity Freedom from Torture. Prior to this Polly worked at Public Law Project (PLP) where she led the organisation's work on access to legal aid. She has been instructed in several judicial review challenges to the legal aid scheme, particularly in relation to the cuts introduced under the Legal Aid, Sentencing and Punishment of Offenders Act 2012 (LASPO). These cases include *Ben Hoare Bell and others v The Lord Chancellor, IS v Director of Legal Aid Casework and The Lord Chancellor* and *The Law Centres Federation v The Lord Chancellor*.

Richard Charlton is a solicitor and specialist in mental health and mental capacity law. He was selected as the first Legal Aid Lawyer of the Year Awards (LALYs) mental health lawyer of the year and was for 15 years chair then president of the Mental Health Lawyers Association. He has also been a senior peer reviewer in mental health for the Ministry of Justice. Currently he is a director at Richard Charlton Solicitors and is an assessor for the Law Society's Mental Health Tribunal and Mental Capacity (Welfate) Panels.

Anthony Edwards was a criminal law solicitor at TV Edwards LLP until his retirement in October 2019. He had been a higher courts advocate and duty solicitor. He remains a visiting professor at Queen Mary, University of London. Anthony writes widely on criminal law. He is on the editorial board of *Blackstones' Criminal Practice*, author of *Advising a Suspect in the Police Station* (Sweet & Maxwell), *Criminal Defence: Good Practice in the Criminal Courts* (Law Society), *Criminal Costs: legal aid costs in the criminal courts* (LAG, 2nd edn, 2019) and *Magistrates Court Handbook* and contributing author to *Blackstone's Criminal Practice* and *Handbook of Youths in the Criminal Courts* (all OUP).

Daniel M Grütters is a pupil barrister at One Pump Court working on immigration, housing and public law matters. Before moving to the Bar, Daniel was an international law adviser at the British Red Cross, where he provided strategic expert advice on public international law, with a focus on international humanitarian law. His work at the British Red Cross also covered refugee and human rights law, as well as compliance with counter-terrorism measures. Daniel is a trustee of English for Action London, a charity that provides ESOL courses (English for Speakers of Other Languages) for adult migrants in communities across London.

Hilton von Herbert is an IAAS accredited supervisor and senior immigration caseworker. His experience in legal aid immigration practice exceed twenty years. For a period of ten years, he was also a trainer in immigration, asylum and nationality law for Citizens Advice throughout the Cambridge and Hertfordshire region. In 2013, Hilton was named immigration lawyer of the year at the LALYs. 2014 saw his appointment as an independent funding adjudicator followed by his appointment as an independent costs assessor. He is currently the immigration supervisor at Ealing Law Centre.

Steve Hynes is a freelance writer and researcher. He was director of Legal Action Group (LAG) from 2007–2019. Steve has written extensively and appeared in the broadcast media commenting on legal aid and access to justice issues. He is author of *Austerity Justice* (LAG, 2012) and co-author, with Jon Robins, of *The Justice Gap* (LAG, 2009). Prior to joining LAG, Steve was director of the Law Centres Federation.

Paul Keeley is a solicitor at South West London Law Centres, a community-based charity that helps local people access justice and uphold their rights. Paul specialises in immigration and asylum. He was appointed as an independent funding adjudicator and independent costs assessor for the Ministry of Justice in 2016, and again in 2019. In that role Paul adjudicates on appeals by legal aid providers against decisions of the Legal Aid Agency. In May 2018 Paul was appointed as an independent peer reviewer, also for the Ministry of Justice, a role in which he assesses the quality of legal advice of immigration legal aid providers.

Samantha Little is a specialist in children law and has been in practice for 25 years. She is a partner in the children and education law team at Russell-Cooke LLP. She advises and represents children, guardians and family members in all areas of children law including public law/care; private law; adoption including international adoption; surrogacy including international surrogacy. She has extensive knowledge and experience of legal aid provision. She is a long-standing member of Resolution's legal aid committee and has engaged on Resolution's behalf with a number of consultations with the Legal Aid Agency and Minitry of Justice about legal aid issues. Samantha is a member of the Law Society's Children Panel (since 1998), and is a Resolution accredited specialist in public law, private law and adoption. She also has her Higher Courts (Civil Advocacy)

Qualification. Samantha provides training for Resolution and has co- presented the annual legal aid update at the ALC conference for some years.

Simon Mullings is a caseworker specialising in housing law at Edwards Duthie Shamash. His work includes homelessness challenges, possession proceedings including extensive court duty desk experience, unlawful eviction, and housing related public law and Equality Act cases. He has served as a trustee at Newham Rights Centre (sadly now defunct), Waltham Forest Citizens Advice and Ealing Law Centre where he was amongst the founders. He speaks on housing law and access to justice issues, is a member of the campaigning group Justice Alliance and writes occasionally for *Legal Action* and other journals.

Silvia Nicolaou Garcia is an associate solicitor at Simpson Millar LLP, where she specialises in public law, human rights and community care cases. She joined Simpson Millar in August 2015 and has a particular interest in assisting trafficked individuals, unaccompanied minors and vulnerable adults. Silvia qualified as a solicitor in September 2013, after completing her training contract at Leigh Day. She then worked at Deighton Pierce Glynn for two years, where she worked on cases concerning age disputed minors in detention, public and private law challenges on behalf of trafficked individuals and on cases against UK corporations in relation to human rights abuses committed in Colombia. Silvia is a regular contributor to *Legal Action*. In 2018 Silvia was shortlisted for the Legal Aid Lawyer of the Year Awards in the children's rights category. In 2018 she was the recipient of the ECPAT UK Children's Champion award.

Jane Pritchard is the founder of Elawvate. Throughout Jane's career as a legal aid lawyer, starting in 1997, Jane developed innovative solutions to deliver digital legal services in the legal aid market. She trained in crime before developing a specialist practice in housing law. She is passionate about paperless practice and enhancing work methods for both case management and client communications. Having left private practice in 2018, Jane's goal is to facilitate a digital revolution, from client inception to billing, keeping legal aid providers in business. Bridging the gap between lawyer and IT systems architect, Jane has an invaluable insight into life at the coal face of legal aid. Jane joined InfoTrack's executive team in 2019, delivering digital law solutions to over 1500 law firms.

Paul Seddon is a regulated costs lawyer and owner of Seddon Costs Law with a wide range of clients including private law firms and law centres. Paul has worked in legal services for 20 years, practising costs law for over 15 years. He spent many years working in-house at law firms in London where he trained as a law costs draftsman before qualifying as a costs lawyer. Paul was chair of the Association of Costs Lawyers legal aid group for five years until 2018, representing the group on the LAA's Civil Contract consultative group, and is still a committee member and member of the LAA's Care Case Fee Scheme focus group. He authors and delivers training to solicitors, barristers and fellow costs professionals on key aspects of procedure and case-law and drafted the Bar Council's guidance *Claiming enhancements for civil (non-family) legal aid work.*

Contents

Table of cases

Table of statutes

Table of statutory instruments

Table of European and international legislation

EU Regulations

EU Directives

Abbreviations

AAF	Advocates Attendance Form
ABH	actual bodily harm
ABP	advocates' bundle payment
ADR	alternative dispute resolution
AGFS	Advocates' Graduated Fee Scheme
AIT	Asylum and Immigration Tribunal
APIL	Association of Personal Injury Lawyers
APPG	All Party Parliamentary Group
ASBCPA	Anti-Social Behaviour, Crime and Policing Act 2014
ASU	Asylum Screening Unit
ATE	after the event
ATP	Agency Transformation Programme
AVMA	Action against Medical Accidents
BACS	Bankers' Automated Clearing Service
BC	Borough Council
CAFCASS	Children and Family Court Advisory and Support Service
CAPA	claims against public authorities
CBA	Criminal Bar Association
CBAM	Criminal Bills Assessment Manual
CBP	court bundle payment
CCA	contract compliance audit
CCFS	Care Case Fee Scheme
CCG	clinical commissioning group
CCLF	Crown Court Litigator Fee
CCMS	Client and Cost Management System
CCRC	Criminal Cases Review Commission
CCU	Complex Crime Unit; or Criminal Cases Unit
CDS	Criminal Defence Service
CFA	Conditional Fee Agreement
CILEx	Chartered Legal Executive
CJSM	Criminal Justice Secure Mail
CLA	Civil Legal Advice
CLAC	Community Legal Advice Centre
CLAN	Community Legal Advice Network
CLAS	Criminal Litigation Accreditation Scheme
CLR	Controlled Legal Representation

CLS	Community Legal Service
CMRF	Consolidated Matter Report Form
CMRH	case management review hearing
CMS	case management system
CPGFS	Care Proceedings Graduated Fees Scheme
CPR	Civil Procedure Rules
CPS	Crown Prosecution Service
CWA	Contracted Work and Administration
DAR	designated accredited representative
DBS	Disclosure and Barring Service
DDVC	Destitution Domestic Violence Concession
DFT	detention fast track
DPA	Data Protection Act 2018
DSCC	Defence Solicitor Call Centre
DWP	Department for Work and Pensions
ECCT	Exceptional and Complex Case Team
ECF	exceptional case funding
ECHR	European Convention for the Protection of Human Rights and Fundamental Freedoms
EEA	European Economic Area
EPA	Environmental Protection Act 1990
ESA	employment and support allowance
EU	European Union
FAQs	frequently asked questions
FAS	Family Advocacy Scheme
FDR	Financial Dispute Resolution
FGFS	Family Graduated Fees Scheme
FGM	female genital mutilation
FLBA	Family Law Bar Association
FOH	Flexible Operating Hours
FOIA	Freedom of Information Act 2000
FTE	full-time equivalent
FTT	First-tier Tribunal
GBH	grievous bodily harm
GDPR	General Data Protection Regulation
GF	graduated fee
GFS	Graduated Fee Scheme
H(FHH)A	Homes (Fitness for Human Habitation) Act 2018
HMCTS	Her Majesty's Courts and Tribunals Service
HMRC	Her Majesty's Revenue and Customs
HPCDS	Housing Possession Court Duty Scheme
HR	hourly rates
IAAS	Immigration and Asylum Accreditation Scheme
IAC	Immigration and Asylum Chamber
IALS	Institute of Advanced Legal Studies
ICA	Independent Costs Assessor
ICC	individual case contract
IFA	Independent Funding Adjudicator
ILR	indefinite leave to remain

IPCC	Independent Police Complaints Commission
IRC	immigration removal centre
KPI	key performance indicator
LAA	Legal Aid Agency
LAB	Legal Aid Board
LAPG	Legal Aid Practitioners Group
LASPO	Legal Aid, Sentencing and Punishment of Offenders Act 2012
LAT	Legal Aid Transformation
LBC	London Borough Council
LCN	Law Centres Network
LGFS	Litigators' Graduated Fee Scheme
LIP	litigant in person
LSC	Legal Services Commission
MHLA	Mental Health Lawyers Association
MHRT	Mental Health Review Tribunal
MHT	Mental Health Tribunal
MI	management information
MIAM	Mediation Information and Assessment Meeting
MoJ	Ministry of Justice
MOU	memorandum of understanding
MPA	multi-party action
NAM	non-asylum matter
NAO	National Audit Office
NASS	National Asylum Support Service
NCVD	National Centre for Domestic Violence
NfP	not-for-profit
NIAA	Nationality, Immigration and Asylum Act 2002
NRM	National Referral Mechanism
OFS	open financial statement
OISC	Office of the Immigration Services Commissioner
PACE	Police and Criminal Evidence Act 1984
PAR	Performance Activity Report
PAS	Prisoners' Advice Service
PD	Practice Direction
PDS	Public Defender Service
PFLRS	Private Family Law Representation Scheme
PIP	personal independence payments
PMS	practice management system
POA	payment on account
POCA	Proceeds of Crime Act 2002
PoD	Point of Dispute
POP	point of principle
PRFD	Principal Registry of the Family Division
PSED	public sector equality duty
PSPO	public spaces protection order
PTE	part-time equivalent
PTPH	pre-trial preparation hearing
QASA	Quality Assurance Scheme for Advocates

QC	Queen's Counsel
QM	Quality Mark
RDCO	Recovery of Defence Costs Order
RSS	really simple syndication
SAAC	Self-Assessment Audit Checklist
SCA	Single Competent Authority
SCCO	Senior Court Costs Office
SCU	Special Cases Unit
SEN	special educational needs
SGO	special guardianship orders
SIAC	Special Immigration Appeals Commission
SMOD	subject matter of the dispute
SMP	standard monthly payment
SQM	Specialist Quality Mark
SRA	Solicitors Regulation Authority
SWL	social welfare law
SWPI	significant wider public interest
TLS	The Law Society
TPIM	Terrorism Prevention and Investigation Measure
UASC	unaccompanied asylum-seeking child
UFN	unique file number
UKVI	UK Visas and Immigration
UT	Upper Tribunal
VHCC	Very High Cost Case
VMP	variable monthly payment
YLAL	Young Legal Aid Lawyers
YOI	Young Offender Institution

Glossary

Advice and Assistance	Funding for advice short of representation in criminal cases, granted by the provider under contract with the LAA.
CCMS	Client and Cost Management System – online portal to submit applications, amendments and claims to the LAA for civil and family licensed work.
CMRF	This used to be an actual paper form (controlled matter report form) used to submit monthly claims for civil and family controlled work and crime lower claims to the Legal Services Commission. The forms have been replaced with the CWA portal; but the expression 'CMRF code' remains in use to describe the codes which are still used. www.gov.uk/government/publications/consolidated-matter-report-forms-civil-codes
Community Legal Service	Holistic provision of civil legal advice and representation under the Access to Justice Act 1999. Concept and branding abolished under LASPO.
Contract Compliance Audit	An audit assessing whether, based on a sample of files, an organisation is complying with the requirements of civil or criminal contracts.
Contract Manager	Official of the LAA with responsibility for managing the contractual relationship between the two parties.
Contract Manager Visit	See Financial Stewardship audit.
Controlled Legal Representation	Representation before the Mental Health Review Tribunal, or in the Immigration Appellate Authority, granted by the provider under contract with the LAA.
Contract Liaison Manager	A member of the organisation's staff designated as the person responsible for quality and contract compliance and the main point of contact for the LAA. This role was previously known as the Quality Representative or Franchise Representative.

Controlled Work Administration (CWA)	Online portal used to submit monthly claims for civil and family controlled work and crime lower. Also used by the LAA for eg execution of contract documentation.
Corrective Action	Action agreed with an LAA auditor to rectify a breach of a QM or contract requirement.
Criminal Defence Service	Provision of Criminal defence advice and representation funded under the Access to Justice Act 1999. Concept and branding abolished under LASPO.
Delegated Function	Delegated function (e.g. to grant emergency representation in civil and family matters) by the LAA's Director of Casework to practitioners. See Devolved Power.
Devolved Power	A power (eg to grant a Representation Certificate) that could be exercised on the LSC's behalf by the provider in certain defined circumstances.
	Known as a 'delegated function' under LASPO.
Escape fee case	Case which would normally be paid by way of fixed fee; but which escapes because the time and item value exceeds a set ratio (the exact ratios differ depending on the scheme).
Exceptional and Complex Cases Unit	Department of the LAA, dealing with individual case contracts in high cost civil cases.
Exceptional case	Previous name under the Access to Justice Act 1999 for an escape fee case. See also below.
Exceptional case funding	Case which would normally be outside the scope of LASPO, but is eligible for funding under Section 10, because failure to do so would breach the client's human rights (or would be likely to do so).
Financial Stewardship audit	Type of audit conducted by a Contract Manager on a provider's premises, focussing on financial issues. Also referred to as 'Contract Manager Visit' from 2011.
Franchise Representative	See Contract Liaison Manager.
Funding Code	The criteria by which the LAA decided whether to grant all levels of civil funding under the Access to Justice Act 1999. Preserved only for cases existing as at 31 March 2013.
Help at Court	An adjunct to Legal Help, which allows representation at particular hearings in defined cases
Individual Case Contract	A separate contract between the LAA and a provider on a particular case, usually because of high costs.

Inter partes costs	The legal costs incurred by a party that another party is ordered or agrees to pay. If the amount to pay cannot be agreed then the costs are assessed by the court, either by way of summary assessment or detailed assessment. Rates higher than legal aid rates can be claimed.
Legal Aid	Legal advice and representation funded by the central government through the LAA and the Courts.
Legal Help	Advice short of representation, granted by the provider under contract with the LAA.
Licensed Work	Civil representation certificates – funding granted by the LAA or under delegated functions by providers.
Matter Start	Also known as a 'new matter start' or NMS, a Matter start is a case started under Legal Help, Help with Mediation or Controlled Legal Representation and Family Help Lower (Public Law) where there has been no previous Legal Help.
McKenzie Adviser	A person who is present at a hearing to advise and assist, but not represent, a party.
Miscellaneous work	Work which falls within LASPO Sch 1 but does not fall within one of the defined categories of work. The work included is listed in the 2018 contract category definitions. All contract schedules include at least five matter starts which can be used for this work, and more can be requested.
Operational Assurance	Department of the LAA, which carries out data analysis and audits to support Contract Managers. Previously known as Provider Assurance.
Prior Authority	A certificate that the LAA considers a disbursement to be reasonable, and therefore that the costs will be paid at the end of the case. May also allow a payment on account.
Peer review	An assessment of the quality of legal work carried out by independent lawyers working under contract with the LAA.
Pro bono	Free legal advice and/or representation.
Procurement area	Geographical area covered by a contract with the LAA, often based on a top tier local authority area; but increasingly on larger geographical areas.
Provider	Term used by the LAA to describe any type of organisation with which it has a contract to deliver services.

Public Defender Service	Solicitors employed by the LAA to do criminal work, in competition with private practice. Four offices in England and Wales.
Quality Concern	A failure to meet a requirement of a Quality Mark. Critical Concerns are more serious than General Concerns. The organisation will be required to put corrective action in place, or in particularly serious cases, will be at risk of SQM termination.
Quality Mark	An accreditation scheme regulating conduct and quality of legal services. Providers of legal services must hold a Specialist Quality Mark (awarded by the LAA) or Lexcel (awarded by the Law Society) in order to be eligible to hold a contract. Compliance may be audited by the LAA or their authorised contractor, Recognising Excellence (from April 2017).
Quality Representative	See Contract Liaison Manager.
Regional Office	Historically, an office of the LAA dealing with all funding and local policy matters within its region. Following restructuring, Regional offices act as a base for staff and may have some processing functions.
Representation Certificate	Funding for representation in civil and family cases, granted by the LAA or in emergencies by the provider.
Representation Order	Funding for representation in criminal cases, granted by the Courts.
Schedule payment limit	The total amount payable to an organisation under a contract.
Special Cases Unit	Former name. See Exceptional and Complex Cases Unit.
Specialist Quality Mark	See Quality Mark.
Standard monthly payment	The monthly payment to an organisation under contract – usually one twelfth of the schedule payment limit (subject to variation during the year). See also variable monthly payment.
Statutory Charge	A charge held by the LAA over property recovered or preserved in funded civil proceedings, intended to allow the LAA to recover the costs of funding the case.
Transaction Criteria	An audit tool, consisting of checklists used to assess whether a file contained required information from the early days of 'franchising'. Superseded by peer review.

Variable monthly payment
An alternative to the standard monthly payment to an organisation under contract, paid to the value of claims submitted.

Very High Cost Cases Panel
A panel of organisations accredited by the LAA to conduct VHCC crime cases. Only accredited organisations may do these cases.

Legal aid advice and litigation

Read this before you start!

continued

Introduction

1.1 This chapter's title is probably a counsel of perfection and will be an unfulfilled aspiration for most caseworkers! However, the point we are trying to make is that there are lots of rules and guidance about how you should do legal aid work; you need to be aware of what they are and consult them where necessary. This is particularly important following the serious cuts in the scope of legal aid from April 2013, which has left it very tightly defined.

1.2 If you don't ensure you are aware of the statutes, regulations, rules and guidance, you may have applications or bills delayed or rejected by the Legal Aid Agency (LAA) for technical errors (and there is a contract key performance indicator[1] (KPI) that limits rejects to five per cent as part of the schedule), or refused because you have not explained your client's case in an appropriate way, or you may have claims for payment disallowed. All these things are important because they may cause your client unnecessary delay, waste your time, and could even threaten the financial viability of your organisation. If you are not sure what to do, look it up and discuss the issue with your supervisor or a colleague.

How legal aid works

1.3 Legal aid is funding, by the state, of individual cases for individual members of the public. It is primarily delivered by lawyers[2] contracted to a government body, the LAA (an agency of the Ministry of Justice). Chapter 2 below gives a brief account of the historical development of the modern legal aid scheme. This section looks at the underlying principles necessary to understand how the scheme works in practice.

1.4 Under the current scheme, the government has decided that it is prepared to fund certain types of legal problem. Broadly speaking, these are:

- advice to and representation of people subject to a police investigation;

---

1 2018 Standard Civil Contract Specification para 2.67.
2 For these purposes, we define lawyers broadly as including not just solicitors, barristers and legal executives and their staff, but also non-qualified advisers working in not-for-profit advice agencies.

- advice to and representation of people being prosecuted in the criminal courts, though generally not for very minor offences;
- advice to and representation of people seeking to appeal criminal convictions;
- advice to and representation of prisoners in respect of their detention;
- advice to people with certain limited types of civil and family legal problems;
- representation of claimants and defendants/respondents in certain types of civil and family cases in courts and some tribunals.

1.5   The LAA only directly pays lawyers or the organisations that employ them. However, those payments will cover both the professional charges of the lawyers involved (usually called profit costs) and expenses they incur in running the case – both out of pocket expenses and the services of other professionals such as expert witnesses (usually called disbursements). Lawyers are paid on the basis of either an hourly rate, a fixed fee per case, or a combination of the two, depending on the type of case.

1.6   The first level of separation within the legal aid scheme is between civil and criminal cases.

1.7   Criminal cases are those involving police investigations;[3] criminal prosecutions and appeals; and the treatment of prisoners. Funding covers:

- advice to those subject to police investigation, including representation at the police station and in interviews under caution;
- representation in court during investigations for things like bail and police applications for extensions of detention time;
- the provision of duty solicitors to advise and represent people at court without their own solicitor – but only for one hearing, not the whole case;
- representation in criminal proceedings and appeals, including:
  - advice on the law and evidence;
  - investigation of defences and interviewing witnesses;
  - commissioning expert witness evidence;
  - advocacy in the court;
- advice and representation to prisoners on matters relating to detention and release

1.8   The main types of funding available in criminal cases are:

---

3   Including investigations by other agencies with similar powers – see chapter 15.

- Advice and assistance – funding for a solicitor and his or her staff or agents to give general advice about criminal matters, including in situations where other types of funding are not available.
- Police station attendance – funding for a solicitor and his or her staff or agents to attend a police station to advise and represent someone who is the subject of a police investigation.
- Advocacy assistance – funding, generally for a solicitor rather than a barrister, to represent someone in court for something other than a prosecution – for example, a police bail application – or in prison disciplinary hearings.
- Representation orders – funding for a solicitor to prepare a defence case where someone is being prosecuted for an offence (or is appealing a conviction), and funding for an advocate (barrister or solicitor) to present the case in court.

1.9 Almost all legal aid funding – civil and criminal – is only available if the applicant for legal aid can show that he or she passes two tests: the means test and the merits test. The means test says that legal aid will only be available to people whose income and capital are below prescribed levels. The merits test in criminal cases says that legal aid will only be available where it is justified, often by the seriousness of the offence and any sentence that might follow. The merits test in civil cases says that legal aid will only be available where it is justified either by the importance of the case or by the chances of it being successful.

1.10 There are exceptions where either the means test, merits test or both do not apply. These cases are generally only what are perceived to be the most important ones – mainly police station representation in crime, mental health detention and taking children into care in civil.

1.11 As well as the means and merits tests, civil cases must pass a scope test. This limits the sorts of civil cases legal aid will fund not by the characteristics of the applicant, but the characteristics of their case. Legal aid is only available if the case is one of those specifically listed in Schedule 1 to the Legal Aid, Sentencing and Punishment of Offenders Act 2012 (LASPO) (see chapter 3 and appendix A for the full list).

1.12 In civil cases, most claims about money are not funded, but cases involving loss of the home, abuses by the state, human rights, detention and liberty and freedom from persecution generally are. For a full discussion of what is and is not funded, see chapter 3 and the subject-specific chapters.

1.13   Cases that are outside the scope of legal aid can still sometimes be funded. Chapter 4 describes the exceptional funding scheme – a discretionary scheme where legal aid may be made available, on a case-by-case basis, in situations where it is generally outside the scope of the scheme.

1.14   If a case is in scope, and qualifies on means and merits (where applicable), there are two main types of funding available:

- Legal Help – this covers general advice on cases which are not (or are not yet) in court, either because proceedings have not started, or because help is needed to apply for funding to cover proceedings. This type of funding does not cover representation in court (except in very limited cases where one-off hearings can be done under an extension of Legal Help called Help at Court).

- Legal Representation – this is only available once court proceedings have been issued (though it is also available to claimants to fund the issuing of proceedings). It allows a solicitor to give advice, prepare the case, commission expert evidence and instruct an advocate, and allows an advocate (either solicitor or barrister) to present the case in court. This type of work is sometimes called certificate or certificated work because the grant of legal aid is signified by the issuing of a legal aid certificate.

1.15   There are some extra types of funding available in certain family cases, immigration cases and mental health – see chapters 7, 10 and 11.

1.16   For both civil and criminal work, the LAA contracts with organisations (mostly solicitors firms and not-for-profit advice agencies but also a few who are regulated by the BSB and OISC) to provide legal aid to the public. The contracts allow organisations to take on cases and be paid for them.

1.17   The contracts provide for fixed or variable monthly payments to be made to the organisation. These payments cover lower value casework. The monthly payments are set off against individual case fees, with the idea that the two balance out over time. Crown Court representation and Legal Representation are paid separately to the monthly contract payments.

1.18   Barristers who do legal aid work are not paid under a contract with the LAA. In the magistrates' court, they are usually paid by solicitors out of their contract payment. In the Crown Court and civil courts, they are paid direct by the LAA on a case-by-case basis.

The LAA Manual

1.19 The LAA Manual was withdrawn from 31 August 2015.[4] The LAA's view is that all necessary guidance is available on their website.

1.20 In this book, wherever possible, we tell you where you can download a document from the LAA's website. We have given website addresses to help you locate what you need, although these are subject to change. Many of the documents are also linked to our website at: www.legalaidhandbook.com/laspo-resources, and we will keep links updated there.

Keeping up to date

1.21 Legal aid can change quickly, as the LAA changes its approach to issues and as challenges to the various cuts are played out in the courts. Everyone involved with legal aid funding needs to keep up with the latest developments. The LAA relies on you to check what is on its website. So – what's the best way of keeping up to date?

1.22 You can sign up to the LAA's email newsletter, which will provide you with updates, announcements and changes. The updates give you a brief summary of the issue, and a link to further information. They make keeping up much easier. You can subscribe through the LAA website at: www.gov.uk. However, if you are really interested in keeping up to date, you cannot beat checking the website, and even particular pages, on a weekly basis, as the LAA does not always alert people to changes.

1.23 The legal aid website is part of the gov.uk network and so follows the standard gov.uk layout and contents structure. This means that it can be hard to find what you need and the search function is often a good place to start, though only if you know the name of the document or page you need.

1.24 Our website has a resources page at: www.legalaidhandbook. com/laspo-resources, which contains links to the various regulations, contracts and most of the guidance documents on the LAA site, so that can be a good place to start if you don't know the location of the item you are looking for.

---

4 www.gov.uk/government/news/civilcrime-news-providers-no-longer-need-to-buy-legal-aid-manual/.

1.25   It is also well worth bookmarking the key pages within the LAA site – such as the forms, contracts and billing pages – so that they are easy to return to.

1.26   One useful feature of the LAA site[5] is the 'latest' section on the front page, which is automatically updated whenever any document or page on the LAA site is added or amended. The 'see all' link contains an RSS feed which can be added to a feed reader to alert you to any changes or newly published material on the LAA site. Our Twitter account (@legalaidhbk) is set automatically to tweet any new news items or content, so following it is another way of staying up to date.

1.27   There is also a public information website on legal aid: www.gov. uk/legal-aid. Other useful public information sites are Advicenow: www.advicenow.org.uk and Adviceguide from Citizens Advice: www. adviceguide.org.uk.

Civil and family – key documentation

The Standard Contract 2018

1.28   Most civil legal aid providers operate under the LAA's Standard Civil Contract 2018 (the main exception is the telephone Civil Legal Advice (CLA) service, for which there is a separate contract).

1.29   The contract contains many detailed provisions concerning the way you work with clients, as well as setting out the formal relationship between your organisation and the LAA. You can download the contract from the LAA website at: www.gov.uk/topic/legal-aid-for-providers/contracts.

1.30   Part A of this book sets out where you can find the main provisions in relation to casework; see Part C: 'Managing legal aid work' for more information on the contractual relationship with the LAA.

The Standard Contract Specification

1.31   The section of the contract that you will need to be familiar with is the Standard Civil Contract Specification. The specification can be downloaded from the webpage noted above. It is split into general rules and category-specific rules; where the two conflict, the category-

---

5 www.gov.uk/government/organisations/legal-aid-agency.

specific rules take precedence.[6] The Specification rules are discussed in detail in chapters 3–14 of this book.

1.32   The Specification contains an introduction to the main workings of the various funding schemes. Section 1 contains general provisions; for example, it explains how to apply regulations and guidance, what is in your contract schedule and rules concerning additional matter starts. Section 2 gives information about service standards, where work can or must be done, supervisor standards, and, crucially, KPIs. Section 3 explains the scope of controlled work and rules applying to it. Section 4 explains how controlled work is paid for. Sections 5 and 6 discuss the scope and main rules applying to licensed work, payment arrangements and the statutory charge (although rates of payment are shown in the Civil Legal Aid (Remuneration) Regulations 2013 and the various regulations amending them – see: www.legalaidhandbook.com/laspo-resources for all the regulations).

1.33   The remaining sections are category-specific, and each specification has its own sections depending on which contract it is part of. Each category-specific section begins with supervisor standards, and then moves on to any additional rules that apply to that category:

- Section 7 – family
- Section 8 – immigration
- Section 9 – mental health
- Section 10 – housing and debt
- Section 11 – community care
- Section 12 – welfare benefits
- Section 13 – claims against public authorities[7]
- Section 14 – public law
- Section 15 – clinical negligence

1.34   There is also a separate Family Mediation Specification and a Housing Possession Court Duty Scheme (HPCDS) Specification.

Guidance

1.35   The LAA has created a series of training modules which cover aspects of legal aid – both scope and how the scheme operates. You do have to be careful with them as they are generally not updated if a scheme is changed; but they are very useful when schemes are new.

---

6 See Standard Contract 2018 Specification para 1.2.
7 The category formerly known as actions against the police etc.

They can be accessed on the LAA website.[8] The LAA also provided some answers to frequently asked questions and guidance in respect of the scope of family, immigration, social welfare law and mental health schemes when the LASPO scheme first came in. They are useful because they deal with a number of queries that arise in day-to-day practice and may well provide the answer to the particular question you have. Unfortunately, they are no longer available on the LAA website, but a copy can be found on our website.[9]

1.36   The Lord Chancellor and the Director of Legal Aid Casework have issued a series of guidance documents using their LASPO statutory powers, including:

- *Lord Chancellor's Guidance on Civil Legal Aid*;
- *Lord Chancellor's Guidance on Exceptional Case Funding* (there are two, one for inquest cases and one for other cases); and
- *Director's Guidance on Evidence Requirements for Private Family Law Matters.*

There is a series of guides and manuals covering general subjects such as financial eligibility and costs assessment, as well as category specific matters like family mediation and housing court duty schemes.[10] There is also guidance for crime practitioners such as *Crown Court Fee Guidance* and the *Criminal Bills Assessment Manual*.

1.37   Links to all guidance documents, as well as other guides and manuals, can be found at: www.legalaidhandbook.com/laspo-resources.

Eligibility guidance

1.38   The legal aid website: www.gov.uk/civil-legal-aid-means-testing has links to guidance materials and the financial eligibility calculator. See chapter 3 of this book for more information about eligibility.

Regulations and guidance

1.39   The regulations create a set of rules that govern whether an individual's case can be funded under legal aid. The key regulations are the Civil Legal Aid (Merits Criteria) Regulations 2013, the Civil Legal Aid (Procedure) Regulations 2012, the Civil Legal Aid (Remuneration)

---

8   http://legalaidtraining.justice.gov.uk.
9   http://legalaidhandbook.files.wordpress.com/2013/04/legal-aid-reform-faq-v3.pdf.
10 www.gov.uk/guidance/funding-and-costs-assessment-for-civil-and-crime-matters/.

Regulations 2013 and the Civil Legal Aid (Financial Resources and Payment for Services) Regulations 2013. Many of these regulations have been amended, and so you should always check the amendment regulations as well as the original ones, as the LAA does not issue updated regulations incorporating the amendments and nor does www.legislation.gov.uk. This is in our view most unfortunate and makes understanding what is already a complex scheme unnecessarily difficult.

1.40   In addition, the LAA has issued the *Lord Chancellor's Guidance on Civil Legal Aid* on the way the regulations should operate. It is a key reference document, whether you are granting legal aid yourself, as controlled work, or under delegated functions (previously known as devolved powers), or whether you are submitting an application for the LAA to decide.

1.41   Links to the regulations and guidance can be found at: www.legalaidhandbook.com/laspo-resources.

Costs assessment guidance

1.42   Many caseworkers focus so hard on achieving the best possible job for their clients that they lose sight of the financial side of the case. This is not sustainable, so it is important to be aware of the rules that govern what you can and cannot claim for.

1.43   The LAA has guidance on claiming, which can be downloaded from:www.gov.uk/funding-and-costs-assessment-for-civil-and-crime-matters. See chapters 16 and 17 of this book for more information about getting paid. There is also a summary of the costs assessment guidance at appendix C.

Fee exemption and remission

1.44   The fee exemption and remission scheme is administered by HM Courts and Tribunals Service (HMCTS) and is not part of legal aid funding. Court fees are a recoverable disbursement under a full legal aid representation certificate, but not under Legal Help or Controlled Legal Representation. Legally aided clients are not automatically exempt from fees, but may apply for exemption or remission on grounds of means where they are not a recoverable disbursement – primarily in Legal Help cases – and where the type of proceedings is covered by fee exemption.

1.45   There is an eligibility checker at: www.gov.uk/get-help-with-court-fees.

Criminal defence – key documentation

The 2017 Crime Contract

1.46   The 2017 Crime Contract came into effect on 1 April 2017. It covers both 'own client' and duty solicitor work. It can be downloaded from 2017: www.gov.uk/government/publications/standard-crime-contract-2017.

1.47   Part A of this book sets out where you can find the main provisions in relation to casework; see Part C: 'Managing legal aid work' for more information on the contractual relationship with the LAA.

The Crime Specification and regulations

1.48   The section of the contract that caseworkers will most need to be familiar with is the Specification. It can also be downloaded from: www.gov.uk/government/publications/standard-crime-contract-2017.

1.49   The Specification covers general rules, among other things: definitions, service standards, qualifying criteria, carrying out and claiming for work, as well as specific provisions for very high cost cases, prison law, appeals and associated civil work. It also provides information about claims assessment and review procedures (although this is not the main source document, see below).

1.50   The crime fees are set out in the Criminal Legal Aid (Remuneration) Regulations 2013 and subsequent amendments – see chapter 15. Other rules are set out in the Criminal Legal Aid (General) Regulations 2013 as well as subsequent amendments and other regulations. You should always check the amendment regulations as well as the original ones, as the LAA does not issue updated regulations incorporating the amendments and nor does www.legislation.gov.uk. This is in our view most unfortunate and makes understanding what is already a complex scheme unnecessarily difficult.

Eligibility guidance

1.51   Advice in the police station is not means tested.

1.52   Representation in the magistrates' court is means tested. There is an eligibility calculator on the legal aid website: www.gov.uk/criminal-legal-aid-means-testing. Clients who are not eligible for legal aid in the magistrates' court and pay for their defence privately can apply to reclaim their costs from Central Funds if they are subsequently acquitted.

1.53   Representation in the Crown Court is also means tested. If clients are found not guilty, their contributions will be repaid. Clients who are not eligible for legal aid in the Crown Court and pay for their defence privately can apply to reclaim their costs from Central Funds if they are subsequently acquitted. The rules and forms can be found at: www.gov.uk/claim-back-costs-from-cases-in-the-criminal-courts. In either case, any refund will be paid at legal aid rates – not the full private costs incurred.

Costs assessment guidance

1.54   Ensuring that you will be paid is as important in criminal defence work as in civil and family, mentioned above.

1.55   The Criminal Bills Assessment Manual (CBAM) elaborates many of the principles in the contract. It can be found at: www.gov.uk/ funding-and-costs-assessment-for-civil-and-crime-matters.

Client and Cost Management System

1.56   A detailed guide to the LAA's Client and Cost Management System (CCMS) is set out in chapter 6. This section provides an introduction for those unfamiliar with it. CCMS is the LAA's system for managing civil cases and dealing with providers.

1.57   CCMS became mandatory for all new civil and family certificate work from April 2016 (February 2016 for Special Children Act cases). The LAA is in the process of replacing the user interface aspect of CCMS with a new digital service called 'Apply'. Details of this are set out in chapter 6.

Training and support

1.58   The LAA has guides to setting up the system and training modules for many common functions: http://ccmstraining.justice.gov.uk/ Getting-Started.

Case management roles

1.59   Users need to be allocated case management roles. The key roles are 'Case management' and 'Case Management Supervisor'. Case management allows for cases to be viewed and amendments and applications to be prepared. Only Case Management Supervisors, who must be 'authorised litigators' (ie solicitors, barristers or Chartered Legal Executives authorised to conduct litigation by their regulatory body), can submit applications, amendments and outcome codes. It is essential that staff are allocated the correct role (and not given privileges which would not be compliant with their job role).

Billing roles

1.60   There are two billing roles: 'Bill Preparation' and 'Bill Supervisor'. 'Bill Preparation' allows bills to be drafted but not submitted. Supporting documents can be submitted as 'Bill Preparation'. A Bill Supervisor must be sufficiently qualified to sign bills. External costs draftsmen can be authorised to prepare but not submit bills.

Office manager

1.61   This role has an overview of all cases, notifications and actions within an organisation, but does not allow the user to create or submit applications or bills.

Making applications and supervision

1.62   CCMS has been created in such a way that the questions asked are dependent on answers to other questions and so the electronic screens do not mirror the paper forms which they replaced.

1.63   CCMS has a significant impact on supervision. A printed summary of an application can be given to the supervisor (authorised litigator) but they must then:

- log in;
- navigate to the correct case; and
- submit the case.

1.64   All communication on a case is done through secure online message boards. This means that supervisors need to be proactive to monitor the way cases are developing. As there is no direct way to pass on an action in the system, good communication is essential. Supervisors will not automatically receive details of the notifications and actions sent to a fee earner. However a 'Case Management Supervisor' can review them by going to 'Your actions/notifications', 'Refine search'.

1.65   It helps to ensure that the LAA reference number (currently a 12-figure number starting with a three) is always clear on a file and in any communication. This ensures that the case can be easily accessed on CCMS.

1.66 The best process for making submissions and other tasks will depend on the supervisor, support staff and fee earner. A number of practitioners report that it can be more effective and efficient if support staff carry out as much work as possible on CCMS before work is checked and submitted by an appropriately qualified fee-earner.

1.67 The majority of the information submitted on CCMS is not then accessible in the same format again. To ensure that it is clear on the file when work was done, it is essential that contemporaneous records are kept on the organisation's own electronic system or paper file. Sometimes the easiest way to do this will be to take a screenshot. For example, when an application is made, the confirmation screen can be captured with the time and date visible.

1.68 One benefit of CCMS is that there is a direct link to the Department for Work and Pensions (DWP), so that when a client is in receipt of a passporting benefit, this can be confirmed automatically. If there is a problem in obtaining electronic confirmation, paper documentation can be uploaded.

Declarations

1.69 Although no paper is sent to the LAA when using CCMS, there is at least one piece of paper that must be held on file – a signed declaration. This declaration is generated by the system only after the application is completed as a draft and it must be signed and retained on the file before submission. This requires a device which can connect to the internet plus access to a printer. If this is not possible, a promissory declaration can be used. It is vital that there is always a signed declaration on the file which can be audited by the LAA. It is never submitted to the LAA, but without it the file is not validated for payment.

Notifications

1.70 Notifications are a key part of the design of CCMS. The system is designed to save LAA caseworkers' time by processing many case management steps through a 'rules engine' incorporated in the software. This means that certain notifications are (or should be) produced automatically. Other types of notification need the consideration of an LAA caseworker.

1.71   For example, when you submit a substantive application, the system will generate a list of evidence requirements which are sent to you. This happens before an LAA caseworker has seen the application. This type of notification is referred to below as an automatic notification. Automatic notifications should never take more than an hour and, if the system is functioning correctly, should arrive in less than 15 minutes.

1.72   CCMS sends one email each day informing you that you have a notification; otherwise all communication to users in firms is through notifications which are accessed through the CCMS portal itself. It is vital that solicitors and caseworkers check, open and deal with their notifications promptly.

Expiry dates

1.73   Emergency certificates will be revoked or nullified if the substantive application is not submitted within five days.

1.74   Unlike paper applications, draft applications, bills and amendments which have not been 'submitted' all automatically delete themselves from CCMS after 28 days (42 days for bills which are to be assessed by the court). This can undo valuable work. To avoid this, access the un-submitted form within this time limit to 'restart the clock'. If someone is going on holiday, they need to ensure the 28 days will not expire when they are away.

Assigning counsel

1.75   All advocates who undertake any work on a case must be assigned to the case on CCMS. The easiest way to assign counsel is to use their LAA reference number. The cost limit assigned to advocates limits the total costs they can claim under a certificate. Advocates still need to submit a bill for the work undertaken, which is reviewed by a caseworker and assessed in the traditional way. An advocate cannot submit a claim for work done until they have been assigned to the case.

Payments on account

1.76   Payments on account (POAs) can be submitted for case costs and for disbursements. You enter 100 per cent of the profit costs incurred to date and then the system calculates 75 per cent of the costs. Once a

POA has been submitted, it will generate a notification allowing supporting documents to be uploaded.

1.77 Some cases, such as high cost case contracts, allow payments on account of 100 per cent of costs as each case stage is reached. CCMS automatically pays 75 per cent of profit costs; to avoid this, these claims should be submitted using the non-expert disbursement claim function rather than the profit costs function, with a full explanation of the costs entitlement included in the narrative section.

Trouble-shooting

1.78 When technical errors occur, it is essential that the LAA's technical team are notified at: online-support@justice.gov.uk. They should be provided with:

- a screenshot of the problem;
- context in relation to what has happened, ie what stage of the application you were at or what was clicked on;
- where necessary, the impact of the potential problem so that it can be triaged and prioritised efficiently; and
- LAA caseworkers may also need to be informed if it affects the handling of the case.

1.79 If you are unable to access CCMS due to a technical issue and you need an urgent decision (needed within 48 hours) on an application or amendment, you can submit a paper application. The LAA will expect you to speak to a member of their Online Support Team before doing so and obtain a contingency reference number – without which the LAA will not consider the application outside CCMS. Contingency cover sheets can be obtained from the Online Support Team if they agree that you can use the process.[11] See chapter 6 for full details.

Logos

1.80 The former Community Legal Service and Criminal Defence Service logos were withdrawn in 2013 and organisations are no longer permitted to use them, but you can use the strapline 'Contracted with the Legal Aid Agency'. If you do not have a contract but do hold

---

11 See the contingency process guide at: http://ccmstraining.justice.gov.uk/__ data/assets/pdf_file/0015/8025/CCMS-Contingency-Process_v1_0.pdf/.

the Specialist Quality Mark (SQM), you can use the descriptor 'Specialist Quality Mark Holder'.[12]

This handbook

1.81   We will keep the *Legal Aid Handbook 2020/21* updated via its supporting website www.legalaidhandbook.com where you can subscribe to receive email alerts of changes to the scheme and other news and developments. You can also follow us on Twitter: @ legalaidhbk for news and updates. Our Twitter feed also automatically tweets all announcements, additions and amendments to the LAA website.

---

12 Specialist Quality Mark Guidance A2.2.

The legal aid framework

Introduction

2.1   This chapter briefly sets out how the legal aid scheme was developed, and how the new scheme was arrived at. It also sets out the legislative framework that underpins legal aid. For more detailed information on the history of legal aid and on the passage of the Legal Aid, Sentencing and Punishment of Offenders Act 2012 (LASPO), see the LAG publications *Austerity Justice* and *The Justice Gap*.[1] For a shorter summary, see Sir Henry Brooke's history written for the Bach Commission.[2]

The development of exclusivity

2.2   From its inception as a relatively widely available state-funded public service in 1948 up to the mid-1990s, the culture of legal aid was that any solicitor who wanted to do so could do legal aid work. Many high street firms offered small amounts of legal aid work, perhaps for divorce or personal injury, alongside their conveyancing and will-writing work.

2.3   As legal aid expanded in the 1960s and 1970s, both in scope and budget, specialist legal aid firms, and legal aid departments in larger firms, came into being. At the same time, the Law Centres movement was growing, and other agencies and voluntary sector groups expanded the provision of advice services.

2.4   By the early 1990s, government policy was changing. Legal aid had moved from being administered by the Law Society to a specialist quasi-governmental body, the Legal Aid Board (LAB). Alongside that, the not-for-profit sector was becoming more significant and taking up a larger share of the overall budget. The LAB wanted to encourage the move to specialisation and introduced a franchise system. The purpose of franchising was to develop a network of specialists accredited as being experts in their type of law, and to ensure that public money was only spent on those who were providing a service of sufficient quality.

2.5   However, the LAB did not have the tools to measure legal quality or competency. It did develop the franchise standard, which was a

---

1   Steve Hynes, *Austerity Justice*, Legal Action Group, 2012; Jon Robins and Steve Hynes, *The Justice Gap: whatever happened to legal aid*, Legal Action Group, 2009.
2   www.fabians.org.uk/wp-content/uploads/2017/09/Bach-Commission-Appendix-6-F-1.pdf.

series of criteria concerned with the management and running of a firm, but not with an assessment of the quality of the work done. Firms that applied for a franchise had to demonstrate that they met the standard, and in return were allowed to describe themselves as franchised and charge a slightly higher hourly rate for the work that they did. However, the franchise system was voluntary, and many firms simply did not apply, and in any event, it offered little insight into the quality of work done.

2.6   Meanwhile, despite periodic attempts to restrict it, expenditure on legal aid was increasing steadily. By the late 1990s, the new Labour government took the view that radical reform was needed and adopted the recommendations of a report commissioned by the previous government and carried out by Sir Peter Middleton.

2.7   The result was a complete overhaul of the system. The LAB was abolished and replaced by the Legal Services Commission (LSC), and the entire legislative basis of legal aid was re-written.

2.8   The basis of the revised scheme was the Access to Justice Act 1999. The Act created the LSC and, within it, two separate funds – the Community Legal Service (CLS) fund for civil work and the Criminal Defence Service (CDS) for crime. Both funds were administered by the LSC, and in practice there was one single legal aid budget with no ring-fencing of either fund (though many called for them to be separated, as criminal and family expenditure took an ever larger share).

2.9   The Access to Justice Act 1999 empowered the LSC to commission and procure legal aid services in such a way as to ensure that they were available to those who needed services in almost any way the LSC considered most appropriate. In practice, the LSC chose to fund services by exclusive contract, and that model continues into the post-LASPO scheme.

2.10   The franchise standard was replaced by the Specialist Quality Mark (SQM) and made compulsory. Legal aid came to be funded by contract – without a contract you could not do legal aid work – and having the SQM or Lexcel is mandatory for being awarded a contract. See chapter 22 for details on the contract award process.

2.11   Therefore, since 2000 (for civil) and 2001 (for crime), legal aid work has been the exclusive preserve of organisations the LSC, subsequently the Legal Aid Agency (LAA), has contracted with to procure services.

2.12   Over the years since the mid-1990s, budgetary control was achieved by holding down eligibility levels and payment rates. The proportion of the population eligible for legal aid steadily shrank, and hourly rates stagnated; the lack of inflationary rises meant an effective cut of around 40 per cent by the time of the LASPO cuts.

The road to LASPO

2.13   When the government changed in 2010, it was the outcome of an election held against the backdrop of a global economic crisis. A coalition of Conservative and Liberal Democrat ministers took power on the basis that the appropriate response to the crisis, and to public expenditure deficits and government debt at home, was a programme of cuts and austerity which would impact on almost all government departments. The Ministry of Justice, by now also including prisons and probation within its remit, was no exception and was required to find savings of about £2 billion annually from its budget. It was decided that the legal aid scheme would have to be cut by about £350 million.

2.14   A consultation paper was issued, to which over 5,000 (overwhelmingly negative) responses were received, proposing drastic cuts focussed primarily on civil and family legal aid. Fees would be cut, the LSC abolished and whole areas of law removed from scope.

2.15   The result of the consultation was very little movement in government policy, and the Legal Aid, Sentencing and Punishment of Offenders Bill (soon to be universally known as LASPO) was published in June 2011. For the full detail of the content of the bill and the government's policy proposals at the time, see: www.legalaid-handbook.com/2011/07/05/legal-aid-reform-overview.

2.16   The passage of the bill was marked by campaigning and lobbying across the legal aid sector and well beyond (a leading voice being the Women's Institute, for example), together with vigorous debate particularly in the House of Lords, which met with almost total government intransigence. Some concessions were made, but LASPO was passed largely intact despite the government losing a record number of votes in the Lords.

Legal Aid, Sentencing and Punishment of Offenders Act 2012

2.17   LASPO repealed the Access to Justice Act 1999, insofar as it dealt with legal aid, and established an entirely new statutory regime. Cases *started before* 1 April 2013 continue to be subject to the Access to Justice Act 1999 regime, and cases *started from* 1 April 2013 are subject to LASPO. Cases under the LASPO regime are covered in this book. Cases started under the Access to Justice Act 1999 are dealt with in a previous edition of this work.[3]

2.18   LASPO is in many parts and covers several aspects of justice policy. The key parts for legal aid are Part 1 (which contains the enabling powers for the new scheme) and Schedule 1 (which sets out what civil work is in scope). Much of the detail of the operation of the scheme is found in regulations made under LASPO, and in contracts entered into using its statutory powers.

2.19   The Act required the Lord Chancellor to make legal aid available in certain categories of case, defines what those cases are, created the LAA (and abolished the LSC) to administer legal aid and empowers the passing of regulations to govern the detail of the scheme.

2.20   In practice, the abolition of the LSC and its replacement with the LAA did not make much difference. Constitutionally, there is a difference since the LSC was an arm's-length body and the LAA is an agency of the Ministry of Justice. This means that the staff are civil servants and the chief executive is more directly accountable to ministers. There was some concern during the passage of the Act that this risked potential political interference in LAA decision-making in respect of individual cases. There are safeguards in the Act which seem to have been largely effective in practice, at least at the level of individual funding decisions.

2.21   However, concerns have been raised about certain contract decisions involving politically contentious firms. Leading commentator Roger Smith has described the LAA as a 'constitutional monstrosity'[4] and pointed out that the safeguards in LASPO relate to decisions on cases – not decisions on contracting or treatment of solicitors.

2.22   Most practitioners carrying out their day-to-day work have not, in the main, seen significant change in the structures surrounding how their work is handled. There are still caseworkers to assess applications for legal aid (though most applications are now made and administered electronically, they are still individually assessed by LAA staff), auditors to conduct audits, and contract managers to manage contracts, though some practitioners report that staff dealing

---

3   *Legal Aid Handbook 2011/12* is available in electronic form from Legal Action Group.

4   www.lawgazette.co.uk/constitutional-monstrosity/5058524.article/.

with cases now tend to be less experienced in the cases they are looking at.

2.23   The Access to Justice Act 1999 created two separate funds for administering legal aid: the CLS and the CDS. Each had their own branding to be used by practitioners as well as the LSC. These were removed, so that now the LAA simply administers a single legal aid fund. There are no longer two separate funds, and there are no specific branding or logos for civil or criminal work. Some practitioners still display the CLS and CDS logos but this is strictly incorrect as these have been withdrawn. The LAA suggests they can state 'contracted with the Legal Aid Agency' instead.[5]

2.24   LASPO vests most of the decision-making powers in respect of legal aid in an official called the Director of Legal Aid Casework. At the date of publication, the Interim Chief Executive is Jane Harbottle. For practical purposes, her powers and responsibilities are delegated to LAA and Court Service staff who make decisions in respect of individual cases.

Life after LASPO

General effects and developments

2.25   The first full financial year after the implementation of LASPO saw a fall in civil expenditure of £150 million. However, that did not tell the whole story. The first year's figures show:[6]

- 50 per cent fewer Legal Help cases were started in the year after LASPO compared to the year before;
- 30 per cent fewer legal aid certificates issued.

In addition to the headline figures, category-based data showed that social welfare cases fell by 80 per cent, housing by 45 per cent, family by 60 per cent and mediation by 40 per cent. This means there were steep drops even in areas that stayed in scope. Even crime was not immune, showing year-on-year falls in both case numbers and expenditure. Most stark of all, the total number of civil providers had halved over five years – and the number of not-for-profit agencies doing legal aid work fell by 90 per cent overnight when LASPO came in.

---

5   See para 1.81 above.
6   For a more detailed discussion of the figures, see our article in the July/August 2014 issue of *Legal Action*.

2.26   The years since have shown a continuation of the trend. The first quarter of 2016 saw a further 13 per cent fall in Legal Help matter starts compared with the same period of 2015, though the number of certificates rose. Overall, Legal Help is now running at under one quarter of 2012/13, the year before LASPO, and about one-sixth of the number of cases in 2002/03. Certificates reduced to two-thirds the year after LASPO came into effect, 2013/14 (the number of applications falling from 191,138 to 117,573). After some minor fluctuations, the last three years have seen applications in the region of 117,000.

2.27   New cases in lower crime work fell from 1,203,906 in 2013/14 to 901,569 in 2018/19, a reduction of a quarter. Crown Court applications fell in that period from 125,013 to 84,223 and prison law reduced to 19,569 cases in 2018/19 from a high of 47,920 in 2009/10.

2.28   There were 1,239 fewer civil providers from 2012/13 to 2018/19 where the number of provider organisations is 2,939. The Legal Aid Agency Annual Report states that 1,578 organisations were awarded a contract under the 2018 Standard Civil Contract which took effect from 1 September 2018. It is important to note that sometimes offices are counted and sometimes organisations – one organisation can have more than one office.

2.29   In the last edition of the Handbook, we reported that there were eight per cent fewer crime providers in 2016 than in 2015. Except for a small increase in 2017/18, the decline continues into 2019.[7] There are 1,050 fewer practices carrying out crime in 2018/19 than in 2012/13.

2.30   Those practitioners who remained in the system reported greater difficulties in getting funding even when work remained in scope, through a combination of falling demand (perhaps because clients believed that all legal aid had been abolished) and ever tighter bureaucratic requirements – implemented by the LAA, some felt, in an arbitrary and heavy-handed way. A particularly contentious example was the introduction, and later mandatory use, of the LAA's online processing system for civil work, the Client and Cost Management System (CCMS). The system has been beset by delays, technical problems and periods when it has been unavailable altogether. Many practitioners report that submitting applications and bills through the system continues to be more difficult and time-consuming than the paper-based system it replaced. However, the system has

---

7 See LAA statistical bulletins at: www.gov.uk/government/statistics?departments%5B%5D=legal-aid-agency/.

become gradually more stable – and slightly more user-friendly – over time. For more on CCMS, see chapter 6.

2.31   Having steered LASPO through parliament, Ken Clarke was replaced as Lord Chancellor by Chris Grayling. Soon after taking office, in April 2013, Grayling announced[8] further cuts to both crime and civil work. He proposed removing a further £200 million from the crime budget through a combination of fee cuts and restructuring of the market. He also proposed further cuts to civil legal aid – this time aimed not at cutting expenditure but 'restoring public confidence'. The measures included restrictions on judicial review, the introduction of a residence test as a qualification for civil legal aid and removing funding from 'borderline' cases, as well as removing the bulk of prison law from scope. Fees in child care cases, and for all non-family civil barristers, as well as experts, were to be cut.

2.32   The subsequent two years saw the professions fight these further cuts, with varying degrees of success. The proposed fee cuts have all been implemented (with the exception of cuts to advocacy fees in the Crown Court, and the second tranche of cuts to solicitor fees in crime, though later changes to the Litigators' Graduated Fee Scheme (LGFS) and Advocates' Graduated Fee Scheme (AGFS) have been implemented).

2.33   However, the government dropped proposals for price competitive tendering and abolishing client choice in crime.[9] Following a series of court cases, the government also dropped a controversial new crime contract, instead implementing a transitional contract that essentially replicated the terms of the old one – but not before many firms had prepared for the new contracts and been through significant upheaval. A fully revised crime contract was issued, though not on a competitive basis, in 2017. Further changes to crime fees in the form of revisions to LGFS and AGFS came into force in 2018. Although the Ministry of Justice stated that they were intended to be cost-neutral, that was not accepted by the profession, which focussed on cuts to payment based on the volume of evidence served. The issue of disclosure has featured in the press. In December 2018 the Ministry of Justice announced a review of criminal legal aid fee

---

8   See: http://legalaidhandbook.com/2013/04/09/government-consults-on-further-legal-aid-cuts for a full list. of the original proposals; and https://legalaidhandbook.com/?s=what+the+government+now+propose for what emerged from consultation.

9   http://legalaidhandbook.com/2013/09/05/transforming-legal-aid-what-the-government-now-propose.

schemes with the final report to be published toward the end of Summer 2020.[10]

2.34   In civil, 'borderline' cases were removed from scope, but later restored as a by-product of litigation over the exceptional funding scheme (see below).

2.35   Since the 2015 general election, Chris Grayling was replaced as Lord Chancellor first by Michael Gove, then in quick succession Liz Truss and then David Lidington. Three separate Lord Chancellors in just over two years led to a lack of detailed reform, and most focussed on other aspects of the justice brief, notably prisons. Gove's main impact on legal aid was to cancel the 2015 crime tender process and postpone the second 8.75 per cent fee cut that would have come in alongside the new contracts. Gove's reforms, combined with litigation, saw an almost total reversal of Grayling's cuts to scope – but not Clarke's, and not a reversal of fee cuts. Following the snap general election in 2017, David Gauke was appointed Lord Chancellor in January 2018, and his tenure lasted until Boris Johnson became Prime Minister. Gauke stood down in July 2019 and was replaced by Robert Buckland.

2.36   The main impact of the rapid turnover of Lord Chancellors was the repeated delaying of the long-awaited full review of LASPO. The review was initially promised for between three and five years after implementation. This then moved to five years (ie by 1 April 2018), then summer 2018. The year-long review commenced in 2018 and was published on 7 February 2019.[11] At the same time, the Legal Support Action Plan[12] was published, which set out the priorities for government action.

2.37   The impact of LASPO on litigants and the courts has been considerable, with a sharp rise in litigants in person, especially in family cases. This has led to a series of expressions of judicial displeasure.[13] One senior judge, the President of the Family Division, Sir James Munby, even tried to create a shadow legal aid scheme by directing the Court Service to fund the representation of some litigants in

---

10 www.gov.uk/guidance/criminal-legal-aid-review.
11 www.gov.uk/government/publications/post-implementation-review-of-part-1-of-laspo.
12 www.gov.uk/government/publications/post-implementation-review-of-part-1-of-laspo.
13 See, for example, https://legalaidhandbook.com/?s=altar+of+public+debt and http://legalaidhandbook.com/2015/03/02/legal-aid-in-mental-health-cases; and more recently www.buzzfeed.com/emilydugan/the-government-tried-to-bury-this-research-showing-judges.

person,[14] but the Court of Appeal made very clear that there was no power to do so.[15] Munby P accepted that there is no such power, but at one point appeared to be contemplating requiring the local authority to fund representation of an otherwise unrepresented parent.[16] However, the higher courts have made clear that local authorities cannot be expected to make up deficiencies in the legal aid fund.[17]

2.38   A further consequence of the rise in litigants in person has been increased judicial and political concern at family cases where alleged perpetrators of domestic abuse have cross-examined their alleged victims in person. The government announced an urgent review of the problem in early 2017. Legislation in the form of the Courts Bill began making its way through parliament but fell because of the 2017 general election. Provisions in the Domestic Abuse Bill stalled in September 2019 with the attempted prorogation of parliament and were finally defeated by the 2019 general election.

2.39   There have been several major parliamentary reports critical of the implementation and effects of LASPO,[18] including by the influential Public Accounts Committee[19] (following on from a report by the National Audit Office[20]). The fight in the House of Lords against LASPO was led by the Labour peer and former justice minister Lord (Willy) Bach. Although no longer a frontbencher, and now an elected police and crime commissioner, he retains a keen interest in legal aid. He was appointed by the Labour leader Jeremy Corbyn to lead an expert commission,[21] which reported in 2017. The report has not yet been adopted as official Labour policy. Its recommendations included a statutory right to access to justice, as well as limited restoration of funding in some areas of civil legal aid, though it doesn't call for the wholesale repeal of the LASPO reforms. The full Bach report

14   *Q v Q; Re B; Re C* [2014] EWFC 31.

15   *Re K and H (children)* [2015] EWCA Civ 543.

16   *M (a child), Re* [2015] EWFC 71 para 12, citing *Re D (a child)* [2014] EWFC 39.

17   A recent example is *M (a child)* [2018] EWCA Civ 240.

18   *Impact of changes to civil legal aid under Part 1 of the Legal Aid, Sentencing and Punishment of Offenders Act 2012*, House of Commons Justice Committee, HC 311, March 2015; *The UK's compliance with the UN Convention on the Rights of the Child*, Human Rights Joint Committee, March 2015.

19   www.parliament.uk/business/committees/committees-a-z/commons-select/public-accounts-committee/news/report-implementing-reforms-to-civil-legal-aid/.

20   www.nao.org.uk/report/implementing-reforms-to-civil-legal-aid/.

21   Members included well-known legal aid lawyers and others, and the commission vice-chair was the late Sir Henry Brooke, a former Court of Appeal judge.

may be found at: https://fabians.org.uk/the-final-report-of-the-bach-commission/, and there is valuable related commentary on the blog of the late Sir Henry Brooke (who served as vice chair) at: https://sirhenrybrooke.me.

The LASPO litigation

2.40   The years since 2012 have seen a series of court cases challenging aspects of the cuts or their implementation.

2.41   A challenge to the reduction in the number of crime contracts lost in both the High Court and Court of Appeal[22] (though the reduction was eventually stopped by Michael Gove as Lord Chancellor), but cases involving civil legal aid have seen more mixed results.

2.42   The only case so far to make it all the way to the Supreme Court concerned the residence test. Originally proposed during Chris Grayling's tenure, the test would have restricted civil legal aid – with certain exceptions – to those who could show 12 months' continuous residence in the UK in the period immediately leading up to their application. The draft regulations implementing the test were laid before parliament but declared unlawful by the High Court.[23] The Court of Appeal[24] allowed the Lord Chancellor's appeal before a seven-justice Supreme Court[25] decided that the test was ultra vires the LASPO powers. A secondary argument, that it amounted to unlawful discrimination, was not considered.

2.43   In the field of family law, a main area of contention has been the domestic violence gateway to private family law funding (see chapter 7). A High Court challenge to the gateway was unsuccessful,[26] but the Court of Appeal found that a requirement that evidence of domestic abuse date from within the 24 months preceding the application, and a failure to cater for other forms of abuse, specifically financial abuse, were unlawful.[27] In response, the Lord Chancellor increased the time limit from two to five years and introduced a

22 *R (London Criminal Courts Solicitors' Association and others) v The Lord Chancellor* [2015] EWHC 295 (Admin); and *R (The Law Society, The London Criminal Courts Solicitors' Association and others) v The Lord Chancellor* [2015] EWCA Civ 230.

23 *R (Public Law Project) v Secretary of State for Justice* [2014] EWHC 2365 (Admin).

24 *Public Law Project v Lord Chancellor* [2015] EWCA Civ 1193.

25 *R (Public Law Project) v Lord Chancellor* [2016] UKSC 39.

26 *R (Rights of Women) v The Lord Chancellor and Secretary of State for Justice* [2015] EWHC 35 (Admin).

27 *R (Rights of Women) v The Lord Chancellor and Secretary of State for Justice* [2016] EWCA Civ 91.

discretion for the Director to accept evidence demonstrating financial abuse.[28] See Explanatory Memorandum.[29] From February 2017 onwards, the government periodically signalled its intention to remove the five-year limit, but only did so in January 2018. See chapter 7 for details of the revised arrangements.

2.44   Most of Chris Grayling's second round of cuts have also featured in litigation. Regulations making payment in judicial review cases conditional on permission being granted were struck down by the High Court,[30] but instead of appealing the Ministry of Justice re-introduced the regulations in a slightly altered form[31] – changed enough to deal with the grounds on which the court found the old regulations unlawful, but still making payment conditional on permission being granted or a roll-up hearing or oral renewal being heard, the defendant conceding, or on a residual discretion to allow payment. See para 15.55 onwards for more information.

2.45   However, a challenge to Grayling's removal of prison law from scope failed in the High Court. The Court of Appeal allowed the appeal in April 2017,[32] and in February 2018 the government brought into force new regulations partially restoring prison law legal aid. See chapter 14.

2.46   In June 2018 the High Court quashed[33] the LAA's tender for Housing Possession Court Duty Scheme (HPCDS). The Law Centres Network argued that the decision to reduce the number of contracts available by increasing the size of scheme areas to cover multiple courts was irrational and in breach of the public sector equality duty (PSED) under the Equality Act 2010. Andrews J was heavily critical of the LAA and Ministry of Justice's approach to decision-making, in particular the gathering of evidence. She found that a series of questionable assumptions had been made without data, and the position of the representative bodies misrepresented. Submissions to ministers were 'woefully inadequate' and necessary enquiries had not been carried out. As a result, the minister making the decision was misled and not properly briefed, and consequently

---

28   www.legislation.gov.uk/uksi/2017/1237/made.

29   www.legislation.gov.uk/uksi/2017/1237/pdfs/uksiem_20171237_en.pdf.

30   *R (Ben Hoare Bell Solicitors and others,) v The Lord Chancellor* [2015] EWHC 523 (Admin).

31   Civil Legal Aid (Remuneration) (Amendment) Regulations 2015 SI No 898.

32   *R (Howard League for Penal Reform and Another) v Lord Chancellor* [2017] EWCA Civ 244.

33   *R (Law Centres Federation Limited t/a Law Centres Network) v Lord Chancellor* [2018] EWHC 1588 (Admin).

reached a decision no minister, properly briefed and in possession of all the facts, could reasonably have reached.

2.47 Following that decision, those with HPCDS contracts were offered a one-year extension to September 2019 with the option to be extended for one more year. The contracts have now been extended to 30 September 2020.[34]

2.48 There have also been a series of challenges to the exceptional funding regime, which are covered in chapter 4.

Regulation of civil work

The statutory foundation

2.49 Civil legal aid, or strictly under the Act, 'civil legal services', is defined by LASPO as only that which is included in Schedule 1 to the Act. In contrast to the Access to Justice Act 1999, which provided that work was in scope unless specifically excluded by the Act, LASPO says that only work explicitly *included* in Schedule 1 is in scope.

2.50 LASPO s8 defines what civil legal aid is. It includes providing:

- advice as to how the law applies in particular circumstances;
- advice and assistance in relation to legal proceedings;
- other advice and assistance in relation to the prevention, settlement or other resolution of legal disputes;
- advice and assistance in relation to the enforcement of decisions in legal proceedings or other decisions by which disputes are resolved.

2.51 Advice and assistance includes both representation and mediation and other forms of dispute resolution.

2.52 LASPO s9 provides that only areas of law expressly listed in Schedule 1 are in scope and can be funded under legal aid. If work is not listed in Schedule 1, it will not be covered by legal aid and you will not be paid for doing it.

2.53 LASPO s10 makes provision for what are known as 'exceptional cases'. Where cases are not covered by the scope rules in Part 1 of Schedule 1 but certain conditions are satisfied, an application may be made to the Director to fund the case even though it is otherwise out of scope. See chapter 4 for more on exceptional cases. Note that these cases should not be confused with Legal Help cases where costs

---

34 www.gov.uk/government/news/legal-aid-agency-extends-housing-possession-court-duty-scheme-contracts.

exceed three times the fixed fee – such cases were previously known as 'exceptional cases' under the Access to Justice Act regime, but are now called 'escape fee' cases.

2.54   LASPO ss11 and 21 provide that legal aid will only be awarded if merits and financial criteria respectively are satisfied. Sections 25 and 26 create the statutory charge and give costs protection and section 27 enables the establishment of the mandatory telephone gateway. As part of the Legal Support Action Plan, the Ministry of Justice committed to closing the Civil Legal Advice (CLA) mandatory telephone gateway in the Education, Discrimination and Debt categories by spring 2020. The LAA hold a tender process for a mixture of specialist telephone and face-to-face CLA services.

2.55   It is under these sections that the relevant regulations are made.

The regulations

2.56   Regulations set out the detail of the scheme. Key regulations are:

- Civil Legal Aid (Procedure) Regulations 2012;
- Civil Legal Aid (Merits Criteria) Regulations 2013;
- Civil Legal Aid (Financial Resources and Payment for Services) Regulations 2013;
- Civil Legal Aid (Costs) Regulations 2013;
- Civil Legal Aid (Remuneration) Regulations 2013;
- Civil Legal Aid (Statutory Charge) Regulations 2013;
- Civil Legal Aid (Procedure) (Amendment) Regulations 2019.

All of the regulations have been amended. A full list of regulations, together with amendments, can be found at: www.legalaidhandbook. com/laspo-resources listed on a single page for easy retrieval. Each has a brief description as some regulation titles are more intuitive than others, and amendment regulations are listed with the regulations they amend to facilitate cross-referencing.

2.57   Regulations deal with the terms on which funding can be granted. They set out the detail of the various means and merits tests to be applied, how costs are dealt with through the statutory charge and costs protection, and not least with the rate you are paid for doing the work.

2.58   The Funding Code made under the Access to Justice Act 1999 was abolished and not replaced. Most of the equivalent provisions are now in the Merits and Procedure Regulations and the Funding Code Guidance has been replaced by the Lord Chancellor's Guidance.[35]

35 See: www.gov.uk/guidance/funding-and-costs-assessment-for-civil-and-crime-matters.

The Procedure Regulations define the various levels of funding, and set out the form of the application, together with appeal procedures against refusal. They also define the terms on which the telephone gateway operates. See chapter 3 for more on the telephone gateway.

The civil contract

2.59 The Standard Civil Contract 2018 governs the relationship between the LAA and organisations holding contracts. The LAA calls such organisations 'providers'. The contract sets out your duties and responsibilities, together with any powers delegated to you. It also governs some of the detail of the operation of individual cases building on what is in the regulations. Unless you have a contract, you will not be permitted to carry out legal aid work.

2.60 The contract consists of three main sections:

- The standard terms govern the relationship between the organisation and the LAA and Lord Chancellor and your obligations as an organisation. See chapter 22.
- The schedule sets out the types of work you are permitted to do, and in the case of Legal Help, Help with Family Mediation and Controlled Legal Representation (CLR), the maximum numbers of matters you are allowed to start per year. It will also specify any additional requirements (such as presence requirements) and will include any commitments you made as part of your tender for the contract (against the selection criteria, for example). Breach of any provision of your schedule, including any commitment you made in your tender, is a breach of contract subject to sanction in the usual way (see chapter 22).
- The specification deals with how you should conduct individual cases, and is dealt with in subsequent chapters.

2.61 Other documents which are referred to in the contract, and which you should follow or take account of (though not technically part of the contract) include:

- Specialist Quality Mark (SQM) or Lexcel (your chosen quality standard);
- Equality and Diversity Guidance;
- Category Definitions (see appendix B below);
- Standard Monthly Payment (SMP) Reconciliation Protocol (see appendix E);
- Independent Peer Review Process;

- Key Performance Indicator (KPI) Outcome Codes;
- Data Security Requirements.

All of these documents are available on the LAA website: www.gov.uk/legal-aid-for-providers/contracts – follow the link to your particular contract.

Regulation of criminal work

The statutory foundation

2.62   The scope of criminal work is defined by LASPO as advice to individuals arrested and held in custody (section 14), involved in investigations which may lead to criminal proceedings, before a court or tribunal in criminal proceedings, or who have been the subject of criminal proceedings (section 16). See chapter 15.

2.63   LASPO s14 defines criminal proceedings as:

- proceedings before a court for an individual accused of an offence;
- proceedings before a court for dealing with an individual convicted of an offence, including proceedings in respect of a sentence or order;
- proceedings or dealing with an individual under the Extradition Act 2003;
- bind-overs;
- appeals under Criminal Appeal Act 1968 s44A (appeal in case of death of appellant);
- references under Criminal Justice Act 1972 s36;
- contempt;
- such other proceedings as may be prescribed.

2.64   Under Criminal Legal Aid (General) Regulations 2013 reg 9,[36] the following have been prescribed as criminal:

(a) civil proceedings in a magistrates' court arising from a failure to pay a sum due or to obey an order of that court where such failure carries the risk of imprisonment;

(b) proceedings under sections 14B, 14D, 14G, 14H, 21B and 21D of the Football Spectators Act 1989 in relation to banning orders and references to a court;

(c) proceedings under section 5A of the Protection from Harassment Act 1997 in relation to restraining orders on acquittal;

---

36 As amended by the Criminal Legal Aid (General) (Amendment) Regulations 2015 and the Civil and Criminal Legal Aid (Amendment) Regulations 2015.

(d), (e) [Revoked.]

(f) proceedings in relation to parenting orders made under section 8(1)(b) of the Crime and Disorder Act 1998 where an order under section 22 of the Anti-social Behaviour, Crime and Policing Act 2014 or a sexual harm prevention order under section 103A of the Sexual Offences Act 2003 is made;

(g) proceedings under section 8(1)(c) of the Crime and Disorder Act 1998 in relation to parenting orders made on the conviction of a child;

(h) proceedings under section 9(5) of the Crime and Disorder Act 1998 to discharge or vary a parenting order made as set out in sub-paragraph (f) or (g);

(i) proceedings under section 10 of the Crime and Disorder Act 1998 in relation to an appeal against a parenting order made as set out in sub-paragraph (f) or (g);

(j) proceedings under Part 1A of Schedule 1 to the Powers of Criminal Courts (Sentencing) Act 2000 in relation to parenting orders for failure to comply with orders under section 20 of that Act;

(ja) proceedings, in a youth court, in relation to a breach or potential breach of a provision in an injunction under Part 1 of the Anti-social Behaviour, Crime and Policing Act 2014 where the person subject to the injunction is under 14.

(k) proceedings under sections 80, 82, 83 and 84 of the Anti-social Behaviour, Crime and Policing Act 2014 in relation to closure orders made under section 80(5)(a) of that Act where a person has engaged in, or is likely to engage in behaviour that constitutes a criminal offence on the premises;

(ka) proceedings under paragraph 3 of Schedule 2 to the Female Genital Mutilation Act 2003 in relation to female genital mutilation protection orders made other than on conviction and related appeals;

(kb) proceedings under paragraph 6 of Schedule 2 to the Female Genital Mutilation Act 2003 in relation to female genital mutilation protection orders made under paragraph 3 of that Schedule;

(l) proceedings under sections 20, 22, 26 and 28 of the Anti-social Behaviour Act 2003 in relation to parenting orders–
(i) in cases of exclusion from school; or
(ii) in respect of criminal conduct and anti-social behaviour;

(m) proceedings under sections 97, 100 and 101 of the Sexual Offences Act 2003 in relation to notification orders and interim notification orders;

(n) proceedings under sections 103A, 103E, 103F and 103H of the Sexual Offences Act 2003 in relation to sexual harm prevention order;

(o) [Revoked.]

(p) proceedings under sections 122A, 122D, 122E and 122G of the Sexual Offences Act 2003 in relation to sexual risk orders;

(q) [Revoked.]

(r) proceedings under section 13 of the Tribunals, Courts and Enforcement Act 2007 on appeal against a decision of the Upper Tribunal in proceedings in respect of–

   (i) a decision of the Financial Conduct Authority;

   (ia) a decision of the Prudential Regulation Authority;

   (ii) a decision of the Bank of England; or

   (iii) a decision of a person in relation to the assessment of any compensation or consideration under the Banking (Special Provisions) Act 2008 or the Banking Act 2009;

(s) proceedings before the Crown Court or the Court of Appeal in relation to serious crime prevention orders under sections 19, 20, 21 and 24 of the Serious Crime Act 2007;

(t) proceedings under sections 100, 101, 103, 104 and 106 of the Criminal Justice and Immigration Act 2008 in relation to violent offender orders and interim violent offender orders;

(u) proceedings under sections 26, 27 and 29 of the Crime and Security Act 2010 in relation to–

   (i) domestic violence protection notices; or

   (ii) domestic violence protection orders;

(ua)   proceedings under sections 14(1)(b) and (c), 15 and 20 to 22 of the Modern Slavery Act 2015 in relation to slavery and trafficking prevention orders;

(ub)   proceedings under sections 23 and 27 to 29 of the Modern Slavery Act 2015 in relation to slavery and trafficking risk orders,

(uc)   proceedings under Part 2 of the Offensive Weapons Act 2019 in relation to a knife crime prevention order or an interim knife crime prevention order;[37]

(ud)   proceedings under sections 1, 4, 5 and 7 of the Stalking Protecting Act 2019 in relation to stalking protection orders and interim stalking protection orders; and

(v) any other proceedings that involve the determination of a criminal charge for the purposes of Article 6(1) of the European Convention on Human Rights.

Sub-paragraph (v) includes contempt other than in the face of the court in the High Court (*King's Lynn and West Norfolk BC v Bunning*[38]) and county court (*Brown v Haringey LBC*[39]).

2.65   LASPO s19 says that determinations about grants of legal aid in criminal proceedings are made by the court. Section 18 says that all

---

37 Inserted by the Offensive Weapons Act 2019. In force from a date to be appointed. See also para 15.71 below.

38 [2013] EWHC 3390 (QB).

39 [2015] EWCA Civ 483.

other determinations are made by the Director, though the contract delegates some of these decisions to you.

2.66   LASPO s17 says that, in determining whether an individual qualifies for legal aid for criminal proceedings, account must be taken of their financial resources and of the interests of justice test. Section 27 gives a right for clients to select a representative of their choice, but that right may be limited and qualified by regulation. This empowers the LAA to, for example, restrict criminal legal aid to those who hold contracts, or provide that certain offences may only receive telephone advice at the police station.

The regulations

2.67   Regulations set out the detail of the scheme. Key ones are:

- Criminal Legal Aid (General) Regulations 2013;
- Criminal Legal Aid (Remuneration) Regulations 2013.

Both have been amended and links to the regulations and subsequent amendments may be found at: www.legalaidhandbook.com/laspo-resources.

The criminal contract

2.68   From April 2017, crime providers operate under the Standard Crime Contract 2017. It is in three main parts:

- The standard terms govern the management of the firm and its relationship with the LAA, and is dealt with in chapter 18.
- The schedule sets out the monthly payment the LAA will make and the types of work the organisation can carry out (also see chapter 20).
- The Specification sets out the rules on conduct of and payment for individual cases, and is dealt with in chapters 14, 16 and 19.

2.69   Other documents which are referred to in the contract, and which you should follow or take account of (though not technically part of the contract) include:

- Specialist Quality Mark (SQM) or Lexcel (your chosen quality standard);
- Equality and Diversity Guidance and Policy;
- Category Definitions;
- Guidance on Category Definitions;
- Monthly Payment Protocol;

- Independent Peer Review Process (the peer review process can be downloaded from: www.gov.uk/guidance/legal-aid-agency-audits#peer-review/);
- Data Security Requirements and Data Security Guidance.

The majority of these documents are available on the LAA for providers section of the gov.uk website (see eg: www.gov.uk/topic/legal-aid-for-providers), but you may need to search for them using your normal search engine and using the exact title of the document.

CHAPTER 3

Taking on civil and family cases

Introduction

3.1   When a client approaches you with a legal problem, there are a number of considerations to bear in mind in deciding whether you can take the case. These include:

- Is the case within the scope of the legal aid scheme?
- Must the client go through the telephone gateway? (To be removed in Spring 2020.)
- Is it covered by your contract?
- If you need to provide advice rather than going straight to court proceedings, do you have sufficient matter starts to be able to take it?
- Is the client financially eligible?
- Does the client's case pass the merits test?
- Is there any other reason why you cannot take it?

Only if the case passes all these tests can it be taken on.

3.2   Note that if you have a case that started pre-1 April 2013, it continues under the provisions of the Access to Justice Act 1999 – see the 2011/12 edition of this Handbook for the operation of the Access to Justice Act scheme.[1]

3.3   In this chapter we will refer to the provisions of the 2018 Standard Civil Contract, as that is now the one that will govern most civil cases.

Scope of the scheme

3.4   Unless Legal Aid, Sentencing and Punishment of Offenders Act 2012 (LASPO) Sch 1 explicitly puts an issue in scope, it is out of scope.[2] See appendix A for the text of Schedule 1.

3.5   Schedule 1 is not easy to understand and requires a certain amount of cross-referencing and double or even triple negatives to be navigated to understand whether a case is in fact in or out of scope. The Schedule is in four parts: Part 1 lists types of proceedings which are in scope but is subject to Part 2 (which excludes certain types of action) and Part 3 (which excludes certain courts and tribunals), as well as the definitions in Part 4. So in order to see whether a case is in scope, you need to check that it is included by Part 1 but not

---

1   *Legal Aid Handbook 2011/12* is available in electronic form from LAG.

2   Previously, legal aid was an inclusionary scheme; unless Schedule 2 to the Access to Justice Act 1999 explicitly put an issue out of scope, it was in scope.

excluded by Part 2, and that your venue is included in Part 3 if you wish to provide advocacy.

3.6   The exclusions in Part 2 of Schedule 1 are:

- personal injury or death;
- negligence;
- assault, battery or false imprisonment;
- trespass to goods or land;
- damage to property;
- defamation etc;
- breach of statutory duty;
- conveyancing;
- making wills;
- trust law;
- a claim for damages for breach of human rights under Human Rights Act 1998 s7;
- company and partnership law;
- matters arising out of a business;
- welfare benefits and social security matters below Upper Tribunal level;
- criminal injuries compensation;
- change of name.

3.7   The Part 2 exclusions always override the Part 1 inclusions unless specifically disapplied. For example, in housing cases, LASPO Sch 1 Part 1 para 33 says that services in relation to loss of a home are in scope, subject to the exclusions in Part 2 but then para 15 of Part 2 says services in relation to benefit matters are out of scope. The result of this is that you can advise and represent in respect of possession proceedings but cannot make representations about housing benefit, universal credit or submit a benefits appeal even where benefit problems are the cause of the arrears underlying the proceedings (see chapter 12 for more information about dealing with housing cases under LASPO).

3.8   Or again, Part 1 para 19 says that services in relation to judicial review are in scope, subject to the exclusions in Part 2. Part 2 para 15 excludes any matter related to welfare benefits but para 19(2)(a) of Part 1 disapplies that exclusion. Therefore, notwithstanding the general exclusion of welfare benefits work, judicial review of welfare benefit decisions is in scope. This allows public law challenges, to the law generally and to the exercise of discretion by benefits authorities but does not allow advice or representation on routine appeals to the Social Entitlement Chamber of the First-tier Tribunal.

3.9   For the purposes of awarding contracts (see more below) the Legal Aid Agency (LAA) divides the work up into categories. The category definitions documents[3] give a reasonable guide to work which is in scope, but for the detail, particularly in borderline or unclear cases or where the Part 2 exclusions may apply (for example, in the case of benefit work within arrears cases, as above), it is always best to refer back to the Act itself. The category definitions can be found on the LAA website.[4]

3.10   The following table gives a summary of the areas of law in scope in each category.

---

3 See appendix B for the 2018 category definitions.
4 https://assets.publishing.service.gov.uk/government/uploads/system/uploads/attachment_data/file/738528/2018_Standard_Civil_Contract_Category_Definitions__August_2018_.pdf.

Category	Type of work	Comments
Claims against public authorities	Where the defendant is a public authority with the power to detain, imprison or prosecute: • abuse of a child or vulnerable adult • abuse of position or power by a public authority where the alleged abuse was deliberate or dishonest and resulted in foreseeable harm • significant breach of human rights • advice to victims of sexual offences Allegations of deliberate abuse of a person in the care of a public authority or institution Exceptional funding in claims against a public authority with the power to detain, imprison or prosecute Exceptional funding on: • applications for compensation following wrongful conviction • applications for criminal injuries compensation • claims for damages for professional negligence in bringing a claim in this category	In each of these causes of action, the LASPO Sch 1 Part 2 exclusions around personal injury and death, negligence, assault, etc are disapplied. See *Director of Legal Aid Casework v R (Sunita Sisangia)* [2016] EWCA Civ 24 for the proper interpretation of LASPO Sch 1 Part 1 para 21(4) (deliberate or dishonest abuse of position or power by a public authority) – something more than an intentional tort is necessary to amount to 'deliberate or dishonest' but whether that threshold is reached in the individual case will be fact specific.
Clinical negligence	Neurological injury to infants causing severe disablement and which happened in the womb, during birth or up to eight weeks after birth Exceptional funding on any matter claiming damages or making a complaint to a professional body alleging breach of duty in the course of clinical or medical services, or claiming damages for professional negligence in the making of such a claim	

Category	Type of work	Comments
Community care	The provision of community care services and of facilities for disabled persons	LASPO Sch 1 Part 1 paras 6 and 7 contain an exhaustive list of statutes and statutory provisions that are in scope; if it is not on the list, it is not in. Para 6(n) was added to include Part 1 of the Care Act 2014.
Debt	Mortgage arrears and possession Orders for sale of the home Involuntary bankruptcy where the home is included in the estate Exceptional funding on any matter relating to proceedings for the payment of monies due or enforcement of orders made in such proceedings Exceptional funding for matters arising out of personal insolvency	At the time of writing, debt is a mandatory gateway category. However, the mandatory gateway will end spring 2020 so check the *Legal Aid Handbook* website – www.legalaidhandbook. com – for further information.
Discrimination	Contravention of the Equality Act 2010 or a previous discrimination statute (a prescribed list is given at LASPO Sch 1 Pt 1 para 43(3), including (but not limited to) cases alleging discrimination before the employment tribunal	This category is not limited to employment cases and includes any matter where discrimination can be pleaded. If it overlaps with another category – for example, alleging discrimination in the provision of community care, housing or education services – work can be done in each category. From 1 September 2019 discrimination became a face to face contract (and was no longer a mandatory gateway category). Transitional provisions are in place until the mandatory element of the gateway is removed in Spring 2020. Check the *Legal Aid Handbook* website www.legalaidhandbook. com for further information.

Education	Special educational needs Discrimination in education provision	All other education work is out of scope. From 1 September 2019 education became a face to face contract (and was no longer a mandatory gateway category). Transitional provisions are in place until the mandatory element of the gateway is removed in Spring 2020. Check the *Legal Aid Handbook* website: www.legalaidhandbook.com for further information.
Family	Public law children work: Child care and supervision Secure accommodation orders Adoption Child abduction and international child abduction Inherent jurisdiction Forced marriage protection and protection from female genital mutilation Domestic abuse and protection from harassment arising out of a family relationship Enforcement of international child maintenance Private law children work and financial provision on relationship breakdown, but only where there is domestic abuse or risk of child abuse – see chapter 7 Child safety orders and parenting orders following conviction of a child	In general, child protection work and work required by the UK's international obligations is in scope but private law work is out of scope. It can be brought back where there is domestic or child abuse, but only where particular prescribed evidence is available. See chapter 7 for more details.

Category	Type of work	Comments
Housing	Possession of a rented home (including most counter-claims in possession proceedings even if they would be out of scope as a stand-alone claim) Unlawful eviction – both injunction and damages Homelessness Allocations where the client is or is threatened with homelessness Provision of accommodation by way of community care services to an individual who is homeless or threatened with homelessness (overlap with the community care category) Disrepair, but only to require carrying out of repairs (solely damages claims are out of scope) and only where the disrepair causes a serious risk of harm Protection from harassment Accommodation and support for asylum-seekers	Damages only unlawful eviction claims may however be caught by the 'suitability for a conditional fee agreement' test – see para 7.16 of the Lord Chancellor's Guidance on Civil Legal Aid and para 12.25 of this book. See chapter 12 of the Guidance for how applications for funding for disrepair will be dealt with.

Immigration and asylum	Asylum	Most mainstream non-asylum immigration work is out of scope.
	Detention (but only advice on the detention and bail, not on the substantive issue unless independently in scope) and residence restrictions pending deportation	LASPO Sch 1 Part 1 para 19, which brings judicial review into scope, contains a number of specific restrictions limiting the circumstances in which a judicial review can be brought in an immigration case.
	Applications for leave to remain under the domestic violence rule	
	Applications for leave by victims of trafficking, slavery, servitude or forced labour	From 25 October 2019, The Legal Aid for Separated Children Order 2019 brought non-asylum immigration and citizenship matters into the scope of legal aid for under-18s who are not in the care of a parent, guardian or legal authority.
	Terrorism prevention and investigation measures	
	Proceedings before the Special Immigration Appeals Commission	
	Judicial review, but not:	
	• where the same issue has been the subject of a previous judicial review or appeal within the last year,	
	• of removal directions where the substantive decision or appeal was made in the last year	
	• of a negative decision on an asylum application where there is no right of appeal to the tribunal	
	Exceptional funding of any immigration or asylum matter	
Mental health	Services in relation to the Mental Health Act 1983, the Mental Capacity Act 2005 and the Repatriation of Prisoners Act 1984 Sch para 5 (2)	This includes claims for breaches of the Human Rights Act 1998 brought within Court of Protection proceedings.

Miscellaneous	Working with children and vulnerable adults Protection from harassment where not arising from a family or housing relationship Proceeds of crime Environmental pollution Advice to victims of sexual offences Abuse of child or vulnerable adult except where in the actions against the police etc category Damages claims by victims of trafficking Gang-related violence injunctions Anti-social behaviour injunctions	This is work that does not fit into any other category. Since all categories became 'exclusive' in 2013 (ie tolerance work is not allowed), you can only take on miscellaneous cases if specifically authorised to do so by your schedule. Some – but not all – contracts include an allocation of miscellaneous matter starts.
Public law	Human rights and public law challenges	Many cases will also be in another category. For example, judicial review of a housing decision falls within both the public law and housing categories.
Welfare benefits	Welfare benefit appeals – but only Upper Tribunal cases, cases in the Court of Appeal, Supreme Court and judicial review only Appeals on a point of law relating to council tax reduction schemes to the High Court and above Exceptional funding on any welfare benefits or council tax reduction scheme matter	Legal Help only for Upper Tribunal cases, and for High Court appeals in council tax reduction scheme cases. Representation including advocacy in all other High Court and above cases.

The telephone gateway

3.11   Up until September 2019 clients with a debt, education or discrimination problem could only seek telephone, not face-to-face, advice unless particular exceptions applied; known as the telephone gateway. Email and webcam advice was also available; when referring to telephone advice the LAA includes all remote electronic means of getting advice.

3.12   From the 1 September 2019 transitional arrangements are in place with the new education and discrimination contracts until the mandatory element of the gateway is removed in spring 2020. The timing may be subject to change however – so check www.legalaidhandbook. com for further information

3.13   The operation of the gateway is dealt with in Part 2 of the Civil Legal Aid (Procedure) Regulations 2012 and para 8.7 onwards of the *Lord Chancellor's guidance on civil legal aid.* Exemptions apply:

3.14   An exempt person can choose whether to go to the gateway or to a face-to-face provider; everyone else must go to the gateway. Exempt persons are:

- a person deprived of their liberty;
- a child (under 18);
- a previously assessed person – that is, someone who the gateway has referred to a face-to-face provider within the last 12 months and returns now with the same or a linked problem.

3.15   Where a client calls the gateway, an operator (who is not legally trained or a specialist caseworker) will assess his or her financial eligibility and if the case is in scope. Having made that determination, the client should then be put straight through to a Civil Legal Advice (CLA) specialist advisor who will assess suitability for remote or face-to-face advice. The specialist advisor is tasked with making an assessment based on a number of factors including the client's circumstances and whether they have expressed a wish for services to be provided by a face-to-face provider. The guidance states that particular emphasis should be placed on any wish expressed for services to be provided on a face-to-face basis.[5]

3.16   In the tender round for 2018 contracts, the LAA did not tender for face-to-face debt work, but every organisation awarded a housing contract also received a notional four debt matter starts and is there-

5   https://assets.publishing.service.gov.uk/government/uploads/system/uploads/ attachment_data/file/828391/CLA_General_Provider_Guidance_V1.6.pdf.

fore also a debt provider (the supervisor standard is a joint one). In practice, any referral for face-to-face advice will be to a housing provider wearing its 'debt hat' rather than a separate contracted debt provider. The effect of the LASPO cuts is that virtually the only debt work in scope is mortgage possession. The transitional provisions from the 1 September 2019 are not in place for debt contracts.

3.17   If you, working in a face-to-face service with a housing and debt contract, are approached by a client with a debt problem, you must refer the client to the gateway unless the client is exempt. If the gateway refers a case to you, you should record the referral, including the reference number, on your file. Face-to-face services cannot take on debt cases, except for exempt persons or as a gateway referral, and any file opened in breach of this rule will be nil assessed. Applications for certificates may be made without going via the gateway, but only when all work that could possibly be done under Legal Help has been completed, the matter is urgent and legal representation is immediately required.[6]

3.18   In December 2014, the government published a review[7] of the operation of the gateway, which found it to be operating effectively, though with scope for improvements to be made. A later independent report by the Public Law Project was more critical.[8] The numbers of recorded referrals for face-to-face advice for discrimination and education had been very low resulting in the new face-to-face contracts in 2019.

3.19   In 2019 the contracts for face-to-face education and discrimination were re-tendered and commenced on the 1 September 2019.

Scope of contracts

3.20   As described above, legal aid cases are divided into categories by the contracts. At the highest level, civil and crime are treated separately, have separate contracts and different funding rules. See chapter 15 for criminal work.

---

6   See para 8.12 of the *Lord Chancellor's guidance on civil legal aid*.
7   The review can be found at: www.gov.uk/government/publications/civil-legal-advice-mandatory-gateway-review and associated data at: www.gov.uk/government/publications/civil-legal-advice-mandatory-gateway-research-findings.
8   www.publiclawproject.org.uk/resources/199/an-independent-review-of-the-mandatory-civil-legal-advice-gateway.

3.21   Until September 2018, there were a number of different contracts for different areas of law:

- The **Standard Civil Contract 2010**: this contract has been super-seded for all categories except family mediation, which continued to operate under an amended version of the 2010 contract following a re-tendering exercise. New contracts took effect from 1 February 2015 and were extended in July 2016.
- The **Standard Civil Contract 2013**: housing and debt; family; immigration and asylum.
- The **Standard Civil Contract (welfare benefits) 2013** from 1 October 2013 – welfare benefits in London and the South East, and the Midlands and the East.
- The **Standard Civil Contract 2014**: from 1 August 2014 – mental health; community care.
- The **Standard Civil Contract 2015**: from 1 November 2015 – actions against the police etc; clinical negligence; public law.
- The **Standard Civil Contract (welfare benefits) 2016**: from 1 November 2016 – welfare benefits advice in the North, South West and Wales.

See the 2017/18 edition of this Handbook for the operation of those contracts.[9]

3.22   With effect from 1 September 2018, there is one single civil contract for all face-to-face work across all categories – the **Standard Civil Contract 2018**. This includes the new education and discrimination face-to-face contracts which commenced on 1 September 2019 (See para 12.72 for the Housing Possession Court Duty Scheme).

3.23   Debt, discrimination and education – until the spring of 2020 – are only available through the telephone gateway, and the providers of this work and those of the telephone housing and family telephone services have a separate contract – the **Civil Legal Advice Contract 2018**. Check the Legal Aid Handbook website – www.legalaidhand-book.com –for further information on when the mandatory element of the gateway ends.

3.24   Within the contract there are general rules and specific rules for each area of work and it is vitally important that you apply the correct rules to the particular category of work you are operating in.

3.25   The definitions of each category are set out in the category definitions. See appendix B.

---

9 *Legal Aid Handbook 2017/18* is available in electronic form from LAG.

Case study

We have a 2018 contract in housing and debt. My client is a homeowner facing possession proceedings. Can I advise her under our housing contract?

Mortgage possession work is categorised as debt work and not included in the housing category. Debt work is gateway work, meaning the client must approach the telephone gateway first (unless she is an exempt person). You should therefore tell her to contact the gateway. Since proceedings have been issued, the gateway may well decide that face-to-face advice and representation is required, but that is a decision for the gateway, not for you or the client. If the gateway does decide that, they will refer the client for face to face advice, and if the case is referred back to you, you will be given a gateway reference number which you must record on your file in order to be paid.

The same applies if you represented the client on a Housing Possession Court Duty Scheme; if ongoing work is required, you should refer it to the gateway, not do it yourself.

However, the mandatory element of the gateway will end spring 2020, so check the Legal Aid Handbook website – www.legalaidhandbook.com – for further information.

3.26   An organisation can only be funded to conduct civil legal aid cases if it has a Standard Civil Contract with the LAA. The contract will specify what cases the organisation can take on.

3.27   Every contract has a schedule, which is the part specific to the organisation. In order to be allowed to take on cases, you must be permitted to work in that category by your schedule. The schedule will specify the number of matter starts of controlled work, and whether licensed work is allowed for each category. Controlled work – Legal Help, Help at Court and Controlled Legal Representation – is funding for advice granted by the organisation; licensed work, also known as legal representation or certificated work, is funding for representation in courts, mainly granted by the LAA.

3.28   The matter starts permitted in your schedule are the maximum number of new controlled work cases in that category of law you are permitted to take on during the life of the schedule (usually a year). You can only take on cases in a category in which you have a supervisor and a contract.

3.29   Licensed work is not restricted by matter starts, so there is no limit on the number of certificate applications you may make in a year, as long as you have a contract in the appropriate category.

3.30   Therefore, provided you have a contract in the relevant category, the matter is in scope and you have sufficient matter starts (where relevant), you can take on the case, if the client is eligible. Under para 1.21 of the 2018 specification, you can self-grant supplementary matter starts in a category of law up to 50 per cent of your existing allocation, but only with the consent of your contract manager.

Exceptional cases

3.31   You may, however, take on cases that would otherwise be excluded but fall within the 'exceptional case' provisions in LASPO.[10] All decisions on exceptional cases are made by the LAA. The test is:

(a) that it is necessary to make the services available to the individual because failure to do so would be a breach of–
   (i) the individual's Convention rights (within the meaning of the Human Rights Act 1998), or
   (ii) any rights of the individual to the provision of legal services that are enforceable EU rights, or
(b) that it is appropriate to do so, in the particular circumstances of the case, having regard to any risk that failure to do so would be such a breach.

3.32   Exceptional cases are dealt with in Part 8 of the Procedure Regulations. An application should be made to the LAA, who will determine whether funding should be granted. Guidance on making exceptional applications can be found on the LAA website: www.gov.uk/guidance/legal-aid-apply-for-exceptional-case-funding.

3.33   Legal aid can be backdated to cover making the application under Civil Legal Aid (Procedure) Regulations 2012 reg 68, but only if legal aid is granted. You may have to make the application pro bono unless the client can pay privately.

3.34   See chapter 4 for more information about making applications and a review of relevant case-law.

---

10 LASPO s10(3).

Financial eligibility

3.35   There are two significant barriers to taking on cases: the means test and the merits test. Every client must qualify financially before their case can be taken on (with very limited exceptions in the family and mental health categories; see chapters 7 and 11), and the case must pass the relevant merits test.

3.36   Financial eligibility is assessed on three separate criteria, all of which the client must satisfy, by being below the threshold on capital, gross income and disposable income.

3.37   The limits on each of these are set out in the Civil Legal Aid (Financial Resources and Payment for Services) Regulations 2013, which are amended periodically. Up to date limits can be found on the LAA website: www.gov.uk/guidance/civil-legal-aid-means-testing.

3.38   In the case of controlled work, you should ascertain the client's resources and calculate eligibility; the decision on whether the means test is met is delegated to you. For licensed work, however, the decision is made by the LAA.

3.39   The LAA has provided guides to assessing eligibility for controlled and certificated work. In relation to certificated work, see the Means Assessment Guidance[11] which is helpful in more complex cases. And the use of the eligibility calculator[12] should ensure that your assessment of whether your client is eligible is accurate.

Case study

Para 3.23 of the 2018 Civil Contract says that satisfactory evidence of the client's means must be provided before we assess eligibility. Our clients rarely bring this evidence with them to the first appointment. Is there anything we can do about this?

You need to explain clearly to clients what evidence they will need to bring with them to their first appointment. Many organisations now train a member of support staff to understand what is and not acceptable and to ensure that clients bring what is necessary to the first appointment. This can be confirmed in a standard letter, and clients can be sent a text message the day before to remind them of the appointment and what they need to bring with them.

---

11 https://assets.publishing.service.gov.uk/government/uploads/system/uploads/attachment_data/file/793462/Means_Assessment_Guidance.pdf.
12 http://civil-eligibility-calculator.justice.gov.uk.

However, if you can justify it to protect your client's position, then you can start work before the client provides evidence, and in very rare cases the LAA may accept that it is not possible for them to provide it at all due to the clients age, mental disability or homelessness make it impracticable (2018 Contract Specification para 3.24). However, the LAA are taking an increasingly strict approach to this provision on evidence of means should have been provided at some point later than the first appointment, the file may be nil assessed. However, a point of principle, CLA59, says that a LAA assessor should only overturn an exercise of discretion allowed by the rules if it was manifestly unreasonable. It is unclear what impact this will have under the 2018 contract, as points of principle can no longer be certified under it; but it may be useful to argue that the LAA should have regard to it (see chapters 16 and 22 for more information).

3.40 Where the client has a partner with whom he or she is living as a couple, you should always aggregate the means of both the client and the partner. Partner means:

- spouse or civil partner;
- person with whom the client lives or ordinarily lives as a couple,

but not where they are separated because of a relationship breakdown likely to be permanent.[13]

3.41 However, if only one partner is seeking advice at your office in person, both are not required to sign the application form. The then Legal Services Commission (LSC) issued guidance in 2009 which clarified the requirement for both to sign only applies to postal and telephone applications.[14]

Passporting benefits

3.42 A client in receipt of passporting benefits automatically qualifies for legal aid on income. However, an assessment of capital will still be

---

13 Civil Legal Aid (Financial Resources and Payment for Services) Regulations 2013 reg 2.

14 Guidance issued by the LSC in 2009. This is available at: http://webarchive. nationalarchives.gov.uk/20121207044149/http://www.LEGALSERVICES.gov. uk/docs/forms/CW1_Client_Certification__Guidance_Nov_2009(1).pdf. It is no longer available on the current LAA website; but equally, we are aware of nothing to suggest that this approach has been changed.

required, and legal aid must be refused if the capital test is not met, even if the client receives a passporting benefit.

3.43   Current income passporting benefits are:

- income support;
- income-based jobseeker's allowance;
- universal credit;
- guarantee pension credit;
- income-related employment and support allowance.

3.44   Support under sections 4 or 95 of the Immigration and Asylum Act 1999 is similarly passported, but only for Legal Help and Controlled Legal Representation in the immigration category.

3.45   For Legal Representation, the evidence requirement for capital is the provision of three months' bank statements or similar. For Legal Help, see para 5.20 below.

Assessment of capital

3.46   Capital is 'every resource of a capital nature belonging to [the client] on the date on which the application is made',[15] either as money or as the realisable value of an asset.[16] It includes money owed to the client, whether or not recovered,[17] and also includes life insurance and endowments if their security can be borrowed upon.[18]

3.47   However, the value of household furniture and effects, a car (unless of exceptional value), clothing and tools of trade is excluded,[19] as is (in the case of controlled work) money the client could realise by selling or borrowing on the strength of any business he or she may own.[20]

3.48   Where the client owns property, the value of that property should be taken into account in the calculation. The value is the client's equity – that is, the current realisable market value.[21] The LAA *Guide to determining financial eligibility for certificated work*,[22] states that a deduction of three per cent should be made from the value, to allow for the cost of selling the property. This does not appear in the equi-

---

15 Civil Legal Aid (Financial Resources and Payment for Services) Regulations 2013 reg 30.
16 Reg 31.
17 Reg 32.
18 Reg 33.
19 Reg 34.
20 Reg 36.
21 Reg 31.
22 www.gov.uk/civil-legal-aid-means-testing.

valent guidance for assessing eligibility for controlled work;[23] but arguably it should as the regulation is the same. From that is taken the value of any outstanding mortgage which is capped at £100,000[24] – so where a property is worth £220,000 and the outstanding mortgage is £120,000, the client's equity should be taken as £120,000. The first £100,000 of equity should also be disregarded.[25] Where the client owns a second property, any unused mortgage disregard may be applied to that property, up to a maximum of £100,000 across all properties. However, no equity disregard can be applied, even if the full amount was not used for the client's home – the mortgage disregard applies across all property owned, but the equity disregard applies only to the client's main dwelling.

3.49   Jointly owned property should be taken into account. Where jointly owned with the client's partner, the entire value will be taken into account because of aggregation of means. Where it is jointly owned with someone else, only the client's share or interest will be taken into account. The default position is that the client's share will be assumed to be 50 per cent, unless there is evidence to the contrary.

3.50   Where any property is the subject matter of the dispute (SMOD), the value of that property may be disregarded from the calculation, up to a maximum of £100,000. It is only the value of the client's interest that is disregarded; the value of the opponent's interest is not taken into account at all.[26] The SMOD disregard is applied after the mortgage disregard, but before the equity disregard. For example:

> A client jointly owns a property worth £400,000 with a mortgage of £170,000. The property is the subject of a dispute with her former husband.
>
> The property value is £400,000 less the maximum mortgage disregard of £100,000 – so £300,000 is taken as being the equity value of the property in dispute. The client's share of the equity is presumed to be 50 per cent of this – £150,000. The SMOD disregard of £100,000 is then applied, leaving a value of £50,000. Finally, the equity disregard is applied, leaving a value of nil to be taken into account on the capital assessment – and so the client is eligible on capital.

23 https://assets.publishing.service.gov.uk/government/uploads/system/uploads/attachment_data/file/793459/Guide_to_determining_controlled_work_.pdf.

24 Reg 37.

25 Reg 39.

26 Reg 38.

3.51   A client applying for an injunction in domestic violence or forced marriage protection proceedings is not subject to the capital threshold[27] and there is no limit on eligibility for capital purposes. However, contributions are not waived, so the practical value of this concession is limited in most cases.

Case study

My client instructs me to advise her regarding financial matters. She qualifies for legal aid because of a history of domestic abuse, and has evidence in the form of a letter from her GP. She and her husband own (as joint tenants) a flat, which has just been valued at £550,000. She wants the flat to be transferred to her. The outstanding mortgage is £150,000. Is she eligible for a certificate?

The value of the property should be taken as £533,500 – that is, £550,000 minus three per cent costs of sale. Disregard the mortgage, capped to £100,000 – so the equity is £433,500.

The client's share of this is £216,750, half of the equity – although the asset is in dispute, there is a presumption of equal shares for the purposes of assessment, and they are joint tenants.

Apply the SMOD disregard of £100,000, which leaves £116,750. Then, as this is the client's main home, apply the equity disregard of £100,000 – leaving capital of £16,750.

As the capital threshold is £8,000, the client is therefore not eligible. Although her case is in scope because she is a victim of domestic violence, the domestic violence capital waiver does not apply to financial matters, only to injunctions.

Clients over 60

3.52   Where a client is aged 60 or over, they are entitled to a further disregard on capital. The level of the disregard is on a sliding scale determined by disposable income (see below) up to a maximum of £100,000 of capital.[28] Using the online calculator[29] will allow you to ensure this is calculated correctly.

---

27 Reg 12.
28 Reg 41.
29 http://civil-eligibility-calculator.justice.gov.uk/.

Contributions from capital

3.53   There are two limits for capital – a lower and upper limit. Where a client is below the lower limit, currently £3,000, the client is eligible on capital with no need to pay a contribution. Where the client is above the lower limit but below the upper limit (currently £8,000), the client must pay a contribution. Any contribution is payable at the start of the case and is the lower of the amount by which capital exceeds £3,000 or the estimated likely total costs of the case. Where the eventual costs are lower than any contribution paid, the balance will be refunded to the client. Capital contributions can cause problems in cases where the only capital is the value of the client's home as it may be difficult for the client to raise funds to cover the contribution quickly or at all.

Assessment of income

3.54   Once you have found the client eligible on capital, you should proceed to the next stage, assessment of income. The client must be eligible on both gross and disposable income, and the thresholds are set on the basis of a calendar month. For example, if the client instructs you on 6 March, you should look at all money received since 7 February.

3.55   'Gross income' means total income from all sources (apart from housing benefit or the housing element of Universal Credit and some benefits and allowances, most commonly disability living allowance/personal independence payment) and universal credit payments on account.[30] It will include salary, benefits, maintenance and any other income.

3.56   You should deduct the following expenses from gross income to arrive at disposable income:

- the amount payable[31] of any rent or mortgage payments, net of any housing benefit – but capped to £545 per month if the client has no dependants;[32]

---

30 Civil Legal Aid (Financial Resources and Payment for Services) Regulations 2013 regs 21 and 24 as amended.

31 Note the amount the client is contractually liable to pay, not the amount they are actually paying. This can be important in housing cases where the client is in arrears and not paying rent. See *R (Southwark Law Centre) v Legal Services Commission; R (Dennis) v Legal Services Commission* [2007] EWHC 1715 (Admin). Although decided on the previous regulations, the same wording is used in reg 28.

32 Civil Legal Aid (Financial Resources and Payment for Services) Regulations 2013 reg 28.

- tax and National Insurance contributions on any earnings;[33]
- childcare costs, but only to the extent that they are incurred because of work or study outside the home and only where reasonable to make a deduction;[34]
- where working, a fixed cost of employment allowance of £45 (for both the client and partner if both are working);[35]
- any maintenance being paid in respect of a child or other dependent relative or former partner not a member of the client's household;[36] and
- fixed dependants' allowances for the partner and each other dependent relative who is a member of the household. (Note that it is a common misconception that the dependants' allowances can only be claimed in respect of the client's children, an impression not dispelled by the wording of the forms which refer to 'child'. The regulations are quite clear that the allowance is claimable for *any dependent relative* who is a member of the client's household.)[37]

3.57   The LAA's eligibility calculator is helpful as it always gets the arithmetic right and applies any allowances and disregards correctly. It can be used online at: www.gov.uk/guidance/civil-legal-aid-means-testing.

Assessment of the means of a child

3.58   You are allowed to accept applications from a child.[38] When deciding on an application for Legal Help, you should assess the means of the child and those of the person(s) who have care and control or are liable to maintain the child or who usually contribute substantially to the child's maintenance. So, in effect, you will often be assessing the means of the parents, with the expectation that they should fund the case if they are able to do so.[39]

3.59   However, you should consider whether it is just and equitable to aggregate the child's means with those of the person(s) liable to

---

33 Civil Legal Aid (Financial Resources and Payment for Services) Regulations 2013 reg 23.

34 Reg 27.

35 Reg 27.

36 Reg 26.

37 Reg 25.

38 Civil Legal Aid (Procedure) Regulations 2012 reg 22.

39 Standard Civil Contract 2018 Specification para 3.27.

maintain them, and if it is not just and equitable you should just assess the means of the child. No guidance is given as to what is 'just and equitable', although the contract says that the presumption is that there should be aggregation but that you can take into account all the circumstances, including the age and resources of the child, and that non-aggregation is more likely to be justified where there is a conflict between the child and the liable person.[40] In the absence of detailed guidance, this is a decision for you as the provider assessing eligibility for Legal Help, and you should therefore keep a detailed file note justifying your decision, especially if it is a decision not to aggregate.

3.60 Where a child applies for a funding certificate, it is generally only the child's means that are taken into account, not those of the litigation friend or any other person liable to maintain the child, and therefore you should only include the child's finances.[41] However, in family cases you should consider whether to aggregate in the same way as for Legal Help.

Legal aid available without regard to means

3.61 Legal aid for the following types of case is not means tested:[42]

- Special Children Act cases and related proceedings (see chapter 8);
- Family Help (Lower) in cases where Children Act 1989 s31 proceedings are contemplated and the client is a parent or person with parental responsibility;
- Mental Health Tribunal cases (see chapter 11);
- certificates in Mental Capacity Act 2005 s21A cases before the Court of Protection where the client is deprived of their liberty;
- terrorism prevention and investigation measure applications, notices and proceedings;
- Hague Convention and European Convention on Child Custody cases;
- various cases concerning international enforcement of child maintenance etc under the United Kingdom's international treaties and obligations;

---

40 Standard Civil Contract 2018 Specification para 3.27.
41 Civil Legal Aid (Financial Resources and Payment for Services) Regulations 2013 reg 16(3) and (4).
42 Reg 5.

- mediation information and assessment meetings and mediation in Hague Convention cases.

3.62   In family cases concerning injunctions for domestic violence and forced marriage the eligibility limits – but not contributions – can be waived. See chapter 7.

3.63   In inquests (where exceptional funding is granted) multi-party actions and cross-border disputes, eligibility limits and contributions can be waived.

Reassessment of means

3.64   The means tests are not one-off tests; if clients' circumstances change during a case, their means should be reassessed. In the case of controlled work, you should reassess means yourself, and if the client is no longer eligible, you may need to withdraw the funding. In the case of licensed work, you should report the change of circumstances to the LAA for them to reassess the means. The LAA *Guide to determining financial eligibility for controlled work*[43] says that it may not be appropriate to reassess the client's means unless they have improved 'dramatically', or the matter is likely to run for some time, suggested as three months or more for controlled work. For certificated work, any change in circumstances must be reported to the LAA and will result in a re-assessment of means provided the criteria below are met.

3.65   Regulation 20 of the Civil Legal Aid (Financial Resources and Payment for Services) Regulations 2013 provides – for all levels of service subject to means assessment – that where:

- disposable income has increased by more than £60 or decreased by more than £25;
- disposable capital has increased by more than £750; or
- the client is no longer in receipt of a passporting benefit,

a reassessment must take place unless it is inappropriate to do so having regard to the period for which legal aid is likely to continue. In the case of controlled work whether it is inappropriate will be a decision for you, applying the guidance set out above. In the case of licensed work for the LAA further contributions from capital may be required. See the Means Assessment Guidance issued by the LAA's legal team for more information.[44]

43   www.gov.uk/civil-legal-aid-means-testing.
44   www.gov.uk/civil-legal-aid-means-testing.

3.66   It is the client's duty to report any change of circumstances to you,[45] and therefore you must always advise clients of the existence of this duty at the first meeting. It should be confirmed in your standard letter.

Merits tests

3.67   Each case must satisfy, and continue to satisfy, the merits test. There are a number of different tests, depending on the nature of the case and the type of funding sought, and they are dealt with in the relevant sections of chapters 5–14 of this book. You should always bear in mind that each merits test should be passed at the start of the case and should continue to be passed throughout its life. If there is insufficient merit in a particular step in the proceedings, you should not take that step; if there is not, or is no longer, sufficient merit in the case as a whole, you should refuse or withdraw funding (controlled work), or report that to the LAA (licensed work).

Other restrictions on taking on cases

Referral fees

3.68   There is an absolute prohibition on referral fees in legal aid work. Clause 6.8 of the Standard Civil Contract 2018 Standard Terms makes clear that no payment or benefit may be made to or received from any third party.

Client has received previous advice

3.69   The Legal Help form requires the client to certify that they have not previously received advice on the same matter, and where they have done so within the last six months requires you to explain why you took on the case. This is because there are specific rules in the contract to prevent the legal aid fund paying out twice for the same matter, and therefore in order to make a claim the second time you must be able to demonstrate that the case meets one of the exceptions allowing you to do so.

---

45 Civil Legal Aid (Financial Resources and Payment for Services) Regulations 2013 reg 18.

3.70   Some of the exceptions apply if you are the client's original provider looking to re-open a case that has been closed; others apply if you are a second provider looking to take over a case from the original organisation.

3.71   In the case of controlled work a second matter start can only be opened on the same case if you are the original provider where:

(a) at least six months has elapsed since there was a claim on the first matter; or

(b) there has been a material development or change in the client's instructions and at least three months has elapsed since there was a claim on the first matter.[46]

3.72   Where you are relying on para 3.35(b) (material development or change), you should note that:

- Giving instructions, following a failure to give instructions, is not a change in instructions.
- A decision or response from any third party to any correspondence, application, appeal, review or other request made in the course of the original matter is not a material development.
- A change in the law that was anticipated in the original matter is not a material development.[47]

However, you can instead re-open the original matter and make a further claim (see chapter 5) in some circumstances.

3.73   Where you are the second provider, looking to take over a case, you can only do so where:

(a) there has been a material change in relevant circumstances since the initial decision to grant Legal Help; or

(b) the client has reasonable cause to be dissatisfied with the first provider; or

(c) the client has moved a distance away from the first provider and effective communication is not practicable; or

(d) the first provider is not making a claim for the work and confirms that in writing.[48]

The contract[49] requires you to make reasonable enquiries of the client as to whether there was previous advice. Where there is a transfer, you must establish that there is good reason, and record that reason on the file.[50]

---

46 Standard Civil Contract 2018 Specification para 3.35.
47 Standard Civil Contract 2018 Specification para 3.36.
48 Civil Legal Aid (Procedure) Regulations 2012 reg 23(4).
49 Standard Civil Contract 2018 Specification para 3.40.
50 Standard Civil Contract 2018 Specification para 3.44.

3.74   However, it is not sufficient for you to take the client's word as to the reasons for transfer. You must seek the client's authority to obtain the file from the previous provider and must then request the file from the previous provider. You cannot start work on the case until you receive the file. Where the client refuses to give you authority, or where you obtain the file and discover that there is in fact no good reason for transfer, you may not make a claim for the case. The sole exception is where there is urgent work that is absolutely necessary to protect the client's position or meet a court deadline, in which case you can do the urgent work and claim for it, even if it later transpires there was no good reason.[51]

3.75   In the case of certificated work, there is no specific rule or guidance on transfer of solicitor. However, to transfer, the second solicitor would have to make an application to the LAA to amend the certificate, and the LAA will consider whether the application is justified. The second solicitor must include work done by the first solicitor on the bill at the end of the case, and therefore the LAA (or court) will be able to see all work done by both solicitors and may disallow on assessment any unjustified duplication.

Permitted work

3.76   So, if your client's case is within the scope of the scheme and your contract, and passes the means and merits tests, you will be able to take it on. However, there are restrictions on what work can be done.

3.77   The Civil Legal Aid (Procedure) Regulations 2012 set out limitations on the work that can be done at each level of legal aid. The definitions in the criteria are important, as they set out in full what can and cannot be done at each level of funding. Where the client's case needs work that is out of the scope of the current level, you will need to make an application for funding at the next level.

Definitions of permitted work[52]

3.78   The main types of funding common to all areas are:

- **Legal Help**, which allows the provision of advice, negotiation and attempts at settlement and resolution, but not acting as a

---

51 Standard Civil Contract 2018 Specification paras 3.42 and 3.43.
52 Civil Legal Aid (Procedure) Regulations 2012 regs 4–10.

mediator, issuing or conducting court proceedings, instruction of an advocate or advocacy;

- **Help at Court**, which authorises help and advocacy for a client at a particular hearing without formally being on the court record as acting for the client;
- **Legal representation**, which allows the provision of representation in proceedings or contemplated proceedings, including the conduct of litigation and advocacy.

3.79   **Controlled Legal Representation** is a form of legal representation at the controlled work level – that is, which is controlled work rather than licensed work, and therefore granted by the provider rather than the LAA. It allows you to represent clients before tribunals, but only in the mental health and immigration categories.

3.80   **Family Help** is a form of funding only available in the family category, and slots in between Legal Help and legal representation. Family Help (Lower) is a form of controlled work, also known as level 2 work, and authorises advice and assistance in attempting to resolve a family dispute through negotiation and settlement. It does not include mediation but can include advice in support of mediation. Family Help (Higher) is licensed work covering all litigation up to but not including a final contested hearing. Final hearings can be covered by Legal Representation (see chapter 7).

3.81   **Help with Mediation** was a new form of funding from 1 April 2013 for legal advice for those who are in, or have participated in, mediation. It is controlled work.

3.82   **Help with Family Mediation** was a new form of funding from 1 April 2013 for legal advice for those who are in, or have participated in, mediation. See chapters 7 and 9.

3.83   **Investigative representation** is a type of licensed work that allows the LAA to issue a certificate that is limited in scope and costs, permitting the solicitor to investigate the strength of a proposed claim but not generally to issue or conduct proceedings.

3.84   More details of the types of work that can be carried out at each funding level can be found in the following chapters.

Exceptional case funding

by Polly Brendon

Introduction

4.1   When the Legal Aid, Sentencing and Punishment of Offenders Act 2012 (LASPO) was passed, the government sought to address concerns that it would result in injustice by making provision, in section 10 of LASPO, for 'exceptional case funding' (ECF) to be granted in limited circumstances where a case was otherwise out of scope for legal aid.

4.2   ECF may be available for civil cases that are not included as in-scope for legal aid under Part 1 Sch 1 to LASPO. It is not available to clients whose case is in-scope, but who are not eligible for legal aid for some other reason. The test for when non-inquest ECF should be granted, as set out in section 10(3) of LASPO, is:

(a) that it is necessary to make the services available to the individual because failure to do so would be a breach of–
  (i) the individual's Convention [European Convention on Human Rights (ECHR)] rights (within the meaning of the Human Rights Act 1998), or
  (ii) any rights of the individual to the provision of legal services that are enforceable EU rights, or
(b) That it is appropriate to do so, in the particular circumstances of the case, having regard to any risk that failure to do so would be such a breach.

4.3   To qualify for ECF, in addition to meeting the test in section 10(3) of LASPO, the client must still meet the financial eligibility criteria to be granted legal aid, and the case must meet the merits criteria that are deemed by the Legal Aid Agency (LAA) 'to be the most appropriate in all the circumstances of the case'.[1]

4.4   During the passage of LASPO, the government estimated that around 6,500 applications for non-inquest ECF Legal Representation would be made each year, with additional applications for ECF Legal Help.[2] However, when LASPO came into force, the Lord Chancellor issued ECF guidance for decision-makers and providers, which made clear that he interpreted its scope very narrowly and expected very few grants.

4.5   In the first year of the ECF scheme, there were only 1,315 applications made with just 16 of them granted – a success rate of less than 1 per cent. Since then, largely as a result of litigation, the grant rate has risen, but numbers of applications remain lower than anticip-

---

1 Civil Legal Aid (Merits Criteria) Regulations 2013 reg 50.
2 Ministry of Justice, 'Legal Aid Reform: Excluded Cases Funding Process Equality Impact Assessment', p9.

ated. The most recent LAA statistics show that in the financial year 2018/19, 2,598 non-inquest ECF applications were made, with a grant rate of 65 per cent. However, the vast majority of those applications, 1,951, were made for immigration cases, for which the grant rate was 77 per cent. The category of law with the next highest number of non-inquest ECF applications was family, at 355 applications, but the grant rate was much lower, at 39 per cent.[3]

4.6 Non-inquest ECF was one of the most litigated area of post-LASPO legal aid. There were two main strands to the litigation: the lawfulness of the tests applied by the LAA in deciding whether ECF was required, and the lawfulness of the process for making applications. In *Gudanaviciene and others v Director of Legal Aid Casework and The Lord Chancellor,*[4] the High Court and the Court of Appeal considered when section 10(3) of LASPO would require ECF to be granted, and the lawfulness of the Lord Chancellor's Exceptional Funding Guidance (Non-Inquests) ('the ECF Guidance'). In *IS (by the Official Solicitor as Litigation Friend) v The Director of Legal Aid Casework and The Lord Chancellor,*[5] one of the original claimants in *Gudanaviciene* continued with a challenge to the LAA's operation of the ECF scheme, as well as challenging the Civil Legal Aid (Merits) Criteria 2013 and continuing to challenge the lawfulness of the ECF Guidance.

When should non-inquest ECF be available: *Gudanaviciene*

4.7 Since the decision in *Airey v Ireland,*[6] it has been accepted that some rights under the European Convention on Human Rights (ECHR) may have an associated right to legal aid so that the rights can be practical and effective. In terms of non-inquest ECF, an ECHR right to civil legal aid is most likely to arise under Article 6 ECHR, the right to a fair hearing, and Article 8 ECHR, the right to respect for private and family life.

4.8 Article 6 ECHR is engaged where there is a civil right and/or obligation to be determined. There is a body of case-law that considers when this will be the case, which will not be set out here. Of note, however, is that Article 6 ECHR will be engaged by most family and

---

3 www.gov.uk/government/statistics/legal-aid-statistics-january-to-march-2019.
4 [2014] EWHC 1840 (Admin), [2014] EWCA Civ 1622.
5 [2015] EWHC 1965 (Admin).
6 (1979–80) 2 EHRR 305.

housing proceedings, save in relation to homelessness applications. It could also be engaged, for example, in certain welfare benefits or employment tribunal cases.

4.9   In *Gudanaviciene*, the Court of Appeal held that the procedural obligations inherent in some ECHR rights, including Article 8 ECHR, can require ECF to be made available. This has been crucial for clients who need ECF for immigration cases, which generally do not engage Article 6 ECHR but will often engage Article 8 ECHR. The procedural obligations under Article 8 ECHR can be engaged at the application stage, not just when a case is before a court or tribunal.

4.10   The relevant provision of European Union (EU) law is Article 47 of the Charter of Fundamental Rights of the European Union which is engaged when the matter for which funding is required falls within the scope of EU law.

4.11   In *Gudanaviciene*, the Court of Appeal confirmed that, in making an ECF determination, it was necessary to consider all the circumstances of the case. Contrary to what was stated in the ECF Guidance, the court found that 'exceptional' is not a test of itself, nor does it necessarily imply that grants will be rare. The Strasbourg case-law does not require representation in all but the most straightforward of cases; but nor does it only require representation in extreme cases.

4.12   Whether or not ECF should be granted is case sensitive – it is not possible to say that a particular class of case will definitely obtain ECF. It will depend on the circumstances and capability of an individual applicant, and the proceedings for which funding is required. The Court of Appeal in *Gudanaviciene* held that, in determining whether funding is required under section 10 of LASPO, the 'critical question' is whether an applicant would be 'able to present their case effectively and without obvious unfairness' (para 56). This test is essentially the same under Articles 6 and 8 ECHR and Article 47 of the EU Charter.

4.13   Relevant to whether the test is met will be 'a) the importance of the issues at stake b) the complexity of the procedural, legal and evidential issues; and c) the ability of the individual to represent himself without legal assistance, having regard to his age and mental capacity' (*Gudanaviciene* para 72).

4.14   Of particular relevance in immigration cases are 'i) there are statutory restrictions on the supply of advice and assistance . . . ii) individuals may well have language difficulties; and iii) the law is complex and rapidly evolving' (*Gudanaviciene* para 72).

4.15   Practitioners making ECF applications for clients will want to consider the Court of Appeal's judgment in *Gudanaviciene* carefully;

although the principles are articulated in the context of the individual claimants' immigration cases, they are relevant to applications for non-inquest ECF in all types of civil case. In addition to explaining when a grant of non-inquest ECF will be required, the Court of Appeal found that the ECF Guidance as it was at the time was unlawful.

The operation of the non-inquest ECF scheme – *IS*

4.16   While the Court of Appeal in *Gudanaviciene* clarified the circumstances in which a grant of non-inquest ECF would be required, there continued to be problems with the operation of the scheme. In addition, the Civil Legal Aid (Merits Criteria) Regulations 2013 had been amended in January 2014 to exclude cases assessed as having 'borderline' prospects of success from legal aid. These issues, and the continuing question of the lawfulness of the ECF Guidance, were considered by the High Court and Court of Appeal in the case *IS*.

4.17   In a detailed judgment, Collins J noted a series of problems with the scheme as it has been implemented by the LAA including:

- Even after *Gudanaviciene*, the success rate for applications was very low (para 29).
- The forms were too complex, for both practitioners and unrepresented applicants, and did not reflect the test in *Gudanaviciene* (paras 43, 54, 55, 56 and 105).
- The system was not meeting needs of unrepresented (paras 43 and 62).
- There was no funding for the initial investigation of whether a potential applicant would be entitled to ECF (para 57).
- The procedure for determining urgent applications for ECF was inadequate (para 78).
- There was no right of appeal to judicial person against a refusal of ECF; the only remedy is to seek judicial review (para 93).
- An applicant was required to provide an unnecessary amount of detail with an application for ECF (para 65).
- It should not be necessary for an applicant to provide full means information for a grant of ECF to be made in principle, subject to full means information being provided, with a grant of funding made once financial eligibility had been determined (para 63).
- It was incorrect to assume that, because Courts and Tribunals have experience of dealing with litigants in person, an unrepresented individual will receive a fair hearing; the extent to which it

is proper for a judge to assist a party to litigation is limited (para 71).

- The way in which the LAA had assessed the merits of cases has been flawed: 'it is not for the LAA to carry out the exercise which the Court will carry out, in effect prejudging the very issue which will be determined by the Court' (paras 72, 96, 97).
- The hurdle to accessing ECF for those lacking capacity, particularly the evidential requirements, was too high (paras 74, 75, 80).

4.18   As a result, Collins J found that the way the LAA was operating the scheme was unlawful as it was 'not properly providing the safety net which s10 [LASPO] is supposed to provide' (para 80). He also declared parts of the Civil Legal Aid (Merits Criteria) Regulations 2013 unlawful, along with parts of the ECF Guidance.

4.19   The Lord Chancellor appealed, and the case came before the Court of Appeal, with judgment given on 20 May 2016.[7] By a majority of 2:1 (Laws and Burnett LJJ, Briggs LJ dissenting), the court found that while there were flaws in the operation of the ECF scheme, they were not sufficient to render it unlawful. The court unanimously allowed the Lord Chancellor's appeal on the issues of the lawfulness of the Civil Legal Aid (Merits Criteria) Regulations 2013 and ECF Guidance.

4.20   Giving the lead judgment, Laws LJ observed that 'systemic failure is not to be equated with proof of a series of individual failures' (para 53), and concluded that the ECF scheme was 'not inherently or systematically unfair' (para 55). In Laws LJ's view, Collins J had not shown how individual criticisms of the scheme added up to systemic unfairness; it was his 'impressionistic' judgment that they did not, and the evidence before the court did not show that the scheme was operating in a way that was so unfair as to be unlawful. However, he also accepted that the court had not read all the evidence filed by the respondent. Notwithstanding his finding that the ECF scheme was operating lawfully, and that there had been improvements, he observed at paragraph 56 of the judgment that 'the extent of the difficulties is . . . troubling'.

4.21   Dissenting, Briggs LJ found that the ECF scheme was unlawful. This conclusion was founded on two key features, its complexity, which was such that it was essentially inaccessible without legal assistance, and the lack of an economic business model that would encourage providers to make ECF applications. In his view, these were inherent flaws in the scheme that rendered it unlawful.

---

7 *IS v Director of Legal Casework and Lord Chancellor* [2016] EWCA Civ 464.

The Lord Chancellor's Guidance: non-inquest ECF

4.22   When making an application for ECF, you must have regard to the Lord Chancellor's guidance and the Provider Pack. They can be found here: www.gov.uk/government/publications/legal-aid-exceptional-case-funding-form-and-guidance. They are to be read in conjunction with the case-law discussed in this chapter.

4.23   Some six months after the Court of Appeal's judgment in *Gudanaviciene*, the Lord Chancellor issued revised Guidance for non-inquest ECF cases, which can be accessed at: www.gov.uk/government/publications/legal-aid-exceptional-case-funding-form-and-guidance. The revised Guidance covers Articles 6 and 8 EHCR and Article 47 of the EU Charter in general terms, and then briefly considers specific categories of law in an annex.

Article 6 ECHR

4.24   The Guidance sets out a three-stage test that LAA decision-makers must consider when determining whether a grant of ECF is required under Article 6 ECHR:

a) Does the case involve the determination of civil rights and obligations?

b) If yes, will withholding legal aid mean the applicant will be unable to present his or her case effectively, or lead to an obvious unfairness in the proceedings?

c) If yes, what are the minimum services required to meet the legal obligation to provide legal aid?

4.25   Further guidance is provided on factors to be taken into account in deciding whether the applicant can present his or her case effectively and without obvious unfairness. These include the importance of the issues at stake, the complexity of law, fact and procedure, and the personal characteristics of the applicant. Specific guidance for adults who lack capacity and children is also given.

4.26   In relation to those factors to be taken into account the Guidance elaborates as follows:

•   **The importance of the issues at stake.** Decision-makers are directed to consider: whether the potential consequences for the applicant are so objectively serious as to add weight to the need for public funds; whether the case is 'merely' a claim for money, or if it is about issues of life, liberty, health, welfare, physical safety or protection from abuse, or about adjustments to medical or other care impacting on the applicant's ability to live independently; and, if the claim is financial, what sums are at stake.

- **The complexity of the legal factual procedural or evidential issues.** Decision-makers are directed to consider: whether the case turns on issues of fact within the applicant's own knowledge; whether there will be a significant number of witnesses or a large volume of evidence will be required; whether expert evidence is required or must be tested, as well as the extent to which the evidence has already been dealt with in earlier hearings or hearings in lower courts or tribunals. It will also include the complexity of the relevant law and procedure, including whether the case is before a specialist court or tribunal and the extent to which it can assist the applicant.

- **The extent to which the applicant is capable of presenting their case effectively without the assistance of a lawyer.** Decision-makers are directed to consider: the complexity of the case; whether the individual has previously had assistance from a lawyer; characteristics of the applicant such as their level of education, level of English language skills, any relevant disabilities, their level of emotional involvement in the case, any special caring responsibilities that could present a barrier to the presentation of the case; the degree to which the court or tribunal is used to assisting litigants in person; and the extent of any other assistance available, including a McKenzie friend. If the applicant is a child, the role of any litigation friend, official solicitor or CAFCASS (Children and Family Court Advisory and Support Service) will be taken into account, as well as the level of the child's maturity and intelligence. Where court rules require a litigation friend and none other than the Official Solicitor is available, this will be 'important (and potentially determinative)'. Similar considerations apply in the case of an adult lacking capacity.

Article 8 ECHR

4.27   The current Guidance acknowledges that the rights under Article 8 ECHR can require ECF to be granted. However, the discussion of Article 8 ECHR in the Guidance is very brief. It directs decision-makers to the factors identified by the Court of Appeal at para 72 of the judgment in *Gudanaviciene,* and to the factors set out elsewhere in the Guidance as relevant to whether ECF is required under Article 6 ECHR.

Extent of services provided

4.28   The Guidance states that where the LAA is satisfied that legal aid is required, it should be limited to the minimum services required to meet the need for funding, through providing only specific levels of service, or through the placing of limitations on certificates. The Guidance requires decision-makers to consider whether full representation is required, or whether advice and the preparation of written submissions using Legal Help would be enough.

4.29   Paragraph six of the Guidance specifically reminds decision-makers that they must have regard to *Gudanaviciene* as well as the Guidance itself. In making applications for ECF where you consider that your case comes within *Gudanaviciene*, but you feel that the Guidance is too restrictive to accommodate your case, it would be good to emphasise paragraph six in your application, and cite the relevant paragraphs from *Gudanaviciene*.

Inquest ECF

4.30   While Legal Help for advice, assistance and preparation in inquests is in-scope, advocacy at inquests is not, and ECF may be required. Section 10(4) LAPSO provides for ECF to be available where:

   (a) the services consist of advocacy in proceedings at an inquest under the Coroners Act 1988 into the death of a member of the individual's family,
   (b) the Director has made a wider public interest determination in relation to the individual and the inquest, and
   (c) the Director has determined that the individual qualifies for the services in accordance with this Part,

(and neither determination has been withdrawn).

4.31   There is specific Lord Chancellor's Guidance for inquest cases, and a Provider Pack, which can also be accessed at: www.gov.uk/government/publications/legal-aid-exceptional-case-funding-form-and-guidance.

4.32   In *R (Letts) v The Lord Chancellor*[8] Mr Justice Green considered the lawfulness of a previous version of the Lord Chancellor's Exceptional Funding Guidance (Inquests) ('Inquest ECF Guidance').[9] After considering carefully the content of the guidance in the light of

---

8   [2015] EWHC 402 (Admin).
9   See: https://assets.publishing.service.gov.uk/government/uploads/system/uploads/attachment_data/file/715441/legal-aid-chancellor-inquests.pdf.

the obligations of the state under Article 2 ECHR (right to life), and reviewing the law relating to Article 2, Green J determined that:

> 94. . . . For the reasons that I have set out above in my judgment this contains a number of errors.
>
> 95. First, the Guidance indicates that there is but one trigger for Article 2, namely evidence of arguable breach by the State: See, eg para [54(iv)] above. This is incorrect in that case law identifies a variety of circumstances and types of case of real public importance and significance where the duty arises independently of the existence of evidence of arguable breach.
>
> 96. Secondly, where the Guidance refers to case types where the test may be modified (for example in the case of death in custody) it persists in articulating the test upon the basis of arguability of breach. Since these case types include cases where the law now makes clear that the duty can arise automatically the reference to the arguability test is wrong in law: See para [54(vii)] above.
>
> 97. Thirdly, and related to the first two errors, is the failure even at a broad level to acknowledge the existence of cases where the test is other than arguability.

4.33   At para 118 of his judgment, Green J concluded that the test for whether the Guidance was lawful was whether it would 'if followed (i) lead to unlawful acts (ii) permit unlawful acts or (iii) encourage such unlawful acts?'. The 'unlawful act' being a refusal of legal aid where it was required, or a failure to consider the right legal basis for determining an application. He concluded that 'for the reasons already given the Guidance would do all of these three things'.

4.34   This led the Lord Chancellor to issue revised guidance taking account of the judgment in *Letts*.[10] The current Inquest ECF Guidance sets out the situations where the Lord Chancellor believes funding should be granted, but also recognises that this is a developing area of the law and says that caseworkers deciding applications should take into account case-law that emerges.

4.35   The Inquest ECF Guidance says that there is a two-stage test in Article 2 ECHR cases: 1) whether the procedural obligation (to investigate whether the state has breached the right to life) arises; and then 2) whether representation at the inquest is necessary to discharge the obligation. The guidance was further revised in June 2018 to make it clearer that the procedural obligation will arise in cases of intentional killing by the state, as well as non-natural deaths

---

10   See: www.gov.uk/government/publications/legal-aid-exceptional-case-funding-form-and-guidance.

(including suicide) of persons detained by the state. However, there remains a relatively high threshold to satisfy the second limb of the test, being the necessity for representation. There is discretion to waive the financial eligibility limits where exceptional funding would otherwise be granted in an inquest case.

Application process: non-inquest and inquest ECF

4.36   Practitioners cannot use delegated functions to grant ECF. All applications must be made to the LAA. The Provider Pack produced by the LAA contains information about the application process.

4.37   The LAA generally expects that applications will come from practitioners with contracts in the relevant category. If you do not hold a contract in that category, or at all, you can apply for an individual case contract at the same time as making the application for funding, but will need to show why the 'effective administration of justice' test is met.[11] The test requires that the Director be satisfied it is necessary for the particular provider to provide the services, having taken into account:

a) the provider's knowledge of the particular case and expertise in providing the legal services which are the subject of the application;
b) the nature and likely length of the case;
c) the complexity of the issues; and
d) the circumstances of the applicant.

4.38   If the LAA grants exceptional funding but does not consider the effective administration of justice test to be met, it will refuse an individual case contract and require you to refer the applicant to a provider with a contract in the relevant category.

4.39   If the case falls outside any of the contracted category definitions, the LAA will award an individual case contract without the need to consider the effective administration of justice test to providers without any civil contract. A provider which holds a civil contract can carry out miscellaneous work under that contract and so an individual case contract will not be necessary.

11   Civil Legal Aid (Procedure) Regulations 2012 reg 31(5).

Forms and the Client and Cost Management System (CCMS)

4.40   If you have a civil contract, and access to CCMS, applications for ECF licensed work should be submitted by CCMS. Otherwise, use the CIV ECF1, which should be submitted with a CW1 (if you are applying for Legal Help), or a CIV APP1 (civil licensed work or special case work) or CIV APP3 (for family licensed work cases) and the applicable means form if you are applying for representation. The appropriate means form must also be submitted, since exceptional funding will only be granted if the applicant passes the means and merits tests applicable for the type of legal aid sought. Applications can also be made through the Client and Cost Management System (CCMS), which should be the default mechanism for existing users of the system.

4.41   The LAA will also consider direct applications for non-inquest ECF from individuals who do not nominate any provider, and in that case will consider any information provided by the individual in whatever form it is provided. The LAA states that it does not require individual applicants to complete the ECF, APP and means forms, though in practice it generally does ask them to do so.

4.42   According to the LAA's website, paper applications should be submitted to the Exceptional Cases Funding Team at: Legal Aid Agency (13.51), 13th Floor, 102 Petty France London SW1H 9AJ; or Legal Aid Agency, DX 161440 Westminster 8. However, the address given in the Provider Pack is slightly different: Legal Aid Agency, Post Point 8.51, Eighth Floor, 102 Petty France London SW1H 9AJ. Applications may also be scanned and submitted by email to: contactECC@justice.gov.uk.

Timescales

4.43   The LAA aims to deal with all applications (inquest and non-inquest) within 20 working days. However, the 20-day period is suspended if the LAA asks the provider or applicant for further information.

4.44   There is now some, limited, provision for the LAA to consider non-inquest ECF applications on an urgent basis. Details of the urgency must be included on p6 of the CIV ECF1 form. This will generally be the expiry of a limitation date, an imminent hearing, or some other reason why delay would prejudice or harm the applicant or their case. If the LAA agrees that the situation is urgent, it will prioritise the application above non-urgent ones and aim to deal with it within five working days. However, the LAA will not guarantee to determine an application before a specific deadline in the case.[12]

Payment

4.45 There is no mechanism for providers to be paid for making an application for non-inquest ECF, unless the application is successful. However, after the judgment of Collins J in *IS* the LAA introduced the possibility of funding being granted to investigate whether a client could be eligible for ECF for a further substantive application.[13] We do not yet have experience of how this process works in practice.

4.46 Grants of ECF will generally be backdated and funding at the usual payment rates for the type of funding will be available from the date it is backdated to. For Legal Help/controlled work, provided the application is submitted within two months of the date when the client signs the controlled work form, the LAA will generally backdate any successful ECF application to the date the client signed the CW1 or CW2 form. For Legal Representation, where the application is submitted within two months from the date on the CIVAPP1 or CIVAPP3 as the date of the client's first attendance/instruction on the matter, the LAA will backdate the certificate to that date.[14]

4.47 Providers granted an individual case contract who do not have a Standard Civil Contract will need to make individual arrangements with the LAA to receive payment.[15]

Review process

4.48 There is no independent appeals process, but you can submit an application for review of an unfavourable decision within 14 days. This is done using form APP9E, which should be completed with grounds for review and any supporting documentation to the ECF Team. The LAA aims to process the application for review within ten working days. There is no right of appeal or any further review process. The review should be considered by a senior caseworker not involved in the original decision.

---

12 Provider Pack section 6.
13 Provider Pack section 5, p5.
14 Provider Pack section 7.
15 Provider Pack section 9.

4.49   However, if a refusal is upheld on internal review, there is no further right of appeal. As there is no alternative remedy it may be necessary to resort to judicial review. A judicial review of a refusal of ECF is in-scope under para 19 of Part 1 of Sch 1 to LASPO. If you have a public law contract, you can, therefore, grant Legal Help and/ or apply for Investigative or Full Representation in the usual way to challenge a refusal of ECF by way of judicial review. There is a helpful discussion of the requirements of such an application and dealing with refusals of it in a paper by John Halford and Francesca Allen of Bindmans LLP.[16]

Public Law Project – help and support for practitioners

4.50   The Public Law Project has produced guides to applying for ECF in various different categories of law, which you can access on their website: www.publiclawproject.org.uk and here:

*   https://publiclawproject.org.uk/wp-content/uploads/2018/07/How-to-get-ECF-in-housing-law.pdf;
*   https://publiclawproject.org.uk/wp-content/uploads/2018/07/PLP-ECF-Immigration-Guide.pdf;
*   https://publiclawproject.org.uk/wp-content/uploads/2018/04/How_to_get_ECF_in_Welfare_Benefits_Cases_web-1.pdf;
*   https://publiclawproject.org.uk/wp-content/uploads/2018/02/ECF_family_for_web-1.pdf.

16 'Physician, Heal Thyself: securing funding from the LAA to challenge its own exceptional funding refusals', available at: https://publiclawproject.org.uk/wp-content/uploads/data/resources/194/JH_FA_physician_heal_thyself.pdf.

Conducting a civil/family case

continued

Introduction

5.1   This chapter deals with the general procedures which apply to most types of civil/family case, where the procedures are very similar. There are separate chapters on family cases (private and public law), immigration and mental health, which cover their own funding schemes and rules, as well as on housing, community care and public law.

5.2   In chapter 3, we saw that there are three key stages in providing legal aid services: to ensure that a) the matter is within scope, b) the client is financially eligible and c) the case meets the merits test. In addition, you need to ensure that an application is made properly in the Client and Cost Management System (CCMS) (see chapter 6) so that funding is obtained.

5.3   This chapter explains how these steps are taken successfully in respect of most civil work. Most references are to the 2018 Standard Civil Contract, because cases still in scope started after 1 September 2018 are governed by that contract. For cases started under previous contracts, see earlier editions of this Handbook.

5.4   See appendix C for a summary of the Legal Aid Agency's (LAA's) Costs assessment guidance, in respect of the most common queries raised by caseworkers.

Legal Help

Scope

5.5   At the most basic level, work must be allowed under the Legal Aid, Sentencing and Punishment of Offenders Act 2012 (LASPO) (see chapter 3 for more information).

5.6   Legal Help allows you to provide advice and assistance in relation to a specific matter, but does not cover issuing proceedings, advocacy or instruction of an advocate (although you may obtain counsel's opinion, where justified in a complex case, but this would be very rare). For information about clients who are outside England and Wales or who are not from England and Wales, see further 'Clients abroad' below.

Other sources of funding

5.7   The Civil Legal Aid (Merits Criteria) Regulations 2013[1] state that Legal Help may only be provided if it is reasonable to do so, having

1 Reg 32.

regard to any other sources of funding available to the client. This means that, for example, you should check whether the client has legal expenses insurance (perhaps as part of home contents cover) or is a member (or the partner of a member) of a trade union.

Forms

5.8 The form is the CW1 Legal Help, Help at Court and Family Help (Lower) form.

5.9 The assessment of means and client's details sections must be fully completed, and signed by the client, normally in the presence of someone from your organisation, before you start doing any legal work.[2]

Case study

I don't really want to stick a Legal Help form under the client's nose and ask them to sign, even before we've said 'Good morning'. Does that mean I will not be able to charge for all my time during the initial interview?

You will be covered for the whole interview, as the Standard Contract 2018 Specification para 3.10(i) confirms all the time in an interview will be allowed, when a client signs the CW1 form at any point.

5.10 The form must be kept on the file and is not sent to the LAA, unless requested for an assessment.[3]

What if the client cannot sign the form?

5.11 There will be occasions when your client is a child or patient, and you may not be satisfied of their capacity to sign the form and give instructions. Sometimes a client will not be physically able to attend your office. Under the 2013 Contract you were unable to use more than ten per cent of your matter starts in any schedule period for clients who cannot attend on you personally. Under the 2018 Contract

---

2 Standard Civil Contract 2018 Specification para 3.10.
3 Standard Civil Contract 2018 Specification para 3.12

this has been increased to 25 per cent of your allocated matter starts in that schedule period.[4]

5.12   Whenever you grant Legal Help to a client in the circumstances described below, you should make an attendance note justifying what you did and tick the appropriate box on page 5 of the Legal Help form.

Applications on behalf of children/protected parties

5.13   You can accept an application direct from a child, if the child is entitled to bring, prosecute or defend proceedings without a litigation friend or equivalent;[5] or there is good reason why one of the persons listed in regulation 22(4) of the Civil Legal Aid (Merits Criteria) Regulations 2013 (see para 5.14 below) cannot apply on the client's behalf and the adviser is satisfied that the child understands the nature of the work and is capable of giving instructions.

5.14   An application can be accepted on behalf of a child from:

- a parent, guardian or other person responsible for the child's care;
- a litigation friend or guardian ad litem; or
- if neither of the above are available, any other person (except anyone who works in your organisation), provided that the other person has sufficient knowledge of all the circumstances to act responsibly in the child's interests and to give proper instructions.

5.15   An application can be made on behalf of a protected party by:

- a person acting or proposing to act as the protected party's litigation friend; or
- any other person (who does not work for your organisation) where there is good reason why a litigation friend or proposed litigation friend cannot make the application.[6]

Applications by post

5.16   You may grant Legal Help to a client by post where there is good reason. Standard Civil Contract Specification 2018 para 3.15 says that this applies 'where the client requests that the application is made in

---

4 Standard Civil Contract 2018 Specification para 3.17. This restriction does not apply if you have accepted the case this way in order to comply with the Equality Act 2010.

5 Civil Legal Aid (Procedure) Regulations 2012 reg 22(2).

6 Civil Legal Aid (Procedure) Regulations 2012 reg 22(4).

this way and it is not necessary for the interests of the client or his or her case to attend in person'.

People resident outside the European Union

5.17 You may not grant Legal Help by post to a client resident outside the European Union (EU) if one of the following applies:[7]

- the client could, without serious disadvantage, delay his or her application until the client had returned to the EU;
- someone resident in the EU could apply on the client's behalf; or
- it would otherwise be unreasonable to accept the application.

This means that applications by post can be accepted from persons outside the EU in certain circumstances. This facility has been particularly useful in immigration cases where clients have been refused entry to the UK, or have been removed or deported, but have a right of appeal that can be exercised from outside the UK. From April 2013 such cases are less likely to be in scope, but clients abroad can apply for legal aid if the work does remain in scope, for example judicial reviews.

Applications by fax

5.18 You can only accept applications by fax if that is specified in your contract schedule. The Standard Civil Contract 2018 Specification para 3.15 says that you can only exercise that power if your client is a child or vulnerable adult and work is urgently required for the client's safety, and you take reasonable steps to obtain the original signed form.

Telephone, webcam and email advice

5.19 You can give, and claim for, advice over the telephone or by email, webcam etc if the client cannot attend your office for a 'good reason' as defined in the Standard Civil Contract 2018 Specification para 3.18, see applications by post above, provided the client is later found to be eligible for Legal Help and signs the form. If the client subsequently fails to sign the form, you cannot claim payment.[8] This can be combined with a postal application, subject to the rules above, meaning that the client does not need to attend your offices to sign the form.

---

7 Standard Civil Contract 2018 Specification para 3.1.
8 Standard Civil Contract 2018 Specification para 3.20.

Financial eligibility

5.20   Clients must be financially eligible on both capital and income. Evidence must relate to the previous calendar month.[9] They must inform you of any change in their means and you may have to stop work if their means change significantly (see chapter 3 for more information). However, there are no contributions to be paid in respect of Legal Help.

5.21   The Standard Civil Contract 2018 Specification para 3.23 states that you can only carry out work for clients who are financially eligible and that you must obtain satisfactory evidence of their means before assessing eligibility. In practical terms, that means, except in exceptional circumstances, you must obtain evidence of a client's means before starting work and retain that evidence on file. Further guidance and a non-exhaustive list of types of satisfactory evidence may be found in section 12 of the *Guide to determining financial eligibility for controlled work and family mediation*.[10] What is required is satisfactory evidence to show that the client is eligible. Where reasonable to do so, you may accept evidence that falls outside the computation period – for example, a letter showing an award of benefits issued before the period.

5.22   Generally the evidence should show the amounts received. However (in a case based on the previous Access to Justice Act rules, which were similarly worded), the High Court has ruled that a nil assessment because a local authority letter showing a client as being in receipt of Children Act 1989 s17 support did not contain the amounts was irrational because it was within the solicitor's knowledge that such support was within eligibility limits. The question that should have been asked was not whether the evidence contained the amounts, but whether it was reasonably sufficient to show eligibility.[11]

5.23   If it is 'not practicable to obtain it before commencing controlled work', you may start without evidence of means, but you need to show that you acted reasonably in assessing eligibility and starting work without evidence. In practice you should record on your initial attendance note:

9   Civil Legal Aid (Financial Resources and Payment for Services) Regulations 2013 Reg 14(2).

10   See: www.gov.uk/government/uploads/system/uploads/attachment_data/file/420970/laa-determine-controlled-work-mediation.pdf/.

11   *R (Duncan Lewis Solicitors) v The Lord Chancellor* [2015] EWHC 2498 (Admin).

- **why** it was reasonable to start work without evidence of means (for example, because the client needed advice urgently due to the imminent expiry of a time limit); and
- **how** you assessed eligibility (eg by making sure that the Legal Help form is properly completed, using the information the client was able to give you from the client's account of what he or she has been living on).

5.24 You must get the evidence as soon as practicable unless the client's circumstances prevent this being done at all at any point in the case, for example due to mental disability, age or homelessness.[12] Where a client states that they have no income or capital, you should assess whether this is credible and note your file accordingly. Where a client has, for example, recently fled domestic violence that may well be the case. You should enquire how they are living day to day and if, for example, financial or other support is being provided by a friend or relative, that person should provide a letter setting out the nature and extent – and any financial amounts – of that support.[13]

5.25 If you act reasonably in granting Legal Help to a client before obtaining evidence of their means and you do not claim any disbursement or report any time after the point where the LAA decides it would have been practicable to obtain satisfactory evidence of means, you can still claim payment for the work.

5.26 However, if the LAA decides that you could have obtained evidence of means at any stage of the case, costs will be 'nil assessed' at any audit. Having files 'nil assessed' can have very serious consequences, so it is strongly advisable to get valid evidence of means prior to starting work in all but emergency situations.

Merits test

5.27 The Legal Help merits test is known as the 'sufficient benefit test', and in full states: 'Help may only be provided where there is sufficient benefit to the client, having regard to the circumstances of the matter, including the circumstances of the individual, to justify the cost of the provision of legal help'.[14] This is not intended to be a

---

12 Standard Civil Contract 2018 Specification para 3.24.
13 *Guide to determining financial eligibility for controlled work and family mediation*, April 2015 v1, para 12.2.16.
14 Civil Legal Aid (Merits Criteria) Regulations 2013 reg 32(b).

high hurdle, at least to initial advice, but will apply to all steps in the case:

> . . . it may well be considered worthwhile for an individual to pay for initial advice, including the advice that the case is not worth pursuing further. The more legal help is provided, however, the more that the benefits deriving from the costs incurred will need to be taken into account.[15]

Previous advice

5.28   Clients are generally only entitled to advice on a matter from one legal aid provider, so you should always ask the client whether he or she has taken previous advice before starting work.

5.29   The Standard Civil Contract 2018 Specification paras 3.40–3.45 set out what you must do if the client has received previous advice, whether that is from your organisation or somewhere else.

5.30   There is a list of particular circumstances in which a new matter start will not be justified at para 3.46 of the Standard Civil Contract 2018 Specification. However, it is worth noting that you can open a new matter if a client faces enforcement proceedings because he or she is alleged to have breached the terms of a suspended or postponed order, or the terms on which proceedings were adjourned.[16]

5.31   You generally cannot open a new matter for a client who has received advice on the same matter within the last six months, unless an exception applies. Exceptions are listed at para 3.35 of the Standard Civil Contract 2018 Specification:

- There has been a material development or change in the client's instructions and at least three months have elapsed since the previous claim was submitted, but:
  - note that if the client has simply failed to give instructions, then returns, that cannot be counted as a change in instructions;
  - change in the law that was anticipated in the original matter cannot count as a material development;
  - a decision, or other response from another party, arising from the first piece of work cannot count as a material development.

---

15   *Lord Chancellor's guidance on civil legal aid* (2018) para 4.2.14.
16   Standard Civil Contract 2018 Specification para 3.48.

- The client has reasonable cause for dissatisfaction with the previous adviser (this must be justified dissatisfaction with the service, not because the client was unhappy about good advice they were given or wants a second opinion).
- The client has moved away and has difficulty communicating with the previous adviser.
- The first adviser is no longer able to act for a good reason relating to professional conduct, eg conflict of interest.
- The first adviser has confirmed that no claim will be made.

5.32   If the client says that he or she is dissatisfied, you must request confirmation of the reasons for transfer, and a copy of the file from the previous organisation. If the client refuses consent, no advice should be given and no claim can be made.[17] No work may be done until the previous file has been received unless absolutely necessary, to protect the client's position or meet a deadline. When you receive the file, if you believe the client was unreasonable in being dissatisfied with the service, you must stop work but can still claim a fixed fee if urgent work was justified before getting the file.[18]

Case study

Can I open a new matter when the client has already received advice on the same problem from my organisation?

Legal Help forms are also known as 'new matter starts' (see chapter 3 for more information about means tests for Legal Help cases).

Matter claimed	Open new matter?
Up to 3 months ago	No
3–6 months	Yes – if there is a material development or change in instructions
6+ months ago	Yes

---

17 Standard Civil Contract 2018 Specification para 3.42.
18 Standard Civil Contract 2018 Specification para 3.43.

Case study

My client says she received advice from the Civil Legal Advice telephone service last month. Can I open a new matter start?

First, check that the category of advice would fall within your contract schedule (ie, family, debt or housing).

It is mandatory for debt work to go through the telephone gateway (note the mandatory element of the gateway will end in spring 2020 so check the Legal Aid Handbook website for further detail: https://legalaidhandbook.com/. As a face-to-face provider, you can only do debt work if the client is exempt (see para 3.11) or the gateway refers it to you.

The other two gateway categories – education and discrimination – will have transitional provisions between from 1 September 2019 until the changes are made.

Having established whether you can take it on in principle, it depends how much work they did for the client. Ask her to show you the confirmation of instructions, advice and action letter which the gateway will have sent under SQM requirement F1.1.

If the client has not signed a Legal Help form, you can open a new matter, as initial telephone advice is not 'controlled work' under the Civil Legal Aid (Procedure) Regulations 2012 reg 2.

Otherwise, you should treat advice from the Civil Legal Advice telephone service as you would advice from any other LAA provider.

Reopening a closed matter

5.33   Although you may not be able to open a new matter, you can (and may be obliged to) do more work on the original matter.[19] The disadvantage is that you cannot claim an additional fixed fee; but there are compensations:[20]

- previous work and additional work after the client comes back, can be counted together towards the escape fee threshold;
- further disbursements can be claimed.

19 Standard Civil Contract 2018 Specification para 3.34.
20 Standard Civil Contract 2018 Specification para 3.37.

> **Case study**
>
> *What is the procedure for reporting a revived Legal Help case to the LAA?*
>
> You complete the appropriate amendment spreadsheet to the LAA (civil, crime, or mediation) and send it with an email to Operational Assurance explaining what you have done: PA-ClaimAmend @legalservices.gsi.gov.uk. You should put your organisation's name and account number in the subject line. Operational Assurance will void the first claim so that you do not claim twice for the same matter. They will confirm the action they have taken and copy to your contract manager for information.

Opening more than one matter

Separate and distinct

5.34 If a client has problems that are 'separate and distinct',[21] you can open more than one matter. Opening more than one matter for a client must be carefully justified in every case if you are not to fall foul of LAA audits. If your organisation is found to have opened matters incorrectly, significant amounts of money may need to be repaid to the LAA, so it is extremely important to get this right.

5.35 It is relatively easy to justify more than one case as 'separate and distinct' if they necessarily fall under different categories of law. So, if a client has a housing problem and needs a divorce, it is likely to be justifiable to open two matters (subject to scope rules).

5.36 It is more difficult to justify opening more than one matter within one overall category of law. The first thing to remember is that the rules contained in the category-specific sections of the Specification take precedence.[22] So, if you are considering whether to open more than one matter within a category, you should look up the category-specific rules first. See chapters 7–14 for more on the rules for individual categories.

Different causes or events

5.37 If your client's circumstances are not explicitly dealt with, it is worth applying the wording in the general Contract Specification, which

---

21 Standard Civil Contract 2018 Specification para 3.30.
22 Standard Civil Contract 2018 Specification para 1.2.

states that matters are 'separate and distinct' 'typically because they arise out of different causes or events'. So, it is a good idea to ask yourself whether the causes or events are separate. For example, if your client has a serious housing disrepair problem and a family law problem, these would be very likely to be separate and distinct.

5.38   It is more difficult if the client has 'more than one separate and distinct legal problem' within a category.[23] You must be able to demonstrate two things:

> If legal proceedings were started, or other appropriate remedies pursued, for each problem it would be appropriate for such proceedings to be both issued and heard separately.
>
> AND
>
> Each problem requires substantial legal work which does not address the other problem(s).

'Substantial legal work' is defined as at least 30 minutes' additional preparation or advice, or separate communication with other parties on legal issues.[24]

Work that does not address the other problem(s)

5.39   If you are going to satisfy the LAA that work on one issue does not address another, this has to be clear in your case recording. If you consistently deal with two or more issues together, it will be very difficult to argue that they were really 'separate and distinct'. You will need to open two separate files and keep separate attendance notes and letters relating to each issue. However, more than one problem may be discussed in one interview with a client as this may be more convenient for them. If so, separate attendance notes should be produced for each and time apportioned between the issues.

5.40   If you consider that the test is satisfied, you can ask the client to sign more than one Legal Help form at the initial meeting, or subsequently.[25]

23 Standard Civil Contract 2018 Specification para 3.30.
24 Standard Civil Contract 2018 Specification para 3.31.
25 Standard Civil Contract 2018 Specification paras 3.29 (c) and 3.32.

More than one client

5.41   The LAA says that you should only use one new matter even if the problem involves more than one client, unless:[26]

- if proceedings were issued, each client would be a party to those proceedings;
- each client has a separate and distinct legal interest in the problem or issue; *and*
- in considering whether there is sufficient benefit for the second or any subsequent client to receive Legal Help, you take into account the fact that Legal Help that is already being provided in relation to the same general problem.

Case study

I have a client who has been unlawfully evicted from his rented property. He doesn't want to go back there but does want to sue the landlord. He also wants to apply to the local authority as homeless. How many Legal Help forms should he sign?

This is two matter starts. They are two separate causes of action, albeit both within the housing category, and were the cases to go to court they would be separate proceedings.

Funding

Fixed fees

5.42   Legal Help is paid under fixed fees, although cases that reach the escape threshold (three times the fixed fee) can be paid in full at hourly rates. Current fees and hourly rates are found in the Civil Legal Aid (Remuneration) Regulations 2013.

5.43   Paragraph 3.30 of the Standard Civil Contract Specification 2018 states that you must not open more than one matter start for a client unless the client has more than one 'separate and distinct' legal problem – see above.

More than one fixed fee

5.44   In some circumstances, you may be able to justify opening more than one Legal Help file for a client. For more information about this,

---

26 Standard Civil Contract 2018 Specification para 3.38.

see para 5.34 onwards above; and comments in relation to individual categories of law, below.

Housing possession schemes

5.45   You cannot ask a client to sign a Legal Help form at a court duty scheme, as this work is funded under a separate schedule, and is paid at a fixed fee per client seen.[27]

5.46   If you make a claim under the Housing Possession Court Duty Scheme (HPCDS) then you cannot provide assistance on the same matter under the Legal Help Scheme, see para 12.65 below.

5.47   If follow-up work is required, then practitioners will want to make sure that a representation certificate under delegated functions is applied for if at all possible.

Disbursements

5.48   You can claim disbursements in addition to the fixed fee,[28] provided that they meet the criteria set out in the contract:

- it is in the best interests of the client to incur the disbursement;
- it is reasonable to incur the disbursement for the purpose of providing controlled work, ie necessary for the purpose of giving advice to the client or progressing the case;
- the amount of the disbursement is reasonable; and
- it is not a disbursement which is specifically prohibited.[29]

See para 16.15 for more information.

Disbursements that may not be claimed under controlled work

5.49   The Standard Civil Contract 2018 Specification para 4.29 provides a non-exhaustive list of disbursements that may not be incurred in the provision of controlled work. Note that the same disbursements are prohibited for licensed work, save that court fees are an allowable disbursement under a certificate.[30] These disbursements are:

27 Standard Civil Contract 2018 HPCDS Specification para 1.10.
28 Standard Civil Contract 2018 Specification para 4.8.
29 Standard Civil Contract 2018 Specification para 4.24 and subject-specific sections.
30 Standard Civil Contract 2018 Specification para 6.61.

- costs of (or expenses relating to) the residential assessment of a child or treatment, therapy, training or other interventions of an educative or rehabilitative nature unless authorised by the LAA;
- Ad Valorem stamp duties;
- capital duty;
- clients' travelling and accommodation expenses save in the circumstances prescribed in the Costs assessment guidance and unless they relate to treatment, therapy, training or other interventions of an educative or rehabilitative nature or to the residential assessment of a child (in the immigration category you may in limited circumstances pay the client's travel expenses to attend to give instructions);[31]
- all fees, charges and costs of child contact centres, including assessments and reports on supervised contact, and of other professional assessments of contact between children and adults;
- court fees unless for a search/photocopies/bailiff service or as part of Controlled Legal Representation or otherwise permitted by Category Specific Rules;
- discharge of debts owed by the client, for example, rent or mortgage arrears;
- fee payable on voluntary petitions in bankruptcy;
- fee payable to implement a pension sharing order;
- fee payable to the Office of the Public Guardian;
- immigration application fees;
- mortgagees' or lessors' legal costs and disbursements;
- passport fees;
- probate fees;
- in the family category of law only, costs of or expenses in relation to the provision of family mediation, conciliation or any other dispute resolution including family group conferences;
- in the family category of law only, costs or expenses of risk assessments within section 16A of the Children Act 1989 (as amended) and undertaken by CAFCASS (Children and Family Court Advisory and Support Service) officers or Welsh family proceedings officers, including assessments of the risk of harm to a child in connection with domestic abuse to the child or another person;
- in the family category of law only, costs of or expenses relating to any activity to promote contact with a child directed by the court under sections 11A–11G of the Children Act 1989 (as

---

31 Standard Civil Contract Specification 2018 para 8.49.

amended) – this includes all programmes, consideration of suitability under section 11E and other work to or with a view to establishing, maintaining or improving contact with a child or, by addressing violent behaviour, to or with a view to enabling or facilitating contact with a child;

- any administration fee charged by an expert including, but not limited to, i) a fee in respect of office space or provision of a consultation room; ii) a fee in respect of administrative support services, such as typing services; iii) a fee in respect of courier services; and iv) a subsistence fee;
- any cancellation fee charged by an expert, where the notice of cancellation was given to the expert more than 72 hours before the relevant hearing or appointment;
- any fees charged for witness intermediary services provided in court, reports in advance of the provision of such services and other work in preparation for or ancillary to court proceedings.

5.50   The LAA limits what it will pay in respect of experts to 45 pence per mile for travelling costs, and £40 per hour travelling time. Substantive work by experts will be limited to the hourly rates/fixed fees for that expertise set out in the remuneration regulations (see paras 5.143 onwards for more).

5.51   Family practitioners should note the Standard Civil Contract 2018 Specification para 7.64, which states that:

> Court fees are an allowable disbursement under Family Help (Lower) only where such fees are incurred for the purpose of obtaining a consent order. In all cases, court fees may only be incurred where they are a reasonable and proportionate step which satisfies the reasonable private paying individual test (regulation 7 of the Merits Regulations).

The enhancement of costs has two stages (threshold and factors) and is found in the Contract[32] and expanded upon under section 12 of the Costs Assessment Guidance.

5.52   This is slightly ambiguous, but it means that consent order fees are the only ones permitted and it must be reasonable to incur them.

5.53   This contrasts with licensed work, where court fees are an allowable disbursement, and with Legal Help, where court fees are never allowable.

---

32   Standard Civil Contract 2018 Specification paras 6.13–6.15.

Help at Court

Scope

5.54 Work must be allowed under LASPO (see chapter 3 for more information). Help at Court is help and advocacy for a client in relation to a particular hearing, without formally acting as legal representative in the proceedings.

'Help at court' means the provision of any of the following civil legal services at a particular hearing–

(a) instructing an advocate;
(b) preparing to provide advocacy; or
(c) advocacy.[33]

However, note that counsel may not be instructed under Help at Court.

5.55 Ongoing representation can only be provided under a legal representation certificate.

5.56 Help at Court is useful for cases where a legal representation certificate would not be available – for example, where a client does not have a defence to a possession claim but does need an experienced adviser to set out repayment proposals to the court. Help at Court can also be used to represent the client on an application for enforcement of an order where the client is the applicant.

5.57 However, it is always preferable to provide representation under a legal representation certificate wherever possible as this provides costs protection for the client (para 5.82) and is better paid (at hourly rates in civil non-family categories).

5.58 See chapter 12 (housing) for more on when Help at Court can be used.

Financial eligibility

5.59 As Legal Help, see above.

Merits test

The sufficient benefit test

5.60 See Legal Help, above.

5.61 The nature of the proceedings and the circumstances of the hearing must be such that representation will be of real benefit to

---

33 Civil Legal Aid (Procedure) Regulations 2012 reg 5.

the client.[34] This means the issue(s) must be more complex than the client could have explained to the court himself or herself.

5.62　You must apply the test before every hearing and note the file with your justification. 'Sufficient benefit test met' is not an adequate justification.

Forms

5.63　The form is the CW1 Legal Help, Help at Court and Family Help (Lower) form (see Legal Help, above).

5.64　If the client has already signed a Legal Help form to cover advice and assistance, he or she does not need to sign another form in relation to Help at Court.[35]

Funding

5.65　Advisers without rights of audience may provide informal advocacy and claim payment under Help at Court, as long as advocacy is justified, and the court agrees to hear them. Counsel may not be instructed.

5.66　There are no additional fixed fees to cover Help at Court. However, the additional work involved may make it more likely that the case will reach the escape threshold (three times the fixed fee).

5.67　Where advocacy is justified, you may claim travel and waiting to/ from and at court, as well as preparation and attendance, where appropriate. See chapter 16 for more information on payment schemes.

Help with Family Mediation

5.68　This level of controlled work was introduced from 1 April 2013 to pay for legal advice to clients who are participating, or have participated, in family mediation – see chapter 9 for more information.

Ending a case

5.69　The Standard Civil Contract Specification 2018 para 3.64 sets out the circumstances in which you can close your file and claim your costs.

34　Civil Legal Aid (Merits Criteria) Regulations 2013 reg 33.
35　Standard Civil Contract 2018 Specification para 1.44.

5.70   Most are obvious: the client decides not to proceed, or decides to take the matter forward himself of herself; a representation certificate is granted, or you cannot act further due to a conflict of interest or other professional conduct issue; or the matter simply reaches a logical conclusion.

5.71   One is less obvious, which is where the client fails to give instructions for three months (unless the matter is on hold, for example, because you are waiting for a third party to act or you have agreed it with the client). You have to watch out for this, because on a costs/contract compliance audit (see chapter 22) the LAA may say that the case terminated at that point and disallow all profit costs and disbursements after it. This is important in escape fee cases.

5.72   You cannot stop work or close a matter simply because the value of your costs is equal to, or more than, the fixed fee.[36] Equally, you should not delay making an application for a certificate that would otherwise be appropriate so that your costs cross the escape fee threshold.[37]

5.73   You should close and claim for your case as soon as you properly can, as apart from anything else, the date of the claim is when time starts to run to open a new matter start if the client subsequently needs further advice.

5.74   You have to submit a claim for controlled work standard fee matters within six months of the ending of the matter.[38]

5.75   Note that claims for escape fee cases have to be submitted within three months of the standard fee claim on that case.[39]

5.76   If you fail to submit claims within time limits 'persistently', you may receive a contract notice, which could lead to contract termination.[40]

Ending a case – monitoring

5.77   The LAA monitors organisations remotely, using the data they supply as a matter of course when applying for funding or claiming at the end of the case.

5.78   The Standard Contract 2018 includes key performance indicators (KPIs). We will deal with all the KPIs in this section for complete-

---

36 Standard Civil Contract 2018 Specification para 3.5.
37 Standard Civil Contract 2018 Specification para 3.6.
38 Standard Civil Contract 2018 Specification para 4.41.
39 Standard Civil Contract 2018 Specification para 4.20.
40 Standard Contract 2018 clause 14.5.

ness, although some relate to controlled work and some to licensed work. Some KPIs apply to all categories of law and a few are category specific. Standard Civil Contract Specification 2018 paras 2.52–2.71 contains the detailed rules.

5.79 Failure to meet KPIs can result in further audit or monitoring and could be taken into account when bidding for a new contract.[41] Therefore, it is important for caseworkers to be aware that their performance under the contract can affect the organisation as a whole.

Key performance indicators

5.80 KPIs are monitored on a rolling three-month basis, rather than on each individual case. They are set out from para 2.52 onwards of the Standard Civil Contract Specification 2018. A summary of the KPIs is as follows:

KPI 1 – Controlled work (non-fixed fee) – assessment reduction – ten per cent max

When your 'escape cases' are assessed (these are the cases that used to be called exceptional cases, where the costs on a time and item basis are 3 × the fixed fee), the costs claimed must not be reduced by more than ten per cent. This includes disbursements but not VAT. This KPI will be calculated across a minimum of three months and a minimum of ten cases.

KPI 2 – Licensed work – assessment reduction – 15 per cent max

This sets a similar target in relation to licensed work cases that are claimed on a time and item basis. This KPI will be calculated across a minimum of three months and a minimum of five cases.

KPI 3 – Fixed fee margin – 20 per cent max

The LAA is concerned that some organisations will select clients with straightforward cases that do not require much work, in order to retain a high surplus under each fixed fee case. This KPI can only be met if the total cost of cases under fixed fees when calculated in minutes and items is at least 80 per cent of the appropriate fixed fees.

This KPI applies to controlled work cases, and Family Private and Public Law Representation Scheme cases that are paid by way of fixed fees.

---

41 Standard Contract 2018 clauses 11.5 and 11.6.

KPI 4 – Rejection rates for licensed work – five per cent max in the schedule period

Rejections are when applications or claims are refused because of technical errors in form completion, or lack of enclosures etc. This applies to applications for legal aid (known as applications for determinations that an individual qualifies for legal aid in the post-LASPO scheme) and claims for payment. There are separate KPIs for applications for funding (KPI 4A) and for claims (KPI 4B).

KPI 5 – Refusal rates for licensed work – 15 per cent max in the schedule period

This applies to applications for legal aid which are refused because the LAA considers that the practitioner has failed to show that they meet the applicable means or merits test.

KPI 6 – Legal Representation outcomes – 30 per cent minimum

This KPI applies to all licensed work except in the Clinical Negligence and Claims Against Public Authorities categories.

KPI 7 – Quality – Post investigative success – substantive benefit – claims against public authorities 50 per cent, clinical negligence 60 per cent

This applies to licensed work which proceed beyond investigation in these two categories.

Legal aid representation certificates

Scope

5.81   Legal aid representation certificates are also known as 'full legal aid certificates'. They authorise the conduct of litigation and the provision of advocacy and representation, and generally – though not always[42] – include steps preliminary and incidental to proceedings, and steps to settle or avoid proceedings.

5.82   Clients in receipt of a legal aid certificate have a high degree of protection against costs being awarded against them.[43] Failure to advise clients of their ability to seek public funding where available

---

42 For example – a certificate is not available in housing possession cases until proceedings have been issued; see chapter 12.
43 LASPO s26 and Civil Legal Aid (Costs) Regulations 2013.

could be a matter of professional misconduct[44] (though there is no obligation on any individual solicitor to take on a case on legal aid as opposed to privately as long as the client is aware they could have got legal aid somewhere else).

Investigative representation

5.83   This is a type of civil legal aid funding certificate (not available in family, mental health or immigration) limited to the investigation of a claim where the prospects of success are unclear without substantial investigative work; but it appears that once the investigative work is completed, the case would meet the merits test for a representation certificate[45] (see below). It is preferable to conduct investigation under this form of funding where possible rather than under Legal Help as it is paid under hourly rates and there is less uncertainty about payment than a Legal Help escape fee claim.

5.84   The *Lord Chancellor's guidance on civil legal aid*[46] suggests that substantial investigative work would be at least six hours of fee earner work or disbursements (including counsel's fees) of £400 or more (ex VAT). Therefore, an application needs to be very clear about the extent of work required. It may be possible to obtain a very brief opinion pro bono from counsel to confirm that merits are not clear, and counsel will need to consider the papers in full before advising on merits. It will not be necessary for counsel to give any advice on the actual details of the case itself at this stage.

Before you apply for a certificate

5.85   You need to ensure that the standard criteria are satisfied (see also para 5.94):

- The case must concern a matter of England and Wales (or Welsh) law, in an area permitted by LASPO (see chapter 3).
- The client must be an individual, and a party or proposed party to the proceedings or potential proceedings.
- You must be permitted by your contract to carry out the case.
- The client must not have acted unreasonably in this or any other application, or in these or any other proceedings (for example, by

---

44 Solicitors Regulation Authority (SRA) Principle 7 '. . . act: in the best interests of each client'.
45 Civil Legal Aid (Merits Criteria) Regulations 2013 reg 40.
46 Lord Chancellor's guidance under section 4 of LASPO (2018) para 6.11.

concealing information or acting dishonestly to obtain funding – this criterion does not refer to a client's general character or notoriety).

- There must be no alternative funding available to the client, for example through an insurance policy or trade union membership, or through another person or organisation the client could approach to fund the case.
- There must be no alternatives to litigation, or the client must have exhausted reasonable alternatives, such as complaints and ombudsman schemes and alternative dispute resolution mechanisms.
- The application should not be premature – that is, funding under Legal Help or Help at Court would not be more appropriate at this stage.
- It must be necessary for the client to be represented in the proceedings, and funding will be refused if it is not necessary, for example if the case is straightforward and parties would ordinarily not be represented, or if the client does not need to be separately represented.
- Funding will be refused for cases allocated to the small claims track in the county court.[47]
- Representation will be refused if the case is suitable for a conditional fee agreement and the client is likely to be able to enter into a Conditional Fee Agreement (CFA), damages-based agreement or other litigation funding agreement.[48] This test is likely to be applied strictly.[49] See para 5.98.

Clients abroad

5.86 Although the case must be a matter of England and Wales (or Welsh) law, the client does not have to be resident in England or Wales to receive funding. Where clients abroad are entitled to access the courts in England and Wales, they remain eligible for legal aid subject to the usual scope, means and merits provisions. For example, legal aid is likely to be refused if any order obtained in England and Wales is likely to be ineffective, for example, if there is no reciprocal judicial protocol.[50]

---

47 Civil Legal Aid (Merits Criteria) Regulations 2013 reg 39.
48 Civil Legal Aid (Merits Criteria) Regulations 2013 reg 2.
49 See para 7.16 of the *Lord Chancellor's guidance on civil legal aid* (2018).
50 Civil Legal Aid (Merits Criteria) Regulations 2013 reg 66(2).

5.87   The proposed residence test[51] has been ruled unlawful by the Supreme Court[52] in the form in which the government intended to implement it. It is now clear that any residence test will require primary legislation, and at the time of writing no further policy announcement had been made.

Clients abroad – procedures

5.88   Where the client is outside the EU (the Channel Islands and Isle of Man counting as part of the EU for these purposes), special procedures must be followed:

- The application must be made in English or French.
- If the client is not a member of UK armed forces posted outside the EU, the application must be sworn before a person authorised under local law to administer oaths or before a British consular official.
- The application must be accompanied by a sworn statement, made by a responsible person who has knowledge of the facts, certifying the client's statement of means as accurate.[53]

Clients from abroad

5.89   Under Home Office guidelines,[54] legal aid is not classed as a 'public fund' for the purposes of those with no recourse to public funds. Legal aid is available regardless of immigration status.

Children

5.90   Where the client is a child, you should note that (unlike controlled work) children cannot apply for funding direct. Where children are parties to litigation in the courts, they should be represented by litigation friends, and it is the litigation friend who should make the application for funding on behalf of the child. However, the application should be in the name of the child. Where the court orders that the child can be a party to the proceedings without a litigation friend, you should make the application on the child's behalf as the child's solicitor.[55]

---

51 https://legalaidhandbook.com/2014/06/17/can-you-prove-it/.
52 *R (Public Law Project) v The Lord Chancellor* [2016] UKSC 39.
53 Civil Legal Aid (Procedure) Regulations 2012 reg 31(3).
54 See: www.gov.uk/government/publications/public-funds.
55 Civil Legal Aid (Procedure) Regulations 2012 reg 30(2)(b).

5.91 The child's own means, not those of the litigation friend, are the means to be assessed, and you should therefore put the child's means into CCMS.[56] In cases where others might have an interest (for example, in special educational needs (SEN) and public law cases), the LAA can require them to make a financial contribution.[57] Therefore, where you are submitting an application on behalf of a child, you should make clear whether you are seeking to justify non-aggregation of means, and if so, explain why it would be inequitable to aggregate, for example because there is a conflict between the child and adult.

Financial eligibility

5.92 See chapter 3. See also para 5.154 'Funding from the client's point of view', below. Where the client declares a bank account on the application, he or she will be required to provide three months' worth of statements. Where the client is in employment, he or she will need to provide three months of wage slips (and an L17 is not required unless the client cannot do so).

Merits test

5.93 Funding will not be granted unless the case passes the merits test. There are a number of different merits tests depending on the type of case – for those that apply in family, immigration and housing cases, see chapters 7, 8, 10 and 12; for all others, see below. The various merits tests are set out in the Civil Legal Aid (Merits Criteria) Regulations 2013, amended by the Civil Legal Aid (Merits Criteria) (Amendment) (No 2) Regulations 2015 and the Civil Legal Aid (Merits Criteria) (Amendment) Regulations 2016, and in each case you must satisfy both the standard criteria and the particular criteria applicable to the case.

The standard criteria

5.94 Before you apply for a certificate, you need to ensure that the standard criteria are satisfied:[58]

56 Civil Legal Aid (Financial Resources and Payment for Services) Regulations 2013 reg 13.
57 Civil Legal Aid (Financial Resources and Payment for Services) Regulations 2013 reg 44(6).
58 Civil Legal Aid (Merits Criteria) Regulations 2013 reg 39.

(a) the individual does not have access to other potential sources of funding (other than a conditional fee agreement) from which it would be reasonable to fund the case;

(b) the case is unsuitable for a conditional fee agreement;[59]

(c) there is no other person other than the individual, including a person who might benefit from the proceedings, who can reasonably be expected to bring the proceedings;

(d) the individual has exhausted all reasonable alternatives to bringing proceedings including any complaints system, ombudsman scheme or other form of alternative dispute resolution;

(e) there is a need for representation in all the circumstances of the case including–

  (i) the nature and complexity of the issues;

  (ii) the existence of other proceedings; and

  (iii) the interests of other parties to the proceedings; and

(f) the proceedings are not likely to be allocated to the small claims track.

5.95   The first criterion requires you to consider whether the client has alternative methods of funding the case at his or her disposal, and you will need to explore with the client and consider whether the client has, for example, trade union membership or legal expenses insurance. Many household insurance policies include legal expenses insurance, and therefore if the client has a policy you will need to consider the certificates to satisfy yourself that the particular case is not covered (you will need to address this on the application form).

5.96   The LAA will ask people unconnected with the case (and possibly even unrelated to the client) to make declarations as to their means. This has forced clients to tell people they might not wish to know about their situation. The difficulty is that Civil Legal Aid (Financial Resources and Payment for Services) Regulations 2013 reg 16(5) allows the LAA to take the resources of persons other than the person applying for legal aid into account if the LAA considers that they may be 'substantially maintaining' the client. However, this power is discretionary, and if there are valid reasons why it should not be applied in a particular case, the LAA should be asked to take these into account.

5.97   The LAA will also investigate this as part of its consideration of the standard criteria – in particular that there is no other person who can reasonably be expected to bring the proceedings. For example, the LAA will want evidence about the means of adults living in a

59   See para 7.16 of the *Lord Chancellor's guidance on civil legal aid* for the approach the LAA will take to suitability for a CFA. See also para 5.98 below.

property if it appears they would benefit from defending possession proceedings and could contribute to legal costs. If they are unable to contribute due to their own circumstances, the reason should be provided as 'extra information' in the means section of the CCMS application.

5.98   The Director of Legal Aid has to consider whether the case is 'unsuitable' for a CFA.[60] You therefore need to make sure you tick the 'yes' box on the CCMS form to confirm the case is *not* suitable for a CFA, bearing in mind the guidance below. The *Lord Chancellor's guidance on civil legal aid* says:

> 7.17 The test of suitability for a CFA is an objective one, rather than a question of whether an individual provider is willing to act under a CFA (although the test cannot be met if there is evidence of a CFA in fact having been offered or put in place for the applicant). In principle a non-family case may be considered suitable for a conditional fee agreement if:
> - Prospects of success are considered at least at 60%
> - The opponent is considered able to meet any costs and/or damages (or other sum of money) that might be awarded
> - After-the-event insurance can be obtained by the applicant
>
> 7.18 An applicant without after-the-event insurance seeking services otherwise considered suitable for a CFA will be expected to provide evidence of attempts to secure such insurance. Even where evidence is provided of refusals of insurance, the Director him/herself may make enquiries of insurers to see if they would support a CFA in the individual circumstances. Moreover, it will not always be sufficient for the applicant to allege that s/he cannot afford the after-the-event premium. If the proposed claim is for damages then the applicant would need to demonstrate that it has not been possible to defer payment of the premium from any damages recovered.
>
> 7.19 If the proposed proceedings do not include a claim for damages or other money, however, particular considerations apply. An applicant for legal aid is unlikely to be able to pay an after-the-event insurance premium or success fee from his/her own resources, and the case should not generally be considered as suitable for a CFA unless both:
> - prospects of success are at least 80% (otherwise it would be unreasonable to expect the legal representative to act at risk in relation to costs without the prospect of a success fee or for the applicant to risk an adverse costs order); and
> - the case will not involve significant expenditure on disbursements (in particular experts' fees).

---

60 Civil Legal Aid (Merits Criteria) Regulations 2013 reg 39.

Of course, if there is no likelihood of either damages or costs being awarded (for instance in seeking an injunction against an impecunious opponent) then there is no basis on which the case could be pursued under a CFA.

7.20 The fact that the applicant may wish to obtain legal aid rather than a CFA because of the potential deduction from damages in respect of a success premium or damages agreement, will not of itself prevent a case being suitable for a CFA. The test is not whether the applicant or provider would prefer legal aid to a CFA, but is, in essence, whether the case could realistically be brought under a CFA in the absence of legal aid. It will be a question of fact on the individual circumstances of the case whether the need to meet an insurance payment from the likely damages would render the proceedings futile.

5.99 You may wish to carry out a pre-emptive 'shopping around' exercise, trying to attempt obtaining after the event (ATE) insurance in a couple of typical scenarios, so that you could use those as examples of why a CFA is not available. If you are a not for profit (NfP) agency that does not offer CFAs, you could try asking a friendly firm whether they would accept some typical case scenarios on a CFA basis and again use their response as evidence that such cases are not commercially attractive. If you are a private firm that does offer CFAs, you could set out your criteria for accepting CFAs and why the particular case does not meet them.

5.100 Two key criteria that must be addressed are the need for representation and the likely track allocation. The effect of these is that legal aid will not be available for the most simple and straightforward cases, including those likely to be small claims.

The various merits tests

5.101 In addition to satisfying the standard criteria, you must be able to demonstrate that your case passes the applicable merits test for the type of work. Most merits criteria are expressed by reference to the **prospects of success test**. In *IS (by the Official Solicitor as Litigation Friend) v The Director of Legal Aid Casework and The Lord Chancellor*,[61] Collins J declared unlawful the part of the merits test which restricted legal aid to cases where the prospects of success were better than 50 per cent, and so the LAA revised the test with effect from 27 July 2015.

---

61 [2015] EWHC 1965 (Admin).

5.102   From that date, the Civil Legal Aid (Merits Criteria) Regulations 2013 were amended by the Civil Legal Aid (Merits Criteria) (Amendment) (No 2) Regulations 2015. However, the Court of Appeal unanimously allowed the Lord Chancellor's appeal against Collins J.[62] This led the Lord Chancellor to issue further regulations, the Civil Legal Aid (Merits Criteria) (Amendment) Regulations 2016. The 2016 regulations amended the merits tests, but not simply to reverse the 2015 changes – instead, further changes were made building on and revising the 2015 changes.

5.103   Unfortunately, the LAA does not make available consolidated sets of regulations, and neither does the official government site: www. legislation.gov.uk. It is therefore necessary to consult and cross-reference all of the 2013, 2015 and 2016 regulations in order to see the full accurate test. There is nowhere publicly available that sets out the full consolidated and up-to-date tests. In our view, this is very unsatisfactory, and we would encourage the LAA to make publicly available a single, definitive and up-to-date set of regulations for the whole scheme.

5.104   Regulation 5 of the 2013 regulations, as amended by reg 2 of the 2015 regulations and reg 2 of the 2016 regulations, sets out the prospects of success – the likelihood of achieving a successful substantive outcome – and categorises them thus:

- very good – 80 per cent or above;
- good – 60 to 80 per cent;
- moderate – 50 to 60 per cent;
- marginal – 45 to 50 per cent;
- poor – less than 45 per cent;
- borderline – it is not possible, because of disputed law, fact or expert evidence, to assign the case to another category but it cannot be categorised as 'unclear'; or
- unclear – the case cannot be assigned to any of the other categories because there are identifiable investigations to be carried out after which the prospects can be estimated.

5.105 The 'borderline' category was removed from the merits tests in 2014 by the Civil Legal Aid (Merits Criteria) (Amendment) Regulations 2014, but it remained in the definitions, and was reinstated to the merits tests by the 2015 amendment regulations and retained by the 2016 regulations. The 2015 regulations separated the then 'poor' (below 50 per cent) category into 'poor' and 'very poor' (below

---

62 *IS v Director of Legal Aid Casework and Lord Chancellor* [2016] EWCA Civ 464.

20 per cent), making funding available in 'poor' cases in limited circumstances. The 2016 regulations replaced the 'poor' and 'very poor' categories with the 'marginal' and 'poor' categories set out above.

5.106　　In *IS* in the High Court, Collins J said that the standard to be applied in assessing the prospects of success is the prospects as they would be with the assistance of competent legal representation, not the prospects on the basis of material available but untested at the time of the application. This is to ensure that cases where competent representation would turn the case in the applicant's favour are not excluded from funding.[63] Although the Court of Appeal overturned his declaration that the merits regulations were unlawful, it did not specifically deal with this point. In our view, and notwithstanding that the wider judgment was overturned, that must be the right approach.

5.107　　Following assessment of the prospects of success, the following will apply:

- Where prospects of success are moderate or better, the prospects of success criterion will be met and so legal aid will be granted (subject to any other criteria that may apply in the individual case).
- Where prospects of success are borderline or marginal, the prospects of success criterion will only be met if the case is of significant wider public interest or of overwhelming importance to the individual.[64] See paras 5.108 and 5.111 below.
- Where prospects of success are unclear, it will generally be more appropriate to grant Investigative Help than full representation, so that investigation can be carried out and the prospects clarified.
- Where prospects of success are poor, representation will be refused.

In addition, the value of the outcome must justify the costs. For damages claims, see below.

5.108　　Besides the prospects of success test, there are other tests:

- The **proportionality test**[65] is met if:

63　[2015] EWHC 1965 (Admin) para 96, per Collins J.

64　Civil Legal Aid (Merits Criteria) Regulations 2013 reg 43, as amended by Civil Legal Aid (Merits Criteria) (Amendment) (No 2) Regulations 2015 reg 2(4).

65　Civil Legal Aid (Merits Criteria) Regulations 2013 reg 8.

... the Director is satisfied that the likely benefits of the proceedings to the individual and others justify the likely costs, having regard to the prospects of success and all the other circumstances of the case.

- The **significant wider public interest test**[66] is met if:

  ... the Director is satisfied that the case is an appropriate case to realise–
  - real benefits to the public at large, other than those which normally flow from cases of the type in question; and
  - benefits for an identifiable class of individuals, other than the individual to whom civil legal services may be provided or members of that individual's family.
- The **reasonable private paying individual test** is met if:

  ... the Director is satisfied that the potential benefit to be gained from the provision of civil legal services justifies the likely costs, such that a reasonable private paying individual would be prepared to start or continue the proceedings having regard to the prospects of success and all the other circumstances of the case.[67]

5.109 The **cost benefit criteria** are (reg 42 of the 2013 regulations, as amended by reg 2(3) of the 2015 regulations and reg 2(3) of the 2016 regulations):

- If the case is primarily a claim for damages or other sum of money and not of significant wider public interest:
  - if prospects are very good, likely damages must exceed likely costs;
  - if prospects are good, likely damages must exceed likely costs by a ratio of 2:1;
  - if prospects are moderate, the ratio must be 4:1.
- If the case is not primarily a claim for damages or other sum of money and not of significant wider public interest:
  - the reasonable private paying client test must be met.
- If the case is of significant wider public interest:
  - the proportionality test must be met.

5.110 The **multi-party action criteria** are:

- The client's claim is the lead claim; and
- the case is of significant wider public interest.

5.111 A case is of **overwhelming importance to the individual** if it is not primarily a claim for damages or other sum of money and relates to the individual's life, liberty or physical safety (or that of a member of the individual's family) or an immediate risk that the individual may

---

66 Civil Legal Aid (Merits Criteria) Regulations 2013 reg 6.
67 Civil Legal Aid (Merits Criteria) Regulations 2013 reg 6.

become homeless.[68] For this to apply, that must be at issue in the proceedings and be more than merely academic. A claim for damages for false imprisonment post-dating release will not satisfy this test since liberty is no longer at stake, but a claim for habeas corpus will. If you are relying on the risk of homelessness to justify funding it must be immediate – so relate to occupation of property, not financial difficulties that may lead to later loss of occupation. Homelessness means lack of physical occupation of property, rather than the wider statutory definition of homelessness in Part 7 of the Housing Act 1996.[69]

5.112   The regulations go on to set out a merits test that applies to general certificated cases, with variations for specific types of cases.

The general merits test for full representation

5.113   The general merits test is set out in the Civil Legal Aid (Merits Criteria) Regulations 2013 reg 41 and applies in all cases except those set out below. The test is that:

- the prospects of success criteria are satisfied;
- the cost benefit criteria are satisfied; and
- if the claim is a multi-party action and is primarily a money claim but likely damages do not exceed £5,000, the multi-party action criteria are satisfied.

5.114   What this means in practice is that the case must fall into one of the following types:

1) A claim for damages or other sum of money with no significant wider public interest and which is not of overwhelming importance to the individual:
   a) prospects of success must be very good and likely damages exceed likely costs;
   b) prospects of success must be good and likely damages exceed likely costs by 2:1; or
   c) prospects of success must be moderate and likely damages exceed likely costs by 4:1.
2) A claim other than for damages or other sum of money, or a defence to a claim, with no significant wider public interest and which is not of overwhelming importance to the individual:
   a) prospects of success must be moderate or better; and
   b) the reasonable private paying client test must be met.

---

68 Civil Legal Aid (Merits Criteria) Regulations 2013 reg 2.
69 *Lord Chancellor's guidance on civil legal aid* (2018), paras 4.2.10–4.2.12.

3) A claim or defence to a claim which has significant wider public interest:
   a) prospects of success must be marginal or better; and
   b) the proportionality test must be met.
4) A case which is of overwhelming importance to the individual:
   a) the prospects of success must be marginal or better; and
   b) the reasonable private paying client test must be met.
5) A multi-party action case: the multi-party action criteria are satisfied.

Public law claims

5.115 For public law claims (defined in reg 2 as judicial review, habeas corpus and homelessness appeals), there are additions to the standard criteria:[70]

- the act, omission or matter complained of appears to be susceptible to challenge; and
- there are no alternative proceedings before a court or tribunal which are available to challenge the act, omission or other matter, except where the Director considers that such proceedings would not provide an effective remedy.[71]

5.116 The merits test for full representation in public law claims is:[72]

- the standard criteria are met (including the additional ones above);
- unless impracticable to do so, a letter before claim has been sent and the defendant given a reasonable time to respond;
- the proportionality test is met; and
- prospects of success are:
  - moderate or better; or
  - borderline or marginal, and:
    - the case is of significant wider public interest;
    - the case is of overwhelming importance to the individual; or
    - the substance of the case relates to a breach of rights under the European Convention on Human Rights (ECHR).[73]

70 Civil Legal Aid (Merits Criteria) Regulations 2013 reg 53 and Civil Legal Aid (Merits Criteria) (Amendment) Regulations 2013.
71 Civil Legal Aid (Merits Criteria) Regulations 2013 reg 53(b) as amended by Civil Legal Aid (Merits Criteria) (Amendment) Regulations 2013 reg 2.
72 Civil Legal Aid (Merits Criteria) Regulations 2013 reg 56 amended by Civil Legal Aid (Merits Criteria) (Amendment) (No 2) Regulations 2015 reg 2(5).
73 See chapter 5 of the *Lord Chancellor's guidance on civil legal aid* (2018).

See para 7.34 of the *Lord Chancellor's guidance on civil legal aid* (2018) and chapter 14 below for detailed guidance on public law claims.

Claims against public authorities

5.117   For claims against public authorities (paras 21 and 22 of Part 1 of Schedule 1 to LASPO), the test is:[74]

- the proportionality test is met; and
- prospects of success are:
  - moderate or better; or
  - borderline or marginal, and:
    - the case is of significant wider public interest;
    - the case is of overwhelming importance to the individual; or
    - the substance of the case relates to a breach of ECHR rights.[75]

Other cases

5.118   For immigration, housing, mental health and family merits tests, see the appropriate chapters of this book.

Changes to prospects of success or cost–benefit

5.119   As the case progresses, inevitably further information and evidence will come to light. If you consider that the merits test is no longer met, the case should be referred to the LAA for decision.

5.120   There is useful guidance on the difference of approach under the LASPO scheme which can be found in the *Lord Chancellor's guidance on civil legal aid*:

> 8.37 Regulation 42 addresses the grounds and procedures for withdrawal of determinations. The grounds for withdrawal are set out at 42(1). These are expanded in comparison with those under the funding code to include the provisions in relation to the domestic violence 'gateway' to civil legal services in family proceedings no longer being satisfied 42(k) and a ground for withdrawal.
>
> 8.38 Regulation 42(3) provides for an equivalent of the 'show cause' procedure under the funding code procedures through notification of an intention to withdraw a determination. The scheme is different in

---

74 Civil Legal Aid (Merits Criteria) Regulations 2013, as amended by the 2015 and 2016 regulations.

75 See chapter 5 of the *Lord Chancellor's guidance on civil legal aid* (2018).

that, if the determination is withdrawn as a result of this procedure, the withdrawal takes place with effect from the initial notification of intention (42(3)). That represents a difference from the position under the funding code in that:

(a) The client will not have cost protection, under the Civil Legal Aid (Costs) Regulations 2013, in the period from when the Director first notified an intention to withdraw the determination;

(b) The provider can carry out work at risk in relation to whether the withdrawal does occur, whereas no work could be carried out within the show cause period under the funding code without express permission irrespective of the ultimate outcome of the show cause.

CCMS and forms

5.121 Applications for certificates for legal representation and for Investigative Help are made to the LAA. Except in certain circumstances where urgent work is required (see below), solicitors do not have the power to grant or amend certificates directly. Special procedures also apply in urgent cases (see below).

5.122 The LAA made its electronic CCMS mandatory for all civil and family applications for certificates from April 2016, a date which was put back several times. There have been considerable difficulties with the system, including criticisms of its functionality. There have also been several extended periods when it has not been available at all. The representative bodies continue to press the LAA for improvements to the system. See chapter 6 for more information about how CCMS works.

5.123 CCMS has been created in such a way that the questions asked are dependent on answers to other questions and so the electronic screens do not mirror the paper forms which they replaced.

5.124 If you are unable to access CCMS due to a technical issue and you need an **urgent** decision (needed within 48 hours) on an **application or amendment**, you can submit a paper application. The LAA guidance is that it should be contacted by telephone for authorisation before contingency protocols can be used. The LAA will give you a contingency reference number which should be quoted in subsequent correspondence.[76]

---

76 https://ccmstraining.justice.gov.uk/__data/assets/pdf_file/0015/8025/CCMS-Contingency-Process_v1_0.pdf.

5.125   This process is not available where you have delegated functions allowing you to grant the application or amendment yourself.[77] For further details, see chapter 6.

5.126   When applying through CCMS, evidence of the client's means covering the last three months will also be required. See chapter 3 for details of financial eligibility. You will need to complete a statement of case, and this should be completed in as much detail as possible, as this is the part of the application that demonstrates that the criteria for granting a certificate are met. Don't forget that your client's statement is not the same as a statement of case. You have to explain to someone at the LAA, who has not met your client, why what the client says amounts to a cause of action and why it should be funded.

5.127   If you are applying for exceptional case funding (see chapter 4 and merits tests above), you can apply through CCMS. There is a CCMS quick guide to making exceptional cases funding (ECF) applications, which will help you to follow the correct procedure. See chapter 4 for more information on ECF.

5.128   Low levels of rejects and refusals are KPIs under the Standard Contract 2018 – see chapter 22 and para 5.80 onwards.

Refusals and appeals

5.129   A refusal of a certificate on the basis of merit can be appealed, within 14 days of the decision – first to a review by the director, then to an independent adjudicator.[78]

5.130   If successful on review, then the certificate will be granted from the date of the successful appeal. There is no provision for backdating to the original application.[79]

5.131   A refusal on financial grounds cannot be formally appealed, though a director's review is available, and a fresh application can be made if circumstances change.

---

77   www.gov.uk/guidance/bringing-civil-legal-aid-processing-online#ccms-contingency-arrangements.

78   Civil Legal Aid (Procedure) Regulations 2012 reg 44.

79   Civil Legal Aid (Procedure) Regulations 2012 reg 44(4).

Funding

5.132   Civil legal aid representation certificates are funded on an hourly rate basis. See chapter 16 for more information.

5.133   In almost every case, a funding certificate is only granted subject to two limitations:

1) a particular step in the proceedings, such as 'all steps up to the filing of a defence and thereafter obtaining counsel's opinion', or 'all steps up to a case management conference'; and
2) a costs limitation – costs limitations include profit costs (and any enhancement or uplift), counsels' fees and disbursements, but not VAT.

5.134   Standard costs limits vary by category:
- claims against public authorities – £6,000;
- community care – £3,500;
- immigration and asylum – £4,500;
- mental health – £5,000;
- special Children Act cases – £9,000;
- all other categories, and judicial review cases in the above categories – £2,250.

The above limits are the standard defaults, but it is open to you to apply for a larger initial limit where justified.

5.135   It is extremely important not to do work outside the scope of either limitation, as you will not be paid for it. It is particularly easy to lose track of counsels' fees and disbursements, and it really helps to keep all documents relating to financial issues together in the file. One of the advantages of CCMS is that you can log on and see claims made by counsel under your certificate, helping to keep track of costs.

5.136   Limitations can be amended on application to the LAA, or under delegated functions in urgent circumstances (see below for more information about delegated functions).

Amendments to scope and costs

5.137   Requests for amendments to either scope or costs limitations are made to the LAA via CCMS. In making a request, the adviser will be obliged to demonstrate that the case continues to satisfy both limitations of the merits test, and state what new scope or costs limitation is required. Therefore, there must be merit not only in the case as a whole but in each step of the proceedings.

5.138   Timing the application for an amendment has to be done with care, as the date an amendment takes effect is the date of the decision. If you leave your application until the last minute, you risk exceeding the current limitation and not being paid. On the other hand, you must justify why the work needs to be done at the particular time, as the LAA will refuse any amendment considered to be premature. It will also refuse an amendment that might become redundant due to some other event taking place.

Use of counsel and amendments for a QC

5.139   A representation certificate allows you to instruct one counsel; but if the case warrants second counsel or a QC, you must apply to the LAA for authority. In general, authority will only be granted in cases of exceptional complexity or importance, and you must be able to show that the interests of the client cannot properly be represented without the authority being granted. There is no automatic presumption that a QC will be granted for an appeal to the Court of Appeal, nor that where another party has a QC or more than one counsel that it will be justified for a legally aided party to have the same level of representation. See the LAA's prior authority guidance for more information.[80]

5.140   Failure to obtain authority will mean that no payment can be made for the second counsel or QC. See also chapter 16.

Disbursements and prior authority

5.141   In many cases, disbursements can be large, and there is a risk to the organisation that they will not be allowed, or allowed in full, on assessment of the bill.

5.142   Therefore, the prior authority scheme allows you to apply to the LAA for authority to incur a disbursement in advance, if it is above £100 and is not an expert fee covered by the standard rates/hours introduced from 3 October 2011 and reduced from 2 December 2013.[81] The application is made via CCMS accompanied by a quote

---

80   Available at: www.gov.uk/government/uploads/system/uploads/attachment_ data/file/543186/legal-aid-narrative-guidance.pdf/.

81   Community Legal Service (Funding) (Amendment No 2) Order 2011 (for Access to Justice Act 1999 cases) and Civil Legal Aid (Remuneration) (Amendment) Regulations 2013 Schedule 2 (for LASPO cases). Expert fees were reduced by 20 per cent on 2 December 2013 and so the rates in Schedule 5 to the 2013 Remuneration Regulations are no longer valid for cases started after that date.

for the disbursement and reasons why it is necessary. The advantage of having authority is that no question as to the validity of the disbursement can be raised on assessment of the bill, unless and to the extent that it exceeds the amount or scope of the authority. Prior authority therefore gives a measure of costs protection for expensive disbursements.

5.143 You may apply for prior authority if:[82]

a) an item of costs is either unusual in its nature or is unusually large;

b) you wish to instruct a QC;

c) prior authority is required under the specification; or

d) you wish to instruct an expert at higher rates than are set out in the Civil Legal Aid (Remuneration) (Amendment) Regulations 2013.

If you do not apply for prior authority and b), c) or d) above applies, you will not be paid in full or at all for the fees incurred.

Experts' fees

5.144 Experts' fees have been codified since October 2011. The Civil Legal Aid (Remuneration) Regulations 2013 set out applicable rates for experts in different areas of expertise. The fees were reduced by 20 per cent by the Civil Legal Aid (Remuneration) (Amendment) Regulations 2013. In some cases, there are fixed fees for reports, in others hourly rates. The hourly rates are a maximum, not a fixed rate.[83] The LAA has issued some useful guidance on experts' fees.[84]

5.145 There are 'London' and 'non-London' rates; which applies is determined by the location of the expert. Where an expert has offices both in and outside London, it is the location of the solicitor that determines the rate.[85]

5.146 The rates cannot be exceeded unless the LAA has granted prior authority in advance. Prior authority will only be granted in exceptional circumstances, defined as being where:[86]

---

82 Standard Civil Contract 2018 Specification para 5.10.

83 The full list of rates can be found in Civil Legal Aid (Remuneration) Regulations 2013 Sch 5 for cases started before 2 December 2013 and in Civil Legal Aid (Remuneration) (Amendment) Regulations 2013 Sch 2 for cases started on or after that date.

84 Guidance on the remuneration of expert witnesses: www.gov.uk/expert-witnesses-in-legal-aid-cases.

85 Costs assessment guidance para 3.46.

86 Standard Civil Contract 2018 Specification para 6.60.

- the expert's evidence is key to the client's case and either:
  - the complexity of the material is such that an expert with a high level of seniority is required; or
  - the material is of such a specialised and unusual nature that only very few experts are available to provide the necessary evidence.

5.147   Applications for prior authority in certificate cases should be made via CCMS. Prior authority cannot be granted in Legal Help cases, and so where you instruct an expert at a higher rate in a Legal Help case you should justify on the file why you have done so. It would be unusual – and risky – to do this in a Legal Help case.

5.148   Where a particular type of expert is not specified in the regulations and therefore there are no codified rates, the LAA will assess rates on a case-by-case basis but will 'have regard to' the codified rates.

5.149   Where either enhanced or non-codified rates are sought, the LAA will expect to see at least three[87] written quotes setting out the hourly rate, number of hours and total fee.

5.150   Where joint experts are instructed and all instructing parties are legally aided, the codified rates apply to the total instruction, not each party's share. Any application for prior authority need only be made by the lead solicitor in the instruction.

5.151   Where joint experts are instructed by both legally aided and non-legally aided parties, the LAA will take a pro rata approach. Where fixed fees are specified, the LAA will pay a share of the fee. Where an hourly rate is specified, the LAA will determine their share on the basis of hours rather than rates. They will pay – in a two-party case – half the time at the codified rate.[88]

5.152   For example, a surveyor is instructed jointly on behalf of a tenant and a landlord. If he takes six hours to do his report, the LAA will pay for three hours, up to the maximum of £115 per hour (in London) – so £345. They will not pay six hours at £115 (£690) where the landlord also agrees to pay six hours at £115 – the approach is that the codified rate is the maximum the expert can charge to the fund and in a joint instruction the LAA will pay half the time taken to prepare the report. The other party can agree to pay the expert more, but that is a matter between them and the expert.

5.153   As a result of these changes, the LAA now require disbursement vouchers with a breakdown of time spent and hourly rates charged to

---

87   Standard Civil Contract 2018 Specification para 4.28.
88   Costs assessment guidance para 3.41.

accompany claims, even those assessed by the court. If the court has assessed an hourly rate higher than the codified rates without prior authority, the LAA will reject it and it will have to go back to the court for re-assessment.[89] Other restrictions on experts' fees include:

- capping travel time to £40 per hour and costs to 45p per mile;
- ban on claiming for administration costs;
- ban on claiming a cancellation fee unless given less than 72 hours' notice of the cancellation;
- requiring experts to time-record and itemise time spent on their invoices.

5.154 The codified rates also apply to attendance at court. Some experts have been in the habit of charging for half or full days for court attendance; now they must charge the hourly rate.

Funding from the client's point of view

Contributions

5.155 Clients on passporting benefits (see para 3.43 above) or with very limited means do not have to make contributions to the cost of their case during its lifetime; but they may need to make payment at the end of their case if money or property is recovered or preserved, under the statutory charge (see below at para 5.160 onwards for more information). It is therefore easy for such clients to be lulled into feeling that their legal aid is going to be free, when it is not, and so it is even more important to ensure they understand the effect of the statutory charge and are given a costs estimate which is revised at every relevant point throughout the case.

5.156 If the client's capital is between the lower and upper thresholds, the client is required to pay a contribution. The amount of the contribution is the lower of: a) the amount by which capital exceeds the lower threshold; and b) the total estimated costs of the case.

5.157 If the client's disposable income is between the lower and upper threshold, a contribution will be payable. The amount of the contribution depends on the amount by which income is above the lower threshold but is a fixed sum plus a percentage of the excess each month for the life of the certificate. The eligibility calculator on the LAA website will show you the level of contribution the client will have to pay.

---

89 See the court-assessed claim checklist at: www.gov.uk/government/publications/civ-claim1-civil-claim-form-not-fixed-fee.

5.158   If the client fails to pay a contribution, you will receive notification from the LAA, and although you do not have to stop work, you
are at risk that legal aid will be withdrawn from the date of the notice[90]
if the client does not make payment.

5.159   Should the amount paid in contributions exceed the final costs as
assessed, the client will be entitled to a refund of the difference.

Changes in circumstances

5.160   Clients must be financially eligible on both capital and income. They
must inform the LAA of any change in their means. A reassessment
will then be carried out.

Statutory charge

5.161   The charge is governed by section 25 of LASPO and by the Civil
Legal Aid (Statutory Charge) Regulations 2013. The statutory charge
under certificates operates at all levels of service, and across all
categories, except family mediation. It operates on both property
recovered and property preserved.[91]

5.162   If a matter is funded by Legal Help *only*, the charge does not arise
in any category.[92]

5.163   If a case is funded initially under Legal Help, Help with Mediation
or Family Help (Lower) and goes on to a certificate, if the charge
arises, it also applies to those costs.[93]

5.164   If money or property is at issue in the proceedings, then the
successful client is at risk of the charge. A claimant client whose
claim succeeds recovers property; a defendant client who resists a
claim preserves property.[94] Even if title to the property is not in issue,
but possession of it is, the charge still arises.[95]

5.165   Where the proceedings result in recovery or preservation for
someone other than the client, the charge arises.[96]

5.166   The charge gives the LAA first call on any money or property
recovered in the proceedings. It is used to repay the costs of funding
the case. You should note that even though damages in disrepair
cases are out of scope under LASPO, the LAA takes the view that if

90 See the Civil Legal Aid (Procedure) Regulations 2012 reg 43.
91 LASPO s25.
92 Civil Legal Aid (Statutory Charge) Regulations 2013 reg 4(1).
93 Reg 4(2).
94 *Hanlon v Law Society* [1980] 2 All ER 199.
95 *Parkes v Legal Aid Board* [1994] 2 FLR 850.
96 LASPO s25(1)(a).

the client has had the benefit of legal aid to enforce repairs, the statutory charge applies to the whole of the proceedings (see chapter 12 and para 5.183 for more information). So, if a claimant in a housing disrepair case wins compensation of £5,000, and costs under the certificate and Legal Help were £1,500, then (assuming no costs were awarded from the other side) the charge would operate and the client would receive only £3,500 (recovery). On the other hand, if the client was defending a claim for a £5,000 share in property and won the case, if the costs were £1,500, he or she would be liable to pay £1,500 (preservation).

5.167   All monies due to a client in legal proceedings must be paid to his or her solicitor if the client is legally aided in any way.[97]

5.168   All property is caught by the charge, unless exempt by regulation. Exempt property is currently limited to:

- periodical payments of maintenance;
- sums paid under:
  - Matrimonial Causes Act 1973 s25B or s25C;
  - Inheritance (Provision for Family and Dependants) Act 1975 s5;
  - Family Law Act 1996 Part 4;
  - Civil Partnership Act 2004 Sch 5 paras 25(2) or 26;
- interim payments in Inheritance Act proceedings;
- the first 50 per cent of a redundancy award;
- the client's clothes, household furniture or tools of the trade (except in exceptional circumstances);
- state benefits and pensions, and any other property subject to a statutory prohibition on assignment.[98]

5.169   Damages recovered from the state for breach of the claimant's human rights are not exempt and caught by the operation of the charge in the same way as all other damages.[99]

5.170   The amount of the charge is calculated to compensate the LAA for funding the case and is therefore the amount of costs as assessed (less any contribution paid by the client), less costs recovered from the other side. Therefore, the amount is the net amount paid to the supplier by the LAA.

5.171   If the charge arises, the client will have a financial interest in the organisation's bill of costs. Clients should be advised of the potential

---

97 Civil Legal Aid (Statutory Charge) Regulations 2013 reg 13.

98 Reg 5.

99 *R (Faulkner) v Director of Legal Aid Casework* [2016] EWHC 717 (Admin).

effect of the charge at the outset of the case, given regular costs updates, and at the end of the case be given a copy of the bill and advised of their right to make representations on the bill, including at any assessment hearing. The only elements of the bill that do not form part of the charge are the costs of assessment and costs of complying with Equality Act 2010 obligations to clients with disabilities[100] as well as any settlement fees in family cases.[101]

Recovery of money

5.172   Civil Legal Aid (Statutory Charge) Regulations reg 13 provides that all monies owing to a funded client should be paid to his or her solicitor, not to the client direct. The only exceptions are periodic payments of maintenance, and money paid into court to be invested for the client's benefit in the limited circumstances set out in reg 11. Regulation 15(1)(a) obliges the solicitor to report any recovery or preservation to the LAA straight away.

5.173   Once money is received, the solicitor may make a judgment as to whether it is exempt property. If it is, it may be paid to the client. If not, it must be paid to the LAA. In cases of doubt, the best course is to pay to the LAA, which can refund the client. If the solicitor fails to protect the LAA's charge and pays the money to the client without deducting it, the solicitor is liable.[102]

5.174   Regulation 15(3) entitles the solicitor to apply to the Director for permission to pay to the client money which is not required to satisfy the charge – for example, if £10,000 is recovered and costs will not exceed £5,000, an application can be made to return the extra £5,000 to the client.

5.175   Unless an application to defer the charge is being made (see below), the solicitor should send a cheque for the value of the money recovered with the final bill to the LAA. The LAA will assess the bill, pay solicitor and counsel, and return the balance to the client.

Recovery of property, and preservation cases

5.176   In such cases, money is unlikely to be paid to the solicitor. Instead, the solicitor will report recovery or preservation to the LAA. The LAA will pay the costs of solicitor and counsel and pursue the client for the costs.

---

100 Civil Legal Aid (Statutory Charge) Regulations 2013 reg 6.
101 Reg 4(4).
102 Standard Civil Contract 2018 Standard Terms clause 14.15.

Enforcement of the charge – the LAA's powers

5.177 The LAA has no power to waive the charge altogether, except in very limited circumstances (basically, where it was recognised as a wider public interest case from the start and the LAA funded this client but not others to act as a test case: reg 9). See also para 5.191.

5.178 In certain circumstances, enforcement of the charge can be postponed under reg 22. The conditions are:

- the property is the client's (or the client's dependant's) family home; or in family cases, money to be used to purchase a home for the client or dependants; and
- the LAA is satisfied that the home will provide sufficient security for the charge; and
- it would be unreasonable for the client to repay the charge.

5.179 If the charge is postponed, simple interest at 8 per cent per annum will accrue from the date of registration. Interest is due on the lower of the value of the charge or the value of the home (reg 25). The charge must be registered at the Land Registry or equivalent steps taken.[103]

5.180 Otherwise, the charge is payable immediately unless the LAA agrees to accept payment by instalment, and the LAA can enforce the charge, if necessary, by enforcement proceedings in the courts.

5.181 The solicitor should report to the LAA using the appropriate ADMIN form if the case is paper-based, or through CCMS as appropriate. There is a quick guide to reporting the statutory charge.[104]

Related proceedings

5.182 The LAA takes the view that the statutory charge applies to the whole of proceedings, whether or not it funds the whole case. LASPO s25 says that the charge arises on 'any property recovered or preserved by the individual in proceedings, or in any compromise or settlement of a dispute, in connection with which the services were provided'.

5.183 There are two particular areas where practitioners have encountered difficulty: i) housing disrepair; and ii) Human Rights Act (HRA) 1998 claims made by children and parents within care and wardship proceedings.

---

103 Civil Legal Aid (Statutory Charge) Regulations 2013 reg 22(2).
104 http://ccmstraining.justice.gov.uk/Quick-guides/Quickguides/closing-cases-and-submitting-bills–1.

5.184   Disrepair claims (the position is different for counter-claims; see chapter 12) are only in scope to the extent that an injunction or claim for specific performance is sought to enforce repairs to a defect that carries a significant risk of harm. Any related damages claim – even if made within the same proceedings – is out of scope, and work done in relation to the damages must not be claimed for on the certificate. However, the LAA will recover the costs of the funded part of the claim – the remedy of the defect – as part of the statutory charge where damages are recovered in the non-funded part. Even though that part of the proceedings was unfunded, the damages were recovered within the proceedings or in settlement of a dispute in connection with which services were provided.

5.185   The effect has been that in any case where damages are more than purely nominal, practitioners bring the entire claim under a conditional fee agreement where practicable to do so.

5.186   There have been a number of cases relating to the welfare and protection of children, including care and wardship proceedings, where a local authority has fallen short in its obligations to the child or parents or both. These have increased recently through judicial displeasure at increased use of – and duration of use of – Children Act 1989 s20 rather than bringing care proceedings. This has led to claims for damages under HRA 1998. There have been a number of reported decisions on bringing claims for damages leading to two important judgments by Mr Justice Cobb – *CZ v Kirklees Council*[105] and *SW & TW (human rights claim: procedure) (No 1)*.[106] These both involved claims arising out of a failure to bring care proceedings. There is another important decision regarding a claim arising in wardship – *P v A Local Authority*,[107] decided by Mr Justice Keehan (see below).

5.187   These cases are essential reading to avoid the pitfalls in these claims, one of which is the fact that any damages award is lost in legal costs and the application of the statutory charge.

5.188   The guidance set out by Mr Justice Cobb makes it clear that the damages claims must be made as civil claims, subject to the Civil Procedure Rules 1998. These claims are then separate, but may run alongside the care case, although CAFCASS cannot be appointed to take this litigation. Any child seeking to claim must bring the case by

105 [2017] EWFC 11.
106 [2017] EWHC 450 (Fam).
107 [2016] EWHC 2779 (Fam).

a litigation friend or the Official Solicitor if there is nobody else to take the claim.

5.189   These cases create a problem with the statutory charge, since the general position in care proceedings is no order for costs, with the costs of the care proceedings coming out of legal aid rather than being awarded against the local authority. However, in civil claims the costs rules are different. There is a risk the losing party has to pay the successful party's costs, although legally aided clients have a significant degree of costs protection and are very unlikely to be ordered to pay costs even if they lose.

5.190   The further problem is that any damages awarded to the child or parents for breach of their human rights will be swallowed up in paying the costs of the care proceedings and the HRA 1998 claims through the statutory charge given that the proceedings are likely to be linked.

5.191   Alternative ways of dealing with these claims that were suggested in the past (eg the local authority paying the costs of the care proceedings and HRA 1998 costs or seeking increased damages to cover costs) need to be re-evaluated in the light of these cases.

5.192   An application to the LAA to waive the statutory charge is an option; but will generally be doomed to failure. The only power to waive the charge is contained in reg 9 of the Statutory Charge Regulations. That power is only exercisable when an application for waiver is made at the same time as the application for funding and is made on the basis that the funded proceedings have a wider public interest for which this case acts as a test case. It would be very unusual for an HRA 1998 claim within care proceedings to meet the second part of the test, and even more unusual for that to have been anticipated and a waiver applied for when funding was first applied for – especially in the many care cases where emergency funding is issued via delegated functions. Even where a separate legal aid certificate is issued for the HRA 1998 claim – as current LAA practice requires – LASPO s25 will still bite as it covers the proceedings not the funding.

5.193   In *P v A Local Authority*, Keehan J (having heard from counsel representing the Lord Chancellor and LAA) considered the principles applying to the statutory charge and the judgment is worth reading for that discussion. The judge found that reg 9 was very limited in scope and so there was no power to waive the charge. However, he concluded that the statutory charge did not apply to the costs for which funding was granted and so would not eat into the HRA 1998 damages. This was because the substantive case – wardship – had concluded by the time the local authority's act which gave rise to the damages claim arose. So the damages claim was brought as a free-standing claim and (because it misunderstood the nature of the claim) legal aid for that claim was refused by the LAA. So, there was no recovery in proceedings in connection with funded services. As a result, LASPO s25 did not apply to the damages and the LAA had no claim on them.

5.194   This is an interesting and useful judgment, but probably confined to its (relatively unusual) facts. The wider situation has not been – and probably cannot be – resolved by the courts. There are competing policy considerations and competing injustices, and ultimately a policy decision will need to be made. If it is not considered right that a child or young person should receive no benefit from damages awarded because of a failure of the state's obligation to protect him or her, an amendment to the statutory charge scheme will be required. The most straightforward way of doing so would seem to be adding such damages to the list of exempt recoveries found in reg 5. Until then, the charge is likely to apply to the care costs unless the damages claim can be brought in wholly separate proceedings.

Ending a case

5.195   Legal aid certificates come to an end in one of three ways: being discharged or revoked, or when a final bill is submitted at the end of the case.

Discharge

5.196   When the LAA decides that a certificate should not continue because changing circumstances indicate that funding is no longer justified on the merits, or because the client is no longer financially eligible, the certificate will be discharged. The effect of this is that the client is no longer in receipt of legal aid. If discharge is at the instigation of the LAA, there is a right to appeal to an independent adjudicator. Once the certificate is discharged, the case is at an end and the file can be billed. At the end of a case, the adviser should usually apply for the certificate to be discharged.

Revocation

5.197   The effect of revocation[108] is not simply to end the funding of a case – revocation retrospectively removes funding from the client, so that he or she never had a valid legal aid certificate at all. The LAA will only

108 Civil Legal Aid (Procedure) Regulations 2012 reg 42(2).

revoke a certificate when information comes to light to suggest that it should never have been issued, for example because a client concealed information about his or her resources because the client was never in fact eligible. The effect of revocation is that the client becomes liable for all costs incurred under the certificate.

Submission of final bill

5.198   See chapter 16. A final bill can only be submitted after first discharging the certificate where there is an order for costs to be assessed.

Urgent cases

Scope

5.199   The LAA defines a case as urgent if it is necessary to carry out work before a substantive application could be made and determined. The LAA aims to process most substantive applications within four weeks. Therefore an emergency certificate is unlikely to be granted unless the work has to be carried out before a substantive certificate could be granted and cannot wait without serious adverse consequences to the client, for example risk to the life, liberty or physical safety of the client or the client's family or the roof over their heads; or the delay will cause a significant risk of miscarriage of justice, or unreasonable hardship to the client, or irretrievable problems in handling the case; and in either case, there are no other appropriate options available to deal with the risk.

5.200   There have been changes to the process for applying for emergency non delegated functions applications which came into force on the 20 February 2019.[109] New powers were introduced to backdate the determination date of legal aid funding but note that this is a discretionary power. See chapter 6 for more details.

5.201   You should also consider whether it would be more appropriate to grant or amend a certificate under delegated functions (see para 5.211 below) before you submit an application to the LAA for decision.

109 www.legislation.gov.uk/uksi/2019/130/contents/made.

Financial eligibility

5.202 See chapter 3. See also 'Funding from the client's point of view', para 5.154 onwards above.

5.203 Emergency representation may be granted without a full means assessment. This clearly has short term advantages for the client, but it creates a financial risk for the legal aid fund.

Revocation

5.204 The client may turn out to be financially ineligible, may not co-operate with the means assessment, or may not accept an offer, should a contribution be required. In all of those circumstances, the emergency certificate will be revoked (ie cancelled and the client treated as though he or she was never in receipt of legal aid).

5.205 The client will be responsible for the full costs of his or her representation. In addition, he or she will not have the protection from opponents' costs provided by a representation certificate. You must therefore advise the client of this and give a costs estimate. If the certificate is revoked, you should submit a bill in the usual way; the LAA will pursue the client for the costs.

Merits test

5.206 The appropriate merits test (see para 5.93 onwards above) must be satisfied, as well as the urgency criteria.

5.207 However, as the situation will be urgent, it may often be that only limited information is available. If so, emergency representation may be granted where it appears likely on the information available that the merits test will be satisfied.

Forms

5.208 Emergency applications for civil legal aid certificates are made via CCMS in the usual way. Emergency amendments to limitations on existing certificates may also be made via CCMS. See chapter 6 for more information about this.

5.209 The LAA must receive the substantive application within five working days of the emergency grant. If you fail to submit the application, the emergency certificate only covers work done within the first five working days, and you will not be paid for work beyond that period.

Funding

5.210   Emergency certificates will usually be limited to £1,350 (profit costs, counsels' fees and disbursements, but not VAT), though you can grant a higher limit, or amend to a higher limit, as long as you do not go above £10,000 and as long as the costs only relate to urgent work.

5.211   Emergency certificates only last for eight weeks, so you must ensure that you are covered by a substantive certificate from that date, or else you will not be paid. This time limit cannot be extended.

Delegated functions

Scope

5.212   The delegated functions used to be listed in the contract specification but have been moved to a separate document.[110]

5.213   The LAA monitors the use of delegated functions and may suspend or terminate them if they have been seriously misused.[111]

5.214   Certificates can be granted for full legal representation in urgent cases. You may not use delegated functions to grant a certificate where there is an outstanding certificate or application at the LAA, or where a previous application has been refused and there is no clear and relevant change of circumstances to suggest that a reapplication would be granted.

5.215   You may not use delegated functions to grant exceptional case funding under section 10 of LASPO (see para 3.30 and chapter 4 for more information), nor for judicial review cases (with limited exceptions mainly for emergency homelessness cases or unless you have specific authorisation). You must comply with any restrictions on your exercise of delegated functions set out in your schedule authorisation.[112]

Steps for granting an emergency certificate

5.216   The LAA has issued guidance on the matter types, standard wordings and limitation codes you will need which can be downloaded

---

110   www.gov.uk/government/uploads/system/uploads/attachment_data/file/448948/civil-procedure.pdf.

111   Funding Code: decision-making guidance section 12.8. Post-LASPO guidance has not been issued.

112   Standard Civil Contract 2018 Specification paras 5.2 and 5.3.

here: www.gov.uk/government/publications/civil-legal-aid-application-forms-supporting-guidance.

1   Select a matter type code.
2   Identify the wording code for the allowable proceedings.
    If there is no appropriate wording code, the relevant LAA processing office must be contacted.
3   Apply an appropriate scope limitation wording.
4   Apply a costs limitation.
    Costs limitations include profit costs, disbursements and counsels' fees, but *not* VAT.
    In emergency applications this will generally be £1,350 and must not exceed £10,000.
5   Submit an application for a substantive certificate within five working days.

Amendments under delegated functions

5.217   Under the Civil Legal Aid (Procedure) Regulations 2012 reg 39(3)(b), you can amend an emergency certificate as long as the LAA has not yet granted a substantive certificate and the amendment is required because of the urgency of the situation. In the event of a delegated function amendment to scope or costs, you can apply through the single step process so that the substantive certificate reflects the amendment you made using your delegated functions. There is a LAA quick guide to this: https://ccmstraining.justice.gov.uk/Quick-guides/Quickguides/making-an-initial-application-1. See also para 6.26 onwards for more information.

Refusals under delegated functions

5.218   A client has no right of appeal against your refusal to grant an emergency certificate.[113]

Financial eligibility

5.219   As 'Urgent cases', above.

Merits test

5.220   As 'Urgent cases', above.

---

113 Civil Legal Aid (Procedure) Regulations 2012 reg 53.

Funding

5.221   As 'Urgent cases', above.

Very expensive cases/special case work

5.222   Civil high cost cases are called 'special case work' under LASPO and are governed under reg 54 of the Civil Legal Aid (Procedure) Regulations 2012.

Scope

5.223   High cost civil cases are dealt with by two teams at the LAA. The Very High Cost Case (VHCC) family team (South Tyneside) deals with single counsel/advocate cases in private and public law family matters. The Exceptional and Complex Case Team (ECCT) family section (London) deals with QC/two-counsel cases in private and public law family matters, all high-cost child abduction and Court of Protection cases, and all civil non-family high cost cases.

5.224   In civil cases, the LAA will agree individual case contracts for cases.

5.225   High cost cases fall into five types:

- individual very high-cost cases: where costs are expected to exceed £25,000, such as Children Act 1989, clinical negligence and judicial review cases;
- cases which might exceed £75,000 if they proceeded to contested trial, final hearing or the conclusion of any appeal stage before the Court of Appeal or Supreme Court;
- multi-party actions (MPAs): these range from 1,000-claimant actions to ten-claimant actions;
- exceptional funding cases: when funding is approved outside LASPO provisions;
- 'community action' cases in relation to individuals who belong to an identifiable geographic community the members of which have a common interest in the proceedings.

5.226   The LAA can treat more than one set of proceedings or certificates as a single case when deciding whether the cost thresholds are reached, for example in public law Children Act 1989 proceedings involving numerous parties.

5.227   Cases can be referred to the South Tyneside Family Team or the Exceptional and Complex Case Team at any stage if it appears that they may meet the criteria.

Family high cost cases – CCFS

5.228   In family, most high cost cases are subject to the 'Care Case Fee Scheme', which is a form of graduated/fixed fee, dependent on the number of hearing days and other events (as outlined in guidance). The benefit of the CCFS is that it avoids multiple revisions to detailed case plans, which is popular with practitioners and is often (but not always) considered preferable to an individually agreed case plan. From 1 October 2015 all single advocate care cases have been paid under CCFS unless you can show you would be paid at least 30 per cent more by claiming hourly rates with a case plan.

5.229   Prior to 3 June 2019, CCFS cases had an immediate limit of £25,000. From that date, the LAA increased the initial limit to £32,000, which applies as soon as the contract documentation is accepted by the LAA. This allows you to claim a payment on account (POA) up to the limitation. If costs will exceed £32,000, you need to apply for an extension. See chapters 8 and 16 for more detail.

Family QC and two counsel cases

5.230   From 12 July 2019, the LAA took a similar approach to Family QC and two counsel cases. Once you are granted prior authority for a QC / two counsel, you should be asked to upload a signed High Costs Contract and Counsel Acceptance Forms (where external counsel are used). If you accept, the case will be costed using CCFS. At the same time, you should submit a cost amendment for £60,000 where the authority covers a fact-finding hearing or a composite hearing. The LAA asks that if counsel is used, they are assigned to the case and allocated appropriate funds.

5.231   The LAA has issued guidance on high cost Family cases: www. gov.uk/guidance/civil-high-cost-cases-family. See also chapters 8 and 16 for more detail.

Financial eligibility

5.232   See chapter 3 and para 5.154 onwards above. The LAA has a limited power to waive eligibility rules in relation to MPAs.[114]

Merits test

5.233   Only three types of case are automatically entitled to funding:

114 Civil Legal Aid (Procedure) Regulations 2012 reg 53.

1) special Children Act proceedings;
2) proceedings in which the client's life or liberty are at risk;
3) judicial review proceedings in which:
   - the court has given permission for the case to continue, and
   - the case:
     - has a significant wider interest; or
     - is of overwhelming interest to the client; or
     - raises significant human rights issues.

5.234 Cases concerning multi-party actions, appeals to the Supreme Court, breaches of ECHR rights (within the meaning of HRA 1998) or a Community Action, may be subject to special controls.[115]

CCMS and forms

5.235 There is a quick guide to how to register a case as high cost using CCMS.[116]

5.236 If you need to submit a fully costed case plan, you need to submit:
- a statement of what the case is about;
- a statement of objectives – what is in issue and what is likely to be secured;
- a case analysis – this must include:
  - issues of law – favourable and unfavourable, setting out how any obstacles will be overcome;
  - issues of fact – favourable and unfavourable, assessing the evidence supporting each;
  - expert evidence required – and why;
  - costs in issue – eg amount of claim for damages – special rules for clinical negligence see below;
  - key events and resources required – likely costs of solicitors, counsel, experts and disbursements;
  - risk analysis – and how to deal with risks identified;
  - statement of prospects of success within the terms of the funding code;
- an assessment – addressing each relevant element of the merits criteria and stating how each is satisfied;
- case theory – a short statement (five sentences or less) explaining why the client will win the case;

115 Civil Legal Aid (Procedure) Regulations 2012 reg 58.
116 http://ccmstraining.justice.gov.uk/Quick-guides/Quickguides/managing-live-cases–1.

- broadly costed overall case plan, including:
  - when counsel and experts will be instructed;
  - when the case management conference will be held;
  - when the trial will take place;
  - forecast of cumulative costs – at key events and appropriate intervals and at 31 March each year;
  - fully costed plan for the next stage of the case, showing an overall price for the stage – also setting out costs of all elements of work to be performed and costs to be incurred;
  - breakdown of costs to date;
  - details of any costs-sharing agreements;
  - details of the person managing the case, and of the team (if any) who will be doing the work;
  - names of person managing the case and the team members;
  - what they will be doing;
  - evidence of their suitability;
  - evidence of the firm's suitability to handle the work to its conclusion.

5.237 There is more information about what to submit (including sample case plans) on the LAA's website at: www.gov.uk/government/publications/high-cost-cases-non-family-civil.

Funding

5.238 The LAA has produced guidance, which can be downloaded from: www.gov.uk/civil-high-cost-cases-family.

5.239 Funding is agreed as set out in the case plan. There is very little flexibility to move costs from one heading to another once they are agreed. It can also be difficult to get amendments to the case plan accepted.

5.240 For a case where inter partes costs are expected to be paid if successful, funding is provided on a risk-sharing basis. If it settles, recovery is at full inter partes rates; but if unsuccessful, the LAA will pay at specified hourly rates with no mark-up (normally £90 for senior counsel, £70 per hour for solicitors and £50 for junior counsel).

5.241 There are specific rates of payment for other contracted cases, which vary depending on the type of case, prospects of success, and any exceptional circumstances.

5.242 Claims can be made, at the hourly rates applying, for costs to date at the start of the contract, and at the end of each stage. If a stage lasts longer than three months, a claim for costs can be made, but not more than twice in any 12-month period. These are applications for POA and made direct to the high costs cases team.

5.243   At the end of the case, claims can be made in the same way as under an ordinary certificate (see chapter 16), though at the hourly rate agreed in the contract. If costs are recovered from the other side, the LAA is entitled to the recoupment of payments on account. High cost case bills are always assessed by the LAA, not the courts.

CHAPTER 6

Client and Cost Management System

by Jane Pritchard

continued

Introduction

6.1   This chapter is intended to provide useful oversight into how to best use the Client and Cost Management System (CCMS), which became mandatory in April 2016 (February 2016 for Special Children Act cases).

6.2   The home page for CCMS training is found at ccmstraining. justice.gov.uk. It contains a wealth of resources and training guides: from introducing you to the system, getting started and making an application to uploading multiple bill submissions from your practice or case management system (PMS/CMS). The training methods vary from quick guides to interactive training sessions using live web chat. For ease of reference, some of the most useful guides are listed during the course of this chapter. Although, there can be no replacement for completing the training and using the website as an initial point of reference.

6.3   Keeping up to date with changes made in CCMS will always be a sound investment. Changes to process are added to 'Quick Guides' accessed through the above CCMS training site. There is a dedicated section for latest news, posted on the same home page.

The logic of CCMS

6.4   It is perhaps the logic of CCMS which has caused so much controversy in its development and application. CCMS was built to facilitate the digital delivery of the application and billing process of civil and family certificated legal aid work, but not to replicate the paper-based system. Despite applying the same regulations, the logic of the build of CCMS is very different, providing a digital platform to communicate the whole application and process.

6.5   Every process designed in CCMS follows the same regulations as the paper-based system, but due to the confines of the build of the digital platform, it has changed the way suppliers process their applications from start to finish. Perhaps the most frustrating element of CCMS when first using it is the linear structure it follows. Using a paper or eform provided the flexibility for suppliers to complete some of the form with their client present, enter further details off-site, and part-prepare forms sufficiently in advance of an event that was likely to occur. With the fast pace of most case work and vulnerability of many applicants for legal aid, paper helped you if you needed to issue emergency, time-sensitive applications without your client present. Front-loaded advice and action, printing off applications in advance of an event, was particularly useful for high-volume emergency work such as housing and immigration.

6.6 It appears there was little insight into how suppliers applied for funding, and why, during the development process of CCMS. As a result, applications are intended to be completed with a client present from start to finish (although promissory declarations can be used in some circumstances – see below) and despite the fantastic potential of a digital portal, unfortunately in practice CCMS restricts the application process.

Introduction of 'Apply' for Legal Aid

6.7 The Legal Aid Agency (LAA) has announced its intention to develop a new digital service for the submission of civil legal aid applications as part of its Agency Transformation Programme (ATP). In its 2018/19 annual report and accounts, the LAA referenced developments to support 'Apply' for Legal Aid ('Apply') which is being beta tested in 2019/20. Initially Apply will focus on solving two problems within CCMS: complex processes; and evidence requirements. The aim is to simplify the application process by using existing information where possible and asking the right person the right question at the right time.

6.8 Perhaps the most radical aspect of Apply will involve the client by submission of digital evidence of means for non-passported applications (see para 3.43 above).[1] The application process, commenced by a provider, will involve a link being sent to a client where they can access and supply proof of means using open banking.

6.9 The roll-out of Apply will be in stages. Not all providers will start using Apply at the same time. It is intended that it will initially be confined to passported applications in a limited number of proceedings. CCMS will still be used for amendments and to communicate decisions.

6.10 The second stage is expected to be opened up to clients who consent to use open banking, who are not self-employed and have no partner income to include. Connecting to Her Majesty's Revenue and Customs (HMRC) for salary information is intended to replace the need for uploading wage slips.

6.11 Eventually the LAA intends to extend the proceedings available; open the application process up for LAA caseworker reviews of evid-

---

1 Applications where a client is not in receipt of passporting benefits and therefore a full assessment of income is required. See chapter 3.43 for a list of passporting benefits.

ence; include a manual update fallback provision and extend the use of Apply to amend existing applications. Simplification of the application process is long overdue, and we hope the LAA's developments deliver real benefits to practitioners and clients. Whether vulnerable clients can or will use the LAA's offered open banking facility will be key to the success of Apply. Updates on the roll out will be provided on the website at: https://legalaidhandbook.com/

How to use CCMS in your practice

6.12   In the light of the restrictions that CCMS places on the application and billing process, it is essential to spend some time getting the operations and set-up of users right. The matrix for roles and responsibilities below is useful to establish the appropriate rights to allocate to each user.

6.13   Whether you are setting up CCMS for the first time, adding new users or perhaps reviewing how it has been working, it is important to ensure you are as efficient as possible at entering data and getting the results you want. Lack of training of new or current users can add delays, increase rejections and ultimately put your costs at risk. Users need to feel confident in what they need to do and the best way to achieve it. Using the wrong code for proceedings, or choosing a more limited scope, can have drastic consequences for an application. Once a certain path has been chosen – dual or single stage – it cannot be easily changed. If you choose the incorrect scope from a drop-down menu, it is highly likely to result in work being unpaid, if it is not noticed and remedied immediately.

6.14   The same was always true with a paper-based application, however practitioners were much less likely to select incorrect proceedings, as solicitors were well-versed in the codes and wordings for proceedings and limitations. Within CCMS, some of the wordings appear slightly different, which can be confusing.

6.15   For example, in Housing Act cases, you should not use the wording 'HO11A' for first-instance section 204 Housing Act 1996 Appeals ('HO011' should be used instead) and you should not use appeal versions of wordings generally, as proceedings are not intended to cover an appeal. 'Enforcement' (HSO11E) should be selected to enforce an original County Court Order.

6.16   Investing in CCMS training as part of every new starter's induction is therefore essential, regardless of whether they are new to the system or have joined you from another practice.

6.17   Work-arounds in CCMS are often solutions identified to existing design defects in the system. Sharing knowledge and the benefit of experience is also essential across your organisation. Often users do not sit in the same rooms, and information exchange within organisations can be sporadic. Adding CCMS updates as agenda items to regular departmental, practice area and supervision meetings is a way to ensure that no one within your organisation is having to work systems out for themselves, or equally has useful knowledge that is not being shared. The development of CCMS will continue, and practitioners must stay up to date.

Who does what within CCMS?

Overview

6.18   It is often helpful for certain preparation work to be completed offline in advance of the application. A straightforward check of the means assessment and merits of the case can save time wasted in an abandoned application. Checking through papers and means evidence without a client present is often the best investment in time at the start of the process.

6.19   The Ministry of Justice (MoJ) means assessment calculator is still available and can be assessed at: http://civil-eligibility-calculator.justice.gov.uk/. Using it before starting in CCMS to undertake a means assessment can save time because of the need to set up the client and the application on the CCMS portal before the means assessment can commence as it avoids the need to go through the process for ineligible clients. At the same time as pausing to consider means and merits, consideration of the type of application to submit can prevent a rejection and the need to start again.

6.20   For legal aid applications, there are two main ways most firms operate; additionally, the LAA modelled CCMS assuming a third way:

1) A paralegal/trainee solicitor completes the majority of the admin process through CCMS in the same way they may have taken basic information essential to an application for funding on a paper form: they create the client, the new application and then fill in all the information up to and including means assessment, but not merits. The solicitor with conduct (who could be in a different location) then logs on to CCMS to add the merits information including the statement of case. In this scenario, the solicitor has the opportunity to prepare a statement of case while

means information is being entered, which can streamline the process, making reference to case papers which the client has provided.

2) It is also possible for a paralegal/trainee solicitor to undertake all of the work necessary in completing an application, all the way up to, but excluding, the submission of the application. The improved navigation within CCMS means you can move back and forward within sections of the application. It has always been good practice for a separate statement of case to be drafted, which can either be uploaded or pasted into CCMS, setting out the facts of the applicant's case, the law and the merits of the application to satisfy the criteria for funding. This could be completed by the solicitor in advance of the application, where possible, preventing the need for the solicitor to be involved at all in data input/form filling. Only an authorised litigator can submit an application in CCMS, and therefore it is necessary for such a person to approve the application, but her or his involvement in CCMS can be limited to the submission only. Often where urgent court work is required, this is the route chosen by practitioners, freeing up the solicitor to concentrate on drafting.

3) The method of submission the LAA assumed when designing CCMS is for a supervising solicitor to approve every application submitted. A solicitor/trainee solicitor/paralegal within a practice completes the application, and the supervising solicitor logs in to approve and submit it. The LAA definition of 'supervisor' within CCMS is not one that corresponds with the way in which supervisors may work in practice, and is not the same as supervision as required by the SQM/Lexcel and the Contract. As can be seen from the table below, anyone who requires access to all areas of CCMS for completing an application requires a **Case Management** role, but the case manager cannot submit applications or bills in CCMS. A user needs the **Case Management Supervisor** role in order to submit an application. It appears it was expected by the LAA that a supervising solicitor would approve all submissions of applications, though that is not common in practice.

6.21   Unless your organisation chooses to require all applications to be approved by a supervising solicitor, you will need to give 'supervisor' rights to every authorised litigator as well as case management rights. They will then be able to create and submit applications. It would perhaps be easier if the LAA had called the supervisor role the 'authorised litigator' role to avoid confusion.

6.22   The **Bill Preparation** and **Bill Supervisor** roles in the matrix below work in the same way for billing as for legal aid applications but perhaps more logically. A biller or costs draftsman, external or internal, is allocated the bill preparation role, and so can draft but not submit the bill on CCMS. A bill supervisor in house needs to approve their bills. If your biller is in-house and needs both to prepare and submit bills, they would need both roles allocated to them. Please note, however, the guidance on bill preparation and submission below.

6.23   Finally, the roles of Office Manager, Cross Office Access and Firm Administrator need to be considered. As with 'supervisor', these are specific roles within the CCMS process and need not correspond with equivalent positions in your organisation.

6.24   The **Office Manager** role simply provides an overview of all cases, notifications and actions within an organisation, but does not allow the user to create or submit applications or bills. This is quite a useful function and could be used to ensure all outstanding notifications across the whole practice have been closed or replied to within the appropriate time limits. It is useful to allocate this role to supervising solicitors, heads of departments and billing managers.

6.25   The **Firm Administrator** role should be allocated to your CCMS administrator, the person who controls the set up and allocation of roles to all users within your practice. The remittance advice/BACS statements for the practice are only sent to the Firm Administrator, though they also need to be allocated the Office Manager role in order to receive them.

6.26   The final role is the **Cross Office Access** role: this is commonly used as an 'add on' privilege for all users to enable anyone entering data into CCMS to first check not just cases opened by them, but any of their colleagues across the organisation. It can be built into your CCMS protocol to complete a wide search for the client across your organisation before entering the client as a new client within CCMS, to prevent duplicate entries if, for example, an existing client of another department returns with a new case. Organisations will often check for existing client entries in their own case management system before submission in routine cases. However, in urgent cases this may not be possible, and having Cross Office Access is another tool that can help prevent duplication and also help avoid conflicts of interest.

CCMS super users

6.27   There is still a huge variance in the time it takes different organisations to complete a CCMS application, with some taking significantly longer where only one person is involved in the process from start to finish. Admin support may not always be available, but planning your application around the availability of support can both reduce fee earner time taken and increase capacity to take on new cases. It can also improve the experience of the client, who will not need to be present while data entry is carried out.

6.28   Creating CCMS 'super users' within every team across the firm can also improve efficiency of creating and submitting applications. Frequent use of CCMS for repeated actions and familiarity of the navigation tools will improve the streamlining of the process. As with any routine, the more you use it the faster you become. CCMS super users could also have responsibility for updating the practice on new releases, trialling new upgrades, and feeding back to the LAA and representative bodies on enhancements needed.

Role	Case Management*	Case Management Supervisor*	Bill Preparation*	Bill Supervisor*	Office Manager
Search for and view cases	•	•	•	•	•
View case details	•		•		
View case attachments	•	•	•	•	•
Search for client	•				
Register client/ Amend client details	•				
Create new applications	•				
View proceedings	•		•		
Add/amend proceedings	•				
View, record and amend outcomes (incl undertaking)	•				
View actions and notifications	•	•	•	•	•
Add/amend case costs	•				

Role	Case Management*	Case Management Supervisor*	Bill Preparation*	Bill Supervisor*	Office Manager
Request prior authority	•				
Submit new applications		•			
Submit amendments to applications/ outcomes		•			
Create bills/ POAs			•		
Submit bills/ POAs				•	
Attach documents/ evidence	•		•		
Submit attached documents	•	•	•	•	•
Submit notifications	•	•	•	•	•
Bulk upload – claim upload pricing only			•		
Bulk upload – claim upload				•	
Accessing remittance advice notifications					•

CCMS Provider: Roles and Responsibilities Guidance – Quick Guide V2.0,13/02/2019

What application should you make?

6.29   Navigating the application process is one of the most troubling issues that users experience (as confirmed by the Legal Aid Practitioners Group (LAPG) 2017 national survey[2]). However, since April 2016 there has been some significant change in how CCMS can be used, and accordingly the information which follows is the up-to-date position at the time of writing. Where in doubt, always make

2   See www.lapg.co.uk.

reference to the CCMS training pages: http://ccmstraining.justice. gov.uk/Quick-guides/Quickguides/making-an-initial-application-1.

6.30   Applications can be made in the following way depending on whether delegated functions can be exercised for all the work involved (see chapter 5 and subject-specific chapters for more on delegated functions):

Applications

1	Delegated functions	Dual stage emergency application
2	Delegated functions	Single stage emergency application
3	Delegated functions	Special Children Act application
4	Non-delegated functions	Emergency application
5	Non-delegated functions	Substantive application
6	Non-delegated functions	Exceptional case funding application

Emergency delegated function applications

6.31   A particular difficulty for many practitioners is the submission of emergency applications. In the table above, this includes numbers 1 and 2 where there is an emergency (urgent work to progress the case is required within four weeks, eg a hearing date or directions to comply with) and you have delegated functions permitted in your schedule authorisation for this type of case.

6.32   The purpose of CCMS in these cases is to communicate to the LAA the use of delegated functions rather than to seek funding. As you have the power to self-grant funding, you are reporting to the LAA that you have done so – not making an application for emergency representation.

6.33   There is a choice of two methods: the more frequently used dual stage application; or the single stage application. Most practitioners have used the dual stage application because in urgent circumstances a client may not have all the documentation to support the application, either for the merits but more often the means stage. As the descriptions suggest, they allow the report of the exercise of delegated functions to be completed in a single stage, or in two stages.

6.34   The training resources available on the CCMS website explain that the dual stage process is useful where you need more time to obtain evidence required in the single stage application but do not list what this evidence is. The resources also explain that one of the benefits of the dual stage process is that the application can be amended before the substantive application is submitted. Wherever possible, you should consider the type of application you are making alongside the nature of the emergency work to be done to minimise the need to amend the emergency application. This can be illustrated by considering examples of different sorts of emergency cases.

6.35   For example, in family proceedings you may make an initial application for a non-molestation order which you will rely on for a later application for linked proceedings. Where the second application is to be heard within five working days of the decision to use delegated functions for the non-molestation order, you can wait for the outcome of the hearing where the non-molestation is granted and then submit one application with both proceedings. The same principle applies to a judicial review application where there will be interim relief and directions sought within five working days.

6.36   However, the main difference is that in family cases, the additional proceedings cannot be added unless you have the evidence required for the domestic violence gateway – which the non-molestation order will provide. However, for the judicial review case the initial limitation to proceedings chosen can reflect all work reasonably expected to be completed within the emergency period so as to avoid the need for emergency amendments in quick succession.

6.37   To take another example, in a housing case you might use a limitation up to a specified hearing date. If you consider the hearing has a likelihood of being adjourned to a date within the four-week emergency period, then add to the wording of the limitation 'any adjournment thereof'. This would then include any work completed for repeated adjournments of the hearing in the emergency period. Clarification of the use of this wider scope should be made in your statement of case.

6.38   If, however, it is predicted that at the hearing an order will require filing of a defence and counter claim, a limitation of all steps up to and including the filing of the defence and counterclaim could be used, as long as the work is predicted to be completed within the emergency four-week period justifying the exercise of delegated functions.

6.39   If you are satisfied that you can exercise delegated functions for the emergency application, your assessment of means and merits is sound, you are authorised to do so under your Contract Schedule and the case meets reg 46 of the Civil Legal Aid (Merits Criteria)

Regulations 2013, then you need the easiest method of submitting the application which communicates your decision through CCMS.

6.40   Where there are no anticipated emergency amendments following the application it is likely that the single stage application is the most appropriate. See the table below which sets out an example of the options available where delegated functions are available:

Situation	Single stage	Dual stage
Client has the necessary evidence of means but limited case papers	Submit a single stage application and advise the LAA in the statement of case that you have been able to decide the merits based on the papers available, how and why. If requested, supply additional papers if they become available.	
Client in receipt of passported benefit and eligible based on capital assessment but doesn't have three months of bank statements	Submit a single stage application, upload the evidence you have available, fill in any gaps when requested at a later date when the application is processed by case workers. If your client is unlikely to be able to provide bank statements, let the LAA know in the statement of case or by a case enquiry to help the LAA caseworker process with the evidence available without asking questions you already know the answers to.	Submit a dual stage application, await bank statements which may not be available before the date when the LAA request you submit the substantive amendment in any event.
Client has all the means and merits evidence needed, but the urgent work required within the initial four-week period of the emergency certificated includes potential changes to scope	Submit a single stage application with the scope limitation predicted for the whole of the emergency period rather than limited to a single stage or application. Explain the situation in your statement of case and why all of the emergency work is required beyond the first hearing.	Submit a dual stage application where you are less certain of what will be the outcome of urgent action and submit an amendment to the dual stage before submitting your substantive application amendment.

Situation	Single stage	Dual stage
Client has all the means and merits evidence needed but there are amendments to proceedings and scope likely at the first hearing taking place within five days of the grant of emergency funding	Wait to make the application within the five working-day period once the hearing has taken place of the further application or when the order has been made, however be aware of the risk you take as a provider that your client will come back to the office to sign the CCMS declaration.	Make a dual stage application and an application for an amendment in quick succession.

Emergency non-delegated functions applications and backdating

6.41   After the Legal Aid, Sentencing and Punishment of Offenders Act 2012 (LASPO) came into force, the LAA restricted delegated functions in many categories of work. The result is an increase in the number of non-delegated function applications being made. The time taken for the LAA to process these often-urgent applications can result in delays, and therefore close attention should be given to the options available. These are discussed below.

6.42   Changes to the process for applying for emergency non-delegated functions applications came into force on 20 February 2019. Previously it had been possible to make what was known as an out of hours application for funding, which commenced outside of CCMS. This process enabled urgent applications to be made and funding granted up to 8pm, often in immigration, community care and public law cases where funding was required to obtain interim relief in the Administrative Court.

6.43   Following the successful challenge in *R (Duncan Lewis Solicitors Ltd) v Director of Legal Aid Casework and the Lord Chancellor*,[3] the LAA introduced discretionary powers to backdate the grant of legal aid funding. Urgent applications can now commence in CCMS, even if a decision is not communicated on funding, before immediate work is carried out.

6.44   However, it is important to note that the backdating power is a discretionary one and as such close scrutiny should always be applied to the regulation that enables the power to be exercised under reg 2 of the Civil Legal Aid (Procedure) (Amendment) Regulations 2019.

3   [2016] EWHC 717 (Admin).

6.45   For non-delegated functions work:

1) **Submitting an emergency dual stage application on CCMS then contacting customer services if the application requires assessment within 48 hours of the application** (the LAA state it takes two hours for the system to upload the information and therefore ask you to wait two hours to call). The process is similar to submitting a delegated functions emergency dual stage application, however when asked you select the drop down for 'no' to the delegated functions box. Once the emergency application is processed, you will have five working days to submit the substantive application. It will be necessary to chase up the application by telephone at regular intervals and obtain clear information on timescales from the LAA.

2) **Making an application where work needs to commence before a determination is likely to be issued – backdating request.** As with all CCMS guidance in this chapter, the onus is on the earliest possible notification to the LAA of the work predicted. Where for example an urgent non-delegated functions application is made, and work will commence for injunctive relief immediately, the full nature of work should be predicted and a request for backdating of the determination included in the initial CCMS application. If in doubt of when the application would be considered and whether therefore a backdate is requested, air on the side of caution and include the backdate request. Target turn arounds for applications vary, where urgent work is predicted, a backdated request is sensible.

   The application type selected will be emergency. The application proceeds as normal until the merits section is reached. When completing the emergency details, you must select from the drop-down menu the reason for the emergency: ie injunctive relief sought/hearing date and then in the text box enter the date you wish to backdate the application and the justification.

   If all the information cannot be included in the further information box, reference can be made to an uploaded statement of case which may detail the chronology of actions taken to date. The Director of Casework at the LAA has discretion to backdate the determination date where the application was made as soon as reasonably practical, it was in the interests of justice for the services to be carried out prior to the date of the determination, and the services could not have been carried out as Controlled Work. Sufficient detail and justification need to be included.

3) **Requesting a backdate for an existing application for funding or amendment to a certificate.** Circumstances may change rapidly where work is required to be carried out which could not have been predicted when the application for funding was submitted on CCMS. In accordance with reg 2(4) of the Civil Legal Aid (Procedure) (Amendment) Regulations 2019, the application for funding must be made as soon as reasonably practical. A case enquiry should be submitted with the same detail as above of the details requested and justification for the backdating.

4) **Monitoring the success of backdated applications.** As with all changes to CCMS practice, practitioners may find it useful to introduce an in-house template making reference to the regulations when justifying the backdate. Due to the risk of commencing work and or proceedings without a legal aid determination, you may want to include an approval process into any backdated application submission. Justifying the basis for backdated applications set against your own protocols is a great method of quality control. Keeping a central record of when backdating is required and responses from the LAA can help improve process for future applications.

Situation	Emergency application	Backdate request
Client needs representation for urgent work within 48 hours but work does not need to commence immediately.	Submit a dual stage emergency non-delegated functions application and contact customer services two hours after the CCMS submission to ask for the application to be expedited.	
Client needs representation the same day your application is being made with immediate work required which cannot be completed under Controlled Work, ie representation at a hearing the same or next day and or applying for interim relief in the Administrative Court.	Submit a dual stage emergency non-delegated functions application and contact customer services two hours after the CCMS submission to ask for the application to be expedited.	Include a fully detailed request for the backdating of the date of the determination. Set out the chronology of action to urgent work to be completed.

An application (initial funding application or amendment request) has been submitted where a backdated request was not made but immediate urgent work is now needed. eg an eviction date has been set, interim relief or an urgent application to maintain the status quo required.		Submit a case enquiry including a fully detailed request for the backdating of the date of the determ-ination. Set out the chronology of action to urgent work to be completed.

Family legal aid cost limits

6.46   In a move to streamline family work, applications from 19 April 2019 are now granted an initial cost limit of £25,000 for some proceedings (see para 7.106 below for a list). All Special Children Act applications within CCMS will have a default cost limit already applied. However, for all other qualifying family proceedings, you should request the £25,000 limit in the Proceedings and Costs section of the applica-tion. In the Requested Cost Limitation box simply overtype the default limitation provided. When you reach the Merits Assessment section you will be asked to justify the additional cost limit, you will need to use the following wording: 'We are applying for the new default cost limit'. The cost limits do not apply for certificates granted before 19 April 2019, however the LAA may grant a single amend-ment to the cost limit up to £25,000 where justified.

Urgent amendments

6.47   As explained above, some emergency amendments can be predicted and to avoid urgent amendments, a wider limitation included in the initial application, whether exercising delegated functions or not. Practitioners have reported that the LAA have discouraged applica-tions for amendments to scope pending a substantive certificate being granted on the basis it can be applied for later and the cost limit will apply retrospectively. Any delay in applying for extensions to cost or scope limits places practitioners at risk. Should the LAA decide a substantive certificate is granted, but only limited to the emergency work, and then discharge the certificate (for example, if new evidence of means comes to light suggesting the client is not eligible), the cost limit would never be amended. Regardless of the ability now to request backdating for determination dates, it is still best practice to ensure amendments are processed in the order they arise, even if this means a delay to a substantive certificate being granted. If the choice is whether to apply for the substantive certificate or increase costs, the cost increase should be pursued first. However, predicting the right cost limit with the initial application, rather than accepting a default limit, can dramatically reduce the need for cost amendments. Note below the changes for family cost limits in CCMS and changes to process needed.

6.48   Where delegated functions have been exercised and emergency work which was not predicted arises after submission of an emergency application and the substantive certificate has not yet been processed, you should contact the LAA customer service team by telephone on 0300 200 2020 to determine what process to follow. It may be that the application is to be granted imminently and you can wait. Or it may be that the LAA will reject your substantive amendment, to enable you to submit an emergency amendment which will be considered before the substantive amendment.

6.49   If you submit a single stage application, the LAA can convert this to a dual stage application, which should result in your substantive amendment information being saved for future use. You can then submit the new emergency amendment to scope, and once this is considered, submit the substantive amendment within the deadline provided in subsequent notifications. This process can be difficult to understand; however, it follows the linear process of CCMS in that multiple amendments are not possible at the same time. They are dealt with in strict order, and so if a new amendment arises which is more urgent than an outstanding one, the outstanding one must be cancelled before the new one can be processed.

6.50   Similarly, you may grant multiple amendments pursuant to your contract schedule using delegated functions, but you can only communicate one at a time to the LAA via CCMS. It is therefore very important to anticipate all work needed in the emergency period from the date of the grant of any delegated functions where possible.

What if the client cannot be present to sign the CCMS application?

6.51   It is a requirement in CCMS that the client be present at the time the application is submitted. With both emergency delegated function applications and non-delegated function applications, there is a limited number of circumstances where a signature is not required before the application is submitted on the basis the client is not present. These are:

1) **Promissory declarations.** To be used only when you are granting an emergency certificate under delegated functions. There is no guidance specific to promissory declarations in the CCMS training materials save for a quick guide, however the guidance given for the use of Declaration Against Instructions will be useful as it provides a procedure you can follow for both methods of submitting applications. The most important part of both processes is the due diligence used to record the means and merits information which enables you to decide whether the applicant is eligible for legal aid. To this end, completing a thorough means assessment and being satisfied on disclosure of evidence of means is crucial. It would be sensible to have an office protocol for a supervisor to check and authorise the use of both declarations as they will be used infrequently. Particularly with promissory declarations where work commences before the CCMS declaration is signed, there is a heightened risk to your costs until the LAA issue a substantive application.

   The promissory declaration can only be used when the client is reasonably unable to attend the office to sign the emergency application declaration in person. Examples given by the LAA include where the client is imprisoned or hospitalised; or there is an LAA system outage formally communicated to you by the LAA which prevents the client from being able to sign the client declaration on the CCMS emergency application. Therefore, the client is in the office but the relevant declaration page of their application cannot be printed off. There will be other circumstances in addition to prison and hospitalisation which could prevent access to CCMS in emergency circumstances. These may include: acting for a client with disabilities who cannot reasonably be expected to travel to the office. It may not be safe for an applicant to travel to the office or an applicant may be homeless and destitute and only able to attend the office of a referrer within their locality, particularly in immigration and homeless cases.

   Ultimately it is for you to decide (and, if necessary, justify on audit) whether the condition of 'unreasonable to travel to the office' is met. A clear attendance note referencing the reasons for your decision to use a promissory declaration and detailing the steps taken is essential.

The LAA does provide a checklist for means to complete with your client to ensure you can fully complete the means application within CCMS later. Search 'means checklist' on the CCMS training site. The checklist includes the mandatory fields in CCMS so that you can answer all means questions. Despite a client not attending the office in person, you still need to have seen adequate evidence to enable you to reasonably assess that your client is likely to be eligible for legal aid. Screen shots using cameras on mobile phones can be a useful resource for clients to send images of either their online bank statements or letters received from the Department for Work and Pensions (DWP) when they cannot attend the office. Email copies may also be used.

In these cases, your client must still sign the CCMS declaration page from the application which must be printed and a hard copy kept on file. The promissory declaration simply means they do not need to sign it at the point of submitting the application on CCMS; it can be completed later.

See chapter 5 for situations where a client cannot reasonably travel to the office at all and you need to use delegated functions. In an emergency case, there may be no time to travel to your client or you may not be able to secure a prison visit. Collating information to complete applications over the phone is never ideal, but where a referral agency, probation or a local advice centre are able to facilitate access to your client, they can be crucial in the process of obtaining a signed promissory declaration.

When submitting your application on CCMS and making the declaration at the end of the merits section, you will need to confirm you do not have a signed form and complete the free text box to set out the circumstances. If the situation is complex, you may want to make reference to the further information contained within your statement of case. Finally, when you complete the application you need to tick the box to confirm you have obtained the necessary signed declarations as the promissory declaration satisfies that criteria.

2) **Declaration against instructions.** The process for promissory declarations is only available for applications where you can use delegated functions to grant emergency funding. The declaration against instructions can be used where the client cannot attend the office for the same reasons detailed above and it is necessary to make the application for legal aid during the period when the client or their partner, for good reason, cannot attend your office

in person, but you cannot use delegated functions. Examples given by the LAA include the imminent expiry of a limitation period or substantial detriment to the client; this could include urgent judicial review applications for example where access to the client and CCMS was not possible and delegated functions were not available due to the nature of the work.

LAA guidance is that the process is designed for use in a non-emergency situation where you attend your client and complete the full paper forms, uploading the information onto CCMS at a later date. Once you have completed the application on CCMS and uploaded the information you relied upon, the application summary needs to be sent to the client to consider within 14 days of submission and any inaccuracies communicated. If there are any inaccuracies a further signed declaration will need to be obtained.

Whereas with the promissory declaration you should tick yes to certify you have the necessary declarations signed before submission on CCMS, you will not have a signature where you are using the declaration against instructions process. Therefore, in the means and merits assessments declaration box you should specify that you will be printing the CCMS Application Summary screen and having the client sign as their declaration. If you answer no to having the signed declaration you will then need to answer questions on how you satisfy the criteria for using the declaration of instructions process.

The LAA scrutinises use of this process, as it is only expected in a small minority of cases. You should keep a full attendance note detailing why and how you have followed the process, including attending your client for instructions and confirming the information provided as this will be crucial in justifying your actions on audit.

Exceptional case funding applications

6.52   CCMS is primarily used for applications for funding which are within the scope of LASPO. If you are applying for exceptional funding, you must use the hyperlink on page 2 of the online application to be presented with the correct options. There is a quick guide on the CCMS training website which sets out the process. Please note that if part of your application for funding falls within scope of LASPO and part would be an exceptional funding application, both applications must be submitted separately, the LAA refers to such applications as 'blended' applications and there is no process within CCMS to submit one application with separate parts.

Billing through CCMS

6.53   A significant benefit of CCMS is the potential for improved cost control. All relevant data for a certificate including limitations, scope, and allocation of costs to counsel are retained in the system. However, there are some additional digital processes which did not exist with a paper bill submission, and which if not dealt with promptly, can slow down bill payment.

6.54   The LAA did not develop CCMS billing functionality to rival existing billing software. You can report through CCMS, but the process is more time consuming than the market-leading software widely available for legal aid billing. Line-by-line cost entry in CCMS is a laborious process which is not intuitive, so that save for the simplest of bills, mistakes may be made with incomplete submissions. If at all possible, you should avoid billing through CCMS and instead use billing software (either your case management software or dedicated digital billing tools) which produce an XML report to upload to CCMS.

6.55   The upload functionality includes a price check before submission to ensure CCMS has matched the fields within your submission to pay what you expect.

6.56   While you will not be able to upload the billing bundle at the same time you submit the claim, it is sensible to prepare your billing bundle when the bill is uploaded. This ensures it is ready to upload when the request for required evidence is received and will prevent delay before the claim can be processed. This will enable you to work to the tight deadline for submission and receive payment sooner.

6.57   When uploading supporting papers, the LAA may list a number of items. Despite the guidance available on the LAA website, it is not necessary to separate out and individually update the documents requested. A paginated bundle with all the documents clearly listed in one upload is satisfactory and can save additional administrative time being added to the process.

6.58   Where you have linked certificates on CCMS, you will need to submit a nil bill for each of the linked certificates at the same time as submitting the bill on the main certificate. If you omit to submit the nil bills, this will delay your main bill being processed and paid.

6.59   When processing claims for travel through CCMS, the LAA regularly seeks clarification of the reason for the travel if it is not clear on the claim. It is sensible to provide any supporting documentation or a word document setting out the reasons for travel to prevent delay to payment of the claim. Anticipating any reasons for further queries, and front loading the information provided, can save valuable weeks in the billing process.

6.60   Before the LAA can process your bill, it needs first to have processed the outcome codes submission for the case. It is essential therefore that the outcome codes are completed as soon as the legal work on the case is concluded rather than waiting for the file to be billed. The LAA processing timetables only apply for billing to cases where the outcome code step has been completed.

6.61   Initially, CCMS would enable you to upload a bill which was outside of scope of your client's funding. The bill would then be rejected at a later date when processed. The same was the case for uploading claims against emergency certificates where means had not yet been assessed. Enhancements to CCMS now prevent any bill upload giving an error message if the claim does not match the scope of the funding or is before a substantive certificate is processed. This should prevent unnecessary rejections.

Contingency plans if CCMS is not available

6.62   Should CCMS be unavailable, the LAA guidance is that practitioners should contact the online support team by telephone for authorisation to be given before contingency protocols can be used. Should the LAA accept the criteria for contingency is met, they will give you a contingency reference number which should be quoted in subsequent contact.

6.63   If the contingency is in regard to an application or amendment and you have access to the case via CCMS, you will be sent a document request via CCMS. You will be expected to return the cover sheet with the relevant paper application by email to: contactcivil@legalaid.gsi.gov.uk marked as 'contingency' in the subject line. You will be expected to keep the original signed form.

6.64   When deciding whether to apply the contingency process, the LAA will consider the urgency of the application and whether delegated functions can be exercised.

6.65   The LAA contingency guidance sets out the circumstances in which the contingency process will be invoked, however it is advisable to take a screen shot of each and every attempt to submit your application on CCMS and contact the LAA at the earliest opportunity. The LAA are alerted to CCMS outages by providers. It is imperative therefore that technical issues are reported and do not delay the grant of Legal Aid.

Technical difficulties

6.66   There are two well-known issues which can frustrate attempts to copy and paste into CCMS applications and access the CCMS platform: browser cache and special characters.

Clearing your browser cache

6.67   Clearing your browser cache can resolve a number of issues. Your browser cache is a temporary storage area on your computer which remembers your recent web browsing history and can take you to frequented pages. Old passwords and temporary internet files can be saved automatically in your browser cache. This has been identified by the LAA technical team as potentially impacting system performance negatively. Pressing Ctrl/shift/delete while in your browser should bring up a window with options for deletion. See the CCMS training site for the guide with more details.

Cutting and pasting text

6.68   When drafting any text to copy and paste into CCMS upload screens, you should avoid the use of any 'special characters'. Only a comma and full stop should be used. Adding any others such as colons, speech marks etc will slow down the process and can be prevent the pasting process altogether. The technical guide on the CCMS training website sets out how you can identify any hidden special characters to remove them. You can also copy and paste text into the note pad programme which removes them before transferring onto CCMS.

CHAPTER 7

Conducting a family private law case

continued

Introduction

7.1 This chapter deals with conducting family private law cases, that is where the issues are between private individuals rather than involving the state (in the shape of social services). There are separate chapters on the general rules that apply to all civil cases, as well as family public law, housing, immigration and mental health, as they have their own funding schemes and rules.

7.2 In chapter 3, we saw that there are three key stages in providing publicly funded services: to ensure that i) the matter is within scope, ii) the client is financially eligible and iii) the case meets the merits test. In addition, you need to ensure that applications are completed correctly and funding is obtained. The Lord Chancellor's guidance under section 4 of the Legal Aid, Sentencing and Punishment of Offenders Act 2012 (LASPO) has a helpful section in relation to how the Act applies: www.gov.uk/guidance/funding-and-costs-assessment-for-civil-and-crime-matters.

7.3 This chapter explains how these steps are taken successfully in respect of family private law. Where appropriate, you will be referred back to chapter 5, as that chapter sets out the general rules.

7.4 See appendix C for a summary of the Legal Aid Agency's (LAA's) Costs – Assessment Guidance, in respect of the most common queries raised by caseworkers.

Scope

7.5 Scope is determined by LASPO. Part 1 of Schedule 1 to the Act lists the services which may generally be provided in the family category.

In scope with no need for evidence of abuse

7.6 The following types of case are within scope without the need to produce evidence of domestic abuse or evidence that a child is at risk of abuse.

Inherent jurisdiction of the High Court

7.7 Inherent jurisdiction of the High Court in relation to children and vulnerable adults (Sch 1 Part 1 para 9) applications for wardship are covered by legal aid.

Unlawful removal of children

7.8   You can prevent removal from the jurisdiction but can only secure return of a child if unlawfully removed within the jurisdiction (Sch 1 Part 1 para 10). Unlawfully means removed by someone who does not have authority to do so, either because they do not have parental responsibility or because of a court order. The following are in scope:

- prohibited steps orders;
- specific issue orders;
- orders for disclosure of a child's whereabouts under Family Law Act 1986 s33, under section 34 for a child's return, and a requirement under section 37 to surrender a passport of, issued to, or containing the particulars of a child.

Domestic abuse

7.9   Advice and representation in relation to home rights, occupation orders and non-molestation orders under Part 4 of the Family Law Act 1996, injunctions following assault, battery or false imprisonment, and inherent jurisdiction of the High Court to protect an adult (Sch 1 Part 1 para 11) are all in scope.

7.10   It is really important to note that this paragraph is not qualified – it is not necessary for the client to show or provide evidence of any previous violence to be eligible for 'civil legal services'. Civil legal services include all forms of legal aid, so advice under Legal Help can be provided in relation to the issues concerning domestic violence itself, and a warning letter drafted, prior to, or instead of, applying to court for an injunction.

Respondents in domestic abuse cases

7.11   Legal aid may still be available to respondents in some cases, but it depends on the facts of the case. See below for an extract from the Lord Chancellor's guidance:

Respondents

10.31 The prospects of success criteria (Merits Regulation 67(2)) and the proportionality test (Merits Regulation 67(3)) are unlikely to be satisfied by a respondent to non-molestation proceedings or a forced marriage protection order only, unless there are very serious allegations which are plausibly denied wholly or substantially. An exception is where there is any question of inability to defend, for example because of mental incapacity or age, in which case a grant is likely to be justified. When considering the proportionality test, the impact on the client of the order sought will be taken into account, including any impact on contact or other related family proceedings.

10.32 In cases where the allegations are less serious or are admitted to a significant extent the main issue may well be whether the respondent should give an undertaking to the court and what form that undertaking should take. Legal help will usually be more appropriate in such cases (regulation 20 of the Merits Regulations).

Other areas within scope without evidence of abuse

7.12   Other areas within scope without evidence of abuse are:

- mediation (Sch 1 Part 1 para 14);
- representation of children who are themselves parties to family proceedings (Sch 1 Part 1 para 15);
- forced marriage cases (Sch 1 Part 1 para 16);
- European Union (EU) and international agreements concerning children (Sch 1 Part 1 para 17);
- EU and international agreements concerning maintenance (Sch 1 Part 1 para 18);
- forced marriage protection orders;
- female genital mutilation (FGM) protection orders.

7.13   Following the LASPO policy implementation review, the Ministry of Justice (MoJ) stated an intention to widen scope to include Special Guardianship Orders, without having to provide evidence of abuse. Implementation fell behind the stated time-table but progress had been made on this issue at the time of writing and we hope to see regulations to enable this early in 2020.

7.14   A further proposal is to extend eligibility for non-means tested legal aid for parents, or those with parental responsibility, who wish to oppose applications for placement orders or adoption orders in public family law proceedings. As far as we are aware, there was no progress on this as we went to press.

In scope with evidence of abuse

7.15   Other than the above, private family law cases are only in scope where the applicant for legal aid can show that he or she is a victim of domestic abuse, or that the services are required to protect a child from an adult other than the applicant for legal aid. In either case, evidence will be required – see para 7.18 below.

Other private law matters arising out a family relationship (Sch 1 Part 1 para 12)

7.16   Legal aid (both advice and representation) for matters arising out of a family relationship is only available to people who can show in very specific ways (set out in Schedule 1 to the Civil Legal Aid (Procedure) Regulations 2012[1]) that they are the victims of domestic abuse. Examples include:

- financial matters and arrangements for children (eg maintenance or other financial arrangement orders, ancillary relief, transfer of tenancy);
- divorce, dissolution or nullity;
- child arrangement orders;
- declaration of parentage;
- parental responsibility orders;
- special guardianship orders;
- prohibited steps orders;
- specific issue orders;
- orders under Family Law Act 1986 ss33 and 34 for disclosure of the child's whereabouts or return unless in relation to the unlawful removal of a child.

7.17   LASPO has the following wide definition of 'domestic violence' and 'abuse':

'domestic violence' means any incident, or pattern of incidents, of controlling, coercive or threatening behaviour, violence or abuse (whether psychological, physical, sexual, financial or emotional) between individuals who are associated with each other;[2]

Protection of children and family matters (Sch 1 Part 1 para 13)

7.18   Legal aid advice and representation is available in specified private family law matters:

- child arrangement orders prohibited steps orders and specific issue orders;
- removal of a father's parental responsibility under Children Act 1989 s4(2A);
- special guardianship orders;

---

1   Schedule 1 to the 2012 Regs, replacing the previous reg 33, was inserted by Civil Legal Aid (Procedure) (Amendment) (No 2) Regulations 2017 reg 2. The full text can also be found in Schedule 1 to the 2017 Regs.
2   Legal Aid, Sentencing and Punishment of Offenders Act 2012 (Amendment of Schedule 1) Order 2013 art 4(1).

- termination of appointment of a guardian under Children Act 1989 s6(7);
- orders under Adoption and Children Act 2002 s51A (post adoption contact); and
- orders under Family Law Act 1986 ss33 and 34 for disclosure of the child's whereabouts or return, unless in relation to the unlawful removal of a child, where a child is at risk from an adult who is not the person receiving legal aid.

7.19 Legal aid is only available to people who can show in very specific ways (set out in Schedule 2 to the Civil Legal Aid (Procedure) Regulations 2012)[3] that the child is at risk of abuse from an adult who is not the applicant for legal aid.

Evidence of domestic abuse

7.20 Acceptable evidence of abuse is listed in Schedule 1 to the Civil Legal Aid (Procedure) (Amendment) (No 2) Regulations 2017 – the culmination (so far) of amendments over the years[4] to permit some additional forms of evidence. The validity of documentary evidence of domestic abuse was extended to 60 months from 25 April 2016, following the Rights of Women judicial review.[5] However, that limitation was removed altogether from 8 January 2018, so that once evidence has been provided, it does not need to be updated, and does not need to be of events that have occurred within five years prior to the application.

7.21 The Director has released detailed guidance on the operation of the evidence requirements, available at: www.gov.uk/guidance/funding-and-costs-assessment-for-civil-and-crime-matters. This specifies in detail what is required for each piece of evidence. It also confirms that full and satisfactory evidence must be provided *before* work starts, otherwise legal aid will be refused or the Legal Help will be nil assessed (para 2.5 of the guidance). Where you are applying for a certificate, you

---

3 Schedule 2, replacing the previous reg 34, was inserted by the Civil Legal Aid (Procedure) (Amendment) (No 2) Regulations 2017. The full text can also be found in Schedule 2 to the 2017 Regs.

4 The original reg 33(2) of the 2012 Regs was amended first by Civil Legal Aid (Procedure) (Amendment) Regulations 2014, then by Civil Legal Aid (Procedure) (Amendment) Regulations 2016, then replaced with a new Schedule 1 by Civil Legal Aid (Procedure) (Amendment) (No 2) Regulations 2017.

5 *R (Rights of Women) v The Lord Chancellor and Secretary of State for Justice* [2016] EWCA Civ 91.

should submit certified copies of the evidence and retain the originals on file (para 1.11).

7.22   Where work on a case covers work automatically in scope (eg an application for a domestic violence injunction) and work only in scope on production of evidence (eg a prohibited steps order), you can only work on the first element until the evidence is obtained (whether through the initial in-scope work or separately) (para 1.8 of the guidance).

7.23   The guidance includes the wording of the relevant regulation as well as a checklist setting out exactly what they look for in each document. As the LAA will reject any document which does not appear to match the wording of the regulation exactly, using this guide can save time and prevent delay.

7.24   Any of the following forms of evidence are acceptable. However, note that Legal Help is not available to assist the client to obtain the evidence or to pay the costs, eg GP's report fees, of obtaining it. The LAA has issued some standard letters which clients can ask the relevant agency to complete. It is advisable that they are used wherever possible, as the regulations are tightly drafted and unless the wording precisely covers all elements of the regulation, the LAA cannot accept it. The letters can be downloaded from: www.gov.uk/government/collections/sample-letters-to-get-evidence-of-domestic-violence.

7.25   You cannot grant Legal Help, nor will the client be eligible for a representation certificate for the private family law services listed at LASPO Sch 1 Part 1 para 12, without one of the following[6]. Note that A is the applicant for legal aid and B is the (alleged) perpetrator – see also children at risk below:

1. Evidence that B has been arrested for a relevant domestic violence offence.
2. A relevant police caution for a domestic violence offence.
3. Evidence of relevant criminal proceedings for a domestic violence offence which have not concluded.
4. A relevant conviction for a domestic violence offence.
5. Evidence of a court order binding over B in connection with a domestic violence offence.
6. A domestic violence protection notice issued under section 24 of the Crime and Security Act 2010 against B.

---

6   The Legal Aid Sentencing and Punishment of Offenders Act (LASPO) 2012 – Evidence Requirements for Private Family Law Matters – Legal Aid Agency. Version 8, January 2018.

7. A relevant protective injunction.
8. An undertaking given in England and Wales under section 46 or 63E of the Family Law Act 1996 (or given in Scotland or Northern Ireland in place of a protective injunction) by B provided that a cross-undertaking relating to domestic violence was not given by A.
9. A copy of a finding of fact, made in proceedings in the United Kingdom, that there has been domestic violence by B.
10. An expert report produced as evidence in proceedings in the United Kingdom for the benefit of a court or tribunal confirming that a person with whom B is or was in a family relationship, was assessed as being, or at risk of being, a victim of domestic violence by B.
11. A letter or report from an appropriate health professional[7] confirming that that professional, or another appropriate health professional–
    (a) has examined A in person; and
    (b) in the reasonable professional judgement of the author or the examining appropriate health professional A has, or has had, injuries or a condition consistent with being a victim of domestic violence.
12. A letter or report from–
    (a) the appropriate health professional who made the referral described below;
    (b) an appropriate health professional who has access to the medical records of A; or
    (c) the person to whom the referral described below was made;
    confirming that there was a referral by an appropriate health professional of A to a person who provides specialist support or assistance for victims of, or those at risk of, domestic violence.
13. A letter from any person who is a member of a multi-agency risk assessment conference (or other suitable local safeguarding forum) confirming that A, or a person with whom A is in a family relationship, is or has been at risk of harm from domestic violence by B.
14. A letter from an independent domestic violence advisor/advocate confirming that they are providing support to A.
15. A letter from an independent sexual violence advisor/advocate confirming that they are providing support to A relating to sexual violence by B.

---

7 Civil Legal Aid (Procedure) (Amendment) (No 2) Regulations 2017 Sch 1 para 22 allows a wide range of registered health practitioners can provide the evidence, including nurses, midwives, dentists and related professionals, paramedics, psychologists, radiographers and social workers.

16. A letter from an officer employed by a local authority or housing association (or their equivalent in Scotland or Northern Ireland) for the purpose of supporting tenants containing–
   (a) a statement to the effect that, in their reasonable professional judgment, a person with whom B is or has been in a family relationship is, or is at risk of being, a victim of domestic violence by B;
   (b) a description of the specific matters relied upon to support that judgment; and
   (c) a description of the support they provided to the victim of domestic violence or the person at risk of domestic violence by B.
17. (1) A letter from an organisation providing domestic violence support services.
   (2) The letter must confirm that it–
   (a) is situated in England and Wales;
   (b) has been operating for an uninterrupted period of six months or more; and
   (c) provided A with support in relation to A's needs as a victim, or person at risk, of domestic violence.
   (3) The letter must contain–
   (a) a statement to the effect that, in the reasonable professional judgment of the author of the letter, A is, or is at risk of being, a victim of domestic violence;
   (b) a description of the specific matters relied upon to support that judgment;
   (c) a description of the support provided to A; and
   (d) a statement of the reasons why A needed that support.
18. A letter or report from an organisation providing domestic violence support services in the United Kingdom confirming–
   (a) that a person with whom B is or was in a family relationship was refused admission to a refuge;
   (b) the date on which they were refused admission to the refuge; and
   (c) they sought admission to the refuge because of allegations of domestic violence by B.
19. A letter from a public authority confirming that a person with whom B is or was in a family relationship, was assessed as being, or at risk of being, a victim of domestic violence by B (or a copy of that assessment).

20. A letter from the Secretary of State for the Home Department confirming that A has been granted leave to remain in the United Kingdom under paragraph 289B of the Immigration Rules.
21. Evidence which the Director is satisfied demonstrates that A has been, or is at risk of being, the victim of domestic violence by B in the form of abuse which relates to financial matters.

7.26 The guidance on evidence issued by the LAA[8] does not specify in detail what they will and will not accept in relation to evidence of financial abuse as the amendment is widely drafted, so other types of evidence should be accepted.

7.27 They suggest the following as non-exhaustive examples, although some seem unlikely to be available to the applicant for legal aid:

• copies of both the victims and the perpetrator's bank statements and or cancelled cheques;
• relevant letters from banks;
• credit card accounts;
• loan documents and statements;
• business financial statements;
• employee benefit records including insurance, stock options and bonuses;
• letter from a domestic violence support organisation;
• money order receipts;
• documentation with regard to any public assistance received;
• emails;
• text messages;
• diary kept by the victim;
• letters from employers or from an education or training institute;
• benefits or welfare history;
• application for Universal Credit Split Payment;
• evidence from foodbank;
• exemption from child maintenance service fees.

Evidence that a child is at risk of abuse

7.28 In relation to the legal services listed in LASPO Sch 1 Part 1 para 13, acceptable evidence is listed in Schedule 2 to the Civil Legal Aid

---

8 https://assets.publishing.service.gov.uk/government/uploads/system/uploads/attachment_data/file/672143/evidence-requirements-private-family-law-matters-guidance-version-8.pdf

(Procedure) (Amendment) (No 2) Regulations 2017. Any of the following are acceptable:

1. Evidence that B has been arrested for a child abuse offence.
2. A relevant police caution for a child abuse offence.
3. Evidence of relevant criminal proceedings for a child abuse offence which have not concluded.
4. A relevant conviction for a child abuse offence.
5. A relevant protective injunction.
6. A copy of a finding of fact made in proceedings in the United Kingdom of abuse of a child by B.
7. A letter from a social services department in England and Wales (or its equivalent in Scotland or Northern Ireland) confirming that the child was assessed as being, or at risk of being, a victim of child abuse by B (or a copy of that assessment).
8. A letter from a social services department in England and Wales (or its equivalent in Scotland or Northern Ireland) confirming that a child protection plan was put in place to protect the child from abuse or a risk of abuse by B (or a copy of that plan).
9. An application for an injunction described in paragraph 5 of this Schedule made with an application for a prohibited steps order against B under section 8 of the Children Act 1989 which has not, at the date of the application for civil legal services, been decided by the court.

For a full list of the work that can be done in the family category, see appendix B.

Controlled work and licensed work

7.29   Controlled work is granted by the solicitor/caseworker according to rules under the Standard Contract 2018. It is called 'controlled' because the LAA controls the number of matter starts which are allowed each year. The kinds of controlled work that are relevant to family practitioners are Legal Help and Family Help (Lower). Help at Court is not available in family work.

7.30   You need a representation certificate, sometimes known as a legal aid certificate, to represent a client in legal proceedings. This is called licensed work, as the organisation has a general licence to do such work, and numbers of matter starts are not limited. Certificates may be granted by the LAA, or in urgent circumstances, granted as a delegated function by the organisation.

Private family law – controlled work

7.31   Under LASPO, much private family law was removed from scope unless the client can demonstrate that he or she is the victim of domestic violence or that a child is at risk of abuse. Check carefully that the case you intend to take on remains in scope before granting controlled work (see the section on scope, above). This is particularly important as if you grant controlled work in an out of scope case, you may be paid for it on your initial claim, as it will be submitted electronically and the LAA may not be able to identify your error through claim codes without seeing the file; but the LAA will seek to recover fees if an error comes to light on audit and could extrapolate the finding across all your claims. You do not want the LAA to recover the fees they have paid and issue your organisation with a contract notice.

Legal Help – level 1

7.32   Legal Help allows you to provide legal advice and assistance in relation to a specific matter, but does not cover issuing proceedings, advocacy or instruction of an advocate (although you can obtain counsel's opinion, where justifiable). If you need to advise your client on issues arising from mediation and arbitration, see Help with Family Mediation.

7.33   Representation is not available in uncontested proceedings for divorce or judicial separation, except in very limited circumstances. Straightforward divorce work, where representation at court is not required, should be done under Legal Help, where it remains in scope for people who are the victims of domestic abuse (see 'Scope' at para 7.5 above for more information).

7.34   Legal Help is also known as level 1 in the family standard fees scheme.

Scope

7.35   See chapter 5 for information on the following:

- whether other funding may be available, and legal aid should therefore not be granted;
- what to do if your client has received previous advice from another organisation;
- what to do if your client has received previous advice from your organisation;

- clients from abroad or clients who are abroad;
- clients who are children.

Legal Help is designed to cover cases which complete after little work beyond the first meeting with the client and covers the consequential letters to the client and any letters to a third party. If you do more work in relation to children or finance issues, you may be able to go on to grant Family Help (Lower) funding (see below).

Domestic abuse and child abduction cases

7.36   These cases are included in the controlled work standard fee scheme as far as level 1. Level 2 is not designed to cover these cases and you will often find that you need to issue proceedings under a certificate very quickly.

7.37   For evidence of domestic abuse which acts as a passport to private family law services, see 'Scope' above.

Wills and change of name cases

7.38   These cases are not in scope under LASPO.

Divorce petitioner cases

7.39   There is a 'stand-alone' fee which applies to divorce, nullity, judicial separation and proceedings to dissolve civil partnerships (assuming the work is brought into scope due to evidence of domestic abuse). This covers cases where the client requires advice to initiate proceedings, they are issued, and there are no children or finance issues that would justify the grant of Family Help (Lower). We will look at this in more detail later on.

Financial eligibility

7.40   See chapter 3 for more information on the following:
- passporting benefits;
- assessment of capital;
- assessment of income;
- reassessment of means.

7.41   See chapter 5 for more information on the following:
- evidence of means;
- when you can start work without evidence of means;
- reassessing the client's eligibility if their means change significantly.

Merits test

7.42   The Legal Help merits test is known as the 'sufficient benefit test', and in full states: 'there is likely to be sufficient benefit to the individual, having regard to all the circumstances of the case, including the circumstances of the individual, to justify the cost of provision of legal help'.[9] The question is whether a reasonable private paying individual would pay for the work.[10] In most family cases remaining within scope, the test will be met.

Forms

7.43   The form is the CW1 Legal Help, Help at Court and Family Help (Lower) form. The assessment of means and client's details sections must be fully completed, and signed by the client, normally in the presence of someone from your organisation, before you start doing any legal work.[11]

How many Legal Help forms?

7.44   You can have more than one Legal Help matter open at the same time, but this is very unusual in family work. It may be permissible if your client has entirely separate family disputes.[12] The LAA gives the example of disputes in respect of different family relationships, where any potential proceedings would be separate. This would apply, for example, where your client was the mother of children with different fathers, each of whom was applying separately for residence.

Funding

7.45   Legal Help – level 1 is paid as two different standard fees.[13] The higher fee is only applicable when your client is the petitioner in a divorce and there are no significant children or finance issues and no other form of civil legal service is provided to your client. The higher fee can be claimed three months after proceedings are issued or when the proceedings are concluded (whichever is sooner).

---

9   Civil Legal Aid (Merits Criteria) Regulations 2013 reg 32(b).
10   Civil Legal Aid (Merits Criteria) Regulations 2013 reg 7.
11   Standard Civil Contract 2018 Specification para 3.9.
12   Standard Civil Contract 2018 Specification para 7.167.
13   Current fees and hourly rates are found in the Civil Legal Aid (Remuneration) Regulations 2013 Sch 1.

7.46   In all other cases, the lower level 1 fee is payable (whether or not combined with a level 2 fee).

7.47   Divorce, child abduction and domestic abuse cases that exceed three times the fixed fee when calculated at hourly rates, can be claimed in full (see chapter 15 for more information about claiming escape fee cases).

7.48   Other level 1 cases cannot be claimed as escape fee cases.

Family Help (Lower) – level 2

Scope

7.49   This covers the provision of ongoing assistance with some kinds of 'Family Dispute'.[14]

Private Family Law – conditions for level 2

7.50   Up to and including 8 May 2011, para 10.55 of the then Family Contract Specification required two meetings with the client in order to justify a level 2 fee. The then Legal Services Commission (LSC) removed the requirement for a second meeting from 9 May 2011, and instead practitioners had to show that 'substantive negotiations' had taken place and that you have been conducting the negotiations. This remains the position under the 2018 Standard Contract. However, practitioners report that it can be difficult to persuade some contract managers that 'substantive negotiations' have taken place, even when considerable work has been done on the file, for example if the other party is acting in person and responds through their ex-partner rather than to the solicitors direct. However, Contract Managers should accept this, see the LAA's costs assessment guidance para 4.10 for more information.

> **Criteria for Family Help (Lower) – meaning of 'significant family dispute' – Family Contract Specification 2018**
>
> 7.58 You may only make a determination that a Client qualifies for Family Help (Lower) where all relevant criteria in the Merits Regulations, Financial Regulations and Procedure Regulations are satisfied including the criteria in Paragraph 35 of the Merits Regulations. In addition, the fee for Family Help (Lower) may only be claimed for those Family Disputes:
>
> (a) which involve more than simply taking instructions from and advising the Client, and providing any follow up written or telephone advice; and

14   Standard Civil Contract 2018 Specification para 7.58.

(b) where you are involved in substantive negotiations with a third party (either by conducting the negotiations yourself or by advice and assistance in support of mediation); and

(c) where the dispute, if unresolved, would be likely to lead to family proceedings; and

(d) which do not primarily concern processing a divorce, nullity, judicial separation or dissolution of a civil partnership; and

(e) which do not primarily concern advice relating to child support.

Family Help (Lower) – children

7.51　This covers all work up to the issue of proceedings. It is not necessary to obtain a consent order to formalise any agreement in respect of children, although if you are claiming a settlement fee (see para 7.53 below), it is advisable to record the agreement in writing, so that the LAA can see that it was a 'genuine settlement to conclude that aspect of the case'.[15]

Family Help (Lower) – finance

7.52　This covers all work including the issue of proceedings and all work required to obtain a consent order.[16]

Family Help (Lower) – children and finance

7.53　Where a case involves children and finance issues meeting the criteria set out above, both the children and finance fees may be claimed. You claim two Family Help (Lower) fees, one for children and one for finance, where the merits criteria are met[17] (see merits test at para 7.85 below).

Forms

7.54　When claiming the level 2 fee you do not need another CW1 Legal Help, Help at Court and Family Help (Lower) form. Simply tick the box at the bottom of page 9 of the original form to confirm that the criteria for level 2 are met.

Funding

7.55　Family Help (Lower) (level 2) is paid under standard fees, although cases that reach the escape threshold (three times the fixed fee at

---

15 Standard Civil Contract 2018 Specification para 7.65(c).
16 Standard Civil Contract 2018 Specification para 7.65(d).
17 Standard Civil Contract 2018 Specification para 7.59.

levels 1 and 2 combined) can be paid in full at hourly rates. For more information about claiming escape fee cases, see chapter 15.

Settlement fees

7.56   Settlement fees can be claimed for cases that conclude at this level, without the issue of proceedings (save to obtain a consent order – Standard Civil Contract Specification 2018 para 7.65). In order to be considered as 'settled', that aspect of the case (ie children or finance) must be fully resolved at that level and the client actively involved in a decision to accept a settlement. The agreement on financial issues must be recorded in writing or in a consent order. It is advisable to record the agreement in respect of children in writing as well.

7.57   If the client ceases to give instructions, dies, or the parties are reconciled, the settlement fee cannot be claimed.[18]

7.58   You must wait for 21 days after the case has been concluded before claiming the settlement fee. In relation to financial issues, if the settlement breaks down, and you become aware of the fact within six months, the settlement fee becomes repayable. In relation to children issues, the period is three months.[19]

Case study

Mrs Brown had been married for 11 years and has two children, James and Jennifer. She came to see us about her divorce. It transpired that her husband had been very controlling, preventing Mrs Brown from contacting her family and only permitting her access to small amounts of money, which had to be fully accounted for. This had resulted in Mrs Brown suffering from anxiety and depression, about which she had consulted her GP within the last two years. She was able to obtain a GP's letter to show that she was eligible on the basis of 'domestic abuse' under LASPO.

Mr Brown refused to attend mediation; and also instructed solicitors on a private paying basis. Eventually we were able to finalise the divorce and obtain agreement to settlements in respect of the arrangements for the children and the finances.

Our office is in Salisbury. What can we claim?

---

18 Standard Civil Contract 2018 Specification para 7.65(c).
19 Standard Civil Contract 2018 Specification para 7.65(b).

You can claim:	
Legal Help level 1	£86.00
Family Help (Lower) (children)	£199.00
Family Help (Lower) (finance)	£208.00
Settlement fee (children)	£119.00
Settlement fee (finance)	£125.00
	Total £737.00

7.59　　For more information about when you can or should close a case, see chapter 5.

Funding from the client's point of view – the statutory charge

7.60　　For information about the statutory charge,[20] see chapter 5. The statutory charge does not apply to cases completing at Legal Help (level 1), but if the case goes beyond level 1, the level 1 costs are included in the costs caught by the charge.

7.61　　The home is exempt from the charge in cases completing under Legal Help, Help at Court or Family Help (Lower). The charge does not apply to maintenance payments. However, even where a lump sum is paid, the statutory charge does not apply to standard fee cases. This is a powerful incentive to clients to settle at level 2, as in most cases their legal aid will be free.

7.62　　However, in escape fee cases, the charge applies, but only to costs above the escape threshold (ie, those costs over three times the standard fee).

7.63　　Where the charge arises only under Legal Help, Help at Court or Family Help (Lower), it is in favour of your organisation. You may apply to the LAA to waive it, if its operation would cause grave hardship or distress to the client, or where it would be unreasonably difficult to enforce.[21]

7.64　　You should collect the appropriate sum from the client and claim the net costs from the LAA.

20　Civil Legal Aid (Statutory Charge) Regulations 2013.
21　Civil Legal Aid (Statutory Charge) Regulations 2013 reg 8.

7.65   But note that at level 3 (certificated work), the charge applies in favour of the LAA and includes the fees at levels 1 and 2.[22]

Help with Family Mediation

Introduction

7.66   LASPO introduced a level of service to allow solicitors to provide legal advice to clients during and immediately following mediation. It is designed to assist the mediation process and give legal effect to any agreement reached. This covers the provision of any of the following legal services in relation to a family dispute:

(a) civil legal services provided in relation to family mediation; or
(b) civil legal services provided in relation to the issuing of proceedings to obtain a consent order following the settlement of the dispute following family mediation.[23]

Scope

7.67   Help with Family Mediation is controlled work.[24] Therefore, you need to use a matter start under your schedule to start a case.

7.68   Help with Family Mediation covers legal advice to a client who is undergoing or who has participated in family mediation within the last three months and can include the issuing of proceedings to obtain a consent order following the settlement of the dispute within family mediation.[25]

Financial eligibility

7.69   See Legal Help above.

Merits test

7.70   The merits test is the sufficient benefit test, see above. You will need evidence on the file that the client is, or has been within the last three months, participating in family mediation.[26]

---

22 Civil Legal Aid (Statutory Charge) Regulations 2013 reg 4(2).
23 Civil Legal Aid (Procedure) Regulations 2012 reg 8.
24 Civil Legal Aid (Procedure) Regulations 2012 reg 21(2).
25 Civil Legal Aid (Procedure) Regulations 2012 reg 8.
26 Standard Civil Contract 2018 Specification para 7.67.

Forms

7.71   The form is the CW5. It has to be signed by the mediator as well as the client.

Funding

7.72   You may not claim for Help with Family Mediation if you have provided Family Help or legal representation in relation to the same family dispute within the previous six months. If a certificate is granted to a client in respect of the same family dispute within six months of your claim, your fee will be recouped.[27]

7.73   You may only claim one Help with Family Mediation fee per case, regardless of the number of clients you represented who took part in the mediation or the number of different issues covered by the mediation.[28]

7.74   There is a fixed fee of £150; but you can also claim a further £200 if you draft a consent order giving effect to a mediated agreement and which is approved by the court. There is no 'escape' from these flat fees.[29]

Certificates – private family law

Scope

7.75   A representation certificate authorises the conduct of litigation and the provision of advocacy and representation, and includes steps preliminary and incidental to proceedings, and steps to settle or avoid proceedings.

7.76   The then LSC introduced a standard fee funding scheme known as the Private Family Law Representation Scheme (PFLRS) from 9 May 2011. Under the PFLRS there are two levels of funding:

- Family Help (Higher) – Level 3: To cover all work up to the preparation for final hearing.
- Legal Representation – Level 4: To cover all work from preparation for a final hearing up to and including all work to conclude a case after the final hearing, eg application to the court of first instance for permission to appeal, and advice on the merits of an appeal against a final order.

27 Standard Civil Contract 2018 Specification para 7.70.
28 Standard Civil Contract 2018 Specification para 7.68.
29 Standard Civil Contract 2018 Specification para 7.3.

7.77   The LSC introduced a standard fee scheme for advocacy, the Family Advocacy Scheme (FAS) from 9 May 2011. For more information on the fee schemes for litigators, see chapter 15. For more on the FAS, see chapter 18.

7.78   Before you apply for a certificate, see chapter 5:

- general criteria;
- clients who are abroad;
- clients from abroad;
- clients who are children.

Mediation

7.79   Mediation is within the scope of legal aid. It is means and merits tested. The merits test is that 'the Director is satisfied that the mediator has assessed that, in all the circumstances of the case, the case is suitable for mediation'.[30] Prior to 2014, there was an obligation only on applicants for legal aid to prove their case was unsuitable for mediation before starting court proceedings; but the Children and Families Act 2014 s10 made it compulsory for all separating couples to attend a Mediation Information and Assessment Meeting (MIAM) before starting proceedings in relation to money or children issues. Practitioners report that enforcement of this requirement varies considerably between different courts.

Domestic violence and abuse

7.80   The LAA does not consider the fact that domestic abuse or violence has taken place should automatically rule out consideration of mediation. They will accept that it is not reasonable to consider mediation if an allegation of domestic abuse has resulted in a police investigation or the issuing of civil proceedings for the protection of the applicant within the last 12 months. In other circumstances, you will need to justify why it is not appropriate to involve the police, for example where this might jeopardise the long-term financial or other interests of the family, or if you have reason to believe that the police will not be able to assist, or if they have been contacted but have failed to respond or to provide adequate assistance in the past.

7.81   It is unlikely that funding will be granted for committal proceedings if criminal proceedings have been instigated by the police. Breach of a non-molestation order became a criminal offence in

---

30 Civil Legal Aid (Merits Criteria) Regulations 2013 Part 4 reg 37.

2007, and the LAA would ordinarily expect the client to report a breach to the police before seeking an amendment to the certificate for committal.

7.82 The LAA normally expects a warning letter to be sent to the respondent. However, this is not an absolute rule, for example if you can show that a warning letter might endanger the client.[31]

Final hearings

7.83 Proceedings up to a final hearing are covered by a form of legal aid called Family Help (Higher). Final hearings are covered by a form of legal aid called 'Legal Representation'. In practice, you need to apply for an amendment to the certificate.

Financial eligibility

7.84 See chapter 3.

Waiver in domestic abuse cases

7.85 The LAA has discretion to waive the upper disposable income and capital limits for victims of domestic abuse seeking protection from the court.[32] It does not apply at Legal Help level. It is important to note that any contribution from income or capital that is applicable under the regulations cannot be waived. If granting a certificate as a delegated function, you can assume the LAA will exercise its discretion in favour of granting a waiver; but when you submit the substantive application, you should make clear that the case is a domestic abuse case, and that you are seeking the waiver.

7.86 You should advise your client that, although the upper limit may be waived, the liability to pay contributions is not. The usual rules on contributions will apply, so the client's funding will be revoked in the event of non-payment. Clients with income much above the upper limit who successfully obtain a waiver can find themselves paying quite substantial contributions, so you should clearly advise the client to expect that. You can provide an indication of how much this will be by using the LAA's eligibility calculator at: http://civil-eligibility-calculator.justice.gov.uk/.

---

31 See the *Lord Chancellor's guidance on civil legal aid* (2018): www.gov.uk/funding-and-costs-assessment-for-civil-and-crime-matters para 10.28.

32 Civil Legal Aid (Financial Resources and Payment for Services) Regulations 2013 reg 12.

7.87   This is particularly important in emergency cases, since if you grant an emergency certificate, and the client is then offered a substantive certificate with contributions and declines the offer, he or she will be liable for the full costs you incur on the emergency certificate.

Merits test – standard criteria

7.88   Before you apply for a certificate, you need to ensure that the standard criteria are satisfied.[33] Those that apply in private family law cases are:

- the individual does not have access to other potential sources of funding from which it would be reasonable to fund the case;
- there is no other person besides the individual, including a person who might benefit from the proceedings, who can reasonably be expected to bring the proceedings;
- the individual has exhausted all reasonable alternatives to bringing proceedings including any complaints system, ombudsman scheme or other form of alternative dispute resolution;
- there is a need for representation in all the circumstances of the case including:
  - the nature and complexity of the issues;
  - the existence of other proceedings; and
  - the interests of other parties to the proceedings.

7.89   The first criterion requires you to consider whether the client has alternative methods of funding the case at their disposal, and you will need to explore with the client and consider whether, for example, the local authority would pay for adoption proceedings. You will need to address any potential sources which are not in fact available, in the application.

Stage 1 – Prospects of success

7.90   All cases must be put into one of the following categories according to its prospects of success (for a discussion of the sequence and reasons behind the amendments see chapter 5):[34]

---

33 Civil Legal Aid (Merits Criteria) Regulations 2013 reg 39.
34 Civil Legal Aid (Merits Criteria) (Amendment) Regulations 2013 reg 5, amended by Civil Legal Aid (Merits Criteria) (Amendment) (No 2) Regulations 2015 reg 2 and Civil Legal Aid (Merits Criteria) (Amendment) Regulations 2016 reg 2.

- very good – 80 per cent or above;
- good – 60 to 80 per cent;
- moderate – 50 to 60 per cent;
- marginal – 45 to 50 per cent;
- poor – less than 45 per cent;
- borderline – it is not possible, because of disputed law, fact or expert evidence, to assign the case to another category but it cannot be categorised as 'unclear'; or
- unclear – the case cannot be assigned to any of the other categories because there are identifiable investigations to be carried out after which the prospects can be estimated.

7.91 In *IS*[35] in the High Court, Collins J said that the standard to be applied in assessing the prospects of success is the prospects as they would be with the assistance of competent legal representation, not the prospects on the basis of material available but untested at the time of the application. This is to ensure that cases where competent representation would turn the case in the applicant's favour are not excluded from funding. Although the Court of Appeal overturned his declaration that the Merits Regulations were unlawful, it did not specifically deal with this point. In our view, and notwithstanding that the wider judgment was overturned, that must be the right approach.

Stage 2 – Cost-benefit/successful outcome

7.92 This varies according to the type of case, see below.

Appealing refusals

7.93 A refusal of a certificate on the basis of merit can be appealed, within 14 days of the decision, to the Independent Adjudicator. A refusal on financial grounds cannot be appealed, though a fresh application can be made if circumstances change.

Private law children cases – merits test

7.94 Private law children cases are proceedings concerning child arrangements, parental responsibility, financial provision for children, and other matters under the Children Act 1989 which are not Special Children Act or other public law proceedings.

---

35 [2015] EWHC 1965 (Admin) para 96, per Collins J.

7.95   You need to show that you are likely to obtain a 'successful outcome' – a significant improvement in the arrangements for children.

7.96   The merits test is as follows:

- Prospects of success are marginal or better or borderline;[36] and
- the reasonable private paying individual test is met:

    ... the potential benefit to be gained from the provision of civil legal services justifies the likely costs, such that a reasonable private paying individual would be prepared to start or continue the proceedings having regard to the prospects of success and all the other circumstances of the case.[37]

CCMS and forms

7.97   The LAA introduced mandatory use of its online Client and Cost Management System (CCMS) for all new applications from April 2016. CCMS has replaced the paper forms which are retained for emergency use only, when authorised as such by the LAA.

7.98   See paras 5.123 and 6.53 onwards for more information about:

- what to do if CCMS is not available; and
- claiming time spent on CCMS that exceeds time taken using a paper form (see appendix C).

7.99   The client should attend an appointment with a mediator (Mediation Information and Assessment Meeting – MIAM) unless any of the exceptions set out in Family Procedure Rules Practice Direction 3A apply.

7.100   Representation will be refused if no reasonable attempts to settle without recourse to litigation (whether by negotiation or otherwise) have been attempted.

7.101   For CCMS cases, the client's signature cannot be obtained until the application is completed and must be done at that time unless CCMS is not available, for example there is no internet access, in which case the client can sign a promissory declaration: see para 6.42 for more information.

---

36   Civil Legal Aid (Merits Criteria) Regulations 2013 reg 68, amended by Civil Legal Aid (Merits Criteria) (Amendment) (No 2) Regulations 2015 reg 2(9) and Civil Legal Aid (Merits Criteria) (Amendment) Regulations 2016 reg 2(11).
37   Civil Legal Aid (Merits Criteria) Regulations 2013 reg 7.

Financial matters – merits test

7.102   You need to show that you are likely to obtain a 'successful outcome' – a significant improvement in financial or other arrangements. The merits test is as follows:[38]

- Prospects of success are:
  - moderate or better; or
  - borderline, marginal or unclear, and the case is of significant wider public interest, of overwhelming importance to the client, or the substance of it relates to a breach of rights under the European Convention on Human Rights.
- Representation will be refused unless the likely benefits justify the likely cost, such that the reasonable private paying individual would be prepared to take or defend the proceedings in all the circumstances.

CCMS and forms

7.103   Again, before applying for funding, the client should attend mediation (unless the exceptions apply) and to have attempted to settle, by negotiation or otherwise. Applications should be made via CCMS. If you need to apply using a paper form because CCMS is not available and this has been authorised by the LAA, use form CIVAPP3 with the appropriate MEANS form.

Funding

7.104   The PFLRS and the FAS have applied since 9 May 2011. For more information on the fee schemes, see chapter 15.

Grant and scope of a certificate

7.105   In almost every case, a certificate is only granted subject to two limitations. First, it is very rare for a certificate to be granted to cover the entirety of proceedings. Usually, it is limited to a particular step in the proceedings. Second, costs will be limited, usually to £2,250 plus VAT in the first instance.

7.106   From 19 April 2019, following a pilot which showed it did not increase final claims, the LAA changed their approach and applied

---

38 Civil Legal Aid (Merits Criteria) Regulations 2013 reg 69, amended by Civil Legal Aid (Merits Criteria) (Amendment) (No 2) Regulations 2015 reg 2(10) and Civil Legal Aid (Merits Criteria) (Amendment) Regulations 2016 reg 2(12).

an initial limit of £25,000 to a specific range of cases. However, if the subject matter of the case also includes an issue which falls outside the list below, the LAA will treat the case as though each aspect has a different limitation, so you will need to keep a careful eye on cost allocation.

Cases covered by the £25,000 limit

Public law	
Care proceedings	Discharge Care
Supervision proceedings	Vary/Discharge Supervision
Emergency Protection Order/ Extend Emergency Protection Order	Contact Child in Care/Refuse Contact Child in Care
Secure Accommodation	Education Supervision Order
Section 37 Order (standalone)	Child Assessment Order
Placement Order (standalone)	Vary/Discharge Placement Order (standalone)
Children	
Parental Responsibility (including vary/discharge)	Prohibited Steps (including vary/discharge)
Specific Issue (including vary/discharge)	Declaration of Parentage
CAO Contact (including vary/discharge)	CAO Residence (including vary/discharge)
Special Guardianship (including vary/discharge)	Adoption (standalone)
Remove Children from Jurisdiction	Enforcement of any Section 8 Order
Disclosure of Child's Whereabouts under section 33	Recovery of a Child under section 34
Domestic Abuse	
Non-Molestation (including vary/discharge)	Occupation (including vary/discharge)
Forced Marriage Protection Order	Female Genital Protection Order

7.107   Costs limitations include profit costs (and any enhancement or uplift), counsel's fees and disbursements, but not VAT. It is extremely important not to do work outside the scope of any limitation, as you will not be paid for it. You should note that payments to counsel under the FAS count towards the financial limitation on certificates.[39] It is particularly easy to lose track of counsel's fees and disbursements and it really helps to keep all documents relating to financial issues

39   Standard Civil Contract 2018 Specification para 6.64.

together if using a paper file. CCMS helps in this area if you apportion part of your costs limit to counsel once instructed. If you have delegated functions, you have the power to amend the financial limitation on an emergency (but not substantive) certificate up to £10,000, but only to allow you to do work that is urgent.[40] If you exercise this power, you should inform the LAA via CCMS, or on form APP8 if CCMS is not available (and you have been authorised to do so by the LAA), that you have done so.

Domestic abuse cases

7.108 Representation is available to apply for an injunction under Family Law Act 1996 Part 4. This is covered by LASPO Sch 1 Part 1 para 11, therefore there is no need to produce evidence of previous domestic abuse as this only applies to services under para 12.

7.109 The merits test is as follows:[41]

- Prospects of success are:
  - marginal or better, or borderline.
- Representation will be refused unless the case meets the proportionality test: 'that the likely benefits of the proceedings to the individual and others justify the likely costs, having regard to the prospects of success and all the other circumstances of the case'.

7.110 The LAA has made detailed guidance available on its website, see the Lord Chancellor's guidance on civil legal aid: www.gov.uk/funding-and-costs-assessment-for-civil-and-crime-matters/.

Applying for a certificate – urgent cases

7.111 You may exercise a delegated function to grant an emergency certificate. See chapter 5 for more information about delegated functions.

7.112 If a substantive certificate is refused (on means or merits), or made conditional on a contribution which the client refuses, the client is liable for all costs incurred under the emergency certificate. The client must therefore be advised of this at or before the time of the grant, and given a costs estimate. In these circumstances, the solicitor should bill the certificate in the usual way; the LAA will pursue the client for the costs.

---

40 Legal Aid Civil (Procedure) Regulations 2012 reg 39(3)(b).
41 Civil Legal Aid (Merits Criteria) Regulations 2013 reg 67, amended by Civil Legal Aid (Merits Criteria) (Amendment) (No 2) Regulations 2015 reg 2(8) and Civil Legal Aid (Merits Criteria) (Amendment) Regulations 2016 reg 2(10).

- **Merits**: Emergency representation may be granted as a matter of urgency where it appears in the interests of justice to do so.[42]
- **Means**: Emergency representation may be provided where there has not yet been a detailed assessment of the client's resources, provided that he or she has provided sufficient financial information to demonstrate that it is likely that he or she will be found to be eligible.[43] In cases of doubt, eg because of complex means, you can submit an urgent application via CCMS. See above for the LAA's power to waive the capital and income limits in domestic abuse cases.
- **Limitations**: You must apply both a scope and a costs limitation (see the standard limitations at: www.gov.uk/government/publications/civil-legal-aid-application-forms-supporting-guidance). Scope should be limited to the steps that need to be taken urgently. The initial scope limitation can be amended, provided the certificate remains limited to steps that need to be taken urgently. Costs will usually be limited to £1,350 plus VAT in the first instance, though this can be exceeded or amended where justifiable.
- **Application for substantive certificate**: The LAA must receive the substantive application within five working days of the emergency grant. In the event of a delegated function amendment to scope or costs, you can apply through the single step process so that the substantive certificate reflects the amendment you made using your delegated functions. There is a LAA quick guide to this: https://ccmstraining.justice.gov.uk/Quick-guides/Quickguides/making-an-initial-application-1. See also para 6.26 onwards for more information.

7.113   It is important to ensure that an emergency certificate is replaced by a substantive certificate within 56 days, as emergency certificates expire at that point and any further work would not be funded. The time limit cannot be extended.

7.114   See chapter 5 for information about:

- amendments to certificates;
- refusals and appeals;
- use of counsel and amendments for a QC;
- changes to prospects of success or cost–benefit;
- disbursements and prior authority;

---

42 Civil Legal Aid (Procedure) Regulations 2012 reg 52(1)(b).
43 Civil Legal Aid (Procedure) Regulations 2012 reg 52(2). Confirmed by Point of Principle (PoP) CLA59, 1 February 2017, Points of Principal Manual: www.gov.uk/guidance/legal-aid-points-of-principle-of-general-importance-pop.

- contributions;
- high-cost cases;
- ending a case;
- discharge of certificate;
- revocation of certificate.

7.115   See chapter 16 for information about getting paid in family cases.

CHAPTER 8

Conducting a family public law case

continued

Introduction

8.1 This chapter deals with conducting family public law cases. There are separate chapters on the general rules that apply to all civil cases, as well as family private law, immigration, housing and mental health, as they each have their own funding schemes and rules.

8.2 In chapter 3, we saw that there are three key stages in providing publicly funded services: to ensure that i) the matter is within scope; ii) the client is financially eligible; and iii) the case meets the merits test. In addition, you need to ensure that forms are completed correctly and funding is obtained. This chapter explains how these steps are taken successfully in respect of family public law.

8.3 See appendix C for a summary of the Legal Aid Agency's (LAA's) costs assessment guidance, in respect of the most common queries raised by caseworkers.

What is public family law?

8.4 Public family law includes Special Children Act proceedings and 'public law children cases'. These are defined in reg 2 of the Civil Legal Aid (Merits Criteria) Regulations 2013. The term 'Special Children Act' covers applications for funding from a child, parent or other person with parental responsibility in cases under Children Act 1989 ss31, 43, 44 and 45, and applications from a child under section 25 (use of accommodation for restricting liberty), but not appeals from final orders made in cases under those sections. The Ministry of Justice (MoJ) announced as part of its policy implementation review of Legal Aid, Sentencing and Punishment of Offenders Act 2012 (LASPO) that it would make legal aid available on a non-means tested basis, with a less stringent merits test (see para 8.39 below), for parents/people with parental responsibility who wish to oppose applications for placement orders or adoption orders by the summer of 2019.[1] The Ministry commented that this would bring such cases into line with care and other cases having a similar effect to 'Special Children Act 1989 cases'. However, there had been no progress on this at the time of writing.

8.5 'Public law children cases' are all other matters described in paras 1 and 9 of Part 1 of Schedule 1 to LASPO, including care, protection and supervision matters that are not Special Children Act, and High

---

1 https://assets.publishing.service.gov.uk/government/uploads/system/uploads/attachment_data/file/777036/legal-support-the-way-ahead.pdf.

Court inherent jurisdiction cases. It also includes parties other than the child or person with parental responsibility who are (or want to apply to be) joined to Special Children Act cases.

8.6   Note that special guardianship orders (SGOs) are private law family (under Children Act 1989 Part II), so clients needed to provide evidence to satisfy domestic violence (Civil Legal Aid (Procedure) Regulations 2012 reg 33) or child protection requirements (reg 34) to be in scope of legal aid. See chapter 7 for a detailed discussion of the requirements. However, the MoJ announced as part of its policy implementation review of LASPO that it would bring SGOs into scope by the autumn of 2019.[2] However, work on this had only just begun by Autumn 2019.

8.7   LASPO Sch 1 Part 1 para 1 brings within scope:

(a) orders under section 25 of the Children Act 1989 ('the 1989 Act') (secure accommodation);
(b) orders under Part 4 of the 1989 Act (care and supervision);
(c) orders under Part 5 of the 1989 Act (protection of children);
(d) approval by a court under paragraph 19 of Schedule 2 to the 1989 Act (arrangements to assist children to live abroad);
(e) parenting orders under section 8 of the Crime and Disorder Act 1998 ('the 1998 Act');
(f) child safety orders under section 11 of the 1998 Act;
(g) orders for contact under section 26 of the Adoption and Children Act 2002 ('the 2002 Act');
(h) applications for leave of the court to remove a child from a person's custody under section 36 of the 2002 Act;
(i) placement orders, recovery orders or adoption orders under Chapter 3 of Part 1 of the 2002 Act (see sections 21, 41 and 46 of that Act);
(j) orders under section 84 of the 2002 Act (parental responsibility prior to adoption abroad).
(k) orders under section 119 of the Social Services and Wellbeing (Wales) Act 2014 ("the 2014 Act") (secure accommodation);
(l) approval by a court under section 124 of the 2014 Act (arrangements to assist children to live abroad).

8.8   LASPO Sch 1 Part 1 para 9 brings within scope:

(1) Civil legal services provided in relation to the inherent jurisdiction of the High Court in relation to children.[3]

See appendix B for a list of work that falls within the Family category under the legal aid standard contract.

---

2 https://assets.publishing.service.gov.uk/government/uploads/system/uploads/attachment_data/file/777036/legal-support-the-way-ahead.pdf.
3 Vulnerable adults are also within scope but not in the family category.

8.9   Where appropriate, you will be referred back to chapter 5, as that chapter sets out the general rules.

Scope

8.10   See chapter 5 for information on the following:

- what to do if your client has received previous advice from another organisation;
- what to do if your client has received previous advice from your organisation;
- clients from abroad or clients who are abroad;
- clients who are children.

For exceptional case funding for cases that are out of scope under LASPO, see chapter 4.

Controlled work and licensed work

8.11   Controlled work is granted by solicitors according to rules under the Standard Contract 2018. It is called 'controlled' because the LAA controls the number of matter starts which are allowed each year. The kinds of controlled work that are relevant to family practitioners are Legal Help and Family Help (Lower). Help at Court is not available in family work.

8.12   You need a representation certificate, sometimes known as a legal aid certificate, to represent a client in legal proceedings. This is called licensed work, as the practice has a general licence to do such work, and numbers of matter starts are not limited. Certificates may be granted by the LAA, or, in urgent circumstances, granted as a delegated function, by the organisation.

Public family law – controlled work

Legal Help – level 1

Scope

8.13   This covers initial (ie pre-proceedings) advice and assistance in relation to any kind of public law family case, including the consequential letters to the client and any letters to a third party.

8.14   However, it is not designed to cover attending child protection conferences as a matter of course. The LAA believes that legal advice is only required in 'exceptional circumstances'.[4] If you attend a child protection conference, you will need to ensure that this is fully justified on your attendance note.

Merits test

8.15   The 'sufficient benefit test' applies to Legal Help: 'there is likely to be sufficient benefit to the individual, having regard to all the circumstances of the case, including the circumstances of the individual, to justify the cost of provision of legal help'.[5] The question is whether a reasonable private paying client would pay for the work.[6] It is hard to think of circumstances where it would not be met in such cases.

Financial eligibility

8.16   Legal Help is means tested, even in relation to care cases. See Family Help Lower, below, where the local authority has given notice of its intention to issue proceedings, as this is not means tested and has its own form.

8.17   See chapter 3 for more information on the following:

- passporting benefits;
- assessment of capital;
- assessment of income;
- reassessment of means.

8.18   See chapter 5 for more information on the following:
- evidence of means;
- when you can start work without evidence of means;
- reassessing the client's eligibility if their means change significantly.

Forms

8.19   The form is the CW1 Legal Help, Help at Court and Family Help (Lower) form (unless the local authority has given written notice of its intention to issue proceedings in which case CW1PL must be used, see below).

---

4 Family Fee Scheme Guidance (excluding advocacy), February 2012 para 3.2. This has since been withdrawn but it is useful to note as it set out the LAA's approach to this level of work.
5 Civil Legal Aid (Merits Criteria) Regulations 2013 reg 32(b).
6 Civil Legal Aid (Merits Criteria) Regulations 2013 reg 7.

8.20 The assessment of means and client's details sections must be fully completed, and signed by the client, normally in the presence of someone from your organisation, before you start doing any legal work.[7]

How many Legal Help forms?

8.21 You can have more than one Legal Help matter open at the same time, but only if they relate to entirely separate family disputes where any proceedings would be issued and heard separately.[8] The LAA gives the example where there is a public law Legal Help matter in relation to concerns raised by the local authority and also a private law matter in relation to a divorce.[9]

Funding

8.22 Legal Help – level 1 is paid as a standard fee.[10] Cases that exceed three times the fixed fee when calculated at hourly rates can be claimed in full (see chapter 16 for more information about claiming escape cases).

Family Help (Lower) – level 2

Scope

8.23 This level of funding covers advice and other work for parents or those with parental responsibility. It is intended that the focus of work at this level is on negotiation with the local authority to resolve disputes under the President's Public Law Outline. Therefore, it covers cases where the local authority has issued a notice of its intention to issue proceedings; but no proceedings have yet been issued.

8.24 The letter before proceedings may suggest that a meeting is held between the client and the local authority to discuss the concerns raised in the letter and level 2 will cover attending this meeting (sometimes called 'a family meeting') with the client.

Extract from the Standard Civil Contract Specification 2018

8.25 The Standard Civil Contract Specification 2018 para 7.35 states:

---

7 Standard Civil Contract 2018 Specification para 3.9.
8 Standard Civil Contract 2018 Specification para 3.30.
9 Costs assessment guidance 2013 Appendix 1 'Family Fee Scheme Guidance (excluding advocacy)' para 2.5.
10 Current fees and hourly rates are found in the Civil Legal Aid (Remuneration) Regulations 2013 as amended.

Payment for Family Help (Lower)

7.35 A determination that a Client qualifies for Family Help (Lower) may only be made where all criteria at Regulation 35 of the Merits Regulations are satisfied. In addition, in Public Law Work remuneration for Family Help (Lower) may only be claimed where the following conditions are satisfied:

(a) the Local Authority has given written notice of potential s31 Care Proceedings in accordance with statutory guidance on court orders and pre-proceedings for local authorities, issued by the Department for Education or Welsh Assembly under the Local Authority and Social Services Act 1970 and regulations, but no proceedings have yet been issued (application for an Emergency Protection Order does not count as issue of proceedings for this purpose);

(b) your Client is a Parent (as defined above) and 'Parent' for this purpose shall include either a mother or father of an unborn child in respect of whom proceedings are contemplated;

(c) your Client requires advice and assistance with a view to avoiding the proceedings, or narrowing and resolving any issues with the Local Authority.

Merits test

8.26 Family Help (Lower) is not merits tested in public family law, as long as the requirements of para 7.35 (reproduced above) are met.

Financial eligibility

8.27 Family Help (Lower) is not means tested in public family law.

Forms

8.28 There is a separate form for level 2 in public family law – the CW1PL. It is designed to be used in relation to advice after the local authority has issued its notice of intention to issue proceedings (advice prior to this is covered under the CW1 Legal Help form). Key points are:

- it is not means tested;
- it has a box that allows you to record that the criteria for advice at level 2 were met;
- the local authority's notice of intention to issue proceedings must be attached to it.

In these cases, you tick the box at the top of page 2 of the Family Help (Lower) Public Law form, and attach a copy of the notice to show that the criteria are met.

Funding

8.29 Family Help (Lower) level 2 is paid as a standard fee. Whether you can claim it depends on the local authority issuing written notice of their intention to issue proceedings. This can be in an email, as long as the wording is unambiguous.

Exceptional cases

8.30 A case escapes the fixed fee in public law matters where the costs of all levels of advice provided at controlled work, calculated at hourly rates,[11] exceed three times the relevant fees. Therefore, where level 1 and level 2 advice has been provided, costs calculated at an hourly rate must exceed three times the level 1 and level 2 fees combined. If advice has only been provided at either level 1 or level 2, the exceptional limit will be three times the fees for that level of service.

Closing controlled work matters

8.31 For information about when you can or should close a case, see chapter 5.

Certificates – public law cases

Scope

8.32 A representation certificate in family public law can only be granted when the local authority issues proceedings, and is therefore usually granted initially as an emergency certificate using delegated functions. It authorises the conduct of litigation and the provision of advocacy and representation.

Certificates

8.33 An application for funding in Special Children Act cases is granted automatically, without reference to means or merits. An application to extend the scope of the certificate to cover related proceedings (for example, to make an application for a residence or contact order within the care proceedings, or to include representation in any other related proceedings which are being heard together) must be made, as the usual form of the certificate only covers proceedings under

11 Set out in Schedule 1 to the Civil Legal Aid (Remuneration) Regulations 2013.

Children Act 1989 ss31, 43, 44 and 45, and applications from a child under s27.

8.34   Apart from 'related proceedings', certificates in this area are kept completely separate from all other work. Therefore, a separate application must always be made – an ordinary certificate cannot be amended to cover Special Children Act proceedings, and a Special Children Act certificate cannot be amended to cover anything else.

8.35   The application includes a question on whether separate representation is appropriate. Once funding has been granted, you have an ongoing duty to report any new information or changes of circumstance which might affect the terms of the certificate.[12]

Financial eligibility

8.36   Certificates in Special Children Act proceedings are not means tested. Certificates in other public law Children cases are means tested, including interim care orders under section 38 of the Children Act 1989.[13]

8.37   See chapter 3 for information about the means test.

Merits test

8.38   Certificates in Special Children Act proceedings are not merits tested.

8.39   Certificates in other public law children cases are subject to a limited merits test:[14]

- representation will be refused if:
  - alternative funding is available (eg in adoption, where the child is placed by the local authority who consent to the adoption, it would be reasonable to expect them to bear the costs of the application);
  - not necessary (for example, because of the involvement of other parties or a professional guardian);
  - it is unreasonable to provide representation, having regard to the importance of the case to the applicant; and

---

12 Civil Legal Aid (Procedure) Regulations 2012 reg 40(1)(a).
13 Civil Legal Aid (Financial Resources and Payment for Services) Regulations 2013 reg 5.
14 Civil Legal Aid (Merits Criteria) Regulations 2013 reg 66, amended by Civil Legal Aid (Merits Criteria) (Amendment) (No 2) Regulations 2015 reg 2(7); and Civil Legal Aid (Merits Criteria) (Amendment) Regulations 2016 reg 2(9).

- if the applicant is making or supporting an appeal or application, the prospects of success of that appeal or application are:
  - marginal or better; or borderline.

CCMS and forms

8.40 As mentioned in chapter 5, the LAA introduced mandatory use of its online Client and Cost Management System (CCMS) for all new applications from April 2016. CCMS has replaced the paper forms explained below but they may be used when CCMS is not available and the LAA authorises the alternative process.

8.41 See paras 5.123 and 6.53 above for more information about:

- what to do if CCMS is not available;
- claiming time spent on CCMS that exceeds time taken using a paper form (see also appendix C).

If you need to use a paper form, you use CIVAPP5 for Special Children Act proceedings and CIVAPP3 in other cases.

8.42 Apart from 'related proceedings', Special Children Act certificates are kept completely separate from all other work. Therefore, a separate application must always be made – an ordinary certificate cannot be amended to cover Special Children Act proceedings, and a Special Children Act certificate cannot be amended to cover anything else.

8.43 See chapter 6 for more on CCMS.

Funding

8.44 Representation in respect of a child, parent or joined party in care and supervision proceedings (Children Act 1989 s31) and related proceedings[15] is covered by a standard fee scheme. The fees are based on the location of the solicitor's office and the nature and number of parties represented.

8.45 Fees refer to the LAA region where the fee earner was based during the case:

- Wales;
- London, Brighton, Reading and Bristol – all claim the 'London and South' fee;
- Birmingham, Nottingham and Cambridge – all claim the 'Midlands' fee;

---

15 Standard Civil Contract 2018 Specification para 7.46.

- Newcastle, Leeds, Liverpool and Manchester – all claim the 'North' fee.

8.46   The standard fee scheme does not apply to other 'Special Children Act proceedings', ie under sections 25–41 (when a child is brought before the court and wishes to be separately represented), section 43 (a child assessment order), section 44 (an emergency protection order) and section 45 (extension or discharge of an emergency protection order).

8.47   It does not apply to other public law family proceedings, including appeals in Special Children Act cases, and proceedings under Parts IV and V of the Children Act 1989, as well as adoption and High Court inherent jurisdiction cases.[16]

8.48   In Children Act 1989 s31 cases, funding under the Graduated Fee Scheme for legal representation certificates covers all stages up to the conclusion of the proceedings in the first instance (including representation on any interim appeal and/or advice on the merits of an appeal against a final order). Where legal representation is granted to defend or bring an appeal against a final order, it is paid by way of hourly rates.[17]

8.49   Other public law family certificated cases are funded under hourly rates; but see below concerning very high cost cases and the Care Cases Fee Scheme.

8.50   The rates were reduced by ten per cent for cases started on or after 22 April 2014, and so the current hourly rates and fees are set out in the Civil Legal Aid (Remuneration) (Amendment) (No 2) Regulations 2014.

Advocacy under standard fees

8.51   The standard fees do not include advocacy. Where advocacy is provided, whether by counsel or a solicitor advocate, the claim is made under the Family Advocacy Scheme (FAS) (see chapter 18 for more information).

8.52   The LAA include the following activities under the definition of advocacy for the purposes of the FAS preparation for advocacy:

- appearances as advocate before the court;
- travel to and from court and waiting time;
- attendances by the advocate at court, including attendance at advocates meetings.

---

16   Standard Civil Contract 2018 Specification paras 7.36 and 7.3.
17   Standard Civil Contract 2018 Specification para 7.52.

8.53   If you are a solicitor carrying out advocacy, it is helpful to keep a separate file for this aspect of the case as it helps you keep track of the advocacy fees to be charged on top of the applicable standard fee for other work. It also helps you identify if you need to apply for an increase in the financial limitation as this includes all profit costs as well as disbursements, advocacy fees and VAT.

Applying for a certificate – urgent cases

8.54   Unless otherwise notified, under para 7.38 of the Standard Civil Contract Specification 2018 you have a delegated function to grant legal representation in Special Children Act cases. If authorised to use the alternative application process to CCMS, you use the CIVAPP5 form and the delegated functions section on page 5 of that form completed, stating the date on which the delegated function was exercised and confirming that the criterion as to separate representation is met.

8.55   See chapter 5 for more information about delegated functions, and also about:

- amendments to certificates;
- refusals and appeals;
- use of counsel and amendments for a QC;
- changes to prospects of success or cost–benefit;
- disbursements and prior authority;
- contributions;
- high cost cases;
- ending a case;
- discharge of certificate;
- revocation of certificate.

Very High Cost Cases

8.56   A Very High Cost Case (VHCC) is a case where total costs and disbursements are expected to be over £25,000 (not including VAT). Most of these cases are dealt with under a single case contract under the Care Case Fee Scheme (CCFS). From 3 June 2019, high cost care cases under the Care Cases Fee Scheme have an immediate limit of £32,500. Once you become aware that the costs are likely to exceed £25,000, you must contact the LAA by general case enquiry informing the LAA of this. The LAA will set up a case plan task on CCMS to which the Provider must upload a signed contract and Counsel Acceptance Form/s (if an external advocate is being used) and separately apply to amend the cost limitation to £32,500. A CCFS Form (case plan) will not be required until the end of the case unless the costs will exceed the increased limit.

Care Case Fee Scheme

8.57   The LAA introduced the CCFS from 1 October 2015 (it was previously known as the 'Events Model'). It covers all single counsel care cases. Payment is made by reference to expected 'events' during the lifetime of the case. Examples of 'events' include the number of hearings, prehearing reviews and counsel conferences. Costs are calculated by totalling up these 'events'.

8.58   Some private law and other child cases, which follow a similar fact-finding route and have main hearings over 10 days, may qualify for the CCFS scheme (on request and agreed by the LAA).

QC and two counsel cases

8.59   From 12 July 2019, once you are granted prior authority for a QC/2 Counsel, you should be asked to upload a signed High Costs Contract and Counsel Acceptance Forms (where external counsel are used). If you accept, the case will be costed using CCFS. At the same time, you should submit a cost amendment for £60,000 where the authority covers a fact finding hearing or a composite hearing. The LAA asks that if counsel is used, they are assigned to the case and allocated appropriate funds.

Exceptions to the CCFS

8.60   If you can show you would be paid at least 30 per cent more by claiming hourly rates with a fully costed case plan rather than using the CCFS model, it can be an exception to the CCFS scheme. This needs to be fully justified with reasons.

8.61   The LAA has issued guidance on high cost Family cases: www. gov.uk/guidance/civilhighcostcasesfamily. See chapter 16 for more information about the CCFS and VHCCs.

Family mediation

Introduction

9.1   This chapter deals with mediation – but mainly from the point of view of a lawyer, rather than a mediator or client. There is increased emphasis on resolving disputes through mediation rather than litigation, regardless of the way that cases are funded.

9.2   Used well, and complemented by legal advice, mediation helps clients find a solution to their problems in a more positive way. From April 2013, when the Legal Aid, Sentencing and Punishment of Offenders Act 2012 (LASPO) took effect, mediation and Help with Family Mediation (see para 7.63 above) are the only legal aid services available to clients seeking to resolve private family disputes, unless the client is the victim of domestic abuse, or likely to be so, or there is evidence of child protection concerns (see chapter 7).

Scope

9.3   There are two types of mediation that can be funded by the Legal Aid Agency (LAA):

1) family mediation, where the LAA funds the mediator directly; and

2) non-family mediation, which can be funded as a disbursement under both Legal Help and representation certificates.[1]

9.4   Paragraph 14 of Part 1 of Schedule 1 to LASPO provides that mediation is only available for a 'family dispute' which is a matter arising out of a family relationship as defined in the Act. LAA guidance[2] states that if there are no significant legal family issues in dispute and the role of the mediation is simply to improve communication and the relationship between the parties then it does not fall within the scope of public funding.

> As part of considering whether mediation is suitable for the dispute, the parties and all the circumstances, the mediator must consider whether the costs of mediation are themselves justified.[3]

9.5   Disputes which the LAA considers to be minor will not pass the merits test. The LAA gives the following list of examples where

---

1   Costs assessment guidance for use with the Standard Civil Contract 2018 para 3.6.

2   *Family mediation guidance manual*, LAA, September 2018, para 3.5.

3   *Family mediation guidance manual*, para 3.4.

issues would be capable of giving rise to court proceedings and so Family mediation would be appropriate:

- Contact arrangements
- Residence and Parental Responsibility
- Child maintenance
- Property
- Finance – savings, debts and pensions.[4]

9.6 The scheme includes the following:

- Mediation Information and Assessment Meetings (MIAMs) (which may be attended by one or both parties);
- mediation:
  - all issues mediation;
  - child mediation;
  - property and financial mediation.

9.7 The Children and Families Act 2014 was implemented on 22 April 2014. This makes it compulsory for people seeking to make applications in certain family proceedings to attend a MIAM before making an application unless they are exempt. The legal requirement is for the applicant to attend, and respondents are expected to do so.

Contract

9.8 Mediation used to have a separate contract; but has been brought under the 2018 Standard Civil Contract with its own specification.

9.9 There is a detailed guidance document (version 5, updated to reflect the 2018 contract at: https://assets.publishing.service.gov.uk/government/uploads/system/uploads/attachment_data/file/738258/Family_Mediation_GuidanceManual_V5_Sep2018.pdf.

Financial eligibility

9.10 In non-family mediation, the means test is carried out as usual for the type of funding – Legal Help or a representation certificate (see chapter 3).

---

4 *Family mediation guidance manual*, para 3.3.

9.11   In family mediation, the mediator carries out the eligibility test. If one of the parties qualifies for legal aid, then the cost of the MIAM will be met by the LAA.

9.12   Family mediation is means tested; but from 3 November 2014, non-financially eligible parties were exempted from the financial means test in respect of the first mediation session where the other party is financially eligible for legal aid.[5] The LAA will pay half a single session fee for the non-eligible party.

9.13   For all subsequent mediation sessions, legal aid is only available for the party eligible for legal aid. The idea is that the free 'taster' session will encourage the non-financially eligible party to fund their own mediation from then on.

Merits test

9.14   Mediation beyond the MIAM will only be provided where the mediator is satisfied that mediation is suitable in all the circumstances of the case.[6] See the LAA's *Family mediation guidance manual* (September 2018) for more information on how the LAA expects mediators to apply the test.

Forms

9.15   Family mediation is controlled work. The application form is the CW5.

9.16   There are no forms for non-family mediation as this is claimed as a disbursement.

Funding

9.17   Where the parties are willing and the issues are suitable, the mediation should be able to deal with all the issues arising, including explanation of the law (but not advice), and disclosure.

9.18   From the client's point of view, family mediation is advantageous, as it is exempt from the statutory charge.

5   Civil Legal Aid (Financial Resources and Payment for Services) (Amendment) (No 2) Regulations 2014.
6   Civil Legal Aid (Merits Criteria) Regulations 2013 reg 37.

9.19 Robert Clerke, solicitor and mediator, has explained the stages of mediation in a typical family case:[7]

- setting the agenda/identification of the issues;
- disclosure;
- identification and exploration of options;
- impasse, and strategies to break through it;
- reality testing;
- recording the outcome – hopefully a memorandum of understanding (MOU) and, where appropriate, an open financial statement (OFS).

9.20 A lawyer is needed to advise on the law and draw up the consent order and statement of information for the court: see Help with Family Mediation, para 7.63 above.

7 *Carter survival handbook*, Quay Books, 2007, chapter 5.

CHAPTER 10

Conducting an immigration case

by Hilton von Herbert

continued

Introduction

10.1   This chapter deals with work funded under the immigration and asylum category of law. You should read it in conjunction with chapters 3, 4 and 5 of this handbook. Chapter 3 deals with general rules about taking on civil cases and applies to work in immigration and asylum as it does to all other work; chapter 4 deals with exceptional cases; and chapter 5 deals with the rules that apply to the conduct of all civil cases. The immigration and asylum-specific rules in this chapter usually build on, rather than replace, the general rules; where they do replace the general rules in chapters 3 and 5 we will say so.

10.2   See appendix C for a summary of the Legal Aid Agency's (LAA's) Costs assessment guidance, in respect of the most common queries raised by caseworkers.

What immigration work is in scope of legal aid?

10.3   Paragraph 39 of the (August) 2018 Category Definitions defines asylum and immigration as work covered by Legal Aid, Sentencing and Punishment of Offenders Act 2012 (LASPO) Sch 1 Part 1 paras 25(1); 26(1), 27(1); 28; 29; 30(1); 32(1); 32A(1); 39; and 24, together with any LASPO s10 exceptional funding granted where the primary problem or issue is an immigration or asylum matter.

10.4   The descriptions within the Category Definitions should be read in conjunction with the exclusions set out in LASPO Sch 1 Part 2. The paragraphs in Part 2 exclude from the services (detailed below) those that are provided, among others, in relation to: personal injury or death; claims in tort in respect of negligence; claims in tort in respect of assault, battery or false imprisonment; claims in tort in respect of trespass to goods or to land; damage to property; defamation or malicious falsehood; claims in tort in respect of breach of statutory duty; claims for damages in respect of a breach of rights under the European Convention on Human Rights (ECHR) by a public authority (if relying on section 7 of the Human Rights Act (HRA) 1998); and compensation under the Criminal Injuries Compensation Scheme.

Separated children: immigration and citizenship matters

10.5   Separated migrant children became eligible for legal aid to help with citizenship and non-asylum immigration applications and appeals from 25 October 2019. The Legal Aid, Sentencing and Punishment of Offenders Act 2012 (Legal Aid for Separated Children) (Miscellaneous Amendments) Order 2019 brings non-asylum immigration and citizenship matters into scope of legal aid for under 18-year-olds who are not in the care of a parent, guardian or legal authority. Existing guidance relating to the 2018 Standard Civil Contract and working with the LAA is expected to be updated and published shortly.

10.6   Transitional arrangements are in place to deal with applications made on CCMS. See: www.gov.uk/government/publications/separated-migrant-children-transitional-guidance.

Immigration-related detention and bail

10.7   Legal aid will be available on matters and all proceedings in relation to immigration-related detention and bail.[1] These provisions refer to detention or control of persons: under the authority of an immigration officer; liable to deportation;[2] awaiting a decision of the secretary of state;[3] having served a period of imprisonment;[4] and granted or refused immigration bail.[5]

10.8   You can provide advice and assistance to an individual solely in relation to detention under immigration powers, such as applications for bail (and conditions on bail). You will not be able to claim for any non-detention work as part of the case unless this is itself in scope of immigration or asylum legal aid.

10.9   You can provide advice and assistance on bail conditions to a person who is liable to or has been released from detention, or to a person who has had conditions imposed on bail such as restriction to reside at a fixed address, reporting and employment.

10.10   In most cases, only the detention issue is in scope, not the substantive immigration case. For example, a person subject to deportation following imprisonment is entitled to legal aid in respect of his or her

---

1   LASPO Sch 1 Part 1 paras 25(1), 26(1) and 27(1).
2   Immigration Act 1971 Sch 3.
3   Nationality, Immigration and Asylum Act 2002 s62.
4   UK Borders Act 2007 s36.
5   Immigration Act 1971 Sch 3 para 2(5).

detention or bail conditions, but not in respect of deportation advice and proceedings themselves. You will need to be careful on your file to justify that work done is genuinely in relation to the in-scope aspects, such as where it is necessary to consider the immigration history or offences leading to the deportation in order to assess bail or conditions.

Victims of domestic violence: applications for indefinite leave to remain and residence cards

10.11   Legal aid will be available on matters and all proceedings in relation to applications by victims of domestic violence for indefinite leave to remain (ILR) and for a residence card under the Immigration (European Economic Area) Regulations 2016.[6] These provisions both rely on the following definition of domestic violence:

> 'domestic violence' means any incident, or pattern of incidents, of controlling, coercive or threatening behaviour, violence or abuse (whether psychological, physical, sexual, financial or emotional) between individuals who are associated with each other (within the meaning of section 62 of the Family Law Act 1996) . . .[7]

10.12   You can provide advice and assistance to a victim of domestic violence in an application for ILR if the person has been granted leave to remain as a spouse or partner of a British citizen or person present and settled in the UK (probationary leave) and the relationship has broken down permanently due to domestic violence. This will include a person who has been granted leave to enter or remain outside the Immigration Rules as a partner or spouse of a British citizen or person present and settled in the UK (eg victims with leave to enter outside the Immigration Rules or with discretionary leave to remain). This is so long as the advice and assistance is solely in relation to an application for ILR under the domestic violence provisions.

10.13   The time you spent advising and assisting a victim with an application under the three-month Destitution Domestic Violence Concession (DDVC) can also be claimed as part of the substantive ILR application.

10.14   You can provide advice and assistance in relation to an application for a residence card to a person who has ceased to be a family member on the termination of a marriage/partnership (ie only if divorced), who was a victim of domestic violence or was a family member of the

---

6 LASPO Sch 1 Part 1 paras 28 and 29, respectively.
7 LASPO Sch 1 Part 1 paras 28(5) and 29(4).

victim and the violence took place during the time that the marriage was subsisting.

10.15   Other than the above, the fact that the applicant is a victim of domestic violence does not generally entitle them to legal aid for immigration advice (eg those not on probationary leave, family members not divorced from their EEA spouse or those in durable relationships who were never married to EEA nationals in the first place).

10.16   Attendance at interviews conducted on behalf of the secretary of state with a view to reaching a decision on applications for ILR and for a residence card under the EEA Regulations, for victims of domestic violence, are not within scope.[8]

Asylum

10.17   Legal aid will be available on matters and all proceedings in relation to rights to enter and to remain in the UK arising from:[9]

(a) the Convention relating to the Status of Refugees and the Protocol to that Convention;

(b) Articles 2 and 3 of the ECHR (ie right to life, and prohibition of torture and inhuman or degrading treatment or punishment, respectively);

(c) the Temporary Protection Directive;[10]

(d) the Qualification Directive.[11]

10.18   The above will include:

(a) Controlled Work done on an asylum issue related to Special Immigration Appeals Commission (SIAC) proceedings;[12]

(b) an application for ILR under the Refugee Settlement Protection policy;

(c) an application for leave to remain on the basis of serious medical conditions which reaches the Article 3 threshold.[13]

---

8 LASPO Sch 1 Part 1 paras 28(3) and 29(3).

9 LASPO Sch 1 Part 1 para 30(1).

10 Council Directive 2001/55/EC of 20 July 2001 on minimum standards for giving temporary protection in the event of a mass influx of displaced persons and on measures promoting a balance of efforts between Member States in receiving such persons and bearing the consequences thereof.

11 Council Directive 2004/83/EC of 29 April 2004 on minimum standards for the qualification and status of third country nationals or stateless persons as refugees or as persons who otherwise need international protection and the content of the protection granted.

12 Standard Civil Contract (August) 2018 Specification para 8.7(b).

13 LASPO Sch 1 Part 1 para 30(1)(b).

10.19   Legal aid for advice and assistance on family reunion for refugees is not generally in scope. However, the Court of Appeal has said that where a claimant's family reunion case was particularly complex such that failure to provide exceptional funding would amount to a breach of Article 8 of the ECHR (right to respect for one's private and family life, home and correspondence), exceptional case funding (ECF) would be appropriate.[14] See chapter 4 for applying for ECF.

10.20   Attendance at interviews conducted on behalf of the secretary of state with a view to reaching a decision on a claim in relation to the rights mentioned in para 10.16 is not within scope, except where regulations provide otherwise.[15]

Victims of modern slavery: applications for leave to enter or remain

10.21   Legal aid will be available on matters and all proceedings in relation to applications for leave to enter or remain in the UK by: i) victims of human trafficking and ii) victims of slavery, servitude or forced or compulsory labour.[16] These categories reflect different provisions within LASPO. However, the Home Office Competent Authority Guidance uses the term 'modern slavery' to refer to human trafficking, as well as slavery, servitude and forced or compulsory labour.[17]

10.22   You can provide advice and assistance in relation to applications for leave to enter or remain by a victim of modern slavery (ie victim of trafficking and/or victim of slavery, servitude, or forced or compulsory labour). However, in order for you to assist, there must either be a conclusive determination that the person is a victim of modern slavery, or there must have been a determination that there are 'reasonable grounds' to believe that the person is a potential victim of modern slavery and there has not been a negative conclusive grounds determination.[18] These conditions reflect the two decisions that need to be made by the Single Competent Authority (SCA) once someone

---

14 *R (Gudanaviciene and others) v Director of Legal Aid Casework and The Lord Chancellor* [2014] EWCA Civ 1622.

15 LASPO Sch 1 Part 1 para 30(3). The Civil Legal Aid (Immigration Interviews) (Exceptions) Regulations 2012 provides for attendance at asylum screening interviews and asylum interviews where the person is a child, or at an asylum interview where the person is either being detained at a specified IRC or lacks mental capacity. See paras 10.87–10.89 (attendance at interviews) below.

16 LASPO Sch1 Part 1 paras 32(1) and 32A(1), respectively.

17 Home Office, *Victims of modern slavery – Competent Authority guidance*, Version 8.0 (02 September 2019), p. 24.

18 LASPO Sch 1 Part 1 paras 32(1)(a) and (b), and 32A(1)(a) and (b).

has been identified as a potential victim and referred to the National Referral Mechanism (NRM).[19] The NRM is the framework by which the UK implements relevant obligations under the 2005 Council of Europe Convention on Action against Trafficking in Human Beings.

10.23   Once a potential victim of modern slavery has been identified by the specified statutory authorities or non-governmental organisations and referred to the NRM, the SCA will make a 'reasonable grounds decision'. If there is a positive 'reasonable grounds decision' then the SCA should go on to make a 'conclusive grounds decision'. After a positive 'reasonable grounds decision' you can provide advice and assistance on applications for leave to enter or remain.

10.24   There is no legal aid available to assist a person in the NRM, except potentially on the basis of ECF (see paras 10.29–10.33 below).[20]

10.25   There is no time restriction on the availability of funding to assist a person who has been determined a victim of modern slavery by the competent authority under Controlled Work. However, in Licensed Work, there is a time restriction of 12 months from the date of the 'conclusive grounds' determination that the person is a victim of trafficking or before the end of any leave outside the rules granted to the victim.[21]

10.26   Where a client has been determined a victim of modern slavery and is also making an asylum claim, you will need to treat the asylum work, and any 'associated' or 'additional' application for leave to remain on human rights grounds, as one asylum matter start under the Immigration specification.

Terrorism Prevention and Investigation Measures

10.27   Legal aid will be available on matters and all proceedings in relation to a Terrorism Prevention and Investigation Measure (TPIM) notice (see para 10.64(k)) relating to the client that is being advised.[22]

---

19   LASPO Sch 1 Part 1 paras 32(6)–(8) and 32A(6), (7) and (10). See also Home Office, *Victims of modern slavery – Competent Authority guidance*, Version 7.0 (29 April 2019), p. 14.

20   *R (Gudanaviciene and others) v Director of Legal Aid Casework and The Lord Chancellor* [2014] EWCA Civ 1622.

21   Civil Legal Aid (Procedure) Regulations 2012 reg 31(8).

22   LASPO Sch 1 Part 1 para 45(1). For authority of the secretary of state to impose TPIM notices, see Terrorism Prevention and Investigation Measures Act 2011 s2.

Claims for damages arising from immigration-related detention and bail

10.28 Legal aid will be available on matters and all proceedings in relation to a claim for damages arising from the powers related to immigration detention and bail, as referred to in paras 10.5–10.8 above.[23] In particular, this relates to civil legal services provided in relation to:

(a) abuse of an individual that took place at a time when the individual was a child or vulnerable adult;[24]
(b) abuse by a public authority of its position or powers;[25]
(c) in respect of an act or omission by a public authority that involves a significant breach of Convention rights by the authority;[26] and
(d) a sexual offence, but only where the services are provided to the victim of the offence, or the victim of the offence has died, and the services are provided to the victim's personal representative.[27]

Special Immigration Appeals Commission

10.29 Legal aid will be available for all proceedings before the SIAC. This will normally involve Controlled Work under Legal Help for any initial advice and Licensed Work for any preparation and representation on an SIAC appeal.[28]

Exceptional case funding

10.30 An ECF application to fund work which is not in scope may be made to the LAA under LASPO s10, but only where you can demonstrate that the following test is met:

(3) . . . (a) that it is necessary to make the services available to the individual (. . .) because failure to do so would be a breach of:
(i) the individual's Convention rights (within the meaning of the Human Rights Act 1998), or
(ii) any rights of the individual to the provision of legal services that are enforceable EU rights, or
(b) that it is appropriate to do so, in the particular circumstances of the case, having regard to any risk that failure to do so would be such a breach.

23 LASPO Sch 1 Part 1 paras 25(1), 26(1) and 27(1).
24 LASPO Sch 1 Part 1 para 3(1).
25 LASPO Sch 1 Part 1 para 21(1).
26 LASPO Sch 1 Part 1 para 22(1).
27 LASPO Sch 1 Part 1 para 39(1).
28 LASPO Sch 1 Part 1 para 24(1) and Part 3 para 21.

10.31   In his original ECF guidance, the Lord Chancellor did not consider that immigration cases would come within the ambit of exceptional funding. However, in *R (Gudanaviciene) v Director of Legal Aid Casework*,[29] the Court of Appeal held that certain paragraphs of this guidance were incompatible with ECHR Article 6(1) and with Article 47 of the Charter of Fundamental Rights of the European Union as well as, in immigration cases, incompatible with ECHR Article 8.

10.32   The court in *Gudanaviciene* also held that whether funding should be granted will depend on the facts of the case, including the importance and complexity of the issues and the person's ability to act on their own without legal assistance and any language difficulties. Since there is no appeal against an exceptional case funding determination, beyond a review by the Director, any challenge on a refusal of funding would be by way of judicial review.

10.33   Following *Gudanaviciene*, the Lord Chancellor issued new guidance which was amended to take account of the Court of Appeal judgment. In particular, the current guidance refers to the Court of Appeal's finding that 'Article 8 may give rise to a right to legal assistance in relation to immigration matters which engage the substantive right to respect for private and family life conferred by Article 8'.[30] In any event, before making any application for exceptional funding you should carefully consider the judgment as well as the revised guidance (see chapter 4 for more on exceptional cases).

Immigration appeals and bail hearings before the First-tier Tribunal and Upper Tribunal

10.34   If an area of immigration or asylum law is in scope, this will also include, aside from Legal Help, Controlled Legal Representation and Legal Representation for appeal work.[31]

10.35   Advocacy in the First-tier Tribunal (FTT) and Upper Tribunal (UT) is in scope for specific proceedings.[32] First, advocacy in appeals of decisions by the secretary of state to refuse a protection or human rights claim (or revoke protection status), is in scope.[33] Second, advocacy is also covered in proceedings before the FTT and UT related

---

29   [2014] EWCA Civ 1622.
30   Lord Chancellor's Exceptional Funding Guidance (Non-Inquests), paras 27–29.
31   Standard Civil Contract 2018 Specification, Category Specific Rules: Immigration and Asylum, para 8.4.
32   LASPO Sch1 Part 3 paras 11–13 and 15.
33   LASPO Sch 1 Part 3 para 11(b); and Nationality, Immigration and Asylum Act 2002 s82(1).

to Immigration Act 1971 Sch 2, ie administrative provisions as to control on entry.[34] Third, advocacy is also available in appeal proceedings in relation to applications for ILR and for a residence card under the EEA Regulations 2006 by victims of domestic violence.[35] Fourth, advocacy is further in scope in appeal proceedings in relation to applications for leave or enter by victims of modern slavery.[36]

10.36 Fifth, advocacy is available in the FTT and UT in appeals where a person is being deprived of British Citizenship under British Nationality Act 1981 s40A and rights of residence under EEA Regulations 2006 reg 26.[37] However, this is only to the extent that the appeal concerns a contravention of the Equality Act 2010. Although the Immigration (EEA) Regulations 2016 replaced the 2006 Regulations from 1 February 2017 in respect of appeal rights, LASPO has not been updated to reflect this.[38]

10.37 If it arises from in-scope work, any advocacy work in the High Court, Court of Appeal and Supreme Court is in scope as Licensed Work.[39]

Judicial review

10.38 Judicial review is in scope, but there are three types of restrictions.[40] First, and these restrictions apply to all categories, the judicial review must have the potential to produce a benefit for the individual, a member of the individual's family or the environment.[41]

10.39 Second, the judicial review may not relate to an issue relating to immigration where:

(a) the same issue, or substantially the same issue, was the subject of a previous judicial review or an appeal to a court or tribunal,

(b) on the determination of the previous judicial review or appeal (or, if there was more than one, the latest one), the court, tribunal or other person hearing the case found against the applicant or appellant on that issue, and

---

34 LASPO Sch 1 Part 3 para 11(a).
35 LASPO Sch 1 Part 3 para 13; and Part 1 paras 28–29.
36 LASPO Sch 1 Part 3 para 13; and Part 1 paras 32(1)–32A(1).
37 LASPO Sch 1 Part 3 para 12.
38 LASPO Sch 1 Part 3 para 12(b).
39 LASPO Sch 1 Part 3 paras 1–3.
40 LASPO Sch 1 Part 1 para 19(1).
41 LASPO Sch 1 Part 1 para 19(3).

(c) the services in relation to the new judicial review are provided before the end of the period of 1 year beginning with the day of that determination.[42]

10.40   Third, the judicial review may not relate to removal directions in respect of an individual where the directions were given not more than one year after the latest of the following:

(a) the making of the decision (or, if there was more than one, the latest decision) to remove the individual from the United Kingdom by way of removal directions;

(b) the refusal of leave to appeal against that decision;

(c) the determination or withdrawal of an appeal against that decision.[43]

10.41   Despite these restrictions, judicial review is still permitted in fresh asylum claims and other certified cases (effectively where there would be no appeal to the immigration tribunal against the decision). The latter two exclusions mentioned above do not apply when services are provided to an individual in relation to:

(a) judicial review of a negative decision in relation to an asylum application (within the meaning of the EU Procedures Directive[44]) where there is no right of appeal to the First-tier Tribunal against the decision;

(b) judicial review of certification under section 94 or 96[45] of the Nationality, Immigration and Asylum Act 2002 (certificate preventing or restricting appeal of immigration decision).[46]

10.42   Further, the latter two exclusions mentioned above do not apply when services are provided in relation to judicial review of removal directions in respect of an individual where prescribed conditions relating to either or both of the following are met:

(a) the period between the individual being given notice of the removal directions and the proposed time for his or her removal;

(b) the reasons for proposing that period.[47]

10.43   It is important to be clear about what funding is being sought in judicial review cases, and to ensure that the work is in scope and is not

---

42   LASPO Sch 1 Part 1 para 19(5).

43   LASPO Sch 1 Part 1 para 19(6).

44   Council Directive 2005/85/EC of 1 December 2005 on minimum standards on procedures in Member States for granting and withdrawing refugee status.

45   Respectively, unfounded human rights or asylum claims or certification on the basis of an earlier right of appeal.

46   LASPO Sch 1 Part 1 para 19(7).

47   LASPO Sch 1 Part 1 para 19(8).

excluded under the above provisions. You will need to ensure that this is clearly spelt out in all funding applications to the LAA.

10.44   It is expected that all internal reviews and appeals are exhausted before any refusal of funding is challenged in court proceedings.[48]

Definition of an immigration or an asylum matter

10.45   Paragraphs 8.7 and 8.8 of the 2018 Standard Civil Contract Specification (**Contract Specification**) divide work in the immigration category into asylum and immigration matter types.

10.46   It is important that you correctly report new matter starts and claims as asylum or immigration, both as part of your contractual obligation but also because the funding limits are different. The **Contract Specification** says:

Contract Work covered by this Specification

8.7 For the purposes of Controlled Work, a Matter should proceed and be reported under this Specification as an 'Asylum Matter' where:

(a) it relates to civil legal services in respect of the rights set out in paragraph 30 of Part 1 of Schedule 1 of the Act ('Immigration: rights to enter and remain');

(b) it relates to an asylum issue and is proceeding under paragraph 24 of Part 1 of Schedule 1 to the Act ('Special Immigration Appeals Commission').

8.8 For the purposes of Controlled Work, a Matter should proceed and be reported as an 'Immigration Matter' where it relates to civil legal services in respect of the rights mentioned in:

(a) paragraph 25 of Part 1 of Schedule 1 to the Act ('Immigration: detention');

(b) paragraph 26 of Part 1 of Schedule 1 to the Act ('Immigration: temporary admission');

(c) paragraph 27 of Part 1 of Schedule 1 to the Act ('Immigration: residence etc restrictions);

(d) paragraph 28 of Part 1 of Schedule 1 to the Act ('Immigration: victims of domestic violence and indefinite leave to remain');

(e) paragraph 29 of Part 1 of Schedule 1 to the Act ('Immigration: victims of domestic violence and residence cards');

(f) paragraph 32 of Part 1 of Schedule 1 to the Act (Victims of trafficking in human beings') insofar as civil legal services relate to an application by the individual for leave to enter, or to remain in, the United Kingdom;

48 *Rrapaj and others v Director of Legal Aid Casework* [2013] EWHC 1837 (Admin).

(g) paragraph 24 of Part 1 of Schedule 1 to the Act ('Special Immigration Appeals Commission') where it relates to an immigration issue;

(h) paragraph 45 of Part 1 of Schedule 1 to the Act ('Terrorism prevention and investigation measures etc');

(i) paragraph 32A of Part 1 of Schedule 1 to the Act ('Victims of slavery, servitude or forced or compulsory labour') in so far as civil legal services relate to an application by the individual for leave to enter, or to remain in, the United Kingdom.

Who can carry out the work?

Individual caseworkers

10.47   Immigration work is unique in legal aid, in being completely subject to an accreditation scheme (ie the Immigration and Asylum Accreditation Scheme (IAAS)).[49] Other areas of legal aid also use accreditation, for example to qualify as a supervisor, and even restrict work by accreditation type, for example criminal police station work, but only immigration funding is subject to a category-wide restriction. Please note that IAAS accreditation is a separate matter from that provided by the Office of the Immigration Services Commissioner (OISC).

10.48   Unless you are IAAS accredited, you will not be paid for doing any legal aid work in the immigration category at all.[50] There are several levels of accreditation:

- Trainee Caseworker (formerly level 1 probationer);
- Casework Assistant (formerly level 1 accredited caseworker);
- Senior Caseworker (level 2 accredited);
- Advanced Caseworker (level 3 accredited); and
- Accredited Supervisor.

10.49   The contract reserves certain types of work to caseworkers of a particular level or above, as set out in the textbox in para 10.49 below.[51] You should note that the **Contract Specification** restricts representation of any child to a senior caseworker[52] who must hold a

---

49 This scheme is now referred to by the Law Society as 'Immigration and Asylum Accreditation' (IAA). However, Standard Civil Contract 2018 Specification para 8.13(a) still refers to it as the 'IAAS'.

50 Standard Civil Contract 2018 Specification para 8.13.

51 Standard Civil Contract 2018 Specification para 8.18.

52 Standard Civil Contract 2018 Specification para 8.20.

valid (ie within two years) enhanced Disclosure and Barring Service (DBS) certificate.[53]

10.50   Under the **Contract Specification**, both Legal Help and Controlled Legal Representation (CLR) cases must be conducted by a senior caseworker. However, individual tasks at both levels can be delegated to assistant and trainee caseworkers (except in cases involving children, detention and mental capacity issues):[54]

Type of contract work	Level of accreditation
Conduct of Legal Help Matters and Legal Representation	Senior Caseworker Trainee Casework Assistants (who have passed the relevant examination required by the IAAS at that level) and Casework Assistants can conduct tasks delegated by the Senior Caseworker, except Reserved Matters
Reserved Matter 1 – Use of Delegated Functions to make a determination that an individual qualifies for CLR; and conduct of CLR cases	Senior Caseworker and above
Reserved Matter 2 – All Contract Work for clients who lack capacity within the meaning of section 2 of the Mental Capacity Act 2005	Senior Caseworker and above
Reserved Matter 3 – All Contract Work carried out for a Child or an unaccompanied asylum-seeking child (UASC)	Senior Caseworker and above
Reserved Matter 4 – All Contract Work for clients detained in IRCs	Senior Caseworker and above
Conduct of any other Contract Work not covered above	Senior Caseworker and above

10.51   What work can be done by caseworkers of each level is defined by the contract and the accreditation work restrictions.

10.52   In this context, 'conduct' means 'having responsibility and control for the progression of the case'.[55] So a casework assistant can carry out tasks on an appeal conducted by a senior caseworker, whereas all work on the file of an unaccompanied child must be carried out by a

53 Standard Civil Contract 2018 Specification para 8.13(c).
54 Standard Civil Contract 2018 Specification para 8.18.
55 Standard Civil Contract 2018 Specification para 8.19.

senior caseworker. In addition to this broad rule, you must comply with the work restrictions, as set out in the textbox in para 10.49 above.

10.53 Work varied out by Advanced Caseworkers attract an uplift of five per cent on the payment rates, but only on Controlled Work paid at hourly rates.[56]

10.54 The **Contract Specification** requires each of your offices to maintain a ratio of at least one full-time equivalent Senior Caseworker for every two Trainee Caseworkers or Casework Assistants.[57]

Organisations with exclusive Immigration Removal Centre contracts

10.55 You may only provide advice and representation to clients in an Immigration Removal Centre (IRC) if you have been granted Schedule authorisation to do so,[58] with the following four exceptions:[59]

   (a) the client is a close family member of an existing client and knowledge of the family's circumstances is material to the new client's case (a close family member for the purpose of this rule is a member of the family who is the client's spouse, partner, child, sibling, parent, grandparent or grandchild); or

   (b) in the case of a client detained in an IRC only, the client is an existing client on whom you have attended in the UK and carried out at least five hours work prior to the client's detention; or

   (c) there are no providers with Schedule authorisation in the IRC Procurement Area where the client is detained; or

   (d) your client has an appeal listed at a designated Fast Track location.

10.56 Unfortunately, the current list of exclusive IRC contract providers does not appear to be available on the LAA website. Providers with authorisation have either a contract to carry out work by way of: i) the Detained Duty Advice Scheme in an IRC; and/or ii) the Detained Fast Track Scheme/Detained Asylum Casework Scheme.[60] The schedule authorisation does not apply to Licensed Work (ie work that is in scope and that is carried out under a funding certificate in higher court proceedings).

56 Standard Civil Contract 2018 Specification para 8.78.
57 Standard Civil Contract 2018 Specification para 8.15.
58 Standard Civil Contract 2018 Specification para 8.44.
59 Standard Civil Contract 2018 Specification para 8.6.
60 Standard Civil Contract 2018 Specification para 8.5.

Clients detained otherwise than in an Immigration Removal Centre

10.57 You can provide advice and representation to clients detained in prisons and other places of detention that are not IRCs without special authorisation.[61] Where you do so, your advice must include advice on bail. Where you act for a client in detention, or who becomes detained during the case, you must continue acting until:

- the client formally ceases to give instructions;
- the client is released from detention;
- the client is dispersed from the area;
- the client is removed from the country; or
- you can no longer act because of conflict of interest or other good professional conduct reason.[62]

Scope

10.58 See chapter 5 for information on the following:

- whether other funding may be available, and public funding should not be granted;
- what to do if your client has received previous advice from another organisation;
- what to do if your client has received previous advice from your organisation;
- clients from abroad or clients who are abroad;
- clients who are children.

Structure of immigration work

10.59 In general, immigration work can be divided into four stages:

1) Advice and assistance on Home Office/entry clearance applications;
2) Advice and representation on appeals to the FTT;
3) Advice and representation on appeals to the UT;
4) Litigation in the UT and higher courts.

---

61 Standard Civil Contract 2018 Specification para 8.44.
62 Standard Civil Contract 2018 Specification para 8.45.

10.60   Stage 1 is funded by Legal Help. Stages 2 and 3 are funded by CLR (though different rules apply and it helps to think of them as different types of work), and stage 4 is funded by a representation certificate.

10.61   The **Contract Specification** does not create any additional rules for certificated work in the higher courts, and this is therefore not dealt with to any great extent in this chapter. See chapter 5 for the general rules that apply.

10.62   The various funding types are consecutive as the case progresses. For example, where a client's application is refused, you should consider whether there is merit for an appeal under CLR, and, if so, grant it. CLR should be applied for as soon as practicable after the right to appeal has arisen. Once CLR is granted or refused, the Legal Help comes to an end and no further Legal Help work may be done on that matter.[63] Post-appeal work will form part of the CLR.[64]

10.63   Where you take an appeal to the Court of Appeal, the issue of a certificate to conduct the appeal brings the Controlled Work matter to an end. If the Court of Appeal then remits the case back to the Immigration and Asylum Chamber (IAC), a new matter start will be required to do the remitted appeal, which will be paid at hourly rates.[65] If during either stage 1 or stages 2 or 3, it is necessary to do work under a certificate while the relevant stage remains pending, then either the Legal Help or the CLR, as applicable, may be kept open to deal with that work.

Fee types

10.64   Immigration work is paid as standard fees or at hourly rates. Different rules apply to standard fee work and hourly rates work. Therefore, it is important to determine at the start of the case which category the work falls into.

10.65   The **Contract Specification** lists all hourly rates work:[66]

(a) Asylum Matters opened under this Contract which relate to an Asylum application (including 'NAM' or 'Legacy'), made to the Home Office prior to 1 October 2007;

(b) a fresh claim/further application for Asylum opened under this Contract where the original Asylum application was lodged, whether concluded or not, prior to 1 October 2007;

---

63 Standard Civil Contract 2018 Specification para 8.62.
64 Standard Civil Contract 2018 Specification paras 8.63(e) and 8.64(g).
65 Standard Civil Contract 2018 Specification para 8.76(i).
66 Standard Civil Contract 2018 Specification para 8.76.

(c) advice in relation to the merits of lodging an application for permission to appeal to the Upper Tribunal (where advice has not been received under Stage 2 of the Standard Fee);

(d) Bail applications;

(e) advice and applying for a determination that a Client qualifies for civil legal services provided as Licensed Work, including complying with any pre-action protocol;

(f) initial advice in relation to an Asylum application prior to claiming Asylum at the Asylum Screening Unit where you then cease to be instructed. This will also apply where the Client returns after attendance at the Asylum Screening Unit but where it is confirmed that the Client will be dispersed and will not continue to instruct you;

(g) Escape Fee Cases under the Standard Fee;

(h) advice in relation to a Client who is an UASC (unaccompanied asylum-seeking child);

(i) cases remitted, reviewed or referred from the Court of Appeal to the Upper Tribunal or the Upper Tribunal to the First-tier Tribunal;

(j) where you hold a Schedule authorisation, any Matters opened under the Detained Duty Advice Scheme or for a Detained Fast Track or a DAC Scheme client;

(k) advice in relation to Terrorism Prevention and Investigation Measures Orders;

(l) applying for a determination that an individual qualifies for civil legal services provided as Licensed Work in relation to Terrorism Prevention and Investigation Measures Orders; and

(m) applying for a determination that an individual qualifies for civil legal services provided as Licensed Work in relation to the Special Immigration Appeals Commission.

10.66 All other work not included in para 8.76 of the **Contract Specification** is payable as standard fees.

10.67 Where the substantive matter is standard fee, nonetheless any bail, UT, remittals, applications for funding certificates, and pre-action work under the same matter will always be paid at hourly rates. In this situation, the hourly rates work is an additional payment. By contrast, where the substantive matter is hourly rates, bail, applications for funding certificates, and pre-action work all fall under the costs limit of the substantive matter. The costs limit for UT and remittals work is explained later in this chapter.

10.68 You should be especially careful when dealing with the case of a UASC. If the child turns 18 before CLR is granted, the CLR work on this matter will be standard fee. The Legal Help work on this matter will still all be hourly rates.[67] If the child turns 18 after CLR is granted, then both the Legal Help and CLR work on this matter will remain at hourly rates.

Matter starts and separate matters

10.69   A 'matter' is all work done on a single case for a client. A matter can pass through Legal Help and CLR and will still be treated as the same matter.

10.70   The following explains when only one matter should be opened and when more than one matter should be opened:

- An application and subsequent appeal is one matter.[68]
- Any human rights application associated with an asylum matter should be dealt with under that asylum matter.[69]
- A fresh application for asylum is a new matter.[70]
- Work in relation to preparation for and applying for a certificate for licensed work (including compliance with any pre-action protocol) may be dealt with under the relevant existing matter or by opening a new matter.[71]
- Where a client applies to enter or remain in the UK under more than one category, or applies to switch status while the first application remains outstanding, this will be one matter.[72] However, where the first application is at appeal stage and a different additional application is made, the second application will be a new matter.[73]
- Where you transfer cases between your own offices, either because of dispersal or other reason, you can continue the case under the same matter start and should not open a new one.[74]
- If you are acting for several clients in relation to the same case, this should generally be one Legal Help matter. For example, where you have an asylum claim with a principal applicant and a

---

67 This is because although both count as same matter start, Legal Help and CLR are two separate services under Controlled Work, see page 68 of Escape Fee Cases Electronic Handbook (version 1.11, 24/07/19), available at: www.gov.uk/government/publications/submit-an-escape-fee-case-claim.

68 Standard Civil Contract 2018 Specification para 8.25.

69 Standard Civil Contract 2018 Specification para 8.27.

70 Standard Civil Contract 2018 Specification para 8.28.

71 Standard Civil Contract 2018 Specification para 8.29.

72 Standard Civil Contract 2018 Specification para 8.32.

73 Standard Civil Contract 2018 Specification para 8.33.

74 Standard Civil Contract 2018 Specification para 8.31.

family member who is dependent, then this should usually be one matter. However, if there needs to be separate applications or appeals for each family member, then separate matters may be opened. To determine that separate applications or appeals are needed, you must consider that each family member has a separate and distinct legal interest for which there is sufficient benefit to justify a separate matter. For example, where the family members are claiming asylum each in their own right, there should normally be separate matters.

10.71 A second matter start for the same client would not be justified on the same case unless:

- at least six months have elapsed since the first matter was closed; or
- there has been a material development or change in the client's instructions and at least three months have elapsed.

10.72 If the client fails to give instructions and you close the file, and then the client returns, that is not a change in instructions. A decision, response, etc from a third party to an application, representations, correspondence etc made in the first matter is not a material development.

10.73 Where further work is justified, but you cannot start a new matter under the rule, new disbursements can be claimed, as can profit costs if the case is an hourly rate case. You may claim new disbursements and profit costs if the case is an hourly rate case, or an escape fee case if the new work plus the old work would make it an escape fee claim. However, note that the previous relevant upper costs and disbursements limits will apply and you will need to apply for extensions where necessary.

10.74 See chapter 3 for further information on how to report further work on a revived case and where a new matter would be justified.

Granting Legal Help

10.75 The means test for Legal Help as set out in chapter 3 must be applied. The only difference in the immigration category is that support granted under section 4 or section 95 of the Immigration and Asylum Act 1999 (referred to as National Asylum Support Service (NASS) support) is treated as a passporting benefit (see para 3.43 above).[75]

---

75 Civil Legal Aid (Financial Resources and Payments for Services) Regulations 2013 reg 6(1).

10.76   In all Controlled Work cases, the means of minors should not be aggregated with those of their foster carer's or social worker's.[76] Proof of means will be required. Many asylum-seekers and migrants without leave who are not in receipt of section 4 or section 95 support may be accommodated and maintained by friends and relatives. Where that is the case, you will need to get proof, usually in the form of a letter signed by the person accommodating the client and setting out the nature and extent of support being given (and quantifying it if it includes money). It is very important that the letter is signed and dated and makes it clear that the support has covered the whole of the month prior to the date the form was signed. Letters that do not specify a time period since the support began have not been allowed as acceptable evidence of means at audit. Alternatively, you may use the LAA's optional form for third parties providing support.[77]

10.77   The merits test is the sufficient benefit test – see chapter 3 for further information on the means test, and chapter 5 for further information on the merits test.

Granting Controlled Legal Representation

10.78   CLR is subject to the means test. The test is the same as for Legal Help, except that the capital limit for CLR is £3,000 for all non-asylum appeal work, rather than the £8,000 that applies to all other levels of civil funding.

10.79   CLR has its own merits test, which should be applied under Legal Help and kept in mind throughout, once CLR has been granted. This test, in addition to the standard criteria (see chapter 5), requires that (emphasis added):

- if the case is not of significant wider public interest, the *reasonable private paying client test* is met; or
- if the case is of significant wider public interest, the *proportionality test* is met; and
- in either of these two scenarios, the prospects of success for the case are:
  (a) very good, good or moderate; or
  (b) *borderline, marginal* or *unclear*, and:
     (i) the case is of *significant wider public interest*;
     (ii) the case is one with *overwhelming importance to the individual*; or

---

76   *LAA Guide to Determining Financial Eligibility for Controlled Work and Family Mediation April 2019*, para 9.2. Please note that the text states that it would 'usually be inequitable' to do so.

77   www.gov.uk/government/publications/cw1-financial-eligibility-for-legal-aid-clients.

(iii)   the substance of the case relates to a breach of Convention rights.[78]

10.80   The italicised terms in the above-mentioned CLR merits test are defined elsewhere in the relevant statutory instrument as follows (emphasis added):

- The *reasonable private paying individual test* is met if the Director is satisfied that the potential benefit to be gained from the provision of civil legal services justifies the likely costs, such that a reasonable private paying individual would be prepared to start or continue the proceedings having regard to the prospects of success and all the other circumstances of the case.[79]

- The *proportionality test* is met if the Director is satisfied that the likely benefits of the proceedings to the individual and others justify the likely costs, having regard to the prospects of success and all the other circumstances of the case.[80]

- '*Borderline*' means that the case is not 'unclear' but that it is not possible, by reason of disputed law, fact or expert evidence, to:
    (i)   decide that the chance of obtaining a successful outcome is 50% or more; or
    (ii) classify the prospects as marginal or poor.[81]

- '*Unclear*' means where there are identifiable investigations which could be carried out, after which it should be possible to give a reliable estimate of the prospects of success.[82]

- '*Marginal*' means a 45% or more chance, but less than a 50% chance, of obtaining a successful outcome.[83]

- A case is of *significant wider public interest* if the Director is satisfied that the case is an appropriate case to realise:
    (a) real benefits to the public at large, other than those which normally flow from cases of the type in question; and
    (b) benefits for an identifiable class of individuals, other than the individual to whom civil legal services may be provided or members of that individual's family.[84]

- A case with '*overwhelming importance to the individual*' means a case which is not primarily a claim for damages or other sum of money and which relates to one or more of the following:

78 Civil Legal Aid (Merits Criteria) Regulations 2013 reg 60(2)–(3).
79 Civil Legal Aid (Merits Criteria) Regulations 2013 reg 7.
80 Civil Legal Aid (Merits Criteria) Regulations 2013 reg 8.
81 Civil Legal Aid (Merits Criteria) Regulations 2013 reg 5.
82 Civil Legal Aid (Merits Criteria) Regulations 2013 reg 5.
83 Civil Legal Aid (Merits Criteria) Regulations 2013 reg 5.
84 Civil Legal Aid (Merits Criteria) Regulations 2013 reg 6.

(a) the life, liberty or physical safety of the individual or a member of that individual's family; or

(b) the immediate risk that the individual may become homeless.[85]

10.81   The merits test applies to both FTT and UT appeals.

10.82   Where you are satisfied that the merits are either very good, good or moderate,[86] you should sign the CLR form – it is your signature (the client having already signed the form) that gives effect to the grant – since you are making the determination on behalf of the Director of the LAA.[87]

Refusing and withdrawing CLR

10.83   Where you believe the merits test is not, or is no longer, satisfied, you should refuse or withdraw CLR as appropriate and complete form CW4 setting out your reasons.[88]

10.84   A copy of the form must be provided to the client within five days of your decision, and you must also advise the client of their right to appeal against your decision.[89]

10.85   Either the client can appeal direct to the LAA or instruct you to do so on their behalf.[90] This work is normally carried out under Legal Help.

Change of supplier

10.86   A person's remedy against a refusal of CLR would be to appeal to the LAA against a provider's decision to refuse or withdraw CLR. If an appeal to the Independent Funding Adjudicator (IFA) is being considered, the applicant will have 14 days by which to submit the appeal to the Director of Legal Aid Casework.

10.87   Where you are asked to take on a transfer following refusal of CLR, you should generally advise the client to appeal to the IFA. However, there may be occasions where your specific experience and knowledge compel you to take a different view on the merits and grant CLR funding on this basis. You will need to follow the usual

---

85   Civil Legal Aid (Merits Criteria) Regulations 2013 reg 2.
86   See Civil Legal Aid (Merits Criteria) Regulations 2013 reg 5(1)(a), (b) and (c) for the respective definitions of these terms.
87   Civil Legal Aid (Merits Criteria) Regulations 2013 reg 3.
88   Standard Civil Contract 2018 Specification para 8.39.
89   Standard Civil Contract 2018 Specification para 8.40.
90   Standard Civil Contract 2018 Specification paras 8.40, 8.42 and 8.43.

rules for transfers of funding (see chapter 5). If you re-assess and decide to grant funding, without your client having to appeal to an IFA, you will need to record details of your revised determination in section A6, page 5 or 6 of the CW2 form.

Conducting the case

10.88 Once you have determined the case is in scope and Legal Help or CLR, as appropriate, has been granted (and assuming there is sufficient merit on an ongoing basis), you can conduct the case.

10.89 You are generally permitted to take instructions, take witness statements, make applications and representations, conduct appeals, and so on.

10.90 There are rules that govern certain aspects of the conduct of cases, which we will look at in this section.

Attendance at interviews

10.91 As mentioned in paras 10.15 and 10.19 above, attendance at interviews is excluded under LASPO unless allowed by regulations. The relevant regulations provide for attendance at: i) asylum screening interviews and asylum interviews where the person is a child;[91] or ii) at an asylum interview where the person is either being detained at a specified IRC[92] or lacks mental capacity.[93] In respect of attendance at interview of a child, a child does not include a child whose age is being disputed at the time of the interview unless the Home Office have said that they are nevertheless going to treat the person as a child for the purpose of the interview.[94]

10.92 Payment for attendance at an interview is not determined by the age of the child at the time of signing Controlled Work but whether the child is a still a child at the time of the actual interview.

---

91 Civil Legal Aid (Immigration Interviews) (Exceptions) Regulations 2012 regs 2 and 3.

92 Following the amendment of the relevant regulations by the Civil Legal Aid (Immigration Interviews) (Exceptions) (Amendment) Regulations 2017, these are, currently, Colnbrook House IRC, Harmondsworth IRC and Yarl's Wood Immigration IRC.

93 Civil Legal Aid (Immigration Interviews) (Exceptions) Regulations 2012 reg 4.

94 Civil Legal Aid (Immigration Interviews) (Exceptions) Regulations 2012 regs 2(b) and 3.

10.93   Where you attend in a standard fee case, you can claim the interview additional fee. In an hourly rate case, the contract says that attendance at a substantive interview is outside the relevant costs and disbursement limits.[95]

Travel to detained clients

10.94   Unless you are attending a Detained Duty Advice Surgery under a Schedule authorisation,[96] you can claim for travel and waiting costs to visit a client in detention.[97] However, travel time is capped to a maximum of three hours for both legs of the journey. Travel and waiting time and associated disbursements are excluded from any applicable costs limit, and in a standard fee case payable on top of the relevant fee.

Bail

10.95   When attending a client in detention you must always advise the client in relation to bail and record the outcome of this advice on the file. You must ensure that the client receives advice on the appropriateness of making an application at any particular time (including when appeal rights have been exhausted).[98]

10.96   Bail applications to the tribunal are covered by CLR funding[99] (Home Office bail and bail restrictions are covered under Legal Help[100]). If you do not already have CLR open for an appeal, you should grant CLR to cover bail.[101] If you are already conducting an appeal, you should extend the scope of CLR to cover the bail application. The merits test for bail is the same for CLR generally, except that it will be specifically related to the prospects of a successful bail application.

10.97   Bail work is always paid at hourly rates.[102] See below for costs limits in bail matters.

95 Standard Civil Contract Specification 2018 para 8.82.
96 Standard Civil Contract Specification 2018 para 8.47.
97 Standard Civil Contract Specification 2018 para 8.46.
98 Standard Civil Contract Specification 2018 paras 8.34–8.35.
99 Standard Civil Contract Specification 2018 para 8.85(b).
100 Standard Civil Contract Specification 2018 para 8.80.
101 Standard Civil Contract Specification 2018 para 8.76(b).
102 Standard Civil Contract Specification 2018 para 8.76(d).

Attendance at hearings

10.98 Appeals work is out of scope of Legal Help but is covered by CLR. You may instruct an advocate (within or outside your organisation) to attend any hearing if CLR has been granted.

10.99 The advocate's time should be included on your claim as if it were your profit costs, and it will be paid at the relevant hourly rate or as part of the standard fee – in a standard fee case, their time will count towards exceptionality. Where an advocate is instructed, you cannot make a claim for time spent accompanying them at the hearing.[103]

10.100 You can apply to the LAA to increase the rates payable to advocates (including advocates employed by you) if the case raises an exceptionally complex or novel point of law (eg country guidance cases) or if there is a significant wider public interest (as defined by the regulations). Any enhanced rates that may be granted apply to advocacy, attendance and preparation only.[104]

10.101 Time spent instructing advocates and in conference is properly claimable if reasonable in the circumstances of the case.

Post-appeal work

10.102 The scope of Legal Help ends at the point of Home Office decision and consideration of CLR merits.[105] Therefore, by definition, Legal Help cannot be used for post-appeal follow-up work, such as chasing of status papers and advice on status.

10.103 The CLR will cover advice on the outcome of the appeal, including on the rights conferred by a grant of status, together with any post-appeal advice and assistance that does not justify a new matter start (see above for rules on matter start boundaries).[106]

Appeals to the Upper Tribunal

10.104 Work on an application for permission to appeal to the UT, and, if granted, the appeal itself and any subsequent remittal back, is Licensed Work and you must apply for a certificate before any work can be done.[107] The work carried out on the initial application to the FTT for permission to appeal to the UT on the application is payable

---

103 Standard Civil Contract Specification 2018 para 8.92.
104 Standard Civil Contract Specification 2018 paras 8.89–8.91.
105 Standard Civil Contract Specification 2018 para 8.62.
106 Standard Civil Contract Specification 2018 para 8.64.
107 Standard Civil Contract Specification 2018 para 8.96.

at the hourly rates set out in the regulations for FTT work. However, work carried out on a direct application to the UT for permission to appeal and all subsequent work in that forum, is payable at the hourly rates specified for Licensed Work in the Higher Courts.[108]

10.105   If you apply for permission to appeal and permission is refused, you may not claim any costs related to the application or appeal, but may claim any disbursements incurred, including interpreters' fees.[109]

10.106   Where the application for permission is lodged by the Home Office, or where the case is subject to the Detained Fast Track Scheme or the Detained Asylum Casework Scheme (see para 10.54 above), work done is not at risk, and is Contract Work not Licensed Work.[110]

Higher Courts litigation

10.107   Onward litigation will usually take the form of an appeal to the Court of Appeal against a decision of the UT. In this case, a full representation certificate is required. See chapter 5 for information on applying for a funding certificate. The issue of the certificate will end the controlled work matter. Therefore, remittal back to the tribunal would be a new matter.

10.108   The main difference in the immigration category to the usual rules on certificate applications is that you do not have the delegated function to grant emergency certificates in judicial review claims unless you have specifically been granted that power by the LAA – the reverse of the position is seen in other categories, where suppliers have the power by default. You therefore need to submit an application for emergency funding to the LAA. All applications must be made via the Client and Cost Management System (CCMS) including, from 1 February 2018, out of hours emergency applications (see chapter 6 for more information about CCMS).

Managing costs

10.109   The amount of any costs limit depends on the stage of the case and the type of funding.

---

108 Standard Civil Contract Specification 2018 para 8.100.
109 Standard Civil Contract Specification 2018 paras 8.96 and 8.98.
110 Standard Civil Contract Specification 2018 para 8.97.

10.110   In standard fee cases, save for disbursements, only the standard fee is payable unless the matter becomes an escape fee case. There is a limit on disbursements. Hourly rate cases are limited by both profits costs and disbursements. Review and reconsideration cases before the UT are not subject to costs limits for either costs or disbursements, since they are subject to assessment on a case-by-case basis by the LAA.

10.111   These are the applicable costs limits:

- Standard fee stage 1 (Legal Help):
  - £400 disbursements;[111]
  - no profit costs limits.
- Standard fee stage 2 (CLR):
  - £600 disbursements;[112]
  - no profit costs limits.
- Hourly rates Legal Help:
  - £800 profit costs (asylum); £500 profit costs (non-asylum);[113]
  - £400 disbursements.[114]
- Hourly rates CLR:
  - £1,600 combined costs and disbursements in asylum;
  - £1,200 combined costs and disbursements in non-asylum.[115]
- Bail work:
  - £500 for all bail work, inclusive of disbursements (where CLR has not already been granted for an appeal; where it has, bail work forms part of the main £1,600/£1,200 limit; if CLR has already been granted for bail, when it is granted for a substantive appeal, the costs already spent on bail count towards the £1,600/£1,200).[116]

10.112 Any of the above limits can be extended on application to the LAA. In addition, there are limits for specific case stages:
   (a) Where a client instructs you prior to making an application at the Asylum Screening Unit (ASU), and following attendance at the ASU you cease to be instructed – £100 including disbursements.
   (b) Where advice is given on the merits of an appeal to the UT under Legal Help (usually because the case has transferred to you at this

---

111 Standard Civil Contract Specification 2018 para 8.67.
112 Standard Civil Contract Specification 2018 para 8.67.
113 Standard Civil Contract Specification 2018 para 8.79.
114 Standard Civil Contract Specification 2018 para 8.83.
115 Standard Civil Contract Specification 2018 para 8.85.
116 Standard Civil Contract Specification 2018 paras 8.85–8.86.

stage, otherwise such advice would be part of CLR stage 2b) – £100 including disbursements.

(c) Where you provide initial advice in relation to an asylum application which the client decides not to make or ceases to provide instructions before making – £100 including disbursements.

The Legal Help Cost Limit set out in subparagraph (a) above cannot be extended. In contrast, the Cost Limits set out in subparagraphs (b) and (c) above may be extended by submitting the relevant Contract Report Form to the LAA. However, costs are only payable within the Cost Limits that applied at the point they were incurred. Cost Limits cannot be extended retrospectively.[117]

10.113   For details of making claims for costs, see chapter 16.

Licensed work

10.114   For the detail of how licensed work operates, see chapter 5.

10.115   The merits tests for Licensed Work in the immigration and asylum category are the same as those for CLR, ie the standard criteria combined with the test set out in paras 10.75 and 10.76.[118]

10.116   In a judicial review in relation to a transfer decision within the meaning of the Dublin III Regulations (ie EU Regulation No 604/2013: establishing the criteria and mechanisms for determining the Member State responsible for examining an application for international protection lodged in one of the member states by a third-country national or a stateless person),[119] the general merits criteria do not apply. Instead the merits test is whether the Director of the LAA is satisfied that the case has a tangible prospect of success.[120]

---

117   Standard Civil Contract Specification 2018 paras 8.79 and 8.81.
118   Civil Legal Aid (Merits Criteria) Regulations 2013, reg 60(2)–(3). The LAA has produced a guidance document (version 1, 21 November 2018): Background Information on the transfer of Immigration and Asylum Upper Tribunal work from Controlled Legal Representation to Licensed Work: https://assets. publishing.service.gov.uk/government/uploads/system/uploads/attachment_data/file/759115/Immigration_and_Asylum_Upper_Tribunal_Background_Information.pdf.
119   Civil Legal Aid (Merits Criteria) (Amendment) (No 3) Regulations 2013 reg 2.
120   Civil Legal Aid (Merits Criteria) Regulations 2013 reg 56A.

CHAPTER 11

Conducting a mental health case

by Richard Charlton

continued

Introduction

11.1   This chapter deals with the funding of mental health cases, and should be read alongside chapters 3, 4 and 5. In this chapter we set out the rules specific to mental health work. You should note that most of those rules are in addition to and build on the general rules applicable to all civil work, set out in chapters 3 and 5. Detailed guidance for costs in mental health work is beyond the scope of this work, but there is a summary of the fee schemes in chapter 16. See also appendix C for a summary of costs issues applicable to all civil work.

11.2   However, some issues arising from the representation of those with mental health issues may be relevant for uplift of costs;[1] and in addition, payment for examination of records, for example in Mental Capacity Act 2005 cases, may be possible notwithstanding the same examination by experts instructed.[2] The Legal Aid Agency (LAA) published useful guidance to common billing errors in 2015.[3] There is also guidance in relation to the Mental Health category specification and billing in the 2018 Standard Civil Contract.[4] This may be updated during the lifetime of the 2018 Contract.

11.3   Peer review guidance to work in this field has been published by the LAA and the fourth edition is to be found at: https://assets.publishing. service.gov.uk/government/uploads/system/uploads/attachment_ data/file/556275/improving-your-quality-guide-mental-health.pdf. In addition, invaluable guidance as to attendance and appropriate work is to be found in the Law Society's Practice Note on Mental Health Tribunals at: www.lawsociety.org.uk/support-services/advice/practice-notes/representation-before-mental-health-tribunals/.

What is mental health work?

11.4   The mental health category of law is defined as:

- Cases under Legal Aid, Sentencing and Punishment of Offenders Act 2012 (LASPO) Sch 1 Part 1 para 5 – services in relation to:

1 Costs Assessment Guidance 2018 para 12.8.
2 Costs Assessment Guidance 2018 para 12.14.
3 www.mentalhealthlaw.co.uk/media/LAA_MH_Common_Errors_v1_ Feb_2015.pdf.
4 https://assets.publishing.service.gov.uk/government/uploads/system/uploads/ attachment_data/file/737489/Mental_Health_Guidance_September_2018_ Update.pdf.

- – Mental Health Act 1983;
- – Mental Capacity Act 2005;
- • Repatriation of Prisoners Act 1984 Sch para 5(2).

11.5   Court of Protection work is permitted by virtue of the inclusion of the Mental Capacity Act 2005, but LASPO Sch 1 Part 3 para 4 says that advocacy in the Court of Protection is only permitted where the proceedings concern:

- • right to life;
- • liberty or physical safety;
- • medical treatment;
- • capacity to marry, enter a civil partnership or enter sexual relations;
- • right to family life.

11.6   For any other matter, advice will be in scope but not representation. Where representation can be justified, an application for exceptional funding can be made (see chapter 4), and the category definitions confirm that will be treated as mental health work.

11.7   Mental health work is governed by the general provisions of the 2018 Standard Civil Contract, and by section 9 of the Specification with effect from 1 September 2018. See chapters 3 and 5 of this book for the general rules.

Who can do the work?

11.8   Under the 2018 Standard Civil Contract, Mental Health Contracts were let by procurement area.

11.9   To do any mental health work at all, you must have a schedule authorisation for at least one procurement area and meet the appropriate Supervisor requirements. All advocates before the Mental Health Tribunal (MHT) except self-employed counsel must be members of the Law Society's Mental Health Accreditation Scheme.[5]

Mental health supervisors

11.10   Under the 2018 Civil Specification there are two legal competence standards for supervisors. These are:

---

5   Standard Civil Contract 2018 Specification para 9.8.

a) the MHT Legal Competence Standard at paras 9.18–9.23 for Supervisors who predominately supervise mental health contract work in relation to the Mental Health Act 1983; and,

b) the Mental Health and Mental Capacity Legal Competence Standard is at paras 9.24–9.31 for supervisors who supervise a mixture of contract work under the Mental Health Act 1983 and Mental Capacity Act 2005.

11.11 You may only rely on an individual qualifying as a supervisor via the Mental Health and Mental Capacity Act Legal Competence Standard at para 9.15(b) to fulfil the requirements of this contract where that individual has been directly involved in the delivery of at least ten new cases (whether delivered under this contract, a previous contract or otherwise), during the 12 months. There are provisions for reducing this to five cases if appropriate work is shown on another five MHT files.

11.12 As previously there needs to be evidence of work on two Legal Help non-tribunal files.

11.13 The Legal Competence Standard for these two different supervisor standards are summarised in the tables below:

Mental health (paras 9.18 – 9.23)	Mental health and mental capacity (paras 9.24 – 9.31)
Member of Law Society MH Accreditation Scheme	Member of Law Society MH Accreditation Scheme
Representation at 10 MHTs (or representation at 5 MHTs and 5 cases where preparation has been completed/conduct of other case in the scope of category)	Representation at 5 MHTs (or representation at 3 MHTs and 2 cases where preparation has been completed/conduct of other case in the scope of the category)
2 Non-MHT cases from list	5 cases files involving under the MCA (including at least 2 CoP applications)
	2 Non-MHT cases from list (can include MCA cases)

Advocacy

11.14 All advocates before the MHT except self-employed counsel, must be members of the Law Society's Mental Health Accreditation Scheme.[6]

---

6 Standard Civil Contract 2018 Specification para 9.8.

11.15   You are required to have a documented list of 'designated accredited representatives' (DARs) who are members of the Law Society's Mental Health Accreditation scheme and are used by you to carry out advocacy before the MHT.[7]

11.16   These DARs must undertake a minimum of 14 hours a week for your firm per week in the category of mental health law. The 14 hours will be calculated rolling across a month to allow for different work patterns.[8]

11.17   DARs must carry out 50 per cent of advocacy before the tribunal in a contract period.[9] For the remaining 50 per cent, you may use another advocate (ie self-employed counsel or another member of the Law Society's Mental Health Accreditation scheme), provided that the advocate has the appropriate skills, experience and knowledge to act for the client in these proceedings and you have ensured as far as possible, that they have taken steps to familiarise themselves with the client's case.[10]

Use of matter starts

11.18   You can take on cases as you see fit, subject to means and merits tests where applicable. However, you must use at least 70 per cent of your matter starts for a procurement area for clients who were physically located in the procurement area at the time the matter start is opened.[11]

Levels of funding

Overview

11.19   The following levels of funding apply to mental health work:

- Legal Help – advice and assistance, but excluding representation before the tribunal;
- Help at Court – funding for representation for victims under the Domestic Violence, Crime and Victims Act 2004;

---

7   Standard Civil Contract 2018 Specification para 9.9.
8   Standard Civil Contract 2018 Specification para 9.10.
9   Standard Civil Contract 2018 Specification para 9.11.
10   Standard Civil Contract 2018 Specification para 9.12.
11   Standard Civil Contract 2018 Specification para 9.13.

- Controlled Legal Representation (CLR) – representation before the tribunal;
- Legal representation (certificate) – appeals to the Upper Tribunal and representation in the higher courts, including the Court of Protection.[12]

Legal Help, Help at Court and CLR granted on the same case all form part of the same matter.

11.20   Mental health work is covered by standard fees for almost all controlled (ie non-certificate) work – the sole exception being Help at Court for victims.[13]

11.21   There are four fees:[14]

- the non-MHT fee, for all work that does not go to the tribunal;
- MHT fee level 1 – initial advice;[15]
- MHT fee level 2 – negotiation and preparation once an application to the MHT has been made;[16] and
- MHT fee level 3 – representation before the MHT, and follow-up work.[17]

11.22   A fee may be claimed for each stage through which the matter passes. Any disbursements incurred are in addition to the fee, but where counsel is instructed, their fees are included in the graduated fee[18] and it is for you to negotiate with counsel which part of the fee you will pay to counsel and which part you will keep. In cases of unusual complexity you can apply to the LAA for prior authority to pay a rate higher than that set for solicitors. This cannot be retrospective.[19] Further fees are payable for adjourned/postponed/cancelled hearings[20] and for travel to any hospital that the LAA has designated on their website as a remote hospital[21] (at the time of writing, none had been designated).

11.23   See chapter 16 for more on payment.

---

12 Standard Civil Contract 2018 Specification para 9.3.
13 Standard Civil Contract 2018 Specification para 9.66.
14 Standard Civil Contract 2018 Specification para 9.66.
15 Standard Civil Contract 2018 Specification para 9.77.
16 Standard Civil Contract 2018 Specification para 9.79.
17 Standard Civil Contract 2018 Specification para 9.84.
18 Standard Civil Contract 2018 Specification para 9.84.
19 Standard Civil Contract 2018 Specification para 9.61.
20 Standard Civil Contract 2018 Specification para 9.85.
21 Standard Civil Contract 2018 Specification para 9.88.

Case study

I have granted CLR to my client. I made an application to the tribunal. I prepared the case and represented my client at a manager's review, but he then decided he didn't want to proceed to a full hearing yet. What can I claim?

All work is covered by the level 2 fee. You can claim for preparation work, and for attendance at meetings and reviews, at this level. You only go on to level 3 if there is an MHT hearing.

Granting Legal Help

11.24   The general rules set out in chapter 3 and 5 apply to the granting of Legal Help in the mental health category. Where the client's condition is such that he or she will not sign the application form, and there is no other person who could sign it on his or her behalf, a supervisor in your organisation can sign it on the client's behalf.[22] The reasons should be noted on file.

Means

11.25   The usual means test for Legal Help will apply – see chapter 3 for details. Note that the guidance on evidence of means, which can be accessed on the legal aid website via the eligibility calculator,[23] states:

> It will often be impracticable to obtain evidence of income from patients with mental health problems who are in hospital (for example, those detained under the Mental Health Act). Practitioners should however attempt to obtain oral or written confirmation of the position (eg type of benefit received) from the ward manager or social worker where practicable.[24]

11.26   However, where the client is a patient whose case is the subject of proceedings or potential proceedings before the MHT, no means test is required[25] – the client is automatically eligible. Where the case

---

22 Standard Civil Contract 2018 Specification para 9.59.
23 http://civil-eligibility-calculator.justice.gov.uk/.
24 *Guide to determining financial eligibility for controlled work and family mediation* April 2018 para 12.2.11.
25 Civil Legal Aid (Financial Resources and Payment for Services) Regulations 2013 reg 5(1)(f); Standard Civil Contract 2018 Specification para 9.32(a).

covers both MHT and non-MHT issues, it will be all one matter and therefore no means test need be carried out.[26]

Merits

11.27 The usual merits test for Legal Help – the 'sufficient benefit test' – will apply. See chapter 5 for details of the sufficient benefit test.

Granting CLR

11.28 CLR is granted by your signature on a form already signed by the client (subject to the same provisions set out above for Legal Help where the client is unable or refuses to sign).[27] Since a grant of CLR is a requirement in any case that goes to the MHT (subject to merit, below), and therefore very much standard practice in most cases, it can become easy to overlook the necessity actually to sign the form and keep it on file. In our experience, some firms have suffered on costs audit as a result. You may wish to consider incorporating a reminder into your file checklist.

Means

11.29 CLR for representation before the MHT is available without the need for a means test.[28]

Merits

11.30 The merits test applicable to CLR in the mental health category is set at a very low threshold, given that the client's liberty is at stake. The test is that the Director (in practice, you) must be satisfied that it is reasonable in the particular circumstances of the case for CLR to be granted.[29] The contract makes clear that it would be unusual for it to be unreasonable to grant CLR.[30] However, the prospects of success will govern how much work should be done. CLR is available to the patient, and if the nearest relative is the applicant to the tribunal, to the nearest relative.[31]

26 Standard Civil Contract 2018 Specification para 9.33.
27 Standard Civil Contract 2018 Specification para 9.59.
28 Civil Legal Aid (Financial Resources and Payment for Services) Regulations 2013 reg5(1)(f); Standard Civil Contract 2018 Specification para 9.32(b).
29 Civil Legal Aid (Merits Criteria) Regulations 2013 reg 51.
30 Standard Civil Contract 2018 Specification para 9.54.
31 Standard Civil Contract 2018 Specification para 9.52.

Conduct of the case

Non-Mental Health Tribunal cases

11.31   All cases that do not concern an application or potential application to the MHT are deemed to be non-MHT cases and attract the non-MHT fee.[32] Only Legal Help is available.

11.32   Where you are acting for a victim, Help at Court for representation is available and claimed at hourly rates on top of the fee.[33]

11.33   Initial advice in a Mental Capacity Act 2005 case is a non-MHT matter,[34] including making an application for a certificate for representation before the Court of Protection.

Mental Health Tribunal cases

11.34   MHT cases divide into three fee levels.

11.35   Level 1 is funded by Legal Help and covers initial advice to the client, including a visit to the client and follow-up work up to and including making an application to the MHT.[35] The scope of the Level 1 (Mental Health Proceedings) Fee level has been clarified to address areas of common confusion. The contract now specifies that the fee

> . . . covers the work done in making an initial visit to the Client, including all advice and assistance provided to the client at your first attendance, and follow up work such as:
> (a) preparing and sending initial letters of instruction;
> (b) making the application to the MHT if none has been made; and/or
> (c) applying to withdraw an existing MHT application if this is agreed as part of the initial advice (e.g. at the first attendance or as part of the immediate follow up work).

The last paragraph means that providers cannot trigger the level 2 Fee using work carried out helping to withdraw an application already made by the client if this action is agreed at the outset of the case.[36]

11.36   Once it becomes clear that the case is to be considered by the MHT, you should grant CLR[37] and continue work at level 2, but you

---

32 Standard Civil Contract 2018 Specification para 9.66.
33 Standard Civil Contract 2018 Specification para 9.100.
34 Standard Civil Contract 2018 Specification para 9.47.
35 Standard Civil Contract 2018 Specification para 9.77.
36 Standard Civil Contract 2018 Specification para 9.77.
37 Standard Civil Contract 2018 Specification para 9.52.

can only go to level 2 having passed through (and done at least 30 minutes of work at) level 1.[38] This stage covers all work up to, but not including, the substantive hearing, including preparation of the case generally and for the hearing, negotiation with third parties, attendance at managers' reviews and other meetings where appropriate, as well as taking instructions from the client and instructing experts.[39]

11.37   Level 3 covers representation at the tribunal hearing, including any adjourned/cancelled/postponed hearings[40] (for which an additional fee is or may be payable if cancelled on the day of the hearing, in some circumstances[41]). Level 3 also includes work done in applying to the tribunal for a review of its decision under Tribunals, Courts and Enforcement Act 2007 s9, or applying for permission to appeal under section 11.[42]

11.38   Where the tribunal sets aside its decision, you are still in stage 3 but may claim an additional adjourned hearing fee.[43] However, where an appeal or review goes to the Upper Tribunal, you will need to apply for a certificate for representation at that stage.[44]

Separate matters

11.39   Each time a client becomes eligible to make an application to the tribunal, the client enters a 'period of eligibility'. This is defined in the preliminaries to the Mental Health Contract Specification as:

> . . . the period during which the Client is eligible to apply to the MHT under the applicable provisions in Part V of the Mental Health Act 1983 relating to their particular circumstances.

All work done for a client within a period of eligibility, on both MHT and non-MHT matters, forms one matter start.[45] However, where more than one set of MHT proceedings are running concurrently during a period of eligibility, you can claim separate fees for each set of proceedings.[46]

---

38 Standard Civil Contract 2018 Specification para 9.81.
39 Standard Civil Contract 2018 Specification para 9.82.
40 Standard Civil Contract 2018 Specification para 9.84.
41 Standard Civil Contract 2018 Specification para 9.85.
42 Standard Civil Contract 2018 Specification para 9.101.
43 Standard Civil Contract 2018 Specification para 9.101.
44 Standard Civil Contract 2018 Specification para 9.3.
45 Standard Civil Contract 2018 Specification para 9.39.
46 Standard Civil Contract 2018 Specification para 9.41(a).

11.40   You may start a new matter, even if you have an existing ongoing matter, when:[47]

- there is more than one set of MHT proceedings within the same period of eligibility (and separate MHT proceedings fees can be claimed for each);
- the client withdraws from the MHT, and within the same period of eligibility applies again in the same period of eligibility and the withdrawal and re-application were carried out in good faith and made with the client's consent and/or in the client's best interests and you have noted down the reasons for withdrawal and re-application on your file.[48]

11.41   You must open a new matter start for any work on a new issue where a client has a statutory entitlement to a new MHT (which does not include any issue that originally arose within a previous period of eligibility).[49]

11.42   However, note that communicating the decision of the MHT, advising the client about it and about aftercare is the same matter as the MHT.[50]

11.43   In addition, any work that 'rolls over' to a previous period of tribunal eligibility, such as a section 20 Hospital Managers review, needs to be incorporated in that earlier period.

Interpretation issues of new matter starts and level 2 work

11.44   Where a Mental Capacity Act matter is open, and then the client is sectioned or otherwise requires MHT advice, a separate MHT matter should be opened.[51]

Disbursements

11.45   Disbursements may be incurred in the usual way in the mental health category.

---

47 Standard Civil Contract 2018 Specification para 9.41.
48 Standard Civil Contract 2018 Specification para 9.41.
49 Standard Civil Contract 2018 Specification para 9.43.
50 Standard Civil Contract 2018 Specification para 9.44.
51 Standard Civil Contract 2018 Specification para 9.48.

11.46   You can make a claim for payment on account of disbursements during the life of a case, but only where the matter has been open for at least six months and, if there has been a previous application for payment on account, at least six months have elapsed since that payment was made.[52]

Use of counsel

11.47   You are entitled to instruct counsel to represent clients before the tribunal. Where you instruct counsel, you will still only be entitled to the level 3 fee, and it is a matter for you to negotiate how much of that fee to pay to counsel. Counsel is not a disbursement.[53]

11.48   In unusually complex cases, you can apply to the LAA to pay counsel at an hourly rate above the standard hourly rates in the contract. The LAA will grant prior authority, specifying the hourly rate and the maximum costs limit if the case poses unusually complex evidential problems, or novel or difficult points of law. The LAA consider it highly unlikely that such issues will arise at MHT level.[54]

Licensed work

11.49   See chapter 5 for the general principles applicable to licensed work.

11.50   The merits test for certificates to be granted for mental capacity work is:[55]

- the standard criteria apply (see chapter 5); and
- the Court of Protection has ordered, or is likely to order, an oral hearing; and
- it is necessary for the individual to be provided with full representation in the proceedings. This means free representation is, however, available for the protected person and his or her Responsible Person's Representative in an application under Mental Capacity Act 2005 s21A.

11.51   Representation is generally only available where the proceedings concern:

- right to life;

---

52 Standard Civil Contract 2018 Specification para 9.68.
53 Standard Civil Contract 2018 Specification para 9.60.
54 Standard Civil Contract 2018 Specification para 9.61.
55 Civil Legal Aid (Merits Criteria) Regulations 2013 reg 52.

- liberty or physical safety;
- medical treatment;
- capacity to marry, enter a civil partnership or enter sexual relationships;
- right to family life.

11.52   Other matters are out of the scope of representation, and an exceptional funding application will be required (see chapter 4 and para 11.6 above).

Potential Restriction on Court of Protection Work

11.53   The 2018 Contract includes a clause that states that the LAA may implement further restrictions on providers carrying out Mental Capacity Act 2005 work in the Court of Protection. These will only be introduced with the express agreement of the Consultative Bodies and providers will be given 12 months' notice of any changes before they come into effect.[56] There has been no indication at the time of publication of when any such 12-month period will commence.

Contact with the Legal Aid Agency

11.54   All work in the mental health category, with the exception of high cost cases, is handled by the Liverpool Office of the LAA. All claims, and applications, including certificate applications, together with any queries, should be directed to:

Mental Health Unit/Immigration and Asylum
Controlled Work and Escaped Fee Claims
Legal Aid Agency
Level 6, The Capital
Union Street
Liverpool L3 9AF
Phone: 0151 235 6750 (option 1)
Email: mhu-ec@legalaid.gsi.gov.uk

---

56 Standard Civil Contract 2018 Specification para 9.7.

CHAPTER 12

Conducting a housing case

by Sue James and Simon Mullings

Introduction

12.1   This chapter deals with work done in the housing category. You should read it in conjunction with chapters 3 and 5. Chapter 3 deals with general rules about taking on civil cases and applies to work in housing as it does to all other work; chapter 5 deals with the rules that apply to the conduct of all civil cases. The housing-specific rules in this chapter usually build on, rather than replace, the general rules; where they do replace the general rules in chapters 3 and 5 we will say so. Out of scope housing cases may be funded as exceptional cases; see chapter 4 for more on exceptional funding.

12.2   Included is advice about counterclaims in housing proceedings. You should keep in mind that when you apply for a representation certificate, a counterclaim is treated as separate proceedings and so you need to add the counterclaim as a proceeding in your application. For example, housing possession proceedings with a disrepair counterclaim should have two sets of proceedings, namely;

- Recover possession – tenant – Housing; and
- Bring a counterclaim – Housing,

and each should have appropriate scope and costs limitations. Please also keep in mind that where there is any damages claim you will need to advise your client of the operation of the Legal Aid Agency's (LAA's) statutory charge (see chapter 5).

12.3   See appendix C for a summary of the LAA's Costs Assessment Guidance, in respect of the most common queries raised by caseworkers.

What housing work is in the scope of legal aid?

Overview

12.4   The Category Definitions 2018[1] define housing work as:

- possession of the home, other than mortgage possession and orders for sale;[2]

---

1   https://assets.publishing.service.gov.uk/government/uploads/system/uploads/attachment_data/file/738528/2018_Standard_Civil_Contract_Category_Definitions__August_2018_.pdf?_ga=2.136894128.149788027.1566817931-1766719165.1529322761.

2   Mortgage possession and orders for sale are in the debt category, and as such required to go through the telephone gateway.

- eviction, including unlawful eviction, and planning eviction and closure orders not arising from criminal conduct;
- provision of accommodation and assistance under Parts 6 and 7 of the Housing Act 1996 (although not mentioned in the Category Definitions, includes Part 2 of Housing (Wales) Act 2014) for an individual who is homeless or threatened with homelessness;
- provision of accommodation by way of community care services to an individual who is homeless or threatened with homelessness;
- accommodation and support for asylum-seekers etc;
- housing conditions and disrepair, to the extent it is in scope;
- applications to vary or discharge an injunction under Housing Act 1996 s153A; (this provision has been repealed and effectively replaced by Anti-Social Behaviour Crime and Policing Act 2014. While the definition has not been updated in the Category Definitions, document guidance makes clear that the new provisions are in scope for legal aid);
- injunctions under the Protection from Harassment Act 1997 arising from housing matters;
- exceptional funding grants on any other matter concerning the possession, status, terms of occupation, repair, improvement, eviction from, quiet enjoyment of, or payment of rent or other charges for premises (including vehicles and sites they occupy) which are occupied as a residence, including the rights of lease-holders, allocation, transfers and the provision of sites for occupation.

Possession cases

Overview

12.5 Defences to claims for possession of the home in cases other than mortgage cases are in scope and in the housing category. Legal Help will be available for initial advice, and you can apply for a certificate for representation in court should that become necessary.

12.6 Possession of 'the home' includes houses, caravans, houseboats and other vehicles that are the individual's only or main residence, together with the land on which they are located.[3]

12.7 Legal aid is not available to defend possession proceedings brought against squatters – that is, where there are no grounds for

---

3 Legal Aid, Sentencing and Punishment of Offenders Act 2012 (LASPO) Sch 1 Part 1 para 33(9) and (11).

arguing that the individual is occupying otherwise than as a trespasser, and no grounds for arguing that their occupation began otherwise than as a trespasser.[4]

12.8   Defences based on whether it is reasonable for a possession order to be made and/or defences on public law/human rights/Equality Act grounds are included. Help at Court and Investigative Help are also available in appropriate cases.

12.9   Mortgage possession claims are also in scope but are in the debt category. Each housing contract is actually a housing and debt contract and includes a notional four debt matter starts per year, as well as a licence to do debt certificated work. At the time of writing Debt is a mandatory gateway category – although the mandatory element will end in Spring 2020.[5] In the meantime, it means that a client needing Legal Help or Help at Court must go through the gateway unless they are exempt (see para 3.13 above). The gateway will attempt to refer clients requiring face-to-face advice and/or representation to practitioners and provide a referral number. If you are approached by a client who needs representation, because proceedings have already been issued and the merits test is met (see below), you can apply for representation without needing to go through the gateway, though you cannot sign a Legal Help form to fund the application unless you contact the gateway and get a referral number. You can exercise delegated functions to grant a debt certificate in appropriate cases.[6]

12.10 Legal Aid, Sentencing and Punishment of Offenders Act 2012 (LASPO) Sch 1 Part 1 para 33 says that civil legal services in relation to court orders for possession are in scope. This does not mean that you have to wait until proceedings are issued before any legal aid becomes available, though there must be a real prospect of proceedings. The LAA has said that 'formal written notification that proceedings will be issued (such as a section 8 or section 21 notice)' will be enough. There is no reason to think that where a tenant has received

---

4 LASPO Sch 1 Part 1 para 33(10).
5 Mortgage work being done under the mandatory gateway has led to a drastic reduction in the amount of mortgage work being undertaken by practitioners. Bringing mortgage work out of the mandatory gateway may lead to this work coming to practitioners more often, and there is a possibility that some may feel de-skilled in this area if training is not updated. See Daniel Clarke, Derek McConnel and Simon Mullings, 'Mortgage possession claims: the changed legal landscape' May 2018 *Legal Action*.
6 FAQ 91, Civil Legal Aid Reform FAQs – no longer on the LAA website, but available at: https://legalaidhandbook.files.wordpress.com/2013/04/legal-aid-reform-faq-v3.pdf.

a letter with a credible threat to bring proceedings they should not receive legal help just because the landlord has erroneously not served a notice. A representation certificate will not be granted, however, until proceedings have actually been issued.[7] Prior to that, you may grant Legal Help.

12.11 Therefore, general advice on the theoretical possibility of possession proceedings, or advice on the implications of a client's rent arrears at an early stage, will be out of scope. However, once the landlord has issued notification of intent to take proceedings, legal aid in the form of Legal Help will be available. Once proceedings have actually been issued, you can apply for a certificate, using delegated functions if necessary, as long as the client has a defence (or a realistic prospect of arguing that it would not be reasonable to make a possession order. If not, you can still attend court to offer mitigation using Help at Court. The timescales of housing possession cases means that Investigative Help is rarely required, but it should be borne in mind that it is available in appropriate cases.

12.12 The merits test for grant of a certificate in possession proceedings is:[8]

- the standard criteria are met (see para 5.94 above);
- the individual has a defence (including that it would be unreasonable for the court to make an order for possession in the circumstances);
- prospects of success are:
  - borderline, or marginal or better; and
  - the proportionality test is met (see para 5.108 above).

12.13 Many possession cases involving rent arrears will have, as the underlying cause or a contributor to it, problems with housing benefit or housing element of Universal Credit. LASPO Sch 1 Part 1 para 33(3) applies the Part 2 exclusions, including the welfare benefits exclusion. The effect of this is that work done in relation to the possession proceedings is in scope, but work done in relation to welfare benefits is out of scope. You can investigate the housing benefit or Universal

---

7 FAQ 98, Civil Legal Aid Reform FAQs – no longer on the LAA website, but available at: https://legalaidhandbook.files.wordpress.com/2013/04/legal-aid-reform-faq-v3.pdf.

8 Civil Legal Aid (Merits Criteria) Regulations 2013 reg 61, amended by Civil Legal Aid (Merits Criteria) (Amendment) Regulations 2014 to provide that the prospects of success test to be applied is that in reg 43 of the 2013 Regulations. Regulation 43 was amended by Civil Legal Aid (Merits Criteria) (Amendment) Regulations 2016 SI No 781 reg 2(4) to allow for grants in the borderline and marginal, but not poor, categories.

Credit position to prepare a defence to the possession matter – which may include preparing witness statements, or even summonsing housing benefits officers – and can seek an adjournment for the client to resolve the benefits matter themselves. However, any work in assisting the client with that resolution will not be claimable.[9] Often work will be done to assist your client to resolve matters and so good, properly apportioned attendance notes will help with costs assessment.

12.14   Judicial review of housing benefit and other local authority financial assistance is in scope, though would fall into the welfare benefits and public law categories. Exceptional case funding (ECF) for welfare benefits cases is possible. Practitioners who apply for this will do well to consult the guidance from the Public Law Project.[10] See also chapter 4.

12.15   Where there is a claim for possession based wholly or in part on allegations of anti-social behaviour, including mandatory grounds, then legal representation to defend the possession proceedings is made in the usual way, selecting the appropriate scope in the Client and Cost Management System (CCMS). However, applications for injunctions under Anti-Social Behaviour Crime and Policing Act 2014 and committal proceedings based on a breach of such injunctions are dealt with separately in this chapter at para 12.45 and following.

12.16   Where a client does not have a full or partial defence to the proceedings (including that it would be unreasonable for the court to make an order for possession in the circumstances and/or on public law/human rights/Equality Act grounds) it is unlikely that a certificate would be justified, though Help at Court may be granted where informal advocacy is justified by way of mitigation at court hearings. The guidance[11] states that this would 'typically will be in possession proceedings where the client has no defence to possession but seeks to influence the discretion of the court in relation to postponing possession or suspending eviction'. Practitioners should consider (a) whether there is a defence and (b) whether that defence has sufficient merits under the rules, rather than be inhibited from applying because a suspended order is a possible outcome. Difficulties sometimes arise when LAA caseworkers misunderstand the nature of a

9   FAQ 107, Civil Legal Aid Reform FAQs – no longer on the LAA website, but available at: https://legalaidhandbook.files.wordpress.com/2013/04/legal-aid-reform-faq-v3.pdf.

10   https://publiclawproject.org.uk/what-we-do/current-projects-and-activities/legal-aid/exceptional-funding-project.

11   *Lord Chancellor's guidance on civil legal aid* (2018) para 6.9. See para 5.54 of this book for more on Help at Court.

defence in possession proceedings, particularly in section 21 Housing Act 1988 cases, and so it is important to set out the nature of the defence carefully in the application and to appeal bad decisions where necessary.

12.17 Where legal aid is required to apply to suspend a warrant of eviction then in all appropriate cases an application for Legal Representation should be made, not least because the certificate affords the client costs protection. Formal representation can be made on behalf of the client, adjournments with directions can be obtained for exchange of statements and relevant medical reports, and the hearing allocated sufficient time for proper judicial consideration.

Counterclaims

12.18 Where legal aid has been granted in possession proceedings, it can also be granted to cover work done on a counterclaim (see para 12.2 above), even if the subject of the counterclaim would otherwise be out of scope as a freestanding claim including discrimination, declaration of tenancy and Equality Act 2010 claims. The Part 2[12] exclusions of assault, battery and false imprisonment claims, trespass to goods and trespass to land, damage to property and breach of statutory duty do not apply to counterclaims in possession proceedings, so all may be pleaded and claimed for.[13] However, from our experience, the LAA considers claims for personal injury (which are excluded by para 2 of Part 2 of Sch 1) are not in scope (because personal injury is not re-included for counterclaims by LASPO Sch 1 Part 1 para 33(6)) and that is the case even when personal injury would be the subject of a counterclaim which is re-included, such as a claim for breach of statutory duty. In that case, exceptional case funding is the only route to litigate a personal injury counterclaim with legal aid funding. There is more on housing conditions and disrepair counterclaims at para 12.52 and following.

Homelessness and allocations

Housing Act 1996 and Housing (Wales) Act 2014

12.19 Both Legal Help and, in appropriate cases, legal representation, are available to individuals who are homeless or threatened with

---

12 LASPO Sch 1 Part 2.
13 LASPO Sch 1 Part 1 para 33(7).

homelessness[14] and seeking assistance under Part 6 or 7 of the Housing Act 1996.

12.20   In Wales, the law on allocations is the same (Part 6 Housing Act 1996) but the law on homelessness is different and contained in Part 2 of Housing (Wales) Act 2014. There is a separate Welsh code of guidance for both Part 6 Housing Act 1996 and Part 2 Housing (Wales) Act 2014. Although homelessness cases in Wales are in scope for legal aid, the LAA's regulations, guidance and CCMS system do not refer to the Housing (Wales) Act 2014. For example, CCMS does not have scope limitations referring to the Welsh Act. Practitioners are forced therefore to 'read across' provisions when dealing with homelessness cases in Wales, eg a section 88 Housing (Wales) Act 2014 appeal is treated as a section 204 Housing Act 1996 appeal.

12.21   LASPO Sch 1 Part 1 para 34 says that 'civil legal services . . . in relation to the provision of accommodation and assistance for the individual' are within scope. This is relatively broad and will cover advice on entitlement and suitability of accommodation for homeless people (although legal aid is not available in relation to allocations and suitability of accommodation to people who do not fall within the definition of 'homeless' as set out above), as well as assistance with making an application and any statutory review and appeal that may follow. All such work should be carried out as part of one matter except when i) as a result of a Housing Act 1996 section 204 appeal (section 88 of the Welsh Act) the matter is, by order or agreement, remitted back to the council for a further decision; ii) the review is a suitability review pursuant to section 202(1)(f) of the Housing Act 1996 (section 85(3) of the Welsh Act); or iii) Judicial Review is contemplated in relation to the council's failure to protect possessions under sections 211 and 212 of the Housing Act 1996 (sections 93 and 94 of the Welsh Act). In those cases a further matter start may be used.[15]

12.22   Legal Help will cover initial advice, the application and any review. The decisions which may be reviewed and therefore which may be the subject of legal help are set out in section 202 of the Housing Act 1996 (as amended) and are the subject of guidance at chapter 19 of the Homelessness Code of Guidance.[16] In Wales the equivalent provi-

---

14 As defined in Housing Act 1996 s175as amended by the Homelessness Reduction Act 2017 s1(2) and the Housing (Wales) Act 2014 s55(4).

15 Standard Civil Contract 2018 Specification para 10.13.

16 https://assets.publishing.service.gov.uk/media/5a969da940f0b67aa5087b93/Homelessness_code_of_guidance.pdf.

sions are at section 85 of the Welsh Act and chapter 20 of the Welsh Code of Guidance.[17]

12.23   A certificate for legal representation will cover an appeal to the county court, or a judicial review. The merits test for homelessness cases is the same as for public law more generally.[18] The test is:

- the standard criteria are met (see para 5.94 above);
- all administrative appeals and alternatives to court have been exhausted;
- a letter before claim has been sent (only relevant to judicial review);
- the proportionality test is met (see para 5.108);
- prospects of success are:
  - moderate or better; or
  - borderline or marginal, and the case of significant wider public interest, of overwhelming importance to the individual or the substance of the case relates to a breach of European Convention on Human Rights (ECHR) rights.[19]

The borderline or marginal criteria will often be satisfied in cases involving homelessness.

12.24   Inexplicably the default scope limitation for a homelessness appeal in CCMS is for Counsel's opinion only and so in order to comply with the 21-day appeal deadline practitioners should add a limitation under delegated functions which covers lodging the appeal.

12.25   There is a lack of clarity as to whether an appeal and/or application under section 204A (section 89 of the Welsh Act) should be progressed under a separate certificate or under the same certificate as the section 204 appeal. In this situation practitioners are advised to telephone the agency for advice and keep a good note of the advice given.

12.26   You can use delegated functions to grant emergency legal aid in homelessness cases, and in judicial review cases involving homelessness.[20]

---

17 https://gweddill.gov.wales/docs/desh/publications/160324-code-of-guidance-for-local-authorities-on-allocation-of-accommodation-and-homelessness-en.pdf.

18 Civil Legal Aid (Merits Criteria) Regulations 2013 reg 2 – see definition of 'public law'.

19 Civil Legal Aid (Merits Criteria) Regulations 2013 reg 56, as amended, most recently by the Civil Legal Aid (Merits Criteria) (Amendment) Regulations 2016.

20 Standard Civil Contract 2018 Specification para 5.2.

Accommodation by way of community care services

12.27   Legal aid (both Legal Help and legal representation) is available in the housing category to provide advice and representation to individuals seeking accommodation under certain community care provisions (as set out at LASPO Sch 1 Part 1 para 5). The main provisions that housing practitioners use include:

- Children Act 1989 s17 for families with children;
- Children Act 1989 s20 for homeless children;
- Children Act 1989 ss22A, 22B, 22C, 23, 23B, 23C, 24, 24A and 24B (the 'leaving care' provisions) for young people previously accommodated by children's services;
- Mental Health Act 1983 s117 (after-care services for individuals previously detained under Mental Health Act 1983 s3);
- Care Act 2014 Part 1 for individuals who have care and support needs.

Organisations that hold housing and community care contracts will be aware that the community care fixed fee for legal help is higher.

12.28   Legal Help will cover initial advice and assistance including consideration of any assessments carried out by local authorities and drafting pre-action letters under the Judicial Review Pre-Action Protocol. A certificate for legal representation will cover a judicial review. The merits test for community care cases is the same as for public law more generally.[21] The test is:

- the standard criteria are met (see para 5.94 above);
- all administrative appeals and alternatives to court have been exhausted;
- a letter before claim has been sent (only relevant to judicial review);
- the proportionality test is met (see para 5.108);
- prospects of success are:
  - moderate or better; or
  - borderline or marginal, and the case of significant wider public interest, of overwhelming importance to the individual or the substance of the case relates to a breach of ECHR rights.[22]

---

21 Civil Legal Aid (Merits Criteria) Regulations 2013 reg 2 – see definition of 'public law'.
22 Civil Legal Aid (Merits Criteria) Regulations 2013 reg 56, as amended, most recently by the Civil Legal Aid (Merits Criteria) (Amendment) Regulations 2016.

12.29   Practitioners do not have delegated functions to grant emergency funding in these cases, save for Children Act 1989 s20 and the provision of urgent services pending completion of an assessment under Care Act 2014 s9(3). If the individual needs emergency funding for other cases (including temporary accommodation under Children Act 1989 s17) the practitioner must make an emergency application for a certificate on the CCMS. It is advisable to ring the LAA, after making the application online, to ask them to make a decision on the application. It is also advisable to be persistent and continue to chase the determination of the application. Full details of the CCMS procedure are outlined in chapter 6 and community care in chapter 13.

Accommodation for asylum-seekers

12.30   Legal Help is available to individuals who apply for accommodation from the Home Office under the Immigration Act 1996 s4 (for destitute failed asylum-seekers) and s95 (those with ongoing asylum claims or failed asylum-seekers with children under 18). This can include advice on making an application, challenging the suitability of the offered accommodation (including location and type), and drafting letters before claim under the Judicial Review Pre-Action Protocol for delays in processing applications or failure to provide appropriate accommodation. Assistance can also be provided to draft a notice of appeal and appeal submissions to the First-tier Tribunal (Asylum Support). However, legal aid is not available for representation at the tribunal itself.

12.31   Legal Help is not available under the housing category to individuals who apply for subsistence-only support under Immigration Act 1996 s98. However, where the Home Office makes an unlawful decision advice and assistance may be provided under the public law category.

12.32   Practitioners do not have delegated functions to grant emergency funding for judicial review in asylum support accommodation cases.

Unlawful eviction

12.33   Legal aid is available for unlawful eviction claims and these include claims for damages only.[23] In most cases, the eviction will have happened and so an emergency grant of legal aid using delegated functions will be appropriate (unless the client is simply seeking

23 LASPO Sch 1 Part 1 para 33.

damages, not reinstatement). However, a 'reasonably alleged' threat of unlawful eviction will be in scope,[24] including by way of withdrawal of services such as utilities,[25] and in such a case, Legal Help to advise and issue a warning letter may be more appropriate.

12.34   That being said, legal representation may be granted under delegated functions in appropriate cases in order to apply to the court for an injunction prohibiting the landlord from carrying out an unlawful eviction where there is a credible threat to do so. Justification should be set out clearly in the application.

12.35   The merits test for legal representation is:[26]

- the standard criteria are met (see para 5.94 above);
- the proportionality test is met (see para 5.108 above);
- prospects of success are:
  - moderate or better; or
  - borderline or marginal, and the case is of significant wider public interest or of overwhelming importance to the individual;
- the landlord or other person responsible for the matter complained of has been notified of the complaint (except where this is impracticable) and, where notice has been given, has had a reasonable opportunity to resolve the matter.

12.36   Where a claim is primarily for damages rather than reinstatement, it is still in scope, but you will need to explain on the legal aid application why a conditional fee agreement is not appropriate. The Lord Chancellor's guidance suggests a Conditional Fee Agreement (CFA) will be considered suitable – and so legal aid refused – if:[27]

- prospects of success are at least 60 per cent;
- the opponent is considered able to meet any costs and damages awarded;
- after the event (ATE) insurance can be obtained;

---

24 FAQ 84, Civil Legal Aid Reform FAQs – no longer on the LAA website, but available at: https://legalaidhandbook.files.wordpress.com/2013/04/legal-aid-reform-faq-v3.pdf.

25 FAQ 105, Civil Legal Aid Reform FAQs – no longer on the LAA website, but available at: https://legalaidhandbook.files.wordpress.com/2013/04/legal-aid-reform-faq-v3.pdf.

26 Civil Legal Aid (Merits Criteria) Regulations 2013 reg 63. Note that the prospects of success criterion is contained in reg 43, which was amended by Civil Legal Aid (Merits Criteria) (Amendment) Regulations 2016 reg 2(4) to allow for grants in the borderline and marginal, but not poor, categories.

27 *Lord Chancellor's guidance on civil legal aid* (2018) para 7.17.

- where you are relying on the non-availability of ATE insurance, you will be expected to provide evidence of having tried and failed to obtain it. (See paras 5.98–5.99 for more information.)

Remember that in any claim for damages you must advise your client as to the operation of the LAA's statutory charge.

Housing conditions and disrepair

12.37 For legal aid purposes, disrepair and housing conditions cases can be considered separately as (i) freestanding claims and (ii) counter-claims respectively. Each has their own distinct rules.

12.38 It is considered that, absent any further rules or guidance issued by the LAA, freestanding claims and counterclaims brought pursu-ant to the Homes (Fitness for Human Habitation) Act (H(FHH)A) 2018 will be in scope for legal aid in the same way and to the same extent as disrepair claims. In this chapter, then, we refer to 'disrepair and housing conditions' to mean traditional disrepair claims *and* claims brought under the amendments to sections 8 to 10 of the Landlord and Tenant Act 1985 by the H(FHH)A 2018.

Freestanding disrepair and housing conditions claims

12.39 Disrepair and housing conditions claims are in scope, but only in limited circumstances. LASPO Sch 1 Part 1 para 35 says:

(1) Civil legal services provided to an individual in relation to the removal or reduction of a serious risk of harm to the health or safety of the individual or a relevant member of the individual's family where–
   (a) the risk arises from a deficiency in the individual's home,
   (b) the individual's home is rented or leased from another person, and
   (c) the services are provided with a view to securing that the other person makes arrangements to remove or reduce the risk.
(2) Sub-paragraph (1) is subject to–
   (a) the exclusions in Part 2 of this Schedule, with the exception of paragraphs 6 and 8 of that Part, and
   (b) the exclusion in Part 3 of this Schedule.
(3) For the purposes of this paragraph–
   (a) a child is a relevant member of an individual's family if the individual is the child's parent or has parental responsibility for the child;
   (b) an adult ('A') is a relevant member of an individual's family if–

> (i) they are relatives (whether of the full blood or half blood or by marriage or civil partnership) or cohabitants, and
>
> (ii) the individual's home is also A's home.
>
> (4) In this paragraph–
>
>   'adult' means a person aged 18 or over;
>
>   'building' includes part of a building;
>
>   'child' means a person under the age of 18;
>
>   'cohabitant' has the same meaning as in Part 4 of the Family Law Act 1996 (see section 62(1) of that Act);
>
>   'deficiency' means any deficiency, whether arising as a result of the construction of a building, an absence of maintenance or repair, or otherwise;
>
>   'harm' includes temporary harm;
>
>   'health' includes mental health;
>
>   'home', in relation to an individual, means the house, caravan, houseboat or other vehicle or structure that is the individual's only or main residence, together with any garden or ground usually occupied with it.

12.40   The merits test for a disrepair claim is:

- the standard criteria are met (see para 5.94 above);
- the proportionality test is met (see para 5.108 above);
- prospects of success are:
    - moderate or better; or
    - borderline or marginal, and the case is of significant wider public interest or of overwhelming importance to the individual; and
- the landlord or other person responsible for the matter complained of has been notified of the complaint (except where this is impracticable) and, where notice has been given, has had a reasonable opportunity to resolve the matter.

12.41   Therefore, legal aid is only available to remove or reduce a serious risk of harm to the client or a member of his or her family. This means that it is available to force repairs to be done, and/or work to make the premises fit for habitation, but not to claim damages.

12.42   In order to be eligible for legal aid, there must at least be a credible allegation that there is such a risk.[28] Once that threshold is crossed, Legal Help will be available to investigate further, including by obtaining expert reports. If after investigation it transpires that there was no serious risk of harm, then legal aid should be withdrawn, though the costs of the investigation will be claimable.

---

28 *Lord Chancellor's guidance on civil legal aid* (2018) para 12.6, Standard Civil Contract Specification 2018 para 10.10.

12.43   The costs of expert reports should be limited to the maximum set out in the remuneration regulations[29] and if they are, you do not need to apply for prior authority. However, if you need to go above those levels, you can apply for prior authority to do so if working under a certificate. There is no way of applying for prior authority in Legal Help cases, and so you should make a note on the file explaining why you believe the exceptional circumstances criteria are met.[30] The criteria are that the complexity of the material is such that an expert with a high level of seniority is required, or the material is so specialised and unusual that only very few experts are available.[31] These criteria are unlikely to be met in most disrepair and housing conditions cases.

12.44   Any expert instructed should generally be a joint expert in accordance with the Housing Disrepair Cases Pre-Action Protocol,[32] though additional medical evidence may be necessary to show that there is a serious risk of harm in the particular client's circumstances. The LAA recognises that the risk may vary from individual to individual – the risk, for example, arising from damp is higher for a tenant with a respiratory illness than a tenant without one.[33] There is, however, no specific evidential requirement to establish a serious risk of harm.[34] If the LAA does not agree that there is a serious risk, and so considers funding is not justified, there is a right to request a review by the Director, but no right of appeal to an independent funding adjudicator.[35] Any further challenge would have to be by way of judicial review.

---

29 The current rates can be found in Civil Legal Aid (Remuneration) (Amendment) Regulations 2013 Sch 2; following the 20 per cent reduction in rates that took place in December 2013, Civil Legal Aid (Remuneration) Regulations 2013 Sch 5 is no longer current for cases started after that date.

30 FAQ 86, Civil Legal Aid Reform FAQs – no longer on the LAA website, but available at: https://legalaidhandbook.files.wordpress.com/2013/04/legal-aid-reform-faq-v3.pdf.

31 Civil Legal Aid (Remuneration) Regulations 2013 Sch 5 para 2.

32 *Lord Chancellor's guidance on civil legal aid* (2018) para 12.7.

33 *Lord Chancellor's guidance on civil legal aid* (2018) para 12.9.

34 FAQ 79, Civil Legal Aid Reform FAQs – no longer on the LAA website, but available at: https://legalaidhandbook.files.wordpress.com/2013/04/legal- aid-reform-faq-v3.pdf.

35 FAQ 80, Civil Legal Aid Reform FAQs – no longer on the LAA website, but available at: https://legalaidhandbook.files.wordpress.com/2013/04/legal-aid-reform-faq-v3.pdf.

12.45   The Lord Chancellor's guidance says that all relevant factors will be taken into account in determining whether there is a serious risk of harm, including the following (non-exhaustive) list of examples:[36]

- whether harm has already resulted;
- whether, as a result of the deficiency, an existing health condition has been exacerbated;
- whether the individual or any family members are in a high risk group, such as the elderly or very young children;
- whether the individual or any family member is vulnerable due to a disability, either because of risk to them, or damage to medical equipment;
- whether there are relevant environmental conditions – such as broken heating in winter;
- whether there are multiple deficiencies that could, taken cumulatively, be of greater seriousness;
- whether a single deficiency poses multiple risks;
- whether a deficiency affects shared rooms or areas;
- whether an instructed expert reports that future deterioration is likely;
- whether the local authority has identified hazards.

12.46   Freestanding damages claims are out of scope under LASPO. Where you claim both for enforcement of repairs and other works and for damages, you should separate the work done on the file and ensure that you do not claim any work done in respect of the damages aspect on your legal aid bill.

12.47   However, it should also be noted that the LAA takes the view that the statutory charge applies to the whole proceedings, not just the funded part.[37] So if you recover damages as part of a case for which you have legal aid, even if the damages part was out of scope and you have made no claim for work done in respect of it, your client will be required to pay the costs of the in-scope part of the case out of any damages recovered. See also para 5.165 in this book, and chapter 4 of Luba, O'Donnell and Peaker, *Housing Conditions: tenants' rights*.[38]

12.48   It may therefore be in the client's best interests to bring a claim where the damages element is more than purely nominal under a

---

36 *Lord Chancellor's guidance on civil legal aid* (2018) para 12.10.

37 FAQ 81, Civil Legal Aid Reform FAQs – no longer on the LAA website, but available at: https://legalaidhandbook.files.wordpress.com/2013/04/legal- aid-reform-faq-v3.pdf.

38 LAG, sixth edition, 2019.

CFA. In any event, the LAA is likely to take the view that a claim involving a substantial damages element is likely to be suitable for a CFA, and so refuse a certificate on that basis. See paras 5.98–5.99 above for more on suitability for a CFA.

12.49 Where a client is eligible for legal aid then the work to gather evidence to consider whether a case is suitable for a CFA or not can usefully be done under Legal Help. It can then be decided what is the best way to progress the claim further.

12.50 Statutory nuisance proceedings under Environmental Protection Act (EPA) 1990 s82 are in scope.[39] However, the combined effect of LASPO Sch 1 Part 1 para 35(2)(b) and Part 3 is to exclude the provision of advocacy services in the magistrates' court.

12.51 It is thought likely that the innovations brought about by the H(FHH)A 2018 may mean that EPA 1990 proceedings may be more utilised than currently, but, given that legal aid is not available for representation in EPA 1990 claims, that would be under legal help with a view to using a CFA for representation.

Disrepair counterclaims

12.52 Disrepair and housing conditions counterclaims in possession proceedings are in scope (see para 12.2 above), and unlike with freestanding claims, counterclaims for damages are included.[40] The Part 2[41] exclusions of assault, battery and false imprisonment claims, trespass to goods and trespass to land, damage to property and breach of statutory duty do not apply to counterclaims in possession proceedings, so all may be pleaded and claimed for.[42] As set out above at para 12.18, Personal Injury counterclaims are excluded and so exceptional case funding would be needed if that were to be pursued.

12.53 However, if a tenant withholds rent in order to provoke possession proceedings, and then counterclaims for disrepair and/or housing conditions, legal aid is likely to be refused.[43] This is because legal aid will only be granted if the Director is satisfied it would be

---

39 FAQ 104, Civil Legal Aid Reform FAQs – no longer on the LAA website, but available at: https://legalaidhandbook.files.wordpress.com/2013/04/legal-aid-reform-faq-v3.pdf.
40 LASPO Sch 1 Part 1 para 33(6)(a).
41 LASPO Sch 1 Part 2.
42 LASPO Sch 1 Part 1 para 33(6).
43 *Lord Chancellor's guidance on civil legal aid* (2018) para 7.4(c).

reasonable to do so in light of the applicant's conduct.[44] It appears that this provision has caused little difficulty in practice.[45]

12.54   The Part 2[46] exclusions of assault, battery and false imprisonment claims, trespass to goods and trespass to land, damage to property and breach of statutory duty do not apply to claims for unlawful eviction, so all may be pleaded and claimed for.[47] Personal injury counterclaims are not re-included for counterclaims and so are not in scope – see para 12.18 above.

12.55   Many practitioners have found bringing a counterclaim a useful way to bring funded disrepair cases (and are likely to do so for housing conditions cases) where there has previously been a possession order but before execution of the warrant. If the counterclaim is successful to the extent of extinguishing the arrears, then an application can be made to discharge the possession order. If a counterclaim exceeds any rent or other set-off, then the statutory charge would apply to the excess amount in the normal way. Because of this, clients must be informed for the potential operation of the statutory charge at the outset of the case.

Harassment

12.56   Legal aid is available to victims of harassment to bring an application for an order under Protection from Harassment Act 1997 s3 or s3A, and to defend against such an application. It will only be in the housing category where the injunction arises out of a housing issue, such as harassment by a landlord or arising out of a neighbour dispute. The merits test for legal representation is:[48]

- the standard criteria are met (see para 5.94 above);
- the proportionality test is met (see para 5.108 above);
- prospects of success are:
  - moderate or better; or
  - borderline or marginal, and the case is of significant wider public interest or of overwhelming importance to the individual; and

---

44   Civil Legal Aid (Merits Criteria) Regulations 2013 reg 11(6).

45   See Jan Luba QC and Sara Stephens, 'Sorting myths from facts over housing cases' November 2014 *Legal Action* 10.

46   LASPO Sch 1 Part 2.

47   LASPO Sch 1 Part 1 para 33(7).

48   Civil Legal Aid (Merits Criteria) Regulations 2013 reg 63. Note that the prospects of success criterion is contained in reg 43, which was amended by Civil Legal Aid (Merits Criteria) (Amendment) Regulations 2016 reg 2(4) to allow for grants in the borderline and marginal, but not poor, categories.

- the landlord or other person responsible for the matter complained of has been notified of the complaint (except where this is impracticable) and, where notice has been given, has had a reasonable opportunity to resolve the matter.

12.57 Legal Help will be available to advise prior to proceedings and to issue a warning letter.

Anti-social behaviour

12.58 Injunctions under the Anti-Social Behaviour, Crime and Policing Act (ASBCPA) 2014 are in scope, but even where they arise out of a housing issue, are in the 'miscellaneous' category. Advice funded by Legal Help, and representation in the County Court or Youth Court by certificate, will be available in the usual way. Even though applications for injunctions against under 18s are dealt with in the Youth Court, they are still deemed to be civil cases for the purposes of legal aid. Where you have general authorisation to do so, you can grant an emergency certificate using delegated functions. If not, you can apply to the LAA in the usual way for a certificate. However, you can only grant Legal Help if you have sufficient 'miscellaneous' matter starts on your contract schedule.

12.59 If the only proceedings are possession proceedings brought on grounds of anti-social behaviour then just as with any other possession proceedings a certificate with the proceeding wording *Recover Possession – tenant – Housing* is all that is required.

12.60 If only ASBCPA 2014 injunction proceedings are in play, then you will simply need a certificate with the *ASBO* proceedings wording.

12.61 If an injunction application is being made in the same proceedings as possession is sought then you will need to apply for a certificate with both *Recover Possession – tenant – Housing* proceeding wording and *ASBO* wording, much like the procedure for applying for *Counterclaim* proceedings alongside *Recover Possession* proceedings as described at para 12.2 above.

12.62 If there are separately issued proceedings for an ASBCPA 2014 injunction on the one hand and possession proceedings on the other, then you will need to apply for a separate certificate for each set of proceedings, each with an appropriate proceedings wording.

12.63 Breach of injunction proceedings, although dealt with in the County Court (for adults) are deemed by the LAA to fall within the crime category and the provisions of the Crime Contract. Civil practitioners whose firm does not have a crime contract can apply for an individual case contract (ICC) to represent an existing individual client. Where there are conjoined injunction and possession proceedings and within those proceedings an application for committal for breach of an ASBCPA 2014 injunction is made the practitioner should apply for a criminal Representation Order from the LAA to be covered for the work carried out on the breach proceedings.

12.64   Funding of breach proceedings are paid by way of a fixed fee under the crime provisions (see chapter 16 for more details). Counsel is assigned automatically and so will be paid at hourly rates. There is no means test for breach proceedings.

12.65   Applications for funding of breach proceedings is by way of CRM14 form online through the LAA online portal or by email in the case of an ICC.[49]

12.66   Civil legal aid only covers Part 1 of ASBCPA 2014 so because closure orders do not come under Part 1 they are excluded. You would need to refer your client to a criminal practitioner to deal with closure order proceedings, although you can grant legal aid under the possession proceedings wordings to defend possession proceedings which rely on Housing Act 1988 Sch 2 ground 7A and Housing Act 1985 s84A.

Other housing work

12.67   All other housing cases are outside the scope of legal aid. However, applications for exceptional funding can be made – see chapter 4.

Housing Possession Court Duty Scheme

12.68   The service involves the provision at court, of emergency 'on-the-day' face-to-face advice, assistance and advocacy to anyone who is faced with a risk of losing his or her home as a result of possession and associated proceedings. Representation at a court duty session is not means or merits tested, but a means assessment must be carried out along with the collection of basic client details on the Housing Possession Court Duty Scheme (HPCDS) Client Monitoring Form. After the hearing, a follow-up advice letter must be sent to the client.

---

49 https://assets.publishing.service.gov.uk/government/uploads/system/uploads/attachment_data/file/620025/part-1-asbcpa-injunction-guidance.pdf.

12.69   Duty scheme advisers can claim a fixed fee for each client seen. If no clients are seen in a session, then one fixed amount is paid for attendance.

12.70   If you make a claim under the HPCD Scheme, then you cannot provide assistance on the same matter under the Legal Help Scheme. Practitioners will therefore want to try to make sure that work following the duty hearing can be done under a representation certificate granted under delegated functions if at all possible.

12.71   If you have advised a client on a duty scheme who was in court for mortgage possession, you will need to refer the client to the telephone gateway unless the client is exempt; or you can go straight to full legal representation in appropriate cases. The mandatory gateway will end in spring 2020, so check the Legal Aid Handbook website – www.legalaidhandbook.com – for further information.

12.72   The HPCD Schemes were re-tendered in 2018, but after a successful challenge by Law Centres Network the decision to 'bundle up' the courts into larger scheme areas (from 113 to 47) was held to be irrational and in breach of the public sector equality duty.[50] The decision was quashed and the matter remitted to the Lord Chancellor for reconsideration which resulted in the original contracts being extended for a further year. In August 2019 contract holders received a further extension for one year to 30 September 2020 pending further consideration by the LAA. This means that the 2013 Civil Contract applies to HPCD Schemes.[51]

Flexible Operating Hours

12.73   On 2 September 2019, two county courts commenced a pilot of Flexible Operating Hours (FOH), at Brentford and Manchester Civil Justice Centre where they will trial extended opening hours. Brentford is piloting early starts (8am–10.30am) and late finishing (4.30pm–7pm) for civil work. Manchester will pilot the later session only for civil and family work. It will run for six months – until the 13 March 2020.

12.74   A participation fee of £100 will be paid to housing duty advisers attending a HCPDS FOH slot in a single court room. If a slot includes HPCDS hearings in two different court rooms, it appears

---

50   *R (Law Centres Federation Limited t/a Law Centres Network) v Lord Chancellor* [2018] EWHC 1588 (Admin).
51   Standard Civil Contract (as amended) 2013.

two fees of £100 can be claimed. These fees are in addition to the normal HCPDS contract fees.[52]

12.75   In respect of all other hearings where a client is represented under legal aid, be it Help at Court or a Representation Certificate, a fee of £50 for a single hearing in a single FOH court room can be claimed in addition to the normal legal aid hourly rate. The fee is claimed by the advocate attending (solicitor or barrister). If a provider attends more than one single hearing within a single FOH session in a single court room, then the maximum number of fees claimable is two (ie 2 x £50). A claim for a fee does not have to wait for the legal aid case to be billed and a claim can be made within the same month as the hearing is listed. If the advocate attends court but the hearing is cancelled at the last minute, then the fee is still claimable.

---

52 Guidance as to the participation fees as well as the claim form can be found at:
https://assets.publishing.service.gov.uk/government/uploads/system/uploads/
attachment_data/file/822666/HMCTS_Flexible_Operating_Hours_-_Pilot_
Participation_Fee_Guidance_v.1a__July_2019_.pdf?_
ga=2.58298410.149788027.1566817931-1766719165.1529322761.

CHAPTER 13

Conducting a community care case

by Silvia Nicolaou Garcia

Introduction

13.1   This chapter deals with work done in the community care category. You should read it in conjunction with chapters 3 and 5. Chapter 3 deals with general rules about taking on civil cases and applies to work in community care as it does to all other work; chapter 5 deals with the rules that apply to the conduct of all civil cases. The community care rules in this chapter usually build on, rather than replace, the general rules: where they do replace the general rules in chapters 3 and 5, we will say so.

13.2   See appendix C for a summary of the Legal Aid Agency's (LAA's) Costs assessment guidance, in respect of the most common queries raised by caseworkers.

What is community care law?

13.3   Community care law covers access to health and social services from the National Health Service (NHS) or local authorities. Community care cases affect adults and children alike. They often relate to an individual's care and wellbeing but can also relate to decisions about policy and strategy such as increased charging or reductions in service provision.[1]

13.4   Most community care cases cover legal advice and challenges relating to:

- the provision of services by local authority social departments, both to children and young people (generally under the Children Act 1989[2]) and to adults, now largely under the framework of the Care Act 2014;
- the provision of services by local authority social services departments and clinical commissioning groups (CCGs) in relation to aftercare services under the Mental Health Act 1983 s117.

13.5   Cases are often sensitive and urgent, and it is important for practitioners to know the community care funding regime and to satisfy themselves that the work is within scope before undertaking community care legal aid work.[3]

---

1 Funding regimes for court of protection cases are outside the scope of this chapter.
2 Excluding matters within the family public law category – see chapter 8.
3 Standard Civil Contract 2018 Specification, Category Specific Rules: Community Care, section 11: www.gov.uk/government/uploads/system/uploads/attachment_data/file/645391/2018-standard-civil-contract-category-specific-rules-community-care_-section_11.pdf.

What community care law is within the scope of legal aid?

13.6   Under Legal Aid, Sentencing and Punishment of Offenders Act 2012 (LASPO) Sch 1 Part 1 para 6, 'community care services' are defined as:

- Part 3 of the National Assistance Act 1948 ('the 1948 Act') (local authority support for children and families);
- section 47 of the 1948 Act (removal to suitable premises of persons in need of care and attention);
- section 48 of the 1948 Act (temporary protection for property of persons admitted to hospital);
- section 45 of the Health Services and Public Health Act 1968 (arrangements for promoting welfare of old people);
- section 117 of the Mental Health Act 1983 (after-care);
- section 17 of the Children Act 1989 ('the 1989 Act') (provision of services for children in need);
- section 20 of the 1989 Act (provision of accommodation for children);
- sections 22A, 22B, 22C and 23 of the 1989 Act (accommodation and maintenance for children in care and looked after children);
- sections 23B and 23C of the 1989 Act (local authority functions in respect of relevant children);
- sections 24, 24A and 24B of the 1989 Act (provision of services for persons qualifying for advice and assistance);
- section 2 of the Carers and Disabled Children Act 2000 (services for carers);
- section 192 of, and Schedule 15 to, the National Health Service (Wales) Act 2006 (functions of local social service authorities);
- Part 1 of the Care Act 2014.

13.7   Examples of community care cases within scope which practitioners often encounter could include:

- a family not getting the help that they need to care for a severely disabled child;
- a 16-year-old who has fled an abusive home and has nowhere to sleep that night;
- a family with no recourse to public funds who have finally exhausted the resources of the friends whose floors they have been sleeping on;
- a trafficked child whose age is disbelieved by the Home Office who is being wrongly treated as an adult and who is homeless and in need of support and accommodation;

- a 17-year-old in a young offender institution who has been approved for early release but has nowhere safe to go;
- a care-leaver who is not being given the support she needs to pursue her education;
- an adult previously detained under Mental Health Act 1983 s3 who has not been provided with adequate aftercare services on discharge.

13.8   This chapter will deal with some of the most common types of community care work in scope in more detail.

Who can do community care law?

13.9   Under the Standard Civil Contract 2018, community care contracts are commissioned by procurement area and require permanent presence.[4] To do community care work at all, you must have a schedule authorisation for at least one procurement area.

Levels of funding for community care work

13.10   Legal Help will cover initial advice and assistance including: taking instructions, consideration of any assessments carried out by local authorities and drafting pre-action protocol letters under the Judicial Review Pre-Action Protocol. A certificate for legal representation (full representation) will cover an application for judicial review. The merits test for a full representation certificate in community care cases is the same as for public law cases more generally.[5] The test is:

- for the standard criteria to be met (see para 5.94 above);
- for a letter before claim to have been sent to the proposed defendant (except where impracticable) and for the defendant to have been given a reasonable time to respond;
- for the proportionality test to be met (see para 5.108 above);
- for the prospects of success to be: very good, good or moderate; or, borderline and for the case to be of significant wider public interest or of overwhelming importance to the individual or the

---

4   Standard Civil Contract Specification 2018 para 2.32.
5   Civil Legal Aid (Merits Criteria Regulations) 2013 reg 56 as amended by the Civil Legal Aid (Merits Criteria) (Amendment) (No 2) Regulations 2015 and the Civil Legal Aid (Merits Criteria) (Amendment) Regulations 2016.

substance of the case relates to a breach of European Convention on Human Rights (ECHR) rights.

13.11 The merits test for an investigative representation certificate in community care cases is the same as for public law cases generally.[6] The test is:

- for the standard criteria in reg 40 to be met (see para 5.94 above): unclear prospects of success and substantial investigative work required before those prospects can be determined; once the investigative work is completed, the case will satisfy the criteria for full representation and will meet the cost benefit criteria; if it is a claim for damages which does not meet £5,000, the case must be of significant wider public interest;
- for the claimant to have notified the proposed defendant of the potential challenge and given reasonable time for the defendant to respond (unless impracticable).

13.12 Some practitioners report that it is very difficult to obtain investigative representation for public law challenges. When applying for investigative representation, practitioners need to show that they are in a position to consider whether or not the prospects of success in relation to a claim for judicial review are unclear (and substantial work needs to be done to ascertain the merits of a case), rather than at the early stage of taking initial instructions from their client, as this initial work would fall under the ambit of the legal help scheme rather than a funding certificate.

How to conduct a community care case

13.13 There are distinct statutory frameworks governing community care for children and for adults. Both, however, follow the same basic pattern: in certain defined circumstances, a local authority will have i) a duty to assess a person's needs; and ii) a duty or a power to formulate and implement a plan to meet certain of those needs by providing services.

13.14 Challenges can be brought regarding:

- a failure to assess needs;
- an inadequate assessment of needs;

---

6 Civil Legal Aid (Merits Criteria Regulations) 2013 reg 57 as amended by the Civil Legal Aid (Merits Criteria) (Amendment) (No 2) Regulations 2015 and the Civil Legal Aid (Merits Criteria) (Amendment) Regulations 2016.

- an unlawful plan to meet needs; or
- a failure to implement a care plan.

13.15   Work will normally be started on a Legal Help file and full represent-ation will be applied for later on, after either sending a pre-action protocol letter, giving the defendant enough time to reply and/or after putting the defendant on notice. If the merits of the case are unclear, and substantial work needs to be done to ascertain the merits of the case, then investigative representation should be applied for (see chapter 5 for further details of investigative and full representa-tion). Where possible, delegated functions should be used.

National Assistance Act 1948

13.16   Part 3 of the National Assistance Act 1948 cases (ss21–36) and ss45, 47 and 48 are in scope and in the community care category. The Care Act 2014 brought together and replaced many of the existing statutes, regulations and guidance, including: the National Assistance Act 1948; Health Services and Public Health Act 1968; Chronically Sick and Disabled Persons Act 1970; Health and Social Services and Security Adjudications Act 1983; Disabled Persons (Services, Consultation and Representation) Act 1986; parts of the NHS and Community Care Act 1990; and parts of the Health and Social Care Act 2001.[7] It is unclear how many 1948 claims will be live since the relevant provisions of the Care Act 2014 came into force.

13.17   The Care and Support statutory guidance makes clear that Part 3 of the National Assistance Act 1948 will be used to determine ordin-ary residence in respect of a period which falls before 1 April 2015.[8] This commonly arises where two local authorities are in dispute about the place of ordinary residence of a person.

13.18   The relevant provisions of the National Assistance Act 1948 have been disapplied in relation to England by the Care Act 2014 and Children and Families Act 2014 (Consequential Amendments) Order 2015. However, under article 3(3) of that order, despite the amend-ments made by that order, provisions of the 1948 Act that operate in relation to, or by reference to, support or services provided, or

---

7   See Care and support statutory guidance, Annex 1 (Repeals and Revocations): www.gov.uk/government/publications/care-act-statutory-guidance/care-and-support-statutory-guidance for full details of the legal provisions and statutory guidance replaced by the Care Act 2014.

8   Care and support statutory guidance para 19.77: www.gov.uk/government/publications/care-act-statutory-guidance/care-and-support-statutory-guidance#AnnexI.

payments towards the cost of support or services made, before or on or after 1 April 2015 and anything done under such provision, continue to have effect for the purposes of that support or those services or payments. Also, by virtue of transitional provisions, any question as to a person's ordinary residence arising under the 1948 Act which is to be determined by the secretary of state on or after 1 April 2015 is to be determined in accordance with section 40 of the Care Act 2014 (disputes about ordinary residence).

Mental Health Act 1983 s117

13.19 Persons who cease to be detained under certain provisions of the Mental Health Act 1983 (ss3, 37, 45A and 48) are entitled to after-care services from the relevant Clinical Commissioning Group (CCG) and local authority, until both organisations are satisfied that the person is no longer in need of such services. After-care services comprise any service within reason necessary to meet a need arising from a person's continued mental disorder including medication, counselling and accommodation plus care and social support. The Care Act 2014 amended the Mental Health Act 1983 s117 to make it clearer which authority bears responsibility for the provision of after-care services.

13.20 Challenges to failures to provide support under the Mental Health Act 1983 s117 are in scope and in the community care category. Legal Help will cover initial advice and assistance including travel to the hospital, taking instructions, considering any assessments and drafting Judicial Review Pre-action Protocol letters. Legal aid (full representation or investigative representation) could then be applied for by making an application on the Client and Cost Management System (CCMS). Delegated functions cannot be used in section 117 cases.[9]

Children Act 1989

Main provisions of the Act

13.21 Legal aid (both Legal Help and legal representation) is available in the community law category to provide advice and representation to individuals seeking accommodation and support under certain community care provisions (as set out in LASPO Sch 1 Part 1 para 6). The main provisions of the Children Act 1989 that are in scope are:

---

9 www.gov.uk/guidance/work-out-who-qualifies-for-civil-legal-aid.

- section 17: provision of services for children in need and their families;
- section 20: provision of accommodation for homeless children;
- sections 22A, 22B, 22C, 23, 23B, 23C, 24, 24A and 24B: the leaving care provisions.

Means in Children Act 1989 cases

13.22   For Legal Help cases, when assessing the means of a child, the resources of a parent, guardian or other person who is responsible for maintaining the child, or who usually contributes substantially to the child's maintenance, must be taken into account, as well as any assets of the child. There is a discretion not to aggregate assets in this way if it appears inequitable to do so, having regard to all the circumstances, including the age and resources of the child and any conflict of interest between the child and the adult(s). For example, it might be inequitable to aggregate the resources of a 17-year-old child who is estranged from his parents and living separately from them and who is fully financially independent from his parents.[10]

13.23   For legal representation cases, financial determination will normally be carried out using the child's resources. However, where the application is made in respect of family proceedings, the resources of a parent, guardian or any other person who is responsible for maintaining the child, or who usually contributes substantially to the child's maintenance, are required to be treated as the child's resources (ie, they are aggregated), unless having regard to all the circumstances including the age and resources of the child and any conflict of interest, it appears inequitable to do so. A legal aid application on behalf of a child must be made by: i) the person who is or proposes to be the child's litigation friend, professional children's guardian or parental order reporter; or ii) the proposed practitioner in proceedings which the child may conduct without a children's guardian or litigation friend in accordance with rule 16.6 of the Family Procedure Rules 2010 or rule 21.2 of the Civil Procedure Rules 1998.[11]

13.24   Practitioners report having mixed experience when working on community care cases on behalf of children. For initial work done on Legal Help, the parent's means will be aggregated, unless there are exceptional reasons as to why this should not be the case, such as a

---

10 Controlled work eligibility guidance para 9: www.gov.uk/government/uploads/system/uploads/attachment_data/file/420970/laa-determine-controlled-work-mediation.pdf.

11 Civil Legal Aid (Procedure) Regulations 2012 reg 30(2).

conflict of interest for example. For legal representation cases, the means for the children should not be aggregated to the parents' means. It is important to note that the LAA will seek to aggregate parental means. Practitioners appealing decisions from the LAA should bear in mind that for the parents' means not to be aggregated, it is important to show that the cause of action will benefit the child and that it is appropriate only for the child to bring the claim, not for the parent. For large-scale policy challenge cases, the LAA will seek to aggregate the parents' means.

Children Act 1989 s17 work

13.25   The provision of services to children 'in need' lies at the heart of local authority duties towards children and families. The duty to provide services to children 'in need' and their families arises following an assessment, which must be concluded in accordance with the relevant statutory guidance.[12] It is only following assessment that a local authority can decide whether or not it is necessary to provide a child or family member with services. Common challenges under Children Act 1989 s17 include: failure to conduct an assessment; failure to accommodate and support pending an assessment; withdrawal of section 17 support; and accommodation out of area.

13.26   Practitioners acting for children and families in need of section 17 support should ensure that they gather enough evidence in relation to the means of their clients. If the clients and their families have been supported by family members, friends or community groups, it will be necessary to get a statement of support from each of these individuals. This will be required for both Legal Help and legal representation work. In September 2018, a change was made to allow the use of delegated functions in Children Act 1989 s17 homeless judicial reviews. The LAA has now clarified its position in relation to the scope of delegated functions to grant emergency representation for urgent homelessness judicial reviews. The position reverts back to the position before September 2018. Delegated functions cannot be used in s17 Children Act 1989 judicial reviews.[13]

---

12 www.gov.uk/government/uploads/system/uploads/attachment_data/file/683115/Changes_to_statutory_guidance-_Working_Together_to_Safeguard_Children.pdf.

13 www.lag.org.uk/article/206294/keeping-up-with-delegated-functions.

Children Act 1989 s20 work

13.27   Children Act 1989 s20 places local authorities under a 'specific' statutory duty to provide accommodation for any child in need within
their area who requires accommodation as a result of:

    a) there being no person who has parental responsibility for the
child;

    b) the child being lost or having being abandoned; or

    c) the person who has been caring for the child being prevented
(whether or not permanently, and for whatever reason) from
providing the child with suitable care accommodation or care.

13.28   The law concerning the duties and powers contained in Children Act
1989 s20 is clear following the landmark House of Lords case of *R
(G) v Southwark LBC*.[14] It is therefore surprising that a decade after
these cases local authorities still misunderstand the nature of the
Children Act 1989 s20 duty. It is often necessary to send a Judicial
Review Pre-action Protocol letter or even issue proceedings, to secure
appropriate accommodation for child clients who are street homeless, 'sofa-surfing' or in unsuitable accommodation (for example,
asylum support accommodation for adults or bed and breakfast
accommodation). There are a number of specific issues arising from
particular categories of children requiring accommodation, such as:

- children in custody;
- children at risk of gang violence;
- unaccompanied asylum-seeking children (UASC);
- trafficked children;
- child victims of sexual abuse; and
- children at risk of going missing.

Because of this, practitioners will be involved in section 20 challenges that often relate to, not just the requirement of a roof over
the child's head, but also to the suitability of the section 20
accommodation.

13.29   Children Act 1989 s20 cases are often very urgent, and practitioners have delegated functions to grant emergency funding in these
cases[15] (see chapter 5).

---

14 [2009] UKHL 26, [2009] 1 WLR 1299.

15 www.gov.uk/government/news/civil-news-delegated-functions-for-emergency-
homelessness-jrs.

Age assessment cases

13.30 Community care practitioners will also often act for children from abroad whose age has not been correctly determined, either by the Home Office or by a local authority.

13.31 Challenges to local authority age assessments (or failure to conduct age assessments) are within scope, given that a failure to conduct a lawful age assessment of the age of an unaccompanied asylum-seeking children will result in no services being provided to the child under the Children Act 1989.[16]

Children Act 1989 leaving care work

13.32 Care leavers are a particularly vulnerable group, more prone to homelessness and unemployment than other young adults. If a child is accommodated by a local authority for 13 weeks between the ages of 14 and 18 with at least one day being on or after the child's 16th birthday, he or she becomes entitled to a wide range of long-term support set out in Children Act 1989 ss23A–23C and Sch 2, and the Care Leavers (England) Regulations 2010.

13.33 Common challenges for practitioners acting for this client group include:

- challenges to the failure of support and accommodation;
- challenges to pathway plans including failure to support and assist to the extent that the young person's education, training or welfare requires;
- failure to appoint a personal adviser; and
- retrospective Children Act 1989 s20 cases, for young adults who should have been looked after under section 20 by a local authority and were not.

13.34 Delegated functions cannot be used for leaving care cases.[17]

Children Act 1989 s24 work

13.35 Many children and young people who spend time in care will not accumulate the requisite period of 13 weeks spent as a 'looked after' child in order to qualify for the full leaving care package. However,

16 Services under Part III of the Children Act 1989 are only available to children under 18 and their families, therefore, the assessment of a young person's age is a central issue for unaccompanied asylum-seeking children claiming to be children.

17 www.gov.uk/government/news/civil-news-delegated-functions-for-emergency-homelessness-jrs.

they may qualify for a more limited form of 'advice and assistance' under Children Act 1989 s24 from the responsible local authority, sometimes referred to as 'aftercare'. This work is in scope.

13.36   Delegated functions cannot be used for Children Act 1989 s24 cases.[18]

Care Act 2014

13.37   Adult social care in England is now largely governed by the Care Act 2014. The preamble to the Act describes it as:

> . . . an Act to make provision to reform the law relating to care and support for adults and the law relating to support for carers; to make provision about safeguarding adults from abuse or neglect; to make provision about care standards; to establish and make provision about health Education England; to establish and make provision about Health Research Authority; to make provision about integrating care and support with health services; and for connected purposes.

13.38   Part 1 of the Care Act is within the scope of legal aid[19] and sets out the general responsibilities of local authorities for care and support, and safeguarding, in relation to adults, carers and children becoming adults. Some sections came into force on 1 October 2014, but most of Part 1 came into force on 1 April 2015. Common challenges community care practitioners will work on are:

- failure to assess an adult's needs for care and support;
- failure to assess a carer's needs for support;
- refusal to assess;
- failure to accommodate and support pending assessment; and
- failure to safeguard adults at risk of abuse or harm.

13.39   Delegated functions can be used for Care Act 2014 s19(3) cases.[20]

Community care for people from abroad

13.40   In the last few years, a number of reported community care cases have involved the interaction of immigration, community care and

---

18 www.gov.uk/government/news/civil-news-delegated-functions-for-emergency-homelessness-jrs.

19 LASPO Sch 1 Part 1 para 6(n).

20 www.gov.uk/government/news/civil-news-delegated-functions-for-emergency-homelessness-jrs.

human rights law.[21] Nationality and immigration status might restrict the community care support clients get from local authorities.[22] In these types of cases, practitioners must ensure that their clients do not fall foul of Schedule 3 to the Nationality, Asylum and Immigration Act 2002. In such cases, practitioners whose clients are excluded by Schedule 3 will have to show that support is necessary to avoid a breach of their client's rights under European human rights law or EU law. In some cases, practitioners will ask local authorities to use their powers under section 1 of the Localism Act 2011 to provide accommodation and support to their clients who are not entitled to accommodation under the Care Act 2014 and who would otherwise have their European Convention of Human Rights (ECHR) breached.[23] These cases will normally be opened as community care cases and not public law cases.

13.41 Challenges to asylum support provided by the Home Office to asylum-seeking clients (also known as asylum support challenges) should be conducted under the housing contract or under the public law contract. See para 12.21 above.

13.42 When seeking evidence of means from clients from abroad for community care cases, it is important to obtain letters or statements of support from individuals supporting the clients before commencing work on the case, even where only non-cash support is being provided to the clients such as food, clothes or travel money. Practitioners report that the LAA are refusing to pay for work unless there is enough evidence of means, including letters or statements of support.

The use of litigation friends

13.43 Many community care clients will require litigation friends. Litigation friends make decisions about a court case for either:

- an adult who lacks the mental capacity to manage their own court case either with or without a solicitor;
- a child.

As such, practitioners need to be aware of the rules that apply to taking instructions from litigation friends, in particular as to who should be signing the legal aid forms and whose resources should be

---

21 *R (SL) v Westminster CC* [2013] UKSC 27; *R (GS) v Camden LBC* [2016] EWHC 1762 (Admin); *R (SG) v Haringey LBC* [2017] EWCA Civ 322; *R (AR) v Hammersmith and Fulham LBC* [2018] EWHC 3453 (Admin).

22 Nationality, Immigration and Asylum Act 2002 Sch 3 para 1.

23 *R (GS) v Camden LBC*, above.

taken into account when assessing financial eligibility. See chapters 3 and 5 for more information.

Community care damages claims

13.44   Claims for damages against social services do not fall within the community care contract and may come within the claims against public authorities or, if it is a claim under the Human Rights Act 1998, within the public law, categories.

CHAPTER 14

Conducting a public law case

by Silvia Nicolaou Garcia

Introduction

14.1   This chapter deals with work done in the public law category. You should read it in conjunction with chapters 3 and 5. Chapter 3 deals with general rules about taking on civil cases; chapter 5 deals with the rules that apply to the conduct of all civil cases. The public law rules in this chapter usually build on, rather than replace, the general rules: where they do replace the general rules in chapters 3 and 5 we will say so. See appendix C for a summary of the Legal Aid Agency's (LAA's) Cost Assessment Guidance, in respect of the most common queries raised by caseworkers.

Public law and judicial review

14.2   Public bodies, such as central and local government, have to obey the law. The type of law governing the conduct of public bodies is known as 'public law'.

14.3   Judicial review is a tool that enables individuals or groups to go to court to hold public bodies to account and determine if decision makers have acted:

- lawfully;
- rationally;
- fairly;
- in good faith;
- only using the powers that they have for their proper purposes; and
- compatibly with the human rights of those affected by their actions.

These are the public law principles which every public decision-maker must respect.

14.4   When a public body acts unlawfully, there are a number of ways in which individuals affected can challenge the decision. These include:

- using a public bodies' complaints procedure or the ombudsman;
- exercising the right of appeal to a tribunal;
- asking a public body to review its decision;
- judicial review proceedings.

14.5 Decision-makers also have to respect laws which protect fundamental rights and interests such as the Human Rights Act 1998, the Data Protection Act 1998, the Equality Act 2010 and European Union (EU) law. These help to ensure that people are treated with dignity, basic freedoms are not overridden, personal information is not misused and that characteristics fundamental to everyone's identity – age, disability, gender reassignment, marriage and civil partnership, pregnancy and maternity, race, religion or belief, sex, and sexual orientation – are respected and do not lead to unfair treatment.

14.6 Of all civil representation applications granted, around 3,000 a year relate to judicial review; 701 in the last quarter. The number granted in January to March 2019 decreased by three per cent compared with the same quarter in 2018. Over a third of judicial reviews were for public law.[1]

Overlaps between categories

14.7 The legal aid categories are drafted to ensure that the majority of cases fall within one category or another. However, some cases arise as a result of a number of different underlying issues so many cases fall within more than one category.[2] For example, sometimes community care work might fall under both the community care and the public law contract. When choosing what category of law to use when opening a file, practitioners should choose the overall substance or predominant issue of the case when taken as a whole.

14.8 Practitioners should be clear when they open legal help and legal aid files what categories of law they are using, as this will have a bearing on many things, including the number of matter starts used and the recoverable rate when billing legal help files.

What public law work is within the scope of legal aid?

14.9 According to reg 2 of the Civil Legal Aid (Merits Criteria) Regulations 2013, a:

> . . . public law claim means any matter which is described in any of the following paragraphs of Part 1 of Schedule 1 to the Act (civil legal services)–

1 Legal Aid Statistics: January to March 2019.
2 Legal Aid Agency: Category Definitions 2018.

(a) paragraph 19 (judicial review);
(b) paragraph 20 (habeas corpus); or
(c) paragraph 34 (homelessness) . . .[3]

Judicial review

14.10   Public law work within the scope of legal aid includes 'judicial review of an enactment, decision, act of omission' of public bodies, as described in para 19 of Part 1 of Sch 1 to the Legal Aid Sentencing and Punishment of Offenders Act 2012 (LASPO). This is subject to the general exclusions under Parts 2 and 3 of LASPO.[4]

14.11   According to para 19(10), 'judicial review' means:

(a) the procedure on an application for judicial review (see section 31 of the Senior Courts Act 1981), but not including the procedure after the application is treated under rules of court as if it were not such an application, and
(b) any procedure in which a court, tribunal or other person mentioned in Part 3 of this Schedule is required by an enactment to make a decision applying the principles that are applied by the court on an application for judicial review . . .

Judicial reviews that benefit the individual and/or the individual's family or the environment

14.12   According to para 19(3) and (4) of Part 1 of Sch 1 to LASPO, services provided to an individual in relation to a judicial review that does not have the potential to produce a benefit for the individual, a member of the individual's family or the environment are excluded from Sch 1 para 19 of LASPO. This does not exclude services provided in relation to a judicial review where the judicial review ceases to have the potential to produce such a benefit after the civil legal services have been provided in relation to the judicial review.[5]

Liberty v Director of Legal Aid Casework[6]

14.13   Paragraphs 19(3), (4) and (10)(a) and (b) of Part 1 of Sch 1 to LASPO have been the subject of recent litigation. In 2018 Liberty brought a judicial review against the Director of Legal Aid Casework for

3 Civil Legal Aid (Merits Criteria) Regulation 2013.
4 With the exception of the paragraphs referred to in LASPO Sch 1 Part 1 para 19(2)(a).
5 LASPO Sch 1 para 19(3) and (4).
6 [2019] EWHC 1532 (Admin).

blocking access to justice for residents seeking to take local authorities to court.[7] Public spaces protection orders (PSPOs) allow councils to ban activities they deem to have a 'detrimental effect' on the lives of others. Many PSPOs have been used to ban rough sleeping. For those who wish to challenge a local authority's decision to introduce a PSPO, section 66 of the Anti-Social Behaviour Crime and Policing Act (ASBCPA) 2014 created a specific statutory appeal route, which must be followed by 'interested persons' (those who live in, work in or regularly visit the relevant area). There is no permission stage. The grounds for such a challenge can be: (a) that the local authority did not have power to make the order or variation, or to include particular prohibitions or requirements imposed by the order; or (b) that a requirement under the statute was not complied with in relation to the order. The ASBCPA 2014 explicitly prohibits interested persons from challenging a PSPO by any route other than the section 66 procedure, but the standard judicial review jurisdiction is still an option for those who do not have interested person status. Anyone seeking to challenge a PSPO faces a significant risk of an adverse costs order if they lose.

14.14   The LAA, in an application by Liberty, had taken the position that statutory appeals under ASBCPA 2014 s66 were not within scope for legal aid purposes for two reasons:

- A section 66 ASBCPA 2014 challenge is not a 'judicial review' within the meaning given to that term in LASPO Sch 1 Part 1 para 19(10).
- The proceedings do not have the potential to produce a 'benefit' for Liberty's client within the meaning given to that term in para 19(3) of Part 1 of Schedule 1 of LASPO.

14.15   On 17 June 2019, Murray J dismissed[8] Liberty's attempt to secure legal aid on behalf of Liberty's client, Ms Ward, so that she could pursue a challenge to a PSPO made by the Borough of Poole. He held that:

  i.   the potential to produce a benefit for an individual or a member of their family was a mixed question of fact and law [43].
  ii.   that the ordinary meaning of the word "benefit" was a broad one and that it was not necessary for the Director or the court to consider the quality of the benefit but that the benefit must be of substance, it must be real, direct and

7 'Legal Aid Agency taken to court for refusing to help rough sleepers', *The Guardian*, 23 October 2018.

8 *R (Liberty) v Director of Legal Aid Casework* [2019] EWHC 1532 (Admin).

material for the individual or a member of her family [44–45].

iii. the elimination of the hypothetical risk that Ms Ward might find herself homeless was not sufficient to constitute a benefit in the sense required by para 19(3) [47].

iv. her experience of working in homelessness services and desire to avoid the criminalisation of the homeless was also an insufficient benefit as it was not sufficiently direct, personal and material to Ms Ward or a member of her family to constitute the sort of benefit that would distinguish the section 66 challenge from what is, in essence, a representative action [53].

14.16   In view of his conclusion, the judge decided it was not necessary for him to decide whether the section 66 challenge fell within the definition of 'judicial review' at para 19(1) for legal aid purposes. Liberty sought permission to appeal this decision in the Court of Appeal. Permission was refused by the Rt Hon Lord Justice Leggatt on 8 October 2019.

14.17   A further judicial review has been issued by Ms Ward against her local authority to determine whether homeless people are being 'criminalised' by fines against begging and leaving bedding in doorways. Permission has been granted.[9] Practitioners will be kept updated on any developments via the *Legal Aid Handbook* website.

Immigration judicial reviews

14.18   Judicial reviews in respect of an issue relating to immigration where the conditions in LASPO Sch 1 Part 1 para 19(5)(a)–(c) are met are also excluded from Sch 1 Part 1 para 19. Similar exclusions apply in judicial review of removal directions,[10] unless they are services provided to an individual in relation to: a judicial review of a negative decision in relation to an asylum application where there is no right of appeal to the First-tier Tribunal against the decision; judicial review of certification under section 94 or 96 of the Nationality, Immigration and Asylum Act 2002; and judicial review of removal directions where the conditions in LASPO Sch 1 Part 1 para 19(8) are met. Practitioners working on immigration judicial reviews should read this chapter in conjunction with chapter 10.

---

9   https://rightsinfo.org/high-court-challenge-begging-fines/.
10 See LASPO Sch 1 Part 1 para 19(7).

Writs of habeas corpus

14.19 'Civil legal cases provided in relation to a writ of habeas corpus ad subjiciendum'[11] are also covered by the public law category, subject to the exclusions in Parts 2 and 3 of Sch 1 to LASPO.

Human Rights Act 1998 claims

14.20 Claims for damages under the Human Rights Act 1998 fall exclusively within the Claims Against Public Authorities category of law or the public law category, depending on the facts of the claim.[12] This includes:

- damages claims made within proceedings not described in Part 1 of Sch 1 to LASPO except para 21 ('Abuse or position of powers by public authority') or 22 ('Breach of Convention [European Convention on Human Rights (ECHR)] rights by public authority');
- all freestanding claims for damages under section 7(1)(a) of the 1998 Act.

14.21 Legal help and all proceedings in relation to: abuse of a child or a vulnerable adult (as described in para 3 of Part 1 of Sch 1 to LASPO); abuse of position of power by a public authority (as described in para 21 of Part 1 of Sch 1 to LASPO); significant breach of ECHR rights by a public authority (as described in para 22 of Part 1 of Sch 1 to LASPO); and sexual offences will fall within the Claims Against Public Authorities category where the conditions set out in para 21 of the LAA Category Definitions August 2018 apply.[13]

Examples of public law cases

14.22 Examples of public law cases within scope which practitioners often encounter could include:

- a judicial review of a council's decision to cut a special educational needs budget without conducting a local consultation and without making sufficient enquiries;
- challenges to central government policies;
- an Article 8 ECHR claim against a local authority for failing to secure a long-term placement for a looked after child;
- an unlawful detention judicial review;

---

11 LASPO Sch 1 para 20(1).
12 Legal Aid Agency: Category Definitions 2018.
13 Legal Aid Agency: Category Definitions 2018 paras 20 and 21.

- a challenge to the home office's failure to give adequate reasons to unaccompanied asylum-seeking children (UASC) not accepted into the UK from the 'Calais Jungle';
- challenges to secure access to the adequacy of financial support victims of trafficking receive;
- a breach of Article 4 of the ECHR for failing to protect a victim of trafficking;
- challenges to secure access to subsistence support for destitute asylum seekers;
- judicial review claims against the Crown Prosecution Service (CPS) and the Independent Police Complaints Commission (IPCC);
- challenges to planning decisions and environmental challenges;
- claims to secure access to medical treatment.

14.23   This chapter will deal with some of the most common types of public law work in scope in more detail.

Who can do public law?

14.24   Under the Standard Civil Contract 2018, public law contracts are let by procurement area and require permanent residence. To do public work at all, practitioners must have a schedule authorisation for at least one procurement area. The 2018 Standard Specification Rules for Public Law must be met.[14]

Levels of funding for public law work

14.25   Legal help will cover initial advice and assistance including: taking instructions from the client; reviewing documentation on the case; and drafting pre-action protocol letters under the Judicial Review Pre-action Protocol. The issue and conduct of legal proceedings is not permitted under legal help.[15]

14.26   A certificate for legal representation (full representation) will cover an application for judicial review. The merits test for full representation in public law cases can be found in reg 53 of the Civil Legal Aid (Merits Criteria) Regulations 2013. See chapter 5 on conducting a civil/family case:

---

14 2018 Standard Civil Contract Specification Category Specific Rules: Public Law.
15 Legal Aid Agency Costs Assessment Guidance: for use with the 2018 Standard Civil Contracts para 6.1.

- for the standard criteria to be met (see para 5.92 above);
- for a letter before claim to have been sent to the proposed defendant (except where impracticable) and for the defendant to have been given a reasonable time to respond;
- for the proportionality test to be met (see para 5.104 above);
- for the prospects of success to be: very good, good or moderate; *or*, borderline and for the case;
- to be of significant wider public interest (SWPI) or of overwhelming importance to the individual or the substance of the case relates to a breach of ECHR rights.

14.27   The merits test for an investigative representation certificate in public law can be found in reg 54 of the Civil Legal Aid (Merits Criteria) Regulations 2013. The test is:

- For the standard criteria in regulation 40 to be met: unclear prospects of success and substantial investigative work required before those prospects can be determined; once the investigative work is completed the case will satisfy the criteria for full representation and will meet the cost benefit criteria; if it is a claim for damages which does not meet £5,000, the case must be of significant wider public interest)
- For the claimant to have notified the proposed defendant of the potential challenge and given a reasonable time for the defendant to respond (unless impracticable).

14.28   Some practitioners report that it is now more difficult to obtain investigative representation for public law challenges. When applying for investigative representation, practitioners need to show that they are in a position to consider whether or not the prospects of success in relation to a claim for judicial review are unclear (and substantial work needs to be done to ascertain the merits of a case), rather than at the early stage of taking initial instructions from their client, as this initial work would fall under the ambit of the legal help scheme rather than a funding certificate.

14.29   Since 2013, practitioners have not had delegated functions to grant emergency application for judicial reviews, though some homelessness housing and community care matters are exempt from this. Delegated functions can only be used in judicial reviews under the following:

- Housing Act 1996 Part VII;
- National Assistance Act 1948 s21;
- Children Act 1989 s20;

- National Health Service and Community Care Act 1990 s47(5);
- Care Act 2014 s19(3); and
- Social Services and Well-Being (Wales) Act 2014 s36.[16]

14.30 Delegated functions (the power that providers have to grant representation using delegated functions for judicial review) can no longer be used in Children Act 1989 section 17 cases (homelessness challenges).[17]

Common reasons for refusal of funding in legal aid cases

14.31 Regulation 39 of the Civil Legal Aid (Merits Criteria) Regulations 2013 states that an individual may qualify for legal representation only if the Director is satisfied that:

- the individual does not have access to other potential sources of funding from which it would be reasonable to fund the case;
- the case is unsuitable for a Conditional Fee Agreement (CFA);
- there is no person other than the individual who can reasonably be expected to bring the proceedings;
- the individual has exhausted all reasonable alternatives to bringing proceedings including any complaints system, ombudsman scheme or other form of alternative dispute resolution.

14.32 Practitioners report that the LAA commonly refuses funding in public law cases where there are alternative sources of funding available.

14.33 The Lord Chancellor's Guidance provides examples of potential sources of funding such as other interested parties, trade unions or insurers.[18] With the cuts to public funding, crowdfunding has arisen as an alternative source of funding in the last few years. Crowdfunding connects litigants with sponsors who are prepared to contribute funds to cases. Some practitioners report that legal aid funding has been refused if no attempts to crowdfund have been made. Practitioners should continue to challenge these refusals of funding.

---

16 Legal Aid Agency, Tables of Delegated Authority.
17 'Keeping up with the new rules on delegated functions', June 2019 *Legal Action* 16, Vicky Ling.
18 Lord Chancellor's Guidance under section 4 of Legal Aid, Sentencing and Punishment of Offenders Act 2012.

According to Crowdjustice, crowdfunding should not be seen as an alternative to legal aid.[19]

14.34 Practitioners also report refusals of funding in public law cases on the basis that that cases should be on CFAs with after the event (ATE) insurance obtained on a deferred basis. Practitioners are encouraged to appeal these decisions by relying on the general lack of ATE funding for judicial reviews. This is because the prospects of success are often difficult to predict and because any relief granted is within the discretion of the Court. ATE insurance premiums are also very expensive.

14.35 Other refusals of funding in public law judicial review cases sometimes refer to the possibility that another body (for example, the Equality and Human Rights Commission) brings the judicial review in question. In human rights cases, the Commission does not need to be a 'victim' of the affected violation. The Commission might bring judicial review cases rather than a victim where the actual or potential victims do not have access to lawyers or the government announces a chance in the law which they believe will lead to violations of people's human rights.

14.36 It will be very difficult in practice for solicitors to obtain evidence of all of the above when applying for emergency public funding or appealing decisions close to limitation deadlines, so practitioners are encouraged to gather generic evidence in support of applications and/or appeals and to liaise with colleague practitioners in relation to this.

14.37 Other common reasons for refusing funding in public law cases include premature applications and/or failure to exhaust all reasonable alternatives to bringing proceedings. In urgent cases or cases issued shortly before limitation deadlines, this will not be appropriate.

How to conduct a public law case

Steps in a judicial review case

14.38 There are various stages to a judicial review case. The first step involves writing a pre-action protocol letter to the proposed defendant, setting out the proposed claim and remedy sought. This is normally done under the Legal Help scheme, although in some very exceptional cases it will be done under the investigative representation scheme.

19 'We're no replacement for legal aid, says crowdfunder pioneer', *Law Gazette*, 22 November 2018.

14.39   A response is normally sought within 14 days. However, in very urgent cases an abridged timescale will be sought. In planning cases, there is a six-week time limit to issue a claim, so a shorter and abridged timescale is also normally sought.

14.40   If the defendant does not concede at this stage, a claim can be lodged in the High Court or the tribunal with the relevant fee. A public funding application for full representation will have to be made on the Client and Cost Management System (CCMS) in order to cover work related to getting the claim issued in court. This will include counsel's fees and the court fee. Full representation is needed in order to issue judicial proceedings.[20] Generally, proceedings cannot be issued on investigative representation, although there are some exceptions to this rule which are set out at reg 18(3) of the Civil Legal Aid (Merits Criteria) Regulations 2013:

- to obtain disclosure of information relevant to the prospects of success of the proceedings;
- to protect the position of the individual or legal persona applying for investigative representation in relation to an urgent hearing; or
- to protect the position of the individual or legal person applying for investigative representation in relation to the time limit for the issue of the proceedings

14.41   The court or tribunal where proceedings are issued must be provided with a copy of the legal aid certificate.[21] Once proceedings are issued, the defendant files its summary grounds of defence to explain why it is unarguable and permission should not be granted. The papers are then sent to a judge for a decision to be made on the papers. The test for permission is that a case is an arguable one. If permission is refused on the papers, it can be 'renewed' in open court. An application will need to be made to the LAA to request that the legal aid certificate covers the renewal hearing.

14.42   If permission is granted, the claim proceeds to a full substantive hearing. A further amendment to the certificate will need to be made at this stage to cover work done between permission and the final hearing and to cover the payment of the permission fee. Sometimes, particularly in urgent cases, a judge may order that both the permission stage and the substantive stage be heard at the same time ('a rolled-up hearing').

---

20 Reg 18(2) of the Civil Legal Aid (Merits Criteria) Regulations 2013.
21 Reg 38 of the Civil Legal Aid (Procedure) Regulations 2012.

Payment for judicial review work

14.43 Payment for work in a judicial review case is dependent on what occurs in the case.

14.44 Regulation 5A of the Civil Legal Aid (Remuneration) Regulation 2013 sets out the circumstances in which legal aid providers are paid for their work having issued a claim for judicial review. When reg 5A first came into force, it provided for a blanket ban on payment when a claim for judicial review had been refused permission to proceed to full judicial review, unless permission was later granted. The regulation was partially amended after the case of *R (Ben Hoare Bell Solicitors and others) v The Lord Chancellor*[22] in 2015, in which the Divisional Court held that the blanket prohibition was unlawful as it included instances where the failure to obtain permission was based on events that occurred 'beyond the control' of the providers and only came to light after the initial merits assessment.

14.45 Following this case, the LAA re-introduced regulations.[23] Duncan Lewis brought a judicial review case challenging the Lord Chancellor's interpretation of the regulations, which settled in December 2018.[24] A copy of the consent order can be found on the Young Legal Aid Lawyers website.[25] As part of the basis of the settlement, the Lord Chancellor undertook to produce a clarification of the effect of reg 5A.[26]

Administrative Court and Judicial Review Guidance

14.46 The latest Administrative Court and Judicial Review Guidance was published in July 2019.[27] Paragraph 3.4.5 of this Guidance deals with the type of legal representation available in civil cases.

14.47 The Guidance also explains (at para 23.10) the issue of cost orders when the claimant has the benefit of legal aid. Costs orders can be made against persons who have the benefit of legal aid. Where the court makes such an order, it will order that the person with the benefit of legal aid must pay the costs of the requesting party and the court may set the amount to be paid, but the court will note that the person

22 [2015] EWHC 523 (Admin).
23 Civil Legal Aid (Remuneration) (Amendment) Regulations 2015.
24 *R (Duncan Lewis Solicitors) v Lord Chancellor* CO/1551/2018.
25 www.younglegalaidlawyers.org/node/2397.
26 Clarification on Payment for Civil Legal Services under Regulation 5A of the Civil Legal Aid (Remuneration) Regulations 2013.
27 The Administrative Court Judicial Review Guide 2019.

with the benefit of legal aid is subject to costs protection in accordance with section 26 of LASPO.

14.48   As a result of the costs protection, the person with the benefit of legal aid is not automatically liable for the costs. However, practitioners acting for individuals from abroad should be aware of the Home Office's Litigation Debt guidance.[28] The latest version of this guidance was published on 13 September 2018, and states that the Home Office has the power to refuse applications for entry clearance, leave to enter or leave to remain on the basis of litigation debt.

Habeas corpus

14.49   Although rarely used nowadays, a writ of habeas corpus is still to be considered a fundamental instrument for safeguarding individual freedom against arbitrary and lawless state action. Writs of habeas corpus are sometimes used in the context of age assessment judicial reviews where the age-disputed child is being detained under immigration powers. This was discussed in the Supreme Court case of *R (AA (Afghanistan)) v Secretary of State for the Home Department*.[29] Practitioners should be wary of applying for writs of habeas corpus when there are other remedies available or to avoid the jurisdiction of the Upper Tribunal.[30]

14.50   If practitioners who are acting for individuals who are being detained send a CW1 legal help form by post or fax to the client, or if they travel out of the office to visit the client, they need to provide the circumstances justifying this in accordance with the relevant rule in the Contract Specification.[31] Only once the declaration has been fully understood and signed by the client can the practitioner open a file and begin work. Detailed guidance as to what evidence of means is required is set out in the LAA Controlled Work guidance. All practitioners should follow this guidance. Further details can be found in chapter 3. It may be impracticable for clients in detention to supply evidence of means. In such cases, eligibility can be assessed without evidence. However, the attendance note must give the reason why evidence could not be obtained and providers must be prepared to justify this on audit if necessary.[32]

28 Litigation Debt guidance version 2.0.

29 [2013] UKSC 49, paras 52–53.

30 See, for example, the case of *R (Ajani and others) v Secretary of State for the Home Department* [2018] EWHC 913 (Admin) where the case was referred to the SRA for full investigation.

31 Legal Help Form, p12.

32 Guide for Determining Financial Eligibility for Controlled Work paras 10–11.

Conducting a criminal case

by Anthony Edwards

continued

Introduction

15.1 The Standard Crime Contract 2017, extended to 31 March 2021 by the Legal Aid Agency (LAA) on 9 July 2019, governs criminal work where representation is granted after 1 April 2017. The contract comprises the Standard Terms and the Specification.

15.2 Criminal work is divided into classes by the contract:[1]

- investigations – work done pre-charge;
- proceedings – post-charge court work appeals and reviews;
- post-conviction work on appeals and reviews of convictions or sentences that do not fall into any other class;
- prison law – work in relation to parole, treatment or discipline in the prison system;
- associated civil work – judicial review, habeas corpus and some Proceeds of Crime Act 2002 work.

In addition, 'Very High Cost Cases' (VHCCs) can be regarded as an extra class of work.

15.3 A case may move through several classes. For example, a client arrested and charged with burglary will start in the investigations class, then move into the proceedings class; if convicted, he or she may have further cases in the appeals and prison law classes. Each of those classes of work has separate rules and funding mechanisms, and we will look at each in turn in this chapter. We will also consider the general rules which apply to all classes of work.

General rules

Unique file numbers[2]

15.4 The contract requires you to assign a unique file number (UFN) to every case. The case will retain the UFN throughout its life as it moves through the classes of work. Where you act for more than one client on the same case, each client will have his or her own UFN, though where you must submit a consolidated claim (see chapter17) it will be under one 'lead' UFN. Where you act for one client on more than one case, each case will have its own UFN.

15.5 All UFNs must be in the format set out in the contract – DDMMYY/NNN, where DDMMYY is the date the client first

---

1 Standard Crime Contract 2017 Specification para 1.3.
2 Standard Crime Contract 2017 Specification paras 4.40 and 4.41.

instructed you on that matter and NNN is a unique three-digit number. It does not matter what that number is, as long as no two clients or cases have the same number.

15.6   So, for example, the first client to instruct you on 1 February 2019 would have the UFN 01022019/001, the second might then be 01022019/002, and so on.

15.7   The purpose of the UFN is to allow the LAA to track and, where necessary, check all work done for a particular client. You are therefore required to record the UFN on file, use it for all applications and claims to the LAA and, since the LAA will use it when communicating with you, ensure that you can search your database against it.

Disbursements

15.8   Disbursements – that is, expenses incurred in the course of a client's case – are generally permitted where it is in the best interests of the client to incur the disbursement for the purpose of giving advice, and the amount of the disbursement is reasonable.[3]

15.9   This amounts to a three-stage test:

1) Is it in the best interests of the client?
2) Is it for the purposes of giving advice or representation?
3) Is the amount reasonable?

15.10   The client's best interests will be served by incurring expenditure that is necessary for you to conduct the case, or that will assist (or may assist) in achieving the best outcome. For example, travel expenses may be in the client's best interests, even though the client does not benefit directly, because it is necessary for you to incur them to get to court. An expert report may or may not assist the client's case – that would depend on what the expert says – but where it has the potential to do so, it would likely be in the client's best interests to obtain it. This test should not be applied with the benefit of hindsight; the question is, what was reasonable based on what was known at the time?

15.11   'For the purpose of advice or representation' describes the nature and purpose of the expense. To use the preceding example, travel expenses to court are justifiable as being for the purpose of providing representation. A medical report to comment on a client's medical situation would be for that purpose, since it is evidence that could be put before the court, but paying for the client to see a medical expert to obtain treatment would not, since it is not necessary for the

---

3 Standard Crime Contract 2017 Specification para 5.38.

purpose of giving advice for the client to be treated, only for you to know what his or her condition is.

15.12 Finally, the amount of the disbursement must be reasonable. The rates for expert witnesses, save in defined exceptional circumstances prescribed by Schedule 5 to the Criminal Legal Aid (Remuneration) Regulations 2013 as amended, are to be found in that schedule. Although it is not mandatory to obtain prior authority to incur disbursements,[4] doing so is advisable where substantial sums are to be incurred as prior authority generally ensures that, unless the scope of the disbursement is not as authorised, it will be paid and not questioned on audit.[5]

15.13 Where disbursements are incurred, you should retain a receipt or invoice on file.[6] Where you incur mileage, the contract rate is 45 pence per mile.[7]

15.14 The LAA has power to fix the maximum payments that may be paid to third parties such as experts.[8] Limits have been set to experts' fees in Schedule 5 to the Remuneration Regulations. These fees may be exceeded only in exceptional circumstances.[9] You must require third parties to keep a record of their time spent on a case if the fees will exceed £250.[10]

15.15 Witness expenses to attend court cannot generally be funded under the contract, unless the court has directed that they may not be recovered from central funds (the usual source of witness expenses, including fees of professional witnesses) and they are not recoverable from any other source.[11]

Work in the investigations class

15.16 Investigations work is work done pre-charge or in the police station, and covers:[12]

4 Standard Crime Contract 2017 Specification para 5.32.
5 Standard Crime Contract 2017 Specification para 5.29.
6 Standard Crime Contract 2017 Specification para 5.40.
7 Standard Crime Contract 2017 Specification para 5.48.
8 Standard Crime Contract 2017 Standard Terms para 3.6 and Specification para 5.37.
9 Criminal Legal Aid (Remuneration) Regulations 2013 as amended, reg 16(2) and (3).
10 Standard Crime Contract 2017 Standard Terms para 3.7.
11 Standard Crime Contract 2017 Specification para 5.47.
12 Standard Crime Contract 2017 Specification para 1.3.

- police station telephone advice;
- police station attendance;
- advice and assistance outside the police station;
- advocacy assistance:
  - on a warrant of further detention;
  - on an application to a magistrates' court to vary police bail conditions or oppose the extension of a bail time limit;
  - at an armed forces custody hearing.

Police station cases

Scope of work

15.17 Police station work will consist of telephone advice, attendance in person at the police station, or both. It is generally available to anyone attending a police station, whether under arrest or as a volunteer, during the course of a criminal investigation.[13] The exceptions to this rule are:

- where the matter falls within the scope of the Criminal Defence Direct scheme (eg arrests for non-imprisonable offences);[14] and
- advice and assistance to a witness (which is covered in certain circumstances by the advice and assistance scheme).[15]

Police station work is not means tested.[16]

15.18 Police station work can also be carried out post-charge, for example to deal with identification procedures, arrest on warrant or for breach of bail, or for caution or re-charge following discontinuance or dismissal. However, only post-charge work carried out at the police station can be claimed under the criminal investigations class of work,[17] rather than as part of the claim in the criminal proceedings.

15.19 For these purposes, a 'police station' is a place where a constable is present, and a 'constable' is an official with a power of arrest conferred by virtue of his or her office.[18] For example, an officer of HM Revenue and Customs (HMRC) is a constable, but a Department for Work and Pensions (DWP) benefit fraud investigator is not; there-

---

13 Standard Crime Contract 2017 Specification para 9.1.
14 Standard Crime Contract 2017 Specification para 9.9.
15 Standard Crime Contract 2017 Specification paras 9.3 and 9.4.
16 Criminal Legal Aid (General) Regulations 2013 Part 2 and Criminal Legal Aid (Financial Resources) Regulations 2013 Part 2.
17 Standard Crime Contract 2017 Specification para 9.105.
18 Standard Crime Contract 2017 Standard Terms para 1.1

fore, a client arrested by HMRC is entitled to police station representation, but a client being interviewed by the DWP is not. However, such a client may be entitled to advice and assistance if the relevant criteria are met. See below for more on advice and assistance.

Case study

One of our clients has been invited to attend the DWP to be interviewed about an allegation that he has been working and claiming benefits. What should I do?

This will be an interview under the Police and Criminal Evidence Act 1984 (PACE) and so a criminal lawyer should attend. Since an officer of the DWP does not have a power of arrest, your client would not be entitled to police station legal aid. However, subject to means, your client would be entitled to advice and assistance. You should get the client to sign a CRM1 and CRM2 and provide proof of means, and then you will be funded to attend the interview with the client. You will have a costs limit of £273.75, but this can be extended on application to the LAA if necessary.

Sources of work

15.20 All requests by persons seeking advice under the police station scheme must, to qualify for public funding, be placed through the Defence Solicitor Call Centre (DSCC).

15.21 The call centre records the basic details of an alleged offence before passing the case on to the own solicitor requested, the duty solicitor or Criminal Defence Direct. Criminal Defence Direct provide telephone advice to clients detained for less serious matters such as drink-driving offences, non-imprisonable offences, breaches of bail and warrants.

15.22 Where an attendance is likely to be necessary, Criminal Defence Direct will not deal with the matter and the case will be passed to the own solicitor (if requested) or the duty solicitor.

15.23 However, you may also be contacted direct by a third party, for example the relative of a client, and requested to take on the case. You may also be contacted by a client direct, for example a client who is aware that the police are looking for him or her and wants to surrender. In such a situation you can take on the case and provide telephone advice and attendance as appropriate, but must, within very short time limits, report to the call centre that you have taken the case.[19]

19 Standard Crime Contract 2017 Specification para 9.20.

Case study

My client's wife phoned to say that he has been arrested for theft and wants me to go to the police station. Can I go?

Yes. You can attend the police station when instructed to do so by a third party. However, you must notify the DSCC that you have taken the case. You must notify them before you contact the client and obtain a reference number. You must notify the DSCC in advance for third party instructions, and within 48 hours where you are at a police station and instructed direct, or where a client instructs you direct to attend a surrender or bail date. The 48-hour time limit, which includes weekends and bank holidays, is strictly enforced.

Permitted work

15.24   Whatever the source of the case, you should consider whether or not to attend the police station. Attendance at the police station is mandatory where:

- the client has been arrested and is to be interviewed;
- there is to be an identification procedure (except a video parade, attendance at which is discretionary[20]);
- the client complains of serious maltreatment by the police.[21]

15.25   You cannot claim for payment for attendance at the police station where:

- the client has been arrested solely for non-imprisonable offences;
- the client has been arrested on a warrant for failure to appear unless you have clear documentary evidence that would result in the client's release, eg a bail form showing that the client is not in fact in breach of a condition;
- the client has been arrested for offences under Road Traffic Act 1988 ss4, 5, 6, 7 and 7A (driving while unfit, drunk in charge of a vehicle, driving with excess alcohol or failure to provide a specimen);
- the client has been detained in relation to breach of police or court bail conditions.[22]

---

20 Standard Crime Contract 2017 Specification para 9.40.
21 Standard Crime Contract 2017 Specification para 9.38.
22 Standard Crime Contract 2017 Specification para 9.9.

15.26 However, attendance in a prohibited case will be permitted (or mandatory, as the case may be) if one of the exceptions apply:[23]

- there is to be an interview or identification procedure;
- the client requires an appropriate adult;
- the client is unable to communicate over the telephone;
- the client complains of serious maltreatment by the police;
- the client is being investigated for an additional offence not covered by the above list;
- you are already at the same police station (but in this case you may only claim the Telephone Advice Fixed Fee);
- the advice relates to an indictable offence;
- the request is identified as a 'Special Request'[24] by the DSCC. A special request will be identified by the DSCC as such; for instance, because Criminal Defence Direct considers an attendance to be required.

In all other cases, attendance at the police station is at your discretion, and you should consider whether the 'sufficient benefit' test is met. This is the merits test for police station work and states that work may only be done where 'there is sufficient benefit to the client, having regard to the circumstances of the matter, including the personal circumstances of the client, to justify work or further work being carried out'.[25]

15.27 The test would be automatically satisfied where the client has a right to advice under PACE, or where the client is a volunteer, or under equivalent military legislation – but only in relation to initial advice; you must apply the test to determine the extent of advice, and particularly whether attendance (as opposed to telephone advice) is necessary.[26]

15.28 Where you intend to attend the police station, and it is not one of the mandatory attendances outlined above, you should be satisfied that the attendance is necessary for the purpose of giving advice that could not be given over the telephone, and is expected to progress the case materially. Specifically, the contract says that it might be reasonable to remain at the police station post-charge to provide advice or make representations on bail, but unless the client is particularly

---

23 Standard Crime Contract 2017 Specification para 9.10.
24 Standard Crime Contract 2017 Specification para 1.2.
25 Standard Crime Contract 2017 Specification paras 1.2 and 3.10–3.16.
26 Standard Crime Contract 2017 Specification para 9.14.

vulnerable it would not be reasonable to stay for photographs, finger-prints and DNA samples.[27]

Who may carry out work?

15.29   Although almost all work comes through the DSCC, there is a distinction between 'own client' and 'duty' work – own client being cases where you or your firm were specifically requested, and duty work where the client requested the duty solicitor and the case was allocated to you.

15.30   In order to carry out police station work, you must be accredited and registered by the LAA. Only an accredited person may undertake duty work.[28] An accredited representative is a person who has passed the police station qualification, which is administered by the LAA and consists of a two-part portfolio of cases, an oral examination known as the critical incidents test and a written examination (which need not be taken by a representative who has a legal qualification).

15.31   To become a probationary representative, you must pass the written examination (if required) and part one of the portfolio; you then have one year to pass the remaining elements to become fully accredited. The accreditation process is no longer bypassed by quali-fication as a solicitor; everyone must be accredited to do duty solicitor police station work. The training and quality assurance of probation-ary and accredited representatives must be documented.[29]

15.32   To do own client work, a person must either be a solicitor or be accredited or a probationary representative. Probationary represent-atives cannot do duty cases, and cannot do cases where the offence under investigation is indictable only; fully accredited representat-ives can do all cases.[30] See chapter 21 for the obligations of those who manage and supervise representatives.

Starting a case

15.33   Police station work is not means tested,[31] and the client is not required to complete any application form.

15.34   A case will be initiated when you are contacted, either by the DSCC or by the client or a third party, and requested to provide advice.

---

27 Standard Crime Contract 2017 Specification para 9.16.
28 Standard Crime Contract 2017 Specification para 9.28.
29 Standard Crime Contract 2017 Specification para 9.33.
30 Standard Crime Contract 2017 Specification paras 9.26–9.37.
31 Standard Crime Contract 2017 Specification para 9.15.

15.35   When you take on a case where the client has been arrested and is at the police station, you must make first contact with the client within 45 minutes of being notified of the case.[32] This is a target set out in the contract which should be met in at least 80 per cent of cases, and to enable monitoring of the target[33] your file should contain a note of the time the case was accepted and the time of first contact, together with a note of why contact was not possible inside the 45 minutes, if applicable.[34]

15.36   Where a client has previously received police station advice on the same matter within the past six months from another firm, you cannot provide further advice on the same matter unless:

- there is a gap in time and a material change in circumstances between the first and second occasions; or
- the client has reasonable cause to transfer; or
- the first supplier confirms they will not make a claim.[35]

15.37   You should make reasonable enquiries of the client to see if there has been previous advice, and if there has been and the exceptions are not met cannot make a claim. Reasonable cause for transfer will not be made out where the client finds sound advice unpalatable and wants a second opinion.[36] Where you take on a transfer case, you should note the reason on the file.

Conducting work

15.38   Once you have accepted a case, you can continue to do such work as is necessary and complies with the requirements above. Where the client is bailed to return to the police station, attendance at the bail to return is funded on the same basis as the initial attendance and will be included in the same fixed fee – you should ensure that the sufficient benefit test is satisfied and that you are permitted to attend.

15.39   There is no costs limitation for police station work.

15.40   Police station work will come to an end at the point the client is charged or cautioned, the police decide to take no further action, or the case is otherwise ended. Uncertainty over cases where a suspect remains under investigation means most firms bill after one month. If the case revives you may not make another claim on the same

---

32 Standard Crime Contract 2017 Specification para 9.23.
33 Standard Crime Contract 2017 Specification para 9.24.
34 Standard Crime Contract 2017 Specification para 9.25.
35 Standard Crime Contract 2017 Specification para 9.67.
36 Standard Crime Contract 2017 Specification para 9.70.

matter until you reach the threshold fee for a full claim to be made. A bill should be submitted at that point[37] – see chapter 17 for details of costs and the billing procedure.

Warrants of further detention

15.41   Where a client is detained and the police seek an extension to the detention under PACE s43 or s44, or under Terrorism Act 2000 Sch 8 para 29 or para 36, you can provide advocacy assistance to represent the client at the hearing of the application.[38]

15.42   Advocacy assistance is not means tested[39] and the client is not required to sign an application form, but you should record on the file that you have granted funding.[40] The scope of advocacy assistance includes any reasonable preparation and follow-up work.[41] However, counsel may only be instructed in applications before the High Court or a senior judge (effectively, only in terrorist cases).[42] There is an extendable upper limit of £1,368.75[43]

15.43   Similar provisions apply to armed forces custody hearings.[44]

Applications in relation to police bail

15.44   In certain circumstances, where the police have the power to impose bail conditions (or 'street bail' conditions), or wish to extend bail time limits, a client can make an application to a magistrates' court to vary the conditions or oppose the extension.[45]

15.45   You can grant advocacy assistance to represent such a client.[46] It is not means tested,[47] and no application form is required, though a note of the grant should be made on the file.[48] The scope of advocacy assistance includes any reasonable preparation and giving of any

---

37   Standard Crime Contract 2017 Specification para 9.104.
38   Standard Crime Contract 2017 Specification para 9.141.
39   Criminal Legal Aid (Financial Resources) Regulations 2013 Part 2; Standard Crime Contract 2017 Specification para 9.143.
40   Standard Crime Contract 2017 Specification paras 9.144–9.146.
41   Standard Crime Contract 2017 Specification para 9.147.
42   Standard Crime Contract 2017 Specification para 9.148.
43   Criminal Legal Aid (Remuneration) Regulations 2013 Sch 4 para 3(2) and (3) as amended.
44   Standard Crime Contract 2017 Specification paras 9.154–9.166.
45   PACE ss30CB and 47(1E).
46   Standard Crime Contract 2017 Specification para 9.167.
47   Criminal Legal Aid (Financial Resources) Regulations 2013 Part 2.
48   Standard Crime Contract 2017 Specification para 9.169–9.170.

advice on appeal.[49] However, counsel may not be instructed.[50] There is an extendable upper limit of £1,368.75.[51]

Advice and assistance

Overview

15.46 Advice and assistance can be given to a client who meets the means and merits tests, to advise and assist in respect of a criminal investigation – that is, before the client is charged, requisitioned or summoned for an offence. It will include representing the client at interviews with non-police agencies, such as the DWP in a benefit fraud matter, as well as general advice, case preparation and related work.

Means test

15.47 In order to qualify for advice and assistance, the client must pass the means test.[52] There are two elements to the test – income and capital – and the client must pass both parts. You are responsible for assessing the client's means and deciding whether the test is met.

15.48 Where the client is directly or indirectly in receipt of any of the following 'passporting' benefits, he or she automatically qualifies for advice and assistance without the need for an assessment of income or capital:

- income support;
- income-based jobseeker's allowance;
- income-based employment and support allowance (ESA);
- guarantee pension credit;
- universal credit paid under Part 1 of the Welfare Reform Act 2012.[53]

A person is indirectly in receipt of a benefit if he or she is included in another person's claim, eg if a partner receives it on the basis of a couple.

15.49 'Capital' means all the client's assets and resources, excluding household furniture and effects, clothes and the tools of the client's trade. Where the client owns property, the value to be taken into account is the equity after disregarding any mortgage, though only

49 Standard Crime Contract 2017 Specification para 9.171.
50 Standard Crime Contract 2017 Specification para 9.172.
51 Criminal Legal Aid (Remuneration) Regulations 2013 Sch 4 para 3(4) as amended.
52 Criminal Legal Aid (Financial Resources) Regulations 2013 reg 8.
53 Criminal Legal Aid (Financial Resources) Regulations 2013 reg 2.

up to the value of £100,000. The first £100,000 of any equity is also disregarded, and the remainder is the capital value.[54] Where the client has a partner, the partner's capital should also be taken into account.

Case study

My client has a flat worth £120,000, with a mortgage of £90,000. He has £650 in savings and his wife has £300 in her account. Is he eligible on capital?

The flat is worth £120,000. Disregard up to £100,000 of the mortgage – so the equity is £30,000. Disregard up to £100,000 of equity – so the capital is nil. Aggregate his and his wife's savings, so the total capital is £950, so the client is eligible on capital.

15.50   'Income' means all income from any source which the client may reasonably expect to receive within the seven days up to and including the day of his or her application[55] – with the following exceptions:

- any tax and National Insurance paid;
- any contributions paid under Part 1 of the Social Security Contributions and Benefits Act 1992;
- disability living allowance;
- attendance allowance;
- constant attendance allowance;
- any payment out of the social fund;
- so much of any back to work bonus received under section 26 of the Jobseekers Act 1995 as is, by virtue of that section, to be treated as payable by way of a jobseeker's allowance;
- any direct payments made under regulations made under Care Act 2014 ss31–33 (direct payments), Children and Families Act 2014 s49(3) (personal budgets and direct payments); Carers and Direct Payments Act (Northern Ireland) 2002 s8(1) (direct payments); or Social Services and Well-being (Wales) Act 2014 ss50–53;
- any reasonable living expenses provided for as an exception to a restraint order under Proceeds of Crime Act 2002 s41;

---

54   Criminal Legal Aid (Financial Resources) Regulations 2013 reg 13.
55   Criminal Legal Aid (Financial Resources) Regulations 2013 reg 6.

- any personal independence payment paid under Part 4 of the Welfare Reform Act 2012;[56]
- any payments made under reg 17 of the Universal Credit (Transitional Payments) Regulations 2014 (reg 17 of the 2016 NI Regs);
- any payment on account of universal credit;
- any personal independence payments (PIPs).

Where the client has a partner, the partner's income should also be taken into account.[57] Where the client has a partner or other dependant member of the household, you should deduct the standard allowance for each member.[58]

15.51   The thresholds for capital and income, and the standard dependants' allowances, can be found on keycard 45A on the LAA website.[59] The levels are very occasionally up-rated, and you should check the website for the most up to date figures.

15.52   Evidence of the client's means will be required, and should be retained on file.[60] This is a key issue on audit. There is a power to assess means without evidence where it is not practicable to obtain it before the form is signed, but it should be obtained at a later stage and if it is not, any claim should be limited to the equivalent of two hours.[61] You cannot make a claim if you do not seek to obtain the relevant evidence. Only in defined exceptional circumstances, may you dispense with evidence altogether, if the client's circumstances make it impracticable to obtain it at any point.[62]

Merits test

15.53   Assuming the client qualifies on means, you should go on to consider whether there is merit. The merits test is the 'sufficient benefit' test – is there 'sufficient benefit to the client, having regard to the circumstances of the matter, including the personal circumstances of the client, to justify work or further work being carried out'.[63]

---

56 Criminal Legal Aid (Financial Resources) Regulations 2013 reg 11.
57 Criminal Legal Aid (Financial Resources) Regulations 2013 reg 9.
58 Criminal Legal Aid (Financial Resources) Regulations 2013 reg 12.
59 www.gov.uk/government/uploads/system/uploads/attachment_data/ file/390542/criminal-keycard-45.pdf. Issued in 2014 and still valid as at the date of writing.
60 Standard Crime Contract 2017 Specification para 9.115.
61 Standard Crime Contract 2017 Specification paras 3.5–3.8.
62 Standard Crime Contract 2017 Specification paras 3.6–3.7.
63 Standard Crime Contract 2017 Specification para 3.10.

15.54   The sufficient benefit test must be applied throughout the case to determine the extent of the advice required,[64] and the provision of advice must cease if it becomes apparent that the test is no longer satisfied.[65]

The application

15.55   The client must complete and sign the application forms – CRM1 and CRM2 – and you should retain the original copies of them on file. Advice and assistance is granted by you, with no application to the LAA required, and so the presence of the signed forms on file is sufficient to effect the grant.

15.56   The usual rule is that the client comes to you to sign the forms. However, there will be situations where that is not possible, and therefore the contract allows for exceptions where certain criteria are met:

- A **postal application** can be accepted where it is reasonable to do so (for example, where there is good reason why the client cannot attend your offices). However, you cannot accept a postal application where a client is temporarily resident outside the European Union and the matter can be delayed until they return, or another person in England and Wales could apply for advice and assistance on the same matter.[66]

- Where the client cannot attend immediately but can telephone you, **telephone advice** can be given before the form is signed[67] and you can claim for that advice. In order to qualify, there has to be good reason why the client cannot attend the office, but the client must later sign the form and be eligible. This power can be combined with one of the others; for example, you could give telephone advice to a client in prison and then post the form to him or her.

- Where the client lacks capacity, you can accept an application on behalf of a child or protected party (a person lacking mental capacity under the Mental Capacity Act 2005)[68] from another person, such as a parent, guardian, deputy or attorney, litigation friend, or any other person where there is good reason why one of the above-named persons cannot make the application. The form will be

---

64 Standard Crime Contract 2017 Specification paras 3.11 and 3.15.
65 Standard Crime Contract 2017 Specification para 3.12.
66 Standard Crime Contract 2017 Specification para 4.31.
67 Standard Crime Contract 2017 Specification para 9.121.
68 Standard Crime Contract 2017 Specification para 4.25.

signed by the authorised person but completed in the name of the client, and it will be the client's means that should be assessed and evidenced.

- You can also accept an application from a child direct[69] where the client is entitled to defend proceedings himself or herself (which is true of almost all criminal work), or where you are satisfied that there is good reason why none of the authorised persons in the previous paragraph can make the application, and the child is old enough to give instructions and understand the nature of the advice, or where the child is seeking police station advice only.

Where a client cannot attend the office for one of the good reasons outlined above, you may claim for outward travel expenses;[70] and where the client is in custody, detention or hospital, travel time[71] for travelling to see the client before the form is signed in order to get the form signed.

15.57   Where a client has received previous advice and assistance on the same matter within the last six months, there are restrictions on where you can accept a further application that would involve a change of solicitor.[72] You cannot accept such an application unless:

- there is a gap in time and a material change in circumstances; or
- the client has reasonable cause to transfer from the first supplier; or
- the first supplier confirms they are making no claim; or
- previous advice and assistance was police station advice only.

You should make reasonable enquiries of the client to find out whether there has been previous advice and assistance. If so, and if you can justify the change of solicitor, there should be a clear note to that effect on the file.

Conducting work

15.58   Once you have confirmed that the client is eligible and the form has been signed, you can proceed to work on the client's case.

15.59   Advice and assistance covers all necessary work (other than work in the police station) up to the point at which the client is charged with, summoned or requisitioned for an offence. It will cover you for attendance and advice to the client, case preparation, taking witness statements

69 Standard Crime Contract 2017 Specification paras 4.28–4.30.
70 Standard Crime Contract 2017 Specification para 9.122.
71 Standard Crime Contract 2017 Specification para 9.123.
72 Standard Crime Contract 2017 Specification para 9.125.

with a view to preserving memory or avoiding charge, and so on. It will also cover attendance at interviews with non-police agencies.

15.60   Costs are limited to £273.75, though an application may be made to the LAA to extend that limit.[73] The limit includes both time and disbursements. Where advice and assistance runs alongside police station work, you may not make a separate claim for the advice and assistance; all work pre-charge is covered by the police station fixed fee. However, the costs limit will continue to apply and you will need to be within the limit or have a granted extension for advice and assistance costs to count towards exceptionality. See chapter 17 for more on getting paid for criminal work.

Separate matters

15.61   All work for a client that constitutes one matter will require one application and will lead to one claim. Where, however, work is a genuinely separate matter, then a separate application and a separate claim will be required.

15.62   All work in respect of a single investigation constitutes one matter and therefore one claim for costs, even if the investigation is subsequently extended to cover other offences. However, work may be treated as a separate matter if it amounts to a generally separate problem requiring separate advice,[74] unless the client requires advice on one occasion only.[75]

Case study

I had a client who was arrested for theft and taken to the police station, where it was found he was also wanted for a separate incident of criminal damage, and he was further arrested for that. Is that one matter or two?

It depends on the outcome of the case. If he were charged with both offences and bailed to the same court date, that would be one matter and one claim. This is because the two allegations required advice on one occasion only. However, if he were charged with theft and bailed to return on the criminal damage, that would constitute two matters, if you could reasonably attend on the bail to return, since they would require separate advice on more than one occasion.

---

73 Criminal Legal Aid (Remuneration) Regulations 2013 Sch 4 para 3(1) as amended; and Standard Criminal Contract 2017 Specification para 9.139.
74 Standard Crime Contract 2017 Specification para 4.43.
75 Standard Crime Contract 2017 Specification para 4.46.

Work in the proceedings class

15.63   The proceedings class runs from the point of charge/summons/requisition and includes all magistrates' court work and most Crown Court proceedings. The main funding types in the proceedings class are:

- advice and assistance/advocacy assistance as court duty solicitor, or in a virtual court;[76]
- representation orders.

15.64   You must be able to work with the Crown Court Digital Case System[77]. This enables you digitally to receive and serve papers and applications.[78]

Court duty solicitor work

15.65   A duty solicitor is a solicitor who has previously been a member of a Scheme under a previous contract or is a current member of the Law Society's Criminal Litigation Accreditation Scheme and undertaken the police station qualification.[79]

15.66   Duty solicitors whose firms have successfully bid in a procurement area will be allocated sessions as a duty solicitor whose role is to advise and assist otherwise unrepresented defendants.

15.67   Technically speaking, two different funding types are available to a court duty solicitor – advice and assistance and advocacy assistance, to advise the client outside court and represent the client in court respectively. In practice, however, there is no distinction and a single consolidated claim is made for all work done for all clients on a duty day.

15.68   Court duty advice is available to clients whose cases qualify for assistance without regard to their means, and no application form is needed. However, a file note of the details of the client and the case will be needed.[80]

15.69   However, clients can only be represented where their case comes within the scope of the scheme:

- The duty solicitor must in all circumstances:[81]

---

76 Standard Crime Contract 2017 Specification paras 10.21–10.35; and see para 15.93.
77   https://crowncourtdcs.caselines.co.uk/.
78   Standard Crime Contract 2017 Standard Terms 7.24 requires the use of CJS online once operational.
79   Standard Crime Contract 2017 Standard Terms 1.1.
80   Standard Crime Contract 2017 Specification para 10.6.
81   Standard Crime Contract 2017 Specification para 10.7. Note the distinctions between advice and representation throughout these provisions.

- advise any client who requests it who is in custody;
- make a bail application where a client in custody requires a bail application and such an application has not previously been made by a duty solicitor;
- advise a client before the court in connection with 'prescribed proceedings' (civil orders deemed to be criminal for legal aid purposes). The full list of prescribed proceedings appears below at para 15.71;[82]
- cross-examine, save in exceptional circumstances, under Youth Justice and Criminal Evidence Act 1999 s38 if appointed to do so by the court.[83]
- The duty solicitor must also:[84]
  - advise and represent any client who is in custody on a plea of guilty and wishes the case to be concluded that day;
  - advise and represent any client before the court for failure to pay a fine or other sum or to obey an order of the court, and such failure may lead to the client being at risk of imprisonment;
  - advise and represent a client not in custody in connection with an imprisonable offence;
  - help a client in making an application for a representation order, whether the nominated solicitor is the duty solicitor or another solicitor;
  - advise and represent a client seeking to vary police-imposed bail conditions pre-charge.
- The duty solicitor must not:
  - represent in committal proceedings (note that although committals have been abolished, the 2017 Contract Specification still refers to committal hearings);
  - represent at a not guilty trial or in relation to a non-imprisonable offence unless within the provisions above;[85]
  - advise or represent a client who has had the services of a duty solicitor at a previous hearing in the proceedings (except where they are before the court this time as a result of failure to pay a fine or other sum or comply with an order imposed previously).[86]

---

82 Criminal Legal Aid (General) Regulations 2013 reg 9.
83 Standard Crime Contract 2017 Specification para 10.15.
84 Standard Crime Contract 2017 Specification para 10.8.
85 Standard Crime Contract 2017 Specification para 10.9.
86 Standard Crime Contract 2017 Specification para 10.10.

As duty solicitor, with the client's permission you are entitled to take on the case and apply for a representation order. However, you must not apply for a representation order where the case concludes on the day of the duty.[87]

Representation orders – magistrates' court

Scope

15.70   A representation order is the main method of funding proceedings in the magistrates' court.

15.71   It covers representation of clients charged or summoned, or requisitioned for criminal offences, and also covers proceedings deemed to be criminal for the purpose of legal aid funding, as set out in Criminal Legal Aid (General) Regulations 2013 reg 9:[88]

(a) civil proceedings in a magistrates' court arising from a failure to pay a sum due or to obey an order of that court where such failure carries the risk of imprisonment;

(b) proceedings under sections 14B, 14D, 14G, 14H, 21B and 21D of the Football Spectators Act 1989 in relation to banning orders and references to a court;

(c) proceedings under section 5A of the Protection from Harassment Act 1997 in relation to restraining orders on acquittal;

(d), (e) [Revoked.]

(f) proceedings in relation to parenting orders made under section 8(1)(b) of the Crime and Disorder Act 1998 where an order under section 22 of the Anti-social Behaviour, Crime and Policing Act 2014 or a sexual harm prevention order under section 103A of the Sexual Offences Act 2003 is made;

(g) proceedings under section 8(1)(c) of the Crime and Disorder Act 1998 in relation to parenting orders made on the conviction of a child;

(h) proceedings under section 9(5) of the Crime and Disorder Act 1998 to discharge or vary a parenting order made as set out in sub-paragraph (f) or (g);

(i) proceedings under section 10 of the Crime and Disorder Act 1998 in relation to an appeal against a parenting order made as set out in sub-paragraph (f) or (g);

(j) proceedings under Part 1A of Schedule 1 to the Powers of Criminal Courts (Sentencing) Act 2000 in relation to parenting orders for failure to comply with orders under section 20 of that Act;

---

87 Standard Crime Contract 2017 Specification para 10.14.

88 As amended by the Criminal Legal Aid (General) (Amendment) Regulations 2015 and the Civil and Criminal Legal Aid (Amendment) Regulations 2015.

(ja) proceedings, in a youth court, in relation to a breach or potential breach of a provision in an injunction under Part 1 of the Anti-social Behaviour, Crime and Policing Act 2014 where the person subject to the injunction is under 14.

(k) proceedings under sections 80, 82, 83 and 84 of the Anti-social Behaviour, Crime and Policing Act 2014 where a person has engaged in or is likely to engage in behaviour that constitutes a criminal offence on the premises;

(ka) proceedings under paragraph 3 of Schedule 2 to the Female Genital Mutilation Act 2003 in relation to female genital mutilation protection orders made other than on conviction and related appeals;

(kb) proceedings under paragraph 6 of Schedule 2 to the Female Genital Mutilation Act 2003 in relation to female genital mutilation protection orders made under paragraph 3 of that Schedule;

(l) proceedings under sections 20, 22, 26 and 28 of the Anti-social Behaviour Act 2003 in relation to parenting orders–
  (i)   in cases of exclusion from school; or
  (ii) in respect of criminal conduct and anti-social behaviour;

(m) proceedings under sections 97, 100 and 101 of the Sexual Offences Act 2003 in relation to notification orders and interim notification orders;

(n) proceedings under sections 103A, 103E, 103F and 103H of the Sexual Offences Act 2003 in relation to sexual harm offences prevention orders and interim sexual harm offences prevention orders;

(o) [Revoked.]

(p) proceedings under sections 122A, 122D, 122E and 122G of the Sexual Offences Act 2003 in relation to sexual risk orders;

(q) [Revoked.]

(r) proceedings under section 13 of the Tribunals, Courts and Enforcement Act 2007 on appeal against a decision of the Upper Tribunal in proceedings in respect of–
  (i)   a decision of the Financial Conduct Authority;
  (ia) a decision of the Prudential Regulation Authority;
  (ii) a decision of the Bank of England; or
  (iii) a decision of a person in relation to the assessment of any compensation or consideration under the Banking (Special Provisions) Act 2008 or the Banking Act 2009;

(s) proceedings before the Crown Court or the Court of Appeal in relation to serious crime prevention orders under sections 19, 20, 21 and 24 of the Serious Crime Act 2007;

(t) proceedings under sections 100, 101, 103, 104 and 106 of the Criminal Justice and Immigration Act 2008 in relation to violent offender orders and interim violent offender orders;

(u) proceedings under sections 26, 27 and 29 of the Crime and Security Act 2010 in relation to–
  (i)   domestic violence protection notices; or
  (ii) domestic violence protection orders;

(ua) proceedings under sections 14(1)(b) and (c), 15 and 20 to 22 of the Modern Slavery Act 2015 in relation to slavery and trafficking prevention orders;

(ub) proceedings under sections 23 and 27 to 29 of the Modern Slavery Act 2015 in relation to slavery and trafficking risk orders,

(uc) proceedings under Part 2 of the Offensive Weapons Act 2019 in relation to a knife crime prevention order or an interim knife crime prevention order;

(ud) proceedings under sections 1, 4, 5 and 7 of the Stalking Protecting Act 2019 in relation to stalking protection orders and interim stalking protection orders; and

(v) any other proceedings that involve the determination of a criminal charge for the purposes of Article 6(1) of the European Convention on Human Rights.

Sub-paragraph (v) includes contempt other than in the face of the court, at all levels of court in all proceedings, including criminal, family, and civil and on appeal. (In the High Court see *King's Lynn and West Norfolk BC v Bunning*;[89] in the county court see *Brown v Haringey LBC*;[90] and in the Court of Appeal and generally see *Devon CC v Kirk*.[91]) Respondents to committal proceedings in courts other than the magistrates' court are entitled to non-means-tested legal aid (*CH v CT* [2018] EWHC 1310 (Fam), approved by *Re O (committal: legal representation)*, [2019] EWCA Civ 1721). Applications for legal aid in the High Court should be made to the Nottingham Office of the Legal Aid Agency; applications in relation to the Court of Appeal are made to that court.

Case study

My client is in arrears on council tax. She has been summoned to appear at the magistrates' court. I cannot represent her. Can I advise her to see the court duty solicitor?

She is in principle eligible to see the duty solicitor, since she is before the court for failure to pay a sum due. Whether she can use the duty depends on whether she is at risk of imprisonment, which is the merits test. That will depend on the facts of her case and is more likely if she is in wilful default or has shown culpable neglect.

15.72   An order also covers advice on appeal, and any related bail proceedings in the Crown Court or High Court.[92]

---

89 [2013] EWHC 3390 (QB).
90 [2015] EWCA Civ 483.
91 [2016] EWCA Civ 1221.
92 Standard Crime Contract 2017 Specification para 10.36.

Financial eligibility

15.73   Representation orders are means tested. Therefore a full application for a representation order (including means information) must be completed in all cases.

15.74   Applications for representation orders are made to the LAA which will apply the means test to decide whether the client is eligible. However, you will need an understanding of the test in order to advise clients whether they are likely to be eligible. You can use the LAA's calculator on its website: www.gov.uk/guidance/ criminal- legal-aid- means-testing.

15.75   The details of the test, together with the eligibility limits applying from time to time can be found in the Criminal Legal Aid (Financial Resources) Regulations 2013 as amended. The eligibility limits are very occasionally amended, and the discussion that follows is based on the limits applying since June 2016. There is guidance in the Criminal Legal Aid Manual and on the LAA website at: www.gov.uk/ guidance/criminal-legal-aid-means-testing.

15.76   Eligibility for a representation order is based solely on income – capital is not taken into account except where there is a conviction at the Crown Court. There are three stages to the test:

1) Is the client under the age of 18, or directly or indirectly in receipt of a passporting benefit? (See para 15.78.)
2) If not, is the client's gross income below the initial test threshold?
3) If not, is the client's disposable income below the full means test threshold?

If the answer to all three questions is no, the client is automatically not eligible.

15.77   The means of the client's partner should always be taken into account, unless the partner has a contrary interest in the proceedings (for example, is a victim or prosecution witness), together with the resources of any other person which have been or are likely to be made available to the client.[93]

15.78   The passporting benefits are:[94]

- income support;
- income-based jobseeker's allowance;
- guarantee state pension credit;
- income-related ESA;
- universal credit.

---

93   Criminal Legal Aid (Financial Resources) Regulations 2013 reg 19.
94   Criminal Legal Aid (Financial Resources) Regulations 2013 reg 2.

If the client is directly or indirectly in receipt of any of these, he or she will automatically be eligible for legal aid. 'Indirectly in receipt' means that the client is included as a dependant on another person's claim.

15.79   If the client is not passported, you will need to proceed to the two-stage means test. If gross income is below the initial threshold, currently £12,457, then he or she is eligible. If gross income is over £22,325, he or she is not eligible.[95] If gross income is between those two figures, then a full means test to determine disposable income will be required. Following that test, if disposable income is less than £3,398 the client will be eligible. All figures are annual.

15.80   'Gross income' is all income from all sources, excluding certain benefits:[96]

- attendance allowance;
- severe disablement allowance;
- carer's allowance;
- disability living allowance;
- constant attendance allowance;
- housing benefit;
- council tax benefit;
- payments out of the social fund;
- direct payments under the Care Act 2014, Children and Families Act 2014, the Carers and Direct Payments Act (Northern Ireland) 2002 and the Social Services and Well-being (Wales) Act 2014;
- exceptionally severe disablement allowance;
- service pensions paid under the Naval, Military and Air Forces Etc (Disablement and Death) Service Pensions Order 2006;
- independent living funds payments;
- financial support paid for the foster care of a child;
- reasonable living expenses provided for as an exception to a restraint order under Proceeds of Crime Act 2002 s41;
- universal credit payments on account;
- PIPs.

15.81   Where the client has a partner or children in the same household, the gross income threshold increases according to the following weighting:[97]

---

95 Criminal Legal Aid (Financial Resources) Regulations 2013 reg 18.
96 Criminal Legal Aid (Financial Resources) Regulations 2013 reg 20.
97 Criminal Legal Aid (Financial Resources) Regulations 2013 Schedule.

Person	Weighting
Partner	0.64
Child 0–1 year	0.15
Child 2–4 years	0.30
Child 5–7 years	0.34
Child 8–10 years	0.38
Child 11–12 years	0.41
Child 13–15 years	0.44
Child 16–17 years	0.59

15.82   To calculate the weighting, add the relevant factors to 1 and divide household income by the result.

Case study

My client earns £25,000 per year. He lives with his partner and their children, aged 6 and 3. Is he eligible for a representation order?

The client has a partner and two children, so the weighting is 1 + 0.64 + 0.30 + 0.34 = 2.28. Weighted income = £25,000 divided by 2.28 = £10,964.91. The gross income threshold is £12,457 and the weighted income is below that, so your client is eligible.

15.83   Where the client is not eligible on gross income, but the (weighted) household income is below the upper threshold, you will need to consider whether the client is eligible on disposable income.[98]

15.84   'Disposable income' is gross income minus:

- tax and National Insurance paid;
- council tax paid;
- rent, mortgage, etc;
- childcare costs;
- maintenance payments;
- living expenses allowance.

15.85   The living expenses allowance is a notional cost of living allowance, currently £5,676 per year. Where the client has a partner and/or children, the allowance is increased using the scale in the table above – so, in the case study, the allowance would be £5,676 x 2.28 = £12,941.28.

---

98 Criminal Legal Aid (Financial Resources) Regulations 2013 reg 18.

15.86 Proof of means will always be required to accompany the application, except where the client is in custody, in which case a statement of truth (now incorporated within form CRM15) should be signed instead, or unless the client's sole income is state benefits, in which case the courts can use their direct computer link with the DWP to check against the client's National Insurance number that the means information is correct.

15.87 Where the client is not financially eligible, but can demonstrate that to pay privately would cause him or her real hardship, an application can be made for hardship funding. This application is made on form CRM16 to the LAA, and whether to grant is at the LAA's discretion.

Merits test

15.88 The merits test for the grant of representation orders is the 'interests of justice' test. The test is set out in Legal Aid, Sentencing and Punishment of Offenders Act 2012 (LASPO) s17(2), which says:

> In deciding what the interests of justice consist of [in relation to any individual], the following factors must be taken into account–
>
> (a) whether, if any matter arising in the proceedings is decided against the individual, the individual would be likely to lose his or her liberty or livelihood or suffer serious damage to his or her reputation,
>
> (b) whether the determination of any matter arising in the proceedings may involve consideration of a substantial question of law,
>
> (c) whether the individual may be unable to understand the proceedings or to state his or her own case,
>
> (d) whether the proceedings may involve the tracing, interviewing or expert cross-examination of witnesses on behalf of the individual, and
>
> (e) whether it is in the interests of another person that the individual be represented.

Note that this list is not exhaustive, merely examples of what can be taken into account. Guidance on the merits test as applied by the courts contains helpful information about factors that are considered.[99] Where reliance is placed on the existence of previous convictions the LAA requires evidence of these either from the IDPC or older files. Significant regard is paid to sentencing guidelines.

---

99 *Interests of Justice: Guidance on the consideration of Defence Representation Order Applications* (May 2018) is available at: www.gov.uk/government/uploads/system/uploads/attachment_data/file/314453/LAA-guidance-consideration-defence-representation-order-applications.pdf.

15.89   Applications for representation orders should be made to the LAA, electronically. There is information about electronic submission of crime forms on the LAA website: www.gov.uk/guidance/legal-aid-crime-eform. Forms CRM14 and CRM15 (where required) should be completed and submitted. If your client is present when you submit the electronic forms, the client can sign the applicant's declaration for online submissions available from the LAA. In all other cases, it is important that the CRM14 and (when relevant) CRM 15 are kept on file for audit purposes. Where your client is not in custody, full evidence of means will be required. Where the client is in custody, the declaration in form CRM15 can be signed instead – this is a statement of truth that the information regarding means is accurate.

15.90   An application should be submitted as soon as possible after charge. Orders are deemed to be granted on the date a properly completed application was received, which will be immediately if submitted electronically.[100]

15.91   Where an application is granted, funding for the magistrates' court element of the case is in place and preparation can begin.

15.92   Where the application is refused on means, there is no right of appeal, although applicants can ask for a recalculation if he or she believes that an error has been made, and a fresh application can be submitted at any time (if, for example, there is a change of circumstances). Where the application is refused on the merits, there is a right of appeal to the magistrates' court, who will either confirm the original decision or grant an order.[101]

Funding in the absence of an order

Virtual courts

15.93   Advocacy assistance is available for work conducted in a virtual court, whether the work is done at the police station or in a court.[102] There is no merits or financial test.[103] Basic information must be recorded.[104] Claims can be made if the case concludes at the first hearing or if the solicitor's representation ends at that hearing.[105] The Virtual Court Appearance Fee must not be claimed if a representation order

100 Criminal Legal Aid (General) Regulations 2013 reg 23.
101 Criminal Legal Aid (General) Regulations 2013 reg 29.
102 Standard Crime Contract 2017 Specification para 10.22.
103 Standard Crime Contract 2017 Specification paras 10.23–10.24.
104 Standard Crime Contract 2017 Specification para 10.26.
105 Standard Crime Contract 2017 Specification para 10.28.

is subsequently granted to the same firm of solicitors.[106] Nor is the fee available if a representation order has already been granted.[107]

Other pre-order costs

15.94 The general rule is that no work can be done and no costs claimed until such time as a representation order has been granted.

15.95 However, an order can be backdated so that a claim can be made for pre-order work where:[108]

- urgent work was required (defined as being a hearing within ten working days of taking initial instructions);
- there was no undue delay in making the application (that is, it was submitted no more than five working days after taking initial instructions); and
- an order is subsequently granted.

If all these conditions are granted, you are able to claim for work done from the time of initial instructions onwards – or if later, from the point of charge onwards.

15.96 Where an order is subsequently refused, you can nevertheless make a claim for work done in certain circumstances:

- Where the application is refused on means, an Early Cover[109] fixed fee of £75 may be claimed if:
  - the application was submitted by 9am on the sixth working day following initial instructions;
  - you have taken all reasonable steps to assist the client to complete the forms and provide appropriate evidence;
  - no decision had been made on the application by the first hearing;
  - you represent the client at the first hearing, and that hearing moves the case forward and any adjournment is justified; and
  - the eventual decision is that the case passes the interests of justice test but the client fails the means test.
- Where the application has been refused on the merits, a Pre-Order Cover[110] claim, limited to one hour's work at preparation rates, may be made if:

---

106 Standard Crime Contract 2017 Specification para 10.29.
107 Standard Crime Contract 2017 Specification paras 10.30–10.31.
108 Standard Crime Contract 2017 Specification para 10.40.
109 Standard Crime Contract 2017 Specification para 10.122.
110 Standard Crime Contract 2017 Specification para 10.115.

- a qualified solicitor documents on file why it was believed the interests of justice test was passed; and
- no claim for early cover is made.[111]
- You can claim a means test form completion[112] fixed fee of £25 where:
  - you complete an application for representation on behalf of the client, whether or not it is actually submitted;
  - you advise the client that although the interests of justice test is in all probability satisfied, the client would fail the means test and the file is marked accordingly;
  - such advice was given within ten working days of charge or summons;
  - the client does not go on to instruct you privately; and
  - you do not make a claim for early cover or pre-order cover.

Disbursements and prior authority

15.97   Disbursements can be incurred in accordance with the general rules – see above. When you are considering large expenditure, you can apply to the LAA for prior authority to incur the disbursement.[113] The effect of prior authority is that, provided the expenditure does not exceed the terms or amount of the authority, no question can normally be raised as to it on assessment – in other words, you are generally guaranteed to be paid.[114] If authority is refused by the LAA, or not granted in full, the application automatically goes before a Costs Assessor, but beyond that there is no appeal – though there is nothing to stop you making a further application at any time.[115]

15.98   If authority is refused, that does not prevent you from incurring the disbursement, it merely means that you do not have the security of knowing it will be paid on assessment.

15.99   Prior authority will be refused, and so will the disbursement if incurred, where it is a disbursement that should have come out of central funds, for example a court ordered report in consideration of

---

111 Standard Crime Contract 2017 Specification para 10.116.
112 Standard Crime Contract 2017 Specification para 10.124.
113 Standard Crime Contract 2017 Specification para 5.27.
114 Standard Crime Contract 2017 Specification para 5.29.
115 Standard Crime Contract 2017 Specification para 5.28.

a Mental Health Act 1983 disposal.[116] Privilege does not attach to such reports, and it is normally preferable for you to obtain the report for which authority may then be given.

15.100 Where an application for prior authority has been made and refused, and the client nevertheless instructs you to incur the expense, you may accept payment from the client or a third party for that expense.[117] This is an exception to the rule that legal aid is complete remuneration for the case and no additional charge may be made to the client or a third party.[118]

Counsel

15.101 A representation order for work in the magistrates' court is usually limited to representation by solicitor only. This does not mean that you cannot instruct counsel at all, it just means that counsel is not assigned by the order and therefore the rules regarding unassigned counsel apply.[119] This means that you are responsible for agreeing and paying counsel's fees.[120]

15.102 In more serious cases, you can apply to the court for counsel (or an independent solicitor advocate) to be assigned. Where counsel is assigned, they are entitled to be paid directly by the LAA at the rates prescribed in the contract, though you should submit their bill with your own[121] – see chapter 17.

15.103 Whether or not counsel is assigned, you must provide them with the UFN and a copy of the representation order when briefing them.[122]

15.104 For more details on the instruction of counsel, please refer to chapter 21.

Separate matters

15.105 All work done in the proceedings class is described by the LAA as a case. Only one bill can be submitted per case.[123] A case is all work done for all clients in respect of:

---

116 Standard Crime Contract 2017 Specification para 5.35(a).
117 Standard Crime Contract 2017 Specification para 8.43.
118 Standard Crime Contract 2017 Specification para 8.41.
119 Standard Crime Contract 2017 Specification paras 10.46–10.55.
120 Standard Crime Contract 2017 Specification para 10.46.
121 Standard Crime Contract 2017 Specification para 10.44.
122 Standard Crime Contract 2017 Specification para 10.43.
123 Standard Crime Contract 2017 Specification para 10.59.

- one offence; or
- more than one offence where the charges are laid at the same time; or
- more than one offence where the charges are founded on the same facts; or
- more than one offence where the charges form a series of offences.[124]

15.106 'Founded on the same facts' covers situations where one charge is withdrawn and replaced by another, or where two charges are laid as alternatives.

15.107 'Series of offences' means offences of a similar nature. For example, where a client is charged with two separate offences which could be tried together, that would constitute one case. Similarly, where two clients are charged with the same offence (assuming you act for both), that would also be one case. There is no hard and fast rule here; the contract does not offer definitive guidance, and it is a matter for your judgment (subject to LAA audit) whether you decide there is one case or two.[125]

Co-defendants and conflict of interest

15.108 Note that the Regulations say that 'where an individual who is granted a right to representation is one of two or more co-defendants whose cases are to be heard together, that individual must select the same litigator as a co-defendant unless there is, or is likely to be, a conflict of interest'.[126] Therefore, if you are making an application for a representation order on behalf of a client whose co-defendant is separately represented, you should ensure that you demonstrate on the application form why there is a potential conflict requiring separate representation.

15.109 There is a practice note on the Law Society's website,[127] which deals with many examples of possible conflict in criminal cases. Although the 2007 Code of Conduct has been superseded, the guidance to the old rule 3 may still be helpful. It stated:

---

124 Standard Crime Contract 2017 Specification para 10.69.
125 Standard Crime Contract 2017 Specification para 10.72; and see chapter 16.
126 Criminal Legal Aid (Determinations by a Court and Choice of Representative) Regulations 2013 reg 13.
127 www.lawsociety.org.uk/support-services/advice/practice-notes/conflict-of-interests-in-criminal-cases/.

... the regulations are not intended to put solicitors in a position where they are asked by the court to act contrary to their professional responsibilities. If asked by the court for your reasons why you cannot act for both defendants, you must not give information which would breach your duty of confidentiality to your client(s). This will normally mean that you can say no more than that it would be unprofessional for you to continue to act.

15.110 Therefore, you do not have to disclose reasons why a potential conflict of interest exists, which prevents you from acting for more than one defendant. However, where such a reason exists, you should make clear on the application that there is a (potential) conflict, to avoid you being appointed for both defendants, or to avoid delay while the court makes further enquiries.

Transfer cases

15.111 Where the client wants to transfer from one solicitor to another, that can only happen if the court agrees to the transfer of the order.

15.112 Transfers are governed by regulation, not by the contract. The regulations say that the court may grant an application to transfer where:

- the solicitor appointed under the order considers himself or herself under a professional duty to withdraw;
- there is breakdown in the relationship between solicitor and client such that effective representation can no longer be provided;
- through circumstances beyond his or her control, the authorised solicitor can no longer represent the client;
- there is some other substantial compelling reason.[128]

15.113 Note that any explanation will be strenuously tested by the courts. Solicitors must exercise a proper and independent judgment when considering the applicant's grounds.[129]

Matter ends

15.114 A matter ends, and a bill must be submitted, when the case comes to an end in the proceedings class. This will happen when:

128 Criminal Legal Aid (Determinations by a Court and Choice of Representative) Regulations 2013 reg 14.

129 *R (Sanjari) v Birmingham Crown Court* [2015] EWHC 2037 (Admin).

- the case has concluded (for example, by acquittal, sentence or committal);
- it is known that no further work will be needed (eg where the client has transferred);
- it is unclear whether further work will be required but at least one month has elapsed since the last work was done;[130]
- the LAA notify you that the case is a VHCC; or
- the representation order is withdrawn.[131]

Representation in the Crown Court

15.115   Cases in the Crown Court are generally funded by representation orders.

The merits test

15.116   The merits test for a Crown Court representation order is the interests of justice test, just as in the magistrates' court – see above.[132]

15.117   Where a case goes from the magistrates' to the Crown Court, except on appeal, the magistrates' court representation order will automatically continue into the Crown Court,[133] and no application to extend or amend the order is required (although additional supporting evidence as to means may have to be provided). If a case is sent to the Crown Court (but not on an appeal) the interests of justice test is deemed to be met.[134] Even if counsel were not assigned under the order in the magistrates' court, once the case goes to the Crown Court the order is deemed to include representation by one junior advocate (that is, any advocate other than a QC) automatically.[135]

15.118   For more information on the instruction of advocates in the Crown Court, see chapter 21.

Means testing

15.119   Representation orders in the Crown Court are means tested. However, the means test takes into account both a client's income and capital.

---

130 Standard Crime Contract 2017 Specification para 10.62.
131 Standard Crime Contract 2017 Specification para 10.56.
132 Criminal Legal Aid (General) Regulations 2013 reg 21; Standard Crime Contract 2017 Specification para 10.144.
133 Criminal Legal Aid (General) Regulations 2013 reg 24.
134 Criminal Legal Aid (General) Regulations 2013 reg 25.
135 Criminal Legal Aid (General) Regulations 2013 reg 18.

15.120   Depending on their means, clients may be:

- granted an order without any financial contribution;
- required to make payments towards the cost of their representation either immediately or following the conclusion of their case, if they are convicted; or
- refused legal aid.[136]

15.121 Certain clients are still passported. These are the same clients who would be passported in the magistrates' court, ie those under 18 or in receipt of income support, income-based jobseeker's allowance, guaranteed state pension credit or income-related ESA or universal credit.

15.122   For those who are not passported, the client's means must be considered. In the Crown Court, unlike in the magistrates' court, this involves assessment of the client's capital as well as income. The means test is the same as in the magistrates' court, save that if the household disposable income is £37,500 or more, the applicant is not eligible for legal aid. The means test can be considered in two stages – income and capital – as follows.

Income

15.123 When the case becomes a Crown Court case, the client who is eligible with a contribution will be required to make monthly contributions towards the cost of his or her representation for the first five months after the case is sent to the Crown Court. The client's annual disposable income will be divided by 12 and the client will be asked to pay 90 per cent of the monthly figure each month for the first five months. Alternatively, the client can pay all five payments up-front in one lump sum.

15.124   Late payment of any of the five monthly contributions will result in an additional month's payment, ie the client will have to pay the same amount again for a sixth month.

15.125   There is a cap on *income* contributions which is determined by the type of offence. If a client's contributions reach the maximum level, the client will be notified and will not be required to make any further income contributions.[137]

15.126   If a client's case concludes within the first five months of being transferred to the Crown Court, the client will not be required to continue paying income contributions.

---

136 Criminal Legal Aid (Contribution Orders) Regulations 2013.
137 Criminal Legal Aid (Contribution Orders) Regulations 2013 reg 16.

15.127   Assuming the case continues beyond five (or six) months from transfer to the Crown Court, the client will not be required to make any further contributions until the conclusion of his or her case.

15.128   If the client is acquitted, the client will not be required to make any further payments at all and the client's income contributions will be refunded in full with interest (currently set at a rate of two per cent annual compound interest). (Note that any costs associated with late payment may be deducted, and very occasionally a client may be required to make a contribution towards his or her defence costs where, for example, the client has misled the prosecution or the court or brought the prosecution on himself or herself by his or her own conduct. This would be a matter for the judge to decide.)

15.129   However, if the client is convicted, the client's position will depend on the costs of his or her case. If the client's income contributions have exceeded the actual costs of the case, the overpayment will be refunded with interest (again, subject to any deduction associated with late payment). However, if the income contributions are less than the actual costs incurred, the client's capital will then be considered.

Capital

15.130 A client will only be required to contribute from his or her capital[138] at the conclusion of his or her case if:

- the client is convicted;
- any payments already made from income do not cover the client's defence costs; and
- the client has more than £30,000 of assets (eg savings, equity in property, shares or Premium Bonds).[139]

Not only can this result in a further payment towards profit costs, but significantly, towards high-cost disbursements.

15.131   A client with less than £30,000 worth of assets will not be required to make any further contribution, even if the client's income contributions have not covered his or her defence costs. (Note, however, that this threshold may be removed if evidence of the client's assets has not been provided.)

15.132   A client with more than £30,000 worth of assets whose income contributions have not accounted for the full costs, will be required to make up the shortfall from his or her assets. The costs may be

---

138 Criminal Legal Aid (Contribution Orders) Regulations 2013 reg 27.
139 Criminal Legal Aid (Contribution Orders) Regulations 2013 reg 28.

recovered in various ways. For example, the LAA may apply an interest-bearing or non-interest-bearing charge to a property or, as a last resort, apply for an order for sale.

15.133 If a client, liable for any contribution either from income or capital, is acquitted of some but not all charges, it is critical that the court is asked to make an apportionment order identifying the percentage of the costs for which the defendant is liable. There is a strict 21-day time limit for applications for such orders.[140]

Applications

15.134 If the order was not granted at the magistrates' court stage, Crown Court means testing means that a complete application for a representation order (forms CRM14 and CRM15 when appropriate) must be submitted to the LAA.

15.135 The same rules apply in the Crown Court as in the magistrates' court regarding applications from children and vulnerable adults.

15.136 A major difference between applications for funding in the magistrates' court and in the Crown Court is that clients who are in custody cannot self-declare as to their means when their case is in the Crown Court.

15.137 This does not mean that all evidence (payslips, bank statements, tax returns, share certificates and so on) must be provided with the initial application, although the CRM15 must contain all of the required information. Provided the completed forms have been submitted, a representation order will be issued. The client then has 14 days in which to provide the required documentary evidence. If the required documents are not provided in this time, sanctions may be imposed with respect to both income and capital:

- If evidence of income is not provided, the client's monthly contribution could increase to £900 or 100 per cent of the client's monthly disposable income, whichever is higher.
- If evidence of capital is not provided (or the information provided is subsequently found to be incorrect), the LAA may remove the £30,000 capital threshold and require a client who has less than this amount in capital to pay towards the costs of their defence.

15.138 Where the evidence required is over and above what would normally be required for a magistrates' court legal aid application, you may be able to claim an evidence provision fee for helping the client to

140 Criminal Legal Aid (Contribution Orders) Regulations 2013 reg 26. *R (Khan) v Director of Legal Aid Casework* [2018] EWHC 3198 (Admin).

provide this evidence. For standard applications a fee of £45 plus VAT can be claimed. For more complex applications, involving five or more pieces of evidence, or a self-employed client whose application is referred to the National Crime Team, a fee of £90 plus VAT can be claimed.

15.139   When the completed application has been assessed, the client will be issued with a Contribution Notice or Order alongside the representation order, detailing how much they will be required to pay and the sanctions for late or non-payment.

15.140   A client can also apply for a review on the grounds of hardship if the client feels that he or she has higher than usual outgoings or would suffer financial hardship as a result of the means assessment. A completed form CRM16 must be submitted. This can be submitted either at the same time as the CRM14 and CRM15 forms, or afterwards.

Assessing case costs

15.141   Case costs in the Crown Court will vary considerably, depending on the type of case, the volume of evidence, the need for expert witnesses and so on. Therefore, at the outset of a case it may be difficult to foresee whether a client's contributions will match the actual case costs.

15.142   The cap imposed on income contributions is intended to prevent clients from paying substantially more than the likely case costs up front, although it should be noted that according to the LAA figures, the cap is well above the average cost to trial in all categories of cases.

15.143   The actual case costs will be calculated at the end of the case and will include the total litigator and advocate fees and any payments to expert witnesses and other disbursements. At the end of the case, this amount will be compared with the amount the client has already paid in income contributions: if the client has already paid more than the actual costs, the difference will be refunded with interest; if the client has paid less, the client may be required to contribute further from capital as described above. The client will be notified of the position and any amount the client owes once the full costs have been established at the end of the case.

Effects of Crown Court means testing

15.144   Because of the potentially high costs of Crown Court cases and the obligation to keep the client informed of the potential costs (Code of Conduct 2011, O1.13) it is essential that the cost implications of any step in the proceedings are thoroughly considered. This will be particularly important in cases where, for example, expert evidence is required: the client should be advised of the cost implications prior to the instruction of any expert and cost considerations may have an impact on the conduct of the case.

15.145   Clients may also be more reluctant to instruct a solicitor at all, and therefore it will be important to advise clients at the outset as to the potential costs (given the type of case), the advantages of being represented and, if appropriate, the possibility of a hardship application. Such an application takes account of the potential private client rates to see if the applicant has sufficient funds to meet them.

15.146   The supporting evidence requirements for a Crown Court legal aid application are more onerous than those in the magistrates' court. Therefore, where a case is sent to the Crown Court and evidence has not already been provided, it is essential that this evidence is obtained as quickly as possible, as failure to provide this evidence within 14 days may have serious financial consequences for the client (see above).

Disbursements

15.147   Disbursements may be incurred in exactly the same way as in the magistrates' court. The test as to whether they are justified is the same, and applications for prior authority may be made.[141] The process is exactly the same as for magistrates' court cases: applications are made directly to the LAA.

15.148   Where the disbursement exceeds £100, you have prior authority and have in fact incurred the disbursement, you can make an application for payment on account of that disbursement at any time. Provided that the amount and scope of the prior authority have not been exceeded, payment should be made.[142] See also chapter 17.

Prescribed proceedings in the Crown Court[143]

15.149   Some civil proceedings have been deemed to be criminal for the purposes of legal aid[144] (designated 'prescribed proceedings'), and where orders are imposed in the magistrates' court, the appeal lies to the Crown Court. Examples include stand-alone parenting orders,

141 Criminal Legal Aid (Remuneration) Regulations 2013 reg 13.
142 Criminal Legal Aid (Remuneration) Regulations 2013 reg 14.
143 Standard Crime Contract 2017 Specification paras 10.131–10.142.
144 Criminal Legal Aid (General) Regulations 2013 reg 9 as amended; see para 15.69 for the full list.

football banning orders, and Sexual Offences Act 2003 orders. The full list is given above (para 15.71).

15.150 Where a standalone order is made by the magistrates' court, and the client wants to appeal it to the Crown Court, this will also be funded on an application by way of a representation order.

15.151 As for other representation orders in the Crown Court, funding for such cases is means tested and the client will need to submit completed forms CRM14 and, if appropriate, CRM15 (if non-passported), in this situation even if a representation order had been granted for the magistrates' court proceedings.

15.152 Claims are made as part of the normal monthly return and not by graduated fees. There is an upper limit to the costs that can be claimed for such work. Unless extended, this is £1,368.75.[145]

Appeals to the Crown Court

15.153 Other appeals to the Crown Court from the magistrates' court, whether against conviction, sentence or other order require a fresh application for funding. The means test is similar to that applied in the magistrates' court.

15.154 Clients who are passported or pass the means test will not be required to pay any contribution towards the cost of their appeal.

15.155 Clients who do not pass the means test will be required to pay a defined contribution in the following appeals:

- £500 if an appeal against conviction is dismissed or abandoned;
- £250 if an appeal against conviction is dismissed but sentence is reduced;
- £250 if an appeal against sentence or order is dismissed or abandoned.

15.156 All applications for funding will also be subject to the interests of justice test.

Recovery of defence costs orders

15.157 Prior to the introduction of Crown Court means testing, Recovery of Defence Costs Orders (RDCOs) were the mechanism used to recover the costs paid out to wealthy defendants who were convicted. RDCOs no longer apply in cases where funding is subject to the Crown Court means testing rules.

---

145 Criminal Legal Aid (Remuneration) Regulations 2013 Sch 4 para 7 as amended.

15.158   However, RCDOs may still be imposed to recover defence costs in the High Court, including the Court of Appeal, as means testing does not apply to these proceedings.

Appeals and reviews

Scope

15.159 Work in the appeals and reviews class covers representation in the High Court on an appeal by way of case stated, advice on an application to the Criminal Cases Review Commission, and advice on appeals to the Court of Appeal.

Case stated

15.160 Where the client seeks an appeal to the High Court by way of case stated, the appeal is funded by a representation order. The original order in the magistrates' court (or as the case may be, the Crown Court) covers advice on appeal,[146] including the application to the magistrates' court to state a case.[147]

15.161   Once the case is lodged at the High Court, an application for representation in the appeal should be made to the High Court.[148] It is an application for a criminal representation order. There is no means test, and the merits test is deemed to be met.[149] If the appeal is unsuccessful, a recovery of defence costs order can be considered by the court.[150]

15.162   Where disbursements are needed, you can make an application to the LAA for prior authority.[151] Counsel may be instructed under the order.[152]

---

146 Standard Crime Contract 2017 Specification para 11.3.

147 Standard Crime Contract 2017 Specification paras 11.44–11.61.

148 Standard Crime Contract 2017 Specification para 11.48; Criminal Legal Aid (Determinations by a Court and Choice of Representative) Regulations 2013 reg 7.

149 Criminal Legal Aid (General) Regulations 2013 reg 21.

150 See the Criminal Legal Aid (Recovery of Defence Costs Orders) Regulations 2013.

151 Standard Crime Contract 2017 Specification para 11.57.

152 Standard Crime Contract 2017 Specification para 11.54.

Advice and assistance in the appeals class

15.163 Advice and assistance may be granted to assist a client with an application to the Criminal Cases Review Commission, or to appeal against conviction and/or sentence.

15.164 The representation order in the magistrates' or Crown Court includes the provision of advice on appeal,[153] up to the point where an appeal is lodged, and therefore where you represented a client in the magistrates' or Crown Court under legal aid, the advice on appeal should be given under the order. It would not be appropriate to grant advice and assistance for that.

15.165 Similarly, where a representation order is available from the Court of Appeal,[154] advice and assistance should not be used as an alternative to, or to supplement, the Court of Appeal's powers to grant a representation order where only counsel has been authorised.[155]

15.166 Therefore, the primary use of advice and assistance is in cases where the client was not represented, or was represented and seeks a second opinion on the appeal. This would apply whether the client is entitled to go direct to the Court of Appeal or would make an application to the Criminal Cases Review Commission (CCRC).

15.167 The general rules on advice and assistance (see the investigations class, above) will apply. The work is means tested[156] and subject to the sufficient benefit test.[157] Costs are limited to £273.75 (£456.25 in the case of a CCRC application) but may be extended on application to the LAA.[158]

15.168 When you are dealing with a CCRC case, the LAA recognises that substantial work may be required, particularly where you are not the solicitor who acted at the trial. This may include obtaining the prosecution and defence files, considering transcripts,[159] commissioning further expert evidence and conducting further investigations. However, you should screen the case at as early a stage as possible,

---

153 Standard Crime Contract 2017 Specification para 11.3.
154 Under the Criminal Legal Aid (Determinations by a Court and Choice of Representative) Regulations 2013 reg 8.
155 Standard Crime Contract 2017 Specification para 11.7.
156 Standard Crime Contract 2017 Specification para 11.9.
157 Standard Crime Contract 2017 Specification para 11.8.
158 Standard Crime Contract 2017 Specification para 11.42 and Criminal Legal Aid (Remuneration) Regulations 2013 Sch 4 para 8.
159 Standard Crime Contract 2017 Specification para 11.23.

and where there is no reasonable prospect it will meet the CCRC's criteria, refuse to carry out further work.[160]

Representation orders in the Court of Appeal

15.169 The Court of Appeal has the power to grant a representation order, but not until notice of appeal or application for leave to appeal has been submitted.[161]

15.170 The court can grant a representation order to an advocate alone,[162] and indeed this is usual practice. Applications for litigators will usually only be granted to undertake some specific step in the proceedings, such as to interview a witness, rather than for the appeal as a whole.

15.171 For Court of Appeal representation orders, the interests of justice test is deemed to be met.[163] There is no means test, but Recovery of Defence Costs Orders may be made.

Prison law work

15.172 Work in the prison law class is divided into two funding types:

1) advice and assistance; and
2) advocacy assistance.

15.173 Assistance under these two categories may be provided to prisoners (including those on remand and those released on licence or parole where appropriate) in the following types of cases:

- sentence cases;
- review of category A classification;
- application of rules 46 and 46A of the Prison Rules 1999 in relation to close supervision centres and separation centres;
- disciplinary cases;

---

160 Standard Crime Contract 2017 Specification para 11.22.
161 The earlier Criminal Defence Service (General) (No 2) Regulations 2001 reg 10(5) was so interpreted in *Revenue and Customs Prosecution Office v The Stokoe Partnership* [2007] EWHC 1588 (Admin): now the Criminal Legal Aid (Determinations by a Court and Choice of Representative) Regulations 2013 reg 8.
162 Criminal Legal Aid (Determinations by a Court and Choice of Representative) Regulations 2013 reg 8.
163 Criminal Legal Aid (General) Regulations 2013 reg 21.

- Parole Board cases, including reconsideration cases;[164]
- review of an individual's classification as a restricted status prisoner or inmate;
- review of the classification of a Young Offender Institution (YOI) inmate's classification as a category A inmate whose escape would be highly dangerous to the public, police or national security and for whom the aim is to make escape impossible.

15.174 The general rules on advice and assistance apply (see above in the investigations class), including the means test[165] and the test that there is a sufficient benefit to the client, having regard to the circumstances of the matter, including the personal circumstances of the client, to justify work or further work being carried out. There should be a realistic prospect of a positive outcome that would be of real benefit to the client.[166]

15.175   There are complex rules on the number of matters that may be opened.[167] An application for Parole Board reconsideration is treated as part of the original Parole Board case but a separate claim should be made if a reconsideration hearing is listed or directed.[168]

15.176   There are restrictive rules on when and how much travel and waiting time can be claimed[169] and a requirement to obtain prior authority to incur a disbursement in excess of £500.[170] There is specific authority to use agents, subject to the rules set out in the Standard Crime Contract 2017,[171] a practice followed by many firms. If counsel is used to give advice and assistance, there are specific rules on how their fees are to be claimed.[172]

15.177   Advice and assistance is limited to a fixed fee of £200.75 unless effective and waiting time costs (calculated at specified hourly rates) exceed £602.25, in which case the costs will be assessed.[173]

15.178   Advocacy assistance for disciplinary cases and Parole Board cases is paid under a standard fee scheme. This is similar to the fee scheme

---

164 Standard Crime Contract 2017 Specification paras 12.68–12.80, 12.81–12.89, 12.90–12.100, 12.101–12.112.
165 Standard Crime Contract 2017 Specification paras 12.13–12.14.
166 Standard Crime Contract 2017 Specification paras 12.5–12.12.
167 Standard Crime Contract 2017 Specification paras 12.23–12.31.
168 Standard Crime Contract 2017 Specification paras 12.114–12.115.
169 Standard Crime Contract 2017 Specification paras 12.32–12.37.
170 Standard Crime Contract 2017 Specification para 12.38.
171 Standard Crime Contract 2017 Specification para 12.40.
172 Standard Crime Contract 2017 Specification paras 12.41–12.44.
173 Criminal Legal Aid (Remuneration) Regulations 2013 Sch 4 para 11 as amended.

for magistrates' court cases, in that you may claim a lower standard fee, a higher standard fee or a non-standard fee depending on whether your profit and waiting time costs (but not travel) fall below, between or above two standard fee limits. Details of the limits are given in the amended Remuneration Regulations at Sch 4 para 11.

15.179   Both advice and assistance and advocacy assistance are granted by you, rather than by application to the LAA.

15.180   The client must complete the relevant forms (CRM1 and CRM2 or CRM3), and must pass the means test. Means are limited by both capital and disposable income, and the eligibility levels can be found on Keycard no 45A on the LAA website.[174] 'Disposable income' means all income received by the client and his or her partner, less tax, National Insurance and the dependants allowances set out on the keycard.

15.181   In all cases within scope, the sufficient benefit test must be satisfied, and in addition advocacy assistance may not be provided in disciplinary cases where:

- it appears unreasonable to grant in the particular circumstances of the case; or
- (where required) permission to be legally represented has not been granted by a Governor or other prison authority where appropriate.[175]

15.182 In all cases, you should record on the file how the merits test has been and continues to be met.[176]

15.183   Counsel may be instructed under advocacy assistance, but you may not claim for accompanying them to a hearing.[177] If you instruct counsel, you are responsible for agreeing a fee with them and paying them directly. There are restrictions on what can be recovered.[178]

Scope of prison law work

15.184 Advice and assistance may be provided regarding reviews of an individual's classification as a restricted status prisoner or inmate and of reviews of the classification of a YOI inmate's classification as a

---

174 www.gov.uk/government/uploads/system/uploads/attachment_data/file/ 390542/criminal-keycard-45.pdf. Dated 2014 but still current as at the date of writing.

175 Standard Crime Contract 2017 Specification para 12.94.

176 Standard Crime Contract 2017 Specification para 12.7.

177 Standard Crime Contract 2017 Specification para 12.47.

178 Standard Crime Contract 2017 Specification paras 12.43 and 12.46.

category A inmate whose escape would be highly dangerous to the public, police or national security and for whom the aim is to make escape impossible. Advice and representation may be provided in sentence cases where the case is about the calculation of the total time to be served before a prison is eligible for automatic release or for consideration of release by the Parole Board;[179] in cases involving the review of category A classification; and the application of rules 46 and 46A in relation to close supervision centres and separation centres.[180]

15.185   Advice and representation is available in all Parole Board cases including reconsideration cases.[181]

15.186   Advice and representation is only available in disciplinary cases that involve the determination of a criminal charge for the purposes of Article 6(1) of the European Convention on Human Rights (ECHR), or where the Governor has exercised the discretion to allow advice and assistance.[182]

Associated civil work

15.187 Associated civil work is civil work arising out of criminal proceedings – for example, judicial review or habeas corpus, the obtaining of anti-social behaviour injunctions in the youth court, or certain civil work under the Proceeds of Crime Act (POCA) 2002. Although you are permitted to do this work if you have a Standard Crime Contract, even if you don't have a Civil Contract, it is fundamentally civil work and the usual civil rules apply.[183] See chapters 3, 5 and 16 for more details of civil funding.

15.188   Criminal offences under POCA 2002 are dealt with in the same way as all other criminal offences. Confiscation as part of criminal proceedings forms part of the criminal case, so where confiscation is sought against a defendant you can deal with that under the representation order.

---

179 Criminal Legal Aid (General) Regulations 2013 reg 12 as amended by SI 2013 No 2790; Standard Crime Contract 2017 Specification paras 12.68–12.80.
180 Criminal Legal Aid (Amendment) Regulations 2017 SI No 1319; Standard Crime Contract 2017 Specification paras 12.81, 12.68–12.80.
181 Standard Crime Contract 2017 Specification paras 12.101–12.112.
182 Criminal Legal Aid (General) Regulations 2013 reg 12 as amended by SI 2013 No 2790; Standard Crime Contract 2017 Specification para 12.90.
183 Standard Crime Contract 2017 Specification paras 13.3 and 13.19.

15.189   Where confiscation is sought as part of criminal proceedings but which affects a third party (for example, someone who jointly owns property with a defendant), that party can apply for civil legal aid to be represented in the confiscation, notwithstanding that it is part of criminal proceedings in the Crown Court.

15.190   The availability of legal aid is now defined by LASPO Sch 1 Part 1 para 40. See appendix A.

Very High Cost Cases

15.191   Criminal proceedings which, if the case were to proceed to trial, would likely last more than 25 days may qualify as VHCC.

15.192   VHCCs may be subject to individual case contracts.[184] If you potentially have such a case, you are obliged to report it to the LAA national courts team within five working days of the earliest date at which the court sets a trial estimate or you identify that the case will be or is likely to be a VHCC.[185]

15.193   If you are required to do so, you can only continue with the case if you enter into a contract with the LAA in relation to the individual case.

15.194   Further information on the arrangements for VHCCs can be found in the standard contract terms and the 2013 VHCC guidance document, all published on the legal aid website at: www.gov.uk/guidance/high-cost-cases-crime.

---

184 Standard Crime Contract 2017 Specification para 7.1.
185 Standard Crime Contract 2017 Specification para 7.3.

CHAPTER 16

Getting paid for civil and family work

by Paul Seddon, Daniel M Grütters
(immigration and asylum fees) and
Richard Charlton (mental health fees)

continued

Introduction

16.1 This chapter deals with billing and payment for civil and family work. You should refer to chapters 2–13 for information on conducting cases.

16.2 This chapter does not deal with contract management (which is covered in Part C), but with the rules and processes for billing individual cases.

16.3 See appendix C for a summary of the Legal Aid Agency's (LAA's) Costs assessment guidance, in respect of the most common queries raised by caseworkers.

16.4 Most payment rates are to be found in the Civil Legal Aid (Remuneration) Regulations 2013. Some of the rates have been amended and so the latest rates are in the following instead:

- Civil Legal Aid (Remuneration) (Amendment) Regulations 2013 – reduced fees for experts for all certificates applied for on or after 2 December 2013, and removed separate hourly rates for controlled work in Upper Tribunal (Immigration and Asylum Chamber) where permission granted to Client (non Fast Track);

- Civil Legal Aid (Remuneration) (Amendment) Regulations 2014 – set rates for welfare benefits work under 2014 contracts including introducing a higher standard (fixed) fee for controlled work;

- Civil Legal Aid (Remuneration) (Amendment) (No 2) Regulations 2014 – implemented remuneration changes arising from the introduction of the single Family Court;

- Civil Legal Aid (Remuneration) (Amendment) (No 4) Regulations 2014 – implemented to apply to bundle payments in Family Advocacy Scheme (FAS) for hearings from 31 July 2014;

- Civil Legal Aid (Procedure, Remuneration and Statutory Charge) (Amendment) Regulations 2014 – set rates for community care and mental health work under 2014 contracts;

- Civil and Criminal Legal Aid (Remuneration) (Amendment) Regulations 2015 – amended the regulations to prescribe payment rates for orders under the Anti-Social Behaviour, Crime and Policing Act 2014 from 24 March 2015;

- Civil Legal Aid (Remuneration) (Amendment) Regulations 2015 – implemented conditional payment for judicial review work done pre-permission for all certificates applied for on or after 27 March 2015;

- Civil and Criminal Legal Aid (Amendment) Regulations 2015 – amended regulations to exclude advocacy services in civil proceedings concerning Female Genital Mutilation Protection Orders from

FAS (non-advocacy family work is also excluded from the Higher Standard Fee Scheme under the contract) for all certificates applied for on or after 17 July 2015;

- Civil Legal Aid (Remuneration and Statutory Charge) (Amendment) Regulations 2016 – set rates for welfare benefits work under 2016 contracts.
- Civil Legal Aid (Procedure, Remuneration and Statutory Charge) (Amendment) Regulations 2018 – set rates for work under the 2018 contract.

16.5   Payment rates not prescribed under the Remuneration Regulations are:
- family counsel fees falling outside the family fixed fee schemes;
- events fees under the Care Case Fee Scheme – these are provided within the Very High Cost Case (VHCC) Contract Guide ('Information Pack') and also now under the Specification to the Individual Case Contract (ICC);
- 'risk rates' paid on Special and High Cost Cases where a costs order against the other side is anticipated. Risk rates (given in the VHCC Information Packs – Non-Family) are agreed under the ICC that the practitioner must sign for such cases.

16.6   Solicitors situated in a London borough receive prescribed rates approximately five to ten per cent higher for non-routine preparation work (and advocacy in family work), as well as routine communications in controlled work.

Terms of assessment and guidance

16.7   Once a case has concluded, the final bill should be submitted to the court or LAA for assessment, as appropriate (see below).

16.8   Assessment of costs is governed by the contracts, the Remuneration Regulations 2013 (as amended) and the Civil Procedure Rules (CPR). Sections 4 and 6 of the Specifications to the contracts are of particular relevance, and provide for the payment and assessment of Controlled Work and Licensed Work, respectively. The transitional provisions of the Specifications (section 1) provide that subject to category-specific rules and the transitional provisions of secondary legislation, they apply to all work done under their particular contract (including procedures for assessment of remuneration). This does not apply to any matter started or certificate applied for before 1 October 2007. This means, for example, that once you start working under a new contract, any disbursements you incur from that date are subject to the list of excluded disbursements under the corresponding specification to that contract. Provisions for interpreters and translators and non-codified disbursements apply to any incurred from the start of the 2018 contract.

16.9   Both the court and the LAA are to refer to the LAA Costs Assessment Guidance (defined under the contract as a 'Costs Assessment Manual') when assessing civil legal aid costs to be paid by the LAA.[1] The guidance provides for how both controlled and licensed work is assessed, including what may be or is un-claimable.

16.10   The court does not have jurisdiction to allow costs falling outside the terms of the contract. Therefore, if the contract and/or documents of contractual authority (such as the Costs assessment guidance) excludes an item of costs whether because it is out of scope of the certificate, claimed at the wrong rate or because the required evidence in support is not on file, then a claim for costs assessed by the court can be rejected or reduced by the LAA on the basis that it is mis-claimed rather than over-claimed.

16.11   Civil legal aid costs to be paid by the LAA (rather than another party) must be assessed on the standard basis.[2] The guidance provides that many of the basic principles governing assessments are contained in the CPR and also cites CPR 44.3(2) (proportionality) and CPR 44.4 (factors to be taken into account in deciding the amount costs, in particular the 'Seven/Eight Pillars of Wisdom').

16.12   The LAA also produces and releases internal guidance on how they will assess Controlled Work and Licensed Work. These are the *Escape cases electronic handbook* (for Controlled Work) and the *Civil finance electronic handbook* (for Licensed Work). While they provide a lot of information and can be very helpful, they are created specifically for LAA caseworkers and are not comprehensive guidance – they are not subject to consultation by the consultative bodies and do not have contractual authority. They refer to authorities and provide the LAA Finance Team's interpretation of them.

1   Standard Civil Contract 2018/CLA Contract 2018/2018 CLA Discrimination Contract/2018 CLA Education Contract Standard Terms Clause 1.1 – see costs assessment manuals.
2   Standard Civil Contract 2018 Specification para 6.9 and CLA Contract 2018 para 8.9.

Exceptional case funding

16.13   Like any other work not within scope under the Legal Aid, Sentencing and Punishment of Offenders Act 2012 (LASPO), you can charge privately for making an application for exceptional case funding (ECF). However, you cannot do this once ECF is granted and you must refund any payment made for costs that become retrospectively covered under ECF.[3]

16.14   There is no special payment scheme for ECF cases, they are paid under the same schemes as non-ECF cases.[4]

16.15   When Legal Help is granted to investigate the possibility of a further ECF application being made to cover substantive services sought, the onus is on you to show that each disbursement is necessary for the work covered, based on the information available to you at the time, rather than for use in potential proceedings for which ECF might be granted. Substantial disbursements will be considered unreasonable unless it has been established that the substantive application likely meets the ECF criteria. An application for Investigative Representation under ECF should be considered if a disbursement would be £400 or more.[5]

Disbursements

16.16   On 3 October 2011, codified (set) rates and fees for experts and other third party suppliers were introduced under secondary legislation and are now found in the Remuneration Regulations. They are commonly referred to as 'expert fees' by the LAA, although not all of them are experts, for example interpreters and process servers. Where a rate is codified, only the LAA have discretion to increase this upon an application for prior authority, and the court can only direct a recommendation and give reasons.[6]

---

3   Standard Civil Contract 2018 Specification para 1.38, CLA Contract 2018 Specification para 9.14, 2018 CLA Discrimination Contract 2018 Specification para 9.4 and amended Specification para 6.30, and CLA Education 2018 Contract Specification para 6.36.

4   Standard Civil Contract 2018 Specification paras 4.51, 5.21, 6.84, 7.1, 8.12, 10.17 and 12.23; CLA Contract 2018/2018 CLA Discrimination Contract 2018 (and amended)/CLA Education 2018 Contract Specification para 5.47.

5   Costs assessment guidance para 3.54.

6   Standard Civil Contract 2018 Specification para 6.60; and *A Local Authority v DS* [2012] EWHC 1442 (Fam).

16.17   The LAA's guidance on the recommended number of hours that experts should incur on a case is also strictly applied (see 'prior authority and payment on account for disbursements' below).

16.18   The codified rates for experts and others outside of London boroughs are generally higher than if they are inside London boroughs. A non-London rate is set by the location of the 'expert' rather than your own office.

16.19   Adequate details should be given on an 'expert's' invoice to show the breakdown of work, including where the expert was travelling from and to when claiming travel time and expenses. Changes to rejection criteria in July 2019 mean that this omission can result in a key performance indicator (KPI) rejection of the claim.

16.20   Under the 2018 Contract you must use interpreters with specified qualifications (listed in the contract) and a note must be placed on the client's case file confirming that the interpreter or the agency through which the interpreter is supplied holds such a qualification and which qualification it is. A 'non-qualified interpreter' can be used in exceptional circumstances (a non-exhaustive list is provided) but you must record on file what these circumstances are and why there was no alternative. The LAA can also require you only to use interpreters under its nominated translation framework upon giving you three months' notice.[7]

16.21   Specified costs and expenses of the expert, including administrative support and subsistence, and cancellation fees where notice is given over 72 hours before the hearing/appointment, will not be paid. Mileage is capped at 45p per mile and travel time is capped at £40 per hour or the codified rate if less.[8] The LAA impose a discretionary cap on travel and waiting time at two-thirds of the codified rate if that rate is under £40 (NB it cannot reject, only assess, a claim that seeks a full codified rate of £40 or under). The LAA imposed this on waiting time for interpreters at court but impracticality forced it to concede to pay the full rate, however, it still seeks to impose a two-thirds rate for interpreters' court waiting time incurred before 1 April 2019.[9] The LAA's only response to objections raised by the Association of Costs Lawyers about imposing this transitional provision date is that assessments reducing rates can be appealed.

---

7 Standard Civil Contract 2018 Specification paras 2.47–2.51.
8 Civil Legal Aid (Remuneration) Regulations 2013 Sch 5 para 4.
9 Section 10.18 page 65 of the Civil Finance Electronic Handbook; and Section 5.16 page 27 of the Escape Case Electronic Handbook.

16.22   Under the 2018 Contract, when you incur a non-codified disbursement you must obtain at least three quotes (unless the LAA agrees this is inappropriate) and select the one that you believe to be the best value for money in the circumstances including but not limited to the need for speed and competence/expertise of the provider. If you cannot do this, then you must advise the LAA and provide them with further information they reasonably require.[10]

16.23   Witness intermediaries have been added to excluded disbursements listed in the contract.[11] The LAA have confirmed that it will not fund assessment reports for the need for witness intermediaries. See para 5.49 for the full list of excluded disbursements.

16.24   When other legal aid practitioners are instructed as legal experts, even when directed by the court, to advise or give evidence on a case, such as immigration advice on the status of children in care proceedings, practitioners' legal aid rates will still apply.[12]

16.25   No payment of fees for client's records requested under a subject access request will be paid, unless the organisation in receipt of the request considers it to be 'manifestly unreasonable or excessive', pursuant to General Data Protection Regulation (EU) No 2016/679 (GDPR) and the Data Protection Act (DPA) 2018. The LAA initially misconstrued the GDPR and the DPA 1998 to mean any request, including police disclosure or medical records even when required by an expert, but it has now changed its internal guidance to better align with them,[13] although providers should still ensure that they properly understand and utilise the provisions of the legislation in particular para 5(2) and (3) of Part 1 of Sch 2 to the DPA 1998.

16.26   With regard to covering travel expenses to court for clients who are destitute, rather than simply eligible for legal aid, the LAA now acknowledge that under Family Procedure Rule 27.3 the parties governed by the FPR must attend any hearing or directions appointment of which they have been notified.[14]

---

10 Standard Civil Contract 2018 Specification paras 4.27; CLA Contract 2018/CLA Discrimination Contract 2018 (and amended)/CLA Education 2018 Contract Specification Annex 3: Payments and Disbursements para 20.
11 Standard Civil Contract 2018 Specification para 4.28; CLA Contract 2018/CLA Discrimination Contract 2018 (and amended)/CLA Education 2018 Contract Specification Annex 3: Payments and Disbursements para 21.
12 Costs assessment guidance para 2.49.
13 Section 10.1 page 58 of the Civil Finance Electronic Handbook and Section 5.4 page 20 of the Escape Case Electronic Handbook.
14 Costs assessment guidance para 3.31.

16.27 The codified rates, number of hours that an expert can incur before a prior authority should be made, specific expert remuneration arrangements and POA of experts, can be found in the LAA's Guidance on the Remuneration of Expert Witnesses. There is also specific guidance on Clinical Negligence Experts and Risk Assessments. These can all be found on: www.gov.uk/guidance/expert-witnesses-in-legal-aid-cases.

16.28 For Civil Legal Advice (CLA) work (including Discrimination and Education), payment of each disbursement is limited to £250 excluding VAT unless approved at discretion the LAA's discretion prior to incurring it, and copies of receipts must be kept at the front of the case file. Some disbursements cannot be claimed. Travel time incurred under disbursements is limited to two hours at the prescribed/codified rate.[15]

16.29 On CLA work, counsel's fees are deemed unusual and claimed as a disbursement but must meet a high threshold to justify instruction. While it is still for you to agree counsel's fees and pay them directly, there is no express exclusion from their prescribed rates and their work is subject to the limits as detailed at para 16.28 above.[16]

Apportionment of experts' fees

16.30 Following the Court of Appeal's decision of *JG v The Lord Chancellor and others*,[17] the Access to Justice Act 1999 and LASPO do not prevent the court from having discretion in private law Children Act 1989 proceedings to depart from the order that it would otherwise have made ('normal order'),[18] in apportioning more or all of joint experts' costs to a legally aided party where other parties (who are not legally aided) cannot afford to pay all or part of their share, if there will be a breach of rights under the European Convention on Human Rights (ECHR). The judgment is also useful in other proceedings where similar situations may arise, eg Court of Protection.

---

15 CLA Contract 2018 Specification/CLA Discrimination Contract 2018 (and amended) Specification/CLA Education 2018 Contract Specification Annex 3: Payments and Disbursements paras 11–25.

16 CLA Contract 2018 Specification/CLA Discrimination Contract 2018 (and amended) Specification/CLA Education 2018 Contract Specification Annex 3: Payments and Disbursements paras 26–27.

17 [2014] EWCA Civ 656.

18 The Court of Appeal found there is no normal rule of equal apportionment of single joint experts' costs in Children Act 1989 proceedings, that FPR 25.12(6) is merely a default position in the absence of the Court directing otherwise, and emphasised the importance of tailoring the order to the facts of the case.

16.31   As with a determination for ECF, the test of exceptionality is that there is (or sometimes might be) a breach of ECHR rights; there is no separate requirement. Further, just because another party will benefit from a report that they have to pay less or nothing at all for, this does not justify a violation of a child's Convention rights by the state refusing to provide legal aid for it. Whether there is a breach will depend on the individual facts and most likely not only the nature of the application but also the nature of the report will be a relevant circumstance.

16.32   In determining impecuniosity, the court does not have to undertake the highly technical analysis of establishing that a non-legally aided party would be financially eligible for legal aid. Although if said party is eligible then this can be indicative, but it is only one relevant factor.

16.33   When a court can reach final determination about whether to depart from a normal order can vary depending on the facts. If reaching that decision will cause harmful delay and the other parties can provide cogent evidence that they cannot pay their share, then the court can order the Guardian to instruct the expert (the costs being met under the child's legal aid certificate) in the first instance, and then the other party be found liable to pay a share, on proper financial information, later by means of a conventional costs order.

16.34   It should also be noted that the judgment recommends that a prior authority should still be obtained.

Controlled Work

16.35   Controlled Work cases are billed individually, but they are paid by way of a monthly payment from the LAA. Each month, the organisation submits claims and receives a monthly payment (known as a 'standard monthly payment' (SMP)), with the aim that bills and payments balance each other out over the course of the financial year, or a 'variable monthly payment' (VMP) based on what it has billed that month. See chapter 22 below for more information on this process (known as reconciliation) and on the management of civil contracts generally. Organisations can opt for the payment system which suits them best. The LAA's *Guidance for reporting Controlled Work and Controlled Work matters* is a substantive guide regarding the various fields and codes for completion via the Contracted Work and Administration (CWA) when submitting Controlled Work. It is found on the LAA's CWA codes guidance page: www.gov.uk/government/publications/cwa-codes-guidance.

16.36   Standard fees are paid for controlled work. These are shown net of VAT and disbursements which may be claimed in addition. You need to submit a claim for the standard fee within six months of the conclusion of a matter,[19] other than CLA matters which is within three months of conclusion or one month in the event of a Determination being made.[20] Standard fees are claimed by submitting an online claim within 20 days of the end of each month.

16.37   Escape fee cases (known under pre-LASPO contracts and their predecessors as 'exceptional cases', are defined as those where costs exceed three times the fixed fee) may be claimed in full.

16.38   You can instruct counsel on Legal Help (not Help at Court) and Family Help (Lower), but their fee cannot be claimed as a disbursement in addition to a standard fee and it cannot be used to escape the standard fee. However, if a case does escape, then their fee can be claimed as a disbursement. Prescribed counsel's hourly rates do not apply. You must record your justification for instruction and counsel must set out details of time spent. You must pay counsel the full fee claimed regardless of any reduction on assessment.[21] See further details of instructing counsel under Controlled Work for family in the 'family' section below. Counsel's fees are deemed a disbursement under CLA and provisions for this are detailed at para 16.29 above (Disbursements).

16.39   In escape cases, you need to submit an EC Claim 1 form (there are separate EC Claim 1 forms for immigration, mental health and CLA work) with your file in order to be credited with the balance above the fixed fee. You must submit claims for escape fee cases within three months of reporting the end of the case and claiming the standard fee.[22] Electronic web-based EC Claim 1 forms were launched in 2017. While there is no change to the assessment process, it is intended that the paper-based forms will eventually be withdrawn.

16.40   If costs are reduced on assessment, you can appeal (see costs appeals, para 16.73 onwards below).

19 Standard Civil Contract 2018 Specification para 4.40.
20 CLA Contract 2018 Specification/CLA Discrimination Contract 2018 (and amended)/CLA Education 2018 Contract Specification Annex 3: Payments and Disbursements para 6.
21 Standard Civil Contract 2018 Specification paras 3.58–3.61; CLA Contract 2018/2018 CLA Discrimination Contract/ 2018 CLA Education Contract Specification paras 5.42–5.44.
22 Standard Civil Contract 2018 Specification para 4.20; CLA Contract 2018 Specification para 6.9.

16.41   Under the 2018 Contract, costs audits have been amended. Findings of 'mis-claiming' and 'over-claiming' have been introduced. 'Mis-claiming' means claiming in a manner that the LAA considers to be 'clearly contrary to the Contract and where no discretion arises as to payment. For instance, claiming using the wrong rates, or incorrectly claiming VAT'. 'Over-claiming' means claiming more than the LAA determines to be reasonable on assessment, but where discretion arises as to the amount allowable.[23]

16.42   A sample of at least 20 files can be requested. For mis-claiming, the sample period has been increased from one year to two (after the claims have been submitted), or up to six years prior where an Official Investigation is underway or the LAA consider it reasonable to do so upon receiving a report. For over-claiming, the period is since the last Contract Compliance Audit, or the 12 months before the date the sample is requested.[24]

16.43   Although the basic systems for claiming immigration/asylum and mental health controlled work fees are the same as other civil and family work, they have more complex fee schemes. Family cases also have their own schemes. There is more information about these below.

Legal aid representation certificates

Rejected claims and erroneous document requests

16.44   Rejected claims (which can include report outcomes) can count against KPIs (see chapter 22 for more information).

16.45   If you believe that your claim should not have been rejected or a non-automated Client and Cost Management System (CCMS) document request is made where information is already provided or is not required as evidence of the claim, then you can use the LAA's Claimfix service to review the rejection/document request and reverse it if they consider it is erroneous. You email laacivilclaimfix@justice.gov.uk. The turnaround is often very fast, usually within 24 hours.

---

23 Standard Civil Contract 2018 and CLA Contract 2018 Specifications definitions.
24 Standard Civil Contract 2018 Specification paras 4.47–4.50; CLA Contract 2018 paras 6.13–6.16; CLA Discrimination Contract 2018 Specification paras 6.7–6.10 and amended paras 6.6–6.10; CLA Education Contract 2018 Specification paras 6.12–6.16.

16.46   In August 2019 the LAA revised the categories of rejects moving many scenarios that would have resulted in a document request to a Non-KPI reject (previously 'priority reject'). This is laid out in the LAA's internal guidance.[25]

Payments on account

16.47 The Standard Contract[26] allows you to claim on account profit costs incurred not earlier than three months after the issue of a legal aid representation certificate. Thereafter, you can apply for further payments on account, provided that you make no more than two applications in any 12-month period which runs from the date that the first profit costs POA is authorised (rather than the anniversary of the certificate). On non-CCMS cases, use form CIVPOA1, which can be submitted as an eform via the LAA CWA online portal.[27]

16.48   Cases where the certificate was applied for through CCMS have to be claimed through CCMS. To claim profit costs payments on account on CCMS, you need to submit a copy of the time ledger, ie full details of the case's running costs incurred to date (unless the case is covered by a standard fee scheme and has not escaped the fee). CCMS sends a notification (document request) for you to upload a copy of the ledger shortly after you have submitted the bill. In family cases, FAS should be included in the claim, neither these nor different fixed fee aspects are claimed separately. The system then calculates 75 per cent of the costs and a caseworker (not CCMS) will check the payments on account value against the supporting evidence. You will be paid the amount to bring the total payments on account made to 75 per cent of your profit costs to date. 100 per cent profit costs payments on account can be paid in CCFS (events) cases (see para 16.167).

16.49   It should be noted that claims for payments on account (whether for profit costs or disbursements) are not assessed and do not form quasi gross sum bills, no matter how much supporting information may be requested for them. Payments on account simply form debit amounts under the certificate which will be deducted from the total amount payable under the interim/final bill, so if the amount allowed under that bill is not greater than or equal to the total amount paid on account then there will be a debit balance owed to the LAA when the

---

25 Civil Finance Electronic Handbook Section 16.

26 Standard Civil Contract 2018 Specification para 6.21 and CLA Contract 2018/ CLA Contract Discrimination 2018 (unamended) Specification para 8.21; Standard Contract 2018 Specification (Family) para 7.25.

27 www.gov.uk/guidance/legal-aid-eforms/.

bill is paid. However, there have been disputes between the LAA (and its predecessors) and practitioners regarding old payments on account and whether final bills were ever received or paid. See 'Recoupment and limitation' below.

16.50   See below for information about payments on account under the family law fee schemes.

Prior authority and payment on account for disbursements

16.51   You can apply to the LAA for authority to incur a disbursement in advance, if it is above £100 and is not covered by the standard rates/ hours for experts introduced from 3 October 2011.[28] The LAA has set out guidance for the number of hours it considers reasonable for different types of expert reports, and will only consider a prior author- ity application if it is for more hours than in the guidance, or of a type not included.[29] The application must include a quote for the disburse- ment and set out the reasons why it is necessary. The application is made via CCMS or using form CIVAPP8A if it is a pre-CCMS case.

16.52   You may apply for prior authority if:[30]

a) an item of costs is either unusual in its nature or is unusually large – this means that it is outside the guidance referred to above;
b) you wish to instruct a QC or more than one counsel;
c) prior authority is required under the specification; or
d) you wish to instruct an expert at higher rates than are set out in the Remuneration Regulations.

If you do not apply for prior authority and b), c), or d) above applies, you may not be paid in full or at all for the fees incurred.

16.53   Payments on account of disbursements can be claimed at any time, subject to disbursements being individually or cumulatively above £100. For non-CCMS cases, the form is the CIVPOA1, as for profit costs above. It can be submitted as a paper form, or as an e-form, using the legal aid online facility. The latter is recommended, not least because payment is made more quickly. See: www.gov.uk/ legal-aid-eforms. In CCMS cases claims are made via CCMS. An

---

28 Community Legal Service (Funding) (Amendment No 2) Order 2011, now in the Civil Legal Aid (Remuneration) (Amendment) Regulations 2013.
29 See *Guidance: Expert witnesses in legal aid cases*: www.gov.uk/guidance/expert-witnesses-in-legal-aid-cases.
30 Standard Civil Contract 2018 Specification para 5.10 and CLA Contract 2018/ CLA Contract Discrimination 2018 (unamended) Specification para 7.17.

invoice showing the hourly rate and number of hours claimed must accompany a claim for expert fees.

Assessment of the final bill

16.54 Once a case has concluded, the final bill should be submitted to the court or LAA for assessment, as appropriate (see below).

16.55 The contract requires certain cases to be assessed by the court. These are principally claims where assessable costs exceed £2,500 excluding VAT ('the assessment limit') in cases where proceedings have been issued and conclude before a judge (rather than a magistrate).[31] Assessable costs are any costs, whether profit costs, counsel's fees or disbursements, that are not subject to standard and graduated fees (ie fixed fees). Unlike FAS, for the purposes of assessment, payments to counsel under the Family Graduated Fees Scheme (FGFS) are considered a disbursement and form assessable costs.[32]

16.56 There are three 'special circumstances' where the assessment limit is disapplied:[33]

1) where the only assessable costs are disbursements – this is the most commonly used special circumstance;
2) where the LAA considers (upon application by the practitioner) that assessment by the court would be against the interests of the legally aided client or would increase the amount under legal aid – in practice, such an application is rarely if ever granted;
3) where a practitioner has been intervened on and the case file is lost, and a notional assessment is required to pay counsel's fees or account to the client for money held.

16.57 There are two further exceptions to the assessment limit:

1) where there is an element of inter partes costs and a detailed assessment of those costs is carried out by the court, in which case the court will also assess the legal aid only costs regardless of the amount;[34]
2) costs under a VHCC contract – these must be assessed by the LAA,[35] even when there are inter partes costs assessed by the

31 Costs assessment guidance paras 14.1–14.10.
32 Costs assessment guidance para 14.2.
33 Costs assessment guidance paras 14.11–14.13.
34 Standard Civil Contract 2018 Specification para 6.36(a) and CLA Contract 2018/ CLA Contract Discrimination 2018 (unamended) Specification para 8.36(a).
35 Individual Case Contract 2018 (High Cost Case) Specification para 5.12.

court and the LAA have authorised that legal aid only costs be paid in addition to them.

16.58 There is provision in the contracts for the LAA to take over assessment of all claims, but it has not yet been brought into force.

16.59 It should be noted that both the LAA and the court require authority to assess the bill. The authority to assess is either a final order requiring costs to be assessed or other authority as detailed in the contract (which mirrors those under CPR 47.7),[36] or in the absence of this a discharged certificate.[37] Therefore, if the final order makes no mention of costs, a discharge should be sought before submitting the bill. If applying to the LAA for assessment, you can apply for discharge at the same time, but if the reasons for discharge are contentious, then the LAA will implement the show cause procedure and return the claim to the practitioner to be resubmitted when the certificate is discharged.[38]

16.60 Where the court is responsible for assessment, you must first submit a detailed bill of costs for assessment by the court; and when that is complete, make a claim for payment from the LAA within three months of the legal aid assessment certificate (HMCTS form EX80A, or EX80B where costs include those subject to/escape family fixed fee(s)) being received from the court.

16.61 Where the LAA is responsible for assessment, you must submit a claim within three months of the right to claim accruing.[39]

16.62 Frequent submission of late claims may lead to contract sanctions.[40] If the client has a financial interest and you fail to submit your claim in time, the LAA may serve notice requiring you to do so within two months. If you then do not submit within two months and do not provide a satisfactory explanation why, the LAA can disallow your claim to the amount of the client's financial interest. You can appeal this disallowance under the costs appeals procedure (see

36 Standard Civil Contract 2018 Specification para 6.33(b)(i)–(iv) and CLA Contract 2018/ CLA Contract Discrimination 2018 (unamended) Specification para 8.33(b)(i)-(iv) (LAA Assessment); Costs assessment guidance paras 15.2–15.3 (Court Assessment).

37 Standard Civil Contract 2018 Specification para 6.33(b)(iv) and CLA Contract 2018/ CLA Contract Discrimination 2018 (unamended) Specification para 8.33(b)(iv) (LAA Assessment); Costs assessment guidance para 15.4 (Court Assessment).

38 Costs assessment guidance para 15.6.

39 Standard Civil Contract 2018 Specification para 6.33 and CLA Contract 2018/ CLA Contract Discrimination 2018 (unamended) Specification para 8.33.

40 Standard Civil Contract 2018 Standard Terms clause 14.5.

below), regardless of whether the LAA has assessed the claim or the court has.[41]

Civil contempt proceedings and Anti-social Behaviour, Crime and Policing Act 2014 breach proceedings

16.63 Civil contempt committal proceedings are classed as criminal under section 14(h) of LASPO and thus the provisions of the Crime Contract apply. Following the decision of *Brown v Haringey LBC*,[42] civil providers can obtain criminal legal aid for contempt committal in civil proceedings, including breaches of Anti-social Behaviour, Crime and Policing Act (ASBCPA) 2014, by way of a Representation Order. The Civil and Criminal Legal Aid (Remuneration) (Amendment) Regulations 2015 amended scope of the criminal regulations to encompass proceedings in the county court and introduced bespoke standard fees and corresponding rates under *Representation in the Magistrates Court* for ASBCPA 2014 breach proceedings[43] dealt with in the county court (for adults). All other civil contempt committal proceedings are paid under hourly rates falling within section 14(h).[44] Counsel is paid under the Criminal Remuneration Regulations also,[45] and is always assigned automatically and so will paid at hourly rates. Further breaches of the same order (whether ASBCPA 2014 or other) count as a series of offences and an amendment is made to the existing Representation Order, thus the date of the original Representation Order determines the applicable rate (eg rates and fees between 1 July 2015 and 31 March 2016 are 8.75 per cent lower). Providers holding a criminal contract claim ASBCPA 2014 via their crime monthly submission/CRM 7. Providers without a criminal contract use the bespoke CRMCLAIM11 (not to be confused with the CRM11) and can use pages 5 and 6 of the CIV CLAIM1 if the schedule of work provided is too small. All other civil contempt committal proceedings are claimed on CRMCLAIM11 regardless of whether the provider has a criminal

---

41 Standard Civil Contract 2018 Specification para 6.35 and CLA Contract 2018/ CLA Contract Discrimination 2018 (unamended) Specification para 8.35.

42 [2015] EWCA Civ 483.

43 Para 5A of Sch 4 to the Criminal Legal Aid (Remuneration) Regulations 2013 (as amended).

44 Para 7 of Sch 4 to the Criminal Legal Aid (Remuneration) Regulations 2013 (as amended).

45 Para 12 of Sch 4 to the Criminal Legal Aid (Remuneration) Regulations 2013 (as amended).

contract. Counsel's fees are claimed using a CRM8 which should be submitted with the CRMCLAIM11.

16.64   Further information on both ASBCPA 2014 and other civil contempt can be found at https://www.gov.uk/guidance/apply-for-legal-aid-for-civil-contempt-cases/.

Enhanced rates

16.65   In certain circumstances, you can apply for payment of the prescribed hourly rate at a discretionary enhanced rate. The LAA/court will consider whether enhancement is justified, and if so will increase the hourly rates for some or all of the work done on the case. It would be very unusual for enhanced rates to be allowed on routine items (short letters and telephone calls) and travel and waiting (this would usually only be applicable for exceptional speed).

16.66   The two-stage criteria for enhancement (threshold and factors) is provided in the Contract[46] and expanded upon under Section 12 of the Costs Assessment Guidance.

16.67   The threshold test for enhancement is one of exceptionality, within the normal meaning of unusual or out of the ordinary,[47] that:

a) the work was done with exceptional **competence, skill or expertise**; or

b) the work was done with exceptional **speed**; or

c) the case involved exceptional **circumstances or complexity**,

compared with the generality of proceedings to which the relevant rates apply.[48] So, the comparison is not just cases within the same category of law, but all cases paid at that rate. However, the exceptional criterion/criteria must have actually had an effect on the fee earner's work in the qualitative or quantitative sense.[49]

16.68   Where the threshold test is met, the LAA may allow a percentage increase to the relevant hourly rate not exceeding 50 per cent, or in cases in the Upper Tribunal, High Court, Court of Appeal and Supreme Court not exceeding 100 per cent.[50] The original allowance

---

46 Standard Civil Contract 2018 Specification paras 6.13–6.15 and CLA Contract 2018/ CLA Contract Discrimination 2018 (unamended) Specification paras 8.13–8.15.

47 Costs assessment guidance para 12.8.

48 Standard Civil Contract 2018 Specification para 6.17 and CLA Contract 2018/ CLA Contract Discrimination 2018 (unamended) Specification para 8.17; and Costs assessment guidance para 12.11.

49 *Re Children Act 1989 (taxation of costs)* [1994] 2 FLR 934, also known as *London Borough of A v M and SF* [1994] Costs LR (Core) 374.

50 Civil Legal Aid (Remuneration) Regulations 2013 reg 6(3).

of 100 per cent and 200 per cent (Senior Courts and Supreme Court) was halved from 3 October 2011/1 February 2012, but this is interpreted as a cap to be applied after the enhancement sought is assessed, rather than a general 50 per cent reduction.[51] Under the 2018 contract, the provision to apply a level of enhancement where the threshold test is met no longer binding on the LAA and is permissive. The amount of the percentage increase will be determined by having regard to seven factors grouped into three areas:

a) the **degree of responsibility** accepted;
b) the **care, speed** and **economy** with which the case was prepared;
c) the **novelty, weight** and **complexity** of the case.

In short: a) is about you and the expertise/experience you brought to the case; b) is about what you had to do and the way you did it; and c) is about the issues affecting the case. These factors are explored in more detail in the Costs Assessment Guidance. It is not only the number of factors present, but the strength of those individual factors that will determine the amount to be claimed on assessment.

16.69   It is rare to apply an enhancement across the board for all pieces of work, but rather enhancements should only be applied to what is affected eg 40 per cent on all work (including routine and travel/waiting) for urgency and complexity up to first hearing, and then 20 per cent for complexity for all non-funding non-routine work (excluding travel/waiting) afterwards. However, preparing appeals to reductions to multi-layered enhancements on CCMS claims can be disproportionately laborious. Every enhancement claim is fact specific and detailed grounds must be given.

Conditional payment for judicial review

16.70   For cases started on or after 22 April 2014, payment for work done between issue of proceedings and grant of permission in judicial review cases was made conditional on either:[52]

- the court granting permission; or
- notwithstanding that no permission was granted, the LAA agreeing to discretionary payment.

16.71   The LAA would only agree to payment of pre-permission work in cases where permission was not granted if the court had neither granted nor refused permission and it considered it was reasonable to

51 Costs assessment guidance para 12.2.
52 Civil Legal Aid (Remuneration) (Amendment) (No 3) Regulations 2014.

pay in the circumstances of the case. Work on interim relief was duly confirmed as payable regardless, to reflect the Ministry of Justice's consultation response on conditional payment in judicial review. This, along with investigative work (including counsel's advice) and reasonable disbursements such as experts' fees (but not including counsel's fees), is clarified in the LAA's pro forma application for discretionary payments (see below) as being paid regardless.

16.72   However, on 3 March 2015 the High Court found the regulations to be irrational in the case of *R (Ben Hoare Bell Solicitors and others) v The Lord Chancellor.*[53] The regulations were quashed on 24 March 2015, meaning that the above amendments to the remuneration regulations were of no effect.

16.73   Rather than appeal the judgment, the Lord Chancellor accepted it but immediately laid new regulations that affected all certificates granted on or after 27 March 2015, which effectively reinstated the quashed regulations with some amendments aimed at alleviating the grounds on which the Court found against them.

16.74   The Civil Legal Aid (Remuneration) (Amendment) Regulations 2015[54] provide that, for all certificates applied for on or after 27 March 2015, payment for judicial review work done pre-permission is conditional on one of the following:

- the court giving permission;
- the defendant withdrawing the decision to which the application for judicial review relates, resulting in the court refusing permission or making no decision on permission;
- the court ordering an oral permission hearing or an oral hearing of an appeal against a refusal of permission;
- the court ordering a rolled up hearing; or
- the court neither granting nor refusing permission but the Lord Chancellor considers it reasonable to pay remuneration in the circumstances of the case, taking into account, in particular:
  - the reason why no costs order or agreement was obtained;
  - the extent to which, and why, the outcome sought was achieved; and
  - the strength of the application for permission at the time it was filed, based on the law and on facts which the provider knew or ought to have known at the time.

---

53 [2015] EWHC 523 (Admin).

54 SI No 898. Reg 2 inserts reg 5A in to the Civil Legal Aid (Remuneration) Regulations 2013.

16.75 In settlement of a judicial review brought by Duncan Lewis, the Lord Chancellor issued a clarification in February 2019 that cases could be paid where permission was refused on papers and oral renewal was sought but the matter then concluded before a decision was made by the court, and further also if the defendant withdraws the decision being challenged either before the court decides on permission on papers or after the matter has moved beyond refusal of permission on papers. This clarification can be found on the same LAA webpage as the 'Judicial review discretion pro-forma' (see below).

16.76 Existing certificates granted before, but to which new judicial review proceedings are added on or after, 27 March 2015, are also subject to these rules, but other judicial review cases under certificates applied for before this must be paid by the LAA without reference to any conditional funding arrangement under the regulations.

16.77 If you want to claim costs that are only payable at the Lord Chancellor's discretion, an application must be made to the LAA for this to be considered and any representations received from counsel should accompany this. Only once such an application is successful should a claim or court bill be prepared.

16.78 Where the certificate is issued under CCMS, a 'JR Discretionary Payment Req'. should be submitted via a Case Enquiry on the CCMS case, and upon receipt of this a document request for any additional supporting paperwork will be made. If it is a pre-CCMS certificate, then an application can be made by using the 'Judicial review discretion pro-forma' letter which also includes guidance on making the application. The letter can be found here: www.gov.uk/government/publications/judicial-review-discretion-pro-forma.

16.79 The Lord Chancellor's discretion is not required for the following work and will be payable regardless:

- work on the earlier stages of a case to investigate the prospects of strength of a claim (including advice from counsel on the merits of the claim) and work under the Pre-action Protocol Procedure for Judicial Review;
- disbursements (but not counsel's fees);
- work carried out on an application for interim relief.

Allowances for CCMS tasks

16.80 After a short consultation process with the Association of Costs Lawyers Legal Aid Group and other representative bodies, allowances were added in September 2018 for time to prepare the means assessment and other CCMS tasks including allocation of costs to counsel.[55]

Assessment of costs by the LAA

Claims to the LAA

16.81   As detailed above, the LAA assesses claims up to £2,500 (excluding VAT) subject to exceptions.

16.82   Claims to the LAA are made via CCMS for certificates granted via CCMS and on form CIV CLAIM1 (or CIV CLAIM1A in certain family cases and CIV CLAIM2 where inter partes costs have also been recovered – see relevant sections below for more details) for pre-CCMS cases. Paper claims must be completed in full. The supporting papers required with a claim (submitted via a document request when a claim is submitted on CCMS) vary:

- Counsels' fee notes are only required with paper claims when FAS/FGFS fees are not being claimed, or on CCMS non-family claims if you and counsel have chosen that the balance fees (after payments on account) will be paid directly to the provider and forwarded to counsel.
- Disbursement vouchers for any disbursement of £20 *including* VAT or more must be provided. For court fees and mileage, the LAA will accept a copy of the accounts ledger instead, although a copy of the covering letter to the court referring to the court fee and amount is usually accepted.
- Where DNA and/or alcohol tests are claimed, copies of the court orders for these are required unless there is prior authority.
- The file of papers is only required on claims for:
  - mental health cases;
  - judicial review and immigration cases if the profit costs excluding VAT exceed £1,000;
  - other cases if the profit costs excluding VAT exceed £2,500 (eg cases where no proceedings have been issued);
  - family cases where costs have escaped the fixed fee.

16.83   There are useful checklists found on each claim form page on the LAA website, to ensure the claim is correctly submitted.

16.84   If the client has a financial interest and wishes to make written objections to the LAA, then the certificate on the Claim form will

---

55 Costs assessment guidance paras 2.61–2.63.

need to be altered (it assumes that the client does not wish to raise objections).

Claims on CCMS

16.85   Where the file of papers is required as detailed above, and the claim is submitted on CCMS, a document request will generally ask for just the preparation notes, file notes and 'third party documents' (documents from a third party to support an unusually high claim eg an unusually high expert's report fee).

16.86   In August 2019, the LAA introduced a checklist for CCMS claims with a two-stage process, with the claim being rejected for amend-ment after one 'fail' on Stage 1 and then rejected for amendment or document request made for additional information at Stage 2. This was introduced in conjunction with the changes to categories of rejects moving many scenarios that would have resulted in a docu-ment request to a Non-KPI reject (previously 'priority reject') as laid out in the LAA's internal guidance.[56]

16.87   There are useful checklists found on each claim form page on the LAA website, to ensure the claim is correctly submitted. There are 'Quick guides' to submitting bills via CCMS on the CCMS Training website: http://ccmstraining.justice.gov.uk/Quick-guides (see the Closing Cases and Submitting Bills section under the respective sections for Providers and Advocates).

16.88   For CCMS cases, unlike paper claims, the outcomes are not included within the claim and are reported separately on CCMS. The outcomes must be reported before a final bill can be submitted on CCMS. Outcomes are not reported when submitting an interim bill for a private family law aspect or transferred case. The final bill will be 'parked' until the outcomes are processed, which may take some time if statutory charge issues have to be investigated. If a CCMS claim is still pending assessment, then omitted costs can be added by submitting an Adjustment Bill. An Adjustment Bill Request must be submitted via a Case Query, and if the LAA grant this then a notification will be sent to submit one – there is a Quick Guide under the Closing Cases and Submitting Bills page for providers on the CCMS Training website. If omitted costs are identified after a CCMS claim is reduced on assessment and an appeal is being made for these, then the omitted costs can be included in the Appeal Bill (see 'Costs appeals' below) but must be identified as such in appeal submissions along with reasons for the omission.

56 Civil Finance Electronic Handbook Section 16.

16.89   Where the client has a financial interest, CCMS will not allow you to prepare the draft claim on its interface without answering that the client has been sent the bill on a specified date, even before the bill itself has been created. This is due to an oversight in the way CCMS has been developed. It is extremely regrettable that the only way around this is to say that you have done something which you cannot possibly have done yet. (The representative bodies have repeatedly made this point to the LAA.) You must then remember to alter this in the bill once the bill has actually been sent to the client together with any response that the client may have made.

16.90   Where multiple certificates cover a family case, the certificates must be linked on CCMS and the claim will be submitted under the lead certificate (which holds the total costs limitation). Currently, outcomes and nil bills must still be submitted on the linked certificates. Where multiple certificates cover a non-family case, these cannot be linked on CCMS. The LAA have confirmed to the Association of Costs Lawyers that as long as there is a sufficient costs limitation under a single certificate, then a single claim can be submitted under it rather than preparing multiple claims apportioning disbursements and time on each line entry.

Use it or lose it – inactivity on CCMS

16.91   Draft claims on the CCMS interface can be left untouched for up to 84 days, but if there is no activity on the claim after this, then it will be deleted from the system and all the data will be lost. If a CCMS claim is submitted and rejected by the assessment team, then a copy will remain on CCMS case billing page indefinitely until it is amended and/or submitted.

When counsel fees are also claimed on CCMS

16.92   Family counsel (whether paid under FAS or hourly rate) must claim their fees on CCMS before solicitors can submit their claim. Significant outstanding balances under their costs allocation will result in queries from the LAA and possibly a rejection of your claim.

16.93   For non-family counsel, unless you have opted that their fees are included within your claim to be paid directly to you and then forwarded to them, once your claim is authorised counsel will be notified to submit their claim for fees on CCMS. You must ensure that they have adequate allocation under the costs limitation before your claim is submitted and authorised.

Costs appeals

Generally

16.94   If costs escape or are not subject to a fixed fee in either controlled work or licensed work are reduced on assessment, you can appeal. You may want to do this, even if the effort of preparing the appeal seems disproportionate to the reduction in fees, if a successful appeal would improve your KPIs (see chapter 23).

16.95   Appeals must be made in writing within 28 days of receipt of the assessment, you can request an extension of up to 14 days if there is a good reason and it is made within 21 days. The appeal must be accompanied by any supporting papers returned with the assessment. An LAA Internal Reviewer will carry out a formal and detailed review of the original decision, and if he or she does not concede to the appeal then it will be referred to an Independent Costs Assessor (ICA). The ICA is an experienced solicitor in private practice, and not a member of the LAA's staff. The ICA may confirm, increase or decrease the amount assessed.

16.96   On pre-CCMS licensed work, an appeal can be made using the APP10 form returned with the assessment, although use of this form is not mandatory and an electronic appeal can be made using the LAA's appeals proforma (see below). On CCMS cases, an Appeal Bill must be completed, and representations are uploaded to the subsequent document request received. A CCMS Appeal Bill must consist of only the balance of work/amounts reduced on the original claim, eg if one hour of preparation is removed from a line entry on assessment then it is that one hour that is entered, or the hearing unit reduction on FAS, or balance disbursement that was reduced. The balance reduced for an enhancement is claimed through the disbursement screen, either as a single-line entry if the same amount is reduced for the same reasons, or multiple lines if different amounts and/or for different reasons. 'Quick guides' are found under the respective Closing Cases and Submitting Bills pages for providers and advocates (counsel) on the CCMS Training website. For providers, a superior quick guide is found under the 'Advanced Billing Guides' (guides produced by the LAA Finance Team) section of the respective page.

16.97   There are optional appeal proformas that can be used for certificated and controlled work. This negates the requirement to return all papers on non-CCMS cases. It can be used as an Appeal submissions document on CCMS appeals (an appeal must still be prepared and submitted on CCMS). For non-CCMS claims it can be emailed to: ContactCivil@Justice.gov.uk and for controlled work emailed to: mhu-ec@legalaid.gsi.gov.uk. The proforma for certificated cases can be found on the LAA's Claim1A form webpage and for controlled work cases the EC Claim 1 form webpage.

16.98   The LAA can make written representations (in addition to those contained in the original assessment) and must send these to you no less than 21 days before the appeal is sent to the ICA. You can provide a written response to these within 14 days of receiving them.

16.99   Any appeal to an ICA is considered on paper, although either party can make a written request (setting out full reasons) to the ICA for an oral hearing. Such requests are rarely granted.

16.100   See the Standard Civil Contract 2018 Specification paras 6.71–6.81 Civil Legal Advice Contract 2018 Specification paras 8.71–8.81; Civil Legal Advice Discrimination Contract 2018 Specification paras 8.71–8.81 and amended paras 6.19–6.29; Civil Legal Advice Education Contract 2018 Specification paras 6.25–6.35 for more information on costs appeals.

Points of principle of general importance

16.101   Under the 2013 and previous civil contracts[57] there was a further right of appeal. Where applicable, you could apply for a point of principle of general importance (POP) to be certified. The provision still applies to cases opened under contracts where there was the right to apply for a POP and this includes the CLA Contract 2018 including pre-amended Discrimination Contract.[58] See the relevant contract for more information. The text of POPs, and the procedure for applying for one, are set out in the POP Manual.[59] It is unclear how the LAA will operate in practice and the extent to which previously certified POPs will bind the LAA's future assessment decisions. Without a further right of appeal to the LAA, the only route to challenge a costs decision would be by way of judicial review.

Assessment of costs by the courts – legal aid only

16.102   Civil and family legal aid costs are assessed by the courts under Part 47 of the CPR (detailed assessment, called taxation pre-CPR), as

---

57   There was no right to apply for POPs under the 2014 or 2015 contracts.
58   CLA Contract 2018 Specification/ CLA Contract Discrimination 2018 (unamended) Specification paras 8.82–8.90.
59   See: www.gov.uk/legal-aid-points-of-principle-of-general-importance-pop.

summarised in sections 4 and 24 of the *Senior Court Costs Office guide*. Part 47 applies to proceedings under other civil court and tribunal procedure rules by those rules delegating to the CPR for detailed assessment.

16.103 The bill must be drawn up in the prescribed form.[60] Although the CPR does not expressly exclude legal aid only court bills in multi-track proceedings subject to a costs budget (CPR Practice Direction 47 Schedule of Costs Precedents: Precedent H) from having to be prepared as a phased bill, and in electronic form for any work done on or after 6 April 2018, it is highly unlikely that the courts will require this when no inter partes costs are being assessed, because the budget (prepared for inter partes recovery only) would not be a useful comparator to refer to. A costs lawyer or draftsman's fee is included in the bill and can be claimed as profit costs falling under solicitor's work.[61]

16.104 Bills are subject to provisional assessment (assessment on papers) under CPR 47.18, which is separate to inter partes provisional assessment under CPR 47.15. The procedure is:

1) Within three months of the right to detailed assessment arising, the bill of costs is lodged for provisional assessment with a request for detailed assessment – HMCTS Form N258A (or D258A for family law proceedings), together with the document giving right to detailed assessment (eg order for detailed assessment or discharged certificate[62]), copies of counsel's and expert's fee notes, written evidence of any disbursement exceeding £500 (if your bill includes the optional certificate as to disbursements of £500 or less), legal aid certificate, a statement of the client's address and contact details should they have a financial interest and wish to be heard on the assessment, and the court fee. An oral detailed assessment will only be listed if the request form asks for a client with financial interest to be heard. The file of relevant papers (as specified under the CPR[63]) must not be lodged unless the court requests them,[64] and contrary to the inclusion on the D258A checklist, this applies to the Senior Court Costs Office (SCCO) which also assesses cases of the Central Family Court (previously the Principal Registry of the Family Division (PRFD)).

---

60 CPR Part 47 Practice Direction paras 5.7–5.22 and Part 44 Practice Direction paras 2.1–2.11.

61 *Crane v Canons Leisure Centre* [2007] EWCA Civ 1352.

62 Costs assessment guidance paras 15.2–15.4.

63 CPR Part 47 Practice Direction para 13.12.

64 CPR Part 47 Practice Direction para 17.2(2).

2) The original assessed bill is returned with an N253 'Notice of Amount Allowed on Provisional Assessment'.

3) You must notify counsel of any reduction to their fees within seven days.[65]

4) If you object to reductions, then you can request a hearing within 14 days of receiving notice of provisional assessment. It is common for written objections to be sent. However, while some courts will list a hearing to hear further submissions if the provider is dissatisfied with the response to written submissions, some may not. Any costs of an appeal will only be payable to the extent that the court hearing it orders.[66]

5) If you object to the outcome of a hearing and wish to proceed further, then you must follow the same route as other costs under CPR Part 47, and appeal under Part 52 or CPR 47.21–24 if heard by an authorised court officer (referred to in the SCCO as costs officer), see para 16.106 for further information.

6) If you consent to the assessment, or after outcome of a hearing and/or appeal, you must return the bill of costs with a completed legal aid assessment certificate HMCTS Form EX80A (or EX80B where costs are subject to or escape family fixed fees). You must retain a copy of the assessed bill. There is no separate court fee for approving the certificate (it was combined with the assessment fee in July 2013).

7) The legal aid assessment certificate is approved (sealed) by the court and returned – the bill of costs is meant to be retained on the court file.

16.105 The costs of detailed assessment (except preparation of the bill of costs) fall outside of the costs limitation and statutory charge.[67] Profit costs which the LAA will recognise as costs of detailed assessment are detailed in their *Civil finance electronic handbook*:

- completing N258A/D258A (request for detailed assessment);
- letter out to court;
- diarising;
- completing EX80A/B/legal aid assessment certificate;
- drawing up the bill of costs following assessment;

---

65 Standard Civil Contract 2018 Specification para 6.43; CLA Contract 2018/ CLA Contract Discrimination 2018 (unamended) Specification para 8.45.

66 Standard Civil Contract 2018 Specification para 6.40; CLA Contract 2018/ CLA Contract Discrimination 2018 (unamended) Specification para 8.40.

67 Standard Civil Contract 2018 Specification para 6.42; CLA Contract 2018 Specification/ CLA Contract Discrimination 2018 (unamended) para 8.44.

- considering points of dispute and preparation of replies;
- attendance on the detailed assessment;
- time spent checking any provisional assessment.

16.106 The contract requires that costs of detailed assessment of legal aid only costs must be assessed within the detailed assessment itself.[68] This means that these costs have to be included within the bill of costs (apart from the court assessment fee). However, this does create a conflict with the CPR which provides that they should not be,[69] because Part 47 is principally for the assessment of inter partes costs, where the liability for costs of detailed assessment must be determined upon the outcome of those proceedings and are summarily assessed. However, for legal aid only assessments the bill is the only available mechanism to recover these costs which you have a right to be paid under the contract.

16.107 The bill and request etc must be lodged at the 'appropriate office' as specified under the CPR.[70] While the practice direction provides that for London County Court proceedings this is the Senior Courts Cost Office (SCCO), this does not apply where there are only legal aid costs, and these are assessed in the county court (unless the SCCO agrees to carry out the assessment instead). In family proceedings the 'appropriate office' is the Designated Family Court for the Designated Family Judge area.[71] However, where there are only legal aid costs, proceedings in the Central Family Court, East London, North London and West London Family Courts are all now assessed by costs officers in the SCCO.

16.108 While there is a sliding scale of court assessment fees for inter partes costs, there is a separate single court fee for detailed assessment of legal aid non-family and family costs respectively.[72] An across-the-board increase to civil proceedings fees on 22 July 2016 has resulted in the assessment fees for non-family cases being ten per cent higher than those for family cases. Any courts demanding the same assessment fee for family cases as civil cases should be referred to the up to date EX50 form.

---

68 Standard Civil Contract 2018 Specification para 6.38; CLA Contract 2018/ CLA Contract Discrimination 2018 (unamended) Specification para 8.38.
69 CPR Part 47 Practice Direction para 5.19.
70 CPR Part 47 Practice Direction paras 4.1–4.3.
71 Family Procedure Rules Part 28 Practice Direction 28A para 4.1.
72 Civil Proceedings Fees Order 2008 (as amended) Sch 1 para 5.1; and Family Proceedings Fees Order 2008 (as amended) Sch 1 para 9.1.

16.109   Once the assessment process is completed, you must then submit your claim for payment of the bill of costs to the LAA. If this is a CCMS case, then a summary level bill is submitted. You can enter a breakdown of disbursements which allows you to enter the hourly rates incurred by the expert if applicable, but this is optional. Solicitor's FAS must be broken down by using the FAS Unit Entry screen the same as a claim assessed by the LAA. The 'Court Assessment Result Date' is the date that the legal aid assessment certificate is sealed. Once the claim is submitted, a document request will be sent asking for:

1) the sealed legal aid assessment certificate;
2) a copy of the assessed bill of costs;
3) counsels' fee notes but only for a non-family case where you and counsel have opted for the balance fees (after payments on account) be paid directly to the provider and forwarded to counsel;
4) expert's invoices and disbursement vouchers exceeding £20 *including* VAT. For court fees and mileage, the LAA will accept a copy of the accounts ledger instead, although a copy of the covering letter to the court referring to the court fee and amount is usually accepted;
5) applicable orders eg for DNA/alcohol testing and directions for family law advocates' meetings where more than two are claimed;
6) disbursement list, number and cross-referenced against the vouchers, court orders, ledgers (only if the disbursements have not been broken down in the CCMS claim).

A quick guide is found under the 'Advanced Billing Guides' (guides produced by the LAA Finance Team) section of the Closing Cases and Submitting Bills page for providers on the CCMS Training website.

16.110   If a pre-CCMS case, then a form CIV CLAIM 1, CIV CLAIM 1A (or CIV CLAIM2 when inter partes costs recovery has also been made) is sent to the LAA together with the documentation detailed above except for the disbursement list but including counsels' fee notes unless counsel has been paid under FAS/FGF.

16.111   Family counsel (whether paid under FAS or hourly rate) must claim their fees on CCMS before you submit your claim. Significant outstanding balances under their costs allocation will result in queries from the LAA and possibly a rejection of your claim.

16.112   For non-family counsel, unless you have opted that their fees are included within your claim to be paid directly to you and then forwarded to them, once your claim is authorised counsel will be notified to submit their claim for fees on CCMS. You must ensure that they have adequate allocation under the costs limitation before your claim is submitted and authorised.

16.113 If the assessed costs (excluding costs of detailed assessment) exceed the costs limit, then you can either limit these when preparing the legal aid assessment certificate, or the LAA state within their *Civil finance electronic handbook* that they will reduce the claim accordingly rather than rejecting the claim and requiring the bill and legal aid assessment certificate to be redrawn. However, if profit costs of detailed assessment have not already been properly split from the rest of the profit costs and claimed as such within your claim, then it is unlikely that the LAA will spend time ringfencing these from the costs limitation for you.

Costs between the parties (inter partes costs)

16.114 The contract requires that you seek costs against another party (inter partes costs) just as you would with any non-legally aided case. An inter partes costs order is an order that one party indemnify another party's loss/liability for legal costs, so if there is no lability there is nothing to indemnify ie there's nothing to pay.[73] This is called the Indemnity Principle, and it limits what can be claimed/recovered inter partes to the terms of the client's retainer. A legal aid provider can recover costs on behalf of their client at market rates rather than legal aid rates, because the Indemnity Principle is disapplied from costs funded under civil legal aid (including family) to the extent of the rates but not the scope.[74] This was first done for Licensed Work in 1994 when civil legal aid rates were first prescribed (at that time these were roughly ten per cent less than market rates), and for Controlled Work in 2000. Today, the disparity between legal aid rates and market rates means that recovering inter partes costs where possible has never been more vital to the survival of many legal aid practices, and there is no reason not to pursue and obtain applicable costs awards for your client even when the paying party is a publicly funded body.[75]

16.115 Debts against the client can be ordered to be set-off against their inter partes costs, such debts are often damages or adverse costs

---

73 *Harold v Smith* (1860) 5 H&N 381.

74 Civil Legal Aid (Costs) Regulations 2013 reg 21(3); and Standard Civil Contract 2018 Specification para 1.40; CLA Contract 2018/CLA Contract Discrimination 2018 (unamended)/CLA Contract Education 2018 Specification para 3.14.

75 *R (Bahta) v Secretary of State for the Home Department* [2011] EWCA Civ 895.

within the same proceedings, but they do not always have to be. An order for set-off against a legally aided party's costs is commonly known as a Lockley Order. Costs protection under legal aid does not prevent a set-off up to the amount of the client's inter partes costs, and the costs order belongs to the client rather than the solicitor or the LAA, even though the client is legally aided.[76] Unfortunately, this means that if there is a set-off against inter partes costs then you can either elect to keep the balance recovered, or pay this into the Fund and claim the costs of the entire action from the LAA at legal aid rates.

16.116   If the order or agreement only allows for a single sum for both damages and costs and does not specify the proportion of that sum which relates to costs, then you cannot keep any of this money for your costs but rather should claim them from the LAA at the applicable legal aid rates/fees.[77]

16.117   Where CPR 44.9 applies, a party is liable to pay costs even when an order is not specifically made by the court eg when a claim is struck out, when a Part 36 offer is accepted, or when the claim is discontinued. Equally, you should try to ensure that there is an order as to costs in every interim order in the case (eg 'Costs in the case'), because (where CPR 44.10 applies) without this no inter partes costs can be claimed in relation to that order (eg costs of the hearing at which the order was made) regardless of the order for costs made at the end of the case, that is unless (in civil cases) it is an order granting permission to appeal or for judicial review or any other order sought without notice which is silent as to costs, in which case these are deemed orders for costs.

Assessment of costs by the courts – inter partes

The procedure

16.118   Civil and family inter partes costs are assessed by the courts under Part 47 of the CPR (detailed assessment, called taxation pre-CPR), as summarised in the *Senior Court Costs Office guide*. Part 47 applies to proceedings under other civil court and tribunal procedure rules by those rules delegating to the CPR for detailed assessment. There is a separate procedure for detailed assessment in the Supreme Court

---

76   *R (Burkett) v Hammersmith and Fulham LBC* [2004] EWCA Civ 1342.
77   Standard Civil Contract 2018 Specification para 1.42; CLA Contract 2018/CLA Contract Discrimination 2018 (unamended)/CLA Contract Education 2018 Specification para 3.16.

including a different form of bill, a requirement to file the bill at court with an upfront court fee at the outset of proceedings with much stricter requirement to do so in time and differing deadlines.[78]

16.119   Inter partes costs funded under legal aid are precluded from summary assessment under the CPR[79] and while this provision does not directly apply to tribunal proceedings, there is case-law that says it should be followed for Licensed Work.[80] However, summary assessments of inter partes costs funded under legal aid are sometimes carried out (usually on interim hearings), and the LAA's *Civil finance electronic handbook* details how such a recovery should be dealt with particularly where legal aid family fixed fees apply.

16.120   Detailed assessment procedure is analogous to the civil fast-track procedure, but with default case management steps as to disclosure and evidence removed:

1) Notice of commencement of detailed assessment proceedings (Claim form);
2) Bill of Costs in the prescribed form[81] (Particulars of Claim);
3) Points of Dispute in the prescribed form[82] (Defence);
4) Optional Replies in the prescribed form[83] (Reply);
5) assessment either by provisional assessment with oral review, or oral detailed assessment (Trial);
6) Final Costs Certificate (Money judgment which can be used for enforcement).

16.121   For cases where proceedings are not issued, and costs are payable pursuant to an agreement and the quantum of those costs is the only issue in dispute, an order for costs must be obtained first. This is done under costs-only proceedings.[84] Applicable cases are usually under Controlled Work and are rare under post-LASPO civil legal aid, so problems have arisen when the parties cannot agree on quantum, or the paying party reneges on the agreement, and the

---

78 Supreme Court Rules 2009 Part 7; and UKSC Practice Direction 13.
79 CPR Part 44 Practice Direction para 9.8.
80 *MG v Cambridgeshire CC (SEN)* [2017] UKUT 172 (AAC).
81 CPR Part 47 Practice Direction paras 5.1–5.1A and 5.7–5.22; and Part 44 Practice Direction paras 2.1–2.11.
82 CPR Part 47 Practice Direction para 8.2; and Schedule of Costs Precedents: Precedent G.
83 CPR Part 47 Practice Direction Schedule of Costs Precedents: Precedent G.
84 CPR 46.14.

LAA refuses to grant legal representation for costs-only proceedings on the basis that they are not within eligible scope.

16.122   Proceedings are commenced by serving the Notice (HMCTS Form N252) and a copy of the bill together with other specified enclosures.[85] Unless a payment of interim costs is sought, or some other application is made, the court is rarely involved until the point that assessment is requested. In the majority of cases a settlement is reached before this point. Commencement is required within three months of the right to costs arising (ie order for costs or deemed order for costs) although this can be extended or shortened either by agreement or the court. The exception to the three-month period is where the right arises in the interim of the principal case, and the general rule is that the principal case must conclude first before detailed assessment proceedings can be commenced. Proceedings are *not* automatically stayed pending an appeal. If the receiving party fails to commence after three months, then the paying party can apply for an unless order disallowing all or part of the costs that would otherwise be allowed if the receiving party fails to commence within a specified time, or if the paying party does not make such an application then the court may disallow interest on costs which can accrue from the date of the costs order, although often only the interest for the period of delay is disallowed. The court can also disallow all or part of the costs claimed on the basis of misconduct but commencing late when this is not deliberate or wilful does not in and of itself meet this criterion.[86] The assessment must be requested within three months of the expiry of the period for commencing proceedings (ie six months after the right to detailed assessment arises) and there are identical sanctions for failure to comply. These are the only applicable sanctions for delay in commencing proceedings and requesting assessment under CPR Part 47.

16.123   The paying party has 21 days to serve Points of Dispute (although this can be extended or shortened by agreement or the court) together with an open offer. The open offer can be nil, and usually any figure given is only for the maximum amount conceded to in the Points of Dispute (PoDs). There are no sanctions for failure to serve an open offer. If the paying party misses the deadline to serve PoDs then a default costs certificate (default money judgment) for the full amount sought in the Notice can be applied for from the court, with fixed

---

85   CPR Part 47 Practice Direction para 5.2.
86   *Haji-Ioannou v Frangos and others* [2006] EWCA Civ 1663.

costs of £80 plus the court fee,[87] and if it is issued before the PoDs are served then it is enforceable. If the PoDs are served out of time then the paying party may not be heard further in the proceedings, unless the court gives permission which it generally will.

16.124   Replies can be served within 21 days of receipt of the Points of Dispute, but these are optional.

16.125   The receiving party recovers costs of detailed assessment unless the court orders otherwise. The amount sought within the Bill does not include these costs (except those exclusive to legal aid only costs as detailed above), which will include costs of negotiations and optional replies. These are usually summarily assessed at the end of the assessment (even when they are a legally aided party's). This distinction between the claim (for costs) and costs of the claim is often overlooked by receiving parties. Part 36 offers may be made within detailed assessment proceedings.[88] However, paying parties will often make non-Part 36 without prejudice save as to costs offers instead, which of course do not carry a predetermined liability for costs of the (detailed assessment) proceedings to be paid. The CPR provides that any offer made within detailed assessed proceedings will include costs of preparing the bill, VAT and interest, unless the offer expressly states otherwise,[89] but the provision omits any reference to inclusion of costs of detailed assessment (apart from preparation of the bill) within the offer. It should be noted that negotiations made on a 'without prejudice' basis (whether oral or on papers) which miss off 'save as to costs', cannot be disclosed to the court after the assessment is concluded. If adverse costs of detailed assessment are made against your client, these will be set off against their costs of the principal case under a Lockley Order (see above).

16.126   If interim costs are agreed or the proceedings are settled, and you are concerned that the paying party will not actually pay, you can apply for an Interim or Final Costs Certificate under CPR 47.10 so that the agreement can be enforced.

16.127   A detailed or provisional assessment is requested on HMCTS Form N258. Claims for costs up to £75,000 (including VAT) are subject to provisional assessment, unless the court orders otherwise. The procedure is under CPR 47.15 and is separate to the procedure for provisional assessment of legal aid only costs under CPR 47.18, although both sets of costs will be assessed by the court and the court

87 CPR Part 47 Practice Direction para 10.7.
88 CPR 47.20.
89 CPR Part 47 Practice Direction para 19.

fee for inter partes assessment covers the legal aid only assessment (at an oral assessment they will be assessed at the end of the hearing[90]). Costs of provisional assessment are capped at £1,500 excluding VAT and court fees. The request for provisional assessment must be lodged with documents specified under CPR Part 47 PD 14.3, which will include your statement of costs (N260) for detailed assessment proceedings, the paying party's open offer, and any Part 36/without prejudice save as to costs offers in a sealed envelope for the court to open when determining the liability of costs of detailed assessment. Under provisional assessment, the rules do not require you to file your file of relevant papers in support of the bill (as specified under the CPR[91]), but the SCCO always requires this and will request it if it is not already lodged with the request for provisional assessment. Other courts may do the same. The provisionally assessed bill will be sent to both parties and they have 14 days to agree the calculation of the assessed figures or make written submissions on any dispute about this. Any dispute as to liability for costs of the provisional assessment process will also be dealt with by written submissions and determined without a hearing. Each party also has 21 days from receipt of notice of provisional assessment to request an oral review of the assessment. The request must specify which items within the bill are to be reviewed and the court can (and does) refuse to review anything that is not specified within the request. Because the oral review is technically not an appeal, it is heard by the same judge or authorised court officer who provisionally assessed the bill. For the requesting party to obtain costs of the oral review and not incur adverse costs of the same, they must vary the total provisionally assessed sum by at least 20 per cent in their favour unless the court orders otherwise. Of course, you will not be successful on review if your costs have been reduced by less than 20 per cent on the provisional assessment. Consequently, you must carefully consider whether it is worth pursuing an oral review, because after incurring further own costs and adverse costs, you may end up worse off even if your claim is increased.

16.128　　　If the assessment is made by an authorised court officer (referred to in the SCCO as a costs officer), their decision is appealed under CPR 47.21–47.24 to a costs judge or a district judge of the High Court. Such appeals do not require permission but must be made no

90　Standard Civil Contract 2018 Specification para 6.46; CLA Contract 2018/CLA Contract Discrimination 2018 (unamended) para 8.51.
91　CPR Part 47 Practice Direction para 13.12.

more than 21 days after the date of the decision being made, the detailed assessment proceedings will be re-heard. An appeal from a judge must be made under Part 52 of the CPR and is limited to review of the decision under appeal rather than a re-hearing of the whole proceedings (CPR 52.21(1)).

The LAA and inter partes costs

16.129 For Licensed Work, there is deemed cover for detailed assessment proceedings under the certificate even after it is discharged,[92] however, since the 2010 contract there has been an express term providing for a conditional funding arrangement meaning that the LAA will not pay you costs of detailed assessed that your client is not awarded when the inter partes costs of the principal case are recovered.[93] Therefore, should costs of detailed assessment not be recovered on a successful inter partes recovery, these cannot be claimed from the LAA even at legal aid rates, although the court fee may be paid.

16.130 Where interest is recovered, you must pay the LAA the proportion of interest on the costs recovered as calculated at legal aid rates, and you may keep any excess.[94] For example, you recover £10,000 costs with interest thereon and at legal aid rates those costs would be worth £3,000, so the proportion of the interest accrued on that £3,000 must be paid to the LAA. When calculating the LAA's share of interest, discretionary enhancements should not be applied to the legal aid rates used to calculate what the costs would be worth.

16.131 Once payment is received from the paying party, if you are not claiming legal aid only costs in addition, then you have two months to report the recovery,[95] however, where multiple recoveries at different times are being made under a certificate, eg where there are costs of the first instance and appellate proceedings, the LAA acknowledge that the recoveries can only be reported after the final recovery. For CCMS cases, you must report the recovery under your outcomes and

---

92 Standard Civil Contract 2018 Specification para 6.38; CLA Contract 2018/CLA Contract Discrimination 2018 (unamended) Specification para 8.38 and Costs assessment guidance para 15.14.

93 Standard Civil Contract 2018 Specification paras 6.39 and 6.41(a); CLA Contract 2018/CLA Contract Discrimination 2018 (unamended) Specification para 8.39 and 8.41(a).

94 Standard Civil Contract 2018 Specification para 6.53; CLA Contract 2018/CLA Contract Discrimination 2018 (unamended) Specification para 8.58.

95 Standard Civil Contract 2018 Specification para 6.48; CLA Contract 2018/CLA Contract Discrimination 2018 (unamended) Specification para 8.53.

any claim for legal aid only costs is made separately with a normal CCMS bill. On non-CCMS cases a form CIV CLAIM2 is used to report the recovery and claim any legal aid only costs.

16.132   There is no deemed cover to enforce the costs certificate if the paying party fails to pay, and an amendment must be sought under the certificate to obtain a retainer to do this.[96] You do not have to carry out enforcement, instead you can claim your costs from the LAA but this will be at legal aid rates. If you have already discharged the legal aid certificate, then you will not be able to obtain cover for enforcement and your only option will be to claim costs at legal aid rates from the LAA and rely upon the LAA to pursue enforcement. You will need to obtain a costs certificate to enable pursuit of enforcement and without this the LAA will not pay your claim. Where a court assessment is required, you will need to lodge your inter partes bill for a legal aid only assessment with an accompanying schedule of the items in the bill calculated at legal aid rates (a legal aid schedule) in the prescribed form.[97] The legal aid assessment certificate must be completed and this is the only time that Box A of the EX80 form is completed to show the costs being paid by the LAA for which an inter partes costs order has been made. For CCMS cases you use the Awards Summary of the outcomes section to report the award, any partial recovery, the paying party's details and amount due. For non-CCMS cases where there is no recovery the form CIV CLAIM2 is not used, but forms CIV CLAIM1 or CIV CLAIM1A instead, which also have relevant pages for awards unrecovered and debtor's details.

Apportioned inter partes costs and legal aid only costs

16.133   In cases where inter partes costs are possible, it is not uncommon for costs to be ordered or negotiated on the basis of payment of part of the costs of the case. If so, it is important that you are clear as to the terms of the order or agreement, because although you can claim the balance from the legal aid fund,[98] if it is a Very High Cost Case (VHCC) then you must specifically apply to the LAA Case Manager for authorisation to do so.[99] The 2018 Standard Civil Contract (and

---

96   Standard Civil Contract 2018 Specification para 1.41; CLA Contract 2018/CLA Contract Discrimination 2018 (unamended)/CLA Contract Education 2018 Specification para 3.15.

97   CPR Part 47 Practice Direction paras 17.6–17.9.

98   Standard Civil Contract 2018 Specification para 6.44; CLA Contract 2018/CLA Contract Discrimination 2018 (unamended) Specification para 8.49.

99   Individual Case Contract 2018 (High Cost Case) Specification paras 5.3–5.11.

previous contracts) allows you to claim from the legal aid fund any costs not payable by another party (legal aid only costs), but only if certain conditions are met.[100]

16.134 The Specification defines 'legal aid only' costs – costs that can be claimed from the legal aid fund even where inter partes costs are recovered – as:

a) contract work not covered by a client's costs order or agreement;
b) costs of completing legal aid forms and communicating with the LAA;
c) certain limited types of costs disallowed or not agreed.

16.135 Where a costs order or agreement specifies that another party should pay a proportion of the client's costs (but not a fixed sum), the same proportion of the total work that is not covered is legal aid only costs.

16.136 To take a practical example, say total costs on the case are £2,000 at legal aid rates and £4,000 at inter partes rates. If the other side agree to pay your costs in the sum of £2,000, that could be expressed in one of three ways:

1) £2,000 as the total agreed costs of the case (you agree it is only worth £2,000 rather than £4,000);
2) agreement to pay costs between x and y dates, totalling £2,000; or
3) agreement to pay 50 per cent of the costs, 100 per cent of this being £4,000 at market rates.

None of the agreed costs include work done relating to legal aid funding, which is solicitor–client/funding work and therefore comes under both categories a) and b) of legal aid only costs (above).

16.137 In each case, you receive £2,000 from the other side. In the first case, that £2,000 represents the total costs of the case, so there are no legal aid costs (apart perhaps from £100 or so for completing the application for legal aid and so on). In the second case, costs outside the agreed dates are not subject to the costs order, so you can claim those costs from the LAA in addition to the £2,000 inter partes costs you have received. In the third case, the other side have agreed to pay 50 per cent of your costs, so the other 50 per cent are legal aid only costs, so you can claim the other 50 per cent from the LAA at legal aid rates plus the full amount for work completing the application for legal etc from the LAA, in addition to the £2,000 from the other side.

---

100 Standard Civil Contract 2018 Specification paras 6.50–6.51 (in para 6.51, para 6.48 is erroneously referred to rather than para 6.50); CLA Contract 2018/CLA Contract Discrimination 2018 (unamended) Specification paras 8.55–8.56.

16.138   Claiming legal aid only costs at a percentage is relatively uncommon and none of the LAA claim forms, both paper and electronic, are designed to cater for this. For a single claim on a non-CCMS case with only one set percentage being claimed, ie 50 per cent with no full costs for solicitor client/funding work, a CIV CLAIM 2 can be used showing the costs at the full claim within the schedules and then an addendum set of figures showing at 50 per cent. If there are multiple percentages and/or it is a CCMS case, then agreement as to how to claim should be sought from the LAA before preparing it. This may be by using separate schedules or forms for each percentage rate. The LAA have accepted paper forms for CCMS cases where there is a percentage claim, because the CCMS pricing system for hourly rates cannot be set at a percentage of the price, let alone multiple percentage rates within a single claim. Splitting the amounts by time – for example, 50 per cent of the full time claimed for each piece of work – is inadvisable, because the full amount must be given in order to assess what is reasonable and proportionate and then the percentage rate applied afterwards.

Recoupment and limitation

16.139   The authority in relation to the limitation period in which the LAA can recover funds paid as payments on account is *Legal Services Commission v Henthorn*.[101] The then Legal Services Commission (LSC) pursued recoupment of payments on account from a retired barrister, Aisha Henthorn. The cases dated back to between 1992 and 1998, with the LSC's claim issued in 2006. Henthorn argued that the six-year limitation period ran from the end of the case, and therefore the LSC were out of time in bringing the case against her. The High Court agreed and the LSC appealed. The Law Society and the Bar Council intervened in the Court of Appeal.

16.140   The Master of the Rolls held that time begins to run not at the end of the case, but only once the assessment process has been completed, and therefore once there has been a determination of how much the LSC owes solicitor/counsel, or how much they owe the LSC by way of recoupment of payments on account. He further held that the LSC's claim was not an abuse of process, nor was it unreasonable in public law terms, and that on the facts of the individual payments, Ms Henthorn had no defence to the claims. The LSC were therefore entitled to recovery of payments on account.

101 [2011] EWCA Civ 1415.

16.141   The effect of this case is that once a final bill is assessed, time starts to run for the purposes of the limitation period and the LAA cannot demand repayment of unrecouped payments on account more than six years after the date of final assessment. However, if no final bill was ever submitted, limitation never starts to run and so the LAA can recover payments on account at any time.

16.142   It is therefore critical that organisations hold good records regarding the discharge and final payments of claims and keep those for at least six years, until claims for the refund of payments on account become statute barred under the Limitation Act 1980.

Pro bono costs orders

16.143 Pro bono is of course no replacement for legal aid, but many legal aid providers find themselves carrying out legal work, including representation, without legal aid to cover fees, and consequently fees for the work cannot be recovered from another party who is ordered to pay costs because of the indemnity principle. If this work and/or period without cover can be identified when the issue of costs liability arises in the applicable court (see below), then you can ask the court to make a pro bono costs order for this work, if costs are awarded to your client or include this within a settlement. In many civil litigation cases this can also avoid the other side being in a position of strength, because they know that they will not be excused from the expense of having to pay your client's costs if they lose.

16.144   Pro bono costs recovered must be paid to the Access to Justice Foundation ('the Foundation') which is the prescribed charity. The Foundation distributes the money to agencies and projects giving free legal help (where legal aid is unavailable) to those in charitable need and can also help fund organisations which further access to justice more broadly. If such a front-line agency recovers costs under a pro bono costs order, they can apply to receive up to 50 per cent of this. The Foundation also provides grants to Legal Support Trusts.

16.145   A pro bono costs order is made pursuant to section 194(3) of the Legal Services Act 2007 and CPR 46.7. Unfortunately, pro bono costs orders are unlikely be made in a tribunal, because section 194(10) of the Act does not include any tribunal under the definition of 'civil court' to which section 194 applies.[102] Courts to which section 194 applies are the Supreme Court when dealing with a relevant appeal

---

102 *Raftopoulou v Revenue and Customs Commissioners* [2015] UKUT 630 (TCC).

(as defined under section 194(10)), the civil division of the Court of Appeal, High Court, the Family Court or County Court. Although in their report of December 2011, 'Costs in Tribunals', to the Senior President of Tribunals, the Costs Review Group recommended that the power to award pro bono costs should be extended to tribunals, to date this recommendation has not been implemented.

16.146　The procedure for obtaining a pro bono costs order is provided under CPR 46.7. A pro bono costs order is like any other order for costs apart from the fact that a) it must provide for payment of pro bono costs to be made to the Access to Justice Foundation, and b) the costs are not restricted by the terms of a retainer. You do not have to put the other party on special notice that you might be seeking a pro bono costs order and you do not have to inform your client either. The factors that determine the making of a costs order are the same, and they can be subject to either summary or detailed assessment. If Part 45 of the CPR applies, then the costs will be limited to the relevant fixed fees.

16.147　If costs are summarily assessed, the prescribed form for other summary assessments (N260) is not required (CPR Part 46 PD 4.1 applies instead) but can be used, although the certificate as to the Indemnity Principle should be removed. The Foundation also provides a guide (*Pro bono passport*) that complies with PD 4.1 and also includes a template order, and this can be used instead.

16.148　If the costs are subject to detailed assessment, then the costs of detailed assessment which can be identified as solely attributable to the pro bono costs cannot be paid to you but can be recovered under a further pro bono costs order and paid to the Foundation.

16.149　CPR 46.7(3) requires you to send a copy of the pro bono costs order to the Access to Justice Foundation within seven days of receipt. There are no sanctions for failing to comply with this rule. The subsequent money judgment (eg Default Costs Certificate) can be enforced as normal. The client can enforce in his or her own name, or alternatively the Foundation will enforce.

16.150　More information and helpful quick guides including guides for litigators and advocates can be found on the Access to Justice Foundation website: www.atjf.org.uk/.

Family

16.151　There are two family payment schemes: public family law and private family law.

Public law

Fee level	Forms of civil legal service	Provided as	Escape threshold
1	Legal Help	Controlled Work	x3 Fixed Fee
2	Family Help (Lower)	Controlled Work	x3 Fixed Fee
3	Legal Representation	Licensed Work	x2 Fixed Fee

Private law

Fee level	Forms of civil legal service	Provided as	Escape threshold
1	Legal Help	Controlled Work	x3 Fixed Fee
2	Family Help (Lower)	Controlled Work	x3 Fixed Fee
3	Help with Family Mediation	Controlled Work	N/A
4	Family Help (Higher)	Licensed Work	x3 Fixed Fee
5	Legal Representation	Licensed Work	x3 Fixed Fee

16.152 The rates and fee amounts are provided under the Remuneration Regulations and the provisions for the schemes are in section 7 of the Contract Specification. All Controlled Work is subject to fixed fees and must 'escape' them before it can be claimed at hourly rates. Most Licensed Work is subject to fixed fees but there are exclusions. Fixed fees do not apply to public family law non-advocacy Licensed Work other than section 31 proceedings (see below). A useful matrix of the non-advocacy fees is provided under para 7.3 of the Section 7 of the Specification. Family advocacy is dealt with separately in chapter 18.

Controlled Work

16.153 Claims for Legal Help and Family Help (Lower) in both private and public family schemes, and Help with Family Mediation claims are paid and claimed as other civil categories, described above.

16.154   In public family law, Controlled Work is provided for work preceding the issue of applications for a care order or supervision order under section 31 of the Children Act 1989. See chapter 8 for more information.

Family – Controlled Work escape fee cases

16.155 The escape threshold for Legal Help and Family Help (Lower) in both private and public family schemes is that profit costs calculated on an hourly rate basis must exceed three times the aggregate fixed fee (combined standard fees) but excluding the settlement fees under the children and finance aspects. The settlement fees cannot be claimed in addition to an escape case claim. The settlement fees under children and finance aspects do not form part of the aggregate fee. Help with Family Mediation cannot escape its standard fee.

16.156   You can instruct counsel on both Legal Help and Family Help (Lower) but their fee cannot be claimed as a disbursement in addition to a standard fee and it cannot be used to escape the standard fee either. However, if a case does escape then counsel's fee can be claimed as a disbursement, but it is limited to the equivalent FAS fee. You must pay counsel within 28 days of receiving their fee note.[103]

Licensed Work

Overview

16.157 The general rules and procedures for claiming licensed work costs are described above. Standard fee claims are submitted to the LAA as above. In cases where proceedings have not been issued, the LAA assesses the costs.

16.158   Where proceedings have been issued, the LAA assesses bills within the assessment limit, ie where assessable costs are up to £2,500 (excluding VAT). The common special circumstance that means the LAA will assess costs over the assessment limit is where the only assessable costs exceeding £2,500 (excluding VAT) are disbursements, eg a section 31 care fixed fee plus substantial disbursements.

16.159   Proceedings that conclude before lay justices (magistrates) are assessed by the LAA regardless of the level of assessable costs. This does not include proceedings concluding before a district judge of the magistrates' court. Further, such judges are now defined as 'judges of district judge level' for the purposes of the family fixed fee scheme[104] and hearings before them attract a higher FAS fee than

103 Civil Standard Contract 2018 Specification paras 7.170–7.172.
104 Civil Legal Aid (Remuneration) (Amendment) (No 2) Regulations 2014 reg 2(1).

they did before the introduction of the single Family Court on 22 April 2014.

16.160 Claims for advocacy under the FAS must be made on an appropriately completed Advocates Attendance Form (EX506). If such form(s) are not completed correctly and submitted, the claim(s) will only be paid at the unit 1 rate for interim hearings and no fee will be paid for a final hearing.

16.161 Private law proceedings heard with public law proceedings or where a private law order is sought within public law proceedings for example an application for a Child Arrangements Order is made within care proceedings, are called 'related proceedings'. Related proceedings are remunerated under public law fees scheme as part of the public law case and no separate standard fee is claimable. The 2018 Contract now expressly clarifies that private law proceedings cannot be related proceedings simply because an order is being sought which may avoid public law proceedings when those public law proceedings do not exist.[105]

16.162 Cases are paid at hourly rates, and are not subject to a fixed fee, if:

a) you are instructed for less than 24 hours;
b) where the client has previously instructed a different provider in respect of the same work and the certificate has not been transferred; or
c) where you act for a client whose application to be joined in proceedings is refused.[106]

16.163 Work on an appeal against a final order is also paid at hourly rates instead of a fixed fee, apart from work up to the conclusion of the first instance proceedings which is within any applicable standard fee and includes:

a) representation on any interim appeal;
b) any advice on the merits of an appeal against the final order; and
c) an application to the court of first instance for permission to appeal.[107]

16.164 Claims for cases on CCMS must be made via CCMS. With non-CCMS cases you must use a form CIV CLAIM1A if the provider's fixed fees are claimed or a case escapes the fixed fee, or a form CIV CLAIM1 if the only fixed fees claimed (if any) are for counsel.

---

105 Standard Civil Contract 2018 Specification paras 7.46–7.47.
106 Standard Civil Contract 2018 Specification para 7.19.
107 Standard Civil Contract 2018 Specification paras 7.48–7.49 and 7.98–7.99.

16.165 Where there are multiple clients on a case and these are under CCMS, then the certificates must be linked. There will be a lead certificate which will hold the costs limitation for all certificates (one full costs limit plus half of that costs limit again for each linked certificate). The claim must be made on the lead certificate, but outcomes must be reported and nil bills submitted on all other certificates.

Family – public law fee scheme

16.166 Within public family law, there is only a non-advocacy standard fee for proceedings under section 31 of the Children Act 1989 – the Legal Representation Standard Fee also known as the Care Proceedings Graduated Fees Scheme (CPGFS). Non-advocacy work in all other public law proceedings is paid at hourly rates.

16.167 The escape threshold for Legal Representation Standard Fee is that profit costs calculated on an hourly rate basis must exceed twice the fixed fee. This calculation cannot include enhancements on the hourly rate, even the guaranteed minimum for panel members. Only once 'base costs' have escaped can you add the percentage enhancement. Don't forget that advocacy is claimed separately and in addition to the fixed fee, so advocacy costs do not count towards reaching the escape threshold.[108]

16.168 The Legal Representation Standard Fee is applied by reference to the level of judge before whom the proceedings conclude (or if you cease to provide the service before conclusion then the relevant level of judge hearing the case at that time),[109] the status of the client in the proceedings and region where the solicitor's office is located.

Parties

16.169 The parties are as follows:

- **'Child'** applies where you represent the child who is the subject of the proceedings.
- **'Parent'** applies where you represent the parent of such a child or a person who has parental responsibility for such a child.
- **'Joined party'** applies to all other clients in section 31 care proceedings (unless the client's application to be joined to the proceedings is refused, in which case must be claimed at hourly rates).

16.170 There is a higher fee where two parents or two+ children are represented. There is one fixed fee per case, not per client, unless the client

108 Standard Civil Contract 2018 Specification paras 7.50–7.52.
109 Standard Civil Contract 2018 Specification para 7.9.

is a joined party to the proceedings (for which there is only a single-party fixed fee available). Where there are separate section 31 care proceedings for another child and these are not consolidated, then a separate Legal Representation Standard Fee is claimable. However, if the proceedings are consolidated, then these are claimed under one fee and if a CCMS case then the certificates will need to be linked.

16.171   Where you act for a client whose status changes during the proceedings, you must claim the higher fee available. For example, if you act for a grandparent, who loses parental responsibility and continues as a joined party, the standard fee (and the relevant escape threshold) for a parent will apply.

Regions

Regional Fee	LAA Regional Office of Provider
North	North Western Region (Manchester)
	North Eastern Region (Newcastle)
	Yorkshire & Humberside Region (Leeds)
	Merseyside Region (Liverpool)
Midlands	West Midlands Region (Birmingham)
	East Midlands Region (Nottingham)
	Eastern Region (Cambridge)
South (including London)	South Eastern Region (Reading)/London Region (London)
	South Western Region (Bristol)
Wales	Wales Region (Cardiff)

16.172 Remember that the region is dictated by the location of the provider's address on the legal aid certificate. As with all costs, it is the retainer that is key, so this is a matter decided by where the client instructs the solicitor.

Family – private law fee scheme

16.173 The Higher Standard Fee Scheme also known as the Private Family Law Representation Scheme (PFLRS) divides private family law into three aspects: 1) domestic abuse; 2) children; and 3) finance. The aspects will be funded under one certificate per client (except child abduction proceedings, which cannot cover any other proceedings[110]).

---

110 Standard Civil Contract 2018 Specification para 7.75.

16.174   There are two levels under the Higher Standard Fee Scheme:

- Level 4 – Family Help (Higher); and
- Level 5 – Legal Representation.

Pre-LASPO these were Level 3 and 4 (Help with Family Mediation was added as Level 3) and are still commonly referred to as such and are still labelled as these on the CCMS Billing interface. Family Help (Higher) is provided in children and finance for all work excluding preparation for and representation at final hearing (any hearing listed to make a final determination). Legal Representation is provided for work up to and including final hearing and is issued from the outset on domestic abuse, although upon initial grant the scope may be limited to the first interim hearing.

16.175   The Higher Standard Fee is applied by reference to the level of judge that the first instance proceedings conclude before (or if you cease to provide the service before conclusion then the relevant level of judge hearing the case at that time),[111] and whether the solicitor's office is located within a London borough.

16.176   The escape threshold for the Higher Standard Fee Scheme is that profit costs calculated on an hourly rate basis must exceed three times the aggregate fixed fee (combined standard fees under a single aspect) but excluding the settlement fee under the finance aspect. Work cannot be combined to escape different aspects. For example, if three times the domestic abuse fee is £1,521 but the domestic abuse work is £500 below this, and three times the children fee is £1,176 and the children work is £501 above this, you cannot combine the two to escape both fees, but rather you must claim the domestic abuse fee and only claim the children work at hourly rates. As above, enhancements (including guaranteed minimum for panel members) cannot be included to escape the fee, only once 'base costs' have escaped can you add the percentage enhancement. Advocacy is also excluded when calculating the escape threshold.

16.177   There are various proceedings excluded from the Higher Standard Fee Scheme,[112] so they are always claimed at hourly rate. The exclusions are identical to those for FAS:

- child abduction proceedings;
- proceedings under the Inheritance (Provision for Family and Dependants) Act 1975;

---

111 Standard Civil Contract 2018 Specification para 7.9.
112 Standard Civil Contract 2018 Specification para 7.74.

- proceedings under the Trusts of Land and Appointment of Trustees Act 1996;
- proceedings in which you provide separate representation of a child in proceedings which are neither Specified Proceedings (as defined in section 41(6) of the Children Act 1989), nor proceedings which are being heard together with Specified Proceedings;
- applications for Forced Marriage Protection Orders under the Forced Marriage (Civil Protection) Act 2007;
- defended proceedings for divorce, judicial separation, dissolution of a civil partnership or for the legal separation of civil partners;
- nullity proceedings (including proceedings for annulment of a civil partnership);
- proceedings under the inherent jurisdiction of the High Court in relation to children;
- applications for Parental Orders under the Human Fertilisation and Embryology Act 2008;
- applications in relation to female genital mutilation protection orders under the Female Genital Mutilation Act 2003.

16.178 Upon settling ongoing litigation with the National Centre for Domestic Violence (NCDV) in December 2018, the LAA have stated that they will not pay providers for the £178.50 plus VAT fee charged by NCDV to produce a bundle of documents including witness statement and draft order. The LAA have also reminded providers that they are prohibited from paying referral fees.

Family – public and private law standard fee schemes: enhancement of hourly rates

16.179 A discretionary enhancement can be claimed on family cases where hourly rates are claimable rather than a fixed fee, as detailed above in enhanced rates.

16.180   In family cases (whether paid under family or non-family remuneration rates), there is a guaranteed minimum enhancement of 15 per cent for all work done (including routine items, travel and waiting) by a member of the following panels:[113]

- Resolution Accredited Specialist Panel;
- the Law Society's Children Panel;*
- the Law Society Family Law Panel Advanced.

---

113 Standard Civil Contract 2018 Specification para 7.23.

* Under previous contracts, a certificate had to include proceedings relating to children in order for a Children Panel member to qualify for the 15 per cent minimum, but this requirement has been removed from the 2018 Contract.

16.181   Where a discretionary higher amount is sought, the 15 per cent minimum cannot be claimed in addition to that amount but rather forms part of it.[114] So, care should be taken when wording the justification in order to avoid any implication of the former, for which the LAA find the claim falls outside the contractual terms and consequently the court's discretion where the court has carried out the assessment.

Family – public and private law standard fee schemes: client transfers

16.182   If your fees on an hourly rates basis (excluding enhancement) are equal to or greater than the standard fee, you claim the standard fee.[115] If your fees on an hourly rates basis are less than the standard fee, you claim half the standard fee. The only exception to this is where you continue to act for one or more clients is a private family law matter, then every provider can claim the full standard fee(s) regardless. You cannot combine the amount of your actual costs with those of the other provider to escape the standard fee.

16.183   Where all clients transfer instructions to you from another provider:

- Where your own actual costs are less *than the full standard fee(s)*, you will claim half of the standard fee.
- Where your own actual costs are *equal to or greater than the full standard fee(s)*, you will claim the full standard fee(s), or hourly rates if your own actual costs reach the escape threshold.

16.184   Where multiple clients instruct you in a private family law case and one or more transfers, and one or more remains:

- One client transfers to another solicitor, and one client remains:
  - First provider gets a full relevant fee unless escapes.
  - Subsequent provider(s) gets a full relevant fee unless escapes (but this may only be a level 5 fee if the case has already moved to level 5, *even* if there is cover for level 4 on the certificate).

16.185   Where multiple clients instruct in section 31 care proceedings and one or more transfers and one or more remains:

114 Costs assessment guidance para 12.23.
115 Standard Civil Contract 2018 Specification paras 7.43 and 7.96.

- First provider gets a full standard fee (which is 2+ fee if more than one client was represented at one or more hearings) unless escapes.
- Subsequent provider(s) get relevant fee which will be half the fee if actual costs are less than the fee, the full fee if actual costs are equal to or greater than the full standard fee, or hourly rates, if the actual costs reach the escape threshold.

Family – public and private law standard fee schemes: advocacy

16.186 The standard fees for both private and public law cases do not include advocacy. The LAA defines 'advocacy' to include not only appearances as advocate before the court, but also any associated travel and waiting time and attendance as advocate at advocates' meetings in public law matters, as well as preparation for advocacy. The exception to this is preparation by a provider when the hearing does not go ahead (so no FAS can be claimed) which can then be claimed under the standard fee. Time spent instructing counsel is part of the standard fee too.[116]

16.187 See chapter 20 for information on FAS.

Family – Very High Cost Cases

16.188 A VHCC is a case where total costs and disbursements are expected to be over £25,000 (not including VAT) and/or one defined as 'Special Case Work'[117] requiring an ICC. If you represent more than one party and the combined costs limitations are more than £25,000 then the LAA will restrict payment to £25,000 unless the case has been notified as a VHCC. However, you need to be aware of the financial limitation (costs limit) when you apply for a case contract (whichever type), because the LAA will not increase it pending approval of the case as exceptional and/or agreement of the case plan/CCFS (Care Case Fee Scheme) form, and if the case is at hourly rates ('Fully costed case plan') then your costs up to the date of registration of the VHCC ('pre-contract costs') will be limited to the costs limit. There is a legislated list of circumstances when an application/amendment for civil legal services will be treated by the LAA as an application for Special Case Work including appeals to the Supreme Court.[118]

16.189 All single-advocate section 31 care cases registered from 1 October 2015 are paid under the CCFS (previously known as the events

116 Standard Civil Contract 2018 Specification paras 7.45 and 7.78.
117 Civil Legal Aid (Procedure) Regulations 2012 Part 6 regs 54–59.
118 Civil Legal Aid (Procedure) Regulations 2012 reg 54(3).

model). This is unless you can show you would be paid at least 30 per cent more by claiming hourly rates (including enhancements) with a fully costed case plan, this is referred to as an 'exceptional case' but should not be confused with a case under ECF (see above). The CCFS model is used in section 31 care cases to avoid multiple revisions to detailed case plans. You can also request your non-section 31 VHCC be paid under CCFS if it follows the Public Law Outline or is being managed in a similar way. If the case concludes before a High Court level judge, then all events will change to High Court events, and vice versa if a case concludes before a judge of a lower level. Costs incurred when a case temporarily escalates (ie for an appeal hearing) are paid at hourly rates rather than events. CCFS is a form of graduated/fixed fee, dependent on the number of hearing days and other events. The event fees are based on detailed analysis of the average costs and hours in these types of expensive/complex cases.

16.190   There is a separate CCFS for cases using two counsel/advocates or leading counsel, which is similar to the one Advocate scheme. Two Counsel CCFS is not mandatory if a two-counsel case becomes high cost, and you can choose to be paid under a fully costed case plan instead, but it must be submitted within 20 working days otherwise the CCFS Two Counsel Model will apply regardless. Upon grant of prior authority for QC or two counsel, the LAA assume that the case will exceed £25,000 and will be subject a VHCC contract unless the provider confirms otherwise. One Advocate (aka Single Counsel) CCFS was calculated using FAS. The Two Counsel CCFS was calculated using the FGFS. The slight differences between how events are triggered on them are detailed below. See chapter 20 for more information about payment for advocacy in family VHCC cases.

16.191   VHCC Contracts are composed of the ICC, ICC Specification, and Contract Guides which are labelled as Information Packs and detail the specific terms of the various schemes.

16.192   A fixed fee is paid to you for each event (eg hearing day or advocates' meeting) based on the predicted case timetable. As the case progresses, revised CCFS forms are submitted for agreement if the case timetable is increased and/or further disbursements are required. At the end of the case, the final costs are adjusted to reflect the final actual timetable. Event fees are paid to counsel only if the main hearing (including split hearings) is listed for more than ten days, otherwise they are paid under FAS on Single Counsel or FGFS on Two Counsel.

16.193   There are slight differences between the Single Counsel and Two Counsel models which can become confusing when alternating between them on different cases:

Event fee	Single Counsel case	Two Counsel case
Hearing day event fee for litigator solicitor	Event fee as shown in the fees matrix.	Only the event fee as shown in the fees matrix *if* the solicitor attends court with the advocate. Otherwise, £900 a day (Section 8 of the Information Pack).
Substantive Conferences with the client	Two event fees available, and then only to the attending advocate, but specific authorisation can be sought for more.	Two event fees available, and then only to the attending advocate, but a further two event fees are available on split hearings at welfare/disposal stage.
Advocates' Meetings	Available for every advocates' meeting ordered in advance by the Court, but they must be evidenced with an order or judicial email.	Two event fees available, even when the Court orders more, unless, like conferences, there is split hearing and then a further two are available at welfare/disposal stage.
Judge's reading day	Only when the advocate is on standby and then called to court. Only then will this count towards a main hearing that exceeds ten days, *unless* in between a group of days that the advocate is ordered to attend court eg not a Monday morning.	Only when the advocate is on standby and then called to court. Only then will this count towards a main hearing that exceeds ten days.
Written submissions	Only if the Judge sets aside a day, and only to the individual advocate preparing the submissions. Will not count towards the ten-day threshold.	Only if the Judge sets aside a day, and only to the individual advocate preparing the submissions. The day set aside must be on a hearing exceeding ten days.

16.194   The information packs and case plans for CCFS were revised on 3 June 2019. At the same time, in response to concerns raised by the Family Law Bar Association (FLBA) regarding large amounts of outstanding fees due to counsel under section 31 VHCCs, an automatic limit of £32,500 for all CCFS cases (regardless of when they were registered) was introduced and this was later extended to

£60,000 for two-Counsel CCFS cases. Upon registration of the section 31 case (or other case deemed by LAA as suitable for CCFS), rather than an interim case plan being prepared, a generic VHCC contract and counsel's acceptance form are downloaded and populated with case details by the provider, signed and uploaded to the Case Plan notification thread on CCMS (see para 16.196 below). An application to increase the case plan to £32,500/£60,000 can then be immediately submitted and will be authorised accordingly. You do not have to submit a case plan under CCFS within the normal four weeks of registration, and you can wait up until three months after the case has concluded to submit your CCFS form. However, your automatic costs limit of £32,500/£60,000 will remain, restricting what you can claim on account and fees that counsel can submit if you exceed it. If you submit a CCFS form before the case has concluded, then the 'FAST' procedure for an interim case plan will apply and you should not have to provide all of the supporting documentation at this point. However, a final case plan with supportive documentation will still need to be provided and agreed before a final claim can be made.

16.195　There are different fees available if you are instructing counsel or doing the advocacy yourself. If you are seeking to agree a single-advocate section 31 case be paid outside CCFS, there are strict deadlines to submit a fully costed case plan and final claim for pre-contract costs.

16.196　If the case is on CCMS, then the case plan and contract will be agreed and uploaded on a case notification thread labelled 'Case Plan'. Previous providers can agree their case plan independently and this will be dealt with through a Case Plan thread activated under the case notifications on their CCMS account. Their final bill will also be submitted via the Billing thread on their CCMS account. However, CCFS was revised before functions on CCMS were considered and communication and co-ordination are needed between the providers. The final provider must apply on CCMS to increase the costs limit once the case plan is agreed (CCMS will not allow the LAA to increase the limit without this) and allocate costs for previous providers and their counsel once the costs limitation is increased. This can be a staggered process because the case plan for each provider will not be agreed at exactly the same time – an established procedure for this is yet to be confirmed by the LAA.

16.197　POAs can be made for all costs and counsels' fees once a VHCC contract is signed and lodged with the LAA, and further POAs can be made every six months or if six events have occurred since the last

POA was paid.[119] 100 per cent POAs will be paid on events but on CCMS cases providers must use the 'Non Expert Disbursement' POA type rather than profit costs[120] and counsel must email a CIV POA1 form to: counsel_events_POA@legalaid.gsi.gov.uk, otherwise only the usual 75 per cent of the claim will paid. Further, the LAA must flag it properly on CCMS.

16.198   The CCFS form includes a final claim page to be added and submitted as a final claim for non-CCMS cases. For CCMS cases, a separate electronic claim must be submitted for the final claim. A quick guide is found under the 'Advanced Billing Guides' (guides produced by the LAA Finance Team) section of the Closing Cases and Submitting Bills page for providers on the CCMS Training site. If there is more than one provider, then interim bills for the previous providers are submitted, then the outcomes are reported by the final provider afterwards and their claim is submitted as the final bill.

16.199   The benefit of the CCFS is that it avoids multiple revisions to detailed case plans, which is popular with practitioners and is often (but not always) considered preferable to an individually agreed case plan. Unlike certificates, you only produce and agree a single case plan (whether CCFS or fully costed) per case, not per client. This is revised as the case changes, in the usual way. The LAA recommends that you consider registration when your fees reach £12,000. It is also worth considering whether to register a case at an earlier stage; but you need to be confident that there are enough 'events' to show costs will exceed £25,000. If it is not clear it will be a VHCC case, the LAA will reject the application as premature.

16.200   All VHCCs are assessed by the LAA. You can find out more information at: www.gov.uk/civil-high-cost-cases-family.

Immigration and asylum

16.201 This section describes payment for Legal Help and Controlled Legal Representation (CLR) cases. For Licensed Work in the immigration category, see the general principles above.

---

119 Section 17 (Interim Payments) of the CCFS Information Packs.
120 CCMS Quick Guide 'Claiming 100% Payment on Account for the Very High Cost Care Case Fee Scheme'.

16.202   Immigration and Asylum Controlled Work is remunerated according to either Standard Fees or Hourly Rates,[121] as set out in the relevant regulations.[122]

Standard Fee cases

16.203 The scope of the Standard Fee scheme is not defined in the contract, except by exclusion. The Specification simply lists Hourly Rates cases, all others – when in scope under LASPO as detailed in chapter 10 – being Standard Fee cases.[123] Therefore, the Standard Fee applies to all cases other than:

  (a) Asylum Matters opened under this Contract which relate to an Asylum application (including 'NAM' or 'Legacy'), made to the UKBA prior to the 1 October 2007;

  (b) a fresh claim/further application for Asylum opened under this Contract where the original Asylum application was lodged, whether concluded or not, prior to 1 October 2007;

  (c) advice in relation to the merits of lodging an application for permission to appeal to the Upper Tribunal (where advice has not been received under Stage 2 of the Standard Fee);

  (d) Bail applications;

  (e) advice and applying for a determination that a Client qualifies for civil legal services provided as Licensed Work, including complying with any pre-action protocol;

  (f) initial advice in relation to an Asylum application prior to claiming Asylum at the Asylum Screening Unit where you then cease to be instructed. This will also apply where the Client returns after attendance at the Asylum Screening Unit but where it is confirmed that the Client will be dispersed and will not continue to instruct you;

  (g) Escape Fee Cases under the Standard Fee;

  (h) advice in relation to a Client who is an UASC (unaccompanied asylum seeking child);

  (i) cases remitted, reviewed or referred from the Court of Appeal or the Upper Tribunal to the First Tier Tribunal;

  (j) where you hold a Schedule authorisation any Matters opened under the Detained Duty Advice Scheme or for a Detained Fast Track or a DAC Scheme Client;

  (k) advice in relation to Terrorism Prevention and Investigation Measures Orders;

---

121 Standard Civil Contract 2018 Specification para 8.55.
122 Civil Legal Aid (Remuneration) Regulations 2013.
123 Standard Civil Contract 2018 Specification para 8.76(a)–(m).

(l) applying for a determination that an individual qualifies for civil legal services provided as Licensed Work in relation to Terrorism Prevention and Investigation Measures Orders; and

(m) applying for a determination that an individual qualifies for civil legal services provided as Licensed Work in relation to the Special Immigration Appeals Commission.

16.204 Exceptional Fee Cases are paid at Hourly Rates rather than through the Standard Fee scheme. However, in the Immigration and Asylum Category, providers must make an application for an Exceptional Fee payment, which can only be made by those with a Schedule authorisation in this Category,[124] unless the case satisfies the effective administration of justice test.[125]

Immigration and Asylum fee stages

16.205 Fees are split into Stage 1, Stage 2(a) and Stage 2(b). While different fees apply at each stage in asylum matters and in immigration (non-asylum) matters, the stages are the same for both.[126] Currently, the Standard Fee for Stages 1, 2(a) and 2(b), in asylum matters are £413, £227 and £567, respectively. The Standard Fee for Stages 1, 2(a) and 2(b), in immigration (non-asylum) matters are £234, £227 and £454, respectively.[127]

16.206 There are additional fees on top of the basic fee for extra work at each stage (see below).[128]

16.207 Stage 1 covers the Legal Help stage of the case, and ends when CLR is granted or refused, or when the matter ends, whichever is earlier.[129]

16.208 Stage 2(a) and 2(b) covers the CLR phase of the matter. Depending on the point at which the matter ends, either the fee for Stage 2(a) or Stage 2(b) (but not both) will be payable. The Stage 2(a) fee will be payable where the case does not proceed to – or, at least, representation is not provided at – a substantive hearing.[130] Stage 2(b) is payable where the case does proceed to a substantive hearing.[131] Stage 2 will end at the point that a determination is made whether the client qual-

---

124 Standard Civil Contract 2018 Specification para 8.12.
125 Civil Legal Aid (Procedure) Regulations 2012 reg 31(5).
126 Standard Civil Contract 2018 Specification para 8.56.
127 Civil Legal Aid (Remuneration) Regulations 2013 Sch 1 table 4(a).
128 Standard Civil Contract 2018 Specification para 8.60.
129 Standard Civil Contract 2018 Specification para 8.62.
130 Standard Civil Contract 2018 Specification para 8.63.
131 Standard Civil Contract 2018 Specification para 8.64.

ifies for Licensed Work in relation to the submission of an application for permission to appeal to the Upper Tribunal or where the matter otherwise ends, whichever is earlier.[132] As detailed in paragraph (e) in 16.177 above, advice on and applying for a determination that a client qualifies for Licensed Work is paid at Hourly Rates.

16.209　See the Standard Civil Contract 2018 Specification paras 8.61–8.65 for full definitions of each stage and examples of what work is included.

16.210　A claim for Stage 1, and either Stage 2(a) or Stage 2(b), must be submitted within six months of the end of each stage.[133] You should not wait until Stage 2(a) or 2(b) is concluded to claim your Stage 1 fee.

Immigration and Asylum – additional fees

16.211 Additional fixed fees are payable on top of the Standard Fee in the following circumstances:[134]

- representation at a Home Office interview where permitted (see chapter 10) (£266);
- advocacy services at a case management review hearing (CMRH) – different fees are payable depending on whether it is an oral (£166) or telephone (£90) hearing;
- advocacy services at a substantive First-tier Tribunal hearing (£302 for asylum, £237 for immigration);
- advocacy services for an additional day for a substantive hearing, including when it has been either part heard or re-listed (£161).[135]

Immigration and Asylum – counsel

16.212 Where counsel is instructed for advocacy services at a hearing, the relevant additional fee, as set out above, will be added to the appropriate Standard Fee paid to the solicitor and it will be for the solicitor to pay counsel.[136] The fees for advocacy services are inclusive of time for travel and waiting.[137]

132　Standard Civil Contract 2018 Specification para 8.65.
133　Standard Civil Contract 2018 Specification para 8.59.
134　Civil Legal Aid (Remuneration) Regulations 2013 Sch 1 table 4(b)–(c).
135　Standard Civil Contract 2018 Specification para 8.66(b).
136　Standard Civil Contract 2018 Specification para 8.66(a).
137　Standard Civil Contract 2018 Specification para 8.66(c).

Immigration and Asylum – disbursements

16.213 All (reasonable) disbursements are payable in addition of the Standard Fee, subject to the relevant disbursement limits. Disbursements at the Legal Help stage should not exceed £400[138] and at the CLR stage should not exceed £600.[139]

16.214 If the case is payable at Hourly Rates, then, at the Legal Help stage, the disbursement limit is still £400.[140] This limit could be extended by submitting the relevant extension request form[141] to the LAA before incurring the costs.[142]

16.215 At the CLR stage, costs and disbursements together should not exceed £1,600 (asylum), £1,200 (immigration)[143] or £500 (bail only).[144] These limits could also be extended by submitting the relevant extension request form to the LAA before incurring the costs.[145] However, the costs of waiting time where there is a significant delay on the day of a hearing, which is no fault of yours or your client, provided you apply for an extension to the Cost Limit as soon as practicable thereafter, can be the basis for retrospective amendment of the cost and disbursement limits.[146]

16.216 A claim can be made in respect of unpaid disbursements. This claim can be made if at least six months have elapsed since the start of the matter and, if you have become entitled to make a Controlled Work claim or have previously applied for payment under this provision (i.e. para 8.95 of the Contract Specification), at least six months have elapsed since that entitlement arose or application was made.[147]

Immigration and Asylum – Escape Fee cases[148]

16.217 Cases may escape the Standard Fee Scheme and become payable solely by Hourly Rates. This will occur when a case, following the

138 Standard Civil Contract 2018 Specification para 8.67(a).
139 Standard Civil Contract 2018 Specification para 8.67(b).
140 Standard Civil Contract 2018 Specification para 8.83.
141 www.gov.uk/government/publications/cw3-extension-of-upper-cost-limit-in-controlled-work-cases.
142 Standard Civil Contract 2018 Specification para 8.84.
143 Standard Civil Contract 2018 Specification para 8.79(b) – (c).
144 Standard Civil Contract 2018 Specification para 8.80.
145 www.gov.uk/government/publications/cw3-extension-of-upper-cost-limit-in-controlled-work-cases.
146 Standard Civil Contract 2018 Specification para 8.87.
147 Standard Civil Contract 2018 Specification para 8.95.
148 Standard Civil Contract 2018 Specification para 8.71.

conclusion of Stage 2(a) or 2(b) or when the matter ends, whichever is earlier, the value of the Controlled Work, when calculated as if it were paid at the appropriate Hourly Rate, exceeds three times the value under the Standard Fee Scheme.[149]

16.218   The calculation for determining whether Escape Fee payments can be made is relatively complicated. You must:

(a) identify the total hours spent on the Matter up to the end of Stage 2 or when the Matter concludes (whichever is earlier), including any advocacy services but excluding services which are outside the Standard Fee and are always payable at Hourly Rates;

(b) calculate the total costs for the hours spent on such services using the Hourly Rates set out in the Remuneration Regulations to determine the 'gross total' (Total A);

(c) from Total A deduct all the claims for additional payments paid or payable, to determine the 'reduced total' (Total B);

(d) identify the Standard Fees claimable for the Matter (note only one Standard Fee is payable at each Stage). Add these Standard Fees together and multiply that total by 3 to determine the 'Escape Threshold' (Total C); and

(e) if Total B exceeds Total C then the Matter has escaped the Standard Fee Scheme and is therefore an Escape Fee Case payable at Hourly Rates.[150]

16.219 Claims for Escape Fee cases are subject to an individual Cost Assessment by the LAA.[151] The claim must be submitted on an EC-Claim 1 IMM form.[152]

Immigration and Asylum – Hourly Rates cases

16.220 All cases excluded from the standard fee scheme (see above) are payable by Hourly Rates.

16.221   In Hourly Rates cases (except those that become so by escaping from the Standard Fee Scheme), there are costs limitations which may be extended on application to the LAA.

16.222   For Legal Help, the limit (excluding VAT and disbursements) is £800 in asylum cases and £500 in (non-asylum) immigration cases.[153]

---

149 Standard Civil Contract 2018 Specification para 8.71 – 72.
150 Standard Civil Contract 2018 Specification para 8.73.
151 Standard Civil Contract 2018 Specification para 8.75.
152 www.gov.uk/government/publications/escape-fee-case-claim-forms. See immigration section in Escape fee cases electronic handbook for guidance: www.gov.uk/government/publications/submit-an-escape-fee-case-claim/.
153 Standard Civil Contract 2018 Specification para 8.79(b)–(c).

16.223   For CLR, the limit (excluding VAT, but including disbursements[154] and counsel) is £1,600 for asylum cases, £1,200 for (non-asylum) immigration cases[155] and £500 for stand-alone bail applications (where a substantive appeal includes a bail application, bail is included in the £1,600/£1,200).[156]

16.224   Legal Help claims must be submitted within six months of submission of a fresh application for asylum (fresh claim cases only), or within six months of the Home Office decision (all other cases), and then within six months of the end of the case. CLR claims should be submitted within six months of the first tribunal decision, and then within six months of the end of the case.[157]

Upper Tribunal cases

16.225 Before any work in connection with applying for an appeal to the Upper Tribunal is carried out, a Licensed Work Certificate must be in place.[158] The costs of interpreters and experts are payable regardless of the outcome of the application.[159] However, the costs of solicitor and counsel are only payable if permission is granted.[160]

16.226   Payment rates will be at the rates set out in the regulations for work in the First-tier Tribunal.[161] Work carried out on the initial application to the First-Tier Tribunal for permission to appeal to the Upper Tribunal, will be paid at the Hourly Rates (specified in the relevant regulations) for Licensed work in the First-Tier Tribunal. However, work carried out on a direct application to the Upper Tribunal for permission to appeal and all subsequent work in that forum, will be paid at the Hourly Rates (specified in the relevant regulations for Licensed Work in the Higher Courts).[162]

16.227   However, where the Home Office applies for permission to appeal, or the case is dealt with under the Detained Fast Track Scheme, you may claim costs under the contract.[163]

154 Standard Civil Contract 2018 Specification para 8.85.
155 Standard Civil Contract 2018 Specification para 8.85(b)–(c).
156 Standard Civil Contract 2018 Specification para 8.86.
157 Standard Civil Contract 2018 Specification para 8.93.
158 Standard Civil Contract 2018 Specification para 8.96.
159 Standard Civil Contract 2018 Specification para 8.98.
160 Standard Civil Contract 2018 Specification para 8.99.
161 Standard Civil Contract 2018 Specification para 8.100.
162 Standard Civil Contract 2018 Specification para 8.100(a)–(b). See also Civil Legal Aid (Remuneration) Regulations 2013 Sch 1 and Sch 2.
163 Standard Civil Contract 2018 Specification para 8.97.

Mental health

16.228 This section summarises provisions in relation to controlled work. For licensed work in the mental health category, see the general principles above.

Mental health fee scheme

16.229 The mental health fee scheme applies to all controlled work in the mental health category of law, except for Help at Court for Victims (which is paid at hourly rates), and is divided into:

- a fee for all non-MHT (Mental Health Tribunal) matters ('non-MHT fee'); and
- three fees for MHT matters ('MHT fees') as follows:
  - MHT fee level 1 (initial advice);
  - MHT fee level 2 (negotiation and preparation); and
  - MHT fee level 3 (representation before the MHT).

You cannot claim both the non-MHT fee and any level of MHT fee in the same matter for a client.

16.230   Help at Court for Victims is not remunerated under the mental health fee scheme but is paid at hourly rates.[164]

Mental health – disbursements

16.231 In general, the cost of all time spent in travel and waiting is included in the fees payable.[165] However, the LAA intends to designate some hospitals as 'remote', and where work is done at these hospitals a remote travel payment will be claimable.[166] Payment of remote travel payments will be generated by completing the appropriate box on the Consolidated Matter Report form (CMRF). At the time of writing, no hospitals had been so designated.

16.232   Other disbursements are paid in addition to the fees.

---

164 Standard Civil Contract 2018 Specification para 9.100.
165 Standard Civil Contract 2018 Specification para 9.88.
166 Standard Civil Contract 2018 Specification para 9.89.

Mental health – transfers

16.233 Where a client transfers his or her case to you, you are entitled to claim the full mental health fee for each of the levels of work you undertake, including initial advice and negotiation/preparation.[167]

Mental health – adjourned hearing fees

16.234 When a hearing is adjourned or is postponed or cancelled on the day at the request of the tribunal or Responsible Medical Officer, or in circumstances where you make a request to adjourn, postpone or cancel, and where you could not have otherwise reasonably avoided making such a request, and you have actually attended the place of the tribunal, you can claim this fee for each additional hearing that is adjourned on the day.[168]

Mental health – escape fee cases

16.235 Where the amount of any claim as calculated on the basis of hourly rates exceeds three times the mental health fee(s) payable, it becomes an escape fee case and is paid at hourly rates.

16.236   For work covered by the non-MHT fee or the MHT fee level 1, the relevant hourly rate is that for Legal Help.

16.237   For work covered by MHT fee Level 2 and MHT fee level 3, the relevant hourly rate is that for CLR.

16.238   When calculating whether a matter or case qualifies as an escape fee case, if the case qualifies for remote travel payment(s) and/or adjourned hearing fee(s), then in order for it to become exceptional its costs need to exceed the total of three times the total of all fee levels payable *plus* the total of all additional payments payable.[169]

16.239   The LAA provides the following example:

In an MHT case with work at levels 1, 2 and 3 and two adjourned hearings, in order to escape the costs would need to be greater than:

(3 × (Level 1 Fee + Level 2 Fee + Level 3 Fee)) + (2 × Adjourned Hearing Fee).[170]

167 Standard Civil Contract 2018 Specification para 9.99.
168 Standard Civil Contract 2018 Specification para 9.85.
169 Standard Civil Contract 2018 Specification para 9.96.
170 Standard Civil Contract 2018 Specification para 9.96.

16.240 Escape fee cases will be remunerated on the basis of the relevant hourly rates. These rates will apply to work carried out by either solicitor or counsel.

Mental health – counsel's fees

16.241 Counsel's fees do not count as a disbursement and you are responsible for agreeing and paying counsel's fees.

16.242   In an unusually complex case you may request prior authority from the LAA for a higher hourly rate. The LAA says this will be highly unusual in MHT cases. Where it is allowed, an hourly rate and a maximum cost limit will be specified. These may not be exceeded without further authority (which will not be granted retrospectively). Where authority is granted but the matter start does not qualify as an exceptional case, then the LAA will pay an additional sum equal to the difference between counsel's fees as authorised by the prior authority and the applicable fees which would have been payable.

CHAPTER 17

Getting paid for criminal work

by Anthony Edwards

continued

Introduction

17.1 This chapter deals with billing and payment for criminal work. See appendix D for a summary of the Legal Aid Agency's (LAA's) *Criminal Bills Assessment Manual,* in respect of the most common queries raised by caseworkers.

17.2 The LAA has also identified a number of regular issues that cause difficulty on audit. These are italicised in the text. They are often raised long after the event, so good record-keeping on file is critical.

17.3 *There must be adequate attendance notes to show how time has been used with some precision as to the work carried out. An explanation should be recorded. If this is longer than might normally be expected (for example, with clients with a disability) then an explanation should be recorded. A lack of adequate notes can cause difficulties on audit when claiming higher standard fees in criminal and prison law cases.*

17.4 *No more can be earned, either as profit costs or as a disbursement, by using a fee earner from a more distant office, or by an agent, or unassigned counsel, than would have been paid had the firm itself undertaken the work from its most local office. This is known by the LAA as the 'maximum fee principle'.*

17.5 *Where travel time is claimed, this must be recorded and justified as the contract limits the amount of travel in a number of circumstances. The use of a private car as opposed to public transport should be explained. The distance cannot exceed that from the provider's office or home, whichever is closer. Explanations should be given for all travel costs so that even if the time cannot be recovered, the justification for the distance is on file.*

17.6 Most criminal work is paid for through the monthly contract payment, the biggest exception being work done in the Crown Court.[1]

17.7 Thus, although contract cases are billed individually, they are not directly paid. Instead, each firm, or office, has a fixed monthly payment set by the LAA. Each month, the firm submits bills which are offset against the payment, with the aim that bills and payments balance each other out over the course of the financial year. See chapter 24 for more information on this process (known as reconciliation); and on the management of criminal contracts generally. Crown Court bills in cases funded by representation orders are individually paid.[2]

---

1 Standard Crime Contract 2017 Standard Terms para 14.8; and Specification paras 5.20 and 5.25.
2 Standard Crime Contract 2017 Specification para 5.25.

17.8   This chapter does not deal with contract management (which is covered in Part C), but with the rules and processes for billing individual cases. For information about conducting criminal cases, see chapter 15.

17.9   This is of necessity a brief overview of a complex subject. The detail is of significance and a full understanding will reduce the number of issues on audit. For more detailed coverage, readers are referred to *Criminal Costs: legal aid costs in the criminal courts.*[3]

Remuneration regulations

17.10   Remuneration rates are set out in the Criminal Legal Aid (Remuneration) Regulations 2013.[4] These have been amended as follows:

- Criminal Legal Aid (General) (Amendment) Regulations 2013[5] – changed the scope of prison law;
- Criminal Legal Aid (Remuneration) (Amendment) Regulations 2013[6] – codified Very High Cost Case (VHCC) rates and reduced expert fees for cases started on or after 2 December 2013;
- Criminal Legal Aid (Remuneration) (Amendment) Regulations 2014[7] – reduced most rates (the main exception being Advocates' Graduated Fee Scheme (AGFS) rates) by 8.75 per cent from 20 March 2014;
- Criminal Legal Aid (Remuneration) (Amendment) (No 2) Regulations 2014[8] – introduced additional interim payments and removed some cases from fixed fees;
- Civil and Criminal Legal Aid (Remuneration) (Amendment) Regulations 2015[9] – prescribed rates for civil injunctions under the Anti-social Behaviour, Crime and Policing Act 2014;
- Criminal Legal Aid (Remuneration) (Amendment) Regulations 2015[10] – prescribed for payments to be made to trial rather than to instructed advocates;

---

3 Edwards and Beaumont, *Criminal Costs: legal aid costs in the criminal courts*, LAG, 2nd edn, 2019.
4 SI No 435.
5 SI No 2790.
6 SI No 2803.
7 SI No 415.
8 SI No 2422.
9 SI No 325.
10 SI No 882.

- Criminal Legal Aid (Remuneration etc) (Amendment) Regulations 2015[11] – imposed a (in the result time limited) further 8.75 per cent cut (again except in AGFS cases) from 1 July 2015 and made amendments to the fee structures applying from 11 January 2016;
- Civil and Criminal Legal Aid (Amendment) Regulations 2015[12] – further provisions on civil injunctions;
- Civil and Criminal Legal Aid (Amendment) (No 2) Regulations 2015[13] – amended definitions;
- Criminal Legal Aid (Remuneration etc) (Amendment) (No 2) Regulations 2015[14] – delays the effect of the Criminal Legal Aid (Remuneration etc) Regulations 2015 above, postponing the second 8.75 per cent fee cut;
- Criminal Legal Aid (Remuneration) (Amendment) Regulations 2016[15] – effectively repeals Criminal Legal Aid (Remuneration etc) (Amendment) Regulations 2015;
- Criminal Legal Aid (Standard Crime Contract) (Amendment) Regulations 2017[16] – extend advice and assistance and advocacy assistance to 'magistrates' court applications relating to police bail' as opposed to bail conditions from 1 April 2017;
- Criminal Legal Aid (Amendment) Regulations 2017– reintroduce some prison law to scope and prescribe the payment rates;
- Criminal Legal Aid (Remuneration) (Amendment) Regulations 2018[17] – amend the fees payable under the AGFS; and Criminal Legal Aid (Remuneration) (Amendment) (No 2) Regulations 2018[18] – further amend the fees payable under the AGFS. It is expected that further regulations increasing the fees payable under the AGFS will be laid shortly.

17.11 *Audits suggest that firms are often not claiming the correct fees.* It is not always easy to work out which rates apply to which cases. You should start with the main 2013 regulations, and then check later regulations to see if there have been amendments relevant to your particular case. Unfortunately, no single consolidated set of rates exists. For cases where the unique file number (UFN) (for advice and assistance

---

11 SI No 1369.
12 SI No 1416.
13 SI No 1678.
14 SI No 2049.
15 SI No 313.
16 SI No 311.
17 SI No 220.
18 SI No 1323.

and advocacy assistance) or the date of the representation order (for representation cases) is on or after 1 April 2016, the rates where set out in this edition are correct at the time of going to print.

Investigations class work

17.12   A bill should be submitted at the end of the investigations class, even if the case continues into proceedings. One bill should be submitted for all work done in the class (subject to the exceptions set out below).

Police station telephone advice only

17.13   Where a client is at the police station and you provide telephone advice but do not attend, you can claim the telephone advice fee.[19]

17.14   The fee is not claimable in a case in which Criminal Defence Direct were involved,[20] and is triggered by a telephone call during which you speak to the client. Only one fee is payable per investigation.[21]

17.15   The value of the fee is set out in the Remuneration Regulations, and is currently £27.60 (£28.70 for London firms). *This fee is deemed to be included in the fixed attendance fee if an attendance is made in the matter, and should not be claimed separately.*

Advice and assistance

17.16   In cases where you provide advice and assistance to a client outside the police station, but do not attend the police station with the client, you can claim for the costs of the advice and assistance at the hourly rates set out in the contract and in addition to a telephone fee. *Where the case also involves attendance at the police station, the costs of advice and assistance are included within the police station fixed attendance fee and must not be claimed separately.*[22]

17.17   A single claim for all work done (except advocacy assistance, which should be claimed separately) in the investigations class should be submitted when:

- the investigation has concluded, whether by charge, summons, requisition or other disposal; or

---

19 Standard Crime Contract 2017 Specification para 9.111.
20 Standard Crime Contract 2017 Specification para 9.110.
21 Standard Crime Contract 2017 Specification para 9.112.
22 Standard Crime Contract 2017 Specification para 9.135.

- it is known no further investigations work will be undertaken for the client; or
- it is unclear whether further work will be required, especially for cases that remain under investigation, but at least one month has elapsed since the last work (unless the client has an outstanding bail back); or
- post-charge work at the police station has been undertaken (in circumstances in which such work is not otherwise funded).[23]

17.18   Where you have acted for more than one client in the same investigation, you should make a separate claim for each client, apportioning the work between them if necessary.[24]

17.19   The hourly rates applicable to this work are set out in the Remuneration Regulations. You should apply the rates to all work done, subject to any costs limit. The costs limit for advice and assistance is £273.75 to cover both profit costs and disbursements; this limit can be extended on application to the LAA.[25]

Police station attendance

17.20   All work done at the police station is subject to a fixed fee regime. The fee is triggered whenever there is attendance upon the client at the police station. However, it does not include attendance for an ineffective bail to return if you did not check whether it would be effective prior to attending.[26]

17.21   *Where triggered, the fee will cover all work done in the investigations class. Therefore, where, for example, you carry out advice and assistance outside the police station for eligible clients (such as between bails to return) or have given telephone advice, that work will also be covered by the fixed attendance fee, until you reach the threshold fee for an escape fee claim to be made.*

17.22   There is a separate fee for each duty scheme area, and the fees are set out in the Remuneration Regulations. Only one fee is payable per client per matter (even if you attend the police station on more than one occasion).[27] Where, however, work is a genuinely separate matter then a separate claim may be made, if you attend the client at the police station on a separate occasion in relation to one of the matters

---

23 Standard Crime Contract 2017 Specification paras 9.104 and 9.136.
24 Standard Crime Contract 2017 Specification paras 9.108 and 9.137.
25 Standard Crime Contract 2017 Specification para 9.139.
26 Standard Crime Contract 2017 Specification para 9.2.
27 Standard Crime Contract 2017 Specification para 9.86.

after another has concluded. *It will be a separate matter if the client has genuinely separate legal problems requiring separate advice*[28] on more than one occasion. This test is carefully applied on audit. *A file note should be made setting out any justification for claiming more than one fixed fee.*[29] If, for example, the client is charged with one offence and you reasonably attend on the bail to return to the police station on another, separate fees should be claimed in relation to each offence.[30]

17.23   A separate Defence Solicitor Call Centre (DSCC) reference number must be obtained for each matter.

Case study

I had a client who was arrested for theft and taken to the police station, where it was found he was also wanted for a separate incident of criminal damage, and he was further arrested for that. Is that one matter or two?

It depends on the outcome of the case. If he were charged with both offences at the same time, that would be one matter and one claim. This is because the two allegations required advice on one occasion only. However, if he were charged with theft and you reasonably attended on the bail to return on the criminal damage, that would constitute two matters since they require separate advice on more than one occasion.

Payment rates and escape fee cases[31]

17.24   Although police station work is payable by fixed fee, you should record all the time spent on the case and report the value of that time at the appropriate hourly rates to the LAA. The applicable rates are set out in the Remuneration Regulations. Where the value of the case at hourly rates exceeds the Escape Fee Threshold for the appropriate area, the case is deemed to be exceptional, and you can apply to the LAA for an additional payment.

17.25   The categories of rates for attendance are:

- own or duty solicitor;
- duty solicitor unsocial hours;
- duty solicitor serious offence social hours;
- duty solicitor serious offence unsocial hours.

28 Standard Crime Contract 2017 Specification para 9.80.
29 Standard Crime Contract 2017 Specification para 9.80.
30 Standard Crime Contract 2017 Specification para 9.82.
31 Standard Crime Contract 2017 Specification paras 9.98–9.100.

Similar categories (except those for serious offences) apply for travel and waiting time.

17.26   For these purposes, social hours are between 9.30am and 5.30pm on a business day – that is, any day other than Saturday, Sunday, Christmas Day, Good Friday or any bank holiday.[32]

17.27   Serious offences are:[33]

- treason;
- murder;
- manslaughter;
- causing death by dangerous driving;
- rape;
- assault by penetration;
- rape of a child under 13;
- assault of a child under 13 by penetration;
- robbery;
- assault with intent to rob;
- arson;
- perverting the course of justice;
- conspiracy to defraud;
- kidnapping;
- wounding/GBH – both sections 18 and 20 of the Offences Against the Person Act 1861;
- conspiracy, solicitation, incitement or attempt of any of the above;
- any offence if the client is also accused of possession of a firearm, shotgun or imitation firearm;
- any offence if the client is detained under Terrorism Act 2000 s41.

17.28   In order to claim duty rates, the case must be a duty case – that is, referred as a duty case by the call centre or conducted during a duty period, and the work done by an accredited fee earner.[34] To claim serious offences rates, the work must be done by a duty solicitor,[35] and you must not be a confirmed category 3 firm (costs audit) in relation to your crime contract.[36]

17.29   To calculate whether the case is exceptional, you calculate the value of all time spent at the appropriate hourly rate. This will include any advice and assistance outside the police station for an eligible

32 Standard Crime Contract 2017 para 1.1 defines Business Hours and Business Day. Unsocial hours are those outside those definitions.
33 Standard Crime Contract 2017 Specification para 9.99(a).
34 Standard Crime Contract 2017 Specification para 9.98.
35 Standard Crime Contract 2017 Specification para 9.99.
36 Standard Crime Contract 2017 Specification para 9.100.

client. You should also include any telephone advice fixed fee[37] or a Criminal Defence Direct acceptance fee[38] (where a former Criminal Defence Direct matter was referred to you for police station attendance). This will give you a total value for the case. If the total value is more than the relevant Exceptional Threshold set out in the Remuneration Regulations, then you can make an application to the LAA to treat it as an escape fee case.[39]

17.30   In order to do that, you should complete the form (form CRM18) and submit it as an e-form through LAA online: https://portal. legalservices.gov.uk/. The LAA will assess the claim, and if following assessment it is confirmed that the case is worth more than the Escape Fee Threshold, the case will be treated as an escape fee case.

17.31   However, you will still not be paid the full value of the case. Instead, you will only be paid the fixed fee, plus the amount by which the case exceeds the threshold.[40]

Case study

I represented a client at a central London police station on a case of murder over a weekend. It was a duty case, and I spent in total 14 unsocial hours in attendance at the police station, plus six hours' travel and waiting (all unsocial). I also incurred a telephone fee. What will I be paid?

The Central London scheme has a fixed fee of £237.25 plus VAT. It was a duty case and a weekend, so London duty unsocial serious case rates apply: £63.01 per hour for attendances, travel and waiting, and telephone attendance fee of £28.70.

Your time is worth (£63.01 × 20) = £1,260.20 + £28.70 = £1,288.90. The fixed fee is £237.25, and the threshold is £803.78. Therefore you are over the threshold and the case is exceptional.

You will be paid (subject to assessment) the value of the fixed fee plus the amount by which the threshold is exceeded: £237.25 + (£1,288.90 − £803.78) = £722.37.

You should send your exceptional claim to the LAA who will assess the bill.

---

37 Standard Crime Contract 2017 Specification para 9.84.
38 Standard Crime Contract 2017 Specification para 9.94.
39 Standard Crime Contract 2017 Specification para 9.95.
40 Standard Crime Contract 2017 Specification paras 9.96–9.97.

17.32   Escape fee cases will not be paid direct. Instead, the value allowed on assessment will count towards your standard monthly payment.

Advocacy assistance

17.33   Advocacy assistance – of whatever type – is the exception to the rule that all investigations work be billed together. Any claim for advocacy assistance should be submitted separately. This work is not subject to fixed fees, and the hourly rates set out in the contract will apply subject to the extendable Costs Limit of £1,369.75. A single claim for all advocacy assistance on a case should be made[41] at the end of the investigations stage.[42] Where police station advice and assistance, or free-standing advice and assistance, has already been provided, the same UFN must be used, although the work must be claimed separately.[43]

Proceedings class work

Virtual court claims[44]

17.34   Rates of remuneration are specified in the Criminal Legal Aid (Remuneration) Regulations 2013 Sch 4 as amended.

Court duty claims[45]

17.35   You should claim any work done as court duty solicitor at the end of the duty session. You should make one claim per session, rather than one claim per client.[46] The applicable payment rates are set out in the Remuneration Regulations.

17.36   *If a claim exceeds eight hours, a special note should be kept for use on audit to explain what had occurred on the day. Similarly, any travel should be justified in accordance with the standard crime contract.*

17.37   You cannot claim for travel time or expenses to get to court, except where you are acting on a non-business day (eg a Saturday or bank holiday sitting), or where you are called to court having not been on

---

41   Standard Crime Contract 2017 Specification paras 9.149, 9.162 and 9.173.
42   Standard Crime Contract 2017 Specification paras 9.150, 9.163 and 9.174.
43   Standard Crime Contract 2017 Specification paras 9.164 and 9.175.
44   Standard Crime Contract 2017 Specification paras 10.21–10.35.
45   Standard Crime Contract 2017 Specification paras 10.1–10.20.
46   Standard Crime Contract 2017 Specification para 10.18.

the rota or having attended on a rota and been released and then asked to return.

Representation orders in the magistrates' court

17.38   See chapter 15 for details on conducting work under a representation order.

17.39   Magistrates' court work should be billed at the end of the magistrates' court stage of the case. No fee is payable if the case is sent to the Crown Court for trial, unless a charge is left in the magistrates' court or a case is remitted to that court. There is no provision for interim payments, so the bill will be submitted when one of the defined end-points occurs:

- the case has concluded;
- it is known that no further work will be required;
- it is unclear whether further work will be required and at least a month has elapsed since the last work was undertaken;[47]
- a warrant of arrest was issued and at least six weeks, but not more than 19 weeks, have elapsed since.[48]

17.40   The exception to this is where sentence is deferred; you may submit a bill when sentence is deferred and another when the client returns to be sentenced.[49] Bills must be submitted within three months of the end of the case.

17.41   Where you act for more than one client in a case, you should submit a single bill covering work done for all clients,[50] though you will need a separate representation order for each one.[51]

Standard fees

17.42   Most magistrates' court work is covered by the standard fee regime. There are three categories of fee – 1A, 1B and 2 – and in each category a lower and a higher standard fee.

17.43   There are two types of fee:

---

47   Standard Crime Contract 2017 Specification para 10.62.
48   Standard Crime Contract 2017 Specification para 10.67.
49   Standard Crime Contract 2017 Specification para 10.66.
50   Standard Crime Contract 2017 Specification paras 10.60 and 10.64.
51   Standard Crime Contract 2017 Specification para 10.37.

1) If your office is in an area designated by the contract, or if it is not but the court named in the representation order is, you should claim the **designated area** standard fee.[52]

2) If not, you should claim the **undesignated area** standard fee.[53]

17.44 The designated areas[54] are the criminal justice areas of:

- Greater Manchester;
- London;
- West Midlands;
- Merseyside; and
- the local authority areas of:
  - Brighton and Hove;
  - Bristol;
  - Cardiff;
  - Derby and Erewash;
  - Kingston upon Hull;
  - Leeds and Bradford;
  - Leicester;
  - Nottingham;
  - Portsmouth;
  - Newcastle-upon-Tyne and Sunderland (including Gateshead, North Tyneside and South Tyneside);
  - Sheffield; and
  - Southampton.

17.45 The difference between designated and undesignated is that in a designated area, the fees are slightly higher but you cannot claim for any travel and waiting time,[55] whereas in an undesignated area you can claim travel and waiting[56] but the standard fees are lower. Even if you cannot claim travel and waiting, you are still required to record the waiting time (though need not record travel).[57]

17.46 In either case, the structure of the fees is the same. Whatever the category of your case, you calculate your core costs (all profit costs except travel and waiting time).[58] If the core costs do not exceed the lower limit for the category of case, you claim the lower standard fee. If core costs are above the lower but do not exceed the higher limit,

52 Standard Crime Contract 2017 Specification para 10.77.
53 Standard Crime Contract 2017 Specification para 10.77.
54 Standard Crime Contract 2017 Specification para 1.2.
55 Standard Crime Contract 2017 Specification paras 10.80 and 10.85.
56 Standard Crime Contract 2017 Specification para 10.83.
57 Standard Crime Contract 2017 Specification para 10.87.
58 Standard Crime Contract 2017 Specification para 10.79.

you claim the higher standard fee. If core costs are above the higher limit, you claim a non-standard fee – that is, you claim your costs in full as incurred.[59]

17.47   You should decide which category of fee to claim based on the nature and outcome of the case.[60] *There are complexities in the correct identification which significantly affects the appropriate fee*:

- Category 1A[61] is:
  - either way guilty pleas (including thefts from a shop of goods valued at under £200);
  - indictable only cases heard in the Youth Court;
  - proceedings relating to either way offences which are discontinued or withdrawn or where the prosecution offer no evidence; and
  - proceedings relating to either way offences which result in a bind over.
- Category 1B[62] is:
  - summary only guilty pleas;
  - uncontested proceedings arising out of a breach of an order of a magistrates' court;
  - proceedings relating to summary offences which are discontinued or withdrawn or where the prosecution offer no evidence;
  - proceedings relating to summary offences which result in a bind over;
  - proceedings arising out of a deferment of sentence (including any subsequent sentence hearing) under section 1 of the Powers of Criminal Courts (Sentencing) Act 2000;
  - proceedings prescribed under reg 9 of the Criminal Legal Aid (General) Regulations 2013 (see para 12.69), except where the case was listed and fully prepared for a contested hearing to decide whether an order should be made; and
  - proceedings relating to either way offences which must be tried in a magistrates' court in accordance with Magistrates' Courts Act 1980 s22.
- Category 2[63] is:

---

59 Standard Crime Contract 2017 Specification para 10.88.
60 Edwards and Beaumont, *Criminal Costs: legal aid costs in the criminal courts*, LAG, 2nd edn, 2019.
61 Criminal Legal Aid (Remuneration) Regulations 2013 Sch 4 para 5.
62 Criminal Legal Aid (Remuneration) Regulations 2013 Sch 4 para 5.
63 Criminal Legal Aid (Remuneration) Regulations 2013 Sch 4 para 5.

- contested trials;
- proceedings which were listed and fully prepared for trial in a magistrates' court but are disposed of by a guilty plea on the day of trial before the opening of the prosecution case;
- proceedings which were listed and fully prepared for trial in a magistrates' court but are discontinued or withdrawn or where the prosecution offers no evidence or which result in a bind over on the day of trial before the opening of the prosecution case;
- contested proceedings relating to a breach of an order of a magistrates' court (including proceedings relating to a breach of a Crown Court community rehabilitation order, community punishment order or suspended sentence);
- proceedings where mixed pleas are entered; and
- proceedings prescribed under reg 9 of the Criminal Legal Aid (General) Regulations 2013 where the case was listed and fully prepared for a contested hearing to decide whether an order should be made (see para 14.71).

17.48 Note that cases sent to the Crown Court under Crime and Disorder Act 1998 s51 are treated as being Crown Court cases from charge – all work should be claimed on the Crown Court bill and no magistrates' court claim can be made (except in the event of a remittal back).[64]

17.49 Where proceedings have not concluded but a warrant of arrest has been issued, the proceedings will be treated as category 1 proceedings.[65]

17.50 Bail applications (including to the Crown Court) and appeals against bail are included in the standard fee of the substantive case.[66]

17.51 Where more than one category is possible, you should select the one that will pay the highest fee.[67]

17.52 On a change of solicitor, the old firm should claim a category 1 fee, and the new firm should claim in the usual way. The exception to this is where the conducting solicitor moves firms and takes the case – if this happens, only the new firm can claim, but should claim for both firms' work. The firms should seek to agree in advance how payments will be distributed between them.[68]

---

64 Standard Crime Contract 2017 Specification para 10.76.
65 Standard Crime Contract 2017 Specification para 10.94.
66 Standard Crime Contract 2017 Specification para 10.73.
67 Standard Crime Contract 2017 Specification para 10.91.
68 Standard Crime Contract 2017 Specification paras 10.92 and 10.93.

17.53   Where you have claimed a fee and then a further claim is required – for example, you claimed a category 1 fee when a client absconds and a warrant is issued, and then continued to represent the client following arrest on the warrant – you should calculate the total costs due for the whole of the case, deduct the amount previously claimed, and claim the balance.[69]

Case study

My office is in Manchester. My client was charged with theft, indicated a not guilty plea and elected summary trial. He was convicted following trial, and sentencing was deferred for six months. What should I claim?

Manchester is in a designated area, so you should be claiming the designated area standard fee. Your client took the case to a trial, so the case is in category 2. You should calculate your core costs (all time excluding travel and waiting) to see whether a lower, higher or non-standard fee is claimable.

When your client comes back to be sentenced in six months' time, you can claim a further category 1B standard fee.

Counsel

17.54   Unassigned counsel are treated as if they were employed by you, and you should include their times on your bill as if they were your profit costs.

17.55   Where counsel is assigned, their costs are separate from yours. Rates for assigned counsel are set out in the Remuneration Regulations, and counsel should prepare a bill at those rates.[70] They will be paid direct by the LAA, but you should submit their bill alongside yours.[71]

Separate matters

17.56   One standard fee is payable per case. A case consists of all work for all clients in respect of:

- one offence; or
- more than one offence, where:

69 Standard Crime Contract 2017 Specification para 10.97.
70 Standard Crime Contract 2017 Specification para 10.44.
71 Standard Crime Contract 2017 Specification para 10.45.

- they are charged at the same time; or
- they are founded on the same facts; or
- they form part of a series of offences.[72]

17.57 Offences 'charged at the same time' is a straightforward test. 'Founded on the same facts' is intended to cover situations where two charges are brought as alternatives, or where one charge is substituted for another – common examples include theft and handling stolen goods, or actual bodily harm (ABH) and common assault.

17.58 A 'series of offences' refers to offences which have similarities or form a pattern of offending, that could be tried together. Each potential series of offences has to be considered on its own facts and definitive guidance cannot be given. However, there is a discussion at section 6.6 of the LAA's *Criminal bills assessment manual* (2020). The key principle is that the offences are sufficiently related to have been tried on the same indictment had they been indictable offences. For example, offences that are based on a system of conduct, are similar in nature, or where evidence of one is admissible at the trial of another, may all form part of a series. Even though some hearings may be held at different times, or in different courts, that would not prevent a series being established. However, cases linked only for sentence do not thereby become a series.

Enhanced rates

17.59 In certain circumstances, you can apply for payment at an enhanced rate. The LAA will consider whether enhancement is justified, and if so will increase the hourly rates for some or all of the work done on the case. It would be very unusual for enhanced rates to be allowed on routine items such as travel and waiting (where payable) or letters and telephone calls.

17.60 The test for enhancement is that:

- the work was done with exceptional competence, skill or expertise; or
- the work was done with exceptional dispatch; or
- the case involved exceptional circumstances or complexity,

compared with the generality of proceedings.[73]

---

72 Standard Crime Contract 2017 Specification para 10.69.
73 Standard Crime Contract 2017 Specification para 10.99.

17.61   Where the test is met, the LAA will allow a percentage increase to the relevant hourly rate not exceeding 100 per cent,[74] except in the case of serious or complex fraud (which are today very unlikely to result in a magistrates' court claim). The amount of the percentage increase will be determined by having regard to:

- the degree of responsibility accepted;
- the care, speed and economy with which the case was prepared;
- the novelty, weight and complexity of the case.[75]

17.62   Enhancement of the hourly rates takes the case out of the standard fee regime, so you should submit an individual bill to the LAA, accompanied by a note setting out why you believe the criteria for enhancement are met and justifying the percentage sought. It is important to remember that what seems obvious to you may not be so to an assessor. So, for example, you should not assume that because the court granted a certificate for counsel that you will automatically obtain an uplift, if you have decided to do the advocacy yourself. You will need to address the criteria explicitly and show how your advocacy was exceptional.

Other contract work

17.63   Advice and assistance in the appeals and prison law classes, and advocacy assistance in the prison law class, is claimed under the contract in the same way as free-standing advice and assistance in the investigations class (see above, and see also sections 11 and 12 of the Contract Specification). *There must be evidence to show that the sufficient benefit test has been met.* The Remuneration Regulations provide details of the fixed fees and standard fees applicable to prison law cases.

17.64   *It is critical correctly to identify the client's eligibility for the work in question. Both income and capital positions must be checked, even for those in prison. The eligibility must be documented.*

17.65   *The scope of prison law has been significantly reduced and then expanded again so the scope rules applicable at the time and section 12 of the Specification should be checked. Where work is within scope, this must be documented, for instance to show that disciplinary proceedings were held before an Adjudicator.*

---

74 Standard Crime Contract 2017 Specification para 10.102.
75 Standard Crime Contract 2017 Specification para 10.101.

17.66   *Similarly the rules on the number of cases that can be claimed, particularly in sentencing cases, are causing difficulty on audit.*[76]

17.67   Representation in judicial review or habeas corpus proceedings, proceedings in the youth court for anti-social behaviour injunctions, or civil proceedings under the Proceeds of Crime Act 2002, is claimed as all other civil legal aid; see chapter 15 and section 13 of the Specification to the Standard Crime Contract.

17.68   Representation in other civil proceedings associated with criminal proceedings (eg where papers from a civil case are relevant to a criminal case) is funded by representation order and requires prior authority. However, it is claimed under the same remuneration provisions as apply to Civil Legal Representation. See sections 10.151–10.162 of the Specification to the Standard Crime Contract.

17.69   Representation on an appeal by way of case stated is funded by representation order (issued by the High Court) and claimed in the same way as in the proceedings class, except that there are no standard fees. See section 11 of the Specification to the Standard Crime Contract.

17.70   Special provision is made by the Standard Crime Contract[77] for representation in proceedings for breach of injunctions under Part 1 of the Anti-Social Behaviour Crime and Policing Act 2014 in whatever court those proceedings take place. Remuneration levels are set out in the Remuneration Regulations. The proceedings at which those injunctions are obtained (including in the youth court) are civil and require civil legal aid. Criminal legal aid however is available in proceedings for breach of these injunctions in all courts. See also chapter 15.

The claiming process

17.71   Contract work is claimed by submitting details of the bills to the LAA. With the exception of magistrates' court non-standard fees, you do not need to send in the file of papers, and bills will not be individually assessed.

17.72   Each month, you should submit form CRM6 to the LAA using the legal aid online portal: https://portal.legalservices.gov.uk. Each line on the CRM6 represents one bill. There is a series of codes you should

---

76 Edwards and Beaumont, *Criminal Costs: legal aid costs in the criminal courts*, LAG, 2nd edn, 2019, paras 4.18–14.22.

77 Standard Crime Contract 2017 Specification paras 10.168–10.178.

use to differentiate between different types of cases, different offences and scheme areas (for police station fee purposes). The LAA then set off each bill against your contract payments, with the overall aim being that payments match claims, within acceptable reconciliation boundaries if you are being paid under standard monthly payments – see chapter 24. The codes can be found on the legal aid website at: www.gov.uk/government/publications/cwa-codes-guidance.

17.73　Non-standard fees in the magistrates' court are subject to individual assessment by the LAA. You should complete form CRM7 with details of the case and the amount claimed, plus justification for the costs, and submit it as an e-form through LAA online: https://portal.legalservices.gov.uk.[78] The LAA will assess the bill and return details of the amount allowed, which will be credited to your contract account rather than paid to you direct.

17.74　If you disagree with the assessment, there is a right of appeal to an Independent Costs Assessor (ICA), who is a solicitor independent of the LAA. The ICA will consider the file, the LAA assessment and your representations and will reduce, confirm or increase the amount allowed by the LAA. There is a 28-day time limit to appeal, and appeals will generally be dealt with on the papers. Full details of the appeal process are set out in the contract.[79] See also chapter 18 for more information on costs appeals.

17.75　There is no right of appeal beyond the Assessor under the 2017 Crime Contract. While ICAs must take points of principle (POPs) published by the LAA into account, no new POPs will be certified from April 2017.

Crown Court – litigator fees

17.76　Although all Crown Court work is included within the scope of the contract, the payment rates and rules are governed by the Criminal Legal Aid (Remuneration) Regulations 2013 as amended. See para 17.10.

17.77　The scheme makes a distinction between fixed fees and graduated fees. There are fixed fees for cases that involve either way offences when the magistrates' court accepted jurisdiction but the defendant elected trial on indictment; and for cases that do not involve trial on indictment, such as committal for sentence, breaches and appeals. Graduated fees apply to all other cases heard on indictment.

78　Standard Crime Contract 2017 Specification para 10.74.
79　Standard Crime Contract 2017 Specification paras 8.19–8.29.

17.78 Graduated fees are determined by a number of factors:

- the classification of the offence – offences are classified into 11 classes (A–K);
- the category (outcome) – whether a guilty plea (plea entered before or at the first hearing at which the defendant enters a plea, a cracked trial (guilty plea or no evidence offered after the first hearing at which the defendant enters a plea) or trial (including Newton hearings);
- the length of the main hearing – the trial or hearing at which pleas were entered;
- the number of pages of prosecution evidence (excluding unused material) served – this can in defined circumstances include pages served electronically;[80]
- the number of defendants represented by you.

To calculate the fee, you should first categorise your case by the offence. Where there is more than one charge on the indictment, select the one which would result in the higher fee.

17.79 For each outcome type, there is a basic fee which varies depending on the classification of the offence, and to which an uplift is added depending on the number of pages of evidence and the length of the main hearing.

17.80 As a result, there are thousands of variables and the tables set out in Schedule 2 to the Remuneration Regulations 2013 and amendments thereto are lengthy and complex. However, the LAA has made available a spreadsheet into which the classification, trial length, page count and outcome can be entered, and which then calculates the appropriate fee – see: www.gov.uk/government/publications/graduated-fee-calculators.

17.81 All work done on a case is covered by the graduated fee; the exceptions are work done in connection with confiscation following conviction,[81] and work classified as 'special preparation' (considering more than 10,000 pages of evidence or exhibits, or electronic evidence which does not qualify as PPE) which is payable at hourly rates in addition to the fee.[82]

---

80 Criminal Legal Aid (Remuneration) Regulations 2013 as amended, Schs 1 and 2 para 1(2)–(5).

81 Criminal Legal Aid (Remuneration) (Amendment) Regulations 2017 Sch 2 para 26.

82 Criminal Legal Aid (Remuneration) (Amendment) Regulations 2017 Sch 2 para 20.

17.82   Claims for litigator fees are to be made through the LAA online billing system.

17.83   Claims are assessed item by item by the LAA, who will compare the information on your claim with that held by the Court Service.

17.84   There is a right to redetermination of an assessment provided for in reg 28 of the Remuneration Regulations 2013. The request must be made in writing within 21 days of receipt of the assessment. You cannot challenge the fee scheme itself, but can challenge the calculation in any individual case, such as by appealing the classification of the offence or the allowed page count. On redetermination, the fee may be confirmed, reduced or increased.

17.85   If you remain dissatisfied with the assessment, you can apply for written reasons within 21 days, and then within 21 days of receipt of the reasons request a hearing before a costs judge.

Payments on account

17.86   Where you have been granted prior authority by the LAA and have incurred a disbursement of more than £100 you can apply for a payment on account of the disbursement at any time.[83]

17.87   A litigator may make a claim for an interim payment of profit costs at one or both of two stages in proceedings.[84]

17.88   The first stage is where a not guilty plea is entered following a pre-trial preparation hearing (PTPH) (unless it was on a defence election), or alternatively, where a retrial is ordered and representation has been transferred to a new litigator. The interim payment at PTPH stage of proceedings is set at 75 per cent of the cracked trial rate plus any uplifts. Where a retrial is ordered and representation transferred to a new litigator, the payment is set at 50 per cent. The determination of the cracked trial rate will depend on the number of pages of prosecution evidence served on the court and the classification of the offence into which the case falls.

17.89   The second stage is where a trial has commenced that is expected to last for ten or more days. The trial is presumed to last one day and the claim is for the fee payable at that stage.

17.90   There is no other provision for payment on account of profit costs unless you can show financial hardship, and even then only if it has been at least six months since the start of the case and it is unlikely

---

83 Criminal Legal Aid (Remuneration) Regulations 2013 reg 14.
84 See Criminal Legal Aid (Remuneration) (Amendment) (No 2) Regulations 2014.

that payment will be received for at least three more months. You will have to provide evidence of hardship, usually in the form of a bank statement or letter from your bank.[85]

Crown Court – advocates' fees

17.91   The scheme for advocates in mainstream criminal cases is similar to that applying to litigators. The applicable rules and fees are set out in Schedule 1 to the Remuneration Regulations 2013 as amended. Further amending regulations are expected to be laid shortly.

17.92   Each case will have a trial advocate, who is responsible for claiming fees on behalf of all advocates instructed in the case. Payment will be made to the trial advocate.

17.93   The scheme provides for a basic fee based on the classification of the offence to which is added an uplift for the length of the trial. There are higher fees for a trial and some cracked trials and a lower fee for guilty plea case. Additional fees can be claimed for other hearings and specified work.

17.94   In prescribed proceedings where criminal legal aid is granted in relation to civil proceedings in accordance with reg 9 of the Criminal Legal Aid (General) Regulations 2013, hourly rates apply subject to an extendable upper fee limit.[86]

Very High Cost Cases

17.95   Cases accepted by the LAA as VHCCs (ie cases in which a representation order was granted on or after 3 October 2011 and, if the case were to proceed to trial, would likely last more than 25 days (60 for advocates)) may be subject to individual case contracts. The rates will depend on the category of case (seriousness) and the level of fee earner (dependent on experience). Standard rates for each category and level of fee earner are set out in the Specification to the VHCC Standard Contract.

17.96   For further information refer to the legal aid website at: www.gov. uk/government/publications/high-cost-case-arrangements-and-contract-documents.

---

85 Criminal Legal Aid (Remuneration) Regulations 2013 reg 21.
86 See paras 12.148–12.152.

Topping up criminal legal aid fees

17.97   Once legal aid has been granted, Legal Aid, Sentencing and Punishment of Offenders Act 2012 s28 (LASPO) provides:

> (2) A person who provides services under arrangements made for the purposes of this Part must not take any payment in respect of the services apart from—
> (a) payment made in accordance with the arrangements, and
> (b) payment authorised by the Lord Chancellor to be taken.[87]

17.98   The Standard Crime Contract 2017 allows[88] for payment by a client, provided that an application for prior authority to incur that expenditure has been refused and express authority has been obtained from the client, to:

> a) prepare, obtain or consider any report, opinion or further evidence, whether provided by an expert witness or otherwise; or
> b) obtain or prepare any transcripts or recordings of any criminal investigation or proceedings, including police questioning; or
> c) instruct counsel other than where an individual is entitled to counsel (as may be determined by the court) in accordance with Criminal Legal Aid (Determinations by a Court and Choice of Representative) Regulations 2013[89] regs 16 and 17.

This paragraph is wider than Criminal Legal Aid (Remuneration) Regulations 2013 reg 9, which restricts payments to a) and b), but appears to amount to an authority, in relation to magistrates' court work, within LASPO s28(2)(b).

---

87   Confirmed by Standard Crime Contract 2017 Standard Terms 7.18 and Specification para 8.41.
88   Standard Crime Contract 2017 Specification para 8.43.
89   SI No 614.

CHAPTER 18

Appeals to Independent Funding Adjudicators and Costs Assessors in civil cases

by Paul Keeley

continued

Introduction

18.1   This chapter deals with appeals to Independent Funding Adjudicators (IFAs) following a determination by the Legal Aid Agency (LAA) that an individual does not qualify for legal aid and appeals to Independent Costs Assessors (ICAs) following a reduction of remuneration by the LAA.

18.2   This chapter also deals with the right to Internal Review of LAA decisions.

When might you need to appeal?

18.3   We will talk about the rights of appeal in more detail below, but first we will set out the scenarios when you might typically appeal:

- You might want to appeal when the LAA refuses to grant a legal aid certificate in a licensed work matter, for example, to bring a judicial review, or an appeal to the Court of Appeal, on the grounds that there are insufficient prospects of success.
- At the end of the case, or after an audit, when the LAA have assessed your costs, you might want to appeal against a decision to reduce payment for some or all of the work carried out. For example, where the LAA decide that you spent too much time on a particular task, or they might decide you were wrong to grant legal aid in the first place.

Appeals to Independent Funding Adjudicators

18.4   IFAs primarily decide appeals against decisions of the LAA to refuse or withdraw funding on the grounds of merits, or related matters such as the cost-benefit ratio.

18.5   IFAs also decide appeals against decisions of suppliers to refuse or withdraw legal aid on merits grounds in some Controlled Legal Representation (CLR) cases (eg asylum appeals).

Before you appeal to an IFA

Can you make a new application?

18.6   Before appealing, you should consider whether you can make a new application. If, for example, you could have provided more evidence to support your application for legal aid, or put your case in different terms, it may be quicker to make a new application. It is usually possible to submit new evidence or arguments as part of an appeal, but it can often take longer to get your case before an IFA than to get a new decision, so making a new application is often the best first step.

Internal Review

18.7 Although you might focus on the appeal, the right of Internal Review process can be just as, if not more, important. That is because, in some cases, there is no right of appeal at all. In cases where there is a right of appeal, it is, in practice, usually the case that if the LAA maintains their decision, the case is automatically passed on to the IFA for a decision,[1] so your grounds for Internal Review, will effectively become your grounds of appeal. You should therefore prepare your application for Internal Review as your grounds of appeal.

18.8 In most cases, the deadline for an Internal Review is 14 days.

Internal review: exceptional case funding decisions

18.9 In matters falling outside the scope of Legal Aid, Sentencing and Punishment of Offenders Act 2012 (LASPO), there is a right of Internal Review of decisions:

a) to refuse to grant exceptional case funding (ECF) generally, either because the LAA decide that case does not meet the exceptional case threshold, or that, for some other reason (such as being financially ineligible), the individual does not qualify for legal aid;

b) that the wider public interest test is not satisfied in relation to inquest matters, or that, for some other reason (such as being financially ineligible), the individual does not qualify for legal aid in such a case;

c) to amend or refuse to amend a limitation or condition attached to a grant of ECF; and

d) to withdraw ECF.[2]

18.10 The deadline to apply for Internal Review on an ECF case is 14 days, and any such application must be made on form APP9E and include written representations in support of the application.[3]

---

1 This is despite LAA policy stating that practitioners should be notified of a decision upheld following an Internal Review: www.gov.uk/guidance/appeals-civil-merits.

2 Civil Legal Aid (Procedure) Regulations 2012 reg 69(1)(b).

3 Civil Legal Aid (Procedure) Regulations 2012 reg 69(2).

18.11   The appeal should be sent to the ECF Team at Legal Aid Agency, Post Point 8.51, Eighth Floor, 102 Petty France, London SW1H 9AJ; Legal Aid Agency, DX 161440 Westminster 8; or by email to contactECC@legalaid.gsi.gov.uk.[4]

18.12   Unless the LAA have specified otherwise, where the decision under review was to withdraw ECF, and that decision is overturned following an Internal Review, the decision takes effect as though the original withdrawal decision had not been made – ie work carried out in the interim would be payable.[5]

18.13   There is no right of appeal to an IFA against a final decision to refuse ECF. The next step would be to apply for judicial review. Judicial review falls within the scope of LASPO, so it may be possible to obtain legal aid to bring such a challenge.

Internal review: licensed work

18.14   Except in cases of Emergency Representation refusals,[6] before reaching a decision to withdraw legal aid on the grounds of means or merits, the LAA must first invite written representations within a specified time-limit and consider those representations before reaching a final decision.[7]

18.15   If the LAA then go on to refuse legal aid, there is a right to Internal Review against decisions:

a)   that a case does not fall within the scope of LASPO;[8]

b)   that an individual does not qualify for the civil aid services (eg on means or merits grounds);[9]

c)   that an individual qualifies for civil legal aid services but not on the terms requested (ie subject to a limitation or condition);[10] and

d)   to amend or refuse to amend a limitation or condition;[11] or

e)   to withdraw legal aid.[12]

18.16   The deadline for Internal Review is 14 days.[13]

---

4 https://assets.publishing.service.gov.uk/government/uploads/system/uploads/attachment_data/file/588924/ecf-provider-pack.pdf.

5 Civil Legal Aid (Procedure) Regulations 2012 reg 69(4).

6 Civil Legal Aid (Procedure) Regulations 2012 reg 50(3).

7 Civil Legal Aid (Procedure) Regulations 2012 reg 42(3).

8 Civil Legal Aid (Procedure) Regulations 2012 reg 44(1)(a).

9 Civil Legal Aid (Procedure) Regulations 2012 reg 44(1)(b).

10 Civil Legal Aid (Procedure) Regulations 2012 reg 44(1)(c).

11 Civil Legal Aid (Procedure) Regulations 2012 reg 44(1)(d).

12 Civil Legal Aid (Procedure) Regulations 2012 reg 44(1)(e).

13 Civil Legal Aid (Procedure) Regulations 2012 reg 44.

18.17   Where the LAA go on to withdraw legal aid, the withdrawal takes effect from the date that the written representations were requested, not at the date of the final decision to withdraw, so any work carried out in the interim would be at risk of non-payment.[14]

Funding appeals: controlled work immigration cases

18.18   In asylum, in-scope immigration and mental health CLR cases, the power to make decisions to refuse or withdraw legal representation[15] lies with you, the practitioner.[16] In such cases, the client has a right of appeal against *your* decision to refuse legal aid. The same would apply to an ECF case where you decided to withdraw CLR after the LAA have decided to grant it.

18.19   Where you have decided to refuse or withdraw CLR (other than on grounds of financial eligibility) you must complete and retain a copy of form CW4.[17] The form must clearly state the date and reason for your decision.

18.20   As soon as possible and, in any event, within five days of the decision, you must provide the client with a copy of the CW4 form and tell the client of their right to appeal your decision and details of how to do this (the form provides the details of how to appeal). You can, if instructed to do this, help your client appeal against your decision.

18.21   There is no deadline for the client to bring such an appeal.

18.22   The powers of the IFA in such cases are the same as in licensed work (see below).

18.23   If you are instructed by a client who has had such a refusal made by another practitioner, you are not prevented from taking on the case in the absence of a successful appeal, because the decision to grant legal aid is yours to make. However, a successful appeal to an IFA would protect you against the LAA stating at the end of case that you were wrong to grant legal aid.

Funding appeals: licensed work

18.24   In licensed work, there is a right of appeal against *all* decisions to refuse or withdraw legal aid, *unless* the decision to refuse is made on the basis that:

14 Civil Legal Aid (Procedure) Regulations 2012 reg 42(4).
15 Civil Legal Aid (Procedure) Regulations 2012 reg 28(1).
16 Immigration Specification 2018 paras 8.39–8.43.
17 https://assets.publishing.service.gov.uk/government/uploads/system/uploads/attachment_data/file/711264/cw4-form.pdf

a) the case does not fall within the scope of LASPO; or
b) the individual does not qualify on the grounds of means.[18]

18.25 In the case of a refusal of Emergency Representation, there is no right of appeal of a decision made on the basis of limited information and documents[19] – ie if the LAA take the view that you have not provided a complete set of papers. There is also no right of appeal against a refusal made solely on the basis that the time limit to bring the case in question has expired.[20]

Powers of the Independent Funding Adjudicator

18.26 On the following matters, an IFA's decision replaces that of the LAA:
a) prospects of success;
b) costs-benefit criteria;
c) whether the case is of overwhelming importance to the individual; and
d) whether a determination that someone qualifies for legal aid should be withdrawn or revoked in light of their conduct.[21]

18.27 In relation to all other appealable decisions, an IFA can only consider whether the decision was unlawful or unreasonable and refer it back to the LAA for a new decision.[22] In such cases, the LAA must reconsider their decision, taking into account the IFA's decision and any new information provided following the review.[23]

18.28 Where the IFA upholds the LAA's decision, the IFA must give written reasons, and the LAA must notify the individual of that decision.[24]

Submission of further information

18.29 Guidance to IFAs makes it clear that additional information submitted at the time of the appeal may be taken into account,[25] although as

---

18 Civil Legal Aid (Procedure) Regulations 2012 reg 45(1).
19 Civil Legal Aid (Procedure) Regulations 2012 reg 53(1)(a).
20 Civil Legal Aid (Procedure) Regulations 2012 reg 53(1)(a).
21 Civil Legal Aid (Procedure) Regulations 2012 reg 46(1)(a), read with reg 47(1).
22 Civil Legal Aid (Procedure) Regulations 2012 reg 46(1)(b), read with reg 47(1).
23 Civil Legal Aid (Procedure) Regulations 2012 reg 48(1).
24 Civil Legal Aid (Procedure) Regulations 2012 reg 47(2).
25 Appeals Manual 2013, p16. This is internal guidance for IFAs and is not on the LAA website.

stated above, if you have additional information, consider whether making a new application may be more advantageous.

Oral hearings

18.30   It is very rare for an oral hearing to be held. The presumption is that appeals to IFAs will be decided without a hearing unless it is in the interests of justice to have a hearing.[26] The regulations envisage that the IFA appeal itself (as opposed to the underlying case) would need to be exceptionally complex. Guidance states that, in reaching a decision to hold such a hearing, the IFA would need to have regard to the intricacy and obscurity of the disputed issues as against common areas of dispute and any unprecedented difficulties faced by the appellant in their attempt to comply with the regulations.[27]

18.31   In such cases, the IFA or LAA may refer the appeal to a panel of two or more adjudicators.

LAA decision upheld for different reasons

18.32   Where, following an appeal to an IFA, the decision of the LAA is upheld but for reasons that are materially different from the reasons for the decision under appeal, you may appeal once again to an IFA, but this may not happen a further time.[28]

Back-dating licensed work: post-20 February 2019

18.33   Unless the LAA specifies otherwise, in all cases where an IFA has overturned a decision to *withdraw* legal aid, work done in the interim is claimable.[29]

18.34   In relation to decisions to *refuse* legal aid, made from 20 February 2019 onwards, it is possible to claim work carried out in the interim – between the refusal and the successful appeal – where:

    a) the application for legal aid was made as soon as reasonably practical;

    b) it was in the interests of justice that work was carried out prior to the final decision;

    c) the work could not have been carried out as controlled work; and

---

26 Civil Legal Aid (Procedure) Regulations 2012 reg 45(2).

27 Appeals Manual. This is internal guidance for IFAs and is not on the LAA website.

28 Civil Legal Aid (Procedure) Regulations 2012 reg 48(4).

29 Civil Legal Aid (Procedure) Regulations 2012 reg 48(5).

d) having regard to all the circumstances, including information that was available to the practitioner when the application for legal aid was made, it is appropriate for payment to be backdated.[30]

Nil assessments appeals in controlled work cases

18.35   What we have called 'nil assessment' appeals are challenges to decisions taken by the LAA at the end of a case or after an audit that you did not carry out a sufficient merits, or, more often, means, assessment. The result being that all the work carried out was not claimable and payment is reduced to nil. Because this happens at the end of a case, it can mean losing payment for considerable work and disbursements. Such decisions occur relatively frequently and can mean the loss of considerable amounts of money. There are some helpful tips to deal with such decisions. For those reasons, we give such appeals specific consideration.

18.36   First, have you been granted ECF? If so, it is the LAA, not you, that made the grant of legal aid. The error, if there is one, is the LAA's, and you are entitled to claim for legal aid granted by the LAA, subject to any changes not made known to the LAA.

18.37   Second, if you are to appeal, it is possible to submit evidence of means that was not available at the time the LAA made the decision to nil assess, so long as a satisfactory reason is given.[31] An example of this could be if the LAA nil assess the claim on account of one payslip being missing in a series of payslips, there are good reasons this was missing at the time, and you can obtain the missing payslip to submit at the time of the appeal. Even if there was no good reason that the payslip was missing, if you can obtain it at the time of the appeal, you should ask that it be considered. Practice shows that the LAA and

30   Civil Legal Aid (Procedure) (Amendment) Regulations 2019 reg 2, amending regs 35 and 37 of the Civil Legal Aid (Procedure) Regulations 2012.
31   This is stated at Point of Principle (POP), CLA 55:

> 3. In any case which on audit is found to have no such evidence on file, the preliminary decision will be to nil assess. A provider appealing or seeking review of such decision will have to provide evidence of eligibility at the time the form was signed and a satisfactory explanation as to why a claim was submitted for payment without such evidence being on file. If these two requirements are fulfilled, the reviewer/ICA will be able to exercise discretion to allow payment in appropriate circumstances.

> The Escape Cases Electronic Handbook v.1.12, at para 9.3, states that, although it is no longer possible to bring new Points of Principle, the PoP Manual can still be relied on. See also the Appeals Manual 2013, p16.

IFAs are generally willing to consider evidence obtained after the grant of legal aid, so long as evidence covers the computation period.

18.38   If you were responsible for the grant of legal aid (in non-ECF Controlled Work cases), the LAA or IFA may only depart from your assessment that the merits test is satisfied where your decision was 'manifestly unreasonable', or where the assessment was:

> . . . plainly unreasonable, such that no reasonably competent solicitor, in light of their then knowledge, could have concluded that the relevant merits test was met rather than because an assessor has simply made a different, although equally valid, decision about merits.[32]

Although this quote from the Cost Assessment Guidance refers to 'merits', to assess merits under the Merits Regulations also includes an assessment as to whether a client has access to other sources of funding – ie an assessment of their means – and so can arguably be relied on in cases where the means test is not satisfied.

18.39   None of this, of course, overrides your duty to carry out an assessment of means and merits according to the relevant regulations, but where there is any element of discretion, such as assessing an individual claim to have no income, the decision lies with you, and so the LAA and IFA should only overturn your decision where it was manifestly unreasonable.

18.40   A sensible approach to the assessment of incomplete means can be seen in *R (Duncan Lewis Solicitors) v The Lord Chancellor*.[33] Although the case in question in *Duncan Lewis* was under the Access to Justice Act 1999, the principles apply equally here.

18.41   Duncan Lewis had assessed their client as being financially eligible for legal aid on the basis of a letter from social services stating that the client was supported financially under the Children Act 1989. The letter stated the amount of money received by the client and, on assessment, was accepted as adequate.[34] However, when the case moved on to another form of legal aid, and an updated letter was provided, it did not state the amount given by social services to the client, but it was clear that support under the Children Act 1989 continued.[35]

18.42   The LAA 'nil assessed' the claim, meaning Duncan Lewis could not claim for work done at the later stage of the case. An IFA upheld

---

32 Cost Assessment Guidance, paras 6.2–6.3; under the 2013 Contract, POP Manual, CLA 56 and 59 are in similar terms.
33 [2015] EWHC 2498 (Admin).
34 Paras 3–4.
35 Paras 4 and 7.

that decision, stating that because the letter did not state the amount received by the client the assessment of means was inadequate.[36]

18.43   When the case went to judicial review, Cranston J held that that the IFA had asked himself the wrong question.[37] While Duncan Lewis had a clear obligation to assess means, the combination of the two letters made it clear that the client was in receipt of support from social services, and in any event Duncan Lewis would have been aware how much is received by such a client supported by social services, which would not have been anywhere near the legal aid financial eligibility threshold.[38]

18.44   The Lord Chancellor accepted that the crux of the case was whether this evidence was satisfactory,[39] and Duncan Lewis had to 'make a judgment whether they had satisfactory evidence', and in doing so they could consider the evidence before them which was to be 'read against the background of their extensive knowledge' of the people on their client's position. The question was not whether the letter stated the specific amount received but whether, when read in light of their extensive knowledge of people in their client's position, the evidence was 'reasonably sufficient'.[40]

18.45   The *Duncan Lewis* case is particularly useful in appeals where the issue is whether you were right to accept a piece of evidence (or right to assess legal aid in the absence of some information or evidence) from the client as to their means.

Appeals to Independent Costs Assessors

18.46   Appeals to ICAs are appeals against decisions of the LAA to reduce payment for work done. They can occur at the end of a case, or, even later, after an audit.

Appeals to ICA: procedure

18.47   Following an assessment of costs made by the LAA at the end of a case, if either you (the supplier) or counsel are dissatisfied with that assessment, there is a right of appeal to an ICA.[41]

36   Para 11.
37   Para 28.
38   Paras 29–30.
39   Para 31.
40   Para 31.
41   Standard Civil Contract 2018, Specification para 6.71.

18.48   The appeal must be made within 28 days of notification of the decision, and must be accompanied by the file. The LAA can extend the time limit for up to 14 days, where an application is made, providing good reason for an extension, and the application itself is made within 21 days.[42]

18.49   If you appeal, the LAA has the right to make additional written representations to the ICA. The LAA must do this 21 days before the appeal is sent to the ICA, providing you with 14 days to provide a written response to them. However, be aware that the LAA often do not provide a copy of such reasons, so you should watch out for this as a ground for further challenge.

18.50   The ICA has the power to review the assessment whether by confirming, increasing or decreasing the amount assessed. In a Controlled Work assessment, the ICA may apply their findings generally across files outside the sample before them.[43] The same or similar powers existed in the 2013 Contract.

18.51   In reaching a decision, the ICA will be bound by the Costs Assessment Guidance, the Standard Contract Terms and the category-specific rules, and must decide what work was reasonably done, the reasonable time to be spent in relation to that work and what reasonable remuneration should be.

18.52   There is a presumption that there will be no right to an oral hearing or to be represented before the ICA, but you may make an application for an oral hearing at the time your appeal, demonstrating exceptional circumstances.[44]

Some tips for appeals to ICAs

18.53   To succeed in appeals before an ICA, or even better, to avoid the need to do so in the first place, there are a few simple tips as follows:

- Always record work done at the time that you did it, even if briefly. If, for example, you read documents while you drafted, note down the documents, and ideally state how long they were, and a brief note on any complexities (eg if medical or technical), or matters that might have added time (eg if the document was handwritten or you needed to cross-refer to other items).

---

42 Standard Civil Contract 2018, Specification para 6.72.
43 Standard Civil Contract 2018, Specification para 6.80.
44 Standard Contract 2018, para 6.74; see also the Appeals Manual at p16 (this is internal guidance for IFAs and is not on the LAA website).

- Refer to the Costs assessment guidance to be clear on what work you can and cannot claim for. See appendix C for common queries in relation to the Costs assessment guidance.
- Compare the work you did, against what the Costs assessment guidance states is reasonable to claim for. Take the example of drafting a two-page letter that took you one hour to draft. The LAA, with little information to go on, might reasonably suggest one hour was too long, and reduce the amount paid. However, had you made clear that you had read 16 pages of complex medical documents and the rate for reading the most simple prepared document is two minutes per page, and the rate for drafting the most straightforward document is 6–12 minutes, it is far easier to justify your work.

Submission of further information

18.54 As with appeals to IFAs, guidance to ICAs makes it clear that additional information submitted at the time of the appeal may be taken into account by the ICA.[45]

Special Casework decisions

18.55 In relation to decision on Special Casework matters, special provisions apply which include that appeals are to a specially appointed panel, not to an IFA.[46]

Family mediation

18.56 In family mediation, there is a right to apply for Internal Review, and no right of appeal to an IFA.[47] No time limit is specified for such an application.

Further challenges

18.57 If you have come to the end of the road with either an Internal Review or a Funding Appeal, the next step is to bring a judicial review.

---

45 Appeals Manual 2013, p16.
46 Civil Legal Aid (Procedure) Regulations 2012 regs 58–59.
47 Civil Legal Aid (Procedure) Regulations 2012 reg 65.

Legal aid advocacy

CHAPTER 19

Advocacy in civil cases

Introduction

19.1   This chapter deals with the conduct of and payment for advocacy in civil cases and the general rules applying to both civil and family cases.

19.2   In general, we use the term 'advocate' to refer to anyone who has a right of audience to appear in the relevant court or who the court is willing to hear where the scheme makes no distinction between solicitor and counsel. Where there is a difference according to whether advocacy is conducted by solicitor or by counsel, we will use the terms 'solicitor' and 'counsel' as appropriate.

19.3   This chapter only deals with the advocacy aspects of cases. For more information on the conduct of litigation, see Part A of this book. For information on the particular rules applying in family and criminal cases, see chapters 20 and 21.

General principles

19.4   Advocacy can only be conducted under the following levels of service:

- Help at Court;
- Controlled Legal Representation (CLR) (immigration and mental health only);
- legal representation (certificated work);
- specific contracts, such as a housing court duty possession scheme contract.

Advocacy can only be carried out by a person who has a general right of audience or who has been given permission to be heard by the court in the specific case.

19.5   Advocacy funded by legal aid can only be carried out in matters before a court and before certain limited tribunals. The full list is set out in Legal Aid, Sentencing and Punishment of Offenders Act 2012 (LASPO) Sch 1 Part 3.

Help at Court

Scope

19.6   Work must be allowed within scope of the scheme (see chapters 3 and 5 for more information).

19.7   Help at Court is help and advocacy for a client in relation to a particular hearing, without formally acting as legal representative in the proceedings or being on the record at the court (Civil Legal Aid (Procedure) Regulations 2012 reg 5, see also para 6.9 of the *Lord Chancellor's guidance on civil legal aid* (2018)). Help at Court only covers informal advocacy, usually by way of mitigation at individual court hearings. Ongoing representation can only be provided under a legal representation certificate.

19.8   Help at Court is particularly useful for cases where a legal representation certificate would not be available, for example where a client does not have a defence to a possession claim but does need an experienced adviser to set out repayment proposals to the court. Note, however, that if it would be unreasonable for the court to make an order for possession in the circumstances, that can be treated as a defence to the claim for possession and a certificate should, assuming means and merits tests are met, be available. See chapter 12 for more information. Help at Court can also be used to represent the client on an application for enforcement of an order where the client is the applicant. It is not a stand-alone level of funding but can only be granted as an add-on to a pre-existing Legal Help matter.

Merits test

The sufficient benefit test

19.9   The merits test is that:

- it is reasonable to provide funding, taking into account the availability of alternative (ie non-legal aid) funding;
- there is likely to be sufficient benefit, having regard to all the circumstances of the case, including the circumstances of the client, to justify the costs; and
- the nature and circumstances of the client, the proceedings and the particular hearing are such that advocacy is appropriate and would be of real benefit.[1]

19.10   You must apply the test before every hearing and note the file with your justification. 'Sufficient benefit test met' is not an adequate justification.

19.11   There are no additional fixed fees to cover Help at Court. However, the additional work involved may make it more likely that the case will reach the Legal Help escape threshold (three times the fixed fee).

---

1 Civil Legal Aid (Merits Criteria) Regulations 2013 reg 33.

19.12   Where advocacy is justified, you may claim travel and waiting to/ from and at court, as well as preparation and attendance, where appropriate. See chapter 16 for more information on payment schemes.

Specific areas of work

Housing cases

19.13   The Funding Code Guidance, at section 19.3, provided specific guidance on the use of Help at Court in housing cases. You may still find it helpful to consult it if your organisation has a pre-LASPO copy of the Legal Services Commission (LSC) Manual (eg that dated December 2012, vol 3). An online version is available in the archived version of the old LSC website.[2]

19.14   Before making an application for a full certificate, you should consider the availability of Help at Court. This may be more appropriate where the client has no defence but seeks to influence the discretion of the court in relation to postponing possession or suspending eviction.[3] In the latter case, Help at Court should not be used where a certificate would be more appropriate (unless one has been applied for and refused) as formal representation can be made on behalf of the client, directions obtained for exchange of statements and relevant medical reports, and the hearing allocated sufficient time for judicial consideration.

19.15   A full certificate should be applied for where the client has a substantive defence to the possession proceedings, or where there is a substantial issue of fact or law or where the client should be formally represented in the proceedings.

19.16   Neither should Help at Court be used where it is not justified, for example because it would achieve no more than would explaining to the client what steps they could take themselves or writing a letter on their behalf under Legal Help.

19.17   See chapter 12 for more information on housing cases.

Who can provide advocacy?

19.18   Solicitors can attend court under Help at Court in circumstances where they have rights of audience; since it will almost always be the

---

2   http://webarchive.nationalarchives.gov.uk/20130403152321/http://www.justice.gov.uk/legal-aid/funding/funding-code/non-family-guidance.

3   Lord Chancellor's guidance on civil legal aid (2018) para 6.9(b).

County Court, that will be most cases. Advisers without rights of audience may provide advocacy and claim payment under Help at Court, as long as advocacy is justified and the court agrees to hear them. Counsel may not be instructed under Help at Court.[4]

Payment for advocacy services

19.19   Advocacy under Help at Court – and associated preparation, attendance, travel and waiting – is claimable as part of the main Legal Help matter. The costs are included within the fixed fee and may be taken into account in determining whether the case becomes an escape fee case – if it does, the costs will be payable at hourly rates.

Controlled Legal Representation

19.20   CLR is only available in the immigration and mental health categories, and advocacy under those levels of service is dealt with in chapters 10 and 11, and payment in chapter 16.

Representation certificates

19.21   Where a certificate is issued to a solicitor covering proceedings before a court, it will in principle be possible to provide and claim for advocacy services under the certificate at all hearings in the case, though like every other step in the proceedings attendance at hearings is subject to there being merit in taking that step. You should also make sure that the particular hearing is within the scope of the certificate; final hearings, for example, are generally not within scope of a certificate as first issued.

19.22   Advocacy under a certificate can be undertaken by a solicitor (subject to rights of audience in the higher courts) or by counsel. An advocate can be employed by your organisation or be in independent practice, either as a freelance solicitor or solicitor agent or as counsel in chambers. Under para 7.3 of the 2018 contract, you must consult your client regarding the use and selection of counsel or in-house advocate, unless it is not practical or appropriate to do so.

---

4 Standard Civil Contract 2018 Specification para 3.61.

19.23   There is general authority to instruct one junior advocate under a certificate;[5] the instruction of more than one junior, or of Queen's Counsel (QC) acting as such, requires an application for prior authority to be made.[6] Unless the authority is granted, no claim can be made by a second advocate appearing at any hearing or by Queen's Counsel for acting as such (it is always open to Queen's Counsel to accept instructions to appear as a junior and to be paid on that basis).[7] In a case where the statutory charge applies, you also require the informed consent of your client to the incurring of the extra costs of instructing a QC or second counsel,[8] and costs officers will be looking to see that on your file.[9]

19.24   Where you instruct counsel, the brief must include a copy of the certificate and a copy of any prior authority to instruct counsel.[10] Where the certificate has not yet been issued, you should provide counsel with a copy within 14 days of receipt.[11]

19.25   You can instruct a solicitor not employed by your organisation to provide advocacy services.[12]

Payment for advocacy services

Work done by a solicitor

19.26   Advocacy work, and associated preparation, attendance, travel and waiting, done by a solicitor is payable at the hourly rates set out in the Civil Legal Aid (Remuneration) Regulations 2013. This is true whether the solicitor is employed by your organisation or whether the solicitor is acting as an independent solicitor-advocate. Their times should be included on your bill along with all other profit costs and will be assessed in the usual way. See chapter 16 for details of the assessment process. The fact that a solicitor has undertaken the advocacy themselves rather than instruct counsel, especially in a complex case, will assist in justifying an enhancement to the hourly rates.

---

5 Standard Civil Contract 2018 Specification para 5.12.
6 Standard Civil Contract 2018 Specification para 5.10(b).
7 Standard Civil Contract 2018 Specification para 6.59(d).
8 *Practice Note (Solicitors: taxation of costs)* [1982] 2 All ER 683.
9 Costs Assessment Guidance: for use with the 2018 Standard Civil Contract para 13.8.
10 Standard Civil Contract 2018 Specification para 5.13(a), (b).
11 Standard Civil Contract 2018 Specification para 5.14.
12 Standard Civil Contract 2018 Specification para 2.5.

Work done by counsel – cases started prior to 2 December 2013

19.27   Barristers' fees are codified in all cases started on or after 3 October 2011. For cases started after that date, but before 2 December 2013, there are hourly rates applicable in all courts and for three categories of barrister – QCs and senior and junior counsel (respectively, ten years' call or more and less than ten years' call). The location of chambers, not the court, determines whether the London or non-London rate should be claimed (only junior counsel in the County Court have separate London and non-London rates).[13] See Schedule 2 to the Civil Legal Aid (Remuneration) Regulations 2013 for the rates. They apply to barristers in independent practice but not solicitor advocates or barristers employed by solicitor firms, both of which claim at solicitor rates.

19.28   There is a discretion for junior counsel in the County Court to be paid at higher rates than those set out in the Remuneration Regulations. The regulations merely say that the Legal Aid Agency (LAA) can do so if it is 'reasonable' to do so. The costs assessment guidance applicable at the time[14] went on to say that the decision lies with the LAA, even if the court has assessed fees at the higher rate, and that factors to be taken into account include:

- the complexity of case – for example, the gravity of the case, points of law or contested evidence;
- novel areas of law – a case requiring unusually specialised knowledge or skill or that is likely to set a precedent or have a wider impact;
- where an opponent has instructed a QC;
- a case requiring considerable amount of out-of-hours work;
- where a client has mental health problems, learning difficulties, social impairment or language difficulties that may impact on the approach taken;
- where the case involves an unusually large number of parties represented at a contested final hearing;
- where a hearing requires the cross-examination of more than one expert on technical issues, for example in clinical negligence cases;
- a fully contested hearing lasting more than two days.

13 Costs Assessment Guidance: for use with the 2013, 2014 and 2015 Standard Civil Contracts para 13.9.

14 This was formerly in Costs Assessment Guidance para 13.12, but has been removed from the current edition, presumably as these provisions are not in force for certificates granted after December 2013.

Work done by counsel – cases started on or after 2 December 2013

19.29   For cases started on or after 2 December 2013, payment rates for counsel were reduced, in most cases, to the rates applicable to solicitors doing the same work where the case is in the High Court or below, or in the Upper Tribunal. The location of chambers, not the court, determines whether the London or non-London rate should be claimed.[15] Where chambers has more than one address, the solicitor's location will be taken into account in determining the applicable rates.

19.30   There are separate rates for counsel appearing in the Court of Appeal and Supreme Court, which depend on the level of counsel's seniority. Those rates also apply to Queen's Counsel acting as such and appearing in any court (assuming authority for a QC has been granted). The rates are set out in Schedule 1 to the Civil Legal Aid (Remuneration) (Amendment) Regulations 2013. There are no prescribed rates for work done in tribunals other than the Upper Tribunal (where in scope or as part of exceptional funding), but in determining the rate paid costs officers should have regard to the prescribed rates.[16]

19.31   Where junior counsel is paid at prescribed rates in the High Court or below, an application for an enhancement of the rates may be made on the bill.[17] The criteria for enhancement are that the work done by counsel (either a particular item of work or hearing, or on the case as a whole):

- was done with exceptional competence, skill or expertise;
- was done with exceptional speed; or
- involved exceptional circumstances or complexity.

19.32   In calculating the percentage enhancement, costs officers will have regard to the degree of responsibility accepted by counsel, the care speed and efficiency with which counsel prepared the case and its novelty weight and complexity. Assessment of the care with which counsel prepared the case includes the skill with which the work was

---

15 Costs Assessment Guidance: for use with the 2018 Standard Civil Contracts para 13.9.

16 Civil Legal Aid (Remuneration) Regulations 2013 reg 7(4) and (4A), as inserted by Civil Legal Aid (Remuneration) (Amendment) Regulations 2013 reg 2(2)(c) and (d).

17 Civil Legal Aid (Remuneration) Regulations 2013 reg 7(3), as inserted by Civil Legal Aid (Remuneration) (Amendment) Regulations 2013 reg 2(2)(b).

carried out and in particular the case shown to a vulnerable client, while the weight of the case means the volume of documentation, the number of issues arising or the importance of the case to the client.[18]

19.33   The percentage enhancement can never exceed 100 per cent in the Upper Tribunal or High Court and 50 per cent in the County Court. In determining what is exceptional, regard is to be had to the generality of proceedings to which the prescribed rate to be enhanced applies.

19.34   In practice, similar considerations apply to the enhancement of counsels' fees as to apply to the enhancement of solicitors'. See chapter 16 for more; and the criteria contained in the costs assessment guidance.[19]

Payment on account of counsel's fees

19.35   Counsel can apply direct to the LAA via Client and Cost Management System (CCMS) for a payment on account of their costs.[20] An application can be made on each anniversary of the issue of the certificate, with a window of two months before and four months after the relevant date.

19.36   An application can also be made at any point if:

- the proceedings have continued for more than 12 months;
- it appears unlikely that an order will be made for the costs of the case to be assessed within the next 12 months; and
- delay in the assessment will cause hardship to counsel.

19.37   An application can also be made if:

- the proceedings have concluded or counsel is otherwise entitled to payment; and
- six months have elapsed since then and counsel has not been paid.

19.38   On application, the LAA will pay up to 75 per cent of counsel's reasonable fees. If the final payment is less than the amount of any payments on account, the outstanding balance will be recouped from counsel.[21]

---

18 Civil Legal Aid (Remuneration) Regulations 2013 reg 7(5), as inserted by Civil Legal Aid (Remuneration) (Amendment) Regulations 2013 reg 2(2)(e).
19 Costs Assessment Guidance: for use with the 2018 Standard Civil Contracts section 12.
20 Civil Legal Aid (Remuneration) Regulations 2013 reg 11.
21 Civil Legal Aid (Remuneration) Regulations 2013 reg 12.

Case study

I am instructed in a case where my solicitor's certificate was issued on 1 April 2019 and the case is still ongoing. When can I make a payment on account application?

You can apply on the anniversary of the issue of the certificate, but there is a window either side to allow some flexibility – two months before and two months after the date. So you could have applied for a payment on account at any point between 1 February and 1 June 2020. If the case continues into 2021 you can apply again at any time between 1 February 2021 and 1 June 2021, and so on into 2022 if applicable.

At any time, you should put your total costs to date into CCMS, and the LAA will pay 75 per cent of that (subject to reasonableness), less any payment you have already received. So, for example, if you were paid £1,000 on account in 2020 and by 1 February 2021 your costs have reached £5,000, you should put £5,000 on the form and will be paid £2,750 (75 per cent of £5,000 = £3,750, less £1,000 already received).

19.39   These provisions do not apply to family proceedings where the Family Advocacy Scheme (FAS) applies – see chapter 20 for FAS.

High cost civil cases

19.40   Where the case is a high cost case (see chapter 5), any advocacy work will also be part of the individual case contract.

19.41   Any contract will be with the solicitor, but where an external advocate is instructed, they will need to agree to the payment rates and case/stage plans.

19.42   The rates payable to counsel depend on the classification of the case. Where there is a possibility that, if successful, inter partes costs will be recovered, the case is deemed to be 'at risk' and the rates will be £50 per hour for junior counsel and £90 per hour for senior counsel. Where prospects of success are only borderline but the case is nonetheless being funded because of its overwhelming importance to the client, wider public interest or significant human rights issues, the rates will be £65 and £117 respectively. Where there is no prospect of inter partes costs, standard remuneration rates will apply.[22] The first £5,000 of counsel's fees will always be paid at standard rates rather than high cost case contract rates.

19.43   See chapter 16 for claiming costs in high cost civil cases.

Unpaid fees

19.44   Counsel can only claim fees through solicitors. In certificated cases, solicitors must include counsel's fees in the bill, and must submit the bill to the court or LAA for assessment within the three-month time limit. See chapter 16 above for details of the process.

19.45   Where the solicitor fails to submit the bill, counsel will not be paid, as there is no provision for counsel to bill the LAA directly. Counsel can, to some extent, protect themselves by using the payment on account scheme to recover 75 per cent of the costs. Counsel can place solicitors on the List of Defaulting Solicitors, and can complain, through the Bar Council, to the Solicitors Regulation Authority (SRA). Note that the Bar Council Standard Terms of Business 2013 do not apply to legal aid work.

19.46   It is a term of the Standard Civil Contract that bills be submitted within the three-month time limit;[23] failure to do so is a breach of contract, and repeated failure may lead to sanctions up to and including termination. Counsel may wish to draw a solicitor's failure to submit a bill to the attention of the LAA. Conversely, solicitors are not paid in CCMS cases if counsel have not submitted their bill, so it is much appreciated if this is done quickly.

Inter partes costs and legal aid only costs

19.47   In cases where inter partes costs are possible, it is not uncommon for costs to be ordered or negotiated on the basis of payment of part of the costs of the case. If so, it is important that you are clear as to the terms of the order or agreement, as in some cases but not others you may be able to claim the balance from the legal aid fund. The Standard Civil Contract allows you to claim from the legal aid fund any costs not payable by another party (legal aid only costs), but only if certain conditions are met – see paras 6.50 and 6.51 of the 2018 Specification.

---

22 Available at: www.gov.uk/government/publications/high-cost-cases-non-family-civil.
23 Standard Civil Contract 2018 Specification para 6.33.

19.48   The Specification defines 'legal aid only' costs – costs that can be claimed from the legal aid fund even where inter partes costs are recovered – as:

- costs of completing legal aid forms and communicating with the LAA;
- certain limited types of costs disallowed or not agreed;
- costs of work not covered by a costs order or agreement.

Where a costs order or agreement specifies that another party should pay a proportion of the client's costs (but not a fixed sum), the same proportion of the total work that is not covered is legal aid only costs.[24]

19.49   To take a practical example, say total costs on the case are £2,000 at legal aid rates and £4,000 at inter partes rates. If the other side agree to pay your costs in the sum of £2,000, that could be expressed in one of three ways:

- £2,000 as the total agreed costs of the case;
- agreement to pay costs between X and Y dates, totalling £2,000; or
- agreement to pay 50 per cent of the costs, being £2,000.

In each case, you receive £2,000 from the other side:

- In the first case, that £2,000 represents the total costs of the case, so there are no legal aid costs (apart perhaps from £100 or so for filling in the APP1 and so on).
- In the second case, costs outside the agreed dates are not subject to the costs order, so you can claim those costs in addition to the inter partes costs you have received.
- In the third case, the other side has agreed to pay 50 per cent of your costs, so the other 50 per cent are legal aid only costs, so you can claim £1,000 (50 per cent of £2,000 at legal aid rates) from the LAA in addition to the £2,000 from the other side.

See also para 16.133 onwards.

---

24 Standard Civil Contract 2018 Specification paras 6.50 and 6.51.

Advocacy in family cases

by Samantha Little

Introduction

20.1 This chapter deals with the particular rules that apply to conduct of and payment for advocacy in family cases. See chapter 16 for the general rules applying to both civil and family cases.

20.2 Advocacy can only be conducted under legal representation certificates in family work as Help at Court and Controlled Legal Representation (CLR) are not available in the family category.

20.3 In general, we use the term 'advocate' to refer to anyone who has a right of audience to appear in the relevant court or whom the court is willing to hear, where the scheme does not make a distinction between solicitor and counsel. Where there is a difference according to whether advocacy is conducted by solicitor or by counsel, we will use the terms 'solicitor' and 'counsel' as appropriate.

20.4 This chapter only deals with the advocacy aspects of family cases. For more information on the conduct of litigation, see Part A of this book. For information on the rules applying in criminal cases, see chapter 21 and chapter 19 for other civil cases.

Merits test

20.5 See chapter 5 for the merits tests relevant to legal representation and chapters 7 and 8 for their operation in family cases.

Family cases started prior to 9 May 2011

20.6 The Family Graduated Fee Scheme (FGFS) continues to apply to these cases. The provisions of the scheme are set out in the Community Legal Service (Funding) (Counsel in Family Proceedings) Order 2001 as amended. It is unlikely that there are many outstanding cases to which this scheme applies, but for details see the 2011/12 edition of this Handbook.

Scope of the FGFS

20.7 The FGFS applies only to counsel. Solicitor advocates claim under the appropriate standard fee or hourly rate scheme, depending on whether the case is public or private law, and whether the case started prior to 1 October 2007.

20.8   Payments under the FGFS are essentially fixed or standard fee payments with a range of base fees for different pieces of work. These fees are set according to the nature of the proceedings, the work to be done, whether junior or leading counsel is employed, and venue. There is also a range of additional payments that may be added to the fee due, to reflect special features and complexity. The permutation of possible payments is quite complex. There is a helpful guidance paper on the national archives website at: http://webarchive. nationalarchives.gov.uk/20130128112038/http://www.justice.gov. uk/downloads/legal-aid/fee-schemes/fgfsrevisedguidance-august2009.pdf.

Family cases started on or after 9 May 2011

20.9   The Family Advocacy Scheme (FAS) applies to cases where the certificate was granted following an application made on or after 9 May 2011. The provisions of the scheme are set out in the Civil Legal Aid (Remuneration) Regulations 2013 Sch 3[1] and in section 7 of the 2018 Standard Civil Contract Specification (specifically Section D).

Scope of the FAS

20.10   The fees apply to most advocacy, and the majority of fees can be claimed equally by solicitors or counsel, although the fees for providing opinions or advising in conference can only be claimed by counsel. The scheme uses the term 'advocate' when any advocate can claim a payment and 'counsel', when only the latter (or a self-employed solicitor or CILEx equivalent) can claim:

> 'Counsel' means either a barrister in independent practice; or a solicitor or Fellow of the Institute of Legal Executives who does not work in a partnership and does not hold a contract with us.[2]

20.11   Solicitors claim payment from the Legal Aid Agency (LAA) in the usual way, and if you instruct a solicitor advocate freelancer or from

---

1 As amended by the Civil Legal Aid (Remuneration) (Amendment) (No 2) Regulations 2014 and the Civil Legal Aid (Remuneration) (Amendment) (No 4) Regulations 2014, which amended the scheme to fit with the new single family court.

2 Civil legal aid cost assessment guidance para 2.1, appendix 2: www.gov.uk/ government/uploads/system/uploads/attachment_data/file/427309/legal-aid-costs-assessment-guidance–2013–2014.pdf. (FILEX – now Chartered Legal Executive – CILEx.)

another firm, they act as an agent and you are responsible for their fees. Counsel claim FAS fees from the LAA direct.[3]

20.12   The advocacy fee includes all preparation for a hearing (including the preparation of a position statement), travel to and waiting at court and time spent in discussions and in advocacy itself. The advocacy fee can only be claimed by the legal representative providing advocacy at a hearing. If a solicitor's representative attends with an advocate, he or she cannot also claim the fee (but can claim the time under the fixed fee for the casework, if justifiable).

20.13   Some types of advocacy are paid under hourly rates because they do not fall under the FAS scheme.[4] Proceedings excluded from the FAS:[5]

(a) Child abduction proceedings;
(b) proceedings under the Inheritance (Provision for Family and Dependants) Act 1975;
(c) proceedings under the Trusts of Land and Appointment of Trustees Act 1996;
(d) proceedings in which you provide separate representation of a Child in proceedings which are neither Specified Proceedings (as defined in section 41(6) of the Children Act 1989) nor proceedings which are being heard together with Specified Proceedings;
(e) applications for Forced Marriage Protection Orders under the Forced Marriage (Civil Protection) Act 2007;
(f) defended proceedings for divorce, judicial separation, dissolution of a civil partnership or for the legal separation of civil partners;
(g) nullity proceedings (including proceedings for annulment of a civil partnership);
(h) proceedings under the inherent jurisdiction of the High Court in relation to the children;
(i) applications for Parental Orders under the Human Fertilisation and Embryology Act 2008;
(j) applications in relation to female genital mutilation protection orders under the Female Genital Mutilation Act 2003.

20.14   The following are also excluded[6]:

• advocacy in relation to appeals against final orders (but note that appeals of interim orders are covered within FAS unless they are in the Court of Appeal or Supreme Court. Applications to the court of first instance for permission to appeal are in the scope of FAS [7]);

3 Standard Civil Contract 2018 Specification para 7.119.
4 Standard Civil Contract 2018 Specification para 7.107.
5 Standard Civil Contract 2018 Specification para 7.107.
6 Standard Civil Contract 2018 Specification paras 7.108 and 7.109.
7 Standard Civil Contract 2018 Specification paras 7.109 and 7.110

- advocacy provided under a high costs case contract;[8]
- advocacy by Queen's Counsel (QCs);
- advocacy before the Court of Appeal or Supreme Court.

20.15 The scheme is split into five categories of case:

1) care and supervision proceedings, including applications made within such proceedings or related proceedings;
2) other public law cases (including adoption);
3) private law children proceedings;
4) finance cases;
5) domestic abuse cases.

Escape fee cases

20.16 There are no escape fee cases or uplifts payable under the FAS, irrespective of the total number of days the hearing lasts. This is because the payments are based on time periods.

Mixed categories

20.17 Where work covers more than one of the categories above within a single set of proceedings, the advocate can choose which fee to claim:[9]

- In family cases, the certificate will often either be issued to cover a number of proceedings or be subsequently amended to add or substitute proceedings during the life of the certificate.
- When the continuing proceedings fall within more than one category, an advocate must, for the purpose of payment under the FAS, choose under which single category they would wish to be paid for all the Advocacy Services performed when making a claim for payment. Usually, an advocate will claim at the category that pays the highest rate. For example, in a Children Act 1989 s8 application that subsequently involves allegations of abuse to a degree that the local authority issues care proceedings, at the point at which a new certificate is issued, an advocate can claim all future work (including issues as to contact) at the higher care proceedings rate.[10]

---

8 But note that in public law cases the LAA will often contract based on the 'events model' rather than at hourly rates and has, in some cases, contracted based on FAS.

9 Cost assessment guidance appendix 2 para 12.2.

10 Cost assessment guidance appendix 2 para 12.2.

- Where an Advocacy Service includes work from two categories but it falls within a single set of proceedings, only one fee will be paid – eg if a single hearing covers both private law children and financial issues, then only one hearing fee will be payable and the advocate can choose which hearing fee to claim.[11]

Hearing fees

20.18   Fees vary according to whether a hearing is interim or final:[12]

Interim and Final Hearings

7.127 A Final Hearing is any hearing which the court has listed for the purpose of making a final determination, either of the whole case or of all issues relating to an Aspect of the case (Domestic Abuse, Children or Finance). Subject to paragraph 7.130, there can only be one Final Hearing per Aspect and a hearing listed only to determine particular facts or issues is not a Final Hearing. A hearing listed with a view to the issues being dealt with under a consent order, or which is otherwise not expected to be effective or contested, is not a Final Hearing. Any hearing which is not a Final Hearing is an Interim Hearing.

7.128 The following hearings are also deemed to be Final Hearings for the purposes of the FAS only:
(a) In Public Law proceedings, if a case is concluded at an Issues Resolution Hearing and therefore does not proceed further, the Issues Resolution Hearing will be treated as a Final Hearing;
(b) Subject to Paragraph 7.129, in Private Law Children proceedings, a hearing listed for the purpose of findings of fact pursuant to the Practice Direction: Residence and Contact Orders: Domestic Violence and Harm issued by the President of the Family Division on 14 January 2009.[13]

7.129 If a Final Hearing is listed for a split hearing in a Public Law matter with certain issues being heard and/or determined in advance of other issues, this must be claimed as a Final Hearing, rather than as an Interim Hearing plus a Final Hearing.

7.130 It is possible for more than one Final Hearing fee to be claimed under a single certificate. In particular this can occur where a Final Hearing has taken place but subsequent enforcement proceedings are listed at first instance. Provided the enforcement issues are listed

---

11 Cost assessment guidance appendix 2 para 12.3.
12 Standard Civil Contract 2018 Specification para 7.127.
13 Note that this practice direction was updated by Practice Direction 12J in December 2017.

to be finally determined at the further hearing, an additional Final Hearing fee may be justified.

20.19 Interim hearings are paid by a series of interim hearing units, final hearings are paid by a fixed daily rate. Bolt on payments may apply to interim and final hearing payments (see below).

Interim hearing units

20.20 The fee payable depends on the length of the hearing. There are two interim hearing units:

- hearing unit 1: one hour or less;
- hearing unit 2: more than one hour but less than 2.5 hours.

If a hearing exceeds 2.5 hours, multiples of unit 2 fees will be paid (rounded up – for example, two unit 2 fees will be paid for a hearing that lasts four hours). You cannot claim multiples of hearing unit 1, or claim both unit 1 and unit 2 for the same hearing.

20.21 The applicable hearing time is the time at which the hearing is listed to start (unless the court specifically directs the advocate to attend earlier) until the time the hearing concludes:[14]

7.131 The fee payable under FAS for an Interim Hearing depends on its length. For this purpose the length of hearing is measured from the time that the hearing is listed at court to start (or such earlier time as the court specifically directs the advocate to attend) to the time that the hearing concludes, disregarding any period in which the court is adjourned overnight or for a lunch break.[15] Time spent when a hearing or resumed hearing is delayed because the court is dealing with other business may however be taken into account. In the case of an Interim Hearing taking place by telephone or video link, time only runs from the time the call is made. If for an emergency hearing the court has not listed a time for the hearing or a time for the advocate to attend and the papers were only issued by the court on the day of the proposed hearing (so that the advocate must wait at court to be heard in the matter), the length of hearing may be measured from the time that the papers were issued.'

20.22 There is additional guidance in relation to interim hearings:[16]

---

14 Standard Civil Contract 2018 Specification para 7.131.
15 Note that the Advocates' Attendance Form now includes a box you must complete if you are at a hearing over lunchtime so that you can claim as part of the hearing time any time spent working over lunch. You need to fill this in even if you are not working over the lunchtime break.
16 Cost assessment guidance appendix 2.

14.6 . . . Where for an emergency hearing the court has not listed a time for the hearing and the papers are only issued by the court on the day of the proposed hearing so that the advocate must wait at court to be heard the length of the hearing will be measured from the time that the papers were issued. If the application is issued and the hearing is then not heard until the next day the hearing time for that day will end when the advocate is informed of this and will start again at the time that they are told to attend for the following day.

14.7 Where a court directs a party to adjourn for further discussions at court then that time will be included in the calculation of the interim hearing fee

14.8 A hearing may take place by any method directed by the court eg by either video or telephone conference without attendance at court. If the court directs an alternative method of hearing then the advocate will receive the appropriate fee as if the hearing had taken place at court. However, in these cases the hearing time will start from the time that the telephone call/video conference is first attempted rather than the time that the hearing was listed. Bolt-ons may be claimed for telephone/video hearings if appropriate although due to the nature of these hearings bolt-ons are less likely to be applicable. It is unlikely, for example, that the criteria for the expert bolt-on would be met. As there will be no Advocates Attendance Form detailed notes of the hearing will need to be recorded and the claim justified on the CLAIM 1A or CLAIM 5A.

14.9 Where a case is resolved at an Issues Resolution Hearing held under the Public Law Outline (PLO) and no further hearings take place then this hearing will be paid as a final hearing.

14.10 In Private Law Children cases where a 'finding of fact hearing' is held in accordance with the Practice Direction 12J of the Family Procedure Rules 2010: Residence and Contact Orders: Domestic Violence and Harm, it will be paid as a final hearing.

Final hearings

20.23   Final hearings are paid under daily rates. A full daily fee is payable, regardless of the length of the hearing on that day.[17] A reading day will not be a hearing day unless the court has also required actual attendance at court for case management issues. The court can designate a hearing day for the writing of submissions, but this must be clearly endorsed on the order.

20.24   Finding of fact hearings in private and public law proceedings will be paid for as final hearings. Issues Resolution hearings in public

17 Standard Civil Contract 2018 Specification para 7.133.

law cases will be paid for as final hearings (if the case concludes at that hearing).[18]

20.25   There is some additional guidance in relation to final hearings:[19]

> 14.11 In care proceedings, the main hearing would be the hearing at which the court determines whether or not a section 31 order is made. If a final hearing is listed for a split hearing with certain issues being heard and/or determined in advance of other issues (for example, findings of fact and/or threshold criteria), this must be claimed as a final hearing rather than an interim hearing plus a final hearing. In ancillary relief proceedings, it is likely to be the hearing at which the court determines the form of relief entitlement and in family injunctions, the on notice hearing which will determine the form and continuation of the without notice injunction order made. The definition includes all preparation or incidental work relating to the hearing including preparation, travel to court and waiting at court as well as the advocacy within the hearing itself.

20.26   See also civil legal aid cost assessment guidance, appendix 2:

> 15.9 A directions hearing that concludes the case does not make the hearing a 'final hearing'.

> 15.10 On the making of an order the court may decide to review the position after an interval of some months. That subsequent review is not a continuation of the final hearing but an interim hearing. The court may make further directions, continue or vary the order. None of these circumstances turn that later hearing into either the continuation of the final hearing or a new final hearing.

> 15.11 It is possible in certain circumstances for more than one final hearing fee to be paid in a case. In particular this can occur where a final hearing has taken place but subsequent enforcement proceedings are issued which are required to be finally determined or where an earlier fact finding hearing has taken place.

Note that if acting in a private law children or finance case, you will not be able to claim for a final hearing if the certificate scope is limited and does not permit attendance at a final hearing.

Cancelled hearings

20.27   Only counsel may claim a fee for cancelled hearings. Counsel must have done at least 30 minutes' preparation in order to claim a hearing unit 1 fee (for interim hearings) or half a final hearing fee (for final

---

18 Standard Civil Contract 2018 Specification para 7.128.
19 Cost assessment guidance appendix 2.

hearings).[20] An employed advocate may not claim a cancellation fee through FAS but may include wasted time in preparation for the hearing as part of the preparation costs of the case and such costs may count towards the case becoming exceptional.[21]

Bolt-ons

20.28   Additional bolt-on fees are available for more complex cases in public and private law children cases. Claims must be verified by the judge, magistrate or legal adviser at the hearing on the Advocates Attendance Form (AAF) either by initial, stamp or court seal.[22] Bolt-on fees cannot be claimed for cancelled hearings. Bolt-ons are not available in finance cases and domestic abuse cases, apart from court bundles in finance cases and exceptional travel in both finance and domestic abuse cases where applicable.[23]

Public law

20.29   In public law cases, bolt-ons are claimable where:
- you are acting for a parent or others against whom allegations of serious harm to a child are made by the local authority;
- the client has difficulty giving instructions/understanding advice;
- expert/s has/have to be cross-examined.[24]

Bolt on payments are cumulative, ie you get 25 per cent uplift for each that applies (thus the total that your fee can be increased in public law is 75 per cent).

Client – allegations of significant harm

20.30   Paragraph 7.145 of the Specification states:

> This Bolt-on Fee is claimable only where your Client is facing allegations that he or she has caused significant harm to a Child. It applies only so long as those allegations remain a live issue in the

20 Standard Civil Contract 2018 Specification para 7.134 and Cost assessment guidance Appendix 2, para 14.15.
21 Cost assessment guidance appendix 2, para 14.16.
22 Note that it is only bolt ons that must be sealed, stamped or initialled next to each bolt on. Aside from the form being signed and dated at the bottom by the Judge/Clerk, nothing else needs stamping/signing or initialling, although we know court staff often then stamp many of the entries on the form, if they do, make sure they don't stamp over your times for an interim hearing.
23 Standard Civil Contract 2018 Specification paras 7.142–7.158.
24 Standard Civil Contract 2018 Specification paras 7.156–7.158.

proceedings. For this purpose only the following conditions constitute significant harm:
(a) death,
(b) significant head and/or fracture injuries,
(c) burns or scalds,
(d) fabricated illness,
(e) extensive bruising involving more than one part of the body,
(f) multiple injuries of different kinds,
(g) other significant ill-treatment (such as suffocation or starvation) likely to endanger life,
(h) sexual abuse.

Client – lack of understanding etc

20.31 Paragraph 7.147 of the Specification states:

This Bolt-on applies to hearings in Public Law proceedings where:
(a) your Client has difficulty in giving instructions or understanding advice,
(b) this is attributable to a mental disorder (as defined in section 1(2) of the Mental Health Act 1983) or to a significant impairment of intelligence or social functioning, and
(c) the Client's condition is verified by a medical report from either a psychologist or psychiatrist.

Cross examination of expert

20.32 This bolt-on applies to all advocates when cross examination is undertaken by any party. It can also be claimed if the expert was stood down within 72 hours of the hearing and preparation has been carried out or if the expert attended the hearing but did not give evidence.

Advocates' meetings

20.33 In public law cases, a separate fee is available for advocates attending an advocates' meeting, where such a meeting is directed by the court in accordance with the Public Law Outline. Where in section 31 care proceedings, advocates are able to discuss all relevant matters without the need for a formal advocates' meeting directed by the court, half the standard fee is payable (without any bolt-ons).[25]

20.34 There is additional guidance in relation to advocates' meetings:[26]

14.18 Although it would usually be expected that two advocates' meetings would take place in accordance with the PLO, provided that the

---

25 Standard Civil Contract 2018 Specification paras 7.135 and 7.136.
26 Cost assessment guidance appendix 2.

advocates' meeting is held as directed by the court and in accordance with the PLO there is no limit to the number of these fees that may be claimed. No fees for advocates' meetings will be payable in Private Law Children cases.

14.19 The definition of Advocates' Meeting includes meetings held by video conference, webcam or telephone where this is appropriate in the circumstances.

14.20 It is not envisaged under the PLO that an advocates meeting would take place on the same day as a hearing. However if an advocates meeting does take place on the same day as an interim hearing then it may be claimed only if the meeting takes place outside of any time period that is taken into account in calculating the fee for the interim hearing.

Private law

20.35   In private law children cases, bolt-ons are claimable where:

- you are acting for a parent or others against whom allegations of significant harm to a child are made;[27]
- expert/s has/have to be substantially challenged in court (but note the uplift is 20 per cent, not 25 per cent as in public law cases).[28]

20.36   In private law finance cases an early resolution fee can be claimed for cases which settle at the first appointment or Financial Dispute Resolution (FDR) Hearing, as long as the advocate materially assisted in the settlement, it is recorded in a consent order and it lasts for six months (as far as you are aware).[29]

Early Resolution Fee

7.152 This Bolt-on Fee is claimable only in Private Law Finance cases which settle at the first appointment or Financial Dispute Resolution ('FDR') hearing. It may only be claimed by an advocate who is entitled to the Hearing fee for that hearing but only if the following conditions are satisfied:

(a) the Finance Aspect of the case has been fully concluded at the first appointment or FDR hearing;

(b) the advocate attending that hearing materially assisted in the settlement;

(c) the Finance Aspect of the case does not proceed further to a new Form of Civil Legal Services within six months of the settlement, either with you or, so far as you are aware, another Provider;

---

27 Standard Civil Contract 2018 Specification para 7.144.
28 Standard Civil Contract 2018 Specification paras 7.156–7.158.
29 Standard Civil Contract 2018 Specification para 7.152.

(d) there has been a genuine settlement to conclude that Aspect of the case, rather than, for example, a reconciliation between the parties or one party dying or disengaging from the case;

(e) the settlement is recorded in a form of a Consent Order approved by the Court, either at the hearing itself or subsequently.

Court bundles

20.37 Additional fees may be claimed for cases involving larger bundles, known as advocates' bundle payments or ABPs:[30]

ABP 1 – over 350 pages (interim and final);
ABP 2 – over 700 pages (interim and final);
ABP 3 – over 1,400 pages (final hearings only).

20.38 Practice Direction 27A (PD27A) sets out the content and format of the court bundle in family proceedings and introduced a maximum 350-page limit on the size of the court bundle in family cases. From that date, the LAA amended the regulations[31] so that bundle payments were claimed by reference to the advocate's bundle rather than the court bundle. The specification continues to refer to 'court bundle payments' and 'CBPs', but claims should be based on the advocate's bundle.

20.39 The amended regulations set out that the advocate's bundle may only include:

- those documents relevant to the case which have been served by the parties to the proceedings to which the hearing relates;
- notes of contact visits if included in the court bundle; and
- a paginated index agreed by the parties to those proceedings.

Advocates must also include a written explanation of how the documents included in the bundle are relevant and necessary to the case. Advocates should keep a copy of the index for the relevant hearing to show the number of pages in the advocate's bundle.

20.40 There are restrictions on the circumstances and number of times within a set of proceedings that a court bundle payment may be claimed for Interim Hearings:[32]

---

30 Standard Civil Contract 2018 Specification para 7.148.

31 Civil Legal Aid (Remuneration) (Amendment) (No 4) Regulations 2014 amended Civil Legal Aid (Remuneration) Regulations 2013 and equivalent amendments to Community Legal Service (Funding) Order 2007, through Community Legal Service (Funding) (Amendment) Order 2014, to cover cases continuing under Access to Justice Act 1999.

32 Standard Civil Contract 2018 Specification para 7.149.

7.149 . . . In Public Law proceedings, court bundle payments may be claimed for no more than two Interim Hearings and each of these must be either a Case Management Conference, an Issues Resolution Hearing or otherwise a hearing which is listed for the hearing of contested evidence. A court bundle payment may never be claimed more than once per hearing.

7.150 In Private Law proceedings court bundle payments may only be claimed at one Interim Hearing per case. For this purpose the Children and Finance Aspects of a case will be treated separately.

7.151 Court bundle payments may not be claimed in Domestic Abuse proceedings, either for Interim or Final Hearings.

An advocate taking on a case part-way through must satisfy themselves as to whether the advocate's bundle payment(s) have already been claimed or are intended to be claimed by an advocate at an earlier hearing.[33]

20.41   There is some additional guidance in relation to court bundles (see above for change in definition from 31 July 2014): Also note that although the 2018 Contract Specification continues to refer to court bundles, the Costs assessment guidance refers – correctly – to advocate's bundles.[34]

14.46 The advocate's bundle will consist of those served documents relevant and necessary to the case, including a paginated index of the contents. The advocate's bundle may include the documents listed in paragraphs 4.2 and 4.3 of PD27A (and which may be included in the court bundle) and other documents relevant to the case which have been served by the parties to the proceedings to which the hearing relates. Notes of contact visits will only be included in the advocate's bundle for the purposes of the FAS if they have been included in the court bundle.

14.47 Verification of the size of the advocate's bundle will be carried out by the judge or person before whom the case is heard by way of a paginated index of documents served in the case that the advocate would be expected to have agreed with the other parties, as appropriate. Additionally, the advocate will need to provide an explanation of why any documents included in the paginated index which do not fall within paragraphs 4.2 and 4.3 of PD27A are relevant and necessary to the case.

14.51 An advocate must obtain certification of the relevant number of pages of the advocate's bundle on the Advocates Attendance Form in order to claim this payment. The Agency may request copies of both

---

33 Costs assessment guidance appendix 2 para 14.52.
34 Costs assessment guidance appendix 2 paras as set out above.

the agreed paginated list and the explanation of why additional documents not referred to in paragraphs 4.2 and 4.3 of PD27A are included either before or after payment is made.

20.42 At the time the changes were implemented, practitioners' representative groups asked the LAA for clarification about what they would require from providers on making claims for bolt on payments relating to advocates' bundles. The advice received by Resolution from the LAA is set out in italics below:

> *You should get certification of the relevant number of pages of the advocate's bundle on the Advocates Attendance Form. You are advised to have available for the judge the agreed paginated index and reasons for why any documents which do not fall within paras 4.2 and 4.3 of PD27A are relevant and necessary.*

Although there is no requirement to do so, some practitioners are seeking to ensure this is covered on the face of the order.

> *Whilst the LAA may ask for a copy of the agreed paginated index with an explanation of why any additional documents were included, there is no intention to do so as a matter of course, the certified AAF will usually be sufficient. Should the LAA make such a request, you would be expected to present the documentation prepared for the judge, but there is no expectation that the judge will have signed anything except the AAF.*

We understand that LAA caseworkers have been instructed not to refuse claims for payment for advocate's bundles with a completed and certified AAF unless there is an unexpected and unusual pattern of claims for payments.

Exceptional travel

20.43 Advocates may claim payments for exceptional travel on each day of the hearing (more than 25 miles each way), as long as it was reasonable for them to be instructed in all the circumstances, rather than someone more local to the court.[35]

20.44 All advocates will need to justify the payment and documents or explanations may need to be uploaded via Client and Cost Management System (CCMS). Counsel should also supply a copy of their brief or instructions with the claim.

Payments for counsel only

20.45 Counsel's fees may be claimed under the FAS:

---

35 Standard Civil Contract 2018 Specification para 7.154.

- for conferences, up to a maximum of two per set of proceedings;[36]
- for opinions, up to a maximum of two per set of proceedings, unless the opinion relates to a proposed appeal against a final order:[37]
  - in private law, counsel may claim two opinions for both the children and finance aspects of a case;
  - no opinion fee may be claimed in domestic abuse proceedings.

20.46 The Costs Assessment Guidance says this about what constitutes a single set of proceedings:[38]

13.1 For particular Advocacy Services only two fees can be claimed per case. In order to determine what is or is not a 'case' for the purposes of determining appropriate claiming, applications to the court constitute a single set of proceedings, irrespective of whether they are made separately or together, where they are heard together or consecutively or are treated by the court as a single set of proceedings. In private law proceedings each aspect of the case (e.g. children and finance), counts as a separate case for the purposes of claiming opinions and conferences.

Conference fees

20.47 There is some additional guidance in relation to conference fees:[39]

14.25 A conference fee is paid for all work carried out in connection with a conference. This can include conferences by telephone or video link or webcam where this is appropriate in the circumstances. Conference fees may only be claimed by Counsel. No bolt-ons may be claimed for conferences.

14.26 Up to two conference fees may be claimed in each single set of proceedings. As for opinions in private law proceedings, if there are separate children and finance proceedings these will be considered separately for these purposes. However, no conference fee may be claimed under FAS in domestic abuse proceedings.

14.27 As only two conference fees may be claimed Counsel will need to designate the conferences for which he or she seeks payment under the FAS.

14.28 No conference fee may be claimed for any conference held on the same day as a Final hearing. Any discussions or negotiations taking place on any day of a final hearing will be covered by the fee for advocacy at that hearing.

---

36 Standard Civil Contract 2018 Specification para 7.141.
37 Standard Civil Contract 2018 Specification para 7.138.
38 Costs assessment guidance appendix 2.
39 Costs assessment guidance appendix 2.

14.29 A conference fee may be claimed for a conference that takes place on the same day as an interim hearing, only if the conference takes place outside of any time period that is taken into account in calculating the fee for the interim hearing. Therefore no conference fee may be claimed for a conference that takes place between the time that the hearing is listed to start and the time that hearing actually starts as this will be claimed as part of the hearing unit.

14.30 Where different Counsel is subsequently instructed and the allowable conference fees have already been claimed, no further claims for conference fees can be made. This is so even in circumstances where the later conference was more substantial. Where one Counsel has replaced another, Counsel must make enquiries as to whether the conference fees payments have been claimed from either the outgoing Counsel, or instructing solicitors.

Opinion fees

20.48 Only counsel (see definition in para 20.10 above) may claim opinion fees.[40] There is some additional guidance in relation to opinion fees:[41]

14.22 Up to two opinion fees may be claimed in each single set of proceedings. If there are separate children and finance proceedings these will be considered separately for these purposes. No opinion fee may claimed under the FAS in domestic abuse proceedings.

14.23 In addition to the two opinions claimed per set of proceedings a further opinion may be claimed in relation to any a proposed appeal against a final order.

14.24 An opinion may include providing advice or drafting pleadings/affidavits after the issue of proceedings.

Assessment

20.49 The LAA assesses all fees due to counsel under the FAS. Solicitors' profit costs (including for advocacy) and disbursements are assessed in the usual way, through assessment either by the LAA or the court. See chapter 15 for more information.

CCMS and forms

20.50 Different forms are submitted depending on whether the claim falls under the FGS (cases started pre 9 May 2011) or the FAS (cases

---

40 Standard Civil Contract 2018 Specification para 7.137.
41 Costs assessment guidance appendix 2.

started after 9 May 2011). The forms, and accompanying guidance on how to fill them out, can be downloaded from: www.gov.uk/government/publications/family-graduated-fee-and-family-advocacy-claim-forms. See para 20.52 below regarding CCMS, which will apply in most cases.

20.51   For older FAS claims, counsel claim on form CIVCLAIM5A and solicitors claim on form CIVCLAIM1A. Claims for advocacy under the FAS must be made on an appropriately completed Advocates Attendance Form (EX506[42]). If such form(s) are not submitted the advocacy claim will be limited to a level 1 hearing unit.

20.52   Cases started since April 2016 (February 2016 for most public law cases and earlier for some firms) are managed through CCMS. Counsel can claim FAS payments through CCMS at the conclusion of each hearing and they will be recorded against the file, assisting the solicitor with the management of the costs of the case. In-house advocates will claim their costs as part of the solicitors' bill. No additional claims can be made for FAS hearings of in-house advocates but they should be included in payments on account claims made during the life of the case. See chapter 16 for details on claiming payments on account.

FAS in high cost cases

20.53   In Family, cases where the costs are anticipated to, or actually do, exceed £25,000 (including all profit costs with enhancement, disbursements and any counsel's fees but excluding VAT) fall under the Special Case Work provisions of Part 6 of the Civil Legal Aid (Procedure) Regulations 2012 (see chapter 5 for more information on Special Case Work). They are referred to the LAA's Very High Cost Case (VHCC) Team. The VHCC family team (South Tyneside) deals with single counsel/advocate cases in private and public law family matters. The Exceptional and Complex Case Team (ECCT) family section (London) deals with QC/two-counsel cases in private and public law family matters, as well as all high cost child abduction cases.

---

42 This is considered to be a Her Majesty's Courts and Tribunals Service (HMCTS) form and so is available via HMCTS form finder rather than on the LAA web pages: http://hmctsformfinder.justice.gov.uk/HMCTS/GetForms.do?court_forms_num=EX506&court_forms_title=&court_forms_category=. And here https://www.gov.uk/government/publications/apply-for-bolt-on-payments-and-advocates-bundle-payments-form-ex506.

20.54   The team will refer to the rates that would have been paid under FAS (if applicable), and if the FAS is not applicable then they may make reference to the rates set out in table 1 of the guidance on VHCC Payments to Counsel in Family Cases,[43] or they will consider the fees paid under the VHCC Care Case Fee Scheme.

---

43 www.gov.uk/government/publications/family-high-cost-cases-forms-and-guidance.

Advocacy in criminal cases

by Anthony Edwards

Introduction

21.1 This chapter deals with the conduct of and payment for advocacy in criminal cases. See appendix D for a summary of the Legal Aid Agency's (LAA's) *Criminal Bills Assessment Manual*, in respect of the most common queries raised by caseworkers.

21.2 In criminal proceedings, advocacy can be conducted under:

- advocacy assistance;
- representation order.

Advocacy may arise at all stages of criminal proceedings, including the investigations stage, where advocacy may arise due to an application for a warrant of further detention or where a client wishes to apply to vary police bail conditions, or oppose a bail time-limit extension.

21.3 In general, we use the term 'advocate' to refer to anyone who has a right of audience to appear in the relevant court or whom the court is willing to hear where the scheme makes no distinction between solicitor and counsel. Where there is a difference according to whether advocacy is conducted by solicitor or by counsel, we will use the terms 'solicitor' and 'counsel' as appropriate.

21.4 Who is entitled to conduct advocacy, and the payment arrangements, will depend on the type of hearing and the stage of the case.

21.5 All qualified solicitors may represent a client at a hearing in the magistrates' court, as may counsel. However, whether or not counsel may be instructed will depend on the type of hearing and whether it is funded by advocacy assistance or a representation order.

21.6 In general, advocacy at Crown Court hearings and above may only be provided by counsel or a solicitor who has higher rights of audience.

Funding[1]

21.7 In general, advocacy in a criminal case is funded by a representation order, which will cover all of the hearings from the first appearance in the magistrates' court up to the final sentencing hearing. A representation order will also generally be required for advocacy in appeals.

21.8 The main stage at which advocacy is not covered by a representation order is the investigations stage. At this stage, funding is

---

1 For more detailed coverage, readers are referred to Edwards and Beaumont, *Criminal Costs: legal aid costs in the criminal courts*, LAG, 2nd edn, 2019.

provided by advocacy assistance. Advocacy assistance is also available to fund representation by the duty solicitor and representation at prison disciplinary and parole board hearings.

Advocacy assistance – investigations stage

Clients detained in custody

21.9 A client who is detained in police (or military) custody may require representation at court if there is an application to extend the custody time limit under Police and Criminal Evidence Act 1984 (PACE) s43 or s44, Terrorism Act 2000 Sch 8 para 29 or para 36, or the relevant military legislation.[2]

21.10 The funding for such hearings is subject to the 'sufficient benefit' test, however the test is automatically deemed satisfied by the circumstances.[3]

21.11 There is no means test[4] and the client is not required to sign any application form.[5] However, you are required to record on the file:

- the client's name and address;
- the unique file number (UFN);
- the date, time and venue of the court appearance; and
- details of the relevant unit of work (as defined by the contract) and how the work falls within the scope of that unit.[6]

These details should be recorded either before the advocacy assistance is provided or as soon as practicable after, if the advocacy is required at short notice.[7]

21.12 Reasonable preparation and follow-up work will be included within the scope of advocacy assistance, as will travel and waiting costs. However, there is an extendable costs limit of £1,368.75.[8]

21.13 There are no fixed fees for this type of work so, subject to the costs limit above, work will be claimed at the hourly rates set out in the Remuneration Regulations. These vary depending on whether the

---

2 Standard Crime Contract 2017 Specification paras 9.141–9.153 and 9.154–9.166.
3 Standard Crime Contract 2017 Specification paras 9.142 and 9.156.
4 Standard Crime Contract 2017 Specification paras 9.143 and 9.157.
5 Standard Crime Contract 2017 Specification paras 9.144 and 9.158.
6 Standard Crime Contract 2017 Specification paras 9.146 and 9.159.
7 Standard Crime Contract 2017 Specification paras 9.144 and 9.158.
8 Criminal Legal Aid (Remuneration) Regulations 2013 Sch 4 as amended.

hearing is before a magistrates' court or judicial authority, or before a High Court or senior judge. There are also different rates for own and duty solicitors, and for unsociable hours.

21.14   Counsel may only be instructed where the application is before the High Court or a senior judge.[9]

Police bail

21.15   A client who is not detained in custody may also require representation at court if there is an application to vary police bail conditions (including 'street bail' conditions),[10] or to oppose an application to extend a bail time limit.[11]

21.16   In this situation there are no qualifying criteria to be met and there is no means test.[12] As above, the client is not required to sign an application form but you must record the same required information on the file.[13]

21.17   Advocacy assistance in this situation includes reasonable preparation, travel, waiting and advocacy at the hearing, and the provision of advice on appeal.[14]

21.18   The same extendable costs limit applies, and the rules on claiming are the same. The applicable fees are set out in the Remuneration Regulations.

21.19   You cannot instruct counsel in this case,[15] and you may not claim under this unit of work if you are acting as duty solicitor.[16] However, you can claim under advocacy assistance if you represented the client as duty solicitor at the police station and you are subsequently instructed in the bail proceedings.

Advocacy assistance – court duty solicitor

21.20   Advocacy assistance is available to cover the representation of clients by the court duty solicitor at the magistrates' court. In practice, it will

---

9   Standard Crime Contract 2017 Specification paras 9.148 and 9.161.
10   Standard Crime Contract 2017 Specification paras 9.167–9.177.
11   Criminal Legal Aid (Standard Crime Contract) (Amendment) Regulations 2017 reg 3(5).
12   Standard Crime Contract 2017 Specification para 9.168.
13   Standard Crime Contract 2017 Specification para 9.170.
14   Standard Crime Contract 2017 Specification para 9.171.
15   Standard Crime Contract 2017 Specification para 9.172.
16   Standard Crime Contract 2017 Specification para 9.167.

be claimed together with advice and assistance, which covers the provision of advice to such clients outside court. The two forms of assistance will be claimed together in a single claim at the end of the duty day.[17]

21.21   Advocacy assistance under this unit of work may only be provided by a qualified duty solicitor (ie one who has previously been a member of a scheme under a previous contract or is a current member of the Law Society's Criminal Litigation Accreditation Scheme and undertaken the police station qualification[18]).

21.22   To qualify for advocacy assistance under this scheme, the client's case must come within the scope of the scheme:

- The duty solicitor must:[19]
  - advise any client who requests it who is in custody;
  - make a bail application where a client in custody requires a bail application and such an application has not previously been made by a duty solicitor;
  - advise a client before the court in connection with 'prescribed proceedings' that is civil orders deemed to be criminal for legal aid purposes (the full list appears at para 15.71)[20] such as:
    - football banning orders;[21]
    - closure orders;[22]
    - sexual offences notification orders;[23]
    - sexual risk orders;[24]
    - restraining orders under section 5A of the Protection from Harassment Act 1997 in relation to a restraining order on acquittal;
    - domestic violence protection orders;[25]
    - knife crime prevention orders;[26]

---

17 Standard Crime Contract 2017 Specification para 10.18.
18 Standard Crime Contract 2017 Standard Terms para 1.1.
19 Standard Crime Contract 2017 Specification para 10.7. Note that the provision makes distinctions between advice, and representation.
20 Criminal Legal Aid (General) Regulations 2013 reg 9.
21 Football Spectators Act 1989 ss14B, 14D, 14G, 14H, 21B and 21D.
22 Anti-social Behaviour, Crime and Policing Act 2014 ss80, 82, 83 and 84 where a person has engaged or is likely to engage in behaviour that constitutes a criminal offence on the premises.
23 Sexual Offences Act 2003 ss97, 100 and 101.
24 Sexual Offences Act 2003 ss122A, 122D, 122E and 122G.
25 Crime and Security Act 2010 ss24–33.
26 Part 2 of the Offensive Weapons Act 2019.

- proceedings in any youth court in relation to the breach of a provision in an injunction under Part 1 of the Anti-social Behaviour, Crime and Policing Act 2014 where the person subject to the injunction is under 14;
- a duty solicitor must also cross-examine under Youth Justice and Criminal Evidence Act 1999 s38 if appointed by the court. Payment will in this case be from central funds.[27]
- The duty solicitor must also, but subject to the exceptions below:[28]
  - advise and represent any client who is in custody on a plea of guilty and wishes the case to be concluded that day;
  - advise and represent any client before the court for failure to pay a fine or other sum or to obey an order of the court, and such failure may lead to the client being at risk of imprisonment;
  - advise and represent a client not in custody in connection with an imprisonable offence;
  - help a client in making an application for a representation order, whether the nominated solicitor is the duty solicitor or another solicitor;
  - advise and represent a client seeking to vary police-imposed bail conditions pre-charge.
- The exceptions are that a duty solicitor must *not*:
  - represent in committal proceedings;[29]
  - represent at a not guilty trial or in relation to a non-imprisonable offence unless with the provisions above;[30]
  - advise or represent a client who has had the services of a duty solicitor at a previous hearing in the proceedings (except where they are before the court this time as a result of failure to pay a fine or other sum or comply with an order imposed previously).[31]

---

27 Standard Crime Contract 2017 Specification para 10.15. The Law Society has issued guidance on when exceptional circumstances may apply so that the appointment should be declined – see 'Rejecting un-remunerative publicly funded criminal work' para 2.4.
28 Standard Crime Contract 2017 Specification para 10.8.
29 Note that, although committal proceedings have been abolished, the Standard Crime Contract 2017 Specification has not been amended at the time of writing.
30 Standard Crime Contract 2017 Specification para 10.9.
31 Standard Crime Contract 2017 Specification para 10.10.

21.23   The sufficient benefit test applies to representation by the duty solicitor (both under advocacy assistance and advice and assistance),[32] but there is no means test and clients are not required to complete an application form.[33] However, you are required to record on the file:

- the client's name and address;
- details of the relevant unit of work;
- whether the client is in custody or charged with an imprisonable offence; and
- the date, time and venue of the court appearance.[34]

These details should be recorded either before the advocacy assistance is provided or as soon as practicable after, if the advocacy is required at short notice.[35]

21.24   The scope of the scheme is limited in terms of the work covered. In addition to the advocacy, you may only claim for reasonable advice and preparation provided during the duty session. This can include advice on the consequences of the outcome and the giving of any notice of appeal or making an application for a case to be stated.[36]

21.25   Claiming for duty solicitor advocacy is done as part of a single claim submitted for the duty session. Hourly rates are set out in the Remuneration Regulations and there is a standard hourly rate for both attendance and waiting. An enhanced rate applies to sessions on non-business days.

21.26   Under the duty solicitor scheme, you cannot claim for travel time other than on a non-business day, unless you are called out having not been on the rota or having been released but then asked to return.

Advocacy assistance – virtual courts

21.27   Special arrangements are made for appearances at virtual courts.[37]

---

32 Standard Crime Contract 2017 Specification para 10.2.
33 Standard Crime Contract 2017 Specification para 10.4.
34 Standard Crime Contract 2017 Specification para 10.6.
35 Standard Crime Contract 2017 Specification para 10.4.
36 Standard Crime Contract 2017 Specification para 10.17.
37 Standard Crime Contract 2017 Specification paras 10.21–10.35. See also para 15.93; and Edwards and Beaumont *Criminal Costs : legal aid costs in the criminal courts*, LAG, 2nd edn, 2019.

Advocacy under a representation order

21.28   All representation orders granted for criminal cases in the magistrates' court and the Crown Court will include the provision of advocacy services. This will include representation at all hearings in the case including bail proceedings in the Crown Court.

21.29   Representation orders in both the magistrates' court and the Crown Court are granted subject to a means test. There is a merits test unless the case is tried in the Crown Court on indictment. For a full discussion of these tests see chapter 15.

21.30   Advocacy under a representation order may be carried out either by a solicitor or by counsel, subject to the requirement for higher rights for advocacy in the Crown Court and above.

Magistrates' court

21.31   A representation order for a magistrates' court case will generally only cover advocacy provided by a solicitor.[38] Payment for advocacy services provided by a solicitor will be claimed within the magistrates' court standard fee regime.

21.32   Advocacy is claimed at the hourly rate prescribed in the Remuneration Regulations, in the same way as all other types of work provided under the representation order.

21.33   Travelling and waiting time can only be claimed if neither the court nor your office is in a 'designated area'. The designated areas[39] are:

- Greater Manchester, London, West Midlands and Merseyside Criminal Justice Areas; and
- the local authority areas of:
  - Brighton and Hove;
  - Bristol;
  - Cardiff;
  - Derby and Erewash;
  - Kingston upon Hull;
  - Leeds and Bradford;
  - Leicester;
  - Nottingham;
  - Portsmouth;

---

38 See Criminal Legal Aid (Determinations by a Court and Choice of Representative) Regulations 2013 reg 16.

39 Standard Crime Contract 2017 Specification para 1.2.

- Newcastle-upon-Tyne and Sunderland (including Gateshead, North and South Tyneside);
- Sheffield;
- Southampton.

Note that you are still required to record the waiting time (but not travel), even if you cannot claim for it.[40]

21.34 The total core costs will then be compared against fee limits for the particular category of case and this will determine whether the standard fee or a non-standard fee is payable.

21.35 For details of the fee structure under representation orders in the magistrates' court, see chapter 17.

Counsel in the magistrates' court

21.36 Although the representation order will usually only provide for advocacy by a solicitor,[41] this does not mean that counsel cannot be instructed in the magistrates' court. It simply means that counsel is usually unassigned and cannot claim their costs from the court or the LAA. Therefore, solicitors are responsible for agreeing a fee with counsel and paying that fee promptly out of their costs. If they fail to pay within 30 days, counsel can apply to the LAA for payment and that payment will be deducted from their monthly payment.[42]

21.37 Unassigned counsel are treated like solicitor agents. From the point of view of the LAA, their work is treated as solicitors work. Their time should be recorded on the bill as if a solicitor had done the work, and counts towards the calculation of the appropriate fee.[43] As for solicitors, counsel's travel and waiting time can only be claimed for cases in 'undesignated areas'.[44]

21.38 You must provide counsel with the UFN and a copy of the representation order when briefing them.[45]

Assigned counsel

21.39 In more serious cases, you can apply to the court for counsel (or an independent solicitor advocate) to be assigned.

---

40 Standard Crime Contract 2017 Specification para 10.87.
41 See Criminal Legal Aid (Determinations by a Court and Choice of Representative) Regulations 2013 reg 16.
42 Standard Crime Contract 2017 Specification paras 10.50, 10.54 and 10.55.
43 Standard Crime Contract 2017 Specification para 10.48.
44 Standard Crime Contract 2017 Specification para 10.83.
45 Standard Crime Contract 2017 Specification para 10.43.

21.40   The regulations say that counsel may be assigned in any case where the charge is an indictable offence (that is, an offence capable of being tried on indictment, including either way offences, not just indictable only offences) or where the case is an extradition matter.[46]

21.41   Indictable only cases involving adults will be sent directly to the Crown Court, so in practice counsel can be assigned in adult either way cases, youth cases where the charge, whether either way or indictable, has not been sent, and extraditions.

21.42   In order to have counsel assigned, you must persuade the court that, because of circumstances which make the case unusually grave or difficult, representation by solicitor and advocate would be desirable.

21.43   In extradition proceedings, you can apply for more than one advocate, or for a QC, to be assigned where you can persuade the court that the defendant cannot be adequately represented except by QC or more than one advocate.[47]

21.44   Where counsel is assigned, they are entitled to be paid directly by the LAA at the rates prescribed in the Remuneration Regulations, though you should submit their bill with your own – see para 17.55.

Crown Court

21.45   Advocacy in the Crown Court must generally be conducted by counsel or a solicitor with higher rights of audience. You must consult the client about the choice of advocate and the alternatives available[48] and keep a record of the discussion.[49]

21.46   Crown Court representation orders automatically allow the instruction of a single junior advocate. Even if counsel was not assigned under the order in the magistrates' court, once the case goes to the Crown Court the order is deemed to include representation by one junior advocate (that is, any advocate other than a QC).[50]

21.47   In more serious and complex cases, an application may be made to the court to amend the order to allow for the instruction of QC or more than one advocate. The court can order representation by:

---

46   Criminal Legal Aid (Determinations by a Court and Choice of Representative) Regulations 2013 reg 16.

47   Criminal Legal Aid (Determinations by a Court and Choice of Representative) Regulations 2013 regs 16 and 17.

48   Standard Crime Contract 2017 Standard Terms para 7.3.

49   Standard Crime Contract 2017 Standard Terms para 7.5.

50   Criminal Legal Aid (Determinations by a Court and Choice of Representative) Regulations 2013 reg 18.

- QC alone;
- two advocates:
  - QC with junior;
  - QC with noting junior;
  - two juniors;
  - junior and noting junior; or
- where three advocates are justified, any of the above plus an additional junior or noting junior.[51]

21.48 In order to persuade the court to make an order for senior or more than one advocate, you must demonstrate that the relevant test is met:

- For QC alone:[52]
  - the case involves substantial novel or complex issues of law or fact which could not be adequately presented except by a QC; and
  - either:
    - the prosecution has instructed QC or senior Treasury counsel; or
    - the case for the defence is exceptional compared with the generality of cases involving similar offences.
- For two junior advocates:[53]
  - the case involves substantial novel or complex issues of law or fact which could not be adequately presented by a single advocate; and
  - either:
    - the prosecution have instructed two or more advocates;
    - the case for the defence is exceptional compared with the generality of cases involving similar offences;
    - the number of prosecution witnesses exceeds 80; or
    - the number of pages of prosecution evidence exceeds 1,000.
- For QC plus junior or noting junior:[54]

---

51 Criminal Legal Aid (Determinations by a Court and Choice of Representative) Regulations 2013 reg 18.
52 Criminal Legal Aid (Determinations by a Court and Choice of Representative) Regulations 2013 reg 18(2).
53 Criminal Legal Aid (Determinations by a Court and Choice of Representative) Regulations 2013 reg 18(3).
54 Criminal Legal Aid (Determinations by a Court and Choice of Representative) Regulations 2013 reg 18(4).

- the case involves substantial novel or complex issues of law or fact which could not be adequately presented except by a QC assisted by a junior advocate; and
- either:
  - the prosecution has instructed QC or senior Treasury counsel and two or more advocates have been instructed by the prosecution; the number of prosecution witnesses exceeds 80; the number of pages of prosecution evidence exceeds 1,000; or
  - the case for the defence is exceptional compared with the generality of cases involving similar offences.
- For three advocates:[55]
  - the case is being prosecuted by the Serious Fraud Office;
  - the court considers three advocates are required; and
  - the conditions for two juniors or QC plus junior are satisfied (as appropriate).

Only defined judges may make the relevant decisions.[56]

21.49   The payment of advocates' fees in the Crown Court is governed by the Advocates Graduated Fee Scheme. The rules and fees applicable to the Advocates Graduated Fee Scheme are set out in Sch 1 to the Criminal Legal Aid (Remuneration) Regulations 2013, as amended, most recently, by the Criminal Legal Aid (Remuneration) (Amendment) (No 2) Regulations 2018 for cases where the representation order is dated on or after 31 December 2018. Further regulations, to increase the fees, are expected during 2020. This scheme applies to all advocates in the Crown Court, whether they are counsel or solicitor advocates.

21.50   Each case will have a trial advocate, who is the advocate responsible for claiming fees on behalf of all advocates instructed in the case.

21.51   The scheme provides for a basic fee based on the classification of the offence to which is added an uplift for length of trial. Additional fees are paid for identified hearings and work. There is a higher basic fee for a trial and some cracked trials and a lower fee for a guilty plea case.

21.52   The full details are set out in Sch 1 to the Remuneration Regulations as amended.

---

55 Criminal Legal Aid (Determinations by a Court and Choice of Representative) Regulations 2013 reg 18(5) and (6).

56 Criminal Legal Aid (Determinations by a Court and Choice of Representative) Regulations 2013 reg 19.

Appeals

21.53 Advice on appeals can, in some circumstances, be provided under the advice and assistance scheme. Advocacy in appeal proceedings can be provided either as advocacy assistance in prescribed proceedings or under a representation order.

21.54 Representation in the crown court in prescribed proceedings[57] is provided for by the Standard Crime Contract 2017[58] and is claimed as part of the normal monthly submission. A representation order must be obtained and there is an extendable fee limit of £1,368.75.[59] Counsel may not be assigned and if instructed a fee must be agreed; the underlying rate must not exceed that payable under the Regulations.[60] The litigator may be paid for preparing counsel's instructions but not for attending them at court.[61]

21.55 Representation in criminal appeal proceedings will require a representation order to be granted for the court in which the appeal is to be heard, be that the Crown Court, (granted by the LAA) High Court (for appeals by way of case stated) or the Court of Appeal. (which both grant their own orders) It is usual for representation orders granted by the Court of Appeal to be granted to an advocate alone.[62]

Advocacy assistance – prison law

21.56 Advocacy in prison law cases may be provided under the advocacy assistance scheme. Representation may be provided in disciplinary cases and in parole board cases, but see chapter 15 for scope.

21.57 You may only represent a client at hearings in these matters if the sufficient benefit test is satisfied, and the contract notes specifically that the LAA would not expect to fund a matter which did not raise a significant legal or human rights issue.[63] In addition, advocacy assistance must not be provided in disciplinary cases where:

57 Defined by regulation 9 of the Criminal Legal Aid (General) Regulations 2013 as amended.
58 Standard Crime Contract 2017 Specification paras 10.131–10.142.
59 Criminal Legal Aid (Remuneration) Regulations 2013 Sch 4 para 10.
60 Standard Crime Contract 2017 Specification para 10.134.
61 Standard Crime Contract 2017 Specification para 10.137.
62 Criminal Legal Aid (Determinations by a Court and Choice of Representative) Regulations 2013 reg 8.
63 Standard Crime Contract 2017 Specification para 12.10.

- it appears unreasonable to grant in the particular circumstances of the case; or
- (where required) permission to be legally represented has not been granted.[64]

In all cases, you should record on the file how the merits test has been and continues to be met.[65]

21.58   In addition, there is a financial eligibility test for both advice and assistance and advocacy assistance in prison law cases. The client must complete the relevant forms (CRM1 and CRM2 or CRM3), and must pass the means test. Means are limited by both capital and disposable income, and the eligibility levels can be found on the Legal Aid website at: www.gov.uk/criminal-legal-aid-means-testing. The completed application forms must be retained on your file.[66]

21.59   Advocacy under this scheme is paid under a system of standard fees.[67] There are two standard fees for each type of case, and two corresponding standard fee limits. If your costs do not exceed either limit, you will be paid the respective standard fee. If your costs fall above the higher limit, you will be paid a non-standard fee for which your costs will be assessed by the LAA. See the Remuneration Regulations for details of the fees and limits.

21.60   Under this form of advocacy assistance, advocacy may be provided by either a solicitor or counsel. However, counsel is effectively 'unassigned' in that they are not able to claim payment directly from the LAA. Counsel's fees must be agreed and paid by the instructing solicitor from the standard fee.[68]

---

64 Standard Crime Contract 2017 Specification para 12.84.
65 Standard Crime Contract 2017 Specification para 12.6.
66 Standard Crime Contract 2017 Specification para 12.15.
67 Standard Crime Contract 2017 Specification para 12.65.
68 Standard Crime Contract 2017 Specification paras 12.45 and 12.48.

Managing legal aid work

CHAPTER 22

Legal aid contracts

Introduction

22.1   This chapter explains the contract documentation, standard terms and obligations imposed by the Standard Contracts and the Civil and Crime Specifications. It also covers how to get additional work under an existing contract, and how to get a new contract with the Legal Aid Agency (LAA).

22.2   It also refers to some of the other contracts offered by the LAA, such as those for telephone triage and advice (Civil Legal Advice (CLA) contracts).

22.3   It is extremely important to become familiar with what your contract allows you to do and prohibits you from doing, since if you overlook something, you could find yourself served with a contract notice. Clause 24 of the Standard Contract allows for termination in relation to 'persistent breaches' – that is, three breaches of the same term in a 24-month period (or six different breaches) – so it is very important to be aware of what you must and must not do.

Civil Standard Contract

22.4   The Standard Civil Contract 2018 replaced six different contracts (issued between 2010 and 2016) from 1 September 2018.

Crime Standard Contract

22.5   The Standard Crime Contract 2017 applied from 1 April 2017.

Elements of the contracts

Overview

22.6   The contracts are divided into the following sections:
- Contract for Signature, Key Information, Tables and Annexes;
- Office Schedule;
- Standard Terms;
- Specification, split into:
  - in the Civil Contract – general rules and category-specific rules;

- in the Crime Contract – sections 1–8 apply to all Classes of Work; sections 9–13 set out the specific rules which apply to each Unit of Work.

All of the above documents form part of the contract, and you are bound by each and every part of them.

Contract for Signature

22.7 As the name suggests, this is the part of the contract that is signed by the organisation and counter-signed by the LAA.

22.8 The contract covers the whole organisation (although it specifies the work that can be done at each office through an Office Schedule). This means that a breach at any office can jeopardise the whole contract. It is only possible for the provider to serve notice on the LAA for the whole contract. However, if a provider wishes to withdraw from an office or category of law, that can be done with the LAA's agreement. The contract for signature also includes any conditions that the LAA has imposed, the office schedules which have been issued, the applicable Quality Standard you must hold (the SQM (Specialist Quality Mark) or Lexcel), and contact details which the LAA will use to deal with you.

22.9 The Crime Contract sets out the types of criminal defence work the organisation is allowed to do, for example, criminal investigations and criminal proceedings, appeals and reviews, prison law. Holders of all types of contract are also authorised to undertake associated civil work.

Office Schedule

22.10 In civil and family, the Office Schedule sets out the details of the work you are allowed to do, including the number of matter starts in each category of work and the monthly controlled work payment.

22.11 The schedule will set out the number of new matter starts allowed, by category.

22.12 Civil Schedules contain the following tables:

- Table 1 gives the start and end dates.
- Table 2 gives the numbers of matter starts you are allowed by category and categories in which you may do licensed work and have delegated functions.

- Table 3 sets out the maximum amount of money the LAA will pay you for Controlled Work[1] while the schedule is in force and the amount of your monthly payment. Sometimes this is shown as £0.00 but for ease of LAA administration only.
- Table 4 sets out exactly what type of service and where you must provide services, and the type of office presence you are required to have, by procurement area.
- Table 5 shows if you have been authorised to carry out work under alternative arrangements in mental health work.
- Table 6 shows any outreaches which have been authorised.
- Table 7 shows any special provisions or restrictions.
- Tables 8 and 9 show Rota weeks under the detained duty scheme and slots under the fast track scheme, respectively.

22.13   The Crime Schedule lists your authorised Duty Schemes. Numbers of cases are not specified and depend on the interests of justice test being met, as defined in the contract (see chapter 15 for more information about conducting criminal cases).

22.14   If you do work outside that authorised under your schedule, you will not be paid for it.

Supplementary matter starts

22.15   Under the 2018 contract, you can self-grant up to an additional 50 per cent of matter starts per year – but you must notify your Contract Manager first.[2] You can apply for further matter starts to the LAA if you need to. You will need to satisfy the LAA that:[3]

a) you are unable to meet an urgent demand from clients for your services from your current matter start allocation; or

b) an urgent need for services arises as a result of another provider in your procurement area ceasing to provide or reducing the provision of such services for any reason; or

c) there is a general increase in demand for services of that type within your procurement area.

If you are granted additional matter starts, the additional matter starts will be reflected in your allocation in the next schedule.[4]

---

1   Standard Civil Contract Specification 2018 para 1.5 Interpretation.
2   Standard Civil Contract 2018 Specification paras 1.21 and 1.22.
3   Standard Civil Contract 2018 Specification para 1.23.
4   Standard Civil Contract 2018 Specification para 1.24.

Standard Terms 2018

22.16 The Standard Terms apply to family, immigration and asylum and housing and debt. Key clauses are summarised below. Changes new to the 2018 contract are shown <u>by underlining</u>:

- **Clause 1: Interpretation.** This clause contains the definitions of expressions which have particular meanings under the contract. These are denoted by the use of capital letters. There are further definitions in the Specification.
  - <u>Good Industry Practice</u>: This is a newly defined term. It is the same as the 2017 Crime contract:

    . . . means that degree of skill, care, diligence, prudence, timeliness, efficiency and foresight which could reasonably and ordinarily be expected from a skilled, experienced and professionally managed provider of legal services similar to those required to be provided under this Contract;

  - <u>Qualifying event</u>: This is new but is a clarification of previous powers to require you to provide the LAA with information about significant changes about your organisation so that they can make decisions about whether the changes impact on whether a contract should continue/be novated. See Clause 2. '"Qualifying Event" means those matters specified in this Contract as being a Qualifying Event'.
- **Clause 2:** You must appoint a Contract Liaison Manager and notify the LAA within five business days if the person is changed. You must monitor the email address which you have given to the LAA 'frequently each business day' and communicate with the LAA electronically where stipulated.
  - <u>Suitability to hold a contract</u> – <u>New provisions</u> so that if any of your answers in a tender document change in relation to suitability question, you must notify them and the LAA can review whether you are still suitable to hold a contract. This ties in with Qualifying Events.
  - The LAA has included a controversial '<u>embarrassment clause</u>' but it has been re-worded following representations by the representative bodies. All the text after and including 'For the avoidance of doubt . . .' has been added to the original draft:

    2.2 You shall ensure that neither you nor any of your Affiliates brings the legal aid scheme into disrepute by engaging in any unprofessional or unlawful conduct which is likely to substantially diminish the trust the public places in the legal aid scheme, regardless of whether or not such conduct is related to your obligations under this Contract. Any operation of this Clause is subject to our obligation to act as a responsible public body and any sanction must be proportionate. <u>For the avoidance of doubt, the engaging by you or any of your Affiliates in any lawful challenge to or criticism or complaint of us or any of our decisions, when acting in clients' best interests or otherwise acting in your professional capacity, is not within the scope of the words "unprofessional or unlawful conduct" under this Clause 2.2.</u>

– <u>Responsibility for personnel</u>: Clarifies that you are responsible for the acts and omissions of all personnel, whether employees or consultants:

2.16 You shall be responsible for the acts and omissions of all personnel who you engage or employ in relation to the fulfilment of your obligations under this Contract.

- **Clause 3:** You cannot subcontract, novate or otherwise delegate any of your obligations under the contract without the LAA's prior written consent. However, you can appoint agents to work for you as long as their work is properly supervised.
  – If an approved third party, agent, counsel or a subcontractor ceases providing services to you, you are responsible for ensuring that you continue to fulfil the obligations under the contract.
  – <u>Payment within 30 days</u>: This requirement has been introduced due to Public Contracts Regulations 2015 reg 113:
    (b) any person pursuant to this Clause 3 you are responsible for ensuring that:
    (i) all payments are made to them for their work within 30 days from receipt of a valid invoice;
  – Clause 3.7 states that if the fees payable by you exceed £250 per matter or case, you must require agents, counsel or subcontractors in connection with contract work, to keep accurate records of the time they spend on the work you have appointed them to do and of the work done. They must also permit the LAA to audit the records.
- **Clause 4:** Accounts must be audited or examined as required by law or professional regulation. You must notify the LAA within 14 days if your accounts are qualified.
  – <u>Clause 4.6 Notify the LAA of changes to directors/members so that they can require indemnities</u> from new ones during the life of the contract. Previously the LAA only asked for indemnities as part of a tender. This is the same as the 2017 Crime Contract.
- **Clause 5:** You must comply with the equality and diversity requirements, and you must have an Equality and Diversity Training Plan.

- **Clause 6:** Restrictions on marketing your services. It is clear that you can neither pay nor receive referral fees nor any other benefit, to any third party for the referral or introduction (directly or indirectly) of any client or potential client.
- **Clause 7:** You must monitor your performance and compliance with the contract and take corrective action if there are problems.
  - Clarification that failure to look after clients (and potential clients) best interests is a fundamental breach of contract.
  - <u>Consulting clients and providing information about the use of in-house counsel</u>: this is very similar to the 2017 Crime Contract:

7.3 Where you instruct Counsel or in-house advocate holding higher rights of audience to conduct advocacy services, before giving such instructions you must consult the Client about the use and the selection of Counsel or in-house advocate and advise the Client of:

(a) the name;
(b) status;
(c) experience; and
(d) suitability,

of this Counsel or in-house advocate to conduct advocacy in each such case having regard to the nature of that case and its complexity and the existence of alternative Counsel or in-house advocate whom the Client may choose to be instructed (subject to availability). In circumstances where you have determined through your reasonable enquiries that there is no alternative Counsel or in-house advocate actually available, you must also advise the Client of that fact.

7.4 Where Counsel or in-house advocate is instructed pursuant to Clause 7.3; if the chosen Counsel or in-house advocate becomes unavailable you must take all reasonable steps to instruct another Counsel or in-house advocate of equivalent standing and, so far as is practicable, advise the Client of the merits and suitability of the proposed replacement.

7.5 You must keep a Record (in accordance with the provisions of Clauses 8.3 and 8.4) to demonstrate your compliance with Clause 7.3.

  - <u>Clause 7.6</u>: There is an obligation to notify a client that they should take independent advice if you become aware of a potentially justified claim against you by a client. A record must be kept on file.
  - You must have access to the LAA online manual: www.gov. uk/guidance/civil-legal-aid-civil-regulations-civil-contracts-and-guidance.

- – IT systems: You must be able to use government secure email, use video conferencing etc.
- **Clause 8:** Requires you to record all the information required by the contract. You are required to keep closed client files (or copies of them) for six years. If you keep electronic files they must contain all the information that they would have if paper files. Documents must be in PDF format.
  - – Use of in-house Counsel: New requirement as 7.5 above.
- **Clause 9:** Concerns access to your premises and information you must provide. Note that you must inform the LAA of the outcome of third party audits and provide them with a copy of the report within seven days of receipt. This clause would apply, for example to Recognising Excellence carrying out an SQM audit.
  - – Time limit to provide information: If the LAA asks for records you have to provide them within 10 business days.
  - – Access to third party premises and records: You have to require sub-contractors to allow the LAA access to their systems (see para 9.4).
  - – You must provide the LAA with access and facilities during any audit by them. Breach would be considered to be a fundamental breach justifying contract termination.
  - – The LAA can carry out mystery shopping exercises and client satisfaction surveys of your clients. They can also obtain reports in connection with any professional misconduct.
- **Clause 10:** Sets out standards of work you must meet, including Peer Review. All work must be performed with reasonable care and skill. You must achieve at least Threshold Competence (3) at Peer Review in order to hold a contract. If you fail a peer review, the LAA may re-charge the cost to you.
  - – You must authorise the LAA to carry out status enquiries in relation to your personnel, if required.
- **Clause 11:** Requires you to meet key performance indicators (KPIs). If you fail to do so, the LAA will first meet with you to agree an action plan to improve performance. The LAA says they may use KPI performance as entry or selection criteria for future contracts (para 11.6) but they have not done so to date due to the difficulty in treating previous contractors and new applicants fairly in the tender process.
- **Clause 12:** Relates to contract documents and precedence.
- **Clause 13:** The LAA may amend the contract to take account of legislation or the justice system. Minor or technical amendments may be made to individual organisations' contracts. If the LAA

wants to make material changes, it has to terminate the contract and issue a new one.

- The clause lists the changes you can request, eg closure or relocation of an office/outreach, temporary or permanent reduction or cessation of contract work; a change to your Quality Standard; the temporary or permanent reduction or cessation of the provision of Duty Solicitor services; or a change in membership of any Consortium. It gives examples of circumstances where the LAA would be justified in refusing your request.

- **Clause 14:** This clause creates a single account for all work done by the organisation which is treated globally. Claims made by you are treated as credits to your account, and any payments made by the LAA as debits. You may be required to reimburse the LAA's reasonable audit costs if you have mis-claimed costs under the Contract.

  - <u>Payment within 30 days of determination of a valid and undisputed claim</u>. This requirement has been introduced due to Regulation 113 of the Public Contracts Regulations (2015). It does not prevent the LAA from subsequently recouping a payment on assessment.
  - <u>You have to notify the LAA</u> within five days if tax non-compliance takes place.

- **Clause 15:** Sets out confidentiality arrangements. Clarification of Freedom of Information Act 2000 (FOIA) disclosure by the LAA. Provisions allowing the LAA to share information on contract performance with other government departments (which must keep it confidential). See para 15.10.

- **Clause 16:** Data protection requirements. <u>The LAA requires you to comply with applicable legislation, particularly The General Data Protection Regulation (Regulation (EU) 2016/679) and the Law Enforcement Directive (Directive EU) 2016/680, being implemented under Part 3 of the Data Protection bill</u>.

  - They require you to notify them within five business days if you receive a request for the following, within LAA or shared data:
    - a data subject request;
    - a request to rectify, block or erase personal data;
    - a complaint or other communication about your or the LAA's handling of data;
    - a communication from the Information Commissioner.
  - You must also indemnify the LAA if it is fined because you fail to comply with the General Data Protection Regulation (GDPR).

- **Clause 17:** FOIA obligations. The LAA may release information about your organisation either following consultation with you, or not, in certain circumstances.
- **Clause 18:** Warranties that the information provided by you and the LAA is true and accurate. Breach of warranties in 18.1 shall be a fundamental breach. This is the same as the 2017 Crime contract.
- **Clause 19:** Indemnity and giving notices.
- **Clause 20:** Giving notices under the contract.
- **Clause 21:** You must notify the LAA as soon as reasonably practicable of any anticipated material constitutional change (within 14 days as a minimum) and any other change that might impact on your ability to do contract work.
  - Clarification of previous powers to require you to provide the LAA with information about significant changes about your organisation so that they can make decisions about whether the changes impact on whether a contract should continue.
  - New clause 21.18 stating that failing to inform them of the matters listed in clause 21 shall be a fundamental breach. It is the same as the 2017 Crime contract.
- **Clause 22: Novations.** The LAA may novate the contract if a practice merges with another. Clarification of previous powers in relation to novations and when a novation will be refused. There is a policy paper on the legal aid website which provides more information (still referring to the 2010 and 2013 contracts at the time of writing): www.gov.uk/government/publications/novation- policy.
- **Clause 23:** Deals with bribery, collusion, false tenders, fraud and unethical behaviour.
- **Clause 24:** Contract sanctions may include; refusal to pay for specified contract work, suspension of payments, or taking on any new matters or cases, exclusion of individuals from being supervisors or performing contract work, suspending or removing your rota allocation (if any) of from holding yourself out as a provider, and termination. If you breach the contract, the LAA may serve a contract notice under clause 24.2, requiring you not to repeat the breach. If you do so, you risk contract termination.
- **Clause 25:** You may terminate the contract at any time on three months' notice (subject to clause 13, which gives you rights to propose amendments). The LAA can terminate the contract at any time on six months' notice.
  - New clause 25.7 allows the LAA to terminate for breach of the Public Contracts Regulations 2015.

- **Clause 26:** Unless the LAA terminates the contract due to your breach, they will authorise you to continue work on existing cases (usually for up to two years).
- **Clause 27:** Reconsidering decisions and reviews of decisions. There is an informal procedure and a formal procedure. Formal reviews may be carried out by the LAA's Chief Executive or the Contract Review Body.
- **Clause 28:** Dispute resolution provisions.
- **Clause 29:** Governing law and jurisdiction.
- **Clause 30:** General provisions.

Crime Standard Terms 2017

22.17 The numbering and subject matter of clauses are the same in the Crime Contract as in the Civil 2018 contract. The only difference is as follows:

- **Clause 7:** The requirements in relation to consulting the client before instructing an advocate apply to Crown Court cases (whether in-house or external Counsel) and advising the client of their name; status; experience; and suitability. Where an advocate becomes unavailable, there is a duty to repeat the above and take all reasonable steps to secure an equivalent advocate. A record of the above must be kept on file. This was regarded as controversial, as it could disadvantage in-house solicitor advocates compared to independent Counsel.

Civil and Crime Specifications

22.18 These contain the detailed rules that apply to the way in which cases are carried out on a day-to-day basis. We cover them in the relevant chapters – see:

- Taking on civil and family cases (chapter 3);
- Conducting a civil/family case (chapter 5);
- Conducting a private family law case (chapter 7);
- Conducting a public family law case (chapter 8);
- Conducting an immigration case (chapter 10);
- Conducting a mental health case (chapter 11);
- Conducting a housing case (chapter 12);
- Conducting a community care case (chapter 13);
- Conducting a public law case (chapter 14);
- Conducting a criminal case (chapter 15); and
- Quality standards and performance monitoring (chapter 23).

22.19   The supervisor standards are in the relevant legal category specifications, but we cover them together in chapter 22, Quality Standards
and performance monitoring.

22.20   Note that prior to 2013, civil payment rates were set out in an
annex to the Contract Specification. This was removed, and payment
rates are only to be found in the Civil (or Criminal) Legal Aid
(Remuneration) Regulations 2013 as amended.

Applying for civil or family contracts

22.21   In civil and family, the LAA allocates funds to geographical areas
using a formula which attempts to estimate the number of potential
legal aid clients who might experience legal problems and remain
within scope. This is called 'indicative spend'.

22.22   The LAA uses the formula as a starting point when considering
where to direct available funding – though only in terms of Legal
Help matter starts made available.

22.23   You should note that although bidding opportunities are expressed
in terms of the numbers of matter starts available, where you provide
services under a schedule, it will also authorise you to undertake an
unlimited number of certificated cases (licensed work).

22.24   If you are an existing provider wanting to add a category, open a
new office, or add a substantial number of new matter starts to your
existing allocation, or if you are an organisation wishing to contract
with the LAA for the first time, you should contact the LAA regional
office that covers your area and make enquiries of the regional
contracts manager. He or she may be able to tell you whether the
LAA plans to issue any tenders in your area. Tender opportunities
are advertised on the LAA's current tenders page: www.gov.uk/
government/organisations/legal-aid-agency/about/procurement.

22.25   We know that the LAA refines its tender process with every round
of tenders it conducts, so it unlikely that the process will be the same
in future; but it is worth considering the requirements of past
tenders, as they give some indication of the LAA's preferences (see
paras 22.27–22.30).

How long contracts last

22.26   In general, LAA contracts last for three years with a power for the
LAA to extend for up to a further two years. It is unusual for the LAA
to tender for face-to-face contracts in between the major tender exer-

cises. The LAA generally exercises its option to extend contracts, so if you miss a tender opportunity, you may have to wait a long time for another.

- The **Standard Crime Contract 2017** started on 1 April 2017 and covers criminal investigations, proceedings, appeal/reviews, associated work, and prison law. It was expected to expire on 31 March 2020; but in July 2019 the LAA announced that it would be extended to 2021.
- The **Standard Civil Contract 2018** started on 1 September 2018 and covers family law; family mediation; housing, debt and welfare benefits; immigration and asylum; mental health; community care; claims against public authorities (previously known as actions against the police etc), clinical negligence and public law. It is expected to expire on 31 August 2021. It can be extended for up to two years.
- In February 2019, the Ministry of Justice published its post-implementation review of the Legal Aid, Sentencing and Punishment of Offenders Act 2012 (LASPO). It decided to remove the mandatory telephone gateway which had restricted access to advice and representation in the Discrimination and Education categories by spring 2020. Face-to-face contracts in these categories were tendered in the summer of 2019 and will also last until 31 August 2021, subject to the LAA's right to extend.

Tenders

22.27 The LAA uses an online tendering process through on online portal – https://legalaid.bravosolution.co.uk/web/login.shtml – hosted by a commercial company, Bravo Solution.

22.28 Bidders usually have to complete a questionnaire (called either a pre-qualification or selection questionnaire) covering basic information about the organisation and its history of compliance with legal and regulatory requirements.

22.29 Bidders have to satisfy the LAA that they meet essential criteria and there is usually a competitive element to tenders including selection criteria based on previous experience of delivering legal services. However, where the LAA perceives there may be a lack of supply, there may be a simple registration process instead. Some tenders (for example, the CLA telephone service) may include price competition.

22.30   Face-to-face contracts for crime and civil face to face legal work starting in 2017 and 2018 respectively were guaranteed to those submitting technically correct bids and meeting minimum requirements. Larger numbers of matter starts were allocated on a pro rata basis to those meeting defined requirements.

Applying for crime contracts

22.31   Under the pressure of a considerable number of legal challenges, the LAA did not go ahead with the two-tier contracting arrangements in 2016 which would have seen only a small number of firms eligible to do police duty solicitor work, which is the life-blood of many criminal defence firms. In the event, the tender for 2017 contracts was mainly a simple registration process, with only firms bidding for larger contracts needing to supply business plan and financial information.

The Public Defender Service

22.32   As well as contracting with private practice to deliver criminal defence work, the LAA also employs a small number of salaried lawyers in the Public Defender Service (PDS). This service was set up to benchmark the cost and quality of services provided by private practice and was never intended to be a nationwide scheme. At the time of writing, there are four PDS offices: Cheltenham, Darlington, Pontypridd and Swansea, as well as an advocacy unit which acts in PDS cases and is able to accept advocacy instructions from private practice.

Crime – very high cost case accreditation

22.33   The LAA's Criminal Cases Unit (CCU) manages membership of the Very High Cost Case (VHCC) scheme. Only firms that are accredited under this scheme can represent clients in VHCC cases – any case where the trial is expected to last for more than 40 days.

22.34   From 14 July 2010, organisations and self-employed advocates wishing to work on cases classified as VHCCs have had to obtain VHCC accreditation. This can be done when you become aware that you have a potential VHCC case and can be submitted at any time.

There is information about the VHCC arrangements and how to apply at: www.gov.uk/high-cost-cases-crime.

Community Legal Advice services

22.35 The Community Legal Service was a concept embodied in the Access to Justice Act 1999. In some areas, the then Legal Services Commission (LSC) contracted with a single provider to deliver a face-to-face legal advice and representation service concentrating on welfare benefits, debt, employment, housing, education and community care (often referred to as social welfare law (SWL) categories), sometimes with family law services. These were known as Community Legal Advice Centres (CLACs) in urban areas, and in rural areas Community Legal Advice Networks (CLANs). LASPO proved fatal to these developments and all those contracts were terminated at the end of March 2013.

Other kinds of contract with the LAA

22.36 The LAA has contracts with organisations for other kinds of service, for example:

- telephone advice, representation and casework for members of the public as part of the CLA telephone service in housing and debt, education (special educational needs), discrimination and family categories. This comprises an operator service which takes initial calls and a specialist adviser service which provides advice, casework and representation;
- telephone advice to people in police stations (Criminal Defence Service Direct).

22.37 Opportunities are publicised on the LAA's tenders page: www.gov. uk/ legal-aid-for-providers/tenders.

CHAPTER 23

Quality standards and performance monitoring

continued

Introduction

23.1   This chapter deals with quality standards and performance monitoring under contracts with the Legal Aid Agency (LAA), from a management perspective. We will cover the Standard Civil Contract 2018, which deals with the main face-to-face categories:

- family (both law and mediation);
- housing;
- debt and welfare benefits;
- immigration and asylum;
- mental health;
- community care;
- claims against public authorities (CAPA) (previously known as actions against the police etc);
- clinical negligence;
- public law;
- discrimination; and education

The last two categories took effect from September 2019. We also cover the Standard Crime Contract 2017. There are also others – see chapter 22.

23.2   Whatever kind of contract you have with the LAA, there is no substitute for reading it! The worst-case scenario is that you overlook something fundamental – for example, your supervisor may not meet the supervisor standards, the LAA discovers this and your contract is terminated – because there is nothing you can do to remedy the historic breach.

Practice management and quality of advice standards

23.3   The LAA has set quality standards for practice management, known as the Specialist Quality Mark (SQM), which applies to professional legal services, with additional requirements for telephone services. The LAA also accepts the Law Society's Lexcel standard in place of the SQM. Until 2018, there was a separate family mediation quality mark; but this has been replaced with standards set out in the family mediation specification. An organisation delivering legal services must be accredited to one of the acceptable standards in order to hold a contract. The SQM standard can be downloaded from the LAA's website: www.gov.uk/guidance/legal-aid-agency-quality-standards/.

23.4   The LAA intended to introduce a Quality Assurance Scheme for Advocates (QASA) for all advocates in criminal courts. This was a controversial scheme from the start and, after several attempts to get it going, was abandoned in 2017.

23.5   The LAA worked with the Institute of Advanced Legal Studies to create a peer review scheme that assesses the quality of legal advice – see: www.gov.uk/legal-aid-agency-audits. If selected for peer review, organisations with face-to-face contracts must reach at least Threshold Competence in order to demonstrate that they meet contractual requirements.

Specialist Quality Mark

23.6   Organisations wanting a contract with the LAA must hold the SQM (or Lexcel – see below) by the date for verification (which is before the contract start date), set in the tender documentation. At the time of writing, the current version of the SQM is V 2.2 dated March 2017.

23.7   The LAA appointed Recognising Excellence to deliver auditing services for the SQM from April 2017. For information about assessment, including cost, see Recognising Excellence's website: www. recognisingexcellence.co.uk/.

Desktop audit

23.8   This is the first stage of assessment. The documentation submitted will be reviewed against the requirements of the Quality Mark. If the documentation is incomplete or so deficient that it is clear the organisation cannot meet the standard, the application will be refused. The documentation will be returned within 28 days with comments so that the organisation knows the issues it needs to address.

23.9   If the organisation passes the desktop audit, and its application for a contract is also successful (see chapter 20 for more information), it will qualify for a contract.

Pre-Quality Mark audit

23.10   Before the SQM is confirmed, an on-site audit will be carried out, usually four to six months after the desk top audit, to make sure that the SQM requirements are in effective operation.

Opening meeting

23.11 The audit will start with an opening meeting at which the auditor will explain its scope and purpose. It is useful to have a copy of the Self-Assessment Audit Checklist (SAAC)[1] to hand, as the auditor is likely to check his or her understanding of procedures and check any queries.

Discussions with the auditor

23.12 If it appears that an auditor is requiring procedures to operate in a certain way, which does not coincide with the organisation's interpretation of SQM requirements (and particularly if it appears that implementing such a system could cause difficulty), it is advisable to ask the auditor to refer you to the requirement in the standard. It may be that the organisation has not understood the requirement; on the other hand, as auditors are human too, they can make mistakes. Many SQM requirements are so detailed that there is a limited number of ways in which they can be met. Auditors can become so used to seeing something being implemented in a certain way that they fail to recognise that an unusual system may still comply. Some auditors conduct assessments against both Lexcel and the SQM – it is not unknown for them to assess against eg a Lexcel requirement which is not in the SQM by mistake. If you both consider the system against the actual wording of the requirement, and any mandatory definition, you are most likely to reach a consensus.

SQM audit procedure and outcomes

23.13 The result will be one of:

- pass;
- pass with acceptable corrective action – usually relating to general quality concerns in non-critical management areas – this is the most common result; or
- fail (recommendation not to award or to terminate the SQM) – this usually relates to critical quality concerns which cannot be addressed.

23.14 There is a representation process which can be invoked if the organisation considers that the audit was not correctly carried out, a critical quality concern should have been disregarded, or any other reasonable grounds.

1 www.recognisingexcellence.co.uk/sqm/how-to-apply-for-an-audit/.

Quality Mark requirements

23.15   First, the standard itself is set out. It is split into 'Requirements', which are mandatory, and 'Definitions'. The definitions are only mandatory where the word 'must' is used. See following page for a compliance aide-memoire, to assist you in maintaining compliance with SQM and contract requirements.

SQM
A: Access to service
Business plan – in detail for one year and outline for two further years. Non-discrimination in the provision of services. Six-monthly review of plan. Providing information about service provision.
B: Seamless service
Signposting – providing the Legal Advisor and Family Mediator finder details: https://find-legal-advice.justice.gov.uk/. Referral – records kept when a client is referred elsewhere on an existing matter.
C: Running the organisation
Staff structure. Key roles and decision-making structure. Financial control. Demonstrate independence.
D: People management
Job descriptions, responsibilities and objectives. Equality and diversity. Open recruitment process. Induction procedure. Annual performance review and feedback. Training plans, training and records. Named supervisors – meeting very detailed technical requirements (see note below for more information). Supervisory skills and conditions for supervision. Limits of individual competence. Legal qualifications or 12 hours' casework per week.
E: Running the service
File management – file lists, conflict of interest, locating files and tracing documents, key dates, solicitor undertakings, monitoring files for inactivity, identifying all matters for one client, logical and orderly files. File reviews for all conducting cases – including legal and procedural issues – by Supervisor with corrective action taken where required (see note below for more information). File review records monitored annually.

F: Meeting clients' needs
Procedures for recording and confirming information and advice at the outset, during and at the end of the case. Keeping clients informed; case plans in complex cases; costs and cost/benefit advice; considering legal aid issues including the statutory charge. Confidentiality and privacy. Use of approved suppliers (eg counsel, experts, interpreters) – selected on the basis of objective assessment, evaluation, consultation with the client, clear instructions.
G: Commitment to quality
Complaints procedure. Quality management – *responsibility for, review of all quality procedures annually, Quality Manual.* Client satisfaction feedback.

Lexcel

23.16 The requirements of Lexcel are more demanding than the SQM and more closely aligned with the Solicitors Regulation Authority (SRA) Standards and Regulations. It is broken down into the following sections:

1. Structure and strategy;
2. Financial management;
3. Information management;
4. People management;
5. Risk management;
6. Client care;
7. File and case management.

23.17 Accrediting to Lexcel makes sense for firms that do non-contentious work or undertake work with a higher risk profile than legal aid. However, firms that have a low risk profile, for example those specialising in criminal defence work only, may find that the simpler SQM standard suits them best.

Supervisors – technical legal competence

23.18 Supervisors in family and civil categories must demonstrate that they have experience in their category of 1,050 casework hours over the preceding three years if full-time, or five years if part-time (supervisors who have been on maternity leave or long-term sick in the last three years can demonstrate the five-year requirement even if they work full-time). In crime, from April 2017, full-time supervisors only need to demonstrate that they have 350 hours experience over the past 12 months if full-time. Requirements for part-time supervisors are the same as in family and civil eg in respect of people who have been on maternity leave or have had long-term sickness absence.

23.19   In some categories, supervisors must be members of a specialist panel, eg family, mental health; in immigration, supervisors must be accredited to that level under the Immigration and Asylum Accreditation Scheme (IAAS), as well as providing evidence of 350 hours' case involvement annually over the preceding 36 months.

23.20   The Supervisor Self-Declaration Forms have caused some confusion. Practitioners should remember that in Case Involvement table (table 4) in many versions boxes (b), (c), (d) and (e) are optional, not mandatory, as long as the individual can show 350 hours' direct personal casework in box (4)(a). Evidence of that experience can be direct casework (which may be easier as that will be time-recorded in any event), or it can include up to 115 hours' supervision, file review, training and research for publication.

23.21   In categories where there is no panel, supervisors must demonstrate that they have closely defined experience of case types. In crime, supervisors have to be members of the Law Society Criminal Litigation Accreditation Scheme (CLAS) and be able to provide case examples. As for panel members, this must be maintained by at least 350 hours' experience in that category annually.

Supervisor standards in the Standard Civil Contract 2018

23.22   The common rules are to be found in the Standard Civil Contract 2018 Specification paras 2.10–2.28.

23.23   **Full-time equivalent (FTE) supervisors:** Under the contract you must (unless category-specific rules specify otherwise – see below for more information) employ at least one FTE supervisor in that category. This means you need at least one FTE in those categories (and you may need more if there are more than four people to supervise or multiple office arrangements mean that is the only practical way to ensure cover). For this purpose, 'full time equivalent' means the equivalent of one individual working five days a week and seven hours on each day (excluding breaks).[2]

---

2 Standard Civil Contract Specification 2018 para 2.10.

23.24　　The contract goes on to say that a supervisor must at all times during his or her working hours (except as required for the proper performance of his or her role, such as attending court and/or clients) work from one of or any combination of your offices.[3] Note this is not exactly the same as requiring the supervisor to be in the office at all times during working hours, and does allow a degree of flexibility.

23.25　　In addition, supervisors must be a sole principal, an employee or a director of or partner in or member of your organisation if your practice is a company, partnership (other than an LLP) or an LLP. Consultants are therefore not permitted to be supervisors.

23.26　　Under the 2017 Crime contract a supervisor may cover up to two offices. A Crime supervisor is restricted to one organisation but a prison law supervisor may work for two providers.[4] A FTE supervisor may supervise up to four caseworkers, unless they only supervise Prison Law, in which case they may supervise up to six.[5]

Under the 2018 Civil contracts, a supervisor must not supervise more than four caseworkers across a maximum of two offices or across two providers with one office each.[6]

23.27　　The LAA will only authorise external supervisors at its discretion and for temporary periods, for example if your supervisor becomes unwell and is unable to discharge his or her duties for no more than six weeks.[7]

23.28　　**Part-time equivalent (PTE) supervisors:** PTE supervisors are acceptable in the following categories of law: welfare benefits, clinical negligence, claims against public authorities, public law, discrimination and education.

Category-specific standards

23.29　These are to be found in the relevant category-specific section of the specification.

23.30　**Family:** See the Standard Civil Contract 2018 Specification section 7.

23.31　Supervisors must be either:

a) a member of the Law Society's Family Law Accreditation Scheme; or

b) a member of the Law Society's Children Law Accreditation Scheme; or

---

3　Standard Civil Contract Specification 2018 para 2.10.
4　Standard Crime Contract Specification 2017 para 2.9.
5　Standard Crime Contract Specification 2017 paras 2.29 and 2.30.
6　Standard Civil Contract Specification 2018 para 2.26.
7　Standard Civil Contract Specification 2018 para 2.24.

c) a Resolution Accredited Specialist or have successfully completed Part I (core assignment) of the Resolution Specialist Accreditation Scheme.[8]

23.32   **Family mediation:** See the Family Mediation Specification.

23.33   Family mediation supervisors must have:

a) at least three years' experience as a mediator;
b) been registered as a supervisor with a member body of the Family Mediation Council;
c) conducted at least 45 hours of mediation sessions (at least 15 of which have been conducted in the year prior to registration as a Supervisor) in each category of work; and
d) successfully completed a mediation supervision training course recognised by a member organisation of the Family Mediation Council;

and must conduct at least 15 hours of mediation sessions per year.[9]

23.34   **Immigration/asylum:** See the Immigration/Asylum Specification section 8.

23.35   Immigration and asylum supervisors must be accredited as an IAAS Senior Caseworker or Advanced Caseworker and have achieved the IAAS Supervising Senior Caseworker level of accreditation.[10]

23.36   **Mental health:** See the Mental Health Specification – section 9.

23.37   There are two legal competence standards for supervisors in this category:[11]

1) the Mental Health Tribunal (MHT) Legal Competence Standard for those who predominately supervise in relation to the Mental Health Act 1983; and
2) the Mental Health and Mental Capacity Legal Competence Standard for Supervisors who supervise a mixture of contract work under the Mental Health Act 1983 and Mental Capacity Act 2005.

23.38   MHT supervisors must hold current membership of either:

* the Law Society Mental Health Accreditation Scheme; or
* (for non-solicitor supervisors only) be assessed by the Law Society as meeting the Mental Health Accreditation Scheme criteria.

---

8 Standard Civil Contract Specification 2018 para 7.159.
9 Standard Civil Family Mediation Specification 2018 para 2.6 and 2.7: www.gov.uk/government/uploads/system/uploads/attachment_data/file/645396/2018-standard-civil-contract-category-specific-rules-family-mediation.pdf.
10 Standard Civil Contract 2018 Immigration/Asylum Specification para 8.16.
11 Standard Civil Contract 2018 Mental Health Specification para 9.15.

23.39   Supervisors must have either:

- provided representation on ten MHT case files in the previous 12 months; or
- provide evidence of representation at five hearings, plus five further cases in which either the preparation for the hearing had been completed and can be demonstrated on file or where you have had conduct of a case which falls within the scope of the category and for which a determination was made that the individual qualifies for civil legal services (legal aid).

Mental Health and Mental Capacity Act supervisors must have been directly involved in the delivery of at least ten new cases where the primary issue related to a matter under the Mental Capacity Act 2005, during the 12 months immediately preceding qualification as a supervisor.

23.40   **Housing and debt** supervisors must maintain a portfolio of specified case types.[12]

23.41   **Community care** supervisors must maintain a portfolio of specified case types.[13]

23.42   **Welfare benefits** supervisors must maintain a portfolio of specified case types.[14] A part time equivalent (17.5 hours a week) is acceptable.[15]

23.43   **Claims against public authorities (CAPA):** A PTE (17.5 hours a week) is acceptable.[16] There are two supervisor standards in this category:

1) the General Standard; and
2) the Abuse in Care Standard.

23.44   Supervisors must maintain a portfolio of specified case types.[17]

23.45   **Public law:** A PTE (17.5 hours a week) is acceptable.[18] Supervisors must maintain a portfolio of specified case types.[19]

23.46   **Clinical negligence:** A PTE (17.5 hours a week) is acceptable.[20] Supervisors must hold current membership of one of the following:

---

12 Standard Civil Contract 2018 Housing and Debt Specification paras 10.1–10.2.
13 Standard Civil Contract 2018 Community Care Specification paras 11.1–11.2.
14 Standard Civil Contract 2018 Welfare Benefits Specification paras 12.1–12.2.
15 Standard Civil Contract 2018 Welfare Benefits Specification para 12.24.
16 Standard Civil Contract 2018 CAPA Specification para 13.12.
17 Standard Civil Contract 2018 CAPA Specification paras 13.2 and 13.7 respectively.
18 Standard Civil Contract 2018 Public Law Specification para 14.6.
19 Standard Civil Contract 2018 Public Law Specification paras 14.1–14.2.
20 Standard Civil Contract 2018 Clinical Negligence Specification para 15.7.

- the Law Society's Clinical Negligence Accreditation Scheme;
- the Action Against Medical Accidents (AVMA) Clinical Negligence Panel; or
- the Association of Personal Injury Lawyers (APIL) Clinical Negligence Accredited Specialist Panel.[21]

23.47 The supervisor must, during any preceding 24-month period, have worked on a minimum number of five cases significantly concerned with claims for damages in respect infant neurological injury.[22]

Education: A PTE (17.5 hours a week) is acceptable.[23] For the period of the 2018 contract, supervisors can meet either the transitional education supervisor standard or the discrimination supervisor standard. The LAA wished to encourage organisations to deliver education law services and so made a less demanding standard available for the initial period.

Discrimination: A PTE (17.5 hours a week) is acceptable.[24] For the period of the 2018 contract, supervisors can meet either the transitional discrimination supervisor standard or the discrimination supervisor standard. The LAA wished to encourage organisations to deliver discrimination law services and so made a less demanding standard available for the initial period.

Supervisor standards in the Standard Crime Contract 2017

23.48 The general requirements are very similar to the 2018 Civil Contract above. The particular issues relating to the Crime Contract are set out below.

23.49 Supervision requirements in the 2017 Contact[25] are significantly different from the 2010 Contract which it replaced. From April 2017, a supervisor can only supervise up to two offices[26] and up to four people (six for prison law[27]). Except in prison law (where it is limited to two), someone can only be a supervisor for one organisation.[28]

---

21 Standard Civil Contract 2018 Clinical Negligence Specification para 15.1.
22 Standard Civil Contract 2018 Clinical Negligence Specification para 15.5.
23 Standard Civil Contract 2018 Education Specification para 16.1.
24 Standard Civil Contract 2018 Discrimination Specification para 17.1.
25 Standard Crime Contract 2017 Specification paras 2.1–2.31.
26 Standard Crime Contract 2017 Specification para 2.8.
27 Standard Crime Contract 2017 Specification paras 2.29–2.30.
28 Standard Crime Contract 2017 Specification paras 2.9–2.10.

Supervisors can supervise more than one class of work (eg investigations, proceedings etc[29]).

23.50 **Crime** supervisors must be accredited to the Law Society's CLAS (either via the Police Station Qualification (PSQ) route or the passporting route for those who qualified under previous schemes); and have held a current non-conditional practising certificate for the previous three years. In the previous 12 months, supervisors must have:

- have undertaken a minimum of six police station advice and assistance cases (of which no more than two can be police station telephone advice where there is no subsequent police station attendance); and
- have undertaken a minimum of 20 magistrates' court representations and advocacy (which may include magistrates' court duty sessions – one session counts as one representation only); or
- ten magistrates' court representations and advocacy and five in the Crown Court.

23.51 **Prison law** supervisors must have, in the previous 12 months, undertaken a minimum of four representations for four clients before the Parole Board or the Independent Adjudicator/Prison Governor. They do not have to be legally qualified.

23.52 **Appeals and reviews** supervisors do have to be legally qualified.[30]

Supervisors – file reviews

23.53 File reviews under the SQM must cover legal and procedural points (Lexcel allows for file reviews limited to procedural points, but that would be risky from the point of view of peer review under the contract). This can cause problems when considering who should review the supervisor's files. If there is another experienced practitioner in the same area of law, they can review each other's files. Where there is not, perhaps because there is no one else who practises in that specialism, the supervisor will have to review his or her own files (as objectively as possible!) for legal issues, and someone else will review it for procedural points. The LAA does not expect an organisation to incur the expense of an external supervisor in these circumstances.

---

29 Standard Crime Contract 2017 Specification para 2.6.
30 Standard Crime Contract 2017 Specification para 2.26.

Key supervision issues from recent audits

- Have file reviews been carried out by the named supervisor (or delegated to a deputy with a training and development plan to meet full supervisor status)?
- Do the management/organisation structure and individual job descriptions agree? *It's amazing how disorganised you can look to an outsider if they don't!*
- If the supervisor has to demonstrate compliance through the portfolio route (as opposed to panel membership), can he or she do so over the last 12 months? *Consider the numbers of hours required and the range of cases.*
- Were independent file reviews undertaken by an appropriate person? *If you are developing a member of staff as a deputy supervisor and delegating aspects of some file reviews to them, make sure this is all properly documented.*
- Are the independent file review records completely up to date? *If there are gaps, eg someone was on maternity leave or on the holiday of a lifetime, are the reasons for them clear?*
- *If you have not been able to do file reviews for a period due to pressures such as sickness absence or additional work demands, catch up later and put a note onto your central record explaining why some file reviews were done late.*
- Is corrective action required recorded on the file review forms, with appropriate dates? Do they also show what action was taken and by when?
- Did file reviews identify any non-compliances with SQM or contract requirements? *If the supervisor is lenient, the LAA cannot be confident that the organisation meets its requirements.*

Peer review

Overview

23.54   Peer review is the measure that the LAA uses to assess quality of advice. It has been developed over many years under the auspices of the Institute of Advanced Legal Studies (IALS). Peer reviewers have carried out thousands of assessments since 2000 and refined the process over the years. There is information about the process at: www.gov.uk/legal-aid-agency-audits.

23.55   There are five possible scores: excellence (1); competence plus (2); threshold competence (3); below competence (4); and failure in performance (5). The LAA has defined the level of skill required under the contract as at least threshold competence. At below competence level, the provider will be given at least six months to improve; if they do not achieve at least threshold competence at their next assessment, their contract will be terminated. An organisation assessed at failure in performance will have its contract terminated quickly, because of the risk to clients.

23.56 The LAA publishes guidance which you can use to benchmark your files and ensure they achieve good peer review scores. These are called 'Improving Your Quality Guides'. There are updated guides in crime, family, housing, mental health and immigration/asylum. They can be downloaded from: www.gov.uk/guidance/legal-aid-agency-audits.

The peer review process

23.57 All peer reviewers are experienced practitioners, trained by the IALS to carry out peer review using their framework. A sample of their own files has to be assessed at competence plus or above. Peer reviewers are consistency-checked against each other and receive regular training. There are various reasons why a review might be carried out – eg random selection, or concern about quality raised by a contract manager – but the reviewer is not told what it is. This ensures that they can approach all peer reviews with an open mind.

23.58 More files are requested than are eventually peer reviewed, of which at least 12 are assessed.[31] The files are selected to cover all the different types of work carried out by the organisation within a category of law and are cases closed during the preceding 12 months. Peer reviewers carry out the assessment away from the practice's office. They do not meet the staff of the organisation being reviewed, which never finds out the identity of its particular reviewer, although they are sent a list of all the reviewers and asked to identify any possible conflict of interest. It usually takes one to two days to do an assessment and write a report.

23.59 The reviewers evaluate issues that relate to quality of advice and service. They do not look at how long was spent on the file and they do not carry out a transaction criteria[32] audit. They apply the 'pick up test', which is the basic question – 'if I, as another fee-earner, picked

---

31 Independent peer review process document 2017 para 2.9.
32 Transaction criteria will be remembered by some legal aid practitioners from the early days of 'franchising'. They enabled the Legal Aid Board (LAB), and later the Legal Services Commission (LSC), to assess the extent to which a lawyer had obtained appropriate information and followed steps associated with best practice. They did not allow any assessment to be made of the quality of legal advice. They were superseded by peer review.

up this file, could I understand what had been done and why, and what remained to be done?'

23.60   They assess individual files and then consider the sample as a whole and form a conclusion about its overall quality. In many cases, this involves a balancing act as some files may be good, others less so. Organisations scoring competence plus tend to have a higher level of consistency. For example, if there is a change of caseworker part-way through the case the peer reviewer would look at the whole case, and in order to score competence plus or excellence, both case-workers would need to achieve that level.

23.61   The reviewers also apply the 'friend and family test', which is simply 'would I refer a friend or family member to this organisa-tion?' If the answer is 'no', the sample will be assessed below threshold competence or worse.

23.62   Peer reviewers use checklists of criteria, which they score indi-vidually; but the overall score is not simply an average of the scores on individual files. Peer reviewers take account of any trends and patterns identified, including evidence of supervision. Having assessed the 15 files, the reviewer compiles a report identifying; positive findings, major areas of concern (if any), areas for develop-ment, suggested areas for improvement and any other comments.

23.63   Reports are checked by IALS to ensure that the score reflects the comments the reviewer has made about the files. So, for example they would pick up a contradiction if the sample scored competence plus but the reviewer had identified major areas of concern, and ask the reviewer to look at the report again. IALS does not double-check the assessment. The provider should receive the final report within 28 days.

Tips for passing peer review

23.64   The peer reviewers emphasise that good practice helps to improve peer review scores, for example:

- file review and supervision support;
- ensuring workload is appropriate;
- training;
- providing appropriate advice on legal and procedural issues on every file;
- confirming the client's initial instructions and your advice in writing.

Standard letters and documentation

23.65   Peer reviewers accept that standard letters have their place; but that it is important to take an individual approach to them. This means ensuring that standard letters should not be 'catch-alls' which try to cover all eventualities, but should be specific to a client's circumstances. So, for example, a letter setting out the different possession proceedings in relation to both owner-occupiers and tenants would not impress a peer reviewer, who would expect the client to be given only the information that applied to his or her case.

23.66   As in all kinds of file-based assessment, it is vital that the file is complete. Some organisations send information leaflets to clients; but do not put a copy of standard information on the file, in order to save paper and printing costs. Peer reviewers advise that if that is the way you work, it is important to include copies of all standard information leaflets with the file sample.

23.67   If your files are digital, you will need to print them out for peer review. It is very important to make sure that the printed copy is complete. If the printed copy looks different from a traditional hard copy file because it was never designed to be printed out, it is worth putting a note on the top of the file, explaining this, and how the file is arranged, to make the peer reviewer's job as easy as possible.

Peer review representations

23.68   Representations can only be made if the assessment is category 4 or 5. The LAA's rationale is that since a category 3 is acceptable for a contract, there is no point in allowing representations when only the organisation's professional pride is at stake.

23.69   Possible grounds are that: you dispute the overall peer review rating; the sample does not appear to be sufficiently representative; any other reasonable grounds.

23.70   Representations must be made on the appropriate form and reach the LAA within 28 days following receipt of the report and the file sample. The representations will be considered by the original peer reviewer and a senior panel member. They may uphold the original rating, revise the original rating, request a new review, or not reach agreement. Where the latter occurs, an external expert who is not a peer reviewer will be asked to help the peer reviewers reach a consensus. Note that, if an appeal is unsuccessful, you may have to pay the costs of the peer review under both civil and crime contracts.

LAA online portal

23.71　The LAA is moving to digital working, which you access through its online portal (not to be confused with the online tendering portal hosted by Bravo Solution). You can download a useful guide to the online portal at: www.gov.uk/government/publications/laa-online-portal-help-and-information.

23.72　There are several significant online applications:

1) **CWA (Contracted Work and Administration):** Through this you submit your monthly claims for Crime lower work, Controlled work, Mediation and notify the LAA of new matters started.

2) **eforms:** Electronic payment on account claims and Crime forms (CRM4/5/7/14).

3) **CCLF (Crown Court Litigator Fee):** claims and disbursements.

4) **Management information (MI):** Financial information about your organisation:

   – **Civil financial statement:** this shows the current financial position of a civil office account ie monthly submissions against payments made (monthly contract payments, adjustments and repayments);

   – **Family mediation financial statement:** this shows the current financial position of a family mediation office account ie, monthly submissions against payments made (monthly contract payments, adjustments / repayments);

   – **Criminal financial statement:** this shows the current financial position of a crime office account ie, monthly submissions (CRM6 and CRM7) against payments made (monthly contract payments, adjustments / repayments);

   – **Financial statement summary:** this provides a summary of the financial position of the entire organisation and includes individual office entries across crime, civil and mediation offices.

5) **CCMS (Client and Cost Management System):** Application through which you apply for, and manage, civil certificated work, including amendments, prior authorities, payments on account and billing. (See chapter 6.)

You can also view your contract for signature and schedule through CWA.

23.73　**Provider Activity Report (PAR):** Towards the end of 2017, the LAA started sending PARs out to practitioners. They provide some key information about contract performance:

- contract status;
- civil and crime fund take;
- claim 1 rejects.

23.74   Unfortunately, it is not possible for organisations to access all MI data to monitor the contract key performance indicators (KPIs) – see below for more information. Therefore, it is a good idea to ask your LAA contract manager to send you this data on a quarterly basis. They can do this and it is regarded as good practice by the LAA senior managers for them to help you in this way.

Key performance indicators

Overview

23.75   Both the civil and crime versions of the Standard Contracts have mandatory KPIs.

23.76   Somebody should be monitoring KPIs, usually a head of department or partner. Some can be monitored at individual file level, others will require the collection of data by department/work type. Contract managers monitor KPI reports, which are flagged as 'red', 'amber' or 'green'. Failing to meet KPIs will not in itself result in sanctions being taken against you or contract notices being raised. However, your contract manager may contact you to ask you to explain the reasons that your organisation is 'out of profile'. If it is an issue which the contract manager thinks should be corrected, then you will be asked to formulate an action plan for doing so. Being 'out of profile' may also trigger an on-site or other type of audit.

23.77   The LAA monitors KPIs on a three-month rolling basis rather than on individual files, with minimum numbers where volumes are low.

Key performance indicators: Standard Civil Contract 2018[33]

KPI 1 – Controlled work escape fee cases – assessment reduction ten per cent max

23.78   When your 'escape cases' are assessed (these are the cases where the costs on a time and item basis are three times the fixed fee), the costs claimed must not be reduced by more than ten per cent. This includes disbursements, but not VAT.

---

33 Standard Civil Contract 2018 Specification paras 2.52–2.72.

KPI 2 – Licensed work – assessment reduction 15 per cent max

23.79   This sets a similar target in relation to licensed work cases that are claimed on a time and item basis.

KPI 3 – Fixed fee margin – 20 per cent max

23.80   The LAA is concerned that some organisations will select clients with straightforward cases that do not require much work, in order to retain a high surplus under each fixed fee case. This KPI can only be met if the total cost of cases under fixed fees when calculated on a time and item basis is at least 80 per cent of the appropriate fixed fees.

23.81   This KPI applies to controlled work cases, and Family Private and Public Law Representation Scheme cases that are paid by way of fixed fees.

KPI 4 – Rejection rates for licensed work – five per cent max in the schedule period

23.82   Rejections are when applications or claims are refused because of technical errors in submission, lack of attachments etc. This applies to applications for legal aid (known as applications for determinations that an individual qualifies for legal aid), and claims for payment. If you think the LAA has made a mistake in rejecting your work, you can use the 'claim-fix' email: laacivilclaimfix@justice.gov. uk so that it doesn't affect your KPI. It also deals with what they call 'secondary requests' where you have already provided documents or documents are not necessary.

KPI 5 – Refusal rates for licensed work – 15 per cent max in the schedule period

23.83   This applies to applications for legal aid which are refused because the LAA considers that the practitioner has failed to show that they meet the applicable merits test.

KPI 6 – Legal representation outcomes – 30 per cent minimum

23.84   You must achieve a substantive benefit for the client in 30 per cent of cases. This applies to clinical negligence and claims against public authorities work only.

KPI 7 – Post investigation success

23.85   This KPI applies to licensed work in clinical negligence and claims against public authorities, in cases which proceed beyond investigation. You must achieve a substantive benefit for the client in 50 per cent of claims against public authorities cases; 60 per cent in clinical negligence cases.

Service standards: civil and family

23.86   Service standards are to be found in the applicable contract specification.

23.87   The general rules under the 2018 contract are set out in the Standard Civil Contract 2018 Specification paras 2.1–2.72.

23.88   **Use of agents and third parties:** You may use agents, counsel and third parties where it is in your client's best interests. The specification allows independent consultants to carry out work under the contract as long as the supervision conditions are met. However, it is important to note that you cannot refer a case to a separate organisation, nor can you use an agent to meet the service standards. So, for example, you cannot use an agent to meet the supervisor standards.

23.89   You must ensure that:

- they comply with data protection and equality and diversity processes;
- they are covered by your insurance.

23.90   **Supervisor standards:** See above for supervisor standards.

23.91   **Authorised litigators:** You must employ an authorised litigator (see glossary for definition), at least on a part-time PTE basis (17.5 hours a week) unless the category specification requires a FTE (35 hours a week[34]). See below for more information.

23.92   **Minimum numbers of matter starts.** Although the specification allows minimum numbers to be specified, usually they are not.

23.93   **Presence in the procurement area.** You must comply with the presence requirements set out in your schedule, that is, your office must comply with the requirements for a permanent or part time presence.[35] You may be allowed to deliver outreach services. If so, these must be noted on your schedule.

23.94   **Referral and signposting arrangements.** You must have referral and signposting arrangements in place. For those categories of law delivered exclusively through the telephone gateway, you must signpost clients or potential clients to the helpline unless that client or potential client is an 'exempted person' as described in the procedure

---

34   Standard Civil Contract 2018 Specification para 2.8.
35   Standard Civil Contract 2018 Specification para 2.32.

regulations. The telephone gateway will cease to be mandatory in Spring 2020.

23.95 The exclusive categories are: debt (post Legal Aid, Sentencing and Punishment of Offenders Act 2012 (LASPO), where the client's owner-occupied home is at risk and involuntary bankruptcy), education (post-LASPO, special educational needs cases) and discrimination (eg consumer and employment cases).

23.96 Exemptions to the mandatory single gateway include where the client is a child or in detention or has previously been assessed by Civil Legal Advice (CLA) as requiring advice face-to-face for this case.

23.97 Telephone advice is also available in those cases remaining in-scope, in housing and family, but is not the mandatory route for clients to access legal aid in those categories.

Additional/variations to service and monitoring requirements

23.98 There are additional service standards for family; immigration/ asylum; housing/debt; welfare benefits; and mental health – see below. Organisations with contracts to deliver housing possession court duty schemes also need additional monitoring systems, also shown below.

Family

23.99 In order to provide services for applicants in child abduction proceedings, your organisation must remain on the Referral List of Specialist Solicitors maintained by the International Child Abduction and Contact Unit.[36]

23.100 You must have appropriate arrangements in operation to enable you, in appropriate cases, to refer clients to local family support services. You should have access to details of such services as are locally available, including: local authority family support services, any providers of family mediation services, any relevant counselling and relationship guidance services, any support services for victims of domestic abuse.[37]

23.101 There are appointment service standards in the family category. When you are contacted by a client for whom you intend to provide services (and have sufficient matter starts) you must offer a first

---

36 Standard Civil Contract 2018 Specification para 7.161.
37 Standard Civil Contract 2018 Specification para 7.162.

appointment to the client within 48 hours of the initial contact in emergency cases, or within ten working days of the initial contact in all other cases.[38]

Immigration and asylum

23.102 The Immigration Specification (paras 8.13–8.20) sets down requirements for caseworkers and supervisors to be accredited under the Immigration and Asylum Accreditation Scheme. It also limits the type of work that can be done by reference to the level of accreditation. For example, only level 2 caseworkers can conduct cases or use delegated functions to grant CLR. Caseworkers acting for children must be enhanced DBS (Disclosure and Barring Service) checked. See chapter 10 for more information.

Mental health

23.103 There are particular presence requirements, which are set out in paras 9.4–9.5 of the 2018 Mental Health Specification. The requirements you have to meet will be recorded in your contract schedule.

23.104 You must employ a FTE Authorised Litigator.[39]

23.105 In addition to the overall requirement to employ a FTE supervisor per four caseworkers in a procurement area, you must employ a supervisor in each procurement area where you have a schedule for at least 17.5 hours a week.

23.106 All advocates before the MHT (except self-employed counsel) must be members of the Law Society Mental Health Accreditation Scheme.[40] You must have a document identifying individuals you have nominated as 'Designated Accredited Representatives' who are members of the Law Society's Mental Health Accreditation Scheme and used by you to provide advocacy before the MHT in 50 per cent of cases.

23.107 In this category, 70 per cent of clients must be physically located in the procurement area in which you have been granted matter starts. Thirty per cent of your matter starts may be used for clients who are not physically located in the procurement area in which you have been granted matter starts. See chapter 11 for more information.

---

38 Standard Civil Contract 2018 Specification para 7.163.
39 Standard Civil Contract 2018 Mental Health Specification para 9.6(a).
40 Standard Civil Contract 2018 Mental Health Specification para 9.8.

Housing/Debt

23.108 Depending on your volume of matter starts you are awarded, you may need to employ a FTE Authorised Litigator at an office. This will be specified in your schedule.[41]

Welfare benefits

23.109 You only need 'access' to an authorised litigator[42] at all times.

Education

23.110 From 1 June 2020, you must provide clients with a choice of advice in person or by remote means (email, telephone, webcam, post or other method as agreed). You must keep a record on the file.[43]

Housing Possession Court Duty Scheme

23.111 Revised Housing Possession Court Duty Scheme (HPCDS) provider guidance came into effect on 1 October 2018 along with a revised client monitoring form and contract report form. They can be downloadedfrom:www.gov.uk/government/publications/housing-possession-court-duty-schemes-hpcds.

If you provide a client with advice at court and subsequently open a new matter start in relation to the same case, then you may not claim payment of the HPCDS fixed fee. However, you can count the work done at Court under the Legal Help matter start, which may help the case to 'escape' the fixed fee.[44]

Key performance indicators: Standard Crime Contract 2017

23.112 The following crime KPIs[45] must be met in any three-month rolling period:

- *Claims for costs must not be reduced on assessment by more than 15 per cent:* police station advice and assistance (escape fee cases); freestanding advice and assistance claims; advocacy assistance

---

41 Standard Civil Contract 2018 Housing/Debt Specification para 10.9.
42 Standard Civil Contract 2018 Welfare Benefits Specification para 12.29.
43 Standard Civil Contract 2018 Education Specification paras 16.19 and 16.21.
44 HPCDS Guidance for use from 01 October 2018 para 2.8.
45 Standard Crime Contract 2017 Specification para 2.65.

claims; magistrates' court non-standard fees; prison law escape fee cases; prison law non-standard fees.

- *You must accept 90 per cent of communications from the Defence Solicitor Call Centre (DSCC)* (and deal with them appropriately) when you are on the rota.
- *You must accept 90 per cent of calls to attend a virtual court hearing* when you are on the rota.
- 95 per cent or more of your cases must conclude before any change of provider under the contract.

Service standards: Standard Crime Contract 2017

23.113 Section 2 of the Crime Specification 2017 contains the service standards for criminal defence work.

23.114 **Supervisors:** You must have at least one person who meets the LAA's standard for supervisors, and they must carry out their duties in accordance with the contract – which contains standards for supervision and file review.

23.115 See 'Supervisors' above for ratios of supervisors to other staff.

23.116 You must designate the staff who work under the Crime Contract and the work they can do. Designating staff means naming the people who do work under the Criminal Contract, ensuring they meet the standards required by the contract, quality standard and duty solicitor requirements set out in the contract[46] and keeping records as shown below.

23.117 Note that the duty solicitor requirements in the 2017 contract were designed to eliminate the phenomenon of 'ghosts', so expect qualifying criteria to be checked.[47] Duty solicitors do not have to be 'employees';[48] but they do have to do 14 hours work for you per week from the office relevant to their slots.[49] There is guidance on the work that may be counted against the requirement in the LAA's Duty Solicitor Guidance 2018, para 3.14 onwards.

23.118 Fee earners should be 'designated', unless they do less than three hours' contract work a month.[50] Those who regularly undertake fee earning criminal work under the contract – crime supervisors,

---

46 Standard Crime Contract 2017 Specification paras 6.15–6.69.
47 Standard Crime Contract 2017 Specification para 6.22.
48 Standard Crime Contract 2017 Specification para 6.21.
49 Standard Crime Contract 2017 Specification para 6.23.
50 Standard Crime Contract 2017 Specification para 2.36.

CILEx supervisors, duty solicitors, accredited and probationary representatives – must be designated.

23.119   The Contract Specification sets out percentages of Crime Contract work which must be performed by designated fee earners:

- Advocacy in the magistrates' court: 50 per cent must be done by designated staff.
- Police station advice and assistance: 80 per cent must be done by designated staff.[51]
- First contact with a client in the police station must be within 45 mins in 80 per cent of cases.[52]

23.120   **Location:** You may only perform contract work from the office(s) specified in your schedule.[53] Offices must be physically accessible for clients from Monday to Friday, and you must have arrangements in place to ensure that during business hours, clients are able to speak to someone by telephone to arrange appointments and to contact you about emergency matters. If you move your office out of your original postcode area, you must ask the LAA's permission. Even if the LAA consents you will not be able undertake work on additional duty schemes which are accessible only by virtue of your new office address.[54]

23.121   **Referral and signposting arrangements:** You must have appropriate arrangements in operation to refer clients or potential clients to another provider if you do not provide the services that the client requires or for some other reason are unable to take on their case.[55]

---

51 Standard Crime Contract 2017 Specification para 2.
52 Standard Crime Contract 2017 Specification para 9.24.
53 Standard Crime Contract 2017 Specification paras 2.41–2.52.
54 Standard Crime Contract 2017 Specification para 2.54d.
55 Standard Crime Contract 2017 Specification para 2.55.

CHAPTER 24

Financial and contract management

continued

Introduction

24.1   This chapter deals with issues that affect an organisation's financial and contractual position: reconciliation; payments on account (POAs); key performance indicators (KPIs); contract compliance audits; contract manager visits; and audits.

24.2   Controlled work in civil and crime 'lower' work (police station and magistrates' court work), is paid by way of a monthly payment under either the Civil or the Crime Contract.

24.3   Each contract has a schedule, which sets out what the Legal Aid Agency (LAA) will pay you each month if you have opted for the standard monthly payment option (see below). At the end of each month, you submit bills for concluded cases via the LAA's online claim portal: https://portal.legalservices.gov.uk/.

Payment for Civil controlled work and Crime Lower

24.4   There are two options for payment of this work. You can opt for variable monthly payments (VMP) reflecting each month's claim, plus the value of any escape fee cases credited to you by the LAA during the month, (sometimes referred to as 'pay as you go'); or you can be paid standard monthly payments (SMP).

24.5   The advantage of 'pay as you go' is that reconciliation of claims against payments should be fairly straightforward. The LAA starts all new contracts on the VMP basis.

24.6   If you opt for an SMP, it will be the amount the LAA expects to pay you over the lifetime of the schedule, divided by that number of months. The advantage is that you get a regular amount, which can help with budgeting; but since it is rare to hit contract targets exactly, it can involve you in complex reconciliation calculations. If you opt for an SMP, you will also have to keep your eye on the reconciliation protocol (see below).

SMP or pay as you go, which is best?

24.7   In many categories of law, post the Legal Aid, Sentencing and Punishment of Offenders Act 2012 (LASPO), there is much less controlled work than there used to be, and it makes less of a contribution to income, so peaks and troughs are easier to manage. If this is the case for your organisation, you may want to opt for VMPs, as it does away with the chore of reconciliation.

24.8   If you are an existing contract-holder, the LAA allows you to choose your payment method; but if you are an existing contract holder and want to change from SMP to VMP, this means reconciling the contract to give the new arrangement a fresh start. If you have a strong cash position, or the LAA owes you money, you may want to opt for 'pay as you go'. However, if you have been paid more money than you have claimed and do not wish to make repayments at once, then you may prefer to stick with the SMP (subject to the reconciliation protocol below). If you are owed money by the LAA, assuming that this figure is less than £20,000, a single ad hoc payment will be made to you. If you owe money to the LAA, then you can choose to make a single payment or spread the payments over a six-month period.

24.9   If you have a Crime Contract and have taken advantage of the one month's 'pull forward' option, that cannot be combined with 'pay as you go'. There is more information about choosing between VMPs and SMPs on the LAA website at: www.gov.uk/government/uploads/system/uploads/attachment_data/file/318538/LAA-variable-monthly-payments-guidance.pdf/.

Reconciliation of contracts

24.10   You should always keep your own figures for the value of your monthly submissions and monitor them against your payments. You can obtain more information and check the LAA's figures at: www.gov.uk/legal-aid-management-information-online. The LAA will do the same, and periodically will seek to adjust the payments to ensure that your contract remains on course. As a result of the adjustment, your payments may go up or down. The purpose is to ensure that at the end of the contract, claims equal payments, or at least that the difference between them is within an agreed band. This process is known as reconciliation, and where parity has been achieved the contract has been successfully reconciled. Where it hasn't, arrangements will need to be made to resolve the outstanding balance, either by payment of a lump sum or recovering the balance during the schedule. The LAA is usually reluctant to allow recovery over more than one schedule or six months; but it can be done.

The reconciliation protocol

24.11   The reconciliation protocol sets out the approach the LAA will take, which can also be downloaded at: www.gov.uk/government/uploads/

system/uploads/attachment_data/file/340267/LAA-monthly-payments-protocol.pdf (or see appendix E). The key is that the target is always reconciliation to 100 per cent – that is, for claims to equal payments over the course of the schedule. It is recognised that in practice it will often work out that 100 per cent is not exactly achieved. Therefore, the LAA will look at the position twice a year – April and September – and determine whether the contract is within the acceptable margin of 90 to 110 per cent (calculated over the shorter of the life of the contract or the last 12 months). Where it is, no action will be taken. Where the contract is outside the acceptable margin, the monthly payment will be revised with a view to paying off any balance within six months.

24.12   It is important to remember that each month you claim less than your SMP, then the closer to the 90 per cent trigger point you will be. You need to try to avoid any cumulative decline in performance that takes you below 90 per cent. Once you go below the trigger point, the reduction happens automatically and the LAA would not warn you about this in advance. The new payment would remain in place for three months to monitor that it would achieve the desired effect. You would have to ensure that claims stayed at or around the level of the previous SMP, otherwise it could trigger a further reduction at the three-month review stage.

Case study

My firm has Criminal and Civil Contracts on the SMP basis. The Civil Contract is currently paid at £10,000 per month. After 12 months, we have claimed £102,000. The Criminal Contract is paid at £5,000 per month and after 12 months we have claimed £64,000. Are we in band? Are the LAA likely to change our payments?

Civil: Total claims = £102,000 over the life of the contract. Payments are £120,000, so the balance on the account is £18,000 owed to the LAA. This is a margin of 82 per cent, so outside the acceptable band (ie below 90 per cent). The payment will be amended. The target is 100 per cent. Average monthly claim is £8,500 (£102,000/12) and you owe the LAA £18,000, which must be repaid over the next six months. The new payment will be £8,500 – (£18,000/6) = £5,500 per month.

Crime: Total claims = £64,000, and payments are £60,000. Ten per cent of claims = £6,400, so the acceptable band is £60,000 ± £6,400 – between £53,600 and £66,400. Therefore you are within band and the LAA will not automatically amend your contract payment. However, you are entitled to ask the LAA to amend your payments at any time and may want to ask for an increase. The LAA do not have to agree, but if you can demonstrate that you are likely to continue to claim more than you are paid, they should do so.

Payments on account

24.13   You are entitled to be paid your costs on civil certificates at the end of the case following assessment by the LAA or court – see chapter 16 for details. In recognition of the fact that such cases often last a considerable time and costs can be substantial, there is provision for you to claim POAs during the life of the case.

24.14   The Standard Civil Contract 2018 entitles you to claim a POA of profit costs at any time, provided that a) you may not apply for the first until three months have elapsed since the certificate was issued; and b) you may not apply more than twice in any 12-month period. Also, cumulatively, you are not entitled to be paid more than 75 per cent of your profit costs to date[1] (or standard fee in applicable family cases[2]). You can make a payment on account for disbursements incurred, or about to be incurred, at any time.[3]

Case study

It is 1 May 2019. I have two certificate files. On the first, the certificate was issued on 1 February 2019 and I have spent £1,000. On the second, the certificate was issued on 1 April 2018. I have spent £5,000 in total, and I received a POA of £2,000 in January. Am I entitled to any POAs? If so, how much?

The first certificate was issued exactly three months ago, so you are entitled to a POA. The second was issued more than three months ago and you have only made one application in the 12 months leading up to today, so you are entitled to a POA. POAs have to be submitted using the Client and Cost Management System (CCMS) where – as here – the case is a CCMS case. You should complete a separate payment on account claim for each certificate. Once you

---

1   Standard Civil Contract 2018 Specification para 6.21.
2   Standard Civil Contract 2018 Specification para 7.25(b).
3   Standard Civil Contract 2018 Specification para 6.20.

have done so, CCMS will send you a notification asking you to upload your running record of costs. This must match your claim exactly. You should upload a copy of the record and mark the notification as 'documents sent' so it is picked up by a caseworker. The LAA will not assess your claim but will check that it matches the running record. Provided it does in each case, you will be paid £750 on the first case and £1,750 on the second (75 per cent of £5,000, less the £2,000 already paid).

If a certificate was issued before CCMS became mandatory (February 2016 for care cases and April 2016 for all other cases) you should send in a single paper POA1 form, completing one line for each case, or you could opt to make a POA application online using an eform: www.gov.uk/legal-aid-eforms. There is no requirement to submit a copy of your record of costs in either case.

24.15   POAs should be paid into your office account (Specification para 6.25).
24.16   POAs are re-payable at the end of the case. When each case concludes and the bill is assessed, the LAA will pay the value of the bill and then recoup the payments on account, so that the net effect is that you are paid only the outstanding balance. Where you receive costs from the other side in part or in full, you should notify the LAA even where you are making no claim for legal aid costs so that payments on account can be recouped.

Unrecouped payments on account

24.17   It is really important to claim or notify the LAA at the end of a case, as the amounts to be recovered can mount up. Repaying historic unrecouped payments on account have caused practitioners serious financial problems and additional work for both themselves and the LAA. From February 2018, the LAA started to send a list of all outstanding certificates every two months, in an effort to make it easier to check your records against theirs and take action promptly where required. One benefit of CCMS is that once all certificates are on the system, it should be much easier to reconcile cases.

Payment on account limits

24.18   Paragraph 6.23 of the Specification entitles the LAA to impose a maximum payment on account limit. This would be set in each individual contract schedule, could vary from category of law to category of law, and indeed from firm to firm.

24.19   The limit would be calculated by comparing the value of debits (payments to you) as against credits (claims received) on your account with the LAA. The maximum amount by which debits would be allowed to exceed credits is the maximum payment on account limit, and once the limit were reached the LAA would refuse to make any further payments on account and would require repayment of the excess.

24.20   However, although this clause is in the contract, no schedules currently specify a limit and the then Legal Services Commission (LSC) undertook not to introduce one without further consultation when the Unified Contract was introduced in 2007. The power in the 2018 Contract is discretionary, and the LAA have, at the time of writing, given no indication of whether or in what circumstances they intend to introduce the limit. The power has not been used in over ten years since it has been in successive contracts.

Key performance indicators

24.21   The LAA monitors organisations remotely, using the data you supply as a matter of course when applying for funding or claiming at the end of the case. You need to be able to monitor your own performance against these.

24.22   The Standard Contracts include key performance indicators (KPIs). See chapter 21 for more information about KPIs.

Service standards

24.23   The Standard Contracts include service standards. You need to comply with them. See chapter 21 for more information about service standards.

Costs audits

Overview

24.24   Historically, cost auditing of controlled work has always been a bone of contention between the LAA and practitioners. Practitioners tend to feel that LAA staff do not understand the work that has been done, and the LAA tends to feel that practitioners are not sufficiently stringent in applying the contract requirements. The LAA has published a list of 14 different types of audit and validation process.[4]

24.25   The LAA's approach is that if, from the management information evidence that they have, it appears that you are complying with contractual requirements, it is likely that you will only have one contract manager visit a year and will not be audited further. The LAA distinguishes between a contract manager visit (which it does not count as a formal audit) and formal audits, carried out by members of the Operational Assurance team. The distinction is lost on many practitioners, who often emerge from whichever process the LAA has used having to repay money. The way to avoid this is by robust supervision and monitoring, especially before final claims for payment are submitted. To ensure all your claims are made correctly, the LAA's Costs assessment guidance is helpful and can be found here: www.gov.uk/funding-and-costs-assessment-for-civil-and-crime-matters.

24.26   The LAA's audits are undertaken to provide the Ministry of Justice with assurance that the legal aid fund has been spent correctly and to eliminate the cause of irregularities and errors identified in the past by the National Audit Office (NAO), which led to the LSC's annual accounts being qualified towards the end of its life. The LAA needs to achieve an overall level of 'materiality of error' of less than one per cent in order to meet NAO targets.

24.27   This means that in the small samples taken by contract managers when they come to visit, you are aiming for a zero per cent error rate. This is not easy!

24.28   The main problem areas are in controlled work (Legal Help, Controlled Legal Representation and Family Help Lower) cases:

- assessing the eligibility of clients incorrectly or retaining insufficient evidence on file;
- incorrect claims for payment for:
  - private law family cases; and
  - immigration and asylum cases;
- travel distances (the LAA prefers a copy of a route planner showing postcodes travelled to/from to be retained on the file).

Therefore, these tend to be the main focus of visits/audits in civil and family categories (see below for crime). In 2016 the LAA issued very

---

4 See: www.gov.uk/legal-aid-agency-audits.

helpful guidance called *Preventing audit issues,* which aims to help practitioners avoid the most common types of error.[5]

24.29   If you disagree with an LAA decision about costs, see costs appeals at para 23.39 below and chapter 18.

Evidence of means

24.30   The contract manager will select at least five Legal Help forms. If even one of them fails (eg due to no or invalid evidence of means), a further sample will be selected. This is then audited by the organisation itself and two files are checked by the contract manager. If three or more of the aggregated sample fail, the organisation may be invited to agree an extrapolation rate across all similar work or may be asked to self-assess all the files which could possibly exhibit the same failing (the latter is more common). In larger organisations this can mean that you are expected to self audit hundreds of files in a short period of time.

Family level 1 and 2 fees

24.31   The contract manager will be checking that level 2 fees have been claimed correctly, see below.

Private family law – conditions for level 2

24.32   Up to and including 8 May 2011, para 10.55 of the Family Contract Specification required two meetings with the client in order to justify a level 2 fee.

24.33   Note also that following certification of PoP CLA 54 – definition of 'meeting' was broadened from 20 December 2010 to include phone calls.

24.34   The LSC removed the requirement for a second meeting from 9 May 2011 and instead practitioners had to show that 'substantive negotiations' had taken place. This remains the position under the 2018 Standard Contract Specification:

> 7.58 You may only make a determination that a Client qualifies for Family Help (Lower) where all relevant criteria in the Merits Regulations, Financial Regulations and Procedure Regulations are satisfied including the criteria in Paragraph 35 of the Merits Regulations. In addition, the fee for Family Help (Lower) may only be claimed for those Family Disputes:

5   See: www.gov.uk/legal-aid-agency-audits.

(a) which involve more than simply taking instructions from and advising the Client, and providing any follow up written or telephone advice; and

(b) where you are involved in substantive negotiations with a third party (either by conducting the negotiations yourself or by advice and assistance in support of mediation); and

(c) where the dispute, if unresolved, would be likely to lead to family proceedings; and

(d) which do not primarily concern processing a divorce, nullity, judicial separation or dissolution of a civil partnership; and

(e) which do not primarily concern advice relating to child support.

Crime

24.35   In crime, contract managers will check:

- evidence of means on CRM1 and 2 cases;
- incorrect claiming of court duty work:
  - claiming under a subsequent representation order as well as court duty for the same case;
  - claiming under a representation order when the case concluded on the same day as a court duty session;
  - incorrect claiming of travel for court duty work (eg other than at a weekend or bank holiday)
- 'duplicate' claims where more than one police station case fee has been claimed, where the contract manager considers that there was a 'series of offences' and only one fee was payable.
- travel distances (the LAA prefers a copy of a route planner showing postcodes travelled to/from to be retained on the file).

Contract notices

Overview

24.36   Up to early 2018, the LAA operated a 'zero tolerance' policy in relation to errors and would issue a contract notice for a single error, even before any review or appeal process had been invoked. In January 2018, the LAA informed the Civil Contract Consultative Group (a regular meeting between the LAA and practitioner representative bodies), that since performance had improved, it would be able take a more risk-based approach. Henceforth, contract notices would be issued when:

- the errors found pose anything other than a low-level risk to the LAA's accounts being qualified by the NAO (to be decided by the Area Contract Manager);
- the provider does not agree that remedial action is needed;
- the contract manager has doubt as to the effectiveness of the provider to make the required changes and a follow-up visit is needed;
- multiple breaches of different aspects on a sample of files, indicating poor reporting practices in the organisation.

24.37 A contract notice requires a significant improvement in performance in relation to the relevant issue within six months, when the contract manager will come back to see whether improvements have been achieved. Clause 24 of the Standard Contract (all versions, both Civil and Crime) allows the LAA to suspend or even terminate contracts for 'persistent breaches', that is three breaches of the same term in a 24-month period (or six different breaches). It is very rare indeed for the LAA to invoke this clause; but it undoubtedly gives practitioners cause for concern.

24.38 The contract manager will also recoup money against any overpayments or ineligible payments.

Appeals

24.39 If you disagree with your contract manager, see 'contract compliance appeals' below.

24.40 You cannot actually appeal against a contract notice as such. It is not an appealable decision under clause 27 of the Standard Contract Terms. What you can do is appeal against any wrong decision which has led to a contract notice, and therefore undermine the basis on which it was issued.

24.41 If you disagree that a contract notice was proportionate in the circumstances, you should write to your contract manager and ask that the issue is considered by the Regional Contract Manager. It may be useful in the long term if the LAA wishes to suspend or terminate your contract under the 'totting up' provisions in clause 24. If all else fails, you can use the LAA's complaints procedure.[6]

---

6 See: www.gov.uk/government/organisations/legal-aid-agency/about/complaints-procedure.

Contract compliance audits

24.42 If they have concerns, the LAA may choose to carry out a contract compliance audit (CCA). However, no CCAs were carried out in 2018 and this form of audit has fallen out of favour with the LAA.

24.43 A minimum of 30 and maximum of 50 files is assessed, depending on the level of claims you have made across the 12-month sample period. The LAA employs a formula devised by the NAO to select samples to test the accuracy of assessments.

24.44 CCAs are carried out off-site on the LAA's premises. They check compliance with the Civil/Crime Contracts, guidance, the criminal bills assessment manual and civil Costs assessment guidance. The LAA assesses whether there is appropriate evidence of eligibility, work done and disbursements on the file, costs incurred are reasonable and the bill is in line with the appropriate guidance.

Contract compliance audit outcomes

24.45 Files are either nil assessed, because the file should not have been funded at all (eg the client was not financially eligible or the matter was out of scope) or reduced by a percentage because a higher fee was claimed than was appropriate (eg a family level 2 fee was claimed when the LAA says it should have been level 1).

24.46 Firms used to be given a categorisation, depending on the outcome of a CCA. The LSC stopped doing that, and the LAA simply applies reductions in fees and takes action as follows:

Final % value assessed down	Action and sanctions	Old rating name
0.00%–10.00%	Recoup or credit value of incorrectly claimed files within audit sample.	Category 1
10.01%–20.00%	Extrapolation of % reduction. Re-audit to be scheduled. Contract notice(s).	Category 2
20.01% or more	Extrapolation of % reduction. Re-audit to be scheduled. Contract notice(s) (further action, including possible termination, to be taken on an individual basis if result of re-audit not improved).	Category 3

Extrapolation

24.47   Extrapolation is one of the reasons that CCAs are dreaded by practitioners as an audit of a relatively small sample can result in significant sums having to be repaid. The Standard Contract[7] allows the LAA to apply the findings of a controlled work costs audit back to the date when the file sample was requested for the previous CCA, or 12 months prior to the date the sample was requested in the current CCA, whichever is the most recent. For example, suppose the file sample of 20 files was requested on 1 July 2019 and the eventual reduction was 25 per cent. For example, if the value of claims 1 July 2019 to 30 June 2018 is £146,000, the recoupment would be 25 per cent of £146,000, ie £36,500.

Contract compliance audit – appeal process

24.48   The appeal process is the same as other types of costs appeal, see below.

Costs appeals

24.49   The first stage of the appeal process (see eg the Standard Contract 2018 Specification para 6.71 onwards; and the Standard Crime Contract 2017 Specification para 8.19 onwards). The substantive provisions in relation to the initial stages are the same in the different contracts (only the paragraph numbers differ). The first is an internal review by another member of the LAA's audit team. You must set out the reasons for the appeal in writing within 28 days and send the file(s) back with the appeal. The LAA suggests that it may be more effective to send only relevant documentation, as it will save time; but whether that would be the best course of action would depend on the nature of the appeal. If you need an extension of time, you must have a 'good reason' and request the extension within 21 days. It is likely to be granted; but only up to a further 14 days. If the initial stage is not successful, you move to independent costs assessment. Independent Costs Assessors (ICAs) are solicitors or barristers who are members of the LAA's Review Panel. They are contracted on a sessional basis and are not LAA employees.

24.50   ICA appeals are generally considered on the papers only, although in exceptional circumstances either party can apply to the assessor

---

7   Standard Civil Contract 2018 Specification para 4.48.

for an oral hearing, although these are rarely granted. The assessor reviews the assessment and may confirm, increase or decrease the amount assessed. However, in contracts issued after 2013, the process ends here. Any further challenge would need to be brought by way of judicial review.

Points of principle

24.51 Under contracts issued up to 2013, it was possible to apply for a 'point of principle of general importance' to be certified if raised by an issue in the costs appeal and overlooked by the ICA. Civil 2018 and Crime 2017 Contracts have no further costs appeal process after the ICA process described above. The only recourse would be by way of judicial review. Points of principle in respect of regulations or contract provisions still applicable or replicated in current rules should, however, be persuasive authority in LAA and ICA decision-making.

Legal aid policy

by Steve Hynes

Introduction

25.1   This chapter gives an overview of the developments in legal aid policy from January 2018 to December 2019. Since the last edition of this Handbook there have also been some significant victories in the courts for legal aid providers against the government and Legal Aid Agency (LAA), as well as some problems with the administration of legal aid, particularly around the tendering system.

25.2   Currently, we are in what might be described as a political limbo. The post legislative review of the Legal Aid, Sentencing and Punishment of Offenders Act 2012 (LASPO), after some delay, has been published, but it seems ministers are waiting for the results of pilots and a major review of criminal legal aid remuneration before they will take any decisions around committing any significant (or insignificant!) sums of new money to the system.

25.3   Much of the chapter is based on articles in Legal Action Group's (LAG's) *Legal Action* magazine, which is also published online. LAG believes it is important to keep practitioners updated on developments in legal aid policy so that they can, hopefully, better plan in order to continue to provide access to justice for the public.

Seventy years of legal aid

25.4   2019 marked the 70th anniversary of the founding of the modern legal aid system. It was on 30 July 1949 that the Legal Aid and Advice Act 1949 received royal assent. The Act introduced the civil legal aid scheme the following year. Until this point, most people with civil legal problems had no recourse if they couldn't afford to pay for the services of a lawyer. Rather like today, there were pro bono services available, but they were overwhelmed and unable to meet demand.

25.5   The 1949 Act also updated the provisions for criminal legal aid in the Poor Prisoners' Defence Act 1903. A publicly funded system for criminal legal aid had been around since that 1903 Act, but it was only after the 1949 legislation that it started to be widely available for anyone accused of a crime.

25.6   LAG believed that the anniversary was an opportunity to celebrate the achievements of the legal aid system, as it upholds the rule of law by ensuring that those accused of a crime receive a fair trial and allows people to enforce their civil rights. We held a celebratory conference in April this year (2019) at which Baroness Hale, President of the Supreme Court, gave the keynote address. Another highlight of the event was a debate and vote on the best legal aid case of the last seventy years.

25.7 Cases discussed in this debate included *Middleton* (*R v HM Coroner for the Western District of Somerset ex p Middleton*[1]), which transformed the law relating to inquests and was advocated for by Henrietta Hill QC of Doughty Street Chambers. However, the case which narrowly won over the majority of the delegates in the vote was not a high-profile precedent-setting one such as this, but a case more typical of those that many of the delegates would be familiar with from their own work in legal aid practices.

25.8 Diane Astin, a LAG author and a solicitor at Deighton Pierce Glynn, argued for a case in which she had represented a 16-year-old homeless asylum-seeker. With the help of legal aid, her client was able to enforce his rights under the Children Act 1989 and turn his life around.[2] Astin believed the case had demonstrated the 'real value' of legal aid, not only to change a client's life, but influence policy (after the case, the local council involved changed its procedures on dealing with asylum-seekers) and by doing so transformed other peoples' lives.

Policy and politicians

Change in leadership at the Ministry of Justice

25.9 Since the vote to leave the European Union (EU) in June 2016, the issue of whether we leave and on what terms has dominated British politics. The politicians' preoccupation with this has meant that other areas of policy have taken a back-seat.

25.10 In part, the fall-out from Brexit has also led to the revolving doors at the Ministry of Justice (MoJ) being rather over-used as new ministers come and go. In the 23 years prior to 2010, we had only four occupants of the post, but since 2010 there have been seven Lord Chancellors. This has led to concerns over a lack of continuity and consistency in justice policy-making.[3]

---

1 [2004] UKHL 10.

2 'Legal Aid at 70: there are reasons to be cheerful', by Catherine Baksi, May 2019 *Legal Action* 8.

3 'Lord Chancellors come and go while the problems with our justice system keep on getting bigger', by Carol Storer, September 2019 *Legal Action* 3.

25.11   David Gauke MP was Lord Chancellor and Secretary of State for Justice for much of the period this chapter covers, which meant that the MoJ was in danger of experiencing some political stability at the top. He was appointed in January 2018 and resigned in July 2019, as he did not want to serve in a cabinet under the Prime Minister, Boris Johnson. Nothing illustrates the parlous state of British politics more than Gauke's fate. In a few short weeks he went from holding one of the most ancient offices of state to being under threat of expulsion from the Conservative Party which he had served as an MP since 2005.

25.12   On 3 September 2019, Gauke voted with 20 other Conservative MPs to block Boris Johnson from allowing the UK to crash out of the EU without a deal on 31 October 2019. At the time of writing (early December 2019), Gauke has lost the Conservative 'whip', which means he cannot stand as a Conservative candidate in the general election which is to take place on 12 December 2019.

25.13   As discussed in the last two editions of this handbook, the post-legislative review of LASPO had been much delayed, again partly due to the upheaval caused by Brexit. The review documents were published in February 2019 and are discussed in the following pages. Robert Buckland QC, who replaced Gauke as Lord Chancellor, will be responsible for continuing to implement the policy changes suggested in the review documents.

25.14   Buckland stepped up from the second ranked post of Minister of State in the MoJ to the post of Lord Chancellor and Justice Secretary. He had previously been the Solicitor General for England and Wales from July 2014 to May 2019. Prior to being elected as an MP in 2010, he was a criminal law barrister practising in Wales.

25.15   The new Lord Chancellor has legal qualifications and experience, which some of the recent incumbents of the post have lacked, and so should be able to get to grips with the challenges facing the justice system quickly. This is provided there is no change of government and he survives the current Brexit political turmoil. In this regard, it is worth noting that he campaigned for 'remain' and is opposed to a no-deal exit from the EU, 'but feels strongly about the need to uphold the result of the referendum'.[4]

Continuing austerity in the justice system

25.16   In less than ten years, civil legal aid has been transformed from a system in which just under 1.5 million people a year received help

---

4 'Brexit update – letter to residents', see: robertbuckland.co.uk, January 2019.

with everyday legal problems, to a rump service assisting fewer than 270,000 per year.[5] While criminal legal aid has not suffered scope cuts in the same way as civil, the gradual chipping away in the real value of fees is leading to a situation in which practitioners take to the streets to protest and, in the case of barristers, strike. Most concerning for the future is the other option they are taking, which is to vote with their feet and leave the system. The problems extend beyond legal aid across most of the justice system, which has suffered disproportionately from successive governments' austerity measures.

25.17   To coincide with Justice Week in 2018, a new event run by the legal professional bodies, the Bar Council published a research paper by Martin Chalkley,[6] a professor of economics at the University of York. The paper shows that in real terms the expenditure on justice has been reduced by 27 per cent since 2008, and for some parts of the system spending cuts were even higher (according to the paper, the legal aid system has been cut by nearly a third).

25.18   Professor Chalkley observes in his report that the UK economy has grown by around 13 per cent in the last ten years and that 'it would not be unreasonable to expect the justice system to grow along with the economy'. He argues it would be fair to conclude that the government 'has taken a conscious decision to substantially withdraw public funding for the support of the justice system and for promoting access to justice'. In contrast, according to Chalkley, other public services have seen substantial increase in their budgets – for example, the NHS has seen growth of 25 per cent in the same period.

25.19   Court closures and the state of repair of the remaining infrastructure of the justice system remain an ongoing concern.[7] According to research carried out by the House of Commons Library, half of all magistrates' courts in England and Wales have closed since 2010.[8] Former judge and LAG author, Nic Madge, believes that the Courts and Tribunals system needs substantial investment in IT systems and that the 'fabric of many court buildings are in a parlous state'. He

---

5 These figures are taken from the quarterly statistical bulletin published by the MoJ see: https://assets.publishing.service.gov.uk/government/uploads/system/uploads/attachment_data/file/533178/legal-aid-statistics-england-and-wales-bulletin.

6 'Funding for Justice 2008 to 2018: Justice in the age of austerity', Professor Martin Chalkley, published for the Bar Council of England & Wales, 1 November 2018.

7 See 'Court closures protest': http://www.lag.org.uk/?id=206443/.

8 https://commonslibrary.parliament.uk/home-affairs/justice/courts/constituency-data-magistrates-court-closures/.

argues that 'Courts appear to have been selected for closure, not on the basis of needs, but rather for the money that sales will generate'.[9]

25.20   In January 2019, severe problems hit the main computer system for the Courts and Tribunals.[10] This led to cancelled hearings and other problems. Practitioners and judges reported to LAG that they were having issues relating to the listing of hearings and the loss of email communication. One of the most-high profile lawyers on social media, The Secret Barrister, said in a tweet on 23 January 2019: 'But this is far from the first time the courts and the public have been let down by the MoJ's abysmal computer system.' The mystery barrister and author questioned, 'how much is this persistent failure costing, and who is going to be accountable?'[11] *The Guardian* newspaper reported that it had seen an internal MoJ document which blamed the IT failure on the 'historical under-investment in ageing IT systems'.[12]

25.21   The MoJ said that the IT problems were unrelated to the digital reform programme for the Courts and Tribunals service. A budget of £1 billion was committed to this in 2016, but the timetable for this has slipped from four to six years (not surprising for such a large IT project). An enquiry by the Justice Committee on the reforms is ongoing. At the launch of this, the chair of the committee, Bob Neil MP, said that while he welcomed the 'intention to modernise the Courts and Tribunal system', concerns about the deliverability of the reforms had already been expressed by the Public Accounts Committee and that his committee was 'worried about the access to justice implications' and was taking the 'opportunity to put those at the heart of our inquiry'.[13]

25.22   Chancellor Sajid Javid told parliament in September 2019 that there would be an increase in spending for government departments. A total of £7.6 billion was announced in extra cash, including a 4.9 per cent increase for the MoJ. According to the government's figures, the MoJ's budget will rise from £7.6 billion in the current financial year (2019/20) to £8.1 billion in the next. While this is of course welcome news, it must be set against the cuts discussed above.[14]

9   'Selling off our silver', Nic Madge, September 2019 *Legal Action* 10.
10 'IT problems hit the courts', February 2019 *Legal Action* 4.
11 https://twitter.com/BarristerSecret/status/1087989691629142016.
12 'Justice ministry knew court IT systems were "obsolete", papers reveal', *The Guardian*, 29 January 2019.
13 'HM Courts and Tribunals Service reforms to be scrutinised', February 2019 *Legal Action* 4.
14 'Spending review: Ministry of Justice receives cash boost', October 2019 *Legal Action* 5.

Considerably more investment will be needed in the justice system if the effects of more than ten years of austerity are to be reversed.

LASPO review

25.23 The post-implementation review of LASPO has been the main hook on which many have hung their hopes for a change in direction from the government – but when it was finally published in February 2019, it met with a downbeat response from practitioners.

25.24 Speaking to *The Guardian*, Richard Atkins QC, chair of the Bar Council, typified the views of many legal aid lawyers. He described the review as a 'wasted opportunity' because the report offered 'little of substance to ease the impact of LASPO on vulnerable individuals seeking justice'. Lucy Frazer, the then justice minister, told the *The Times* that £5 million of cash had been set aside for 'innovative forms of legal support'. She also offered some hope for the future telling *The Guardian* they were 'aiming to put forward a package to the Treasury for the next spending review armed with more evidence for our spending [on legal aid]. We will be making a bid in due course'.[15]

25.25 Three documents were published:

- a review report dealing with legal aid;[16]
- a companion paper, 'Legal support: the way ahead – an action plan to deliver better support to people experiencing legal problems';[17] and
- a paper dealing with Part 2 of LASPO.[18]

25.26 The following two sections include commentary on the LASPO review and its potential impact on civil and criminal legal aid.

Civil legal aid

Civil legal aid tenders

25.27 The latest civil tender process proved to be a rather drawn-out affair. The procurement process was announced in September 2017 with

---

15 See: www.lag.org.uk/article/206047/muted-response-to-laspo-review.
16 *Post-implementation review of Part 1 of the Legal Aid, Sentencing and Punishment of Offenders Act 2012*, MoJ, 7 February 2019.
17 CP 40, MoJ, February 2019.
18 Part 2 of LASPO concerns the reforms relating to Sir Rupert (then Lord Justice) Jackson's 2010 Review of Civil Litigation (civil litigation costs and funding).

the contracts due to commence on 1 September 2018, but it was hit by some glitches.

25.28   Additional tender rounds were announced in March 2018 to plug gaps in services. These included re-tenders for face-to-face contracts in 39 procurement areas for housing and debt advice; six procurement areas for immigration and asylum advice; and seven procurement areas for family work. Vicky Ling, who co-edits this publication, said it was 'unprecedented for the LAA to be re-advertising such a large number of contracts so soon after the tender process has closed'. Head of Justice at the Law Society, Richard Miller, said that it confirmed the profession's view which is that 'the civil legal aid contracts are not viable'.[19]

25.29   In a surprise announcement, the LAA then re-opened tenders for all the main civil legal aid face-to-face contracts in June 2018[20] with a deadline of 10 August for firms and other providers to apply. This second bite at the full tendering cherry, though, was not due to gaps in provision.

25.30   David Gilmore of DG Legal, a firm of consultants which specialises in management consultancy with legal aid firms, told *Legal Action*: 'It would seem that some family law legal aid firms applied for a public law contract in error, believing they were applying for a contract to undertake public law family work.' Vicky Ling believed that some firms might have merged or changed their legal status after they were awarded a contract which would invalidate their bids. According to Ling: 'Running the tender round again is perfectly sensible if two or three significant providers messed-up their original tenders as this is not going to affect anyone adversely.' The re-opening of tenders was also welcomed by LAG.[21]

25.31   The second full tendering round appeared to be at the root of some severe administrative problems which hit the start of the new contracts for civil legal aid providers. While the contracts were due to commence on 1 September, around 350 providers did not have contracts in place by then. This was due to delays in the verification process which providers had to complete before being awarded a contract. It seems that some providers did not realise that bidding in the additional procurement round would invalidate their first-round

---

19 'Advice deserts in civil legal aid provision set to grow as LAA tender rounds fail to attract bids', May 2018 *Legal Action* 4.

20 See: https://assets.publishing.service.gov.uk/government/uploads/system/ uploads/attachment_data/file/722487/Further_Face_to_Face_procurement_ process___Information_For_Applicants.pdf.

21 'The Legal Aid Agency has made the right call in announcing a further civil legal aid bid round', Steve Hynes, July/August 2018 *Legal Action* 13.

bids for contracts due to commence on 1 September (contracts in the additional round were due to start a month later).

25.32   Chris Minnoch, CEO of the Legal Aid Practitioners Group (LAPG), told LAG that 'some firms misunderstood' what was required of them from the LAA and that there were 'lessons to be learnt from both sides' over the timetables and information about the bid rounds. Another well-informed source was less conciliatory than LAPG. They told LAG that they believed that the LAA 'had been inconsistent and vindictive in their treatment of firms' and that '80% of the blame' for the confusion over the civil contracts lay with the LAA.[22]

25.33   A successful judicial review brought by the Law Centres Network in June 2018 led to the tender exercise for the Housing Possession Court Duty Scheme (HPCDS) tenders being scrapped. The LAA had sought to reduce the number of schemes from 113 to 47.[23]

25.34   Duncan Lewis, one of the largest legal aid firms in the country, was also successful in its judicial review of the LAA's policy of not backdating legal aid certificates. This led to an amendment to the Civil Legal Aid (Procedure) Regulations 2012 to allow backdating.[24]

25.35   According to figures published in March 2019, there are a total of 2,424 civil legal aid contracts, which is a slight increase on the previous year (there were 2,283 in March 2018). It should be noted that there were over 4,000 contracts prior to the implementation of the LASPO scope cuts in April 2013.[25]

LASPO review and civil legal aid

25.36   LASPO mainly impacted on civil legal aid due to the cuts in scope falling exclusively on civil law. The review document shows that, in most of the areas of civil law affected, the decline in case numbers has been greater than originally projected – for example, civil representation in housing cases has fallen by 36 per cent in the period 2012/13 to 2017/18, as against the 11 per cent which was predicted.[26]

25.37   While in the review documents there is no commitment to reverse the LASPO scope cuts, there were some positive changes announced

---

22 'Confusion over civil legal aid contracts', October 2018 *Legal Action* 4.

23 'Law Centres win housing legal aid case', July/August 2018 *Legal Action* 4.

24 www.gov.uk/government/news/civil-news-backdating-powers-in-civil-cases-to-be-introduced.

25 *Legal aid statistics England and Wales tables January to March 2019.* Details of the number of providers are contained in the tables document – see section 9.1.

26 See p88 of the Part 1 Review document and figure 44.

which have now been implemented. These were extending legal aid to:

- special guardianship orders;
- non-means tested legal aid in public law family cases; and
- migrant children separated from their families.

A review of eligibility criteria and thresholds for legal aid was also promised, and this is currently ongoing.

25.38   On the controversial exceptional case funding (ECF) scheme, the MoJ committed itself to consider simplifying the application process. Take-up of the ECF has always been much lower than predicted. In the review document, the MoJ admit in the first year of the scheme only 130 applications were granted as against the 'circa 3,700' which had been anticipated.[27] They are playing rather fast and loose with the figures here, as the original estimate was in fact 5,000–7,000 cases.[28]

Telephone gateway and low take-up of mediation

25.39   In a move which vindicated the criticisms of many, including LAG, the review announced a change of policy on the mandatory telephone gateway. Due to a lack of providers willing to bid, the LAA had experienced difficulties with the tender process for special educational needs (SEN) and discrimination law[29] and has committed itself to reviewing the service (the gateway also includes debt advice). This was not the only mea culpa from the MoJ contained in the report. The most notable was the admission of failure to shift more private law family law cases into mediation services.[30]

25.40   The report concedes that the low take-up of mediation has been caused by the lack of legal aid resulting in individuals bypassing alternative dispute resolution (ADR) and instead heading straight to court. This has led to an increase in litigants in person (LIPs). The government, though, does not accept that the solution is to increase access to lawyers to assist the public in family cases, arguing that this 'is not always the correct or most affordable answer'.[31] The MoJ seems to be suggesting that a combination of its digital led reforms

---

27 *Post-implementation Review of Part 1 LASPO* p136.

28 See para 31 of *Impact of changes to civil legal aid under Part 1 of the Legal Aid, Sentencing and Punishment of Offenders Act 2012,* Justice Committee report published by the House of Commons, 4 March 2015.

29 See 'News', March 2018 *Legal Action* 4.

30 See p142 of the review report.

31 See p153.

to the court system and an increase in cash for services aimed at LIPs is the solution.

25.41   A total of £6.5 million in additional hard cash was also announced in the review documents. Lucy Frazer (in the *Guardian* article above) was referring to a £5 million fund to be spent on encouraging legal tech innovation. A separate amount of £1.5 million has been earmarked for enhanced support for LIPs. These are parsimonious sums when considered against the cut of around £400 million which was stripped from the civil legal aid budget due to LASPO.

Early advice

25.42   The strategy document commits the government to a face-to-face pilot for social welfare law. For some time, a policy head of steam has been building around the need for early advice to prevent problems escalating. Early advice was a raised in a special debate on legal aid in the House of Commons in November 2018. Andy Slaughter, the Labour MP for Hammersmith and Fulham, initiated the Westminster Hall debate, which takes place away from the main chamber, to 'consider the future of legal aid'.

25.43   Slaughter, who as shadow justice minister led the opposition to the LASPO legislation in the Commons, told MPs that the aim of the Act had been 'to reduce the legal aid budget by £350m, but last year spending was £950m less than in 2010'. He called on the government to restore legal aid for early advice, as the lack of this meant that 'simple problems are left to escalate'. There was heavyweight cross-party support for a re-think of the government's approach from the Chairman of the Justice Committee, Bob Neill, Conservative MP for Bromley and Chislehurst. In the debate, he described 'early advice as essential' and admitted that he believed that the government had allowed the pendulum to 'go too far the other way' with the reductions in legal aid.

25.44   An evaluation of funding and co-location of legal services, such as those based in health settings, is also promised.[32] This is recognition from the MoJ of the arguments from the Low Commission and others, about the need for early legal advice and the consequential savings in other public services such as health.

---

32   See p25: https://assets.publishing.service.gov.uk/government/uploads/system/uploads/attachment_data/file/777036/legal-support-the-way-ahead.pdf.

Criminal legal aid

25.45 As a former criminal barrister, the new Lord Chancellor, Robert Buckland, will have some insight into the problems in the criminal legal aid system. He will need it. Over the last year or so, his predecessor has tried to keep the lid on an ongoing battle over remuneration rates.

Advocates' Graduated Fee Scheme

25.46 Both barristers and solicitor advocates are paid under the Advocates' Graduated Fee Scheme (AGFS) for Crown Court work. Most of this work is undertaken by self-employed barristers, who are represented by the Criminal Bar Association (CBA).

25.47 In May 2018, the CBA called off its planned boycott of returns (cases taken at short notice) after the government pledged a further £15 million to fund a revised version of AGFS, but this deal began to unravel almost immediately as, according to the CBA, the government calculations were inaccurate and only an extra £8.6 million of new money had in fact been allocated.

25.48 The MoJ made further concessions to the Bar over the AFGS in November 2018. David Gauke announced an extra £8 million in cash, to be targeted to the junior end of the Bar, bringing the total of additional cash, he argued, to £23 million.[33] Discontent among the advocates continued though, and the issue of fees for prosecution work was added to their grievances over remuneration.

25.49 A day of action planned for 1 July 2019, which would have brought the criminal courts system to a standstill, seems to have concentrated minds at the MoJ. A deal agreed between the Bar and government included the fixed fees for prosecution work rising to the same level as AFGS. The government also agreed to accelerate work on three aspects of fees, ahead of the full review of criminal fees announced in the LASPO review (see below). These are payments in high volume evidence cases; cracks (trials which don't proceed at the last minute as the defendant changes their plea); and reviewing material which is eventually not used in the trial.[34]

25.50 It would be fair to say that the deal was not welcomed with unqualified joy by some in the legal aid world. Christine Blacklaws, the then Law Society President, in response to the announcement of the deal said: 'Good firms are collapsing. Young lawyers are rejecting this

---

33 See MoJ press release dated 24 November 2018 at: www.gov.uk/government/news/increased-fees-for-criminal-defence-advocates.

34 'Criminal bar strike deal with government', July/August 2019 *Legal Action* 4.

area of law. In parts of the country, the criminal defence solicitor is going extinct, and the possibility of a fair trial is critically endangered. The government needs to listen to more than just the loudest voices if it is serious about addressing this impending catastrophe.'[35]

Litigators' Graduated Fee Scheme

25.51   Solicitors are paid for preparing Crown Court cases through the Litigators' Graduated Fee Scheme (LGFS) In December 2017 the government introduced changes to the scheme aimed at saving between £26 million to £36 million by altering the formula for the fee paid for reviewing pages of evidence. Unlike the Bar, as they contract directly with the LAA, solicitors are afraid of their firms being subject to legal action if they refuse to take on cases (hence the rather barbed comment from Blacklaws on the AGFS deal above).

25.52   In response to the MoJ's action, the Law Society brought a judicial review against the government. The court's judgment was especially damning of the MoJ's rationale for making the changes to the scheme. The LAA in the course of the case had to make the humiliating admission that it had got its sums wrong in calculating the costings.[36] Lord Justice Leggatt said of the government's defence of its consultation process: 'It is difficult to express in language of appropriate moderation why we consider these arguments without merit.'[37]

25.53   In another judicial review, the government was defeated on the issue of fees in a complex fraud case, which fell into the definition of a very high cost case (VHCC). The case concerned the cost of reviewing pages of evidence by the defence team.[38] Vicky Ling argues the case 'demonstrates the difficulties the LAA has in setting fair remuneration in complex cases', and that it has been 'overtaken by technology' in trying to grapple with setting fees to review large amounts of evidence held digitally.[39]

LASPO review and criminal legal aid

25.54   In December 2018, just prior to the publication of the LASPO review documents, the government announced a comprehensive review of

---

35 www.lawgazette.co.uk/news/secret-negotiations-discontent-over-criminal-legal-aid-fees-deal/5070619.article.

36 See *R (Law Society) v The Lord Chancellor* [2018] EWHC 2094 (Admin) para 117.

37 See para 93.

38 *R (Ames) v Lord Chancellor* [2018] EWHC 2250 (Admin).

39 See 'Legal Aid Agency loses judicial review on fees in complex cases', September 2018 *Legal Action* 4.

criminal fees. The LASPO Review (Part 1) report confirms there have been big reductions in case volumes and expenditure on criminal legal aid. Spending has fallen from about £1.18 billion in 2010/11 when the coalition government came to power, to £890 million in 2017/18.[40]

25.55   Proposals for the reform of Legal Aid (LAR) published in November 2010 changed the system of remuneration for payment in trials. Changes to the fee structure were aimed at preventing anomalies in the system such as paying more for cases in which the defendant entered a guilty plea later in a case.[41] Other changes included harmonising payments for cases which could be heard in either the Crown Court or magistrates' courts (referred to as 'either way' cases); aligning fees paid for murder and manslaughter cases; and combining fees for dishonesty cases.[42] The MoJ estimate that the changes cut around £140 million from the budget but acknowledge that due to the other factors affecting costs in the system this can only be a rough estimate.[43]

25.56   The Legal Aid Transformation (LAT) programme, published in September 2013, attempted to introduce a 17.5 per cent cut to solicitors' fees and a further policy paper sought to introduce competitive tendering for police and magistrates' court work. The then Lord Chancellor, Michael Gove, reversed the second 8.75 per cent tranche of the fee cut in January 2016 and went on to reverse a decision to introduce competitive tendering for police station work.

25.57   As is so well documented by the Secret Barrister, there are clearly profound problems in the criminal justice system caused by cuts. Overall there are 14 per cent fewer solicitor firms providing criminal legal aid and the Law Society presented evidence to the review that the cohort of police station duty solicitors is aging and not being replaced.[44]

25.58   The MoJ estimate there has been a 12 per cent drop in criminal advocates since 2012/13.[45] The ongoing review of criminal fees promises to publish findings on an accelerated work stream by the end of 2019, but the overall review is a complex process which is not scheduled to complete until 2021.[46] Such is the mood among

---

40 See para 846 p202.

41 See p206.

42 See pp207–208.

43 See para 890 p214.

44 See para 968 p239.

45 See para 972.

46 The plans are outline in a document published on the MoJ's website – see: https://assets.publishing.service.gov.uk/government/uploads/system/uploads/attachment_data/file/799661/criminal-legal-aid-programme-overview.pdf.

practitioners that the government might well have to make further concessions before then.

Thoughts on the future

25.59   Much reflection on the future of legal aid boils down to one thing: money. The realpolitik of the situation is that there will have to be a significant increase in fees for Crown and other higher court work. Experience shows that the Treasury will argue that this needs to be contained within the legal aid budget envelope. It's clear from ministers' comments around the LASPO review that they see their main task in legal aid policy is to persuade the Treasury to loosen the purse strings. They will need to be successful in this if they are to head-off knock-on cuts to other parts of the legal aid budget to pay for increases in criminal legal aid fees.

25.60   Continual budget reductions and the negative press they generate is leading to a situation in which legal aid feels like a blighted service. Recruiting and retaining talented lawyers is becoming increasing difficult. Particularly in specialisms such as housing law, despite much of it remaining in scope, there are no longer lawyers around to fill vacancies or to establish new firms or other providers to meet demand. Again, a large part of this is about the demand for an increase in remuneration, but there is also a need for investment in training – one of the early budget cuts was the ending of support for training contracts for the next generation of legal aid lawyers.

25.61   While the LASPO review was disappointing in respect of any substantial reversal of the scope cuts, it does mark an important change in the rhetoric from ministers around legal aid policy. They are no longer talking-up the necessity to control the legal aid budget, but have responded to some of the access to justice lobby's arguments, such as the need for early advice and extending scope to vulnerable groups such as migrant children. Significantly, in *Legal Support: The Way Ahead*, the strategy document published by the MoJ in February 2019, the importance of making people 'aware of their entitlement to legal assistance' was also emphasised.[47]

25.62   The more positive mood music around legal aid policy needs to continue if we are to secure the substantial investment of public money the system needs.

47 See p6.

APPENDICES

Legal Aid, Sentencing and Punishment of Offenders Act 2012 Sch 1[1]

SCHEDULE 1: CIVIL LEGAL SERVICES

PART 1: SERVICES

Care, supervision and protection of children

1(1) Civil legal services provided in relation to–
- (a) orders under section 25 of the Children Act 1989 ('the 1989 Act') (secure accommodation);
- (b) orders under Part 4 of the 1989 Act (care and supervision);
- (c) orders under Part 5 of the 1989 Act (protection of children);
- (d) approval by a court under paragraph 19 of Schedule 2 to the 1989 Act (arrangements to assist children to live abroad);
- (e) parenting orders under section 8 of the Crime and Disorder Act 1998 ('the 1998 Act');
- (f) child safety orders under section 11 of the 1998 Act;
- (g) orders for contact under section 26 of the Adoption and Children Act 2002 ('the 2002 Act');
- (h) applications for leave of the court to remove a child from a person's custody under section 36 of the 2002 Act;
- (i) placement orders, recovery orders or adoption orders under Chapter 3 of Part 1 of the 2002 Act (see sections 21, 41 and 46 of that Act);
- (j) orders under section 84 of the 2002 Act (parental responsibility prior to adoption abroad).
- (k) orders under section 119 of the Social Services and Well-being (Wales) Act 2014 ('the 2014 Act') (secure accommodation);
- (l) approval by a court under section 124 of the 2014 Act (arrangements to assist children to live abroad).

(2) Civil legal services provided in relation to an order under an enactment made–
- (a) as an alternative to an order mentioned in sub-paragraph (1), or
- (b) in proceedings heard together with proceedings relating to such an order.

Exclusions

(3) Sub-paragraphs (1) and (2) are subject to the exclusions in Parts 2 and 3 of this Schedule.

Definitions

(4) In this paragraph 'children' means persons under the age of 18.

Special educational needs

2(1) Civil legal services provided in relation to–
  (a) matters arising under Part 4 of the Education Act 1996 or Part 3 of the Children and Families Act 2014 (special educational needs);
  (b) assessments relating to learning difficulties under section 140 of the Learning and Skills Act 2000.

Exclusions

(2) Sub-paragraph (1) is subject to the exclusions in Parts 2 and 3 of this Schedule.

Abuse of child or vulnerable adult

3(1) Civil legal services provided in relation to abuse of an individual that took place at a time when the individual was a child or vulnerable adult, but only where–
  (a) the services are provided to the individual, or
  (b) the individual has died and the services are provided–
    (i) to the individual's personal representative, or
    (ii) for the purposes of a claim under the Fatal Accidents Act 1976 for the benefit of the individual's dependants.

General exclusions

(2) Sub-paragraph (1) is subject to–
  (a) the exclusions in Part 2 of this Schedule, with the exception of paragraphs 1, 2, 3, 8 and 12 of that Part, and
  (b) the exclusion in Part 3 of this Schedule.

Specific exclusions

(3) The services described in sub-paragraph (1) do not include services provided in relation to clinical negligence.
(4) The services described in sub-paragraph (1) do not include services provided in relation to a matter arising under a family enactment.

Definitions

(5) In this paragraph–
  'abuse' means physical or mental abuse, including–
  (a) sexual abuse, and
  (b) abuse in the form of violence, neglect, maltreatment and exploitation;
  'child' means a person under the age of 18;
  'clinical negligence' means breach of a duty of care or trespass to the person committed in the course of the provision of clinical or medical services (including dental or nursing services);
  'family enactment' has the meaning given in paragraph 12;
  'personal representative', in relation to an individual who has died, means–
  (a) a person responsible for administering the individual's estate under the law of England and Wales, Scotland or Northern Ireland, or
  (b) a person who, under the law of another country or territory, has functions equivalent to those of administering the individual's estate;

'vulnerable adult' means a person aged 18 or over whose ability to protect himself or herself from abuse is significantly impaired through physical or mental disability or illness, through old age or otherwise.

Working with children and vulnerable adults

4(1) Civil legal services provided in relation to—

    (a) the inclusion of a person in a barred list or the removal of a person from a barred list;

    (b) a disqualification order under section 28, 29 or 29A of the Criminal Justice and Court Services Act 2000 (disqualification from working with children);

    (c) a direction under section 142 of the Education Act 2002 (prohibition from teaching etc).

Exclusions

(2) Sub-paragraph (1) is subject to the exclusions in Parts 2 and 3 of this Schedule.

Definitions

(3) In this paragraph 'barred list' means a list maintained under—

    (a) section 2 of the Safeguarding Vulnerable Groups Act 2006 (persons barred from regulated activities relating to children or vulnerable adults);

    (b) section 81 of the Care Standards Act 2000;

    (c) section 1 of the Protection of Children Act 1999.

Mental health and mental capacity

5(1) Civil legal services provided in relation to matters arising under—

    (a) the Mental Health Act 1983;

    (b) paragraph 5(2) of the Schedule to the Repatriation of Prisoners Act 1984;

    (c) the Mental Capacity Act 2005.

General exclusions

(2) Sub-paragraph (1) is subject to the exclusions in Parts 2 and 3 of this Schedule.

Specific exclusion

(3) The services described in sub-paragraph (1) do not include services provided in relation to—

    (a) the creation of lasting powers of attorney under the Mental Capacity Act 2005, or

    (b) the making of advance decisions under that Act.

(4) Sub-paragraph (3) does not exclude services provided in relation to determinations and declarations by a court under the Mental Capacity Act 2005 as to the validity, meaning, effect or applicability of—

    (a) a lasting power of attorney that has been created, or

    (b) an advance decision that has been made.

Community care

6(1) Civil legal services provided in relation to community care services.

Exclusions

(2) Sub-paragraph (1) is subject to the exclusions in Parts 2 and 3 of this Schedule.

Definitions

(3) In this paragraph—

'community care services' means services which a relevant person may provide or arrange to be provided under–
(a) [repealed.]
(b) [repealed.]
(c) [repealed.]
(d) [repealed.]
(e) section 117 of the Mental Health Act 1983 (after-care);
(f) section 17 of the Children Act 1989 ('the 1989 Act') (provision of services for children in need);
(g) section 20 of the 1989 Act (provision of accommodation for children);
(h) sections 22A, 22B, 22C and 23 of the 1989 Act (accommodation and maintenance for children in care and looked after children);
(i) sections 23B and 23C of the 1989 Act (local authority functions in respect of relevant children);
(j) sections 24, 24A and 24B of the 1989 Act (provision of services for persons qualifying for advice and assistance);
(k) [repealed.]
(l) [repealed.]
(m)[repealed.]
(n) Part 1 of the Care Act 2014 (local authority's functions of meeting an adult's needs for care and support);
(o) section 15 of the Social Services and Well-being (Wales) Act 2014 ('the 2014 Act') (preventative services);
(p) Part 4 of the 2014 Act (local authority's functions of meeting a person's needs for care and support);
(q) section 76 of the 2014 Act (provision of accommodation for children);
(r) sections 79, 80 and 81 of the 2014 Act (accommodation and maintenance for children in care and looked after children);
(s) sections 105 to 116 of the 2014 Act (local authority support for certain children);
'relevant person' means–
(a) a district council;
(b) a county council;
(c) a county borough council;
(d) a London borough council;
(e) the Common Council of the City of London;
(f) a Primary Care Trust established under section 18 of the National Health Service Act 2006;
(g) a Local Health Board established under section 11 of the National Health Service (Wales) Act 2006;
(h) any other person prescribed for the purposes of this paragraph.

Facilities for disabled persons

7(1) Civil legal services provided in relation to grants under Part 1 of the Housing Grants, Construction and Regeneration Act 1996 for the provision of facilities for disabled persons.

Exclusions

(2) Sub-paragraph (1) is subject to the exclusions in Parts 2 and 3 of this Schedule.

Definitions

(3) In this paragraph 'disabled person' has the meaning given in section 100 of the Housing Grants, Construction and Regeneration Act 1996.

Appeals relating to welfare benefits

8(1) Civil legal services provided in relation to an appeal on a point of law to the Upper Tribunal, the Court of Appeal or the Supreme Court relating to a benefit, allowance, payment, credit or pension under–

(a) a social security enactment,

(b) the Vaccine Damage Payments Act 1979, or

(c) Part 4 of the Child Maintenance and Other Payments Act 2008.

Exclusions

(2) Sub-paragraph (1) is subject to–

(a) the exclusions in Part 2 of this Schedule, with the exception of paragraphs 1 and 15 of that Part, and

(b) the exclusion in Part 3 of this Schedule.

Definitions

(3) In this paragraph 'social security enactment' means–

(a) the Social Security Contributions and Benefits Act 1992,

(b) the Jobseekers Act 1995,

(c) the State Pension Credit Act 2002,

(d) the Tax Credits Act 2002,

(e) the Welfare Reform Act 2007,

(f) the Welfare Reform Act 2012, or

(g) any other enactment relating to social security.

Inherent jurisdiction of High Court in relation to children and vulnerable adults

9(1) Civil legal services provided in relation to the inherent jurisdiction of the High Court in relation to children and vulnerable adults.

Exclusions

(2) Sub-paragraph (1) is subject to the exclusions in Parts 2 and 3 of this Schedule.

Definitions

(3) In this paragraph–

'adults' means persons aged 18 or over;

'children' means persons under the age of 18.

Unlawful removal of children

10(1) Civil legal services provided to an individual in relation to the following orders and requirements where the individual is seeking to prevent the unlawful removal of a related child from the United Kingdom or to secure the return of a related child who has been unlawfully removed from the United Kingdom–

(a) a prohibited steps order or specific issue order (as defined in section 8(1) of the Children Act 1989);

(b) an order under section 33 of the Family Law Act 1986 for disclosure of the child's whereabouts;

(c) an order under section 34 of that Act for the child's return;

(d) a requirement under section 37 of that Act to surrender a passport issued to, or containing particulars of, the child.

(2) Civil legal services provided to an individual in relation to the following orders and applications where the individual is seeking to secure the return of a related child who has been unlawfully removed to a place in the United Kingdom–

(a) a prohibited steps order or specific issue order (as defined in section 8(1) of the Children Act 1989);

(b) an application under section 27 of the Family Law Act 1986 for registration of an order relating to the child;

(c) an order under section 33 of that Act for disclosure of the child's whereabouts;

(d) an order under section 34 of that Act for the child's return.

Exclusions

(3) Sub-paragraphs (1) and (2) are subject to the exclusions in Parts 2 and 3 of this Schedule.

Definitions

(4) For the purposes of this paragraph, a child is related to an individual if the individual is the child's parent or has parental responsibility for the child.

(5) In this paragraph 'child' means a person under the age of 18.

Family homes and domestic violence

11(1) Civil legal services provided in relation to home rights, occupation orders and non-molestation orders under Part 4 of the Family Law Act 1996.

(2) Civil legal services provided in relation to the following in circumstances arising out of a family relationship–

(a) an injunction following assault, battery or false imprisonment;

(b) the inherent jurisdiction of the High Court to protect an adult.

Exclusions

(3) Sub-paragraphs (1) and (2) are subject to–

(a) the exclusions in Part 2 of this Schedule, with the exception of paragraphs 3 and 11 of that Part, and

(b) the exclusion in Part 3 of this Schedule.

Definitions

(4) For the purposes of this paragraph–

(a) there is a family relationship between two people if they are associated with each other, and

(b) 'associated' has the same meaning as in Part 4 of the Family Law Act 1996 (see section 62 of that Act).

(5) For the purposes of this paragraph, the Lord Chancellor may by regulations make provision about when circumstances arise out of a family relationship.

Victims of domestic violence and family matters

12(1) Civil legal services provided to an adult ('A') in relation to a matter arising out of a family relationship between A and another individual ('B') where–

(a) there has been, or is a risk of, domestic violence between A and B, and

(b) A was, or is at risk of being, the victim of that domestic violence.

General exclusions

(2) Sub-paragraph (1) is subject to the exclusions in Part 2 of this Schedule, with the exception of paragraph 11 of that Part.

(3) But the exclusions described in sub-paragraph (2) are subject to the exception in sub-paragraph (4).

(4) The services described in sub-paragraph (1) include services provided in relation to conveyancing, but only where–

  (a) the services in relation to conveyancing are provided in the course of giving effect to a court order made in proceedings, and

  (b) services described in that sub-paragraph (other than services in relation to conveyancing) are being or have been provided in relation to those proceedings under arrangements made for the purposes of this Part of this Act.

(5) Sub-paragraph (1) is subject to the exclusion in Part 3 of this Schedule.

Specific exclusion

(6) The services described in sub-paragraph (1) do not include services provided in relation to a claim in tort in respect of the domestic violence.

Definitions

(7) For the purposes of this paragraph–

  (a) there is a family relationship between two people if they are associated with each other, and

  (b) 'associated' has the same meaning as in Part 4 of the Family Law Act 1996 (see section 62 of that Act).

(8) For the purposes of this paragraph–

  (a) matters arising out of a family relationship include matters arising under a family enactment, and

  (b) (subject to paragraph (a)) the Lord Chancellor may by regulations make provision about when matters arise out of a family relationship.

(9) In this paragraph–

  'adult' means a person aged 18 or over;

  'domestic violence' means any incident, or pattern of incidents of controlling, coercive or threatening behaviour, violence or abuse (whether psychological, physical, sexual, financial or emotional) between individuals who are associated with each other;

  'family enactment' means–

  (a) section 17 of the Married Women's Property Act 1882 (questions between husband and wife as to property);

  (b) the Maintenance Orders (Facilities for Enforcement) Act 1920;

  (c) the Maintenance Orders Act 1950;

  (d) the Maintenance Orders Act 1958;

  (e) the Maintenance Orders (Reciprocal Enforcement) Act 1972;

  (f) Schedule 1 to the Domicile and Matrimonial Proceedings Act 1973 (staying of matrimonial proceedings) and corresponding provision in relation to civil partnerships made by rules of court under section 223 of the Civil Partnership Act 2004;

  (g) the Matrimonial Causes Act 1973;

  (h) the Inheritance (Provision for Family Dependants) Act 1975;

  (i) the Domestic Proceedings and Magistrates' Courts Act 1978;

   (j) Part 3 of the Matrimonial and Family Proceedings Act 1984 (financial relief after overseas divorce etc);

   (k) Parts 1 and 3 of the Family Law Act 1986 (child custody and declarations of status);

   (l) Parts 1 and 2 of the Children Act 1989 (orders with respect to children in family proceedings);

   (m) section 53 of, and Schedule 7 to, the Family Law Act 1996 (transfer of tenancies on divorce etc or separation of cohabitants);

   (n) Chapters 2 and 3 of Part 2 of the Civil Partnership Act 2004 (dissolution, nullity and other proceedings and property and financial arrangements);

   (o) sections 54/54A of the Human Fertilisation and Embryology Act 2008 (applications for parental orders).

   (p) section 51A of the Adoption and Children Act 2002 (post-adoption contact orders).

Protection of children and family matters

13(1) Civil legal services provided to an adult ('A') in relation to the following orders and procedures where the child who is or would be the subject of the order is at risk of abuse from an individual other than A–

   (a) orders under section 4(2A) of the Children Act 1989 ('the 1989 Act') (removal of father's parental responsibility);

   (b) orders under section 6(7) of the 1989 Act (termination of appointment of guardian);

   (c) orders mentioned in section 8(1) of the 1989 Act (child arrangements and other orders);

   (d) special guardianship orders under Part 2 of the 1989 Act;

   (e) orders under section 33 of the Family Law Act 1986 ('the 1986 Act') (disclosure of child's whereabouts);

   (f) orders under section 34 of the 1986 Act (return of child).

   (g) orders under section 51A of the Adoption and Children Act 2002 (post-adoption contact).

Exclusions

(2) Sub-paragraph (1) is subject to the exclusions in Parts 2 and 3 of this Schedule.

Definitions

(3) In this paragraph–
'abuse' means physical or mental abuse, including–
   (a) sexual abuse, and
   (b) abuse in the form of violence, neglect, maltreatment and exploitation;
'adult' means a person aged 18 or over;
'child' means a person under the age of 18.

Mediation in family disputes

14(1) Mediation provided in relation to family disputes.

(2) Civil legal services provided in connection with the mediation of family disputes.

Exclusions

(3) Sub-paragraphs (1) and (2) are subject to the exclusions in Part 2 of this Schedule, with the exception of paragraph 11 of that Part.

(4) But the exclusions described in sub-paragraph (3) are subject to the exception in sub-paragraph (5).

(5) The services described in sub-paragraph (2) include services provided in relation to conveyancing, but only where–

    (a) the services in relation to conveyancing are provided in the course of giving effect to arrangements for the resolution of a family dispute, and

    (b) services described in that sub-paragraph or sub-paragraph (1) (other than services in relation to conveyancing) are being or have been provided in relation to the dispute under arrangements made for the purposes of this Part of this Act.

(6) Sub-paragraphs (1) and (2) are subject to the exclusion in Part 3 of this Schedule.

Definitions

(7) For the purposes of this paragraph–

    (a) a dispute is a family dispute if it is a dispute between individuals about a matter arising out of a family relationship between the individuals,

    (b) there is a family relationship between two individuals if they are associated with each other, and

    (c) 'associated' has the same meaning as in Part 4 of the Family Law Act 1996 (see section 62 of that Act).

(8) For the purposes of this paragraph–

    (a) matters arising out of a family relationship include matters arising under a family enactment, and

    (b) (subject to paragraph (a)) the Lord Chancellor may by regulations make provision about when matters arise out of a family relationship.

(9) In this paragraph–

'child' means a person under the age of 18;

'family enactment' has the meaning given in paragraph 12.

Children who are parties to family proceedings

15(1) Civil legal services provided to a child in relation to family proceedings–

    (a) where the child is, or proposes to be, the applicant or respondent;

    (b) where the child is made a party to the proceedings by a court under rule 16.2 of the Family Procedure Rules;

    (c) where the child is a party to the proceedings and is conducting, or proposes to conduct, the proceedings without a children's guardian or litigation friend in accordance with rule 16.6 of the Family Procedure Rules.

Exclusions

(2) Sub-paragraph (1) is subject to the exclusions in Parts 2 and 3 of this Schedule.

Definitions

(3) For the purposes of this paragraph–

    (a) proceedings are family proceedings if they relate to a matter arising out of a family relationship,

    (b) there is a family relationship between two individuals if they are associated with each other, and

    (c) 'associated' has the same meaning as in Part 4 of the Family Law Act 1996 (see section 62 of that Act).

(4) For the purposes of this paragraph–
   (a) matters arising out of a family relationship include matters arising under a family enactment, and
   (b) (subject to paragraph (a)) the Lord Chancellor may by regulations make provision about when matters arise out of a family relationship.
(5) In this paragraph–
'child' means a person under the age of 18;
'family enactment' has the meaning given in paragraph 12.

Female genital mutilation protection orders

15A(1) Civil legal services provided in relation to female genital mutilation protection orders under paragraph 1 of Schedule 2 to the Female Genital Mutilation Act 2003.

Exclusions
(2) Sub-paragraph (1) is subject to the exclusions in Parts 2 and 3 of this Schedule.

Forced marriage

16(1) Civil legal services provided in relation to forced marriage protection orders under Part 4A of the Family Law Act 1996.

Exclusions
(2) Sub-paragraph (1) is subject to the exclusions in Parts 2 and 3 of this Schedule.

Transitional EU Arrangements and international agreements concerning children

17(1) Civil legal services provided in relation to–
   (a) an application made to the Lord Chancellor under the 1980 European Convention on Child Custody for the recognition or enforcement in England and Wales of a decision relating to the custody of a child;
   (b) an application made to the Lord Chancellor under the 1980 Hague Convention in respect of a child who is, or is believed to be, in England and Wales;
   (c) the recognition or enforcement of a judgment in England and Wales in accordance with Article 21, 28, 41, 42 or 48 of the 2003 Brussels Regulation.

Exclusions
(2) Sub-paragraph (1) is subject to the exclusions in Parts 2 and 3 of this Schedule.

Definitions
(3) In this paragraph–
'the 1980 European Convention on Child Custody' means the European Convention on Recognition and Enforcement of Decisions concerning Custody of Children and on the Restoration of Custody of Children which was signed in Luxembourg on 20 May 1980;
'the 1980 Hague Convention' means the Convention on the Civil Aspects of International Child Abduction which was signed at The Hague on 25 October 1980;
'the 2003 Brussels Regulation' means Council Regulation (EC) No 2001/2003 of 27 November 2003 concerning jurisdiction and the recognition and

enforcement of judgments in matrimonial matters and the matters of parental responsibility.

(4) For the purposes of this paragraph, an application is made to the Lord Chancellor if it is addressed to the Lord Chancellor or transmitted to the Lord Chancellor in accordance with section 3 or 14 of the Child Abduction and Custody Act 1985.

Transitional EU Arrangements and international agreements concerning maintenance

18(1) Civil legal services provided in relation to an application under the following for the recognition or enforcement in England and Wales of a maintenance order–

(a) the 1968 Brussels Convention;
(b) the 1973 Hague Convention;
(c) the 1989 Lugano Convention;
(d) the 2000 Brussels Regulation;
(e) the 2007 Lugano Convention.

(2) Civil legal services provided in relation to an application under Article 56 of the EU Maintenance Regulation (applications relating to maintenance decisions).

(3) Civil legal services provided to an individual in relation to proceedings in England and Wales relating to the recognition, enforceability or enforcement of a maintenance decision in circumstances in which the individual falls within Article 47(2) or (3) of the EU Maintenance Regulation (parties who benefited from free legal aid etc in Member State of origin).

(3A) Civil legal services provided in relation to an application under Article 10 of the 2007 Hague Convention (applications relating to maintenance decisions).

(3B) Civil legal services provided to an individual in relation to proceedings in England and Wales relating to the recognition or enforcement of a maintenance decision in circumstances in which–

(a) Article 17(b) of the 2007 Hague Convention (free legal assistance for persons who benefited from such assistance in State of origin) applies to the proceedings by virtue of Article 37(2) of that Convention (direct request to competent authority of Contracting State), and
(b) the individual falls within Article 17(b) as so applied.

Exclusions

(4) Sub-paragraphs (1) to (3B) are subject to–

(a) the exclusions in Part 2 of this Schedule, with the exception of paragraph 11 of that Part, and
(b) the exclusion in Part 3 of this Schedule.

Definitions

(5) In this paragraph–

'the 1968 Brussels Convention' means the Convention on jurisdiction and the enforcement of judgments in civil and commercial matters (including the Protocol annexed to that Convention) signed at Brussels on 27 September 1968;

'the 1973 Hague Convention' means the Convention on the recognition and enforcement of decisions relating to maintenance obligations concluded at The Hague on 2 October 1973;

'the 1989 Lugano Convention' means the Convention on jurisdiction and the enforcement of judgments in civil and commercial matters (including the Protocols annexed to that Convention) opened for signature at Lugano on 16 September 1988 and signed by the United Kingdom on 18 September 1989;

'the 2000 Brussels Regulation' means Council Regulation (EC) No 44/2001 of 22 December 2000 on jurisdiction and the recognition and enforcement of judgments in civil and commercial matters;

'the 2007 Hague Convention' means the Convention on the international recovery of child support and other forms of family maintenance concluded at The Hague on 23 November 2007;

'the 2007 Lugano Convention' means the Convention on jurisdiction and enforcement of judgments in civil and commercial matters, between the European Community and the Republic of Iceland, the Kingdom of Norway, the Swiss Confederation and the Kingdom of Denmark signed on behalf of the European Community on 30 October 2007;

'the EU Maintenance Regulation' means Council Regulation (EC) No 4/2009 of 18 December 2008 on jurisdiction, applicable law, recognition and enforcement of decisions and co-operation in matters relating to maintenance obligations;

'maintenance order', in relation to a convention or regulation listed in this paragraph, means a maintenance judgment within the meaning of that convention or regulation.

Judicial review

19(1) Civil legal services provided in relation to judicial review of an enactment, decision, act or omission.

General exclusions

(2) Sub-paragraph (1) is subject to–

    (a) the exclusions in Part 2 of this Schedule, with the exception of paragraphs 1, 2, 3, 4, 5, 6, 8, 12, 15, 16 and 18 of that Part, and

    (b) the exclusion in Part 3 of this Schedule.

Specific exclusion: benefit to individual

(3) The services described in sub-paragraph (1) do not include services provided to an individual in relation to judicial review that does not have the potential to produce a benefit for the individual, a member of the individual's family or the environment.

(4) Sub-paragraph (3) does not exclude services provided in relation to a judicial review where the judicial review ceases to have the potential to produce such a benefit after civil legal services have been provided in relation to the judicial review under arrangements made for the purposes of this Part of this Act.

Specific exclusions: immigration cases

(5) The services described in sub-paragraph (1) do not include services provided in relation to judicial review in respect of an issue relating to immigration where–

    (a) the same issue, or substantially the same issue, was the subject of a previous judicial review or an appeal to a court or tribunal,

(b) on the determination of the previous judicial review or appeal (or, if there was more than one, the latest one), the court, tribunal or other person hearing the case found against the applicant or appellant on that issue, and

(c) the services in relation to the new judicial review are provided before the end of the period of 1 year beginning with the day of that determination.

(6) The services described in sub-paragraph (1) do not include services provided in relation to judicial review of removal directions in respect of an individual where the directions were given not more than 1 year after the latest of the following—

(a) the making of the decision (or, if there was more than one, the latest decision) to remove the individual from the United Kingdom by way of removal directions;

(b) the refusal of leave to appeal against that decision;

(c) the determination or withdrawal of an appeal against that decision.

(7) Sub-paragraphs (5) and (6) do not exclude services provided to an individual in relation to—

(a) judicial review of a negative decision in relation to an asylum application (within the meaning of the EU Procedures Directive) where there is no right of appeal to the First-tier Tribunal against the decision;

(b) judicial review of certification under section 94 or 96 of the Nationality, Immigration and Asylum Act 2002 (certificate preventing or restricting appeal of immigration decision).

(8) Sub-paragraphs (5) and (6) do not exclude services provided in relation to judicial review of removal directions in respect of an individual where prescribed conditions relating to either or both of the following are met—

(a) the period between the individual being given notice of the removal directions and the proposed time for his or her removal;

(b) the reasons for proposing that period.

Definitions

(9) For the purposes of this paragraph an individual is a member of another individual's family if—

(a) they are relatives (whether of the full blood or half blood or by marriage or civil partnership),

(b) they are cohabitants (as defined in Part 4 of the Family Law Act 1996), or

(c) one has parental responsibility for the other.

(10) In this paragraph—

'EU Procedures Directive' means Council Directive 2005/85/EC of 1 December 2005 on minimum standards on procedures in Member States for granting and withdrawing refugee status;

'an issue relating to immigration' includes an issue relating to rights described in paragraph 30 of this Part of this Schedule;

'judicial review' means—

(a) the procedure on an application for judicial review (see section 31 of the Senior Courts Act 1981), but not including the procedure after the application is treated under rules of court as if it were not such an application, and

(b) any procedure in which a court, tribunal or other person mentioned in Part 3 of this Schedule is required by an enactment to make a decision applying the principles that are applied by the court on an application for judicial review;

'removal directions' means directions under–

(a) paragraphs 8 to 10A of Schedule 2 to the Immigration Act 1971 (removal of persons refused leave to enter and illegal entrants);

(b) paragraphs 12 to 14 of Schedule 2 to that Act (removal of seamen and aircrew);

(c) paragraph 1 of Schedule 3 to that Act (removal of persons liable to deportation);

(d) section 10 of the Immigration and Asylum Act 1999 (removal of certain persons unlawfully in the United Kingdom);

(e) [repealed.]

Habeas corpus

20(1) Civil legal services provided in relation to a writ of habeas corpus ad subjiciendum.

Exclusions

(2) Sub-paragraph (1) is subject to the exclusions in Parts 2 and 3 of this Schedule.

Abuse of position or powers by public authority

21(1) Civil legal services provided in relation to abuse by a public authority of its position or powers.

General exclusions

(2) Sub-paragraph (1) is subject to–

(a) the exclusions in Part 2 of this Schedule, with the exception of paragraphs 1, 2, 3, 4, 5, 6, 8 and 12 of that Part, and

(b) the exclusion in Part 3 of this Schedule.

Specific exclusion

(3) The services described in sub-paragraph (1) do not include services provided in relation to clinical negligence.

Definitions

(4) For the purposes of this paragraph, an act or omission by a public authority does not constitute an abuse of its position or powers unless the act or omission–

(a) is deliberate or dishonest, and

(b) results in harm to a person or property that was reasonably foreseeable.

(5) In this paragraph–

'clinical negligence' means breach of a duty of care or trespass to the person committed in the course of the provision of clinical or medical services (including dental or nursing services);

'public authority' has the same meaning as in section 6 of the Human Rights Act 1998.

Breach of Convention rights by public authority

22(1) Civil legal services provided in relation to–

(a) a claim in tort, or

(b) a claim for damages (other than a claim in tort),

in respect of an act or omission by a public authority that involves a significant breach of Convention rights by the authority.

General exclusions

(2) Sub-paragraph (1) is subject to—
 (a) the exclusions in Part 2 of this Schedule, with the exception of paragraphs 1, 2, 3, 4, 5, 6, 8 and 12 of that Part, and
 (b) the exclusion in Part 3 of this Schedule.

Specific exclusion

(3) The services described in sub-paragraph (1) do not include services provided in relation to clinical negligence.

Definitions

(4) In this paragraph—
 'clinical negligence' means breach of a duty of care or trespass to the person committed in the course of the provision of clinical or medical services (including dental or nursing services);
 'Convention rights' has the same meaning as in the Human Rights Act 1998;
 'public authority' has the same meaning as in section 6 of that Act.

Clinical negligence and severely disabled infants

23(1) Civil legal services provided in relation to a claim for damages in respect of clinical negligence which caused a neurological injury to an individual ('V') as a result of which V is severely disabled, but only where the first and second conditions are met.

(2) The first condition is that the clinical negligence occurred—
 (a) while V was in his or her mother's womb, or
 (b) during or after V's birth but before the end of the following period—
  (i) if V was born before the beginning of the 37th week of pregnancy, the period of 8 weeks beginning with the first day of what would have been that week;
  (ii) if V was born during or after the 37th week of pregnancy, the period of 8 weeks beginning with the day of V's birth.

(3) The second condition is that—
 (a) the services are provided to V, or
 (b) V has died and the services are provided to V's personal representative.

General exclusions

(4) Sub-paragraph (1) is subject to—
 (a) the exclusions in Part 2 of this Schedule, with the exception of paragraphs 1, 2, 3 and 8 of that Part, and
 (b) the exclusion in Part 3 of this Schedule.

Definitions

(5) In this paragraph—
 'birth' means the moment when an individual first has a life separate from his or her mother and references to an individual being born are to be interpreted accordingly;
 'clinical negligence' means breach of a duty of care or trespass to the person committed in the course of the provision of clinical or medical services (including dental or nursing services);

'disabled' means physically or mentally disabled;
'personal representative', in relation to an individual who has died, means–
(a) a person responsible for administering the individual's estate under the law of England and Wales, Scotland or Northern Ireland, or
(b) a person who, under the law of another country or territory, has functions equivalent to those of administering the individual's estate.

Special Immigration Appeals Commission

24(1) Civil legal services provided in relation to proceedings before the Special Immigration Appeals Commission.

Exclusions

(2) Sub-paragraph (1) is subject to the exclusions in Parts 2 and 3 of this Schedule.

Immigration: detention

25(1) Civil legal services provided in relation to–
(a) detention under the authority of an immigration officer;
(b) detention under Schedule 3 to the Immigration Act 1971;
(c) detention under section 62 of the Nationality, Immigration and Asylum Act 2002;
(d) detention under section 36 of the UK Borders Act 2007.

Exclusions

(2) Sub-paragraph (1) is subject to the exclusions in Parts 2 and 3 of this Schedule.

Immigration: temporary admission

26(1) Civil legal services provided in relation to temporary admission to the United Kingdom under–
(a) paragraph 21 of Schedule 2 to the Immigration Act 1971;
(b) section 62 of the Nationality, Immigration and Asylum Act 2002.

Exclusions

(2) Sub-paragraph (1) is subject to the exclusions in Parts 2 and 3 of this Schedule.

Immigration: residence etc restrictions

27(1) Civil legal services provided in relation to restrictions imposed under–
(a) paragraph 2(5) or 4 of Schedule 3 to the Immigration Act 1971 (residence etc restrictions pending deportation);
(b) section 71 of the Nationality, Immigration and Asylum Act 2002 (residence etc restrictions on asylum-seekers).

Exclusions

(2) Sub-paragraph (1) is subject to the exclusions in Parts 2 and 3 of this Schedule.

Immigration: victims of domestic violence and indefinite leave to remain

28(1) Civil legal services provided to an individual ('V') in relation to an application by V for indefinite leave to remain in the United Kingdom on the grounds that–
(a) V was given leave to enter or remain in the United Kingdom for a limited period as the partner of another individual present and settled in the United Kingdom, and

(b) V's relationship with the other individual broke down permanently because V was the victim of domestic violence.

General exclusions

(2) Sub-paragraph (1) is subject to the exclusions in Parts 2 and 3 of this Schedule.

Specific exclusion

(3) The services described in sub-paragraph (1) do not include attendance at an interview conducted on behalf of the Secretary of State with a view to reaching a decision on an application.

Definitions

(4) For the purposes of this paragraph, one individual is a partner of another if–
   (a) they are married to each other,
   (b) they are civil partners of each other, or
   (c) they are cohabitants.

(5) In this paragraph–
   'cohabitant' has the same meaning as in Part 4 of the Family Law Act 1996 (see section 62 of that Act);
   'domestic violence' means any incident, or pattern of incidents, of controlling, coercive or threatening behaviour, violence or abuse (whether psychological, physical, sexual, financial or emotional) between individuals who are associated with each other (within the meaning of section 62 of the Family Law Act 1996);
   'indefinite leave to remain in the United Kingdom' means leave to remain in the United Kingdom under the Immigration Act 1971 which is not limited as to duration;
   'present and settled in the United Kingdom' has the same meaning as in the rules made under section 3(2) of the Immigration Act 1971.

Immigration: victims of domestic violence and residence cards

29(1) Civil legal services provided to an individual ('V') in relation to a residence card application where V–
   (a) has ceased to be a family member of a qualified person on the termination of the marriage or civil partnership of the qualified person,
   (b) is a family member who has retained the right of residence by virtue of satisfying the conditions in regulation 10(5) of the Immigration (European Economic Area) Regulations 2006 (SI 2006/1003) ('the 2006 Regulations'), and
   (c) has satisfied the condition in regulation 10(5)(d)(iv) of the 2006 Regulations on the ground that V or a family member of V was the victim of domestic violence while the marriage or civil partnership of the qualified person was subsisting.

General exclusions

(2) Sub-paragraph (1) is subject to the exclusions in Parts 2 and 3 of this Schedule.

Specific exclusion

(3) The services described in sub-paragraph (1) do not include attendance at an interview conducted on behalf of the Secretary of State with a view to reaching a decision on an application.

Definitions
(4) In this paragraph–
 'domestic violence' means any incident, or pattern of incidents, of controlling,
 coercive or threatening behaviour, violence or abuse (whether psychological, physical, sexual, financial or emotional) between individuals who
 are associated with each other (within the meaning of section 62 of the
 Family Law Act 1996);
 'family member' has the same meaning as in the 2006 Regulations (see regulations 7 and 9);
 'family member who has retained the right of residence' has the same
 meaning as in the 2006 Regulations (see regulation 10);
 'qualified person' has the same meaning as in the 2006 Regulations (see
 regulation 6);
 'residence card application' means–
  (a) an application for a residence card under regulation 17 of the 2006
  Regulations, or
  (b) an application for a permanent residence card under regulation 18(2)
  of the 2006 Regulations.

Immigration: rights to enter and remain
30(1) Civil legal services provided in relation to rights to enter, and to remain in,
 the United Kingdom which–
 (a) arise from–
  (i) the Refugee Convention; or
  (ii) Article 2 or 3 of the Human Rights Convention; or
 (b) are conferred by–
  (i) immigration rules, insofar as they implemented the Qualification
  Directive; or
  (ii) any other provision of retained EU law which implemented the
  Qualification Directive.

General exclusions
(2) Sub-paragraph (1) is subject to the exclusions in Parts 2 and 3 of this
 Schedule.

Specific exclusion
(3) The services described in sub-paragraph (1) do not include attendance at an
 interview conducted on behalf of the Secretary of State with a view to reaching a decision on a claim in respect of the rights mentioned in that sub-
 paragraph, except where regulations provide otherwise.

Definitions
(4) In this paragraph–
 'the Human Rights Convention' means the Convention for the Protection of
 Human Rights and Fundamental Freedoms, agreed by the Council of
 Europe at Rome on 4 November 1950 as it has effect for the time being in
 relation to the United Kingdom;
 'Immigration rules' has the meaning given by section 33(1) of the Immigration
 Act 1971;
 'the Qualification Directive' means Council Directive 2004/83/EC of 29 April
 2004 on minimum standards for the qualification and status of third

country nationals or stateless persons as refugees or as persons who otherwise need international protection and the content of the protection granted;

'the Refugee Convention' means the Convention relating to the Status of Refugees done at Geneva on 28 July 1951 and the Protocol to the Convention.

Immigration: accommodation for asylum-seekers etc

31(1) Civil legal services provided in relation to the Secretary of State's powers to provide, or arrange for the provision of, accommodation under–

(a) section 4 or 95 of the Immigration and Asylum Act 1999 (accommodation for persons temporarily admitted and asylum-seekers);

(b) section 17 of the Nationality, Immigration and Asylum Act 2002 (support for destitute asylum-seekers).

Exclusions

(2) Sub-paragraph (1) is subject to the exclusions in Parts 2 and 3 of this Schedule.

Immigration, citizenship and nationality: separated children

31A(1) Civil legal services provided in relation to a relevant application where the services are provided to an individual who, at the time of applying for those services, is a separated child.

(2) A relevant application is–

(a) an application made by the separated child or another person under the immigration rules for the grant of entry clearance, leave to enter or leave to remain in the United Kingdom (whether under or outside of the immigration rules),

(b) an application made by the separated child outside of the immigration rules for the grant of leave to remain in the United Kingdom, or

(c) an application made by the separated child for registration under the British Nationality Act 1981 as–

(i) a British citizen,

(ii) a British overseas territories citizen,

(iii)a British Overseas citizen, or

(iv) a British subject.

Exclusions

(3) Sub-paragraph (1) is subject to the exclusions in Parts 2 and 3 of this Schedule.

Definitions

(4) In this paragraph–

'child' means an individual–

(a) who is under the age of 18, or

(b) whose age is uncertain, but who is treated by the Director as being under the age of 18;

'entry clearance' has the same meaning as in the Immigration Act 1971;

'immigration rules' has the same meaning as in the Immigration Act 1971;

'leave to enter' and 'leave to remain' are to be construed in accordance with the Immigration Act 1971;

'separated', in relation to a child, means–

(a) not being cared for by a parent,

(b) not being cared for by a person with parental responsibility for the child (within the meaning of section 3 of the Children Act 1989), or

(c) looked after by a local authority (within the meaning of section 107(6)).

Victims of trafficking in human beings

32(1) Civil legal services provided to an individual in relation to an application by the individual for leave to enter, or to remain in, the United Kingdom where–

(a) there has been a conclusive determination that the individual is a victim of trafficking in human beings, or

(b) there are reasonable grounds to believe that the individual is such a victim and there has not been a conclusive determination that the individual is not such a victim.

(2) Civil legal services provided in relation to a claim under employment law arising in connection with the exploitation of an individual who is a victim of trafficking in human beings, but only where–

(a) the services are provided to the individual, or

(b) the individual has died and the services are provided to the individual's personal representative.

(3) Civil legal services provided in relation to a claim for damages arising in connection with the trafficking or exploitation of an individual who is a victim of trafficking in human beings, but only where–

(a) the services are provided to the individual, or

(b) the individual has died and the services are provided to the individual's personal representative.

Exclusions

(4) Sub-paragraph (1) is subject to the exclusions in Parts 2 and 3 of this Schedule.

(5) Sub-paragraphs (2) and (3) are subject to–

(a) the exclusions in Part 2 of this Schedule, with the exception of paragraphs 1, 2, 3, 4, 5, 6 and 8 of that Part, and

(b) the exclusion in Part 3 of this Schedule.

Definitions

(6) For the purposes of sub-paragraph (1)(b) there are reasonable grounds to believe that an individual is a victim of trafficking in human beings if a competent authority has determined for the purposes of Article 10 of the Trafficking Convention (identification of victims) that there are such grounds.

(7) For the purposes of sub-paragraph (1) there is a conclusive determination that an individual is or is not a victim of trafficking in human beings when, on completion of the identification process required by Article 10 of the Trafficking Convention, a competent authority concludes that the individual is or is not such a victim.

(8) In this paragraph–

'competent authority' means a person who is a competent authority of the United Kingdom for the purposes of the Trafficking Convention;

'employment' means employment under a contract of employment or a contract personally to do work and references to 'employers' and 'employees' are to be interpreted accordingly;

'employment law' means an enactment or rule of law relating to employment, including in particular an enactment or rule of law conferring powers or imposing duties on employers, conferring rights on employees or otherwise regulating the relations between employers and employees;

'exploitation' means a form of exploitation described in section 4(4) of the Asylum and Immigration (Treatment of Claimants, etc) Act 2004 (trafficking people for exploitation); section 3 of the Modern Slavery Act 2015 (meaning of exploitation for purposes of human trafficking offence in section 2 of that Act);

'personal representative', in relation to an individual who has died, means–
  (a) a person responsible for administering the individual's estate under the law of England and Wales, Scotland or Northern Ireland, or
  (b) a person who, under the law of another country or territory, has functions equivalent to those of administering the individual's estate;

'the Trafficking Convention' means the Council of Europe Convention on Action against Trafficking in Human Beings (done at Warsaw on 16 May 2005);

'trafficking in human beings' has the same meaning as in the Trafficking Convention.

Victims of slavery, servitude or forced or compulsory labour

32A(1) Civil legal services provided to an individual in relation to an application by the individual for leave to enter, or to remain in, the United Kingdom where–
  (a) there has been a conclusive determination that the individual is a victim of slavery, servitude or forced or compulsory labour, or
  (b) there are reasonable grounds to believe that the individual is such a victim and there has not been a conclusive determination that the individual is not such a victim.

(2) Civil legal services provided in relation to a claim under employment law arising in connection with the conduct by virtue of which an individual who is a victim of slavery, servitude or forced or compulsory labour is such a victim, but only where–
  (a) the services are provided to the individual, or
  (b) the individual has died and the services are provided to the individual's personal representative.

(3) Civil legal services provided in relation to a claim for damages arising in connection with the conduct by virtue of which an individual who is a victim of slavery, servitude or forced or compulsory labour is such a victim, but only where–
  (a) the services are provided to the individual, or
  (b) the individual has died and the services are provided to the individual's personal representative.

Exclusions

(4) Sub-paragraph (1) is subject to the exclusions in Parts 2 and 3 of this Schedule.

(5) Sub-paragraphs (2) and (3) are subject to–
  (a) the exclusions in Part 2 of this Schedule, with the exception of paragraphs 1, 2, 3, 4, 5, 6 and 8 of that Part, and
  (b) the exclusion in Part 3 of this Schedule.

Definitions

(6) For the purposes of sub-paragraph (1)(b) there are reasonable grounds to believe that an individual is a victim of slavery, servitude or forced or com-

pulsory labour if a competent authority has determined that there are such grounds.

(7) For the purposes of sub-paragraph (1) there is a conclusive determination that an individual is or is not a victim of slavery, servitude or forced or compulsory labour when a competent authority concludes that the individual is or is not such a victim.

(8) For the purposes of this paragraph 'slavery', 'servitude' and 'forced or compulsory labour' have the same meaning as they have for the purposes of article 4 of the Human Rights Convention.

(9) The 'Human Rights Convention' means the Convention for the Protection of Human Rights and Fundamental Freedoms, agreed by the Council of Europe at Rome on 4 November 1950, as it has effect for the time being in relation to the United Kingdom.

(10) The definitions of 'competent authority', 'employment', 'employment law' and 'personal representative' in paragraph 32(8) also apply for the purposes of this paragraph.

Loss of home

33(1) Civil legal services provided to an individual in relation to–
  (a) court orders for sale or possession of the individual's home, or
  (b) the eviction from the individual's home of the individual or others.

(2) Civil legal services provided to an individual in relation to a bankruptcy order against the individual under Part 9 of the Insolvency Act 1986 where–
  (a) the individual's estate includes the individual's home, and
  (b) the petition for the bankruptcy order is or was presented by a person other than the individual,

including services provided in relation to a statutory demand under that Part of that Act.

General exclusions

(3) Sub-paragraphs (1) and (2) are subject to the exclusions in Part 2 of this Schedule, with the exception of paragraph 14 of that Part.

(4) But the exclusions described in sub-paragraph (3) are subject to the exceptions in sub-paragraphs (5) and (6).

(5) The services described in sub-paragraph (1) include services provided in relation to proceedings on an application under the Trusts of Land and Appointment of Trustees Act 1996 to which section 335A of the Insolvency Act 1986 applies (application by trustee of bankrupt's estate).

(6) The services described in sub-paragraph (1) include services described in any of paragraphs 3 to 6 or 8 of Part 2 of this Schedule to the extent that they are–
  (a) services provided to an individual in relation to a counterclaim in proceedings for a court order for sale or possession of the individual's home, or
  (b) services provided to an individual in relation to the unlawful eviction from the individual's home of the individual or others.

(7) Sub-paragraphs (1) and (2) are subject to the exclusion in Part 3 of this Schedule.

Specific exclusion

(8) The services described in sub-paragraph (1) do not include services provided in relation to–

(a) proceedings under the Matrimonial Causes Act 1973;

(b) proceedings under Chapters 2 and 3 of Part 2 of the Civil Partnership Act 2004 (dissolution, nullity and other proceedings and property and financial arrangements).

Definitions

(9) In this paragraph 'home', in relation to an individual, means the house, caravan, houseboat or other vehicle or structure that is the individual's only or main residence, subject to sub-paragraph (10).

(10) References in this paragraph to an individual's home do not include a vehicle or structure occupied by the individual if—

(a) there are no grounds on which it can be argued that the individual is occupying the vehicle or structure otherwise than as a trespasser, and

(b) there are no grounds on which it can be argued that the individual's occupation of the vehicle or structure began otherwise than as a trespasser.

(11) In sub-paragraphs (9) and (10), the references to a caravan, houseboat or other vehicle include the land on which it is located or to which it is moored.

(12) For the purposes of sub-paragraph (10) individuals occupying, or beginning occupation, of a vehicle or structure as a trespasser include individuals who do so by virtue of—

(a) title derived from a trespasser, or

(b) a licence or consent given by a trespasser or a person deriving title from a trespasser.

(13) For the purposes of sub-paragraph (10) an individual who is occupying a vehicle or structure as a trespasser does not cease to be a trespasser by virtue of being allowed time to leave the vehicle or structure.

Homelessness

34(1) Civil legal services provided to an individual who is homeless, or threatened with homelessness, in relation to the provision of accommodation and assistance for the individual under—

(a) Part 6 of the Housing Act 1996 (allocation of housing accommodation);

(b) Part 7 of that Act (homelessness).

(c) Part 2 of the Housing (Wales) Act 2014 (homelessness).

Exclusions

(2) Sub-paragraph (1) is subject to the exclusions in Parts 2 and 3 of this Schedule.

Definitions

(3) In this paragraph 'homeless' and 'threatened with homelessness' have the same meaning –

(a) as in section 175 of the Housing Act 1996 in cases where sub-paragraph (1) applies in relation to the provision of accommodation and assistance under—

(i) Part 6 of that Act as it relates to England;

(ii) Part 7 of that Act;

(b) as in section 55 of the Housing (Wales) Act 2014 in cases where sub-paragraph (1) applies in relation to the provision of accommodation and assistance under–

(i)   Part 6 of the Housing Act 1996 as it relates to Wales;

(ii) Part 2 of the Housing (Wales) Act 2014.

Risk to health or safety in rented home

35(1) Civil legal services provided to an individual in relation to the removal or reduction of a serious risk of harm to the health or safety of the individual or a relevant member of the individual's family where–

(a) the risk arises from a deficiency in the individual's home,

(b) the individual's home is rented or leased from another person, and

(c) the services are provided with a view to securing that the other person makes arrangements to remove or reduce the risk.

Exclusions

(2) Sub-paragraph (1) is subject to–

(a) the exclusions in Part 2 of this Schedule, with the exception of paragraphs 6 and 8 of that Part, and

(b) the exclusion in Part 3 of this Schedule.

Definitions

(3) For the purposes of this paragraph–

(a) a child is a relevant member of an individual's family if the individual is the child's parent or has parental responsibility for the child;

(b) an adult ('A') is a relevant member of an individual's family if–

(i)   they are relatives (whether of the full blood or half blood or by marriage or civil partnership) or cohabitants, and

(ii) the individual's home is also A's home.

(4) In this paragraph–

'adult' means a person aged 18 or over;

'building' includes part of a building;

'child' means a person under the age of 18;

'cohabitant' has the same meaning as in Part 4 of the Family Law Act 1996 (see section 62(1) of that Act);

'deficiency' means any deficiency, whether arising as a result of the construction of a building, an absence of maintenance or repair, or otherwise;

'harm' includes temporary harm;

'health' includes mental health;

'home', in relation to an individual, means the house, caravan, houseboat or other vehicle or structure that is the individual's only or main residence, together with any garden or ground usually occupied with it.

Anti-social behaviour

36(1) Civil legal services provided to an individual in relation to an application for, or proceedings in respect of, an injunction against the individual under section 1 of the Anti-social Behaviour, Crime and Policing Act 2014.

Exclusions

(2) Sub-paragraph (1) is subject to the exclusions in Parts 2 and 3 of this Schedule.

Protection from harassment

37(1) Civil legal services provided in relation to–

(a) an injunction under section 3 or 3A of the Protection from Harassment Act 1997;

(b) the variation or discharge of a restraining order under section 5 or 5A of that Act.

Exclusions

(2) Sub-paragraph (1) is subject to the exclusions in Parts 2 and 3 of this Schedule.

Gang-related violence and drug-dealing activity

38(1) Civil legal services provided in relation to injunctions under Part 4 of the Policing and Crime Act 2009 (injunctions to prevent gang-related violence and drug-dealing activity).

Exclusions

(2) Sub-paragraph (1) is subject to the exclusions in Parts 2 and 3 of this Schedule.

Sexual offences

39(1) Civil legal services provided in relation to a sexual offence, but only where–
  (a) the services are provided to the victim of the offence, or
  (b) the victim of the offence has died and the services are provided to the victim's personal representative.

Exclusions

(2) Sub-paragraph (1) is subject to–
  (a) the exclusions in Part 2 of this Schedule, with the exception of paragraphs 1, 2, 3, 8 and 12 of that Part, and
  (b) the exclusion in Part 3 of this Schedule.

Definitions

(3) In this paragraph–
  'personal representative', in relation to an individual who has died, means–
  (a) a person responsible for administering the individual's estate under the law of England and Wales, Scotland or Northern Ireland, or
  (b) a person who, under the law of another country or territory, has functions equivalent to those of administering the individual's estate;
  'sexual offence' means–
  (a) an offence under a provision of the Sexual Offences Act 2003 ('the 2003 Act'),
  (b) an offence under section 1 of the Protection of Children Act 1978 ('the 1978 Act') (indecent photographs of children)' and
  (c) an offence under section 2 of the Modern Slavery Act 2015 (human trafficking) committed with a view to exploitation that consists of or includes behaviour within section 3(3) of that Act (sexual exploitation)].

(4) The references in sub-paragraph (1) to a sexual offence include–
  (a) incitement to commit a sexual offence,
  (b) an offence committed by a person under Part 2 of the Serious Crime Act 2007 (encouraging or assisting crime) in relation to which a sexual offence is the offence which the person intended or believed would be committed,
  (c) conspiracy to commit a sexual offence, and
  (d) an attempt to commit a sexual offence.

(5) In this paragraph references to a sexual offence include conduct which would be an offence under a provision of the 2003 Act or section 1 of the 1978 Act

but for the fact that it took place before that provision or section came into force.

(6) Conduct falls within the definition of a sexual offence for the purposes of this paragraph whether or not there have been criminal proceedings in relation to the conduct and whatever the outcome of any such proceedings.

Proceeds of crime

40(1) Civil legal services provided in relation to–

(a) restraint orders under section 41 of the Proceeds of Crime Act 2002 ('the 2002 Act') including orders under section 41(7) of that Act (orders for ensuring that restraint order is effective);

(b) orders under section 47M of the 2002 Act (detention of property);

(c) directions under section 54(3) of the 2002 Act (distribution of funds in the hands of a receiver);

(d) directions under section 62 of the 2002 Act (action to be taken by receiver);

(e) orders under section 67A of the 2002 Act (realising property), including directions under section 67D of that Act (distribution of proceeds of realisation);

(f) orders under section 72 or 73 of the 2002 Act (compensation);

(g) applications under section 351 of the 2002 Act (discharge or variation of a production order or order to grant entry);

(h) applications under section 362 of the 2002 Act (discharge or variation of disclosure order);

(i) applications under section 369 of the 2002 Act (discharge or variation of customer information order);

(j) applications under section 375 of the 2002 Act (discharge or variation of account monitoring orders).

General exclusions

(2) Sub-paragraph (1) is subject to–

(a) the exclusions in Part 2 of this Schedule, with the exception of paragraph 14 of that Part, and

(b) the exclusion in Part 3 of this Schedule.

Specific exclusions

(3) Where a confiscation order has been made under Part 2 of the 2002 Act against a defendant, the services described in sub-paragraph (1) do not include services provided to the defendant in relation to–

(a) directions under section 54(3) of that Act (distribution of funds in the hands of a receiver), or

(b) directions under section 67D of that Act (distribution of proceeds of realisation),

that relate to property recovered pursuant to the order.

(4) Where a confiscation order has been made under Part 2 of the 2002 Act against a defendant and varied under section 29 of that Act, the services described in sub-paragraph (1) do not include services provided in relation to an application by the defendant under section 73 of that Act (compensation).

Inquests

41(1) Civil legal services provided to an individual in relation to an inquest under the Coroners Act 1988 into the death of a member of the individual's family.

Exclusions

(2) Sub-paragraph (1) is subject to–

    (a) the exclusions in Part 2 of this Schedule, with the exception of paragraph 1 of that Part, and

    (b) the exclusion in Part 3 of this Schedule.

Definitions

(3) For the purposes of this paragraph an individual is a member of another individual's family if–

    (a) they are relatives (whether of the full blood or half blood or by marriage or civil partnership),

    (b) they are cohabitants (as defined in Part 4 of the Family Law Act 1996), or

    (c) one has parental responsibility for the other.

Environmental pollution

42(1) Civil legal services provided in relation to injunctions in respect of nuisance arising from prescribed types of pollution of the environment.

Exclusions

(2) Sub-paragraph (1) is subject to the exclusions in Parts 2 and 3 of this Schedule.

Equality

43(1) Civil legal services provided in relation to contravention of the Equality Act 2010 or a previous discrimination enactment.

Exclusions

(2) Sub-paragraph (1) is subject to–

    (a) the exclusions in Part 2 of this Schedule, with the exception of paragraph 15 of that Part, and

    (b) the exclusion in Part 3 of this Schedule.

Definitions

(3) In this paragraph 'previous discrimination enactment' means–

    (a) the Equal Pay Act 1970;

    (b) the Sex Discrimination Act 1975;

    (c) the Race Relations Act 1976;

    (d) the Disability Discrimination Act 1995;

    (e) the Employment Equality (Religion or Belief) Regulations 2003 (SI 2003/1660);

    (f) the Employment Equality (Sexual Orientation) Regulations 2003 (SI 2003/1661);

    (g) the Equality Act 2006;

    (h) the Employment Equality (Age) Regulations 2006 (SI 2006/1031);

    (i) the Equality Act (Sexual Orientation) Regulations 2007 (SI 2007/1263).

(4) The reference in sub-paragraph (1) to contravention of the Equality Act 2010 or a previous discrimination enactment includes–

    (a) breach of a term modified by, or included by virtue of, a provision that is an equality clause or equality rule for the purposes of the Equal Pay Act 1970 or the Equality Act 2010, and

    (b) breach of a provision that is a non-discrimination rule for the purposes of the Equality Act 2010.

Cross-border disputes

44(1) Civil legal services provided in relation to proceedings in circumstances in which the services are required to be provided under Council Directive 2002/8/EC of 27 January 2003 to improve access to justice in cross-border disputes by establishing minimum common rules relating to legal aid for such disputes.

No exclusions

(2) Sub-paragraph (1) is not subject to the exclusions in Parts 2 and 3 of this Schedule.

Terrorism prevention and investigation measures etc

45(1) Civil legal services provided to an individual in relation to a TPIM notice relating to the individual.

(2) Civil legal services provided to an individual in relation to control order proceedings relating to the individual.

Exclusions

(3) Sub-paragraphs (1) and (2) are subject to the exclusions in Parts 2 and 3 of this Schedule.

(4) In this paragraph–
'control order proceedings' means proceedings described in paragraph 3(1)
(a) to (e) of Schedule 8 to the Terrorism Prevention and Investigation Measures Act 2011 ('the 2011 Act');
'TPIM notice' means a notice under section 2(1) of the 2011 Act.

Extension of time for retention of travel documents

45A(1) Civil legal services provided in relation to proceedings under paragraph 8 of Schedule 1 to the Counter-Terrorism and Security Act 2015.

Exclusions

(2) Sub-paragraph (1) is subject to the exclusions in Parts 2 and 3 of this Schedule.

Connected matters

46(1) Prescribed civil legal services provided, in prescribed circumstances, in connection with the provision of services described in a preceding paragraph of this Part of this Schedule.

Exclusions

(2) Sub-paragraph (1) is subject to–
(a) the exclusions in Parts 2 and 3 of this Schedule, except to the extent that regulations under this paragraph provide otherwise, and
(b) any other prescribed exclusions.

PART 2: EXCLUDED SERVICES

The services described in Part 1 of this Schedule do not include the services listed in this Part of this Schedule, except to the extent that Part 1 of this Schedule provides otherwise.

1   Civil legal services provided in relation to personal injury or death.
2   Civil legal services provided in relation to a claim in tort in respect of negligence.

3   Civil legal services provided in relation to a claim in tort in respect of assault, battery or false imprisonment.

4   Civil legal services provided in relation to a claim in tort in respect of trespass to goods.

5   Civil legal services provided in relation to a claim in tort in respect of trespass to land.

6   Civil legal services provided in relation to damage to property.

7   Civil legal services provided in relation to defamation or malicious falsehood.

8   Civil legal services provided in relation to a claim in tort in respect of breach of statutory duty.

9   Civil legal services provided in relation to conveyancing.

10   Civil legal services provided in relation to the making of wills.

11   Civil legal services provided in relation to matters of trust law.

12(1)   Civil legal services provided in relation to a claim for damages in respect of a breach of Convention rights by a public authority to the extent that the claim is made in reliance on section 7 of the Human Rights Act 1998.

   (2)   In this paragraph–
   'Convention rights' has the same meaning as in the Human Rights Act 1998;
   'public authority' has the same meaning as in section 6 of that Act.

13   Civil legal services provided in relation to matters of company or partnership law.

14   Civil legal services provided to an individual in relation to matters arising out of or in connection with–
   (a)   a proposal by that individual to establish a business,
   (b)   the carrying on of a business by that individual (whether or not the business is being carried on at the time the services are provided), or
   (c)   the termination or transfer of a business that was being carried on by that individual.

15(1)   Civil legal services provided in relation to a benefit, allowance, payment, credit or pension under–
   (a)   a social security enactment,
   (b)   the Vaccine Damage Payments Act 1979, or
   (c)   Part 4 of the Child Maintenance and Other Payments Act 2008.

   (2)   In this paragraph 'social security enactment' means–
   (a)   the Social Security Contributions and Benefits Act 1992,
   (b)   the Jobseekers Act 1995,
   (c)   the State Pension Credit Act 2002,
   (d)   the Tax Credits Act 2002,
   (e)   the Welfare Reform Act 2007,
   (f)   the Welfare Reform Act 2012, or
   (g)   any other enactment relating to social security.

16   Civil legal services provided in relation to compensation under the Criminal Injuries Compensation Scheme.

17   Civil legal services provided in relation to changing an individual's name.

18(1)   Civil legal services provided in relation to judicial review of an enactment, decision, act or omission.

   (2)   In this paragraph 'judicial review' means–

(a) the procedure on an application for judicial review (see section 31 of the Senior Courts Act 1981), but not including the procedure after the application is treated under rules of court as if it were not such an application, and

(b) any procedure in which a court, tribunal or other person mentioned in Part 3 of this Schedule is required by an enactment to make a decision applying the principles that are applied by the court on an application for judicial review.

PART 3: ADVOCACY: EXCLUSION AND EXCEPTIONS

The services described in Part 1 of this Schedule do not include advocacy, except as follows–

(a) those services include the types of advocacy listed in this Part of this Schedule, except to the extent that Part 1 of this Schedule provides otherwise;

(b) those services include other types of advocacy to the extent that Part 1 of this Schedule so provides.

Exceptions: courts

1   Advocacy in proceedings in the Supreme Court.

2   Advocacy in proceedings in the Court of Appeal.

3   Advocacy in proceedings in the High Court.

4   Advocacy in proceedings in the Court of Protection to the extent that they concern–

(a) a person's right to life,

(b) a person's liberty or physical safety,

(c) a person's medical treatment (within the meaning of the Mental Health Act 1983),

(d) a person's capacity to marry, to enter into a civil partnership or to enter into sexual relations, or

(e) a person's right to family life.

5   Advocacy in proceedings in a county court.

5A   Advocacy in proceedings in the family court.

6   Advocacy in the following proceedings in the Crown Court–

(a) proceedings for the variation or discharge of an order under section 5 or 5A of the Protection from Harassment Act 1997,

(aa) proceedings on an appeal under section 10(1)(b) of the Crime and Disorder Act 1998 against the making of a parenting order where an injunction is granted under section 1 of the Anti-social Behaviour, Crime and Policing Act 2014,

(b) proceedings under the Proceeds of Crime Act 2002 in relation to matters listed in paragraph 40 of Part 1 of this Schedule,

(c) proceedings on an appeal under section 46B of the Policing and Crime Act 2009,

(d) proceedings on an appeal under section 15 of the Anti-social Behaviour, Crime and Policing Act 2014, and

(e) proceedings for the variation or discharge of an order under paragraph 1 of Schedule 2 to the Female Genital Mutilation Act 2003.

7   Advocacy in a magistrates' court that falls within the description of civil legal services in any of the following provisions of Part 1 of this Schedule–
  (a) paragraph 1(1)(e),
  (b) paragraph 1(2) so far as relating to paragraph (1)(1)(e), and
  (c) paragraphs 11(2), 12, 13(1)(e), 15][, 17 (1)(a) and (b), 36 and 38.

8   Advocacy in the following proceedings in a magistrates' court–
  (a) [Repealed.]
  (b) proceedings in relation to–
      (i) bail under Schedule 2 to the Immigration Act 1971, or
      (ii) arrest under Schedule 2 or 3 to that Act,
  (c) proceedings for the variation or discharge of an order under section 5 or 5A of the Protection from Harassment Act 1997, and
  (d) proceedings under the Proceeds of Crime Act 2002 in relation to matters listed in paragraph 40 of Part 1 of this Schedule, and
  (e) proceedings for the variation or discharge of an order under paragraph 1 of Schedule 2 to the Female Genital Mutilation Act 2003].

Exceptions: tribunals

9   Advocacy in proceedings in the First-tier Tribunal under–
  (a) the Mental Health Act 1983, or
  (b) paragraph 5(2) of the Schedule to the Repatriation of Prisoners Act 1984.

10   Advocacy in proceedings in the Mental Health Review Tribunal for Wales.

11   Advocacy in proceedings in the First-tier Tribunal under–
  (a) Schedule 2 to the Immigration Act 1971,
  (b) Part 5 of the Nationality, Immigration and Asylum Act 2002, or
  (c) Schedule 10 to the Immigration Act 2016.

12   Advocacy in proceedings in the First-tier Tribunal under–
  (a) section 40A of the British Nationality Act 1981, or
  (b) regulation 26 of the Immigration (European Economic Area) Regulations 2006 (SI 2006/1003),
  but only to the extent that the proceedings concern contravention of the Equality Act 2010.

13   Advocacy in the First-tier Tribunal that falls within the description of civil legal services in paragraph 28, 29, 31A, 32(1) or 32A(1) of Part 1 of this Schedule.

14   Advocacy in proceedings in the First-tier Tribunal under–
  (a) section 4 or 4A of the Protection of Children Act 1999 (appeals and applications relating to list of barred from regulated activities with children or vulnerable adults),
  (b) section 86 or 87 of the Care Standards Act 2000 (appeals and applications relating to list of persons unsuitable to work with vulnerable adults),
  (c) section 32 of the Criminal Justice and Court Services Act 2000 (applications relating to disqualification orders), or
  (d) section 144 of the Education Act 2002 (appeals and reviews relating to direction prohibiting person from teaching etc).

15   Advocacy in proceedings in the Upper Tribunal arising out of proceedings within any of paragraphs 9 to 14 of this Part of this Schedule.

16   Advocacy in proceedings in the Upper Tribunal under section 4 of the Safeguarding Vulnerable Groups Act 2006.

17   Advocacy in proceedings in the Upper Tribunal under section 11 of the Tribunals, Courts and Enforcement Act 2007 (appeals on a point of law) from decisions made by the First-tier Tribunal or the Special Educational Needs Tribunal for Wales in proceedings under–
(a) Part 4 of the Education Act 1996 (special educational needs),
(b) the Equality Act 2010, or
(c) Part 3 of the Children and Families Act 2014 (children and young people in England with special education needs or disabilities).

18   Advocacy in proceedings which are brought before the Upper Tribunal (wholly or primarily) to exercise its judicial review jurisdiction under section 15 of the Tribunals, Courts and Enforcement Act 2007.

19   Advocacy where judicial review applications are transferred to the Upper Tribunal from the High Court under section 31A of the Senior Courts Act 1981.

20   Advocacy in proceedings in the Employment Appeal Tribunal, but only to the extent that the proceedings concern contravention of the Equality Act 2010.

Other exceptions

21   Advocacy in proceedings in the Special Immigration Appeals Commission.

22   Advocacy in proceedings in the Proscribed Organisations Appeal Commission.

22A Advocacy in proceedings before a District Judge (Magistrates' Courts) under paragraph 8 of Schedule 1 to the Counter-Terrorism and Security Act 2015.

23   Advocacy in legal proceedings before any person to whom a case is referred (in whole or in part) in any proceedings within any other paragraph of this Part of this Schedule.

24   Advocacy in bail proceedings before any court which are related to proceedings within any other paragraph of this Part of this Schedule.

25   Advocacy in proceedings before any person for the enforcement of a decision in proceedings within any other paragraph of this Part of this Schedule.

PART 4: INTERPRETATION

1   For the purposes of this Part of this Act, civil legal services are described in Part 1 of this Schedule if they are described in one of the paragraphs of that Part (other than in an exclusion), even if they are (expressly or impliedly) excluded from another paragraph of that Part.

2   References in this Schedule to an Act or instrument, or a provision of an Act or instrument–
(a) are references to the Act, instrument or provision as amended from time to time, and
(b) include the Act, instrument or provision as applied by another Act or instrument (with or without modifications).

3   References in this Schedule to services provided in relation to an act, omission or other matter of a particular description (however expressed) include services provided in relation to an act, omission or other matter alleged to be of that description.

4   References in this Schedule to services provided in relation to proceedings, orders and other matters include services provided when such proceedings, orders and matters are contemplated.

5(1)   Where a paragraph of Part 1 or 2 of this Schedule describes services that consist of or include services provided in relation to proceedings, the description is to be treated as including, in particular–

(a) services provided in relation to related bail proceedings,

(b) services provided in relation to preliminary or incidental proceedings,

(c) services provided in relation to a related appeal or reference to a court, tribunal or other person, and

(d) services provided in relation to the enforcement of decisions in the proceedings.

(2) Where a paragraph of Part 3 of this Schedule describes advocacy provided in relation to particular proceedings in or before a court, tribunal or other person, the description is to be treated as including services provided in relation to preliminary or incidental proceedings in or before the same court, tribunal or other person.

(3) Regulations may make provision specifying whether proceedings are or are not to be regarded as preliminary or incidental for the purposes of this paragraph.

6   For the purposes of this Schedule, regulations may make provision about–

(a) when services are provided in relation to a matter;

(b) when matters arise under a particular enactment;

(c) when proceedings are proceedings under a particular enactment;

(d) when proceedings are related to other proceedings.

7   In this Schedule 'enactment' includes–

(a) an enactment contained in subordinate legislation (within the meaning of the Interpretation Act 1978), and

(b) an enactment contained in, or in an instrument made under, an Act or Measure of the National Assembly for Wales.

Standard Civil Contract 2018 Category Definitions

CATEGORY DEFINITIONS 2018

Introduction

1. These are the Category Definitions 2018 as referred to in the 2018 Standard Civil Contract. Definitions of terms set out in those Contracts also apply to these Category Definitions.

2. In these Category Definitions:

    (a) References to 'Legal Help' include Help at Court and in the Family Category only, Family Help (Lower) and Help with Family Mediation;

    (b) References to 'proceedings in a Category' cover the provision of Legal Representation (including Controlled Legal Representation) in that Category and, in the Family Category only, Family Help (Higher).

3. Services within the crime Category are automatically excluded from all Civil Categories, except for the specific overlaps between Categories specified at paragraph 17 of this document.

Legal Aid, Sentencing and Punishment of Offenders Act 2012

4. The Legal Aid, Sentencing and Punishment of Offenders Act 2012 (hereafter referred to as "the Act" in this document) sets out the matters for which civil and criminal legal services may be provided.

5. The Category Definitions show into which Category cases will fall but providers will need to satisfy themselves before undertaking work for any individual client that it is within the scope of the Act or that an application for exceptional funding has been approved.

6. Descriptions in this document of matters within scope of Part 1 of Schedule 1 to the Act should be read subject to the full provisions in that Part. For example, services referred to in Part 1 of Schedule 1 to the Act may be subject to exclusions in Parts 2 and 3 of Schedule 1 to the Act.

    Where a specific paragraph of Part 1 of Schedule 1 to the Act is referred to in a Category Definition then the services covered by that Category are at most only as wide as described in the given paragraph. For example, paragraph 37(a) of Immigration Category Definition allows the detention matters listed in paragraph 25 of Part 1 of Schedule 1 to fall within Immigration but not damages claims arising from such detention.

Exceptional Funding

7. Civil legal services that do not fall within the scope of Part 1 of Schedule 1 to the Act will fall to be funded under section 10 if the Director makes either: (i) an exceptional case determination (under section 10(2)(a) of the Act), or (ii) a wider public interest determination (under section 10(4)(b) of the Act).

8. Matters that are funded by virtue of a determination of the Director under section 10 of the Act will be classified as falling within the Category to which the primary problem or issue relates or, in the case of matters that are wholly unrelated to in-scope categories, as Miscellaneous Work. The extent to which a Category of Law encompasses services made available under section 10 of the Act is set out within each individual Category Definition.

Overlaps between Categories

9. The Categories are drafted to ensure that the majority of cases clearly fall within one Category or another. However, there will be some cases which genuinely fall within more than one Category. For example, certain work under the Mental Capacity Act 2005 falls under both the Mental Health Category of Law and Community Care.

10. Some cases will arise as the result of a number of different underlying issues, which may either be in scope or the subject of an exceptional funding application, and in those instances classification to a Category will depend upon the overall substance or predominant issue of the case when taken as a whole.

11. The following civil legal services fall into the Category of Law that relates to the underlying substance of the case as referenced by the widest Category Definition:

   (a) Public law challenges to the acts, omissions or decisions of public bodies by way of judicial review (as described in paragraph 19 of Part 1 of Schedule 1 to the Act). These cases are also covered by the Public Law Category

   (b) Civil legal services provided in relation to a writ of habeas corpus ad subjiciendum (as described in paragraph 20 of Part 1 of Schedule 1 to the Act). These cases are also covered by the Public Law Category

   (c) Cases involving a contravention of the Equality Act 2010 or previous discrimination enactment (as described in paragraph 43 of Part 1 of Schedule 1 to the Act). These cases are also covered by the Discrimination Category

   (d) Cross-border disputes where the civil legal services are required to be provided under Council Directive 2003/8/EC (as described in paragraph 44 of Part 1 of Schedule 1 to the Act). If these services do not fall within any Category of Law they are classified as Miscellaneous Work.

12. For the purposes of paragraph 11, the widest Category Definition includes those services that can only be made available via exceptional funding. For example, a judicial review would fall into the Housing Category of Law where the challenge was related to issues described in either paragraph 35 or 36 of the Housing Category Definition.

Damages under the Human Rights Act 1998

13. There are special provisions for claims for damages under the Human Rights Act 1998 (to the extent these are in scope by virtue of paragraphs 21 or 22 of Part 1 of Schedule 1 to the Act). A claim for damages made in reliance on section 7(1)(b) of the 1998 Act within existing proceedings described in

Part 1 of Schedule 1 to the Act falls exclusively within the Category of Law that includes the primary proceedings being heard.

14. Other claims for damages under the Human Rights Act 1998 fall exclusively within either the Claims Against Public Authorities Category or the Public Law Category (depending on the facts of the claim). This includes damages claims made within proceedings that are not listed within Part 1 of Schedule 1 to the Act, and all freestanding claims for damages under section 7(1)(a) of the 1998 Act.

Inquests

15. Civil legal services in relation to an inquest under the Coroners Act 1988 will fall into the Category of Law which relates most closely to the underlying subject matter of the inquest, taking into the specific legal issues that will be raised in the inquiry, the place and manner of the individual's death, and the classification of any separate proceedings that are dependent on the outcome of the inquest.

16. As with paragraphs 10–11 above, the widest definition of each Category should be used to determine classification of the case, including services that can only be provided via exceptional funding. For example, Legal Help for an inquest where the client died in prison will be funded in the Claims Against Public Authorities Category given that this Category includes all matters relating to "death in custody" (see paragraph 19 below). Where an inquest does not fall within one of the Categories, it will be classified as Miscellaneous Work.

Minor Civil/Criminal Overlaps

17. Work falling within the crime Category is generally excluded from any civil Category, but there are some minor exceptions:

(a) Enforcement proceedings in the magistrates court arising out of the breach of an order of that court made in family proceedings where there is a risk of imprisonment also fall within the Family Category;

(b) Civil proceedings in the magistrates' court arising out of the breach of a financial order of that court where there is a risk of imprisonment also fall within the Debt Category;

(c) Proceedings against a child for a Sexual Harm Prevention Order and any associated Parenting Order, and for a Parenting Order made on the conviction of a child where the parent cannot be reasonably represented by the child's solicitor also fall within the Family Category; and,

(d) Committal applications for civil contempt of court arising out of proceedings described in Part 1 of Schedule 1 also fall under the civil Category of Law covering the underlying proceedings, or where the underlying proceedings do not fall within a Category of Law, are classified as Miscellaneous Work.

18. The exceptions in paragraph 17 can be carried out under the 2018 Standard Civil Contract as well as by criminal practitioners under the 2017 Standard Crime Contract.

CATEGORY DEFINITIONS

Claims Against Public Authorities Category

19. Legal Help and all proceedings in relation to:

(a) abuse of a child or a vulnerable adult (as described in paragraph 3 of Part 1 of Schedule 1 to the Act

(b) abuse of position or power by a public authority (as described in paragraph 21 of Part 1 of Schedule 1 to the Act

(c) significant breach of convention rights by a public authority (as described in paragraph 22 of Part 1 of Schedule 1 to the Act)

(d) sexual offences (as described in paragraph 39 of Part 1 of Schedule 1 to the Act)

to the extent specified in paragraph 20.

20. A case listed in paragraph 19 will only fall within the Claims Against Public Authorities Category where at least one of the following conditions apply:

(a) The defendant is a public authority with the power to prosecute, detain or imprison and the claim arises out of, or is closely related, to the exercise of such a power; or,

(b) The claim is for personal injury based on allegations of deliberate abuse of a person while in the care of a public authority or other institution, or the failure of such a body to take a person into care.

21. To the extent that any relevant grant of exceptional funding is made (in accordance with section 10 of the Act) this Category also includes all other Legal Help and related proceedings concerning assault, trespass, false imprisonment, wrongful arrest, interference with goods, malicious prosecution, personal injury, wrongful conviction or death in custody, misfeasance in public office or other abuse of authority or neglect of duty against any body or person, private or public, with the power to detain, imprison or prosecute and the claim arises out of, or is closely related, to the exercise of such a power.

Clinical Negligence Category

22. Legal Help and all proceedings in relation to a claim for damages in respect of clinical negligence which caused a neurological injury to an infant as a result of which they are now severely disabled (as described in paragraph 23(1) of Part 1 of Schedule 1 to the Act).

23. To the extent that any relevant grant of exceptional funding is made (in accordance with section 10 of the Act) this Category also includes Legal Help and all proceedings in relation to a claim for damages or a complaint to a relevant professional body in respect of an alleged breach of duty of care or trespass to the person committed in the course of the provision of clinical or medical services (including dental or nursing services); or a claim for damages in respect of alleged professional negligence in the conduct of such a claim.

Community Care Category

24. Legal Help and related proceedings in relation to:

(a) the provision of community care services (as described in paragraph 6 of Part 1 of Schedule 1 to the Act);

(b) the provision of facilities for disabled persons (as described in paragraph 7 of Part 1 of Schedule 1 to the Act); and,

(c) the inherent jurisdiction of the High Court in relation to vulnerable adults (as described in paragraph 9 of Part 1 of Schedule 1 to the Act);

(d) the inherent jurisdiction of the High Court in relation to children (as described in paragraph 9 of Part 1 of Schedule 1 to the Act) where the case relates to a decision on medical treatment; and

(e) a person's capacity, their best interests (health and welfare), and deprivation of liberty issues under the Mental Capacity Act 2005 (as described in subparagraph 5(1)(c) of Part 1 of Schedule 1 to the Act).

25. To the extent that any relevant grant of exceptional funding is made (in accordance with section 10 of the Act), this Category also includes all other Legal Help and related proceedings concerning the provision of services or facilities in the community, nursing accommodation or hospital arranged by social services or a public health authority, excluding services falling within the Welfare Benefits or Clinical Negligence Categories. It also covers advocacy in the Court of Protection for matters arising under the Mental Capacity Act 2005 listed at paragraph 23(e) above that are not described by paragraph 4 of Part 3 of Schedule 1.

Debt Category

26. Legal Help and all proceedings in relation to:
    (a) Court orders for sale of an individual's home (as described in 33(1)(a) of Part 1 of Schedule 1 to the Act);
    (b) Court orders for possession of an individual's home arising out of failure to make payment due under a mortgage (as described in paragraph 33(1)(a) of Part 1 of Schedule 1 to the Act)[1]; and,
    (c) A bankruptcy order against the individual under Part 9 of the Insolvency Act 1986 where the estate includes the individual's home and where the petition for bankruptcy was not presented by the client, including in relation to a statutory demand under Part 9 of that Act (as described in paragraph 33(2) of Part 1 to Schedule 1 to the Act).

27. To the extent that any relevant grant of exceptional funding is made (in accordance with section 10 of the Act), this Category includes Legal Help and all proceedings:
    (a) For the payment of monies due or the enforcement of orders in such proceedings (excluding any matter which falls within the Housing Category); and,
    (b) Arising out of personal insolvency, including bankruptcy, administration, Debt Relief representation or IVA proceedings, but excluding representation in proceedings against parties in default of a fine or other order in criminal proceedings in the magistrates' court who are at risk of imprisonment.

Discrimination Category

28. Legal Help and proceedings in relation to:
    (a) Contravention of the Equality Act 2010 (as described in paragraph 43(1) of Part 1 of Schedule 1 to the Act);
    (b) Contravention of a previous discrimination enactment (as described in paragraph 43(3) of Part 1 of Schedule 1 to the Act), namely;
       i. The Equal Pay Act 1970;
       ii. The Sex Discrimination Act 1976;
       iii. The Race Relations Act 1976;
       iv. The Disability Discrimination Act 1995;
       v. The Employment Equality (Religion or Belief) Regulations 2003 (S.I. 2003/1660);

---

1 Possession of the home arising out of any matter other than failure to make payments on a mortgage fall within the Housing Category.

Education Category

29. Legal Help and all proceedings in relation to:
    (a) matters arising under Part 4 of the Education Act 1996 (Special Educational Needs) (as described in subparagraph 2(1)(a) of Part 1 of Schedule 1 to the Act);
    (b) matters arising under Part 3 of the Children and Families Act 2014 (as described in subparagraph 2(1)(a) of Part 1 of Schedule 1 to the Act);
    (c) assessments relating to learning difficulties under sections 140 of the Learning and Skills Act 2000 (as described in subparagraph 2(1)(b) of Part 1 of Schedule 1 to the Act); and,
    (d) any other matter within the scope of Part 1 of Schedule 1 to the Act where the primary problem or issue relates to the provision of, or failure to provide, education or funding for education.

30. For the avoidance of doubt, the Education Category includes brief advice and assistance on the social care provision and health care provision that have been included, or ought to be included, in an Education, Health and Care plan prepared under section 37 of the Children and Families Act 2014. However, where substantive advice is required to resolve any dispute concerning such provision this work falls under Community Care.

31. To the extent that exceptional funding is granted (in accordance with section 10 of the Act) this Category includes all other Legal Help and proceedings in relation to any matter where the primary problem or issue relates to the provision of or failure to provide education or funding for education.

Family Category

32. Legal Help and all proceedings in relation to:
    (a) orders under section 25 of the Children Act 1989 (as described in subparagraph 1(1)(a) of Part 1 of Schedule 1 to the Act);
    (b) orders under Part 4 and Part 5 of the Children Act 1989 Act (as described in subparagraphs 1(1)(b) and 1(1)(c) of Part 1 of Schedule 1 to the Act);
    (c) approval by a court under paragraph 19 of Schedule 2 to the Children Act 1989 Act (as described in subparagraphs 1(1)(d) of Part 1 of Schedule 1 to the Act);
    (d) parenting orders under sections 8 of the Crime and Disorder Act 1998 (as described in subparagraphs 1(1)(e) of Part 1 of Schedule 1 to the Act);
    (e) child safety orders under section 11 of the Crime and Disorder Act 1998 (as described in subparagraphs 1(1)(f) of Part 1 of Schedule 1 to the Act);
    (f) applications under the Adoption and Children Act 2002 (as described in subparagraphs 1(1)(g) to 1(1)(j) of Part 1 of Schedule 1 to the Act);
    (g) orders under an enactment made as an alternative to an order mentioned in subparagraphs (a) to (f) above (as described in subparagraph 1(2) of Part 1 of Schedule 1 to the Act);
    (h) orders under an enactment made in proceedings heard together with proceedings relating to an order mentioned in subparagraphs (a) to (f) above (as described in subparagraph 1(2) of Part 1 of Schedule 1 to the Act);
    (i) the inherent jurisdiction of the High Court in relation to children (as described in paragraph 9 of Part 1 of Schedule 1 to the Act);

(j) the orders and requirements listed in subparagraph 10(1) of Part 1 of Schedule 1 to the Act in relation to unlawful removal or potential unlawful removal of children from the United Kingdom;

(k) the orders and applications listed in subparagraph 10(2) of Part 1 of Schedule 1 to the Act in relation to the return of children unlawfully removed to a place in the United Kingdom;

(l) home rights, occupation orders and non-molestation orders under Part 4 of the Family Law Act 1996 (as described in paragraph 11(1) of Part 1 of Schedule 1 to the Act);

(m) injunctions following assault, battery and false imprisonment in circumstances arising out of a family relationship (as described in paragraph 11(2)(a) of Part 1 of Schedule 1 to the Act);

(n) the protection of an adult in proceedings under the inherent jurisdiction of the High Court in circumstances arising out of a family relationship (as described in paragraph 11(2)(b) of Part 1 of Schedule 1 to the Act);

(o) the mediation of family disputes (as described in subparagraph 14(2) of Part 1 of Schedule 1 to the Act);

(p) services provided to a child under paragraph 15 of Part 1 of Schedule 1 to the Act in relation to family proceedings where the child:
  i. is, or proposes to be, the applicant or respondent;
  ii. is made a party to the proceedings by a court under rule 16.2 of the Family Procedure Rules; or
  iii. is a party to the proceedings and is conducting, or proposing to conduct, the proceedings themselves in accordance with rule 16.6 of the Family Procedure Rules;

(q) female genital mutilation protection orders under paragraph 1 of Schedule 2 to the Female Genital Mutilation Act 2003 (as described in paragraph 15A of Part 1 of Schedule 1 to the Act);

(r) forced marriage protection orders under Part 4A of the Family Law Act 1996 (as described in paragraph 16 of Part 1 of Schedule 1 to the Act);

(s) the following EU and international agreements concerning children (as described in paragraph 17 of Part 1 of Schedule 1 to the Act):
  i. an application made to the Lord Chancellor under the 1980 European Convention on Child Custody for the recognition or enforcement in England and Wales of a decision relating to the custody of a child;
  ii. an application made to the Lord Chancellor under the 1980 Hague Convention in respect of a child who is, or is believed to be, in England and Wales;
  iii. the recognition or enforcement of a judgment in England and Wales in accordance with Article 21, 28, 41, 42 or 48 of the 2003 Brussels Regulation.

(t) the following EU and international agreements in relation to an application for the recognition or enforcement in England and Wales of a maintenance order (as described in paragraph 18 of Part 1 of Schedule 1 to the Act):
  i. the 1968 Brussels Convention;
  ii. the 1973 Hague Convention;
  iii. the 1989 Lugano Convention;
  iv. the 2000 Brussels Regulation;
  v. the 2007 Lugano Convention;

vi. the EU Maintenance Regulation;

vii. the 2007 Hague Convention;

(u) Proceedings under section 3, 3A, 5 or 5A of the Protection from Harassment Act 1997 (as described in paragraph 37 of Part 1 of Schedule 1 to the Act) arising out of a family relationship;

33. Legal Help and all proceedings in relation to matters arising out of a family relationship where the client has been, or is at risk of being, a victim of domestic violence (as described by paragraph 12 of Part 1 of Schedule 1 of Part 1 to the Act), including matters under the following enactments:

  (a) section 17 of the Married Women's Property Act 1882;

  (b) the Maintenance Orders (Facilities for Enforcement) Act 1920;

  (c) the Maintenance Orders Act 1950;

  (d) the Maintenance Orders Act 1958;

  (e) the Maintenance Orders (Reciprocal Enforcement) Act 1972;

  (f) Schedule 1 to the Domicile and Matrimonial Proceedings Act 1973 (staying of matrimonial proceedings) and corresponding provision in relation to civil partnerships made by rules of court under section 223 of the Civil Partnership Act 2004;

  (g) the Matrimonial Causes Act 1973;

  (h) the Inheritance (Provision for Family Dependants) Act 1975;

  (i) the Domestic Proceedings and Magistrates=' Courts Act 1978;

  (j) Part 3 of the Matrimonial and Family Proceedings Act 1984;

  (k) Parts 1 and 3 of the Family Law Act 1986;

  (l) Parts 1 and 2 of the Children Act 1989;

  (m) section 53 of, and Schedule 7 to, the Family Law Act 1996;

  (n) Chapters 2 and 3 of Part 2 of the Civil Partnership Act 2004;

  (o) section 54 of the Human Fertilisation and Embryology Act 2008

  (p) section 51A of the Adoption and Children Act 2002

  (q) applications for an order under section 14 of the Trusts of Land and Appointment of Trustees Act 1996 arising out of a family relationship

34. Legal Help and all proceedings in relation to the following orders and procedures where the child involved is at risk of abuse (as described in paragraph 13 of Part of Schedule 1 to the Act):

  (a) orders under section 4(2A) of the Children Act 1989 (removal of father's parental responsibility);

  (b) orders under section 6(7) of the Children Act 1989 (termination of appointment of guardian);

  (c) orders mentioned in section 8(1) of the Children Act 1989 (child arrangement orders and other orders);

  (d) special guardianship orders under Part 2 of the Children Act 1989;

  (e) orders under section 33 of the Family Law Act 1986 (disclosure of child's whereabouts);

  (f) orders under section 34 of the Family Law Act 1986 (return of child)

  (g) orders under section 51A of the Adoption and Children Act 2002 (post-adoption contact)

35. To the extent that any relevant grant of exceptional funding is made (in accordance with section 10 of the Act) this Category also includes all other Legal Help and related proceedings arising out of family relationships, including proceedings in which the welfare of children is to be determined

Housing Category

36. Legal Help and proceedings in relation to:
    (a) Possession of an individual's home (other than mortgage possession) (as described in subparagraph 33(1)(a) of Part 1 of Schedule 1 to the Act)[2];
    (b) Eviction from an individual's home of the individual or others, including unlawful eviction and planning eviction matters and closure orders not arising out of criminal conduct (as described in subparagraph 33(1)(b) of Part 1 of Schedule 1);
    (c) The provision of accommodation and assistance under Parts 6 and 7 of the Housing Act 1996 for an individual who is homeless or threatened with homelessness (as described in paragraph 34 of Part 1 of Schedule 1 to the Act)[3];
    (d) The provision of accommodation by way of community care services as specified in paragraph 6 of Part 1 of Schedule 1 to the Act, in relation to an individual who is homeless or threatened with homelessness;
    (e) Housing disrepair matters described in paragraph 35 of Part 1 of Schedule 1 to the Act, namely removing or reducing a serious risk of harm to the health or safety of the individual or relevant family member where the risk arises from a deficiency in the individual's rented or leased home and the legal services are provided with a view to securing that the landlord makes arrangements to remove or reduce the risk. This includes Legal Help for applications under section 82 of the Environmental Protection Act 1990 for a statutory nuisance, where the application falls within the terms of paragraph 35 of Part 1 of Schedule 1;
    (f) Applications to vary or discharge an injunction under section 153A of the Housing Act 1996;
    (g) Injunctions under the Protection from Harassment Act 1997 arising from matters within paragraphs 37 and 38 of these Category Definitions (paragraph 37 of Part 1 of Schedule 1 to the Act); and
    (h) The powers of the Secretary of State to provide or arrange to provide accommodation under section 4 or 95 of the Immigration and Asylum Act 1999 and section 17 of the Nationality, Immigration and Asylum Act 2002 (as described by paragraph 31 of Part of Schedule 1 to the Act).

37. To the extent that any relevant grant of exceptional funding is made (in accordance with section 10 of the Act) this Category also includes all other Legal Help and related proceedings in relation to matters which concern the possession, status, terms of occupation, repair, improvement, eviction from, quiet enjoyment of, or payment of rent or other charges for premises (including vehicles and sites they occupy) which are occupied as a residence, including the rights of leaseholders under the terms of their lease or under any statutory provision (including enfranchisement). Cases including allocation, transfers and the provision of sites for occupation are also included.

---

2 Possession arising from mortgage arrears and court orders for sale of the home fall within the Debt Category.

3 References to Part 7 of the Housing Act 1996 (or to provisions within Part 7 of the Housing Act 1996) include reference to Part 2 of the Housing (Wales) Act 2014 (or equivalent provisions within Part 2 of the Housing (Wales) Act 2014.

Immigration and Asylum Category

38. Legal Help on matters and all proceedings in relation to:
    (a) Immigration-related detention powers referred to in paragraph 25(1) of Part 1 of Schedule 1 to the Act;
    (b) Temporary admission to the UK under provisions referred to in paragraph 26(1) of Part 1 of Schedule 1 to the Act;
    (c) Restrictions imposed on an individual under the provisions referred to in paragraph 27(1) of Part 1 of Schedule 1 to the Act;
    (d) An application for indefinite leave by a victim of domestic violence (as described in paragraph 28 of Part 1 of Schedule 1 to the Act);
    (e) A residence card application by a victim of domestic violence (as described in paragraph 29 of Part 1 of Schedule 1 to the Act);
    (f) Rights to enter and to remain in the United Kingdom under the provisions referred to in paragraph 30(1) of Part 1 of Schedule 1 to the Act;
    (g) An application by a victim of human trafficking for leave to enter or remain in the United Kingdom (as described in subparagraph 32(1) of Part 1 of Schedule 1 to the Act);
    (h) A Terrorism Prevention and Investigation Measure notice (as described in paragraph 45 of Part 1 of Schedule 1 to the Act);
    (i) An application by a victim of slavery, servitude or forced or compulsory labour for leave to enter or remain in the United Kingdom (as described in subparagraph 32A(1) of Part 1 of Schedule 1 to the Act).
39. Legal help and all proceedings before the Special Immigration Appeals Commission (as described in paragraph 24 of Part 1 of Schedule 1 to the Act).
40. To the extent that any relevant grant of exceptional funding is made (in accordance with section 10 of the Act) this Category includes all other Legal Help and proceedings in relation to any matter where the primary problem or issue is an immigration or asylum matter.

Mental Health Category

41. Legal Help and all proceedings in relation to:
    (a) cases under the Mental Health Act 1983, the Mental Capacity Act 2005, and paragraph 5(2) of the Schedule to the Repatriation of Prisoners Act 1984 (as described in paragraph 5 of Part 1 of Schedule 1 to the Act);
    (b) the inherent jurisdiction of the High Court in relation to vulnerable adults (as described in paragraph 9 of Part 1 of Schedule 1 to the Act);
    (c) the inherent jurisdiction of the High Court in relation to children (as described in paragraph 9 of Part 1 of Schedule 1 to the Act) where the case relates to a decision on medical treatment; and
42. For the avoidance of doubt, except as permitted by paragraph 13 above the Mental Health Category does not include any civil legal services made available under paragraphs 21 or 22 of Part 1 of Schedule 1 to the Act, including, but not limited to, matters arising from an individual's detention under the Mental Health Act 1983 or the Mental Capacity Act 2005. Nor does it include services under the Mental Health Act 1983 that are required to be made available under sections 13, 15 and 16 of the Act (criminal legal aid).
43. To the extent that any relevant grant of exceptional funding is made (in accordance with section 10 of the Act), this Category also includes advocacy for matters arising under the Mental Capacity Act 2005 (as described in

paragraph 5 of Part 1 of Schedule 1 to the Act) that are not listed in paragraph 4 of Part 3 of Schedule 1 to the Act.

Public Law Category

44. Legal Help and related proceedings in relation to:
    (a) public law challenges to the acts, omissions or decisions of public bodies by way of judicial review or habeas corpus (as described in paragraphs 19 and 20 of Part 1 of Schedule 1); and
    (b) any claim described in paragraph 21 or 22 of Part 1 of Schedule 1 to the Act concerning the human rights of the client or a dependant of the client (other than matters that fall within the definition of another Category).

Welfare Benefits Category

45. Legal Help in relation to appeals on a point of law in the Upper Tribunal, Court of Appeal and Supreme Court for all welfare benefits (including housing benefit, war pensions, state pensions and other similar benefits under a social security enactment, the Vaccine Damage Payments Act 1979 or Part 4 of the Child Maintenance and Other Payments Act 2008) (as described in paragraph 8 of Part 1 of Schedule 1 to the Act)

46. Legal Help in relation to appeal on a point of law relating to a council tax reduction scheme from the Valuation Tribunal England and the Valuation Tribunal Wales to the High Court, Court of Appeal and Supreme Court (as described in paragraph 8A of Part 1 of Schedule 1 to the Act)

47. Legal representation for appeals to the Court of Appeal and the Supreme Court on a point of law in relation to all welfare benefits (including housing benefit, war pensions, state pensions and other similar benefits under a social security enactment, the Vaccine Damage Payments Act 1979 and Part 4 of the Child Maintenance and Other Payments Act 2008) and appeals on a point of law relating to a council tax reduction scheme to the Court of Appeal and Supreme Court (as described in paragraphs 8 and 8A of Part 1 of Schedule 1 to the Act).

48. To the extent that any grant of exceptional funding is made this Category includes Legal Help in relation to all welfare benefits (including council tax reduction scheme appeals, housing benefit, war pensions, state pensions and vaccine damage payments or similar payments), and in relation to proceedings before any welfare benefit review or appeal body any subsequent or related proceedings before a court.

Miscellaneous Work

49. Civil legal services that are not included within any Category of Law are classified as "Miscellaneous Work". For ease of reference, the following matters or proceedings that are described in Part 1 of Schedule 1 to the Act are likely to fall outside all Civil Categories and thus be classified as Miscellaneous Work.

Working with children and vulnerable adults

50. Legal Help and all proceedings in relation to:
    (a) The inclusion of a person in a barred list or the removal of a person from a barred list (as described in paragraph 4(1)(a) of Part 1 of Schedule 1 to the Act);

(b) A disqualification order under section 28, 29, or 29A of the Criminal Justice and Court Services Act 2000 (disqualification from working with children) (as described in paragraph 4(1)(b) of Part 1 of Schedule 1 to the Act);

(c) A direction under section 142 of the Education Act 2002 (prohibition from teaching etc) (as described in paragraph 4(1)(c) of Part 1 of Schedule 1 to the Act).

Protection from Harassment

51. Legal Help and all proceedings in relation to:

(a) An injunction under section 3 or 3A of the Protection from Harassment Act 1997 (as described in paragraph 37(1)(a) of Part 1 of Schedule 1 to the Act);

(b) The variation or discharge of a restraining order under section 5 or 5A of that Act (as described in paragraph 37(1)(b) of Part 1 of Schedule 1 to the Act),

(other than where they are included in the Family or Housing Categories of Law by virtue of paragraphs 33(u) and 37(g) of the Category Definitions respectively.).

Proceeds of Crime

52. Legal Help and proceedings in relation to:

(a) Restraint orders under section 41 of the Proceeds of Crime Act 2002 (POCA) including orders under section 41(7) of POCA (orders for ensuring that restraint order is effective) (as described in paragraph 40(1)(a) of Part 1 of Schedule 1 to the Act);

(b) Orders under section 47M of POCA (detention of property) (as described in paragraph 40(1)(b) of Part 1 of Schedule 1 to the Act);

(c) Directions under section 54(3) of POCA (distribution of funds in the hands of a receiver) (as described in paragraph 40(1)(c) of Part 1 of Schedule 1 to the Act);

(d) Directions under section 62 of POCA (action to be taken by receiver) (as described in paragraph 40(1)(d) of Part 1 of Schedule 1 to the Act);

(e) Orders under section 67A of POCA (realising property), including directions under section 67D of POCA (distribution of proceeds of realisation) (as described in paragraph 40(1)(e) of Part 1 of Schedule 1 to the Act);

(f) Orders under section 72 or 73 of POCA (compensation) (as described in paragraph 40(1)(f) of Part 1 of Schedule 1 to the Act);

(g) Applications under section 351 of POCA (discharge or variation of a production order or order to grant entry) (as described in paragraph 40(1)(g) of Part 1 of Schedule 1 to the Act);

(h) Applications under section 362 of POCA (discharge or variation of disclosure order) (as described in paragraph 40(1)(h) of Part 1 of Schedule 1 to the Act);

(i) Applications under section 369 of POCA (discharge or variation of customer information order) (as described in paragraph 40(1)(j) of Part 1 of Schedule 1 to the Act);

(j) Applications under section 375 of POCA (discharge or variation of account monitoring orders) (as described in paragraph 40(1)(j) of Part 1 of Schedule 1 to the Act).

53. Note that where a confiscation order has been made against a defendant under Part 2 of POCA, civil legal services provided to the defendant in relation to directions under section 54(3) or section 67D of POCA that relate to property recovered pursuant to the order are not within scope of Part 1 of Schedule 1 to the Act.

54. Note that where a confiscation order has been made under Part 2 of POCA against a defendant and varied under section 29 of POCA, civil legal services provided in relation to an application by the defendant under section 73 of POCA are not within scope of Part 1 of Schedule 1 to the Act.

Environmental Pollution

55. Legal Help and all proceedings in relation to injunctions in respect of nuisance arising from pollution of the environment (as described in paragraph 42(1) of Part 1 of Schedule 1 to the Act).

Sexual offences

56. Legal help and all proceedings in relation to a sexual offence where the client is the victim of the offence, including incitement to commit a sexual offence, encouraging or assisting a sexual offence which the person intended or believed would be committed, conspiracy to commit a sexual offence, and an attempt to commit a sexual offence (as described in paragraph 39 of Part 1 of Schedule 1 to the Act) other than where these matters are included in the Claims Against Public Authorities Category.

Victims of trafficking in human beings or modern slavery

57. Legal Help and all proceedings in connection with:
    (a) a claim for damages arising in connection with the trafficking or exploitation of an individual who is a victim of human trafficking (as described in subparagraph 32(3) of Part 1 of Schedule 1 to the Act);
    (b) claims under employment law arising in connection with the exploitation of an individual who is a victim of human trafficking (as described in subparagraph 32(2) of Part 1 of Schedule 1 to the Act);
    (c) a claim under employment law arising in connection with the conduct by virtue of which an individual who is a victim of slavery, servitude or forced or compulsory labour is such a victim (as described in subparagraph 32A(2) of Part 1 of Schedule 1 to the Act); and,
    (d) a claim for damages arising in connection with the conduct by virtue of which an individual who is a victim of slavery, servitude or forced or compulsory labour is such a victim (as described in subparagraph 32A(2) of Part 1 of Schedule 1 to the Act)

Injunctions to prevent gang-related violence

58. Legal Help and all proceedings in relation to injunctions to prevent gang-related violence under Part 4 of the Policing and Crime Act 2009 (as described in subparagraph 38(1) of Part 1 of Schedule 1 to the Act).

Abuse of child or vulnerable adult

59. Legal Help and all proceedings in relation to abuse of an individual that took place at a time when the individual was a child or vulnerable adult (as described in paragraph 3(1) of Part 1 of Schedule 1 to the Act other than where these matters are included in the Claims Against Public Authorities Category.

Anti-social behaviour injunctions

60. Legal Help and proceedings in relation to an injunction in respect of anti-social behaviour or alleged anti-social behaviour under Part 1 of the Anti-social Behaviour, Crime and Policing Act 2014 and related parenting orders (as described in paragraph 36(1) of Part 1 of Schedule 1 and paragraph 1(1)(e) of Part 1 of Schedule 1.)

Civil costs: what you can claim for

A quick reference guide

This is a summary of the LAA's Costs Assessment Guidance for use with the 2018 Standard Civil Contracts, September 2018, in respect of the most common queries raised by caseworkers. Paragraph numbers are from the Guidance, which can be found on the website at https://www.gov.uk/guidance/funding-and-costs-assessment-for-civil-and-crime-matters

Admin work

Opening and setting up files, maintaining time costing records and other time spent in complying with the requirements of the Standard Contract are not chargeable (paras 2.1 and 2.10). Letters confirming appointments etc with no legal content are administrative if sent by a non fee-earner. They may be allowable if considered by a fee-earner to be appropriate in the particular circumstances of a client. (para 2.18).

Advocacy

Normally (and where claimable), this is time on your feet before a court or tribunal; but note that in the Family Advocacy Scheme advocacy also includes travel to court, waiting time and attendance at advocates' meetings. The Costs assessment guidance states that where you do your own advocacy, it is reasonable to claim for preparing a brief to yourself (para 2.39).

Agents

They stand in your shoes and their costs are part of your profit costs. You cannot claim their fees as a disbursement. A London rate will only apply if the agent is based in London (paras 2.48–2.51).

Attendance

This is the conventional legal costing term for interviewing someone face-to-face, or speaking to them on the telephone (see below for more details on telephone calls).

All claims for attendance must be justified in an attendance note. The longer the time claimed, the more detail is expected.

You may be able to justify more than one caseworker being present; but this would be exceptional, for example, in a complex case, where different aspects of it have been split between different people (para 2.36). In a complex case you may be able to justify the time of two caseworkers in the same category of law where you would be able to justify claiming legal research (see Legal research for more details). You may be able to justify the time of two caseworkers in different categories of law if a difficult or unusual point arises and it would be reasonable. Supervision is a generally considered to be an overhead and not chargeable (para 2.37).

You can claim for attendance on the client or conference during the lunchtime adjournment if at court (para 2.55). A lower rate applies if you are attending with counsel.

Bundles

Fee earners must prepare master bundles for court, and often for counsel. Identifying the documents for the master bundle and drafting the index is fee-earner work. Making up or copying of additional bundles is not chargeable. Where the bundles are above average size it is reasonable for fee earners to check that copies have been properly collated and reproduced (para 2.16). See also chapter 16 for bundle payments under the Family Advocacy Scheme.

CCMS

Prior to the issue of updated guidance below in September 2018, the only way to claim additional fees due to CCMS was to cost the extra time and submit a claim through the LAA's complaint and compensation scheme[1].

The LAA has confirmed that the updated guidance was clarification of the existing position rather than substantive change. As such, these principles apply to all assessments which take place after the revised guidance was issued on 3 September 2018, regardless of when the certificate was granted.

New guideline times are shown below with the previous guidelines they replace but don't forget that additional time may be justified on a case by case basis.

It worth noting how much longer they are in every case where they replace previous guidance. There are also new allowances for processes introduced by CCMS and simply didn't exist before.

Where a provider sends a message on CCMS (and by implication receives one where allowable), this is treated as equivalent to sending an e-mail or letter to the LAA and may be claimed as such (2.31).

Non-merits tested application (previously – no specific time) new guideline – 30min (2.61)

Merits tested application (previously – no specific time) new guideline – 48min (2.61)

The guidance goes on to say that for CCMS claims additional time may be claimed for inputting the means information into CCMS.

Where this is done in the client's presence it will form part of the costs of the attendance on the client. Where the information is input into CCMS by the

---

1   https://www.gov.uk/government/organisations/legal-aid-agency/about/complaints-procedure

fee earner without the client being present 30 minutes will generally be considered reasonable. (2.61)

For allocation of costs to Counsel 12 to 18 minutes will usually be considered reasonable. (2.63)

Amendments (previously – 6min) new guideline – 24-30 min (2.63)

Disbursement POA (previously – 6min) new guideline – 12min (2.63)

Profit costs POA (previously – 6min) new guideline – 12min (2.63)

CCMS outcome codes with no costs recovery/statutory charge – new guideline – 12min (2.63)

CCMS outcome codes with costs recovery/statutory charge – (previously – 12-18 min) new guideline – 24min (2.63)

Hourly rate bill claims – (previously – 30-60 min up to £2500, more than 60min over £2500) new guideline – 48min per page of 10 items (2.63)

Court assessed bills with FAS – (previously – 12-18min) new guideline – 54 - 60min (2.63)

Court assessed bills without FAS – (previously – 12-18min) new guideline – 30-36min (2.63)

Congestion charge
This is claimable where incurred exclusively in relation to the case but not where your journey to work would have meant you incurred the charge anyway (para 3.20).

Consideration of documents
See Perusal.

Disbursements
This means counsel's fees, experts' fees, court fees, travelling and witness expenses and other out of pocket expenses properly incurred by a fee earner which would be properly chargeable to a client. They must be reasonably incurred and reasonable in amount (para 3.1). Some are explicitly excluded under the contract specification, where they are listed (see Paragraph 4.29 of the Specification in relation to controlled work and Paragraph 6.61 of the Specification in relation to licensed work (2018 Specification). Most communication support professionals' fees are regarded as a reasonable adjustment under the Equality Act 2010 and therefore an overhead which cannot be charged for; but sign language interpreters' costs can be claimed. They must be accounted for separately as they are excluded from the statutory charge (para 3.7). See also chapter 14 for information about guideline rates and amounts for experts' fees.

Distant clients
No extra costs can be claimed that arise because you are in a location that is distant from your client, where it would be reasonable for the client to instruct someone closer (para 2.46) (see also Travel time). However, vulnerable clients are not expected to make exhaustive searches for closer providers. If you are within 10 miles of the relevant Court-Tribunal, it will be considered reasonable to instruct you, even though the client may be distant from you.

Drafting documents

As a guideline, 6–12 minutes' preparation time would be expected per page of a straightforward document, but more complex documents will take longer (para 2.16). It is reasonable to re-examine the core documents to consider their effect on the case. However, the degree to which this will be justified depends entirely on the complexity of the issues (para 2.9).

Emails

See Letters.

Enhancements

It is up to you to justify any enhancement of your costs on certificated cases. You cannot apply an enhancement in order to escape any fixed fee (Standard Contract Specification 2018 para 6.12). You may be able to argue for an enhancement of 50% or 100% in High Court, Upper Tribunal, Court of Appeal or Supreme Court cases.

First you must be able to demonstrate one of the following features:
(a) the work was done with exceptional competence, skill or expertise;
(b) the work was done with exceptional speed; or
(c) the case involved exceptional circumstances or complexity.

If accepted, the caseworker will go on to consider the percentage enhancement to apply (12.4).

The LAA caseworker will consider:
(a) the degree of responsibility accepted by the fee earner;
(b) the care, speed and economy with which the case was prepared; and
(c) the novelty, weight and complexity of the case (12.5).

A guaranteed minimum enhancement of 15% is available in respect of work carried out by a fee-earner on the Resolution Accredited Specialist Panel, the Law Society's Children Panel (in respect of proceedings relating to children) or the Law Society Family Law Panel Advanced. This is not paid in addition to any other enhancement which may be justified (para 12.23).

Faxes

These are treated as letters; but you cannot claim for sending a copy by post as well as the fax. See Letters for more detail.

Form completion – see also CCMS

Generally not claimable; but there are exceptions (paras 2.58–2.63):
CW1 where the client is eligible;
CLR in Immigration cases;
application forms for certificates (30 minutes is standard but may be exceeded where justifiable);
applications for amendments to certificates;
POA claims;
applications to increase financial limitations on certificates;
Claim 1, Claim 1A and Claim 2 (12–18 minutes);
POA 1 (6 minutes).

Completion of forms on behalf of clients is only claimable where legal assistance is justified.

See also CCMS for time which may be claimed for time spent when using CCMS.

Legal research

Not claimable unless on a novel, developing or unusual point of law or the impact of new legislation to the particular case (para 2.5). However, it may still be reasonable for time for checking on the application of established law or procedural rules to individual circumstances to be claimed, provided the reasons are recorded (para 2.6).

Letters in

You can only claim for reading routine letters received in Family Licensed Work cases paid at family rates, otherwise CPR 47 PD 5.22(1) applies. Payment for reading the letter is deemed to be included in the charge for a routine letter out (para 2.22). You can only charge for reading routine letters received in Family proceedings (para 2.22). You can charge for reading non-routine letters received in all categories.

Letters out

These are either 'routine' and claimed at the item rate, because they are standard letters or take up to six minutes to write, or they are preparation rate letters, because they take longer to write than six minutes (para 2.17).

You cannot charge for administrative letters, eg confirming an appointment sent by a non-fee-earner. You may be able to charge if the fee earner has considered the letter appropriate in the circumstances of a particular client. You cannot charge for multiple letters sent to the same client or party on the same day, unless there is a good reason that justifies it. You cannot charge for a letter correcting your own mistake (para 2.18).

Office overheads

The following are office overheads and not claimable: costs of postage, stationery, faxes, scanning, typing and the actual cost of telephone calls and most photocopying, but see below for exceptional photocopying costs (para 3.37). Supervision is generally considered to be an overhead (para 2.37).

Overnight expenses

These can only be claimed in exceptional circumstances, where it would be unreasonable to travel the distance there and back and carry out whatever was required in one day (para 3.18).

Perusal

This is also known as consideration of documents. An initial brief perusal of all the documents to identify which documents are relevant is reasonable. Later detailed consideration of documents may also be reasonable (para 2.8). As a very rough guide it takes approximately two minutes per A4 page to read the most simple document. Time taken will depend on the quality and layout of the document, eg whether handwritten or typed, single- or double-spaced, large or small font, etc. More complex documents may take a longer (para 2.12).

Photocopying
Photocopying in-house is generally an overhead expense, but if there are 'unusual circumstances', or documents are unusually numerous (as a rule of thumb, 500 pages), you may claim the lowest commercial photocopying rate as a disbursement, even when carried out in-house (para 3.38).

Preparation
Includes drafting of documents, consideration of documents and evidence provided by the client or other parties, and general consideration of strategy, evidence needed and evidence to be put forward and whether to make or accept offers to settle a case, and 'thinking time' (para 2.7).

Reviewing files
You are expected to be familiar with your own files, so you would need to justify any claim for reading a file, eg prior to seeing a client when you had not dealt with the file for some time (para 2.40). You cannot charge for reviewing a file when it is reallocated from one caseworker to another, unless this is due to unforeseeable circumstances, eg the client needs to give urgent instructions and the first caseworker is not available (para 2.41).

Telephone calls
These are either 'routine' and claimed at the item rate, because they take up to six minutes, or they are attendance rate calls, because they take longer than six minutes (para 2.23). You can claim for an unsuccessful call; but if you make repeated calls to the same number, you would have to justify it. You can claim a routine call for leaving a message on an answering machine. If you are put 'on hold', after the first six minutes on the call, you can charge the waiting time at the waiting rate (para 2.26). However, bear in mind that it may be more efficient to write a letter or send an email.

Texts
These are treated as telephone calls. See Telephone calls for more detail.

Transferring files between fee earners
See Reviewing files.

Travel time
The general rule is that if the round trip travel time is five hours or more, it is usually more reasonable to instruct an agent than to go yourself. However, in some circumstances it may be reasonable to go (para 2.44):
(a) court applications, other than those that are straightforward;
(b) conference with counsel;
(c) interviewing a witness where the fee earner will wish to test the witnesses credibility for him or herself;
(d) because of the specialised nature of the case, the fee earner's close personal understanding of the matter or the nature of the client,
(e) where there is a lack of suitably qualified agents in the area concerned. The reason for making the journey must be recorded on the file.

Travel time to clients
Usually, the client should come to you; but if e.g. the client is housebound, in hospital or detention, it may be reasonable for you to travel to the client (para

2.47). See also the Standard Civil Contract Specification 2018, para 2.38c which says you may provide contract work at the client's location for 'good reason', which is not defined further. If you need to travel to a client before a CW1 Legal Help Form is signed, where this is justified and the client subsequently signs the form and is eligible, you can claim the outward travel (para 2.47). The reason must always be recorded on the file.

Travelling expenses (caseworkers')

Caseworkers' travelling expenses can be claimed where the journey was necessary and the most appropriate form of transport used (para 3.11). The LAA considers that public transport should normally be used; but time saved will be considered as well as travel fares or mileage. Taxis may be justified, eg when transporting heavy bundles. You will need to give justifiable reasons for using other than public transport. Local travelling expenses to court cannot be claimed (eg within a ten-mile radius) unless public transport is known to be poor. Documentary evidence must support claims over £20 (except mileage) (para 3.17). Note that the LAA expects mileage details to include the postcodes of the start and end location. If you had to use a different route from that indicated on a standard route planner (e.g. Google Maps), it is recommended to download the route you took and explain why (e.g. roadworks, accident etc.).

Travelling expenses (clients')

You can pay clients' expenses to attend court and claim them back from the LAA as a disbursement (documentary evidence is required as for caseworkers). The client's presence must be 'necessary'. The Family Procedure Rules 2010 (r.27.3) require that parties to proceedings attend any hearing or directions appointment of which they have notice, unless the court has directed otherwise (para 3.31).

Prior authority can be sought for a clients' travelling expenses to an expert where the client cannot afford them and a report is essential for the proper conduct of proceedings, as the request would be considered 'unusual in nature' (para 3.27). Client's travel to their lawyer can be claimed in asylum cases (Standard Civil Contract 2018 Specification para 8.48).

Travelling expenses (experts')

Note that the LAA expects mileage details of experts' journeys, including the postcodes of the start and end location, as they do for fee-earners (see above).

Waiting

You should not normally arrive at court more than 30 minutes before a hearing. If you have to, perhaps due to transport timetables, you should record the reason on file (para 2.53). You cannot claim waiting time during the lunchtime adjournment; but you can claim for attendance or conference undertaken during that time (2.55).

Waiting on the telephone

If you are out 'on hold', after the first six minutes on the call, you can charge the waiting time at the waiting rate (para 2.26).

Criminal costs: what you can claim for

A full discussion of all the relevant issues is contained in *Criminal Costs: legal aid costs in the criminal courts*, LAG, 2nd edn. 2019.

A quick reference guide

This is a summary based on the LAA's Costs assessment guidance for criminal defence work, in respect of the most common queries raised by caseworkers. Appropriate comments have been added. Paragraph numbers are from the Criminal Bills Assessment Manual, January 2020 edition. The manual is occasionally not wholly accurate or up to date but it explains the training received by LAA staff.

Admin work

Opening and setting up files, taxes, postage, stationery, typing, faxing, and telephone bills are not chargeable (para 3.1.1). Letters written by a non fee-earner which are not fee earner work are administrative (para 3.8.14).

Advocacy

Normally (and where claimable), this is time on your feet before a court, including time while the bench (or jury) has retired (para 6.7.38), as long as the solicitor has not been released from the court.

Agents

They stand in your shoes and their costs are part of your profit costs. You cannot claim their fees as a disbursement (para 3.6.3).

Attendance

All claims for attendance must be justified in an attendance note. The longer the time claimed, the more detail is expected. Time spent dictating an attendance note may be allowed as long as it is reasonable (or typing it up if the fee-earner is self servicing) (3.3.3).

You may be able to justify more than one caseworker being present; but this would be exceptional, for example, in a complex case, where different aspects of it have been split between different people (para 3.5.1)or appropriate delegation or supervision (3.5.4 and 3.5.5).

Congestion charge

This is claimable where incurred exclusively in relation to the case but not where your journey to work would have meant you incurred the charge anyway (para 3.9.33–34).

Consideration of documents
See Perusal.

Disbursements
Must be reasonably incurred and reasonable in amount. See section 7 CBAM for disbursements generally.

Distant clients
No extra costs can normally be claimed that arise because you are in a location that is distant from your client, where it would be reasonable for the client to instruct someone closer. Different considerations apply to travel to counsel experts witnesses or site inspections (para 3.9.7) (see also Travel time).

Drafting documents
As a guideline, 6–12 minutes' preparation time would be expected per page of a straightforward document, but more complex documents will take longer (para 3.3.2). You charge for the time actually taken but test reasonableness against that standard. The longer you take, the greater the explanation that is needed.

Emails
See Letters.

Faxes
These are treated as letters; but you cannot claim for sending a copy by post as well as the fax. See Letters for more detail (para 3.8.24).

Legal research
Not claimable unless on a novel, developing or unusual point of law or the impact of new legislation to the particular case (para 3.4.2-3). However, you should be paid for the application of established law or procedural rules to individual circumstances).

Letters in
You cannot normally claim for reading routine letters received (para 3.8.10) but it becomes an item of preparation when time is reasonably taken on a more detailed letter.

Letters out
Letters sent will not automatically allowed. It has to be reasonable to send them (para 3.8.2). Letters are either 'routine' and claimed at the item rate, because they are standard letters or are the equivalent of the item rate (para 3.8.1), or you can charge for non-routine items at the preparation rate (para 3.8.8). The LAA describes such letters as a preparation item because they take longer than six minutes, although confusingly the guidance suggests that timed letters should take more than 12 minutes (para 3.8.8). You should consider preparation rates at around the 12 minute point if substantive issues were considered.

You cannot charge for multiple letters sent to the same recipient on the same day, unless there is a good reason that justifies it. You cannot charge for a letter correcting your own mistake (para 3.8.3).

Office overheads

The following are office overheads and not claimable: costs of postage, stationery, faxes, scanning, typing and the actual cost of telephone calls and most photocopying, (para 3.1) but see below for exceptional costs. Supervision is an overhead unless required by the needs of a particular case. (3.5.5).

Overnight expenses

These can only be claimed in exceptional circumstances, where it would be unreasonable to travel the distance there and back and carry out whatever was required in one day (para 3.9.31-32).

Perusal

This is also known as consideration of documents. An initial perusal of all the documents to identify which documents are relevant is reasonable. Later detailed consideration of relevant documents will be reasonable. As a very rough guide the LAA allows approximately one to two minutes per A4 page to read the simplest document. Time taken will depend on the quality and layout of the document e.g. whether handwritten or typed, single- or double-spaced, large or small font etc. The time to be claimed is the amount actually taken but the reasonableness will be tested against this time. If longer is taken an explanation should be recorded. More complex documents may take a longer time to consider (para 3.3.10).

Photocopying

Photocopying in-house is generally an overhead expense but if there 'unusual circumstances' or documents are unusually numerous (usually over 500 pages), you may claim the lowest commercial photocopying rate as a disbursement, even when carried out in-house (para 7.14.1).

Preparation

Includes drafting of documents, consideration of documents and evidence provided by the client or other parties, and general consideration of strategy, evidence needed and evidence to be put forward and 'thinking time'.

Reviewing files

You are expected to be familiar with your own files, so you would need to justify any claim for reading a file, e.g. prior to seeing a client when you had not dealt with the file for some time.

Telephone calls

These are either 'routine' and claimed at the item rate, because they take up to six minutes, or they are attendance rate calls, because they take longer than the item charge (again, as for letters CBAM says more than 12 minutes) (para 3.8.16). Consider an item of preparation when the call progresses the case and is around 12 minutes in length. You cannot claim for an unsuccessful call, ie where it is not answered and no message is left. You can claim a routine call for leaving a message on an answering machine (para 3.8.19).

Texts

These are treated as telephone calls. See Telephone calls for more detail.

Transferring files between fee earners
See Reviewing files but the LAA will not pay for duplicated work caused by changes at the firm

Travel time
A useful rule of thumb is that if the round trip travel time is more than two hours, it would not be reasonable and you should instruct a local agent or the client should instruct someone more local to them. In some circumstances you may be able to justify greater travelling times (para 3.9.8), eg–
a) There is no other more local contractor available.
b) The client's problem is so specialised that, in the solicitor's reasonable view, there is no more local contractor with the expertise to deal with the case.
c) The solicitor has significant previous knowledge of the case or dealings with the client in relation to the issues raised by the case so as to justify renewed involvement even though the client is at a distance.
d) The local court or the remand centre where the client is located is more than one hour's travelling time away.
The reason for making the journey must be recorded on the file.

Travel time to clients
Usually, the client should come to you; but if the client is housebound, in hospital or detention, it may be reasonable for you to travel to the client if for instance a telephone call or video link will not enable you to take proper instructions(para 3.9.14).

Travelling expenses (caseworkers)
Caseworkers' travelling expenses can be claimed where the journey was reasonable and the most appropriate form of transport used (see para 3.9 generally). The LAA takes as a starting point that public transport should normally be used; but you should consider the time saved as well as travel fares or mileage (para 3.9.5). The Standard Crime Contract 2017 sets a contractual mileage rate of £0.45 (standard crime contract specification para 5.48) for cases other then in the Crown Court. Travel expenses will not normally accepted if the Court is within walking distance, although issues such as the need to transport bulky files or sensitivity of documentation may be taken into consideration. Taxis may be justified, eg for an out-of-hours attendance at a police station. Documentary evidence must support claims, eg ticket or print out from the internet (except mileage) over £20.00 (para 3.9.22).

Travelling expenses (clients)
You can in exceptional circumstances pay clients' expenses to attend court and claim them back from the LAA as a disbursement using eform CRM4 submitted electronically (documentary evidence is required as for caseworkers) (para 7.3). Prior authority can be sought for a client's travelling expenses to an expert where the client cannot afford them and a report is essential for the proper conduct of proceedings (para 7.3.2).

Waiting
If at court, you cannot claim waiting time whilst taking lunch. Para 3.9.27-29 overstates the case as a solicitor may work through much of the lunch break.

Standard monthly payment reconciliation process[1]

1 Introduction

The Legal Aid Agency (LAA) offers providers a choice as to how they are paid for Civil (Legal Help) and Crime (Lower) work. Providers can be paid a Standard Monthly Payment (SMP) or can opt for a Variable Monthly Payment (VMP).

2 Standard Monthly Payments

The Standard Monthly Payment reconciliation process implements the Protocol set out in the Deed of Settlement as agreed between the Ministry of Justice and the Law Society in 2008. The information in this section provides a guide on how the LAA applies the process.

The aim is to reconcile accounts (claims versus payments) to a 100% balanced position.[2] The contract position percentage is calculated using the following formula:

$$\frac{\text{Claims in last 12 months}}{\text{Total payments aligned to last claim} - (\text{Total Claims} - \text{Claims in last 12 months})} \times 100\%$$

Where an account is within the 90%–110% band no action will be taken to change the SMP. Where an account is below 90% (meaning payments exceed claims by a variance of more than 10%) we will take action to adjust the SMP with the aim of recovering the balance over a period of 6 months to return the contract position to 100%. Likewise where an account is in excess of 110% we will adjust the payment upwards with the aim of bringing the account back to 100% in 6 months.

The new SMP is calculated by taking the average claim value over the preceding 6 months and adding or subtracting 1/6th of the current balance (whether overpaid or underpaid at the time of the review).

---

1 Contract Payments (Legal Help and Crime Lower Work) March 2014. Available at: www.gov.uk/government/uploads/system/uploads/attachment_data/file/340267/ LAA-monthly-payments-protocol.pdf.

2 Criminal legal aid providers who have requested a pull forward of 7.5% (of previous 12 months claims) will have a balance target of 92.5% instead of 100% (of previous 12 months claims) for the purposes of setting future payment levels.

Although this initial action is intended to return the account to 100% balanced, it may not have the desired effect due to fluctuations in claims. Prior to the setting of the 6th payment following the initial review, if the account is still outside of the 90%–110% band further action will be taken to clear the remaining balance over a 3-month period. This is achieved by setting the SMP to the 6 month average claim figure with a series of 3 credits or debits (depending on whether the account is underpaid or overpaid).

If at any time the contract position is less than 50% or in excess of 150% action will be taken to clear the balance over a 3-month period (as above).

Any proposed change to your SMP will be communicated one month in advance of the date of the first SMP at the revised amount.

Every account will be reconciled in accordance with this process, but there may be exceptional circumstances where it is appropriate to vary the action required to reconcile an account. Any exceptions are subject to agreement on a case by case basis with the Operational Assurance Reconciliation team. Examples of such exceptions may include (please note this is not an exhaustive list):

- Novations
- Mergers/Acquisitions
- Significant balance discrepancies
- Significant increase in number of Duty Solicitors

New accounts will be paid for the value of work claimed for the first six months and then providers have the option of requesting an SMP or remaining on a Variable Monthly Payment (further details below).

When a Legal Aid provider's contract ends, and is not replaced, the right to an SMP also ends.

3 Variable Monthly Payments

If you elect to receive a Variable Monthly Payment (VMP) this is calculated using the amount of the latest monthly submission plus or minus any changes to claims since the previous payment, for example, claim amendments and escape fee case assessments.

All other aspects of the contract payments process including the payment dates and submissions deadlines will remain the same.

The intention of VMP is to make a balancing payment each month so there may be a period of transition required in order to achieve a zero account balance.

On transition if an account is underpaid the balance will be cleared in a single payment and VMPs will commence from the following month.

If an account is overpaid on transition the balance will generally be recovered over a period of six months by reducing the variable payments by 1/6th of the balance. Providers have the opportunity to discharge the balance by making a single payment or by requesting payments are stopped until the account moves into a position of credit, or by a combination of these options. Providers should contact the Operational Assurance Reconciliation team to discuss transitional arrangements.

When a Legal Aid provider's contract ends, and is not replaced, the right to a VMP also ends.

Contact Details

By email: reconciliation@legalaid.gsi.gov.uk

By telephone: 0191 428 3738

By DX: Operational Assurance Reconciliation Team, Legal Aid Agency, DX 742350, Jarrow 2

By Post: Operational Assurance Reconciliation Team, Legal Aid Agency, South Tyneside Office, Berkley Way, Viking Business Park, Jarrow, NE31 1SF

Index